ירמיה

JEREMIAH

SONCINO BOOKS OF THE BIBLE
EDITOR: REV. DR. A. COHEN, M.A., Ph.D., D.H.L.

Jeremiah

HEBREW TEXT & ENGLISH TRANSLATION
WITH AN INTRODUCTION
AND COMMENTARY

by

RABBI DR. H. FREEDMAN, B.A., Ph.D.

*Hear the word of the LORD, O ye nations,
And declare it in the isles afar off, and say :
' He that scattered Israel doth gather him,
And keep him, as a shepherd doth his flock.'*
JEREMIAH XXXI. 9.

THE SONCINO PRESS
LONDON

"TEMPLE ISRAEL"

FIRST EDITION 1949
SECOND IMPRESSION 1959
THIRD IMPRESSION 1961

PUBLISHERS' NOTE

Thanks are due to the
Jewish Publication Society of America
for permission to use their very beautiful
English text of the Scriptures

PRINTED IN GREAT BRITAIN
BY THE CHESHAM PRESS, CHESHAM, BUCKS

FOREWORD BY THE GENERAL EDITOR

OF all the Hebrew prophets, with the exception of Moses, the fullest biography we possess is that of Jeremiah as contained in the Book that bears his name. It also provides valuable material which throws light upon the psychology of prophecy. The present volume is accordingly one of exceptional interest.

The series is distinctive in the following respects :

(*i*) Each volume contains the Hebrew text and English translation together with the commentary. (*ii*) The exposition is designed primarily for the ordinary reader of the Bible rather than for the student, and aims at providing this class of reader with requisite direction for the understanding and appreciation of the Biblical Book. (*iii*) The commentary is invariably based upon the received Hebrew text. When this presents difficulties, the most probable translation and interpretation are suggested, without resort to textual emendation. (*iv*) It offers a *Jewish* commentary. Without neglecting the valuable work of Christian expositors, it takes into account the exegesis of the Talmudical Rabbis as well as of the leading Jewish commentators.

All Biblical references are cited according to chapter and verse as in the Hebrew Bible. It is unfortunate that, unlike the American-Jewish translation, the English Authorized and Revised Versions, although made direct from the Hebrew text, did not conform to its chapter divisions. An undesirable complication was thereby introduced into Bible study. In the Hebrew the longer headings of the Psalms are counted as a separate verse; consequently Ps. xxxiv. 12, e.g., corresponds to verse 11 in A.V. and R.V. It is also necessary to take into account a marginal note like that found against 1 Kings iv. 21, 'ch. v. 1 in Heb.', so that the Hebrew 1 Kings v. 14 tallies with iv. 34 in the English.

It is hoped that this Commentary, though more particularly planned for the needs of Jews, will prove helpful to all who desire a fuller knowledge of the Bible, irrespective of their creed.

A. COHEN

v

CONTENTS

INTRODUCTION

THE period of Jeremiah's ministry extends from the thirteenth year of Josiah's reign (625 B.C.E.) until after the destruction of the Temple and the overthrow of the Judean State in 586.

Josiah had come to the throne at the tender age of eight, after the fifty-two years' reign of his father, Manasseh. He did not succeed him directly, but followed his brother Amon who was assassinated after being on the throne less than two years (637). Manasseh's reign had been marked by political and religious retrogression. Politically the country was forced to submit to the suzerainty of Assyria. Religiously the reforms inaugurated by Hezekiah had lost their effect and the people reverted to idolatry, with all its impure orgies and gruesome rites practised at the rural sanctuaries *on every high hill and under every leafy tree.* Superstition ran riot: augury and divination raised their heads again, and human sacrifice was re-introduced, Manasseh himself making his own son pass through the fire to Molech. The Mosaic religion was vigorously suppressed. Small wonder, then, that the Torah, the Mosaic Book of the Law, completely disappeared.

Such was the sorry state of affairs which obtained at the time of Josiah's accession. The Assyrian power, though on the decline, was still to be reckoned with. Western Asia had suffered an invasion by Scythian hordes, and it is probable that some of the pictures of devastation in the Book of Jeremiah were occasioned by this event.

In the eighteenth year of Josiah's reign (621) the Temple was being repaired, when beneath an accumulation of rubbish a copy of the Torah was found by Hilkiah, the High Priest, who handed it to Shaphan the scribe, who in turn read it to the king. He was deeply stirred, because he now realized the full extent of the people's apostasy. He also feared the retribution of his outraged God, and forthwith determined to purify the land from its alien worship. All idolatrous symbols in the country were destroyed. The rural sanctuaries were dismantled and their priests disqualified from officiating in the Temple, though to prevent them from fomenting a religious secessionist party, and perhaps also on humanitarian grounds, they were granted an allowance. The Temple was purified and the Feast of Passover reinstituted.

It was a thorough reform, but it affected externals only. A royal fiat, even if made ostensibly with the agreement of the people (or rather, of their leaders), could not produce a change of heart and truly eradicate the popular form of religion, which was idolatry. Jeremiah had no doubt enthusiastically welcomed the reform, but he was soon chagrined on realizing its superficial character and how quickly the people reverted to their idolatrous malpractices.

In the meantime the political scene had changed. In face of the Scythian peril, the ancient rivals, Egypt and Assyria, had joined hands. Moreover, a new Power was coming on the scene—Babylonia—which threatened both. Nineveh, the capital of Assyria, was overthrown in 612 by a coalition of Babylonians, Medes and Scythians. A new capital was established in Haran, but this too the Assyrian king was compelled to evacuate. In 609 Pharaoh-neco II joined forces with the Assyrians to march on Haran. The Egyptian army advanced up the coast of the Land of Israel. Josiah, who saw his independence endangered if the Assyrians regained power, sought to block their advance. Battle was joined at Megiddo: the Judeans were defeated and Josiah was mortally wounded. He was taken to Jerusalem and buried there (607). This event was more than a political reverse. The devotees of idolatry saw in it judgment upon Josiah of the gods banished by him, and so his defeat and death further undermined his reforms and gave renewed impetus to idol-worship.

He was succeeded by his son Jehoahaz,

who was placed on the throne by *the people of the land*. His reign was brief: after three months he was deposed by Pharaoh-neco and exiled to Egypt where he died. His brother Jehoiakim (607-597) was appointed his successor by the king of Egypt presumably because he was pro-Egyptian. Judea was politically in a dangerous situation, but official circles relied upon the sanctity of the Temple and Jerusalem which, they believed, would render the city and therefore the country inviolable. At the risk of his life Jeremiah proclaimed that so long as they persisted in their way of life, even the Temple might be destroyed like the shrine at Shiloh before it. For uttering such thoughts he was arraigned on the capital charge of treason, and but for the intervention of the princes would undoubtedly have been executed. Another prophet, Uriah by name, who preached the same doctrine, was in fact put to death.

Assyria had by now lost her pre-eminence, and Babylon was embarking upon her career of conquest. In 605 Nebuchadnezzar became king of the new empire. He was immediately hailed as *the servant of the LORD* by Jeremiah who, seeing in him God's chosen instrument for punishing Judea, declared that all nations must submit to him. Jehoiakim, appreciating that Egypt could no longer be relied upon for assistance, swore allegiance to him, but broke away after three years. He was immediately attacked by the armies of the neighbouring countries in conjunction with Babylonian troops and lost his life fighting against them (597). His son Jehoiachin continued the struggle, but when Nebuchadnezzar arrived in person three months later to direct operations, he surrendered and was deported to Babylon, accompanied by his court, the nobility, seven thousand citizens together with their families, and a thousand craftsmen (597). This was the first breach in the Judean State which was to lead to its ultimate collapse.

The final scene in this tragedy was enacted in the reign of his ill-fated successor, Zedekiah, another son of Jehoiakim, and the last king of Judea. He repeated the oath of fealty to Babylon;

and all might have been well had not Egypt continued to stir up trouble, aided from within by a pro-Egyptian party. Wishful thinking did the rest. A wave of optimism swept the nation: they had but to revolt and their hated subjection would be ended. In this dangerous delusion they were encouraged not only by many of the civilian leaders, but also by a prophetic group who, claiming to speak in God's name, assured them of success. They went even farther and raised false hopes of a speedy collapse of the Babylonian empire, and the return of the captives together with the sacred vessels which had been carried away at the same time. Jeremiah now appeared in the streets of Jerusalem with a wooden yoke around his neck, to symbolize the continued domination of Babylon. Hananiah, one of the false prophets, broke the yoke in sight of the people. Jeremiah countered by predicting that instead of a wooden yoke, the nation would soon have an iron yoke fastened upon them. About the same time he sent his famous letter (chapter xxix) to the captives in Babylon, counselling them to settle down in the land of exile, and even to pray for the welfare of the cities where they were residing. But his counsels in Judea were disregarded.

Ultimately Zedekiah, probably against his will, was induced to join an anti-Babylonian coalition consisting of Edom, Ammon, Moab, Tyre, Sidon and Judea. In vain Jeremiah implored him to keep aloof from foreign entanglements and remain faithful to his oath of allegiance: the pro-Egyptian party was too strong for the vacillating king. Nebuchadnezzar dealt energetically with the revolt. Despatching part of his army against Tyre, he laid siege in person to Jerusalem in the winter of 588-7. The advance of an Egyptian army compelled him temporarily to raise the siege. Jeremiah took advantage of this respite to leave Jerusalem for his home in Anathoth, but he was arrested and charged with desertion. In spite of his protestations of innocence, he was thrown into prison. Secretly visited by the king, he again urged him to make a timely surrender to save the city. But

matters were gone too far, and it is doubtful whether the king had the necessary authority even if he so desired. The hopeless revolt moved to its inevitable conclusion.

The Egyptians were repulsed by Nebuchadnezzar who resumed the siege. On the ninth of Tammuz in the year 586 a breach was made in the wall of Jerusalem. Zedekiah fled but was overtaken at Jericho. He was conveyed to Riblah, the enemy's headquarters, where, after being compelled to witness the killing of his sons, he was blinded, put into chains and taken to Babylon. A month later Nebuzaradan, the Babylonian Commander-in-Chief, acting on orders, destroyed Jerusalem. The Temple, the royal palace, and many great mansions were set on fire, and the walls rased to the ground. A large part of the population was deported to Babylon (586), and the overthrow of the Jewish State was complete.

Gedaliah, son of Ahikam and grandson of Shaphan the scribe, was appointed governor over the remnant that was left behind. But the unhappy community was still not to have rest. Baalis, king of Ammon, who resented the existence even of this small and enfeebled community, probably because he had designs upon Judea himself, dealt the final blow. Using Ishmael son of Nethaniah, of the defunct royal house, as his tool, he had Gedaliah murdered. The assassination availed Ishmael but little, for he fled to Ammon; but it wrote an appendix, as it were, to the tragedy. Those who were left in Judea feared the vengeance of Nebuchadnezzar, and in spite of the urgent advice and even threats of Jeremiah, fled to Egypt, forcing the prophet to accompany them. This was the third (but this time voluntary) exile of the Jewish people, and it finally extinguished any sort of autonomous community in Judea. The lights had gone out and were not to be relit for many years.

LIFE AND CHARACTER OF JEREMIAH

Of all the prophets of the Bible Jeremiah is probably the most interesting, because the most self-revealing. None

have told us so much about themselves, their feelings and emotions, as this tragic figure, so strangely compounded of intrepid boldness, which makes him brave the fierce animosity and hatred of people and leaders alike, and a diffident shrinking from his task of telling them the doom which inexorably awaits them —a task which he fain would abandon altogether if he could, but must perform despite himself. Other prophets delivered their messages, but have revealed little of what they felt in doing so. Jeremiah goes farther: he reveals the psychology of the prophet, lays bare the emotion of the man singled out to be the mouthpiece of God. We might have expected a feeling of elation; instead Jeremiah feels poignant sorrow, at times even rebelliousness against his Divinely ordained mission.

The son of Hilkiah, of a priestly family in Anathoth in the land of Benjamin (i. 1), his ministry, as stated above, covered a period of black disaster, culminating in the greatest catastrophe which had as yet befallen the nation. It might well tax the courage of the bravest man to insist that the comforting messages of the popular prophets were false—that for her sins Jerusalem must drink the cup of bitterness to the dregs. Jeremiah was not made of stern stuff. Only the consciousness of having been predestined for his task, the sense of dedication, and the overpowering urge of God's word within him, enable him to rise to the heights of his call. Highly significant is the statement in the first chapter: *And the word of the LORD came unto me saying: Before I formed thee in the belly I knew thee, and before thou camest forth out of the womb I sanctified thee; I have appointed thee a prophet unto the nations . . . Then the LORD put forth His hand, and touched my mouth; and the LORD said unto me: Behold, I have put My words in thy mouth* (verses 4f., 9).

It is instructive to compare his reaction to his call with that of Moses and Isaiah. An overpowering conviction of man's unworthiness in the face of the awe-inspiring majesty and holiness of God fills the latter; yet when he hears

the Divine voice say, *Whom shall I send, and who will go for us?* he unhesitatingly replies, *Here am I; send me* (Isa. vi. 8), although he had not been called by name. Moses, too, perhaps experienced similar feelings when God appeared to him at the Burning Bush, when he hid his face in fear of looking upon the Divine splendour. But here the similarity ends. He, unlike Isaiah, was called by name, and his first reaction was one of personal unfitness: *Who am I, that I should go unto Pharaoh, and that I should bring forth the children of Israel out of Egypt* (Exod. iii. 11). The same humility and distrust of his powers characterized Jeremiah's response: *Ah, Lord GOD! behold, I cannot speak; for I am a child* (i. 6).

Jeremiah, then, may have been the weaker vessel as compared with Isaiah, but his task was far more difficult. In the supreme moment of Judea's trial, when Sennacherib's army lay encamped about Jerusalem, Isaiah had the grateful duty of assuring Hezekiah that the city would *not* fall. It is pleasant to say what one's listener desires to hear. But when more than a century later the Holy City was again menaced, this time by Nebuchadnezzar's forces, Jeremiah had to face obloquy and hatred, taunts of cowardice and defeatism and an accusation of treason when he had to advise submission to the conqueror. The difference in the two messages was not due to difference of theological outlook, as is sometimes argued. Each spoke the words which God had put into his mouth, and each was corroborated by the outcome of events.

Small wonder, then, that Jeremiah movingly bewails his fate. He has no desire to be the harbinger of evil, but he must; and he laments his lot: *Woe is me, my mother, that thou hast borne me a man of strife and a man of contention to the whole earth! I have not lent, neither have men lent to me; yet every one of them doth curse me* (xv. 10). *For as often as I speak, I cry out, I cry: 'Violence and spoil'; because the word of the LORD is made a reproach unto me, and a derision, all the day . . . Cursed be the day wherein I was born; the day wherein my mother bore me, let it not be blessed . . . Where-*

fore came I forth out of the womb to see labour and sorrow, that my days should be consumed in shame? (xx. 8, 14, 18).

This outburst reminds one of Job's (Job iii. 2f.), and it was equally justified. True, he did not suffer the physical calamities which had crushed Job; but for a man of his shrinking temperament the mental anguish which seared his soul was no less overwhelming. He would have preferred to lay aside the mantle of prophecy and live the life of an ordinary citizen, seeing all and saying nothing. But a force stronger than himself drives him on: *O LORD, Thou hast enticed me, and I was enticed, Thou hast overcome me, and hast prevailed . . . And if I say: 'I will not make mention of Him, nor speak any more in His name,' then there is in my heart as it were a burning fire shut up in my bones, and I weary myself to hold it in, but cannot* (xx. 7, 9).

How did a prophet feel when uttering the dire threats of doom which read so impressive in the pages of the Bible? Some picture these men as fierce and vindictive, joyfully contemplating the destruction of sinners, self-righteously exulting over the fate of the wicked. The Bible does not tell us much on this point, but what it does tell is sufficient to show that this picture is far from the truth. With heavy heart they uttered their predictions, and with still heavier heart did they see the fulfilment. The eleventh chapter of Ezekiel records how the prophet, then in Babylon, was lifted up by a spirit and brought to the Temple gate, where he was bidden to prophesy the destruction of the princes who had misled the people. Unlike most other prophecies, the fulfilment in this instance was immediate: *And it came to pass, when I prophesied, that Pelatiah the son of Benaiah* (one of the princes concerned) *died.* What was the prophet's reaction? Did he display exultation? *Then fell I down upon my face, and cried with a loud voice, and said: 'Ah Lord GOD! wilt Thou make a full end of the remnant of Israel?'* (Ezek. xi. 13).

In no prophet is this sympathy with the condemned seen so strongly as in Jeremiah. Taunted and jeered at, he avers that he does not desire the evil that

he must foretell: *Behold, they say unto me: 'Where is the word of the LORD? let it come now.' As for me, I have not hastened from being a shepherd after Thee; neither have I desired the woeful day; Thou knowest it* (xvii. 15f.). Far from wishing it, he earnestly pleaded with God for leniency on behalf of the people, asserting that they had been deceived by false leaders. In a moment of rebelliousness he goes so far as almost to throw the blame upon the Almighty Himself: *Then said I : 'Ah, Lord GOD! surely Thou hast greatly deceived this people and Jerusalem, saying: Ye shall have peace; whereas the sword reacheth unto the soul'* (iv. 10). The theology may be faulty, but the humanity is remarkable.

In that spirit he laments for the people: *My bowels, my bowels! I writhe in pain! The chambers of my heart! My heart moaneth within me! I cannot hold my peace!* . . . *Destruction followeth upon destruction, for the whole land is spoiled; suddenly are my tents spoiled, my curtains in a moment* (iv. 19f.). Repeatedly he displays his tenderness, fervently praying for the people, agonizedly bewailing their cruel fate: *For the hurt of the daughter of my people am I seized with anguish; I am black, appalment hath taken hold on me. Is there no balm in Gilead? Is there no physician there? Why then is not the health of the daughter of my people recovered? Oh that my head were waters, and mine eyes a fountain of tears, that I might weep day and night for the slain of the daughter of my people!* (viii. 21-23; cf. ix. 16ff., etc.). He acknowledges the necessity of judgment, yet prays that it be tempered (x. 23). For His own sake God must help. In his simple and direct approach to God He is almost brought down to man's level, familiarly addressed as a Friend, rather than as an awe-inspiring Monarch: *O Thou hope of Israel, the Saviour thereof in time of trouble, why shouldest Thou be as a stranger in the land, and as a wayfaring man that turneth aside to tarry for a night?* (xiv. 8).

But the people, or rather the priests and prophets, were deaf to all this pleading. They heard only his predictions of woe, and they hated him. They plotted against his life. Jeremiah repeatedly speaks of these personal attacks. He became the object of nefarious schemes, and it is not surprising that mild and gentle though he was, he was goaded to execration and prayer for the death of his enemies. It must have been particularly distressing to him that his own class was foremost in these attacks. He was a priest and a prophet; yet against priest and prophet he had to inveigh, and they repaid him by scheming to take his life. His cup of bitterness was further added to when his own family joined the circle of conspirators, though it is not stated that they sought to kill him.

In fact, his life was more than once in danger. His blunt prophecies of the destruction of the Temple and Jerusalem led to his being arraigned and charged with a capital offence. In general it appears that, at least in the earlier stages of his career, his chief antagonists were the priests and prophets, whilst the princes were more ready to protect him. Charged with treason, he put up a bold defence, insisting that the Lord had sent him to prophesy thus, yet again pleading with them to repent, whereupon He would annul His intentions of evil. Quite simply he admitted that his life was in his accusers' hands, but warned them that should they take it, they would be committing murder (xxvi. 12ff.).

Although of a shrinking nature, he did not lack courage which he displayed not only in braving the fury of the people, but by his vigorous denunciation of their leaders, not even stopping at the king (viii. 1, xxii. 1-5). Allied to that courage was his faith in God in time of trouble, repeatedly expressed (xvi. 19, xvii. 5-11, etc.). In that faith he committed a symbolic act, viz. the purchase of land in the besieged country, though knowing —none better than he—that Judea must fall under the domination of the conqueror; but even as he had predicted disaster, so was he certain of ultimate restoration, and this certainty he manifested so signally by his act (xxxii. 6ff.),

On the other hand, this long-range faith did not blind him to the immediate hopelessness of the position. **Concern-**

ing the first deportation in 597 false prophets gave a comforting assurance that the exile would be short. Jeremiah's endeavours to counter this view were of no avail: perhaps naturally, since men believe what they want to believe, the Judeans cherished hopes of the speedy return of the sacred vessels of the Temple and of the exiles then languishing in Babylon. In one of the most famous chapters of the Book, Jeremiah strongly counselled the exiles to make their peace with their captors, settle in the land of their captivity, and pray and work for the welfare of their new country (xxix. 1-7). This passage is often cited as proving the Jew's loyalty to and care for the land of his adoption, even though he regard himself as in exile. It does. But when Jeremiah wrote his letter the position was very different: the exile had only begun and the nation was locked in a life or death struggle with Nebuchadnezzar who had ordered it. The prophet must have known that his advice would render him liable to a charge of treason, and it needed tremendous courage, as well as unshakable conviction, to tender it.

During the period of his first imprisonment he committed his prophecies to writing through his amanuensis, Baruch the son of Neriah. He had them read to the people on a public fast day, in the hope that they might still effect a reformation, but in vain. When the words were read before Jehoiakim, one of his courtiers showed his anger by burning the scroll. Jeremiah had them rewritten.

In Zedekiah's reign the tragedy was drawing to its close. It is not surprising that as the siege dragged on and the position steadily worsened, his teachings were held to be dangerous, as they must have undermined the morale of the people, and he was imprisoned a second time. There he remained until the fall of the city. But long ere now his status as a man of God had been recognized, and Zedekiah secretly consulted him. Jeremiah once again counselled submission and all would yet be well. But the king was no longer master of the situation, and the war had to proceed to its inevitable dénouement.

Jeremiah was fated to see his prophecies fulfilled. When the city fell he was given the choice of going to Babylon, where he would be well treated, or remaining with the remnants of the people in the desolated country. A true patriot, he chose the latter. After the murder of Gedaliah he urged the people to stay instead of fleeing to Egypt. Even as he had earlier foretold disaster, so now, when his predictions were fulfilled, he comforted the people and assured them of restoration and rehabilitation in the land of their fathers. There was, of course, nothing contradictory in this assurance. The stern moralist must become the loving comforter when disaster has come to pass. His advice was disregarded, and he was forced to leave Judea with the remnants and fly to Egypt. There he made a last attempt to cure the people of their idolatrous practices, but to no effect.

At this point history loses track of him. Doubtless he died in Egypt.

Jeremiah has been called a pessimist. His very name has become symbolic of gloom. Yet nothing could be farther from the truth. His lines were not cast in pleasant places. He was fated to see the utter destruction of his beloved country, and his prophecies must be viewed in that light. It is more correct to describe him as a realistic optimist: 'realistic,' because he would not be lulled, nor allow the people to be lulled, into a false sense of security; 'optimist,' because beyond the immediate blackness he saw brightness for his people, spiritually purified by their sufferings, restored to their homeland, a reunited nation living on their own soil.

'Jeremiah is the spiritual heir of the great prophets that preceded him. He combines the tenderness of Hosea, the fearlessness of Amos, and the stern majesty of Isaiah. Like them, he is first of all a preacher of repentance: threatening judgment and, at the same time, holding out the promise of restoration. But even in his darkest moments, when he utterly despairs of the future of the Jewish State, his faith and trust in God do not desert him. . . . That (Israel) did not disappear (after his

overwhelming disaster) was due to the activity of two men—Jeremiah and his disciple Ezekiel' (Hertz).

RELIGIOUS AND SOCIAL CONDITIONS

The Book of Jeremiah provides us with a very dark picture of the religious and social conditions of the time. Josiah's Reformation had been both incomplete and superficial. His reforms did not long survive him, and even during his lifetime the nation had not returned to God *with her whole heart, but feignedly* (iii. 10). Bitterly the prophet inveighed against the prevalent idolatry, contrasting the loyalty of other peoples to their deities, though these were not gods, with the faithlessness of Israel to the Lord (ii. 10f.). Incense was offered to the *queen of heaven*, primarily by women, but with the full connivance of their husbands. Indeed, the people attributed the misfortunes of the country to the cessation of these observances during the period of the Reformation; and when Jeremiah appealed to them in Egypt, whither they had fled after the overthrow of Judea, to cease these practices, they refused (xliv. 15-19). Superstition was rife: men worshipped the sun, moon and stars (viii. 2), and sought omens and portents for their guidance (x. 2ff.).

Apparently these abominations were not all committed in the name of idol-worship, but also through perversion of the true faith. Thus Jeremiah accuses the scribes of having falsified the Torah: *How do ye say: 'We are wise, and the Law of the LORD is with us'? Lo, certainly in vain hath wrought the vain pen of the scribes* (viii. 8; see note in the Commentary for the translation). This implies that some at least defended themselves against Jeremiah's indictment by insisting that they were obeying the Law of God. But there was even worse. Human sacrifices were offered, and the prophet's vigorous denunciation of them as a perversion of true religion suggests that they were defended on such grounds.

The social picture is no brighter. The people are stigmatized as adulterers and treacherous, false to God and man alike. Slander and deceit make it impossible for one to trust even a neighbour or a brother, for *one speaketh peaceably to his neighbour with his mouth, but in his heart he layeth wait for him* (ix. 7). They are strong, but only to commit falsehood and *proceed from evil to evil* (ix. 2).

What of the leaders? They were the *shepherds* of the people, and in their refusal to seek God had misled their charges; they themselves had not prospered, whilst their flocks were scattered (x. 21). Instead of warning the people of their plight, so as to rouse them to ward off the evil which threatened them, they adopted a complacent attitude, healing the grievous sickness of the nation by glibly denying that there was anything wrong: *They have healed also the hurt of My people lightly, saying: 'Peace, peace,' when there is no peace* (vi. 14). They had gone further: they had actively helped in the ruin of their country (xii. 10). Jeremiah's frequent castigation of the leaders suggests that his sympathies were strongly with the people, and at an early stage of his work he already looked forward to better leaders who would direct them in the will of God: *I will give you shepherds according to My heart, who shall feed you with knowledge and understanding* (iii. 15). But this was a vision for the ideal future. In the unhappy present, oppression and injustice marked the relationship of the rich and powerful toward the poor and defenceless (vii. 6, etc.).

The position of slaves was a special problem. The Mosaic law enjoined that slaves should be freed after six years of service. This law had been a dead letter; but apparently after strong agitation they had been freed, the princes, officials, priests and people having entered into a solemn covenant to that effect. But they had soon re-enslaved them, and because they had violated the liberty of their brothers God proclaimed *liberty unto the sword, unto the pestilence, and unto the famine* (xxxiv. 17).

Social injustice has often been the concomitant of a luxurious civilization. A small group, the Rechabites, recognized this fact, and in obedience to the

command of their ancestor, Jonadab the son of Rechab, had forsaken the complicated urban life of their time, living in tents instead of houses, possessing *no vineyard, or field or seed* (xxxv. 9). Jeremiah commended their faithfulness to their founder's teachings, which example was powerless to stem the rampant evil and only threw it into bolder relief.

JEREMIAH'S RELIGIOUS TEACHINGS

GOD. Like all prophets, Jeremiah starts from the standpoint of God. At a time when the land was overrun with idolatry, to which his pages give mournful testimony, Jeremiah insists that He alone is deserving of worship, He alone is all-powerful, all-seeing and all-knowing, in contrast to the idols which are lifeless. He is the Lord of Nature, and as the universal Creator has the right to dispose of all nations as He wills. This is stressed not as a mere theological concept, but as a truth whose practical consequences are of world import. As universal Creator He now orders all nations to submit to Nebuchadnezzar (xxvii. 5f.), and woe betide them if they prove recalcitrant!

Notwithstanding His infinite might, He is no arbitrary Monarch ruling by whims and caprice. On the contrary, He delights in justice and righteousness whilst Himself practising love on earth (ix. 23). The dark days through which the nation was passing did not shake Jeremiah's faith in Divine justice, and sadly he asked the age-old question why the wicked prosper and are so firmly established (xii. 1f.). This problem did not shake his conviction that God sees all and rewards and punishes (xvi. 17f.). A careful study of the passages where this thought occurs reveals that the prophet was thinking of the nation as a whole rather than of the individual.

To know God is man's highest aim and supreme achievement, in which alone he may take pride (ix. 22f.). By this 'knowing' Jeremiah does not mean abstruse metaphysical profundities about Him, attainable only by the philosopher and scholar. The knowledge required

is of the simplest nature and accessible to all: the awareness that He exercises *mercy* (*chesed*, the better equivalent is 'love'), *justice and righteousness*, for in these virtues He delights.

It is the duty of the Jew to worship and reverence Him alone, and not the idols—but not only the Jew's duty. All peoples must acknowledge Him, otherwise they will inevitably be destroyed (x. 10). In doing this He would not be acting arbitrarily but according to the dictates of justice: *For the LORD hath a controversy with the nations, He doth plead with all flesh* (xxv. 31). The simile is of a law-court where the plaintiff must prove his charge against the defendant; and though God be the Accuser, as Judge He must act in righteousness before condemning or acquitting.

But there is a more tender side to His nature. Though Israel has sinned, He remembers the affection of better days when, in the infancy of their history, the people showed unquestioning love by following Him into the wilderness (ii. 2). If Israel will but return He will show Himself merciful, for He will not nurse His anger against them for ever. He is Father and Friend, and reminds the people how but yesterday they had called Him by these terms (iii. 4, 19).

As He is omnipotent, so is He omnipresent. He can be approached even in exile. In the famous letter to the exiles Jeremiah assured them that they could seek and find Him in captivity; He would hear their supplication and bring them back to their country (xxix. 12f.).

GOD AND ISRAEL. One of the most strongly marked of Jeremiah's teachings is that a bond exists between God and Israel. This bond is in the form of a covenant—an agreement whereby God has chosen Israel as His people in consideration of the latter's acceptance of Him in a peculiar sense as their Deity. It was the prophet's sad duty to urge Israel's submission to Nebuchadnezzar under penalty of utter defeat and destruction. Perhaps for that reason he emphasized the eternal

nature of the bond between God and His people. It is certainly remarkable that Jeremiah and Ezekiel, the prophets of the exile, give most prominence to the idea of a covenant, just because the catastrophic nature of the time might have led people at that stage of religious immaturity to point to current events as proof that the bond was broken.

This covenant idea is developed along two lines. Firstly, it imposes a special obligation of loyalty upon Israel. Upon this concept Jeremiah repeatedly bases his appeal that they abandon idolatry and return to God. On the other hand, though the nations destroy Israel, the special relationship which this covenant implies will not be broken.

He begins his prophetic teaching by reminding Israel of this relationship. In a beautiful simile to which he often returns Israel is depicted as God's 'bride,' consecrated to Him: *Go, and cry in the ears of Jerusalem, saying: Thus saith the LORD: I remember for thee the affection of thy youth, the love of thine espousals; how thou wentest after Me in the wilderness, in a land that was not sown. Israel is the LORD'S hallowed portion, His first-fruits of the increase; all that devour him shall be held guilty. Evil shall come upon them, saith the LORD* (ii. 2f.).

This bond or covenant is urged on historical grounds. God's liberation of Israel from Egypt gave Him a claim on their gratitude and worship, which was reinforced by His care of them in the wilderness, *a land of deserts and of pits . . . a land of drought and of the shadow of death.* He had brought them unscathed through all those dangers *into a land of fruitful fields, to eat the fruit thereof and the good thereof* (ii. 6f.). How base, then, is their ingratitude and forgetfulness when they turn away from Him to serve idols! Moreover, the covenant made with the patriarchs and renewed at the exodus was an essential pre-requisite for the fulfilment of God's promise that the land would belong to their children (xi. 2-5).

The duties which the covenant entails are not enumerated in detail, but it involved refraining from the abomina-

tions of idolatry (xxii. 9) and observing God's *laws, statutes and judgments,* swearing by His name and in general showing allegiance to Him. Two matters, however, are singled out. One is the Sabbath (xvii. 21f.). 'Covenant' is not explicitly mentioned in that passage, but it strongly emphasizes that the land will remain intact only if Israel keep the Sabbath; and since Israel's possession of the land was part of the covenant, it may be regarded as implied. The other was the freeing of slaves after their six years of bondage, in accordance with the Mosaic law (Exod. xxi. 2). In a lengthy passage this is explicitly made part of the covenant, for the violation of which princes, officials, priests and people are all bitterly castigated and threatened with the destruction of their country (xxxiv. 13ff.). That this protection of the rights of the weak should be singled out for special mention is characteristic of prophetical teaching.

The covenant did not confer immunity. On the contrary, it is repeatedly stressed that precisely because they enjoyed God's favour they will be punished in the event of disobedience. One may cite Amos iii. 2: *You only have I known of all the families of the earth; therefore I will visit upon you all your iniquities.* Notwithstanding that *evil shall come upon them* who devour Israel, the nations have been called upon to attack Judah, for whose sins he shall be destroyed and his land laid desolate. This is a cardinal feature of Jeremiah's teaching; hence his Book abounds in predictions of calamity. Naturally such a view aroused violent resentment: the very thing upon which they relied was held up as a cause of their downfall! It was so revolutionary a concept that to many it appeared nothing less than blasphemy.

Yet from the point of view of the nations, that did not mean that the covenant was now obsolete; it was still valid. Although they were carrying out God's purpose (Nebuchadnezzar is actually referred to as *My servant*), they would be punished. The theological problem why the nations should be penalized for carrying out God's designs presented no

difficulty to the prophets. God uses many instruments to bring His decrees to fruition, *for all things are Thy servants* (Ps. cxix. 91). But the delegated nations had no thought of a mission: they were nothing else than rapacious conquerors. Isaiah has given clearest expression to this view: *O Asshur, the rod of Mine anger . . . I do send him against an ungodly nation, and against the people cf My wrath do I give him a charge . . . Howbeit he meaneth not so, neither doth his heart think so; but it is in his heart to destroy, and to cut off nations not a few* (Isa. x. 5ff.).

As with other great teachers, the theologian and the man are sometimes at war with each other, which is not surprising since emotions often triumph over strict logic. So Jeremiah insists that the covenant does not confer immunity; yet when the country was smitten with a drought of extraordinary severity, he eloquently appealed to God, as Israel's hope, to send relief *for Thy name's sake*, reminding Him that they are His people and that His name is called upon them, though they have sinned (xiv. 1ff.). The prophet plaintively asks, *Hast Thou utterly rejected Judah? Hath Thy soul loathed Zion?* (verse 19), and goes on to plead: *Do not contemn us, for Thy name's sake, do not dishonour the throne of Thy glory; remember, break not Thy covenant with us* (verse 21). The misfortunes of His people seemed to reflect upon His honour, for was He not bound to protect them? Moreover, the covenant is here apparently regarded as binding upon God though Israel had been faithless to it. From the theological standpoint this contradicts his other teaching that Israel did not enjoy immunity, and indeed his plea is answered uncompromisingly: *Though Moses and Samuel stood before Me, yet My mind could not be toward this people; cast them out of My sight, and let them go forth* (xv. 1; cf. xi. 8). That the plea was made at all is quite understandable, since Jeremiah's love for his people outweighed his consistency.

Notwithstanding this uncompromising attitude here and elsewhere, which after

all is his final teaching, the covenant was an assurance that in spite of the people's coming overthrow, they would never be wholly destroyed. A terrible picture is given of the havoc which the invader will wreak, yet it is coupled with the assurance that Judah will not be annihilated: *And they shall eat up thy harvest and thy bread, they shall eat up thy sons and thy daughters, they shall eat up thy flocks and thy herds, they shall eat up thy vines and thy fig-trees; they shall batter thy fortified cities, wherein thou trustest, with the sword. But even in those days, saith the LORD, I will not make a full end with you* (v. 17f.).

The covenant had not been a success since Israel had broken it. And so God promises a new covenant, not like the one which He made with them when they left Egypt, but a more durable one which He would write upon their hearts, so that all, from the humblest to the greatest, would know Him (xxxi. 31ff.). God's bond was with Israel as a whole, and with David and the priesthood in particular; and Jeremiah repeated the assurance, in spite of his scathing criticism of the king and the priests, that God's covenant with both was as permanent as the phenomena of Nature (xxxiii. 20ff.).

When his dire threats were fulfilled, Jerusalem captured and the Temple gone up in flames, and the last vestige of independence lost with the deportation of the blinded king Zedekiah and the people to Babylon, he felt the necessity to inspire his countrymen with hope. And Jeremiah, the so-called pessimist, gave new life to them and lifted them out of their despair by assuring them that God would build the nation up again in their own land (xlii. 10ff.), if they would but remain there and not flee to Egypt. On their insisting, he warned them that destruction would overtake them; yet even then a remnant would escape the sword and return to the land of Judah (xliv. 28), because the bond between God and Israel could never be finally broken.

The eternal nature of this bond was not due to an arbitrary favouring of Israel over other peoples. Earlier he

had taught that all nations would come to serve God, but this would only throw Judah's sin in stubbornly clinging to idolatry into bolder prominence (xvi. 19f.). In the final analysis Jeremiah, like all other prophets, was convinced that the people of Israel would refind its better self. If other nations suffer total destruction while Judah would arise out of his defeat, it was because in spite of everything Judah would know how to purify himself from sin in his hour of trial: this alone would ensure his restoration (xxxiii. 4-8).

GOD AND THE NATIONS. At the outset of his ministry Jeremiah strikes the note of universalism: *I have appointed thee a prophet unto the nations* (i. 5). Hence the Book contains a number of messages addressed to the non-Israelite peoples. From chapter xliv onwards it is almost entirely concerned with other nations and only in a minor degree with Judah and Israel. In the earlier chapters there are also several passages of this kind (cf. i. 10, ix. 25, xxv. 15f., xxvii. 2ff., etc.). In the main these are predictions of their ultimate fate, rather than, as in the case of Israel, ethical and religious messages and calls to repentance. It may well be that prophecies or messages of a similar nature were addressed also to them but have not been preserved, on the Rabbinical principle that only prophecies of value for all time were placed on permanent record.

Notwithstanding his teaching that the other nations, and particularly Babylon, had been summoned by God to punish Judah for his sins, Jeremiah naturally felt bitter towards them. He calls on God to pour out His wrath on the nations that know Him not, *for they have devoured Jacob . . . and have laid waste his habitation* (x. 25). That imprecation he follows with the threat that God will destroy the evil neighbours who have consumed Israel's heritage (xii. 14). Israel's oppressors are destined to be punished (xxx. 16). On the other hand, the nations would be built up amidst the people of Judah if they learn to swear by the name of the

Lord instead of Baal's (xii. 16). In a moment of exaltation Jeremiah confidently anticipates that eventually all peoples will recognize Him alone as God: *Unto Thee shall the nations come from the ends of the earth, and shall say: 'Our fathers have inherited nought but lies, vanity and things wherein there is no profit'* (xvi. 19).

In the last chapters he prophesies the doom of several nations, including the Philistines, Moab, Ammon and Elam. Contrary to what we might have expected, he displays deep sympathy with them; yet in speaking of the Philistines he insists that their doom is inevitable, since God has commanded it. Perhaps he had been finally convinced that they were past repentance and improvement. By contrast he tempers his prophecies against Elam by predicting its ultimate restoration (xlix. 39).

JERUSALEM, THE TEMPLE AND ITS SACRIFICES. In popular belief the inviolability of Jerusalem and the Temple was axiomatic. Both were sacred to the people and to Jeremiah. How else could he declare: *At that time they shall call Jerusalem The throne of the LORD; and all the nations shall be gathered unto it, to the name of the LORD, to Jerusalem* (iii. 17)—a prophecy which would be meaningless if he did not acknowledge its sanctity? Very movingly he represents God as saying: *I have forsaken My house, I have cast off My heritage; I have given the dearly beloved of My soul into the hand of her enemies* (xii. 7).

This belief, nevertheless, constituted a danger, material and spiritual. It gave the people a false sense of security: surely God will protect His own! It also gave them a sense of spiritual wellbeing, smug and complacent, which was wholly unjustified. Jeremiah energetically combated these illusions. The mere possession of the Temple and Jerusalem could not save them: *Trust ye not in lying words, saying: 'The temple of the LORD, the temple of the LORD, the temple of the LORD, are these'* (vii. 4). Since the people were so wedded to this belief, they must be taught that even the

Holy City was not inviolable; and his prophecy that the Temple would be destroyed even as Shiloh (verse 14) inflamed the populace who demanded his death. He had earlier preached to them of defeat and destruction, but only in general terms. To specify Jerusalem and the Temple savoured of treason, and the priests formally arraigned him on this charge (xxvi. 8f.). Notwithstanding his narrow escape he continued to teach in the same strain, saying bitterly of Jerusalem: *For this city hath been to Me a provocation of Mine anger and of My fury from the day that they built it even unto this day, that I should remove it from before My face* (xxxii. 31). This second attack was in the tenth year of Zedekiah's reign, much later than the first which occurred in the beginning of Jehoiakim's reign. Nevertheless we may assume that it too, like the first, was only conditional since repentance would avert the evil decree (cf. xxvi. 3).

To deduce, as many scholars have done, that Jeremiah was antagonistic to the ritual of the Temple, is to read into his words a thought which he would have indignantly repudiated. True he uttered the Divine message: *Your burnt-offerings are not acceptable, nor your sacrifices pleasing unto Me* (vi. 20). Isaiah, and long before him Samuel, had stressed that obedience was preferable to sacrifice (cf. 1 Sam. xv. 22f.; Isa. i. 11ff.). Much has been made of vii. 22: *For I spoke not unto your fathers, nor commanded them in the day that I brought them out of the land of Egypt, concerning burnt-offerings or sacrifices.* Some have gone so far as to maintain that this is a repudiation of the Levitical Code. It is certainly far-fetched to make such a sweeping claim on the basis of a single sentence. It should be remembered that national liberation from Egypt had been accompanied by the institution of the Paschal sacrifice: would it then be argued that Jeremiah rejected the version of the exodus? And if so, how did he look upon Josiah's reinstitution of the Passover rite? Did he consider it an innovation based on the falsification of history? It is clear that he, like the other teachers of Israel, denounced sacrifices only when they were brought in the wrong spirit; but he certainly approved of them when offered in genuine contrition. Hence he looked forward to the permanence of the Priestly and Levitical houses (xxxiii. 18), whose function was the maintenance of the ritual of the Temple.

THE EXILE. A most prominent feature of Jeremiah's teaching is his frequent prediction that the Judeans were going into exile. In modern times this is sometimes interpreted as proving that he, and the other prophets of the period, had reached the stage of religious development where they saw that God could be worshipped equally well in all places, and so it was necessary for Israel to be driven from his land and scattered in order that the artificial barrier between God and His people, which was raised by the belief in a special spiritual virtue attaching to the land of Canaan, might be broken down. Thereby the people would be brought nearer to Him, and at the same time diffuse the knowledge of Him among all nations.

This is a distortion of the prophet's teaching. He predicted exile, not as something beneficial either to Israel or to other peoples (although it proved so to the latter), but solely as punishment which would be terminated as soon as Israel repented. Nothing would have been more alien and incomprehensible to Jeremiah than to think of exile as a blessing to other peoples or as a means of bringing Israel closer to God. In one of his earliest utterances he describes exile as divorce between God and Israel (iii. 8; cf. Isa. l. 1). It is a cause for shame, an occasion for lamenting, the destruction of the tent of Israel, a punishment for Israel's forsaking God and His Torah and the practice of idolatry (ix. 16ff., x. 19f., xvi. 12f.).

As strongly as he threatened exile he foretold a restoration. He could hold out no hope for the speedy termination of the captivity and insisted that it must run its full course (xxix. 8f.). Indeed, those already exiled (viz. Jehoiachin and the people deported with him in 597) would be more fortunate than those who

had remained in Judea (xxix. 16ff.), since the full weight of God's wrath was yet to be experienced by the latter. But that was because he saw more hope in the former upon whom he trusted the exile would have a remedial effect (xxiv). He was certain that in captivity they would be purified and learn to seek God with all their heart (xxix. 12, xxxiii. 4-8, l. 4f.).

Another effect of the exile would be the repudiation of the doctrine of ancestral responsibility with the substitution of individual responsibility, according to which a man is punished only for his own sins and not for those of his parents. This idea is elaborated in Ezekiel xviii. Jeremiah declares more briefly: *In those days they shall say no more: 'The fathers have eaten sour grapes, and the children's teeth are set on edge.' But every one shall die for his own iniquity; every man that eateth the sour grapes, his teeth shall be set on edge* (xxxi. 28f.).

Beyond the exile he eagerly looked forward to the restoration, his faith in which he demonstrated so dramatically by buying land in the besieged area (xxxii). So deep rooted was this hope that, in contemplating the exile of Judah, his mind went back to that of the Northern Kingdom more than 130 years earlier, and he apparently expected its restoration too (xxx. 3, l. 4). The restoration would be preceded by a period of great distress and suffering (xxx. 7). Again and again he returns to this theme, which is most beautifully expressed in the picture of Rachel weeping for her children: *Thus saith the LORD: A voice is heard in Ramah, lamentation, and bitter weeping, Rachel weeping for her children; she refuseth to be comforted for her children, because they are not. Thus saith the LORD: Refrain thy voice from weeping, and thine eyes from tears; for thy work shall be rewarded, saith the LORD; and they shall come back from the land of the enemy. And there is hope for thy future, saith the LORD; and thy children shall return to their own border* (xxxi. 14ff.).

Not only from Babylon, but from all the countries of their exile, would they be brought up to dwell in their land (xxiii. 3). When later, in spite of his pleading, they insisted on fleeing to Egypt, he predicted a dire fate for them, but even of those a small number would be saved to return (xliv. 28).

The teeming life of the big cities, their restless surge, the craving for luxury and ease which was productive of oppression and misery—these were not conducive to the purity of worship and social justice which should be the remedial effects of the exile. Jeremiah therefore seems to look forward to a more simplified life after the restoration in the form of a pastoral rehabilitation, coupled with the purification of the House of David: *Thus saith the LORD of hosts: Yet again shall there be in this place . . . and in all the cities thereof a habitation of shepherds causing their flocks to lie down . . . In the cities of the hill-country, in the cities of the Lowland, and in the cities of the South, and in the land of Benjamin, and in the places about Jerusalem, and in the cities of Judah, shall the flocks again pass under the hands of him that counteth them . . . In those days, and at that time, will I cause a shoot of righteousness to grow up unto David; and he shall execute justice and righteousness in the land* (xxxiii. 12ff.).

JEREMIAH'S STYLE

The Book consists of both prose and poetry, the latter slightly exceeding the former in quantity. Jeremiah's style is clear and lucid, direct and concise, and easily understood. His poetry lacks the vigour and crispness of Isaiah, but makes up for it by a lyric quality which combines pathos with picturesque imagery. While he can be and often is fiercely denunciatory, as often as not much of his teaching is in the form of urgent appeals; and in spite of the dread predictions of disaster, one receives the impression that he speaks in sorrow rather than in anger.

His pathos and simplicity and tender appeal are evident in his earliest addresses: *Go, and cry in the ears of Jerusalem, saying: Thus saith the LORD: I remember for thee the affection of thy youth, the love of thine espousals; how*

thou wentest after Me into the wilderness, in a land that was not sown (ii. 2). It would be difficult to express Israel's early trust in God more beautifully and simply than by this picture of a loving bride trustfully following her bridegroom into unknown perils and known hardships for the love of him. Or again: *Thus saith the LORD: What unrighteousness have your fathers found in Me, that they are gone far from Me, and have walked after things of nought, and are become nought?* (verse 5). It is a simple appeal, all the more impressive because in it God, as it were, places Himself on the defensive.

The same elegiac and melting quality is shown in: *Thus saith the LORD of hosts: Consider ye, and call for the mourning women, that they may come; and send for the wise women, that they may come; and let them make haste, and take up a wailing for us, that our eyes may run down with tears, and our eyelids gush out with waters. For a voice of wailing is heard out of Zion: 'How are we undone!'* (ix. 16ff.).

Israel's love for God was reciprocated. This is stated with masterly simplicity: *Thus saith the LORD: The people that were left of the sword have found grace in the wilderness, even Israel, when I go to cause him to rest. 'From afar the LORD appeared unto me.' 'Yea, I have loved thee with an everlasting love; therefore with affection have I drawn thee'* (xxxi. 1f.). There is a lyric quality in the strongly anthropomorphic picture of the relationship between God and His people: *Is Ephraim a darling son unto Me? Is he a child that is dandled? For as often as I speak of him, I do earnestly remember him still; therefore My heart yearneth for him, I will surely have compassion upon him, saith the LORD* (verse 19). This, of course, is the familiar theme of God's Fatherhood, but what could so bring out the close intimacy of that relationship as the humanizing touch of God playing with His darling child, a Father Whose love triumphs over all other feelings so that, notwithstanding His child's waywardness, His heart yearns for him whenever He speaks of him? Another bold anthropomorphism, though in a dif-

ferent vein, is: *The LORD doth roar from on high, and utter His voice from His holy habitation; He doth mightily roar because of His fold; He giveth a shout, as they that tread the grapes, against all the inhabitants of the earth* (xxv. 30).

Similes and picturesque imagery abound. These are often drawn from Nature or from the daily scenes with which the people were familiar. Out of numerous instances only a few need be cited: *For My people have committed two evils: they have forsaken Me, the fountain of living waters, and hewed them out cisterns, broken cisterns, that can hold no water* (ii. 13, cf. xvii. 13). A similar idea, but drawn directly from Nature, is: *Doth the snow of Lebanon fail from the rock of the field? Or are the strange cold flowing waters plucked up? For My people hath forgotten Me* (xviii. 14f.). Again: *I will utterly consume them, saith the LORD; there are no grapes on the vine, nor figs on the fig-tree, and the leaf is faded* (viii. 13)—a simple yet vivid picture of desolation which eats up everything, while 'the faded leaf' adds just the touch of neglect and decay necessary to complete the picture.

From the similes of Nature in which the Book abounds the following illustrate his powers of graphic imagery and his intimate knowledge of animal life: *Know what thou hast done; thou art a swift young camel traversing her ways; a wild ass used to the wilderness, that snuffeth up the wind in her desire; her lust, who can hinder it? All they that seek her will not weary themselves; in her month they shall find her* (ii. 23f.). *Yea, the stork in the heaven knoweth her appointed times; and the turtle and the swallow and the crane observe the time of their coming; but My people know not the ordinance of the LORD* (viii. 7). *As the partridge that broodeth over young which she hath not brought forth, so is he that gathereth riches, and not by right; in the midst of his days he shall leave them, and at his end he shall be a fool* (xvii. 11).

Then there is a passage reminiscent of the first Psalm: *Cursed is the man that trusteth in man . . . For he shall be like a tamarisk in the desert, and shall not see when good cometh; but shall inhabit the*

parched places in the wilderness, a salt land and not inhabited. Blessed is the man that trusteth in the LORD . . . For he shall be as a tree planted by the waters, and that spreadeth out its roots by the river, and shall not see when heat cometh, but its foliage shall be luxuriant; and shall not be anxious in the year of drought, neither shall cease from yielding fruit (xvii. 5-8).

As he is familiar with Nature, so is he also with the scenes of everyday life which he employs to advantage: *The bellows blow fiercely, the lead is consumed of the fire; in vain doth the founder refine, for the wicked are not separated. Refuse silver shall men call them, because the LORD hath rejected them* (vi. 29f.). His simile of the potter fashioning and refashioning his clay (xviii. 2ff.) is too well known to need quoting. This last is also an instance of how he taught directly from the things he saw. Other examples are the almond-rod (i. 11f., the play on words there is noteworthy), the seething pot (verses 13f.), the girdle and its marring (xiii. 1ff.), the bottles filled with wine (verse 12), the four modes of destruction (xv. 3, though this rather belongs to a different category), the straw and the wheat (xxiii. 28), and the basket of figs (xxiv. 1ff.).

Though he lacks the biting satire of Isaiah, he can be satirical when necessary: *And thou, that art spoiled, what doest thou, that thou clothest thyself with scarlet, that thou deckest thee with ornaments of gold, that thou enlargest thine eyes with paint? In vain dost thou make thyself fair; thy lovers despise thee, they seek thy life* (iv. 30). And finally, his powers of graphic vividness are well displayed in the following: *I beheld the earth, and, lo, it was waste and void; and the heavens, and they had no light. I beheld the mountains, and, lo, they trembled, and all the hills moved to and fro. I beheld, and, lo, there was no man, and all the birds of the heavens were fled. I beheld, and, lo, the fruitful field was a wilderness, and all the cities thereof were broken down at the presence of the LORD, and before His fierce anger* (iv. 23ff.). Or again: *For death is come up into our windows, it is entered into our palaces, to cut off the*

children from the street, and the young men from the broad places (ix. 20).

SYNOPSIS OF THE BOOK

Jeremiah's prophecies cover a period of about forty years. They are not arranged in chronological order but according to subject matter. The following is a synopsis of the Book:

I. i-xlv. Prophecies dealing with current history and events at home. These may be subdivided thus:

i-xx. Prophecies between Jeremiah's call (625) and the fourth year of Jehoiakim (604).

xxi-xxv. 14. Prophecies concerning the kings of Judah and the false prophets.

xxv. 15-38. A brief summary of the prophecies against the other nations which appear in xlvi-li.

xxvi-xxviii. Prophecies of the fall of Jerusalem, with several historical notices.

xxix. Letter to the captives in Babylon, deported in 597.

xxx-xxxi. Messages of comfort.

xxxii-xliv. History of the two years before the downfall of the Judean State.

xlv. A message to Baruch.

II. xlvi-li. Prophecies relating to foreign nations. These may be subdivided as follows:

xlvi, against Egypt; xlvii, against the Philistines; xlviii, against Moab; xlix, against Ammon (1-6), Edom (7-22), Damascus (23-27), Kedar and Hazor (28-33), and against Elam (34-39).
l and li, against Babylon.

III. lii. A supplementary and historical appendix relating the collapse of Judea and ending with a message of comfort intended as *athchalta di-geulah*, 'the beginning of the redemption,' conveyed by the fact that in the thirty-seventh year of his captivity, Jehoiachin was freed from prison and shown favour by the king of Babylon who *set his throne above the throne of the kings that were with him in Babylon* (verse 32).

JEREMIAH

1. THE words of Jeremiah the son of
Hilkiah, of the priests that were in
Anathoth in the land of Benjamin,
2. to whom the word of the LORD
came in the days of Josiah the son of
Amon, king of Judah, in the thirteenth year of his reign. 3. It came
also in the days of Jehoiakim the son
of Josiah, king of Judah, unto the
end of the eleventh year of Zedekiah
the son of Josiah, king of Judah, unto the carrying away of Jerusalem
captive in the fifth month.

1 דִּבְרֵי יִרְמְיָהוּ בֶּן־חִלְקִיָּהוּ
מִן־הַכֹּהֲנִים אֲשֶׁר בַּעֲנָתוֹת
2 בְּאֶרֶץ בִּנְיָמִן: אֲשֶׁר הָיָה
דְבַר־יְהֹוָה אֵלָיו בִּימֵי
יֹאשִׁיָּהוּ בֶן־אָמוֹן מֶלֶךְ יְהוּדָה
בִּשְׁלֹשׁ־עֶשְׂרֵה שָׁנָה לְמָלְכוֹ:
3 וַיְהִי בִּימֵי יְהוֹיָקִים בֶּן־
יֹאשִׁיָּהוּ מֶלֶךְ יְהוּדָה עַד־
תֹּם עַשְׁתֵּי־עֶשְׂרֵה שָׁנָה
לְצִדְקִיָּהוּ בֶן־יֹאשִׁיָּהוּ מֶלֶךְ
יְהוּדָה עַד־גְּלוֹת יְרוּשָׁלַםִ
בַּחֹדֶשׁ הַחֲמִישִׁי:

v. 1. הפטרת ואלה שמות וגם הפטרת ראשי המטות

CHAPTER I

1-3 INTRODUCTION

1. *words.* The Hebrew *dibhrē* may also
mean 'matters, incidents, affairs.' Kimchi
renders accordingly, and the opening
phrase indicates both the *words*, i.e.
prophecies of Jeremiah, and historical
incidents in his life.

Jeremiah. Various explanations have
been given of the name, such as 'the
Lord hurls,' 'the Lord founds,' 'appointed of the Lord.' Perhaps it is a
shortened form of *yarum yah*, 'the Lord
is exalted.' The name is borne by
several other persons in the Bible (cf. 2
Kings xxiii. 31; Neh. x. 3; 1 Chron.
v. 24).

Hilkiah. There was a High Priest of
that name (2 Kings xxii. 4), but it is
unlikely that he was Jeremiah's father.

of the priests that were in Anathoth.

Special cities were set aside for residence
by the Levites and priests (cf. Josh. xxi).
Anathoth is the modern Anata, a small
village lying on the highway from
Jerusalem about three miles to the north-
east.

2. *in the thirteenth year of his reign.* From
this year until the end of the period mentioned in the next verse was forty years.
Josiah ascended the throne in 637 B.C.E.;
so Jeremiah's call occurred about 625.
Josiah reigned another eighteen years,
and was followed by Jehoahaz (three
months), Jehoiakim (eleven years), Jehoiachin (three months), and Zedekiah
(eleven years). Jehoahaz and Jehoiachin
are omitted in verse 3, doubtless because
their tenure of the throne was negligible.

3. *in the fifth month.* Of the year 586
B.C.E. In that month Nebuzaradan burnt
the Temple and the houses in Jerusalem
(2 Kings xxv. 8f.).

I

4. And the word of the LORD came
unto me, saying:

5 Before I formed thee in the belly I
knew thee,

And before thou camest forth out
of the womb I sanctified thee;

I have appointed thee a prophet
unto the nations.

6. Then said I: 'Ah, Lord GOD!
behold, I cannot speak; for I am a
child.' 7. But the LORD said unto
me:

Say not: I am a child;

For to whomsoever I shall send
thee thou shalt go,

And whatsoever I shall command
thee thou shalt speak.

8 Be not afraid of them;

For I am with thee to deliver thee,

4 וַיְהִי דְבַר־יְהֹוָה אֵלַי לֵאמֹר׃

5 בְּטֶרֶם אֶצּוֹרְךָ בַבֶּטֶן יְדַעְתִּיךָ
וּבְטֶרֶם
תֵּצֵא מֵרֶחֶם הִקְדַּשְׁתִּיךָ
נָבִיא לַגּוֹיִם נְתַתִּיךָ׃

6 וָאֹמַר אֲהָהּ אֲדֹנָי יֱהֹוִה הִנֵּה
לֹא־יָדַעְתִּי דַּבֵּר כִּי־נַעַר
אָנֹכִי׃

7 וַיֹּאמֶר יְהֹוָה אֵלַי
אַל־תֹּאמַר נַעַר אָנֹכִי
כִּי עַל־כָּל־אֲשֶׁר אֶשְׁלָחֲךָ
תֵּלֵךְ
וְאֵת כָּל־אֲשֶׁר אֲצַוְּךָ תְּדַבֵּר׃

8 אַל־תִּירָא מִפְּנֵיהֶם
כִּי־אִתְּךָ אֲנִי לְהַצִּלֶךָ

ע. 5. ו' יתירה

4-10 GOD'S CALL TO JEREMIAH

5. *before I formed*, etc. Jeremiah commences his prophetic labours with the
consciousness of having been predestined
for his mission. This consciousness
must have sustained him and enabled
him to triumph over the moods of
despondency to which he was subject.

I knew thee. I had regard to and chose
thee as My messenger. For the use of
the verb in this sense, cf. Nahum i. 7;
Ps. i. 6.

I sanctified thee. Destined thee for this
task (Rashi).

a prophet unto the nations. Hebrew
prophecy, like Judaism, was univer-
salistic in its scope. God's message is to
all peoples and for all times (cf. xxv.
15-29 and chapters xlvi-li).

6. *behold, I cannot speak.* It is not his

youth and lack of experience that make
him hesitate, but 'the consciousness of
insignificance, the shrinking of a sensi-
tive and timid nature, which God re-
bukes in His reply (verses 17-19)'
(Peake).

a child. The Hebrew *naar* may mean 'a
child, infant' (cf. Exod. ii. 6; 1 Sam.
iv. 21), but also 'a young man' (cf. Gen.
xiv. 24, xxxiv. 19). The latter, of course,
is intended here, and the word is better
rendered by 'a youth.'

7. *to whomsoever I shall send thee*, etc.
God gives His servants the strength to
carry out their appointed tasks. The
translation *to whomsoever* is preferable to
R.V. margin 'on whatsoever errand,'
the Hebrew preposition *al* having here,
as elsewhere in the Bible, the force of *el.*

8. *I am with thee.* God is with His

2

Saith the LORD.

9. Then the LORD put forth His hand, and touched my mouth; and the LORD said unto me:

Behold, I have put My words in thy mouth;

10 See, I have this day set thee over the nations and over the kingdoms,

To root out and to pull down,

And to destroy and to overthrow;

To build, and to plant.

11. Moreover the word of the LORD came unto me, saying: 'Jeremiah, what seest thou?' And I said: 'I see a rod of an almond-tree.'

12. Then said the LORD unto me: 'Thou hast well seen; for I watch over My word to perform it.'

נְאֻם־יְהֹוָה׃

9 וַיִּשְׁלַ֨ח יְהֹוָ֜ה אֶת־יָד֗וֹ וַיַּגַּ֣ע עַל־פִּ֔י וַיֹּ֥אמֶר יְהֹוָ֖ה אֵלַ֑י הִנֵּ֛ה נָתַ֥תִּי דְבָרַ֖י בְּפִֽיךָ׃

10 רְאֵ֣ה הִפְקַדְתִּ֣יךָ ׀ הַיּ֣וֹם הַזֶּ֗ה עַל־הַגּוֹיִם֙ וְעַל־הַמַּמְלָכ֔וֹת לִנְת֥וֹשׁ וְלִנְת֖וֹץ וּֽלְהַאֲבִ֣יד וְלַהֲר֑וֹס לִבְנ֖וֹת וְלִנְטֽוֹעַ׃

11 וַיְהִ֤י דְבַר־יְהֹוָה֙ אֵלַ֣י לֵאמֹ֔ר מָה־אַתָּ֥ה רֹאֶ֖ה יִרְמְיָ֑הוּ וָאֹמַ֕ר

12 מַקֵּ֥ל שָׁקֵ֖ד אֲנִ֥י רֹאֶֽה׃ וַיֹּ֧אמֶר יְהֹוָ֛ה אֵלַ֖י הֵיטַ֣בְתָּ לִרְא֑וֹת כִּֽי־שֹׁקֵ֥ד אֲנִ֖י עַל־דְּבָרִ֖י

---

servants in the mission He entrusts to them (cf. Exod. iii. 12).

to deliver thee. The form of the assurance is significant. In his mission Jeremiah will not be free from danger and hardship; but God will be his Rescuer.

9. *Then the LORD . . . my mouth.* An anthropomorphism; the action symbolized that henceforth he would speak with the tongue (authority) of God, the Divine holiness having been communicated to him by the contact.

10. *to root out . . . and to plant.* Not that the prophet would himself have the power to do this, but it would be his mission to announce what God was about to do. The ultimate purpose of his prophecy would be *to build, and to plant*; but, as so often happens, much would have to be destroyed before reconstruction could commence.

11-12 VISION OF THE ALMOND-TREE

Following soon on his call, Jeremiah beholds two visions which create within him an awareness that momentous events affecting the Kingdom of Judah are imminent.

12. *for I watch*, etc. The message of the vision is conveyed through the resemblance of the Hebrew for *almond-tree* (*shakëd*) and the verb meaning *watch* (or 'wakeful') (*shokëd*). Two thoughts are suggested: first, the almond-tree is the first to blossom; so will God *hasten* to perform His words (Rashi, Kimchi). Second, 'in Palestine the almond-tree is the harbinger of spring, awaking first from the winter sleep. Amid all the spiritual and moral deadness around God is awake; indications may seem scarce and the time long, yet God's word and judgment will certainly be fulfilled; the winter of moral desolation cannot last for ever; the Lord *is* wakeful' (Pickering).

13. And the word of the LORD came unto me the second time, saying: 'What seest thou?' And I said: 'I see a seething pot; and the face thereof is from the north.' 14. Then the LORD said unto me: 'Out of the north the evil shall break forth upon all the inhabitants of the land. 15. For, lo, I will call all the families of the kingdoms of the north, saith the LORD; and they shall come, and they shall set every one his throne at the entrance of the gates of Jerusalem, and against all the walls thereof round about, and against all the cities of Judah. 16. And I will utter my judgments against them touching all their wickedness; in that they

13 לַעֲשׂתוֹ: וַיְהִי דְבַר־יְהֹוָה |
אֵלַי שֵׁנִית לֵאמֹר מָה אַתָּה
רֹאֶה וָאֹמַר סִיר נָפוּחַ אֲנִי
רֹאֶה וּפָנָיו מִפְּנֵי צָפוֹנָה:
14 וַיֹּאמֶר יְהֹוָה אֵלַי מִצָּפוֹן
תִּפָּתַח הָרָעָה עַל כָּל־יֹשְׁבֵי
15 הָאָרֶץ: כִּי | הִנְנִי קֹרֵא לְכָל־
מִשְׁפְּחוֹת מַמְלְכוֹת צָפוֹנָה
נְאֻם־יְהֹוָה וּבָאוּ וְנָתְנוּ אִישׁ
כִּסְאוֹ פֶּתַח | שַׁעֲרֵי יְרוּשָׁלַ͏ִם
וְעַל כָּל־חוֹמֹתֶיהָ סָבִיב וְעַל
16 כָּל־עָרֵי יְהוּדָה: וְדִבַּרְתִּי
מִשְׁפָּטַי אוֹתָם עַל כָּל־רָעָתָם

13-16 VISION OF THE BOILING CALDRON

13. *seething.* lit. 'blown upon'; the embers under the pot are fanned into flame.

from the north. The direction from which danger threatens Judah.

14. *the evil.* In the sense of calamity; here it denotes the invasion of the land.

break forth. lit. 'opened,' i.e. become revealed.

15. A similar prophecy of the gathering of the nations against Judah is contained in Isa. xvii. 12ff.

families. 'Each kingdom was composed of a mixture of races, here called *families*' (Streane). But *mishpachah* is also used in the sense of 'nations' (cf. Amos iii. 2).

they shall set every one his throne. The prophet does not think of the siege of Jerusalem, but of the sequel when the

city has been captured. The victorious chieftains will proceed to sit in formal judgment (for this use of *throne*, cf. Ps. ix. 5, cxxii. 5) upon the inhabitants, *at the entrance of the gates* where trials were held, to determine what was to be done to the defeated population and their towns.

16. 'Viewed in one light, war is the boiling caldron of human passion, upset by hazard, and bringing only ruin in its course; in the other, it is God sitting in judgment, with the kings of the earth as His assessors, solemnly pronouncing sentence upon the guilty' (Payne Smith).

I will utter my judgments. The initial letter of *my* should be printed with a capital, the reference being to God Whose agents the conquerors are and Whose verdict they will execute.

all their wickedness. Specified in the second half of the verse: desertion of the

have forsaken Me, and have offered unto other gods, and worshipped the work of their own hands. 17. Thou therefore gird up thy loins, and arise, and speak unto them all that I command thee; be not dismayed at them, lest I dismay thee before them. 18. For, behold, I have made thee this day a fortified city, and an iron pillar, and brazen walls, against the whole land, against the kings of Judah, against the princes thereof, against the priests thereof, and against the people of the land. 19. And they shall fight against thee; but they shall not prevail against thee; For I am with thee, saith the LORD, to deliver thee.'

אֲשֶׁר עֲזָבוּנִי וַיְקַטְּרוּ לֵאלֹהִים
אֲחֵרִים וַיִּשְׁתַּחֲווּ לְמַעֲשֵׂי
17 יְדֵיהֶם: וְאַתָּה תֶּאְזֹר מָתְנֶיךָ
וְקַמְתָּ וְדִבַּרְתָּ אֲלֵיהֶם אֵת
כָּל־אֲשֶׁר אָנֹכִי אֲצַוֶּךָּ
אַל־תֵּחַת מִפְּנֵיהֶם פֶּן־
18 אֲחִתְּךָ לִפְנֵיהֶם: וַאֲנִי הִנֵּה
נְתַתִּיךָ הַיּוֹם לְעִיר מִבְצָר
וּלְעַמּוּד בַּרְזֶל וּלְחֹמוֹת נְחֹשֶׁת
עַל־כָּל־הָאָרֶץ לְמַלְכֵי
יְהוּדָה לְשָׂרֶיהָ לְכֹהֲנֶיהָ וּלְעַם
19 הָאָרֶץ: וְנִלְחֲמוּ אֵלֶיךָ וְלֹא־
יוּכְלוּ לָךְ כִּי־אִתְּךָ אֲנִי
נְאֻם־יְהוָה לְהַצִּילֶךָ:

true God, offering sacrifices to false gods and idol-worship. Forsaking the true God does not merely leave a vacuum. It is inevitably followed by the worship of false gods. Thus to eschew the good means in practice to cultivate the bad.

17-19 MESSAGE OF ENCOURAGEMENT TO JEREMIAH

17. gird up thy loins. Gather up the long flowing robe which was worn, preparatory to taking active measures.

be not dismayed at them. Courage, moral and physical, is an essential attribute of the true prophet; cf. Nathan's fearless accusation of David, *Thou art the man* (2 Sam. xii. 7) and Elijah's dauntless

rebuke to Ahab, *Hast thou killed, and also taken possession?* (1 Kings xxi. 19).

18. Jeremiah would, indeed, have to plough a lonely furrow, with all sections of the nation against him. For that reason God assures him of the strength wherewith He will fortify him.

the kings of Judah. The plural, *kings*, signified that his career would extend through several reigns.

the princes. i.e. officers of the State.

the priests. Even from them he would meet with opposition.

19. they shall not prevail against thee. The meaning is, not finally prevail; he would suffer many setbacks, but they would be only temporary.

2   CHAPTER II   ב

1. And the word of the LORD came
to me, saying: 2. Go, and cry in the
ears of Jerusalem, saying: Thus
saith the LORD:
  I remember for thee the affection
    of thy youth,
  The love of thine espousals;
  How thou wentest after Me in the
    wilderness,
  In a land that was not sown.
3 Israel is the LORD's hallowed por-
    tion,
  His first-fruits of the increase;

וַיְהִי דְבַר־יְהֹוָה אֵלַי לֵאמֹר׃ 1
הָלֹךְ וְקָרָאתָ בְאָזְנֵי יְרוּשָׁלַם 2
לֵאמֹר כֹּה אָמַר יְהֹוָה
זָכַרְתִּי לָךְ חֶסֶד נְעוּרַיִךְ
אַהֲבַת כְּלוּלֹתָיִךְ
לֶכְתֵּךְ אַחֲרַי בַּמִּדְבָּר
בְּאֶרֶץ לֹא זְרוּעָה׃
קֹדֶשׁ יִשְׂרָאֵל לַיהֹוָה 3
רֵאשִׁית תְּבוּאָתֹה

CHAPTER II

1-3 GOD REMEMBERS ISRAEL'S LOVE FOR
HIM IN THE PAST

1. the word of the LORD came to me.
This first prophecy of Jeremiah extends
to the end of chapter vi. Its main theme
is the implicit confidence which the
people of Israel displayed in God during
the early stage of the national existence
and its contrast with the present state
of backsliding.

2. for thee. i.e. in thy favour.

affection. Hebrew *chesed* which denotes
both God's love for Israel and Israel's
love for God. Here the latter is meant.

youth. The time of the nation's beginnings in Egypt and the wilderness.

the love of thine espousals. By his trust
in departing from Egypt, a land of comparative plenty (cf. Num. xi. 5), into the
wilderness (*a land that was not sown*),
Israel sealed his ties of close kinship with
God. With beautiful and tender imagery
that act of trust is described as Israel's
espousals, comparable with a bride following her husband to a strange country.

The loving confidence in God shown by
the nation in its youth is remembered by
God in its favour and leads to His
promise in verse 3. It is unlikely that
Jeremiah had forgotten, or desired to
gloss over, the many instances of lack
of faith in the wilderness when the
Israelites murmured against God. But
these could not efface their praiseworthy
trust in embarking upon such a venture,
even though the hardships of the desert
subsequently dimmed their glowing
faith.

3. the LORD'S hallowed portion. In a
special sense Israel is dedicated to God,
just as the first-fruits belonged to the
priests as His representatives. The
people are therefore under His direct
protection, and woe to them who seek
to destroy them. Though it is the prophet's thesis that these nations are
carrying out God's designs, he knew
that they are not actuated by any high
or noble motive. For them it was simply
a matter of aggression and lust for conquest, for which they would be punished.

His first-fruits of the increase. As the
first-fruits of a field are sacred, so is

All that devour him shall be held
  guilty,
Evil shall come upon them,
Saith the LORD.

4 Hear ye the word of the LORD, O
  house of Jacob,
  And all the families of the house of
  Israel;

5 Thus saith the LORD:
  What unrighteousness have your
  fathers found in Me,
  That they are gone far from Me,
  And have walked after things of
  nought, and are become nought?

כָּל־אֹכְלָיו יֶאְשָּׁמוּ
רָעָה תָּבֹא אֲלֵיהֶם
נְאֻם־יְהֹוָה: *

4 *שִׁמְעוּ דְבַר־יְהֹוָה בֵּית
יַעֲקֹב
וְכָל־מִשְׁפְּחוֹת בֵּית יִשְׂרָאֵל:

5 כֹּה ׀ אָמַר יְהֹוָה
מַה־מָּצְאוּ אֲבוֹתֵיכֶם בִּי עָוֶל
כִּי רָחֲקוּ מֵעָלָי
וַיֵּלְכוּ אַחֲרֵי הַהֶבֶל וַיֶּהְבָּלוּ:

v. 3. קמץ בז"ק   v. 3. ע"כ   v. 4. הפטרת מסעי

Israel, the 'first-fruits of humanity'
(Philo), sacred to God. The mention of
first-fruits implies that He expects a later
harvest, i.e. while Israel is the first
people whom He chose, God looks to the
ingathering of all other peoples too,
who in the fulness of time would come to
acknowledge Him.

evil shall come upon them. The assurance given to the patriarchs (Gen. xii. 3,
xxvii. 29) held good also of their descendants. 'The story of European
history during the past centuries teaches
one uniform lesson. That the nations
which have received and in any way dealt
fairly and mercifully with the Jew have
prospered; and that the nations that
have tortured and oppressed him have
written out their own curse' (Olive
Schreiner).

4-13 JUDAH'S UNGRATEFUL FOLLY

4. *Israel.* Only the Kingdom of Judah
was left, that of Israel having come to
an end more than a century earlier (in
722 B.C.E.). But Jeremiah regards Judah

as representative of the whole nation.
Moreover, he may intentionally have
addressed himself also to the exiles of the
Northern Kingdom, as well as to some
Israelite families who may have been left
in Samaria.

5. *what unrighteousness,* etc. As often
in the Bible, the question expresses an
emphatic negative: no unjust act on
God's part can account for the nation's
infidelity.

things of nought. A strong and forth-
right characterization of idolatry: with
all its pomp and pageantry it is mere
nothingness, utterly futile and empty.

and are become nought. The worship of
such futility inevitably renders the worshippers like itself, emptying them of all
spiritual content (cf. Ps. cxv. 8).

6f. Only by deliberately and ungrate-
fully shutting out from their minds
God's manifold favours, His deliverance
of them from Egypt and His loving
protection in the wilderness, could they
have grown so unfaithful to Him.

7

6 Neither said they:
　　'Where is the LORD that brought
　　　us up
　　Out of the land of Egypt;
　　That led us through the wilder-
　　　ness,
　　Through a land of deserts and of
　　　pits,
　　Through a land of drought and of
　　　the shadow of death,
　　Through a land that no man passed
　　　through,
　　And where no man dwelt?'
7 And I brought you into a land of
　　　fruitful fields,
　　To eat the fruit thereof and the
　　　good thereof;
　　But when ye entered, ye defiled
　　　My land,
　　And made My heritage an abomi_
　　　nation.
8 The priests said not: 'Where is the
　　　LORD?'
　　And they that handle the law knew
　　　Me not,

6 וְלֹא אָמְרוּ
אַיֵּה יְהוָֹה הַמַּעֲלֶה אֹתָנוּ
מֵאֶרֶץ מִצְרָיִם
הַמּוֹלִיךְ אֹתָנוּ בַּמִּדְבָּר
בְּאֶרֶץ עֲרָבָה וְשׁוּחָה
בְּאֶרֶץ צִיָּה וְצַלְמָוֶת
בְּאֶרֶץ לֹא־עָבַר בָּהּ אִישׁ
וְלֹא־יָשַׁב אָדָם שָׁם:
7 וָאָבִיא אֶתְכֶם
אֶל־אֶרֶץ הַכַּרְמֶל
לֶאֱכֹל פִּרְיָהּ וְטוּבָהּ
וַתָּבֹאוּ וַתְּטַמְּאוּ אֶת־אַרְצִי
וְנַחֲלָתִי שַׂמְתֶּם לְתוֹעֵבָה:
8 הַכֹּהֲנִים לֹא אָמְרוּ אַיֵּה יְהוָֹה
וְתֹפְשֵׂי הַתּוֹרָה לֹא יְדָעוּנִי

---

6. *pits.* Holes in the treacherous sands which may cause serious accidents.

the shadow of death. The Hebrew word used in Ps. xxiii. 4. Its meaning is 'deep darkness' (so Rashi and R.V. margin). 'The pathless desert is as bewildering as would be profound darkness' (Streane).

7. *a land of fruitful fields.* lit. 'a land of the Carmel.'

ye defiled. 'By idol-worship' (Hertz).

My land . . . My heritage. The land chosen by God for His particular purpose (Kimchi), and therefore a conse-crated land.

an abomination. By pagan rites per-formed in it, the Holy Land is become loathsome in the sight of God.

8. Jeremiah's indictment of the national leaders (whom he evidently holds respon-sible for the people's apostasy) is very comprehensive, and embraces both the spiritual and temporal rulers.

the priests. Whose duty is to teach the ways of God (cf. Mal. ii. 7).

they that handle the law. The religious officials who administer and interpret the Torah.

knew Me not. Men studied the Torah without the desire really to know and imitate the ways of God (Kimchi).

And the rulers transgressed against Me;
The prophets also prophesied by Baal,
And walked after things that do not profit.

9 Wherefore I will yet plead with you, saith the LORD,
And with your children's children will I plead.

10 For pass over to the isles of the Kittites, and see,
And send unto Kedar, and consider diligently,
And see if there hath been such a thing.

11 Hath a nation changed its gods, Which yet are no gods?
But My people hath changed its glory
For that which doth not profit.

12 Be astonished, O ye heavens, at this,

וְהָרֹעִים פָּשְׁעוּ בִי
וְהַנְּבִיאִים נִבְּאוּ בַבַּעַל
וְאַחֲרֵי לֹא־יוֹעִלוּ הָלָכוּ׃

9 לָכֵן עֹד
אָרִיב אִתְּכֶם נְאֻם־יְהֹוָה
וְאֶת־בְּנֵי בְנֵיכֶם אָרִיב׃

10 כִּי עִבְרוּ אִיֵּי כִתִּיִּים וּרְאוּ
וְקֵדָר שִׁלְחוּ וְהִתְבּוֹנְנוּ מְאֹד
וּרְאוּ הֵן הָיְתָה כָּזֹאת׃

11 הַהֵימִיר גּוֹי אֱלֹהִים
וְהֵמָּה לֹא אֱלֹהִים
וְעַמִּי הֵמִיר כְּבוֹדוֹ
בְּלוֹא יוֹעִיל׃

12 שֹׁמּוּ שָׁמַיִם עַל־זֹאת

---

the rulers. lit. 'the shepherds,' i.e. the secular rulers.

the prophets. 'Jeremiah felt most keenly the wickedness of both priest and prophet, since in his own person he represented both orders' (Streane; see on v. 31). In this sweeping indictment, which does not spare even the highest, Jeremiah displays that fearlessness which he had been bidden to maintain (i. 17) in spite of his diffident nature.

things that do not profit. The idols.

9. *plead.* i.e. contend. The Hebrew verb *rib* always means 'to plead' in a legal sense, i.e. contend, and never 'to beseech' or ' make intercession.'

10. *isles of the Kittites.* Cyprus and the neighbouring islands, including also the coastlands of Italy and Greece. In Gen.

x. 4 *Kittim* is reckoned among the sons of Javan (Greece).

Kedar. A son of Ishmael (Gen. xxv. 13), here denoting Arabia in general. The sense is: Go wherever you will, east or west, and you will find no parallel to your conduct.

11. *a nation.* i.e. a heathen nation.

which yet are no gods. A reason why these should have been changed.

its glory. The Almighty, Who is Israel's glory (Rashi). Cf. *Thus they exchanged their glory for the likeness of an ox that eateth grass* (Ps. cvi. 20).

12. As Nature is summoned to attest the prophetic admonition and Divine arraignment of Israel (cf. Deut. xxxii. 1; Isa. i. 2), so is she bidden to show her horror at the people's faithlessness.

And be horribly afraid, be ye exceeding amazed,
Saith the LORD.

13 For My people have committed
two evils:
They have forsaken Me, the
fountain of living waters,
And hewed them out cisterns,
broken cisterns,
That can hold no water.

14 Is Israel a servant?
Is he a home-born slave?
Why is he become a prey?

15 The young lions have roared
upon him,
And let their voice resound;
And they have made his land
desolate,

וְשַׂעֲרוּ חָרְבוּ מְאֹד
נְאֻם־יְהוָֹה׃
13 כִּי־שְׁתַּיִם רָעוֹת עָשָׂה עַמִּי
אֹתִי עָזְבוּ מְקוֹר | מַיִם חַיִּים
לַחְצֹב לָהֶם בֹּארוֹת
בֹּארֹת נִשְׁבָּרִים
אֲשֶׁר לֹא־יָכִלוּ הַמָּיִם׃
14 הַעֶבֶד יִשְׂרָאֵל
אִם־יְלִיד בַּיִת הוּא
מַדּוּעַ הָיָה לָבַז׃
15 עָלָיו יִשְׁאֲגוּ כְפִרִים
נָתְנוּ קוֹלָם
וַיָּשִׁיתוּ אַרְצוֹ לְשַׁמָּה

v. 14. פתח בס״פ

be ye exceedingly amazed. lit. 'be exceedingly dried up'; the heavens should lose
their moisture in horror of such perfidy.

13. *the fountain of living waters.* 'The
perennial spring of water that leaps and
flashes as though it were a living thing,
breaking ceaselessly forth from a hidden
source, is the best image of that higher life
bestowed on him to whom God has
unveiled His face' (Hort.).

cisterns, broken cisterns. 'No comparison could more keenly rebuke the mad-
ness of a people who changed their
glory for that which doth not profit. The
best cisterns, even those in solid rock,
are strangely liable to crack . . . and if by
constant care they are made to hold, yet
the water collected from clay roofs or
from marly soil has the colour of weak
soapsuds, the taste of the earth or the

stable, is full of worms, and in the hour
of greatest need it utterly fails' (Thomson).

14-30 THE FAITHLESSNESS OF ISRAEL

14. *is Israel a servant?* The prophet is
thinking more particularly of the Northern Kingdom which had been devastated and the population taken as
captives to Assyria, and asks, 'Is their
servile condition natural to the people?'
The answer expected is negative; a
different explanation accounts for their
lowly state.

a home-born slave. The child of a bond-
woman and so born into slavery.

a prey. To depredatory neighbours.

15. *the young lions.* Israel's enemies, the
Assyrians; for the imagery, cf. Isa. v. 29.

His cities are laid waste,
Without inhabitant.

16 The children also of Noph and
Tahpanhes
Feed upon the crown of thy head.

17 Is it not this that doth cause it
unto thee,
That thou hast forsaken the LORD
thy God,
When He led thee by the way?

18 And now what hast thou to do in
the way to Egypt,
To drink the waters of Shihor?
Or what hast thou to do in the
way to Assyria,
To drink the waters of the River?

19 Thine own wickedness shall correct thee,

עָרָיו נִצְּתָה
מִבְּלִי יֹשֵׁב׃

16 גַּם־בְּנֵי־נֹף וְתַחְפַּנֵס
יִרְעוּךְ קָדְקֹד׃

17 הֲלוֹא־זֹאת תַּעֲשֶׂה־לָּךְ
עָזְבֵךְ אֶת־יְהוָה אֱלֹהַיִךְ
בְּעֵת מוֹלִיכֵךְ בַּדָּרֶךְ׃

18 וְעַתָּה מַה־לָּךְ לְדֶרֶךְ מִצְרַיִם
לִשְׁתּוֹת מֵי שִׁחוֹר
וּמַה־לָּךְ לְדֶרֶךְ אַשּׁוּר
לִשְׁתּוֹת מֵי נָהָר׃

19 תְּיַסְּרֵךְ רָעָתֵךְ

v. 15. v. 16. נצתו ק׳ ותחפנחס ק׳

---

are laid waste. The verb may mean 'are burnt' (so A.V., R.V.).

16. *Noph.* Memphis, near modern Cairo; further alluded to in xliv. 1, xlvi. 14, 19.

Tahpanhes. Mentioned again in xliii. 7ff., xliv. 1, xlvi. 14. The Greek Daphnae Pelusii, an important fortress on the eastern branch of the Nile, commanding the road to Palestine.

feed upon the crown of thy head. Even Egypt, upon whom Israel relied for help, was merely exploiting them for her own benefit, and would not scruple to rob them, when it suited her convenience (as happened in the reign of Jehoiakim, 2 Kings xxiii. 35). The figure seems to be of cattle grazing in a field.

17. *thou hast forsaken the LORD.* This answers the question in verse 14.

when He led thee by the way. Either in the way of the wilderness (so most

moderns), or in the way of goodness and virtue (Rashi, Kimchi).

18. *what hast thou to do . . .?* The rulers of Judah and Israel had vacillated between the two great Powers, Egypt and Assyria. Menahem, king of Israel, sought Assyria's assistance against Egypt; Hoshea reversed his policy and invoked Egypt against Assyria; while Josiah died fighting against Egypt in support of Assyria. None of these alliances had benefited them. These are the *broken cisterns* referred to in verse 13. Israel's only salvation lay in a return to God.

Shihor. The Nile. *Shihor* probably means 'dark,' and describes the turbid waters of that river.

the River. The Euphrates, on which Babylon was situated. It symbolizes Assyria.

19. *wickedness . . . backslidings.* The bitter

11

And thy backslidings shall re-
prove thee:
Know therefore and see that it is
an evil and a bitter thing,
That thou hast forsaken the LORD
thy God,
Neither is My fear in thee,
Saith the Lord GOD of hosts.

20 For of old time I have broken
thy yoke,
And burst thy bands,
And thou saidst: 'I will not trans-
gress';
Upon every high hill
And under every leafy tree
Thou didst recline, playing the
harlot.

21 Yet I had planted thee a noble
vine,
Wholly a right seed;
How then art thou turned into
the degenerate plant
Of a strange vine unto Me?

וּמְשֻׁבוֹתַ֖יִךְ תּוֹכִחֻ֑ךְ
וּדְעִ֤י וּרְאִי֙ כִּי־רַ֣ע וָמָ֔ר
עָזְבֵ֖ךְ אֶת־יְהֹוָ֣ה אֱלֹהָ֑יִךְ
וְלֹ֤א פַחְדָּתִי֙ אֵלַ֔יִךְ
נְאֻם־אֲדֹנָ֥י יֱהֹוִ֖ה צְבָאֽוֹת׃
20 כִּ֤י מֵעוֹלָם֙ שָׁבַ֣רְתִּי עֻלֵּ֔ךְ
נִתַּ֖קְתִּי מוֹסְרוֹתַ֑יִךְ
וַתֹּאמְרִ֖י לֹ֣א אֶעֱב֑וֹד
כִּ֣י עַל־כָּל־גִּבְעָ֣ה גְּבֹהָ֗ה
וְתַ֙חַת֙ כָּל־עֵ֣ץ רַֽעֲנָ֔ן
אַ֖תְּ צֹעָ֥ה זֹנָֽה׃
21 וְאָֽנֹכִי֙ נְטַעְתִּ֣יךְ שׂוֹרֵ֔ק
כֻּלֹּ֖ה זֶ֣רַע אֱמֶ֑ת
וְאֵיךְ֙ נֶהְפַּ֣כְתְּ לִ֔י
סוּרֵ֖י הַגֶּ֥פֶן נָכְרִיָּֽה׃

v. 19.   v. 20. קמץ בז״ק   אעבור ק׳

results of these acts will show them the
folly of their ways.

My fear. i.e. fear of Me.

20. *I have broken . . not transgress.* If
this rendering is correct, the meaning is
that God had delivered Israel on various
occasions in the past, and after each of
them Israel had promised no more to
transgress His word (Rashi, Kimchi).
R.V. margin reads 'thou hast broken . . .
I will not serve' (*shabarti* and *nittakti*
are then the archaic forms of the second
person feminine and not the usual first
person singular, whilst the *kethib*, *eëbod*,
is retained). This is preferred by modern
commentators as being more in keeping
with the general tenor of the context.

high hill. The location of idolatrous
worship.

under every leafy tree. In whose shade
lewd rites were practised.

playing the harlot. The language is
metaphorical. Israel's infidelity to God,
to Whom he was espoused (cf. verse 2),
is likened to an act of adultery. There
is also an allusion to the gross immorality
which formed part of idolatrous cults.

21. *a noble vine, wholly a right seed.*
Israel was descended from Abraham;
from such seed good fruit might assuredly have been expected; cf. Isa. v. 1-7.

unto Me. To My sorrow.

22 For though thou wash thee with
    nitre,
   And take thee much soap,
   Yet thine iniquity is marked be-
    fore Me,
   Saith the Lord GOD.

23 How canst thou say: 'I am not
    defiled,
   I have not gone after the Baalim'?
   See thy way in the Valley,
   Know what thou hast done;
   Thou art a swift young camel
    traversing her ways;

24 A wild ass used to the wilderness,
   That snuffeth up the wind in her
    desire;
   Her lust, who can hinder it?
   All they that seek her will not
    weary themselves;
   In her month they shall find her.

25 Withhold thy foot from being
    unshod,
   And thy throat from thirst;

כִּי אִם־תְּכַבְּסִי בַּנֶּ֫תֶר 22
וְתַרְבִּי־לָךְ בֹּרִית
נִכְתָּם עֲוֺנֵךְ לְפָנַי
נְאֻם אֲדֹנָי יֱהֹוִה׃
אֵיךְ תֹּאמְרִי לֹא נִטְמֵאתִי 23
אַחֲרֵי הַבְּעָלִים לֹא הָלַכְתִּי
רְאִי דַרְכֵּךְ בַּגַּיְא
דְּעִי מֶה עָשִׂית
בִּכְרָה קַלָּה מְשָׂרֶכֶת דְּרָכֶֽיהָ׃
פֶּרֶא | לִמֻּד מִדְבָּר 24
בְּאַוַּת נַפְשָׁהּ שָׁאֲפָה רוּחַ
תַּאֲנָתָהּ מִי יְשִׁיבֶ֑נָּה
כָּל־מְבַקְשֶׁיהָ לֹא יִיעָ֑פוּ
בְּחָדְשָׁהּ יִמְצָאֽוּנְהָ׃
מִנְעִי רַגְלֵךְ מִיָּחֵף 25
וּגְרוֹנֵךְ מִצִּמְאָה

v. 24. נפשה ק׳   v. 25. וגרונך ק׳

---

22. Even though you perform righteousness outwardly, this does not conceal
from Me your secret iniquity (Metsudath
David).

nitre. The mineral alkali, natron, obtained from soda-lakes in Egypt.

soap. The Hebrew noun, *borith*, signifies a vegetable alkali.

marked. lit. 'stained,' indelibly.

23. *I have not gone . . . Valley.* Probably
in self-defence the Israelites maintained
that the rites they observed were performed in the service of God, not of the
false gods, Baalim. To this the prophet
retorts that by their horrible nature these
rites, which included human sacrifice

in the Valley of Hinnom (cf. vii. 31),
could be ascribed to nought else than the
cult of Baalim.

traversing her ways. lit. 'entangling her
ways': running hither and thither, cross-
ing and recrossing her own path, driven
by lust. So Israel eagerly sought one
god after another.

24. *a wild ass.* Cf. the description of
this animal in Job xxxix. 5-8, distinguished by refusal to be restrained.

will not weary . . . find her. In the month
of mating, her sires need not weary
themselves in seeking her; on the contrary, she eagerly seeks them out. Similarly Israel turns eagerly to idolatry.

25. *withhold . . . thirst.* Do not become

But thou saidst: 'There is no hope;
No, for I have loved strangers,
   and after them will I go.'
26 As the thief is ashamed when he
   is found,
   So is the house of Israel ashamed;
   They, their kings, their princes,
   And their priests, and their prophets;
27 Who say to a stock: 'Thou art my
   father,'
   And to a stone: 'Thou hast
   brought us forth,'
   For they have turned their back
   unto Me, and not their face;
   But in the time of their trouble
   they will say:
   'Arise, and save us.'
28 But where are thy gods that thou
   hast made thee?

וַתֹּאמְרִי נוֹאָשׁ
לוֹא כִּי־אָהַבְתִּי זָרִים
וְאַחֲרֵיהֶם אֵלֵךְ׃
26 כְּבֹשֶׁת גַּנָּב כִּי יִמָּצֵא
כֵּן הֹבִישׁוּ בֵּית יִשְׂרָאֵל
הֵמָּה מַלְכֵיהֶם שָׂרֵיהֶם
וְכֹהֲנֵיהֶם וּנְבִיאֵיהֶם׃
27 אֹמְרִים לָעֵץ אָבִי אַתָּה
וְלָאֶבֶן אַתְּ יְלִדְתָּנִי
כִּי־פָנוּ אֵלַי עֹרֶף וְלֹא פָנִים
וּבְעֵת רָעָתָם יֹאמְרוּ
קוּמָה וְהוֹשִׁיעֵנוּ׃
28 וְאַיֵּה אֱלֹהֶיךָ אֲשֶׁר עָשִׂיתָ לָּךְ

v. 27. ילדתנו ק׳

---

barefooted and parched, do not spend yourselves, in these pursuits. Rashi and Metsudath David explain: Do not persist in your idolatry, for which you will ultimately be punished by going into captivity unshod and parched.

there is no hope. Israel retorts that it is vain to try to turn him away from his chosen paths. He is determined to follow after strange gods.

26. *as the thief is ashamed when he is found.* The Targum and Kimchi render: 'as one is ashamed when he is found out as a thief, after having posed as an honest man.' Since the Hebrew term *gannab* denotes a professional thief, Ehrlich suggests that the verse describes the thief's disappointment rather than his shame on being caught. Instead of profiting, he suffers loss, because he has to restore what was stolen plus a fine of a fifth of, or double, its value (cf. Exod. xxi. 37, xxii. 3).

so is the house of Israel ashamed. Shame and confusion will cover them when they ultimately realize the folly of their ways. Kimchi renders: 'so should Israel have been ashamed of his evil ways.' On Ehrlich's explanation: the house of Israel suffers disappointment in experiencing loss instead of gain.

they. The masses.

their kings, etc. See on i. 18.

27. *stock . . . stone.* From which their idols are fashioned; or the reference may be to the sacred pole (*asherah*) and pillar (*matstsebah*) which were worshipped by idolaters.

thou art my father. Standing in relation to its devotee as guardian and protector.

they will say. To the true God; they will then understand the futility of the worship of idols, their helplessness to render aid in a crisis.

14

Let them arise, if they can save
  thee in the time of thy trouble;
For according to the number of
  thy cities
Are thy gods, O Judah.

29 Wherefore will ye contend with
  Me?
  Ye all have transgressed against
  Me,
  Saith the LORD.

30 In vain have I smitten your chil-
  dren—
  They received no correction;
  Your sword hath devoured your
  prophets,
  Like a destroying lion.

31 O generation, see ye the word of
  the LORD:
  Have I been a wilderness unto
  Israel?

יָקוּמוּ אִם־יוֹשִׁיעוּךָ
בְּעֵת רָעָתֶךָ
כִּי מִסְפַּר עָרֶיךָ
הָיוּ אֱלֹהֶיךָ יְהוּדָה׃

29 לָמָּה תָרִיבוּ אֵלָי
כֻּלְּכֶם פְּשַׁעְתֶּם בִּי
נְאֻם־יְהוָה׃

30 לַשָּׁוְא הִכֵּיתִי אֶת־בְּנֵיכֶם
מוּסָר לֹא לָקָחוּ
אָכְלָה חַרְבְּכֶם
נְבִיאֵיכֶם כְּאַרְיֵה מַשְׁחִית׃

31 הַדּוֹר אַתֶּם רְאוּ דְבַר־יְהוָה
הֲמִדְבָּר הָיִיתִי לְיִשְׂרָאֵל

28. *according to the number*, etc. 'You have so many!' is God's ironical reply. 'In May, 1929, two French archæologists, MM. Schaeffer and Chenet, in digging among the ruins of Ras Shamra in North Syria opposite the island of Cyprus, came across some clay tablets inscribed with a new kind of cuneiform writing . . . These tablets indicate that some fifty gods, and half as many goddesses, were particularly associated with Ras Shamra. This abundance of deities recalls the bitter taunt made by Jeremiah, the prophet, many centuries later, to the Jews: *According to the number of thy cities are thy gods, O Judah*' (Marston). The phrase is repeated in xi. 13.

29. *contend*. Why do you expostulate and complain that I desert you in your crisis, seeing that you rebel against Me? (Kimchi).

30. *in vain . . . correction.* God's punishment has been of no avail; they refused to be instructed.

your prophets. The true messengers of God to be distinguished from the false prophets mentioned in verse 26. Rashi and Metsudath David comment: This alludes to Zechariah the son of Jehoiada (cf. 2 Chron. xxiv. 20f.) and Isaiah (who, according to tradition, suffered a martyr's death in the reign of Manasseh).

31 37   THREATENED PUNISHMENT
OF ISRAEL

31. *see ye the word of the LORD.* Take note of it; pay heed to it.

have I been a wilderness unto Israel? Have I failed to provide for his needs?

Or a land of thick darkness?
Wherefore say My people: 'We
   roam at large;
We will come no more unto
   Thee'?

32 Can a maid forget her ornaments,
Or a bride her attire?
Yet My people have forgotten
   Me
Days without number.

33 How trimmest thou thy way
To seek love!
Therefore—even the wicked
   women
Hast thou taught thy ways;

34 Also in thy skirts is found the
   blood
Of the souls of the innocent poor;
Thou didst not find them break-
   ing in;
Yet for all these things

אִם־אֶרֶץ מַאְפֵּלְיָה
מַדּוּעַ אָמְרוּ עַמִּי רַדְנוּ
לוֹא־נָבוֹא עוֹד אֵלֶיךָ׃
הֲתִשְׁכַּח בְּתוּלָה עֶדְיָהּ 32
כַּלָּה קִשֻּׁרֶיהָ
וְעַמִּי שְׁכֵחוּנִי
יָמִים אֵין מִסְפָּר׃
מַה־תֵּיטִבִי דַּרְכֵּךְ 33
לְבַקֵּשׁ אַהֲבָה
לָכֵן גַּם אֶת־הָרָעוֹת
לִמַּדְתִּי אֶת־דְּרָכָיִךְ׃
גַּם בִּכְנָפַיִךְ נִמְצְאוּ דַּם 34
נַפְשׁוֹת אֶבְיוֹנִים נְקִיִּים
לֹא־בַמַּחְתֶּרֶת מְצָאתִים
כִּי עַל־כָּל־אֵלֶּה׃

v. 31.   v. 33. טעמים ב׳ למדת ק׳

thick darkness. Hebrew *mapelyah*, lit.
'darkness of the Lord,' like *shalhebethyah*,
a very flame of the LORD (Cant. viii. 6).
God did not leave Israel to grope in the
dark without guidance.

we roam at large. At our own sweet will,
declining to accept direction from God.

32. *attire.* The noun *kishshurim* occurs
in Isa. iii. 20 where it is translated
sashes. It denotes the girdle worn by a
bride to mark her status as a married
woman.

have forgotten Me. Though I am as
indispensable to Israel, and indeed the
Source of his glory (cf. verse 11), as are
these adornments to a maid or bride.

33. *how trimmest thou thy way.* lit. 'how
makest thou thy way good,' i.e. how you

carefully plan your way to achieve your
evil object.

therefore. Better, 'verily'; the Hebrew
lachen introduces an oath of affirmation,
explains Rashi.

even the wicked . . . ways. Thou art a
master in wickedness even to the wicked.
Peake renders: 'therefore to evil things
thou hast accustomed thy ways.'

34. *of the souls.* i.e. the persons.

thou didst, etc. This translation construes the verb *metsathim* as the poetic
form of the second person singular, not
the usual first person.

breaking in. Which might have justified
an act of homicide (cf. Exod. xxii. 1).

yet for all these things. If this rendering

35 Thou saidst: 'I am innocent;
    Surely His anger is turned away
        from me'—
    Behold, I will enter into judg-
        ment with thee,
    Because thou sayest: 'I have not
        sinned.'
36 How greatly dost thou cheapen
        thyself
    To change thy way?
    Thou shalt be ashamed of Egypt
        also,
    As thou wast ashamed of Asshur.
37 From him also shalt thou go
        forth,
    With thy hands upon thy head;
    For the Lord hath rejected them
        in whom thou didst trust,
    And thou shalt not prosper in
        them.

35 וַתֹּאמְרִי֙ כִּי נִקֵּ֔יתִי
אַ֛ךְ שָׁ֥ב אַפּ֖וֹ מִמֶּ֑נִּי
הִנְנִי֙ נִשְׁפָּ֣ט אוֹתָ֔ךְ
עַל־אָמְרֵ֖ךְ לֹ֥א חָטָֽאתִי׃
36 מַה־תֵּזְלִ֥י מְאֹ֖ד
לְשַׁנּ֣וֹת אֶת־דַּרְכֵּ֑ךְ
גַּ֤ם מִמִּצְרַ֙יִם֙ תֵּב֔וֹשִׁי
כַּאֲשֶׁ֥ר בֹּ֖שְׁתְּ מֵאַשּֽׁוּר׃
37 גַּ֣ם מֵאֵ֥ת זֶה֙ תֵּֽצְאִ֔י
וְיָדַ֖יִךְ עַל־רֹאשֵׁ֑ךְ
כִּֽי־מָאַ֤ס יְהֹוָה֙ בְּמִבְטַחַ֔יִךְ
וְלֹ֥א תַצְלִ֖יחִי לָהֶֽם׃

is correct, the clause has to be connected with the next verse, as in A.J. (so also Kimchi). R.V. has 'I have not found it at the place of breaking in, but upon all these'; the meaning is: I did not find their blood in a hidden place (where a thief might attempt to break in), which would have indicated that you were ashamed of your misdeeds, but upon your garments (*thy skirts*), openly flaunted (Metsudath David).

35. *thou saidst.* Or, 'yet thou saidst' (R.V.).

surely His anger, etc. All is well with me: this proves my innocence, since I evidently enjoy God's favour.

36. *how greatly dost thou cheapen . . . way?* Another proposed translation is: 'Why makest thou so light of changing thy way?'

to change thy way. To forsake God and seek help from Egypt (Rashi). Or, ever seeking different allies, now Egypt, now Assyria (Kimchi).

thou shalt be ashamed of Egypt also. i.e. disappointed in Egypt who will prove treacherous; for the fulfilment of this prophecy, cf. xxxvii. 5.

as thou wast ashamed of Asshur. This occurred in the reign of Ahaz, who stripped the Temple and his own palace of their treasures in order to enlist the help of the king of Assyria, but with the opposite result (cf. 2 Chron. xxviii. 20).

37. *him.* The king of Egypt.

shalt thou go forth. Empty-handed at a time when his help is required.

with thy hands upon thy head. In shame and lamentation (cf. 2 Sam. xiii. 19).

3   CHAPTER III   ג

1   . . . saying:
If a man put away his wife,
And she go from him,
And become another man's,
May he return unto her again?
Will not that land be greatly pol
   luted?
But thou hast played the harlot
   with many lovers;
And wouldest thou yet return to
   Me?
Saith the LORD.
2 Lift up thine eyes unto the high
   hills, and see:
Where hast thou not been lain
   with?
By the ways hast thou sat for
   them,
	1 לֵאמֹר
	הֵן יְשַׁלַּח אִישׁ אֶת־אִשְׁתּוֹ
	וְהָלְכָה מֵאִתּוֹ
	וְהָיְתָה לְאִישׁ־אַחֵר
	הֲיָשׁוּב אֵלֶיהָ עוֹד
	הֲלוֹא חָנוֹף תֶּחֱנַף
	הָאָרֶץ הַהִיא
	וְאַתְּ זָנִית רֵעִים רַבִּים
	וְשׁוֹב אֵלַי
	נְאֻם־יְהוָה:
	2 שְׂאִי עֵינַיִךְ עַל־שְׁפָיִם וּרְאִי
	אֵיפֹה לֹא שֻׁגַּלְתְּ
	עַל־דְּרָכִים יָשַׁבְתְּ לָהֶם

שכבת ק׳   v. 2.

CHAPTER III

1-5 THE CONSEQUENCE OF INFIDELITY

1. *saying*. Modern commentators either delete the word or hold that an introductory clause, such as 'and the Lord spake unto me,' has dropped out; but M.T. is supported by the Targum. Kimchi connects *saying* with *the LORD hath rejected them*, etc., in the preceding verse.

may he return unto her again? Remarriage in these circumstances is forbidden by the Mosaic legislation (cf. Deut. xxiv. 1-4).

will not . . . polluted? As stated in Deut. xxiv. 4.

played the harlot. Deserted God for numerous idolatrous forms of worship.

and wouldest thou yet return to Me? According to this translation the meaning is: Israel must definitely decide his allegiance once and for all; he cannot play fast and loose with his loyalties. Yet, though this seems the most natural rendering and fits in best with the next verse, it apparently contradicts the urgent pleas of Jeremiah (as, indeed, of all prophets) that, no matter how deeply Israel has sunk, he should repent and return to God. A.V. and R.V. therefore seem preferable: 'yet return again to Me'; in spite of everything, God is ready to receive the people back, although this would be unlawful in marital relationship (so Rashi and Metsudath David).

2. *high hills*. See on ii. 20.

by the ways, etc. Like a harlot to lure men (cf. Gen. xxxviii. 14; Prov. vii. 12).

As an Arabian in the wilderness;
And thou hast polluted the land
With thy harlotries and with thy
    wickedness.
3 Therefore the showers have been
    withheld,
And there hath been no latter
    rain;
Yet thou hadst a harlot's forehead,
Thou refusedst to be ashamed.
4 Didst thou not just now cry unto
    Me: 'My father,
Thou art the friend of my youth.
5 Will He bear grudge for ever?
Will He keep it to the end?'
Behold, thou hast spoken, but hast
    done evil things,
And hast had thy way.
6. And the LORD said unto me in
the days of Josiah the king: 'Hast

כְּעַרְבִי בַּמִּדְבָּר
וַתַּחֲנִיפִי אֶרֶץ
בִּזְנוּתַיִךְ וּבְרָעָתֵךְ׃
3 וַיִּמָּנְעוּ רְבִבִים
וּמַלְקוֹשׁ לוֹא הָיָה
וּמֵצַח אִשָּׁה זוֹנָה הָיָה לָךְ
מֵאַנְתְּ הִכָּלֵם׃
4 הֲלוֹא מֵעַתָּה קָרָאתי לִי אָבִי
אַלּוּף נְעֻרַי אָתָּה׃
5 הֲיִנְטֹר לְעוֹלָם
אִם־יִשְׁמֹר לָנֶצַח
הִנֵּה דִבַּרְתְּ
וַתַּעֲשִׂי הָרָעוֹת וַתּוּכָל׃
6 וַיֹּאמֶר יְהוָֹה אֵלַי בִּימֵי יֹאשִׁיָּהוּ

v. 4. יתיר י׳

as an Arabian in the wilderness. Being out in the open, he is ready to meet any caravans or passers-by. So is Israel eager to embrace every form of idolatry.

3. *the showers.* Perhaps the opposite of *the latter rain,* and therefore equivalent to *the former rain* in Deut. xi. 14, which is the heavy rains that occur about the end of October (so Kimchi).

latter rain. Which falls during March and April.

a harlot's forehead. Brazen and shameless.

4. The meaning of A.J. is: You have only just been appealing to Me, protesting your affection for Me, and asserting your confidence that the forgiving God will not always be angry; yet you are already forsaking Me again. But A.V. (following

Rashi) is preferable: 'Wilt thou not from this time cry unto Me, 'My father . . . youth?' The prophet appeals to Israel to acknowledge God even at this late hour, and gives the assurance that He will surely not retain His anger for ever. Yet even as he makes this appeal, he sadly adds that the people have demonstrated their will to persist in their wickedness.

5. *thou hast spoken.* The words which precede, testifying to the beneficence of God which had been manifested to Israel.

and hast had thy way. lit. 'and hast been able.' Perhaps the meaning is 'and hast prevailed' (as in Gen. xxxii. 29) in evil.

6-13   THE GUILT OF JUDAH

6. *in the days of Josiah.* For the years of his reign, see on i. 2. As the Northern

thou seen that which backsliding Israel did? she went up upon every high mountain and under every leafy tree, and there played the harlot. 7. And I said: After she hath done all these things, she will return unto Me; but she returned not. And her treacherous sister Judah saw it. 8. And I saw, when, forasmuch as backsliding Israel had committed adultery, I had put her away and given her a bill of divorcement, that yet treacherous Judah her sister feared not; but she also went and played the harlot; 9. and it came to pass through the lightness of her harlotry, that the land was polluted, and she committed adultery with stones and with stocks; 10. and yet for all this her treacherous sister Judah hath not returned unto Me

הַמֶּלֶךְ הֲרָאִיתָ אֲשֶׁר עָשְׂתָה
מְשֻׁבָה יִשְׂרָאֵל הֹלְכָה הִיא
עַל־כָּל־הַר גָּבֹהַּ וְאֶל־תַּחַת
כָּל־עֵץ רַעֲנָן וַתִּזְנִי־שָׁם:
7 וָאֹמַר אַחֲרֵי עֲשׂוֹתָהּ אֶת־כָּל־
אֵלֶּה אֵלַי תָּשׁוּב וְלֹא־שָׁבָה
וַתֵּרֶא בָּגוֹדָה אֲחוֹתָהּ
8 יְהוּדָה: וָאֵרֶא כִּי עַל־כָּל־
אֹדוֹת אֲשֶׁר נִאֲפָה מְשֻׁבָה
יִשְׂרָאֵל שִׁלַּחְתִּיהָ וָאֶתֵּן אֶת־
סֵפֶר כְּרִיתֻתֶיהָ אֵלֶיהָ וְלֹא
יָרְאָה בֹּגֵדָה יְהוּדָה אֲחוֹתָהּ
9 וַתֵּלֶךְ וַתִּזֶן גַּם־הִיא: וְהָיָה
מִקֹּל זְנוּתָהּ וַתֶּחֱנַף אֶת־
הָאָרֶץ וַתִּנְאַף אֶת־הָאֶבֶן
10 וְאֶת־הָעֵץ: וְגַם־בְּכָל־זֹאת
לֹא־שָׁבָה אֵלַי בָּגוֹדָה אֲחוֹתָהּ

v. 7. ותרא ק'

Kingdom was overthrown and destroyed in 722 B.C.E., Israel had by then been in exile nearly a hundred years.

Israel. i.e. the ten tribes of the north. *Backsliding Israel* is lit. 'apostasy Israel,' as if Israel were the embodiment of that sin.

she went up, etc. Cf. ii. 20.

7. *and I said.* I hoped that, in spite of all Israel's sinning, he would return to Me. God is not only ever ready, but anxious, to receive the penitent. Jeremiah's intense conviction of this truth leads him to represent even God as mistaken in His hopes. The prophet is here the teacher of his people rather than the pedantic theologian, and does not concern himself with such questions as God's omniscience and foreknowledge.

saw it. This is the translation of the *kethib* (*watirëhah*); the *kerë* is simply 'saw.'

8. *given her a bill of divorcement.* Sent the people into captivity in Assyria.

9. *the lightness of her harlotry.* i.e. she thought lightly of such infidelity to God (so the Targum).

the land was polluted. More lit. 'she was polluted with the land.'

with stones and with stocks. See on ii. 27.

with her whole heart, but feignedly, saith the LORD—11. even the LORD said unto me—backsliding Israel hath proved herself more righteous than treacherous Judah. 12. Go, and proclaim these words toward the north, and say:

Return, thou backsliding Israel,
Saith the LORD;
I will not frown upon you;
For I am merciful, saith the LORD,
I will not bear grudge for ever.

13 Only acknowledge thine iniquity,
That thou hast transgressed against the LORD thy God,
And hast scattered thy ways to the strangers
Under every leafy tree,
And ye have not hearkened to My voice,
Saith the LORD.

יְהוּדָה בְּכָל־לִבָּהּ כִּי אִם־
11 בְּשֶׁקֶר נְאֻם־יְהֹוָה׃ וַיֹּאמֶר
יְהֹוָה אֵלַי צִדְּקָה נַפְשָׁהּ מְשֻׁבָה
12 יִשְׂרָאֵל מִבֹּגֵדָה יְהוּדָה׃ הָלֹךְ
וְקָרֵאתָ אֶת־הַדְּבָרִים הָאֵלֶּה
צָפוֹנָה וְאָמַרְתָּ
שׁוּבָה מְשֻׁבָה יִשְׂרָאֵל
נְאֻם־יְהֹוָה
לוֹא־אַפִּיל פָּנַי בָּכֶם
כִּי־חָסִיד אֲנִי נְאֻם־יְהֹוָה
לֹא אֶטּוֹר לְעוֹלָם׃
13 אַךְ דְּעִי עֲוֹנֵךְ
כִּי בַּיהֹוָה אֱלֹהַיִךְ פָּשָׁעַתְּ
וַתְּפַזְּרִי אֶת־דְּרָכַיִךְ לַזָּרִים
תַּחַת כָּל־עֵץ רַעֲנָן
וּבְקוֹלִי לֹא־שְׁמַעְתֶּם
נְאֻם־יְהֹוָה׃

10. with her whole heart, but feignedly. A great religious reform took place during the reign of Josiah, and an earnest endeavour was made to stamp out idolatry (cf. 2 Kings xxiii). Nevertheless, as appears from this verse, the people were not sincere in their conversion.

11. more righteous. Either, by comparison (Kimchi); or, since the Kingdom of Israel did not have the example of punishment before their eyes, as did Judah in the destruction of the ten tribes (Rashi).

12. toward the north. i.e. Assyria, whither the ten tribes had been deported.

I will not frown. lit. 'I will not cause My face to fall,' paraphrased by R.V. as 'I will not look in anger upon you.'

13. only acknowledge thine iniquity. Admission of sin must be the first step to repentance and recovery of God's favour.

and hast scattered thy ways. The phrase is usually understood as a variant of *traversing her ways* (ii. 23). But, as Ehrlich points out, the verb *pizzer* signifies 'to spend lavishly' (cf. Ps. cxii. 9; Prov. xi. 24), and he explains: thou wast free with thy love for strange gods.

14. Return, O backsliding children, saith the LORD; for I am a lord unto you, and I will take you one of a city, and two of a family, and I will bring you to Zion; 15. and I will give you shepherds according to My heart, who shall feed you with knowledge and understanding. 16. And it shall come to pass, when ye are multiplied and increased in the land, in those days, saith the LORD, they shall say no more: The ark of the covenant of the LORD; neither shall it come to mind; neither shall they make mention of it; neither shall they miss it; neither shall it be made any more. 17. At that time they shall call Jerusalem The throne of the LORD; and all the nations shall be gathered unto it, to the name of the

14 שׁוּבוּ בָנִים שׁוֹבָבִים נְאֻם־
יְהֹוָה כִּי אָנֹכִי בָּעַלְתִּי בָכֶם
וְלָקַחְתִּי אֶתְכֶם אֶחָד מֵעִיר
וּשְׁנַיִם מִמִּשְׁפָּחָה וְהֵבֵאתִי
15 אֶתְכֶם צִיּוֹן: וְנָתַתִּי לָכֶם
רֹעִים כְּלִבִּי וְרָעוּ אֶתְכֶם דֵּעָה
16 וְהַשְׂכֵּיל: וְהָיָה כִּי תִרְבּוּ
וּפְרִיתֶם בָּאָרֶץ בַּיָּמִים הָהֵמָּה
נְאֻם־יְהֹוָה לֹא־יֹאמְרוּ עוֹד
אֲרוֹן בְּרִית־יְהֹוָה וְלֹא יַעֲלֶה
עַל־לֵב וְלֹא יִזְכְּרוּ־בוֹ וְלֹא
17 יִפְקֹדוּ וְלֹא יֵעָשֶׂה עוֹד: בָּעֵת
הַהִיא יִקְרְאוּ לִירוּשָׁלַם כִּסֵּא
יְהֹוָה וְנִקְווּ אֵלֶיהָ כָל־הַגּוֹיִם

14-18 EXHORTATION TO REPENTANCE

14. *children . . . I am a lord.* The verb *baalti* is derived from the noun *baal* which means both 'lord' and 'husband'; R.V. 'I am a husband.' 'The confusion is only verbal, and the twofold relationship gives a double certainty of acceptance. As children they were sure of a father's love, as a wife they might hope for a revival of past affection from the husband of their youth' (Payne Smith).

one of a city, and two of a family. Family probably signifies here 'a clan,' hence a larger group than a city (see on i. 15 and cf. viii. 3, xxv. 9 where the term obviously means whole tribes or peoples). The intention is: even if only a very small number repent, God will not let them be swallowed up in the exile, but bring them back to Zion.

15. *shepherds.* See on ii. 8.

16. *in those days.* When a new covenant is made by God with the people.

they shall say no more: The Ark, etc. The city of Jerusalem as a whole will be filled with the Divine Presence, so that the ark will lose its special significance.

neither shall it be made any more. A tangible and visible symbol of God's Presence will no longer be necessary. Metsudath David comments: Though you be multiplied and increased, you will not arouse the envy of your neighbours, so that there will be no need for you to come and pray before the ark of the Lord for protection; such a petition will never be thought of again. Kimchi's interpretation is somewhat similar.

17. *The throne of the LORD.* Jerusalem, as the centre of God's kingdom and of

LORD, to Jerusalem; neither shall
they walk any more after the stubbornness of their evil heart. 18. In
those days the house of Judah shall
walk with the house of Israel, and
they shall come together out of the
land of the north to the land that I
have given for an inheritance unto
your fathers.'

19 But I said: 'How would I put
    thee among the sons,
And give thee a pleasant land,
The goodliest heritage of the
    nations!'
And I said: 'Thou shalt call Me,
    My father;
And shalt not turn away from
    following Me.'
20 Surely as a wife treacherously
    departeth from her husband,

לְשֵׁם יְהֹוָה לִירוּשָׁלִַם וְלֹא־
יֵלְכוּ עוֹד אַחֲרֵי שְׁרִרוּת לִבָּם
הָרָע׃ 18 בַּיָּמִים הָהֵמָּה יֵלְכוּ
בֵית־יְהוּדָה עַל־בֵּית
יִשְׂרָאֵל וְיָבֹאוּ יַחְדָּו מֵאֶרֶץ
צָפוֹן עַל־הָאָרֶץ אֲשֶׁר
הִנְחַלְתִּי אֶת־אֲבוֹתֵיכֶם׃
19 וְאָנֹכִי אָמַרְתִּי
אֵיךְ אֲשִׁיתֵךְ בַּבָּנִים
וְאֶתֶּן־לָךְ אֶרֶץ חֶמְדָּה
נַחֲלַת צְבִי צִבְאוֹת גּוֹיִם
וָאֹמַר אָבִי תִּקְרְאִו־לִי
וּמֵאַחֲרַי לֹא תָשׁוּבוּ׃
20 אָכֵן בָּגְדָה אִשָּׁה מֵרֵעָהּ

v. 19. תקראי ק'   v. 19. תשובי ק'

His worship, will take the place of the
ark, and all peoples will be attracted to it.

18. The reunion of Israel and Judah was
the fervent dream and hope of the prophets, both before their overthrow and
after (cf. ii. 4; Isa. xi. 12; Ezek. xxxvii.
16ff.; Hos. ii. 2).

19-20 THE PEOPLE FRUSTRATED GOD'S
      HOPES FOR THEM

19. *but I said.* Better, 'now I had said.'
The verse describes God's intentions
and hopes concerning Judah which,
however, were not realized.

among the sons. God would single Judah
out from among His other sons, viz. the
other nations. The words, incidentally,
assert the universality of God's Fatherhood. The verse is differently explained
by modern commentators. Judah is

referred to in this verse in the feminine.
'According to Hebrew law, daughters
were usually unable to inherit. Judah,
addressed as a daughter, could claim no
right to receive Divine mercy, yet
figuratively she will be regarded as
worthy of a son's portion. God is
gracious ' (Pickering).

the goodliest heritage of the nations.
Judah's heritage would be outstandingly
glorious, by having the Divine Presence
specially manifest in it (Metsudath
David).

and I said. Better, 'and I had said,'
a continuation of the first words of the
sentence.

thou shalt call Me, My father. Cf. verse 4.

20. *surely.* Better, 'but surely', 'but in
truth': the contrast between God's hopes
and what actually happened.

23

So have ye dealt treacherously
with Me, O house of Israel,
Saith the LORD.

21 Hark! upon the high hills is heard
The suppliant weeping of the
children of Israel;
For that they have perverted their
way,
They have forgotten the LORD
their God.

22 Return, ye backsliding children,
I will heal your backslidings.—
'Here we are, we are come unto
Thee;
For Thou art the LORD our God.

23 Truly vain have proved the hills,
The uproar on the mountains;
Truly in the LORD our God
Is the salvation of Israel.

24 But the shameful thing hath devoured

כֵּן בְּגַדְתֶּם בִּי
בֵּית יִשְׂרָאֵל נְאֻם־יְהֹוָה:

21 קוֹל עַל־שְׁפָיִים נִשְׁמָע
בְּכִי תַחֲנוּנֵי בְּנֵי יִשְׂרָאֵל
כִּי הֶעֱווּ אֶת־דַּרְכָּם
שָׁכְחוּ אֶת־יְהֹוָה אֱלֹהֵיהֶם:

22 שׁוּבוּ בָּנִים שׁוֹבָבִים
אֶרְפָּה מְשׁוּבֹתֵיכֶם
הִנְנוּ אָתָנוּ לָךְ
כִּי אַתָּה יְהֹוָה אֱלֹהֵינוּ:

23 אָכֵן לַשֶּׁקֶר
מִגְּבָעוֹת הָמוֹן הָרִים
אָכֵן בַּיהֹוָה אֱלֹהֵינוּ
תְּשׁוּעַת יִשְׂרָאֵל:

24 וְהַבֹּשֶׁת אָכְלָה

v. 21. קמץ בז״ק v. 22. כצ״ל

---

house of Israel. This signifies the whole
nation, including Judah.

21-25 ISRAEL'S REMORSE

A picture of the nation's repentance
and confession of sin. This is either a
description of what ought to happen
(Kimchi); or perhaps the prophet here
gives utterance to his conviction of
Israel's ultimate repentance, no matter
how unpropitious the signs in the present.

21. *the high hills.* The same place where
God had been faithlessly forsaken for
idolatry (verse 2). 'The scene of her
idolatry is the scene also of her penitence'
(Peake).

22. *return, ye backsliding children.* The
Hebrew words, though diametrical oppo-
sites, are similar, and the idea conveyed

is: instead of being *shobabim* (*backsliding*),
let them be *shabim* (penitents).

here we are, etc. The eager response of
the people to the call to return.

23. *the hills . . . mountains.* Idolatry,
practised on the hills and mountains, has
been proved vain and futile.

the uproar (*hamon*). The wild orgies
which accompanied idol-worship. It
may perhaps refer to the 'multitudes'
worshipping on the mountains (Kimchi).
Metsudath David explains similarly,
but relates 'multitudes' to the idols,
i.e. the numerous images worshipped
there.

24. *the shameful thing.* viz. Baal-worship, idolatry (cf. Hos. ix. 10).

hath devoured, etc. As a punishment for

The labour of our fathers from
our youth;
Their flocks and their herds,
Their sons and their daughters.

25 Let us lie down in our shame,
And let our confusion cover us;
For we have sinned against the
LORD our God,
We and our fathers,
From our youth even unto this
day;
And we have not hearkened
To the voice of the LORD our
God.'

אֶת־יְגִיעַ אֲבוֹתֵינוּ מִנְּעוּרֵינוּ
אֶת־צֹאנָם וְאֶת־בְּקָרָם
אֶת־בְּנֵיהֶם וְאֶת־בְּנוֹתֵיהֶם׃
25 נִשְׁכְּבָה בְּבָשְׁתֵּנוּ
וּתְכַסֵּנוּ כְּלִמָּתֵנוּ
כִּי לַיהוָֹה אֱלֹהֵינוּ חָטָאנוּ
אֲנַחְנוּ וַאֲבוֹתֵינוּ
מִנְּעוּרֵינוּ וְעַד־הַיּוֹם הַזֶּה
וְלֹא שָׁמַעְנוּ
בְּקוֹל יְהוָֹה אֱלֹהֵינוּ׃

---

4   CHAPTER IV   ד

1 If thou wilt return, O Israel,
Saith the LORD,
Yea, return unto Me;
And if thou wilt put away thy
detestable things out of My
sight,
And wilt not waver;

1 אִם־תָּשׁוּב יִשְׂרָאֵל ׀
נְאֻם־יְהוָֹה
אֵלַי תָּשׁוּב
וְאִם־תָּסִיר שִׁקּוּצֶיךָ
מִפָּנַי וְלֹא תָנוּד׃

---

idolatry we and our fathers have lost all
our possessions; or these had been
sacrificed to Baal.

their sons and their daughters. Cf. v. 17.
It possibly alludes to human sacrifice.

25. *let us lie down in our shame.* Perhaps
on the ground in remorse (cf. 2 Sam. xii.
16, xiii. 31).

let our confusion cover us. So intense will
the feeling of shame be that it will appear
to enshroud us; cf. *and shall put on their
own shame as a robe* (Ps. cix. 29).

CHAPTER IV

1-4 THE CONSEQUENCE OF REPENTANCE

1. *return . . . return.* If you will return
(repent) and confess your guilt (this is a
continuation of iii. 22-25), then you will
return to your former splendour and
be My people once more (Rashi, Metsudath David).

detestable things. Idolatrous worship
and impure rites.

waver. Wander away from God. A.V.,
following Rashi and Kimchi, renders:

2 And wilt swear: 'As the LORD
liveth'
In truth, in justice, and in righteousness;
Then shall the nations bless themselves by Him,
And in Him shall they glory.

3 For thus saith the LORD to the
men of Judah and to Jerusalem:
Break up for you a fallow ground,
And sow not among thorns.

4 Circumcise yourselves to the LORD,
And take away the foreskins of
your heart,
Ye men of Judah and inhabitants
of Jerusalem;
Lest My fury go forth like fire,

² וְנִשְׁבַּעְתָּ חַי־יְהֹוָה
בֶּאֱמֶת בְּמִשְׁפָּט וּבִצְדָקָה
וְהִתְבָּרְכוּ בוֹ
גּוֹיִם וּבוֹ יִתְהַלָּלוּ׃

³ כִּי־כֹה ׀ אָמַר יְהֹוָה
לְאִישׁ יְהוּדָה וְלִירוּשָׁלַַם
נִירוּ לָכֶם נִיר
וְאַל־תִּזְרְעוּ אֶל־קוֹצִים׃

⁴ הִמֹּלוּ לַיהֹוָה
וְהָסִרוּ עָרְלוֹת לְבַבְכֶם
אִישׁ יְהוּדָה וְיֹשְׁבֵי יְרוּשָׁלָָם
פֶּן־תֵּצֵא כָאֵשׁ חֲמָתִי

'then shalt thou not remove', i.e. wander
into captivity. But A.J. correctly construes the clause as still governed by the
introductory *if* and part of the protasis.

2. *and wilt swear.* When the necessity
arises. The phrase does not advocate
swearing, even by the name of God.

as the LORD liveth. Swearing by the
Lord (and not by an idol) implied sincere
allegiance to Him (cf. Deut. vi. 13).

in truth, etc. Otherwise the oath would
be blasphemous. The Rabbis interpret:
Only when a man has truth, justice and
righteousness is he worthy of swearing
by the name of God.

then shall the nations, etc. Israel's genuine repentance will by force of example
lead the other nations also to God. While
Judaism does not advocate active prosely-
tization, it does look forward to the time
when all peoples, spontaneously and of
their own accord, will acknowledge Him
(cf. Isa. ii. 3, lxv. 16).

3. *break up.* Cf. Hos. x. 12. 'The
ground of their heart is hard. It needs,
as it were, the plough and the harrow.
Moreover, it is overgrown with thorns.
These must be removed' (Streane).

and sow not among thorns. First abandon
your wickedness and idolatry, and then
approach Me in prayer. The metaphor
is taken from real life. 'These farmers
all need the exhortation of Jeremiah. . . .
They are too apt to neglect this, and the
thorns, springing up, choke the seed, so
that it cannot come to maturity' (Thomson).

4. *circumcise . . . your heart.* Remove the
hard excrescence which has grown over
your heart and prevents you from being
influenced by God's exhortations (cf.
Deut. x. 16).

*ye men of Judah and inhabitants of Jeru-
salem.* Ryder Smith suggests that the
inhabitants of Jerusalem, as city dwellers,
formed a distinct class within Judah.

And burn that none can quench it,
Because of the evil of your doings.

5 Declare ye in Judah, and publish
in Jerusalem,
And say: 'Blow ye the horn in the
land';
Cry aloud and say:
'Assemble yourselves, and let us
go into the fortified cities.'

6 Set up a standard toward Zion;
Put yourselves under covert, stay
not;
For I will bring evil from the
north,
And a great destruction.

7 A lion is gone up from his thicket,
And a destroyer of nations

וּבָעֲרָה וְאֵין מְכַבֶּה
מִפְּנֵי רֹעַ מַעַלְלֵיכֶם:
5 הַגִּידוּ בִיהוּדָה
וּבִירוּשָׁלַ͏ִם הַשְׁמִיעוּ
וְאִמְרוּ וְתִקְעוּ שׁוֹפָר בָּאָרֶץ
קִרְאוּ מַלְאוּ וְאִמְרוּ
הֵאָסְפוּ וְנָבוֹאָה
אֶל־עָרֵי הַמִּבְצָר:
6 שְׂאוּ־נֵס צִיּוֹנָה
הָעִיזוּ אַל־תַּעֲמֹדוּ
כִּי רָעָה אָנֹכִי
מֵבִיא מִצָּפוֹן וְשֶׁבֶר גָּדוֹל:
7 עָלָה אַרְיֵה מִסֻּבְּכוֹ
וּמַשְׁחִית גּוֹיִם

v. 5. תקעו ק׳   v. 5. המ׳ בפתח

5-31 JUDGMENT IMMINENT UPON JUDAH
A picture of the impending disaster.
Flight to the protection of the walled
cities; terror and dismay spread over the
land; the enemy swoops down on the
doomed country; the prophet's grief at
the horror of it all, particularly as it is
occasioned by the people's insensate
folly; a graphic vision of the earth waste
and void reeling under God's anger;
Zion cries out in the extremity of her
distress. This and the prophecies in the
following chapters may have been written
with reference either to the Scythian
(c. 625 B.C.E.) or the Babylonian invasion.
The latter is more probable; see on
verse 7.

5. declare ye. The danger is at hand;
warn the people to take refuge in the
fortified cities.

blow ye the horn. The signal of danger
and alarm (cf. Amos. iii. 6).

cry aloud. lit. 'cry, fill,' i.e. cry out with
the fulness of your strength.

let us go, etc. Streane quotes as a
parallel the crowding of the inhabitants
of Attica within the walls of Athens on
the occasion of a Spartan invasion.

6. *set up a standard.* As a signpost.

toward Zion. To guide the fleeing refugees. *Zion* here denotes the city of
Jerusalem.

put yourselves under covert. The verb
hëiz means 'to bring one's family, or
possessions, to a place of safety' (cf.
Exod. ix. 19).

7. *a lion.* A designation for Nebuchadnezzar, king of Babylon.

a destroyer of nations. The words

Is set out, gone forth from his
place;
To make thy land desolate,
That thy cities be laid waste, without inhabitant.

8 For this gird you with sackcloth,
Lament and wail;
For the fierce anger of the LORD
Is not turned back from us.

9 And it shall come to pass at that
day,
Saith the LORD,
That the heart of the king shall
fail,
And the heart of the princes;
And the priests shall be astonished,
And the prophets shall wonder.

10. Then said I: 'Ah, Lord GOD!
surely Thou hast greatly deceived
this people and Jerusalem, saying:
Ye shall have peace; whereas the

נָסַע יָצָא מִמְּקֹמוֹ
לָשׂוּם אַרְצֵךְ לְשַׁמָּה
עָרַיִךְ תִּצֶּינָה מֵאֵין יוֹשֵׁב׃
8 עַל־זֹאת חִגְרוּ שַׂקִּים
סִפְדוּ וְהֵילִילוּ
כִּי לֹא־שָׁב
חֲרוֹן אַף־יְהֹוָה מִמֶּנּוּ׃
9 וְהָיָה בַיּוֹם־הַהוּא
נְאֻם־יְהֹוָה
יֹאבַד לֵב־הַמֶּלֶךְ
וְלֵב הַשָּׂרִים
וְנָשַׁמּוּ הַכֹּהֲנִים
וְהַנְּבִיאִים יִתְמָהוּ׃
10 וָאֹמַר אֲהָהּ ׀ אֲדֹנָי יְהֹוִה אָכֵן
הַשֵּׁא הִשֵּׁאתָ לָעָם הַזֶּה
וְלִירוּשָׁלַ͏ִם לֵאמֹר שָׁלוֹם יִהְיֶה

emphasize both the might and ruthless-
ness of the attacker.

8. *gird you with sackcloth.* A mark of
intense distress and mourning.

is not turned back from us. God is still
angry with His people because they have
not repented, or their penitence has not
been sincere.

9. *king . . . princes.* Who should be the
first to encourage and strengthen the
people in the crisis. *Heart* signifies
'courage.'

astonished . . . wonder. They will be
bewildered by the extent of the disaster,
and not know what advice to give to the
stricken nation.

10. *surely Thou hast greatly deceived . . .
peace.* A very daring charge! Kimchi
explains: The false prophets assured the
people of peace, and God, as it were,
must be held responsible, in that they
were not immediately punished by Him.
Most moderns alter *then said I* to 'and
they said' or 'saying,' making the
sentence the exclamation of the faithless
priests and prophets of verse 9. But
it is probable that we have here one of
many instances in the Bible where 'God
is said to have done Himself that evil
which in point of fact He has only
permitted to occur' (Streane). Cf. the
hardening of Pharaoh's heart.

sword reacheth unto the soul.'

11 At that time shall it be said of this
   people and of Jerusalem:
   A hot wind of the high hills in the
      wilderness
   Toward the daughter of My
      people,
   Not to fan, nor to cleanse;

12 A wind too strong for this shall
      come for Me;
   Now will I also utter judgments
      against them.

13 Behold, he cometh up as clouds,
   And his chariots are as the whirl-
      wind;
   His horses are swifter than
      eagles.—
   'Woe unto us! for we are un-
      done.'—

14 O Jerusalem, wash thy heart from
      wickedness,
   That thou mayest be saved.

לָכֶם וְנָגְעָה חֶרֶב עַד־הַנָּפֶשׁ:

11 בָּעֵת הַהִיא יֵאָמֵר לָעָם־הַזֶּה
וְלִירוּשָׁלַ͏ִם
רוּחַ צַח שְׁפָיִם בַּמִּדְבָּר
דֶּרֶךְ בַּת־עַמִּי
לוֹא לִזְרוֹת וְלוֹא לְהָבַר:

12 רוּחַ מָלֵא מֵאֵלֶּה יָבוֹא לִי
עַתָּה גַם־אֲנִי
אֲדַבֵּר מִשְׁפָּטִים אוֹתָם:

13 הִנֵּה ׀ כַּעֲנָנִים יַעֲלֶה
וְכַסּוּפָה מַרְכְּבוֹתָיו
קַלּוּ מִנְּשָׁרִים סוּסָיו
אוֹי לָנוּ כִּי שֻׁדָּדְנוּ:

14 כַּבְּסִי מֵרָעָה לִבֵּךְ יְרוּשָׁלַ͏ִם
לְמַעַן תִּוָּשֵׁעִי

---

whereas the sword, etc. Or, 'and so the
sword,' etc.; because the people were so
beguiled, they are now in this terrible
plight (Metsudath David).

unto the soul. i.e. to the destruction of
life.

11. *shall it be said of this people.* Ehrlich
understands *a hot wind* to be the subject
of the verb and translates: 'a hot wind
will be appointed for this people and for
Jerusalem.' For this force of the verb
amar, cf. 1 Kings xi. 18, *and appointed
him victuals.*

not to fan, nor to cleanse. The foe will
swoop down on Israel, not like a gentle
wind separating the grain from the chaff,
but wholly destructive like *a hot wind.*
'The air (in a sirocco) becomes loaded
with fine dust, which it whirls in rainless
clouds hither and thither at its own wild

will. . . . The eyes inflame, the lips
blister, and the moisture of the body
evaporates, under the ceaseless application of this persecuting wind' (Thomson).

12. *too strong for this.* i.e. for winnowing.
for Me. In My service.

now will I also, etc. Hitherto I have
spoken to the people only through the
prophets; now I Myself will speak—
through the foe coming in punishment
(Metsudath David).

13. *he.* viz. the enemy. Similar com-
parisons are found in other prophets;
cf. Ezek. xxxviii. 16 for *cloud*, Isa. v. 28,
lxvi. 15 for *whirlwind*, and Hab. i. 8 for
eagle (better 'vulture').

14. *that thou mayest be saved.* There is
still time to avert the doom, for all prophecies of punishment are conditional.

How long shall thy baleful
thoughts
Lodge within thee?

15 For hark! one declareth from
Dan,
And announceth calamity from
the hills of Ephraim:

16 'Make ye mention to the nations:
Behold — publish concerning
Jerusalem—
Watchers come from a far coun-
try,
And give out their voice against
the cities of Judah.'

17 As keepers of a field
Are they against her round about;
Because she hath been rebellious
against Me,
Saith the LORD.

18 Thy way and thy doings have
procured
These things unto thee;
This is thy wickedness; yea, it is
bitter,
Yea, it reacheth unto thy heart.

עַד־מָתַי תָּלִין בְּקִרְבֵּךְ
מַחְשְׁבוֹת אוֹנֵךְ׃
15 כִּי קוֹל מַגִּיד מִדָּן
וּמַשְׁמִיעַ אָוֶן מֵהַר אֶפְרָיִם׃
16 הַזְכִּירוּ לַגּוֹיִם
הִנֵּה הַשְׁמִיעוּ עַל־יְרוּשָׁלַ͏ִם
נֹצְרִים בָּאִים מֵאֶרֶץ הַמֶּרְחָק
וַיִּתְּנוּ עַל־עָרֵי יְהוּדָה קוֹלָם׃
17 כְּשֹׁמְרֵי שָׂדַי
הָיוּ עָלֶיהָ מִסָּבִיב
כִּי־אֹתִי מָרָתָה
נְאֻם יְהוָה׃
18 דַּרְכֵּךְ וּמַעֲלָלַיִךְ
עָשׂוֹ אֵלֶּה לָךְ
זֹאת רָעָתֵךְ כִּי מָר
כִּי נָגַע עַד־לִבֵּךְ׃

v. 18. קמץ בז״ק

15. Dan. On the northern border of
Palestine.

the hills of Ephraim. The range that
divides Ephraim from Judah, only about
ten miles from Jerusalem. The force of
the verse is: the sands are running out;
the foe is rapidly approaching the capital,
and repentance is urgent if the land is
to be spared devastation.

16. *to the nations.* The Divine visitation
which is about to take place has a universal significance, that retribution is the
sequel to sin; let the neighbouring peoples
take heed.

watchers. Besiegers, who will watch for
the opportunity to storm the city.

17. *as keepers of a field.* Who maintain
a close guard upon it on all sides.

18. *thy wickedness.* i.e. the effect of thy
wickedness.

it reacheth unto thy heart. It deals a fatal
blow.

19ff. Jeremiah's many prophecies of
disaster and punishment were not the
utterances of a vindictive and ruthless
moralist who derives a self-righteous
pleasure in contemplating the sufferings
of the wicked. His urgent warnings and
gloomy predictions were born of his
intense love for his people. He was a
true patriot; and here in an outpouring
of tenderness he identifies himself completely with the agonies of his country.

19 My bowels, my bowels! I writhe
   in pain!
   The chambers of my heart!
   My heart moaneth within me!
   I cannot hold my peace!
   Because thou hast heard, O my
      soul, the sound of the horn,
   The alarm of war.

20 Destruction followeth upon de-
   struction,
   For the whole land is spoiled;
   Suddenly are my tents spoiled,
   My curtains in a moment.

21 How long shall I see the standard,
   Shall I hear the sound of the
      horn?

22 For My people is foolish,
   They know Me not;
   They are sottish children,
   And they have no understanding;
   They are wise to do evil,
   But to do good they have no
      knowledge.

19 מֵעַי ׀ מֵעַי ׀ אוֹחִילָה
קִירוֹת לִבִּי
הֹמֶה־לִּי לִבִּי
לֹא אַחֲרִשׁ
כִּי קוֹל שׁוֹפָר שָׁמַעַתְּ נַפְשִׁי
תְּרוּעַת מִלְחָמָה׃

20 שֶׁבֶר עַל־שֶׁבֶר נִקְרָא
כִּי שֻׁדְּדָה כָּל־הָאָרֶץ
פִּתְאֹם שֻׁדְּדוּ אֹהָלַי
רֶגַע יְרִיעֹתָי׃

21 עַד־מָתַי אֶרְאֶה־נֵּס
אֶשְׁמְעָה קוֹל שׁוֹפָר׃

22 כִּי ׀ אֱוִיל עַמִּי
אוֹתִי לֹא יָדָעוּ
בָּנִים סְכָלִים הֵמָּה
וְלֹא נְבוֹנִים הֵמָּה
חֲכָמִים הֵמָּה לְהָרַע
וּלְהֵיטִיב לֹא יָדָעוּ׃

v. 19. אוחילה ק׳ v. 19. שמעת ק׳ v. 22. קמץ בז״ק

19. *my bowels.* Thought of by the
Hebrews as the seat of the emotions.

the chambers of my heart. Better, 'the
walls of my heart.' 'Under the stress of
his anguish he feels his wildly throbbing
heart beating against its walls' (Peake).

20. *is spoiled.* The prophet envisages
the invasion as though it were actually
taking place.

my tents. In moments of deep distress
it is not unusual for men to hark back to
the happier days of their youth. By the
use of the word *tents* the prophet thus
recalls, perhaps with nostalgia, the early
days of his people. They had by now
long left behind their nomadic life when
they had lived in tents. Cf. *I will yet
again make thee to dwell in tents* (Hos.
xii. 10).

curtains. Tent-hangings (cf. Isa. liv. 2).

21. *sound of the horn.* Urging the people
to flee from the oncoming enemy.

22. *children.* They are indeed children
of God, but foolish. This verse is God's
reply to Jeremiah's question in the last
verse.

23 I beheld the earth,
  And, lo, it was waste and void;
  And the heavens, and they had
    no light.

24 I beheld the mountains, and, lo,
  they trembled,
  And all the hills moved to and
    fro.

25 I beheld, and, lo, there was no
  man,
  And all the birds of the heavens
    were fled.

26 I beheld, and, lo, the fruitful field
  was a wilderness,
  And all the cities thereof were
    broken down
  At the presence of the Lord,
  And before His fierce anger.

27 For thus saith the Lord:
  The whole land shall be desolate;
  Yet will I not make a full end.

רָאִ֨יתִי֙ אֶת־הָאָ֔רֶץ 23
וְהִנֵּה־תֹ֖הוּ וָבֹ֑הוּ
וְאֶל־הַשָּׁמַ֖יִם וְאֵ֥ין אוֹרָֽם׃
רָאִ֙יתִי֙ הֶֽהָרִ֔ים וְהִנֵּ֖ה רֹעֲשִׁ֑ים 24
וְכָל־הַגְּבָע֖וֹת הִתְקַלְקָֽלוּ׃
רָאִ֕יתִי וְהִנֵּ֖ה אֵ֣ין הָאָדָ֑ם 25
וְכָל־ע֥וֹף הַשָּׁמַ֖יִם נָדָֽדוּ׃
רָאִ֕יתִי וְהִנֵּ֥ה הַכַּרְמֶ֖ל הַמִּדְבָּ֑ר 26
וְכָל־עָרָ֗יו
נִתְּצוּ֙ מִפְּנֵ֣י יְהוָ֔ה
מִפְּנֵ֖י חֲר֥וֹן אַפּֽוֹ׃
כִּי־כֹה֙ אָמַ֣ר יְהוָ֔ה 27
שְׁמָמָ֥ה תִהְיֶ֖ה כָּל־הָאָ֑רֶץ
וְכָלָ֖ה לֹ֥א אֶעֱשֶֽׂה׃

23-28. The previous verse describes the
spiritual and moral deterioration of the
people. It is followed by a passage of
singular power, describing vividly and
graphically how, in the physical world,
cosmos has reverted to chaos—the inevitable result of the former evil. Peake
considers it 'one of the finest, most
powerful descriptions in the prophetic
literature.'

23. *waste and void*. The state of primeval
matter before the spirit of God moulded
it into order and form (Gen. i. 2).

24. *moved to and fro*. Perhaps A.V.
'moved lightly' comes nearer the meaning, the root of the verb signifying
'lightness.' Despite their massive weight,
they swayed like something light.

25. *and all the birds*, etc. The last word
in desolation.

26. *the fruitful field . . . the cities*, etc.
Town and country alike are completely
devastated.

27. *yet will I not make a full end*. This
clause is apparently out of place in a
picture of utter destruction, and, moreover, it breaks the connection between
verses 27 and 28. Nevertheless, to regard
it as an interpolation or spurious is to
misunderstand the teachings of Jeremiah
and, indeed, of the prophets in general.
Even in their darkest predictions and
gloomiest moments, they retained the
profound conviction that no matter how
widespread the destruction, a residue
would be left to form the nucleus of a
better people, faithful in their allegiance
to God. Without this conviction their
life's work would, in fact, be meaningless
(cf. v. 10, 18; Isa. vi. 11-13; Amos **ix.** 8).

28 For this shall the earth mourn,
And the heavens above be black;
Because I have spoken it, I have
purposed it,
And I have not repented, neither
will I turn back from it.

29 For the noise of the horsemen
and bowmen
The whole city fleeth;
They go into the thickets,
And climb up upon the rocks;
Every city is forsaken,
And not a man dwelleth therein.

30 And thou, that art spoiled, what
doest thou,
That thou clothest thyself with
scarlet,
That thou deckest thee with
ornaments of gold,
That thou enlargest thine eyes
with paint?
In vain dost thou make thyself
fair;
Thy lovers despise thee, they seek
thy life.

עַל־זֹאת תֶּאֱבַל הָאָרֶץ 28
וְקָדְרוּ הַשָּׁמַיִם מִמָּעַל
עַל כִּי־דִבַּרְתִּי זַמֹּתִי
וְלֹא נִחַמְתִּי
וְלֹא־אָשׁוּב מִמֶּנָּה׃

מִקּוֹל פָּרָשׁ וְרֹמֵה קֶשֶׁת 29
בֹּרַחַת כָּל־הָעִיר
בָּאוּ בֶּעָבִים
וּבַכֵּפִים עָלוּ
כָּל־הָעִיר עֲזוּבָה
וְאֵין־יוֹשֵׁב בָּהֶן אִישׁ׃

וְאַתִּי שָׁדוּד מַה־תַּעֲשִׂי 30
כִּי־תִלְבְּשִׁי שָׁנִי
כִּי־תַעְדִּי עֲדִי־זָהָב
כִּי־תִקְרְעִי בַפּוּךְ עֵינַיִךְ
לַשָּׁוְא תִּתְיַפִּי
מָאֲסוּ־בָךְ עֹגְבִים
נַפְשֵׁךְ יְבַקֵּשׁוּ׃

ואת ק׳ v. 30.

28. *for this.* The calamity which has befallen the land of Judah.

the earth mourn. The soil will not produce its fruits.

the heavens above be black. With dark clouds, as if in mourning.

29. *the whole city.* *City* stands here for 'land.' Or, perhaps, it is used generically: the whole (of every and any) city.

30. Completely unimpressed by the seductive wiles of Zion's inhabitants, their captors will not abate their harshness in the least.

enlargest thine eyes. A common practice in the East in Biblical times and later (cf. 2 Kings ix. 30; Ezek. xxiii. 40).

thy lovers. They whose friendship was courted (the Chaldeans) are now the implacable enemies of Judah. The Hebrew word *ogebim* is a term of scorn and denotes an adulterous paramour. Thus here, too, Jeremiah emphasized that in seeking alliances with Egypt and Asshur (ii. 33f.) they had, as it were, acted adulterously, since God was their 'Spouse' (iii. 1).

33

31 For I have heard a voice as of a
   woman in travail,
The anguish as of her that bring-
   eth forth her first child,
The voice of the daughter of
   Zion, that gaspeth for breath,
That spreadeth her hands:
'Woe is me, now! for my soul
   fainteth
Before the murderers.'

31 כִּי קוֹל כְּחוֹלָה שָׁמַ֫עְתִּי
צָרָה כְּמַבְכִּירָה
קוֹל בַּת־צִיּוֹן
תִּתְיַפֵּחַ תְּפָרֵשׂ כַּפֶּיהָ
אוֹי־נָא לִי
כִּי־עָיְפָה נַפְשִׁי לְהֹרְגִים׃

5   CHAPTER V   ה

1 Run ye to and fro through the
   streets of Jerusalem,
And see now, and know,
And seek in the broad places
   thereof,
If ye can find a man,
If there be any that doeth justly,
   that seeketh truth;
And I will pardon her.
2 And though they say: 'As the
   LORD liveth,'
Surely they swear falsely.

1 שׁוֹטְט֞וּ בְּחוּצוֹת יְרוּשָׁלַ֫ם
וּרְאוּ־נָא וּדְעוּ
וּבַקְשׁוּ בִרְחוֹבוֹתֶ֫יהָ
אִם־תִּמְצְאוּ אִישׁ
אִם־יֵשׁ עֹשֶׂה מִשְׁפָּט
מְבַקֵּשׁ אֱמוּנָה
וְאֶסְלַח לָהּ׃
2 וְאִם חַי־יְהוָֹה יֹאמֵ֑רוּ
לָכֵן לַשֶּׁקֶר יִשָּׁבֵעוּ׃

v. 2. סבירין אכן

---

31. *that spreadeth her hands.* Appeal-
ingly, crying out in anguish, *Woe is me.*

CHAPTER V

JERUSALEM'S DEPRAVITY

1-9 NO GROUND FOR GOD'S PARDON

1. *streets . . . broad places.* Men of
justice and truth were to be found in
Jerusalem; but they had to shut themselves up in their homes, afraid to appear
in the streets and public squares through
fear of the wicked (Kimchi). It is an
exaggeration to interpret the verse as

declaring that there was not one God-
fearing man in the city, although it is so
understood by many moderns.

a man. Worthy of being so called.

truth. Or, 'faithfulness.' This virtue
(*emunah*) unites in itself faithfulness towards God (constancy), towards man
(integrity), towards oneself (genuineness).

2. *and though . . . swear falsely.* Their
oaths are false, even when supported by
the most solemn mention of God's name.

surely. The Hebrew *lachen* means
'therefore.' A number of Hebrew MSS.

3 O Lord, are not Thine eyes upon
    truth?
  Thou hast stricken them, but
    they were not affected;
  Thou hast consumed them, but
    they have refused to receive
    correction;
  They have made their faces harder
    than a rock;
  They have refused to return.
4 And I said: 'Surely these are poor,
  They are foolish, for they know
    not the way of the Lord,
  Nor the ordinance of their God;
5 I will get me unto the great men,
  And will speak unto them;
  For they know the way of the
    Lord,
  And the ordinance of their God.'
  But these had altogether broken
    the yoke,
  And burst the bands.

3 יְהֹוָה עֵינֶיךָ הֲלוֹא לֶאֱמוּנָה
  הִכִּיתָה אֹתָם וְלֹא־חָלוּ
  כִּלִּיתָם מֵאֲנוּ קַחַת מוּסָר
  חִזְּקוּ פְנֵיהֶם מִסֶּלַע
  מֵאֲנוּ לָשׁוּב:
4 וַאֲנִי אָמַרְתִּי אַךְ דַּלִּים הֵם
  נוֹאֲלוּ כִּי לֹא יָדְעוּ דֶּרֶךְ יְהֹוָה
  מִשְׁפַּט אֱלֹהֵיהֶם:
5 אֵלְכָה־לִּי אֶל־הַגְּדֹלִים
  וַאֲדַבְּרָה אוֹתָם
  כִּי הֵמָּה יָדְעוּ דֶּרֶךְ יְהֹוָה
  מִשְׁפַּט אֱלֹהֵיהֶם
  אַךְ הֵמָּה יַחְדָּו שָׁבְרוּ עֹל
  נִתְּקוּ מוֹסֵרוֹת:

read *achen, surely*; but Ehrlich defends
M.T. by explaining the verse: Though
they swear by the name of God, since
they do not seek truth, etc., therefore
they swear falsely.

3. are not Thine eyes upon truth? Thou
lookest for truth and faithfulness in men.
Rashi explains: dost Thou not look for
faithful men to deal well with them?
Kimchi's rendering is: 'Are not Thine
eyes upon what is enduring?' i.e. God's
acts are meant to be of lasting and stable
worth. But His punishment of Judah
has not been of enduring value, because
despite the fact that He has stricken
them, they were not induced to repent.
Why, then, persist in smiting them?

Thou hast consumed them. God has
almost destroyed them completely.

4. poor. The prophet is referring to the
mass of the people. Some excuse may be

made for them in that their poverty and
lack of education lead them to depart
from God's ordinance. It is more difficult to make them amend their ways.
they are foolish, etc. Sin can only be due
to ignorance and folly, which keep men
from knowing the way of God. Cf. the
Talmudic maxim, 'No man sins unless
a spirit of folly has entered into him'
(Sotah 3a).

5. Perhaps, thinks the prophet, he may
have more success with *the great men*, the
leaders. They will surely listen, since
they must have a knowledge of *the way of
God.* With them, too, he is disappointed.
broken the yoke. Of the Torah; they
violated God's commandments.
the bands. The image is of the ropes
which fasten the yoke upon the neck of
the animal. The leaders have thrown off
their allegiance to God to be free of His
control.

<table>
<tr><td>

6 Wherefore a lion out of the forest
doth slay them,
A wolf of the deserts doth spoil
them,
A leopard watcheth over their
cities,
Every one that goeth out thence is
torn in pieces;
Because their transgressions are
many,
Their backslidings are increased.
7 Wherefore should I pardon thee?
Thy children have forsaken Me,
And sworn by no-gods;
And when I had fed them to the
full, they committed adultery,
And assembled themselves in
troops at the harlots' houses.
8 They are become as well-fed
horses, lusty stallions;
Every one neigheth after his neigh-
bour's wife.

</td><td dir="rtl">

6 עַל־כֵּן הִכָּם אַרְיֵה מִיַּעַר
זְאֵב עֲרָבוֹת יְשָׁדְדֵם
נָמֵר שֹׁקֵד עַל־עָרֵיהֶם
כָּל־הַיּוֹצֵא מֵהֵנָּה יִטָּרֵף
כִּי רַבּוּ פִּשְׁעֵיהֶם
עָצְמוּ מְשֻׁבוֹתֵיהֶם׃
7 אֵי לָזֹאת אֶסְלַח־לָךְ
בָּנַיִךְ עֲזָבוּנִי
וַיִּשָּׁבְעוּ בְּלֹא אֱלֹהִים
וָאַשְׂבִּעַ אוֹתָם וַיִּנְאָפוּ
וּבֵית זוֹנָה יִתְגֹּדָדוּ׃
8 סוּסִים מְיֻזָּנִים מַשְׁכִּים הָיוּ
אִישׁ אֶל־אֵשֶׁת רֵעֵהוּ יִצְהָלוּ׃

</td></tr>
</table>

v. 7. אסלח ק׳   v. 7. קמץ בז״ק   v. 8. מיוזנים ק׳

---

6. *lion . . . wolf . . . leopard.* Typical of the various nations which from time to time attacked and despoiled them. The metaphor is suggested by the wild beasts which were an actual danger in the land (cf. 1 Sam. xvii. 34; 1 Kings xiii. 24). 'There can be little doubt that it was from this verse that Dante borrowed the three beasts which appear in the first Canto of the *Inferno*: the " leopard . . . whose skin full many a dusty spot did stain, the lion, and the she-wolf, with all ill greed defiled" ' (Binns).

7. *thy children.* The inhabitants of Jerusalem. God addresses the nation.

and sworn by no-gods. Swearing *by no-gods* was a profession of belief in idolatry. For the term *no-gods (lo-elohim)*, cf. Deut. xxxii. 17 *(lo-eloah)* and 21 *(lo-el)*.

when I had fed them to the full. Cf. the Talmudic proverb: 'The lion does not growl over a heap of straw, but over a heap of flesh' (Ber. 32a), i.e. satiety produces haughtiness. The prosperity

which God granted to them, instead of making them grateful, led to depravity (cf. Deut. xxxii. 15).

they committed adultery. This may be a metaphor for apostasy (cf. iii. 1), but perhaps also to be understood in its literal sense.

and assembled themselves in troops. Bereft of shame, they make no attempt to avoid publicity in their immoral conduct. The phrase may have an allusion to the obscene orgies which characterized certain idolatrous cults.

8. The first clause is variously translated. A.V. and R.V. have: 'they were as fed horses in the morning' (so Rashi and Metsudath David), i.e. having been filled with food in the night they are lustful in the morning. R.V. margin renders: 'roaming at large,' which derives *mashkim* from a root *shachah*. A.J., *lusty stallions* construes *mashkim* as an abbreviated form of *maashichim*, a denominative of *eshech*, 'testicle.'

36

9 Shall I not punish for these things?
Saith the LORD;
And shall not My soul be avenged
On such a nation as this?

10 Go ye up into her rows, and
destroy,
But make not a full end;
Take away her shoots;
For they are not the LORD's.

11 For the house of Israel and the
house of Judah
Have dealt very treacherously
against Me,
Saith the LORD.

12 They have belied the LORD,
And said: 'It is not He,
Neither shall evil come upon us;
Neither shall we see sword nor
famine;

13 And the prophets shall become
wind,
And the word is not in them;

9 הַעַל־אֵלֶּה לוֹא־אֶפְקֹד
נְאֻם־יְהֹוָה
וְאִם בְּגוֹי אֲשֶׁר־כָּזֶה
לֹא תִתְנַקֵּם נַפְשִׁי׃

10 עֲלוּ בְשָׁרוֹתֶיהָ וְשַׁחֵתוּ
וְכָלָה אַל־תַּעֲשׂוּ
הָסִירוּ נְטִישׁוֹתֶיהָ
כִּי לוֹא לַיהֹוָה הֵמָּה׃

11 כִּי בָגוֹד בָּגְדוּ בִּי
בֵּית יִשְׂרָאֵל וּבֵית יְהוּדָה
נְאֻם־יְהֹוָה׃

12 כִּחֲשׁוּ בַּיהֹוָה
וַיֹּאמְרוּ לוֹא־הוּא
וְלֹא־תָבוֹא עָלֵינוּ רָעָה
וְחֶרֶב וְרָעָב לוֹא נִרְאֶה׃

13 וְהַנְּבִיאִים יִהְיוּ לְרוּחַ
וְהַדִּבֵּר אֵין בָּהֶם

9. *shall not My soul be avenged?* This is anthropomorphism: just retribution for sins which, as it were, affront God's purity and holiness is spoken of as Divine 'vengeance.'

10-19 THE DESTROYING ENEMY IS SUMMONED

10ff. Since the people have thrown off their allegiance, God disowns them and bids the nations come and attack them.

10. *into her rows.* Of vines. A.V. and R.V., 'go ye up upon her walls,' follow Rashi and Kimchi.

but make not a full end. See on iv. 27.

shoots. Continuing the metaphor of the vineyard; but A.V. has 'battlements' and R.V. 'branches.'

12. *it is not He.* Who is responsible either for our well-being or for our ills. We need therefore fear nothing (Targum, Rashi, Kimchi). Or: this picture of doom which the prophets give us is untrue; *it is not He* Who has authorized such a declaration. Rather, as the God of the covenant with us, He is pledged to support us, and all descriptions of Him as the God Who condemns us are figments of the imagination. Possibly this was a popular saying (Duhm).

13. *and the prophets,* etc. This continues

Thus be it done unto them.'

14 Wherefore thus saith the LORD,
the God of hosts:
Because ye speak this word,
Behold, I will make My words in
thy mouth fire,
And this people wood, and it
shall devour them.

15 Lo, I will bring a nation upon
you from far,
O house of Israel, saith the LORD;
It is an enduring nation,
It is an ancient nation,
A nation whose language thou
knowest not,
Neither understandest what they
say.

16 Their quiver is an open sepulchre,
They are all mighty men.

17 And they shall eat up thy harvest,
and thy bread,
They shall eat up thy sons and
thy daughters,

כֹּה יַעֲשֶׂה לָהֶם:

14 לָכֵן כֹּה־אָמַר יְהֹוָה
אֱלֹהֵי צְבָאוֹת
יַעַן דַּבֶּרְכֶם אֶת־הַדָּבָר הַזֶּה
הִנְנִי נֹתֵן דְּבָרַי בְּפִיךָ לְאֵשׁ
וְהָעָם הַזֶּה עֵצִים וַאֲכָלָתַם:

15 הִנְנִי מֵבִיא עֲלֵיכֶם גּוֹי מִמֶּרְחָק
בֵּית יִשְׂרָאֵל נְאֻם־יְהֹוָה
גּוֹי | אֵיתָן הוּא
גּוֹי מֵעוֹלָם הוּא
גּוֹי לֹא־תֵדַע לְשֹׁנוֹ
וְלֹא תִשְׁמַע מַה־יְדַבֵּר:

16 אַשְׁפָּתוֹ כְּקֶבֶר פָּתוּחַ
כֻּלָּם גִּבּוֹרִים:

17 וְאָכַל קְצִירְךָ וְלַחְמֶךָ
יֹאכְלוּ בָּנֶיךָ וּבְנוֹתֶיךָ

the rejoinder of the people. The prophets of doom are empty windbags,
falsely claiming to speak God's word,
and their threatening predictions will be
fulfilled only in themselves.

14. *the God of hosts.* A frequent designation of the Almighty, especially used by
Isaiah. It represents His irresistible
power as the Disposer of forces which
none can withstand.

thy mouth. i.e. Jeremiah's.

it shall devour them. The prophecies of
woe will certainly be fulfilled.

15. *from far.* Cf. Isa. v. 26.

house of Israel. Used here of the whole
nation, Judea included.

an enduring nation. The adjective
describes a stream whose waters do not
fail; here it describes the enemy as a
people which does not fail in the purpose
it undertakes.

an ancient nation. Alluding to the antiquity of the Babylonians with their long
record of military prowess.

whose language thou knowest not. They
were 'barbarians' in the original sense
of the term, a fact which increases the
terror they arouse (cf. Deut. xxviii. 49;
Isa. xxviii. 11).

16. *their quiver is an open sepulchre.* Their
arrows are deadly (cf. Ps. v. 10).

17. *they shall eat up thy sons.* To be
understood metaphorically. A.V. and

They shall eat up thy flocks and
 thy herds,
They shall eat up thy vines and
 thy fig-trees;
They shall batter thy fortified
 cities,
Wherein thou trustest, with the
 sword.

18 But even in those days, saith the
 LORD,
 I will not make a full end with
 you.

19. And it shall come to pass, when
 ye shall say: 'Wherefore hath the
 LORD our God done all these things
 unto us?' then shalt Thou say unto
 them: 'Like as ye have forsaken Me,
 and served strange gods in your land,
 so shall ye serve strangers in a land
 that is not yours.'

20 Declare ye this in the house of
 Jacob,
 And announce it in Judah, saying:

21 Hear now this, O foolish people,
 and without understanding,
 That have eyes, and see not,

יֹאכַל צֹאנְךָ וּבְקָרֶ֔ךָ
יֹאכַל גַּפְנְךָ וּתְאֵנָתֶ֑ךָ
יְרֹשֵׁשׁ עָרֵי מִבְצָרֶ֙יךָ֙
אֲשֶׁר אַתָּ֖ה
בֹּטֵחַ בָּהֵ֑נָּה בֶּחָֽרֶב׃

18 וְגַם בַּיָּמִים הָהֵמָּה נְאֻם־יְהֹוָ֔ה
לֹא־אֶעֱשֶׂה אִתְּכֶם כָּלָֽה׃

19 וְהָיָה כִּי תֹאמְרוּ תַּחַת מֶ֤ה
עָשָׂה יְהֹוָה אֱלֹהֵינוּ לָנוּ אֶת־
כָּל־אֵלֶּה וְאָמַרְתָּ אֲלֵיהֶ֔ם
כַּאֲשֶׁר עֲזַבְתֶּם אוֹתִי֙ וַתַּֽעַבְדוּ֙
אֱלֹהֵי נֵכָר בְּאַרְצְכֶ֔ם כֵּ֣ן
תַּעַבְדוּ זָרִים בְּאֶרֶץ לֹ֥א
לָכֶֽם׃

20 הַגִּידוּ זֹאת בְּבֵית יַעֲקֹ֑ב
וְהַשְׁמִיעוּהָ בִּיהוּדָה לֵאמֹֽר׃

21 שִׁמְעוּ־נָא זֹאת
עַם־סָכָל וְאֵין לֵ֑ב
עֵינַיִם לָהֶם וְלֹא יִרְא֔וּ

R.V. render: 'which thy sons and thy
daughters should eat' (so Metsudath
David).

18. See on iv. 27.

19. *in a land that is not yours.* 'Such
an expression as this would by no means
have been suitable, if the enemy threatened by the prophet were the Scythians,
who were a roving people, having no
fixed habitation' (Streane). The Babylonian captivity is evidently predicted.

20-31 CAUSE OF THE IMPENDING
 CALAMITY

20. *Jacob . . . Judah.   The house of Jacob*
is the Northern Kingdom; again the
whole nation is addressed.

21. *understanding.* lit. 'heart.'

that have eyes, etc. lit. 'they have eyes,'
etc. The change from the second to the
third person indicates that this is a
parenthetical reflection by the prophet.

That have ears, and hear not:

22 Fear ye not Me? saith the LORD;
  Will ye not tremble at My pres-
    ence?
  Who have placed the sand for the
    bound of the sea,
  An everlasting ordinance, which
    it cannot pass;
  And though the waves thereof
    toss themselves, yet can they
    not prevail;
  Though they roar, yet can they
    not pass over it.

23 But this people hath a revolting
    and a rebellious heart;
  They are revolted, and gone.

24 Neither say they in their heart:
  'Let us now fear the LORD our
    God,
  That giveth the former rain, and
    the latter in due season;
  That keepeth for us
  The appointed weeks of the
    harvest.'

25 Your iniquities have turned away
    these things,

אָזְנַיִם לָהֶם וְלֹא יִשְׁמָעוּ׃

22 הַאוֹתִי לֹא־תִירָאוּ
נְאֻם־יְהֹוָה
אִם מִפָּנַי לֹא תָחִילוּ
אֲשֶׁר־שַׂמְתִּי חוֹל גְּבוּל לַיָּם
חָק־עוֹלָם וְלֹא יַעַבְרֶנְהוּ
וַיִּתְגָּעֲשׁוּ וְלֹא יוּכָלוּ
וְהָמוּ גַלָּיו וְלֹא־יַעַבְרֻנְהוּ׃

23 וְלָעָם הַזֶּה הָיָה
לֵב סוֹרֵר וּמוֹרֶה
סָרוּ וַיֵּלֵכוּ׃

24 וְלֹא־אָמְרוּ בִלְבָבָם
נִירָא נָא אֶת־יְהֹוָה אֱלֹהֵינוּ
הַנֹּתֵן גֶּשֶׁם וֹירֶה וּמַלְקוֹשׁ בְּעִתּוֹ
שְׁבֻעוֹת חֻקּוֹת קָצִיר
יִשְׁמָר־לָנוּ׃

25 עֲוֹנוֹתֵיכֶם הִטּוּ־אֵלֶּה

v. 22. ק׳ יורה v. 24. קמץ בז״ק

The phrase occurs *verbatim* in Ps. cxv. 5f.
where it refers to idols. Possibly it was
proverbial, and is here applied by Jeremiah to the people, on the line of reasoning that idolatry (although we have no
particular reference to it) makes its
devotees like the idols themselves (see
on ii. 5).

22. The omnipotence of God is so
obviously attested by Nature; will it have
no effect upon the people?

23. *but this people*, etc. Inanimate
Nature, even when rebellious, cannot
overstep its appointed bounds. Yet this
people has defied God and ignored the
purpose for which He chose them!

24. As His infinite power does not arouse
fear of Him within them (verse 22), they
also blind themselves to their dependence
upon Him for their sustenance.

the former rain, and the latter. See on
iii. 3; they determine plenty or famine
in the land.

that keepeth for us . . . harvest. Who
preserves the harvesting period (about
the latter half of April and May) as a
dry season, since rain at that time would
harm the crops.

25. *these things . . . good.* The aforemen-
tioned blessings. Or, the understanding

And your sins have withholden
    good from you.
26 For among My people are found
    wicked men;
    They pry, as fowlers lie in wait;
    They set a trap, they catch men.
27 As a cage is full of birds,
    So are their houses full of deceit;
    Therefore they are become great,
    and waxen rich;
28 They are waxen fat, they are be-
    come sleek;
    Yea, they overpass in deeds of
    wickedness;
    They plead not the cause, the
    cause of the fatherless,
    That they might make it to
    prosper;
    And the right of the needy do
    they not judge.
29 Shall I not punish for these
    things?
    Saith the LORD;
    Shall not My soul be avenged
    On such a nation as this?

וְחַטֹּאותֵיכֶ֔ם
מָנְע֥וּ הַטּ֖וֹב מִכֶּֽם׃
26 כִּֽי־נִמְצְא֥וּ בְעַמִּ֖י רְשָׁעִ֑ים
יָשׁ֨וּר֙ כְּשַׁ֣ךְ יְקוּשִׁ֔ים
הִצִּ֥יבוּ מַשְׁחִ֖ית אֲנָשִׁ֥ים יִלְכֹּֽדוּ׃
27 כִּכְל֣וּב מָ֤לֵא עֹ֔וף
כֵּ֥ן בָּתֵּיהֶ֖ם מְלֵאִ֣ים מִרְמָ֑ה
עַל־כֵּ֥ן גָּדְל֖וּ וַֽיַּעֲשִֽׁירוּ׃
28 שָׁמְנ֣וּ עָֽשְׁת֗וּ
גַּ֚ם עָֽבְר֣וּ דִבְרֵי־רָ֔ע
דִּ֣ין לֹא־דָ֗נוּ דִּ֤ין יָתֹום֙ וְֽיַצְלִ֔יחוּ
וּמִשְׁפַּ֥ט אֶבְיוֹנִ֖ים לֹ֥א שָׁפָֽטוּ׃
29 הַֽעַל־אֵ֥לֶּה לֹֽא־אֶפְקֹ֖ד
נְאֻם־יְהוָ֑ה
אִ֚ם בְּג֣וֹי אֲשֶׁר־כָּזֶ֔ה
לֹ֥א תִתְנַקֵּ֖ם נַפְשִֽׁי׃

v. 25. ר׳ יתיר

---

of these things (viz. God's power and
bounty) and the good sense to draw the
right conclusions from them.

26. *wicked men.* 'Men of such great
wickedness as to infect all' (Streane).

they pry. The verb is singular; each one
of them pries.

as fowlers. Cf. Mic. vii. 2.

27. *deceit.* Ill-gotten wealth.

28. *that they might make it to prosper.*
Or, 'and yet they prosper'; in spite of
their misdeeds (Kimchi).

29. Repetition of verse 9 as though it
were a refrain.

shall not My soul be avenged? Such acts
of injustice are not merely a wrong
against one's fellow-men, but also an
affront to God which must be avenged.
That evil against man is also evil against
God was one of the great messages of the
prophets. 'God Himself, we have always
understood, hates sin with a most authen-
tic, celestial and eternal hatred. A hatred
and hostility inexorable, unappeasable,
which blasts the scoundrel, and all
scoundrels ultimately, into black annihilation and disappearance from the sum
of things. The path of it is the path of
the flaming sword: he that has eyes may
see it, walking inexorably, divinely
beautiful and divinely terrible, through
the chaotic gulf of human history, and
everywhere burning, as with unquench-
able fire, the false and the deadworthy

30 An appalling and horrible thing
Is come to pass in the land:
31 The prophets prophesy in the
service of falsehood,
And the priests bear rule at
their beck;
And My people love to have it so;
What then will ye do in the end
thereof?

30 שַׁמָּה וְשַׁעֲרוּרָ֔ה
נִהְיְתָ֖ה בָּאָֽרֶץ׃
31 הַנְּבִאִים֙ נִבְּא֣וּ בַשֶּׁ֔קֶר
וְהַכֹּהֲנִים֙ יִרְדּ֣וּ עַל־יְדֵיהֶ֔ם
וְעַמִּ֖י אָ֣הֲבוּ כֵ֑ן
וּמַה־תַּעֲשׂ֖וּ לְאַחֲרִיתָֽהּ׃

6   CHAPTER VI   ו

1 Put yourselves under covert, ye
children of Benjamin,
Away from the midst of Jerusalem,
And blow the horn in Tekoa,

ו הָעִ֣זוּ ׀ בְּנֵ֣י בִנְיָמִ֗ן
מִקֶּ֙רֶב֙ יְר֣וּשָׁלִַ֔ם
וּבִתְק֙וֹעַ֙ תִּקְע֣וּ שׁוֹפָ֔ר

---

from the true and lifeworthy; making all human history, and the biography of every man, a God's Cosmos in place of a Devil's Chaos' (Carlyle).

30. The mode of life among the nation has become normal with them, but in the sight of God it is *an appalling and horrible thing*.

31. Not only the temporal rulers (referred to in verse 28), but also the spiritual leaders, are corrupt. What hope is there then? 'When Amos and Isaiah attacked the priesthood of Judah, they still felt that there remained the prophets on whom the nation could fall back. But when Jeremiah mourned for Israel, he felt that there was no reserve in Judah. And when the priesthood closed in hostile array around him, he felt that, as far as Jerusalem was concerned, the prophets were no supporters' (Stanley). Many modern Biblical scholars assume a conflict between the prophets and the priests, basing their assumption on the frequent criticism of the latter by the former. Jeremiah was both, and he denounced both. The conflict is imaginary: the

true prophets censured the corrupt priests as they denounced the false prophets, but were not antagonistic to the priesthood as such.

at their beck. In their interest and at their pleasure.

My people love to have it so. The masses submitted without protest to the misrule.

in the end thereof. When retribution comes.

CHAPTER VI

1-8 SOUND THE ALARM!

1. *put yourselves under covert.* For the verb, see on iv. 6.

ye children of Benjamin. The city of Jerusalem was located in the territory of Benjamin, and for that reason the population was in special danger since the enemy would make for the capital. Possibly Jeremiah addressed himself to the Benjaminites because he belonged to that tribe.

Tekoa. About twelve miles south of Jerusalem. It was the home of Amos.

And set up a signal on Beth-
cherem;
For evil looketh forth from the
north,
And a great destruction.

2 The comely and delicate one,
The daughter of Zion, will I cut
off.

3 Shepherds with their flocks come
unto her;
They pitch their tents against her
round about;
They feed bare every one what is
nigh at hand.

4 'Prepare ye war against her;
Arise, and let us go up at noon!'
'Woe unto us! for the day declineth,
For the shadows of the evening are
stretched out!'

וְעַל־בֵּית הַכֶּרֶם שְׂאוּ מַשְׂאֵת
כִּי רָעָה נִשְׁקְפָה מִצָּפוֹן
וְשֶׁבֶר גָּדוֹל ׃

2 הַנָּוָה וְהַמְּעֻנָּגָה
דָּמִיתִי בַּת־צִיּוֹן ׃

3 אֵלֶיהָ יָבֹאוּ רֹעִים וְעֶדְרֵיהֶם
תָּקְעוּ עָלֶיהָ אֹהָלִים סָבִיב
רָעוּ אִישׁ אֶת־יָדוֹ ׃

4 קַדְּשׁוּ עָלֶיהָ מִלְחָמָה
קוּמוּ וְנַעֲלֶה בַצָּהֳרָיִם
אוֹי לָנוּ כִּי־פָנָה הַיּוֹם
כִּי־יִנָּטוּ צִלְלֵי־עָרֶב ׃

The name involves a play on the verb
tikeu, blow (the horn), and the town is
probably specified for the assonance.
For another example of this, cf. Zeph.
ii. 4.

a signal. Perhaps 'a beacon' (cf. Judg.
xx. 38).

Beth-cherem. 'To be identified with a
conical-shaped hill called the Frank
mountain, between Bethlehem and Tekoa,
so named as having been used for military
purposes in the Crusades, a very suitable
spot for a beacon station' (Streane). It
is mentioned again in Nehem. iii. 14.

evil. The catastrophe of invasion.

from the north. See on i. 13.

2. *the comely and delicate one.* Zion is
compared to a beautiful and delicately
reared woman (so Kimchi, Metsudath
David, R.V., and some moderns). Rashi
explains the phrase as 'the meadow, yea
the luxuriant one,' and Peake remarks:
'This sense harmonizes with the context,

which represents the enemy under the
figure of shepherds coming with their
flocks to graze the country.'

will I cut off. The tense of the Hebrew
verb is the prophetic perfect, literally
'I have cut off'; so certain is the destruction that it is described as having taken
place.

3. *shepherds.* For this image of invaders,
cf. xii. 10.

they feed bare, etc. Each commander
will ravage a part of the country.

4. *prepare ye.* The verse is spoken to the
enemy. The verb is literally 'sanctify';
entry upon war was regarded as a solemn
act and observed by the offering of
sacrifices.

at noon. The heat of the day when an
enemy on the march usually rests. It
denotes, therefore, a surprise attack.

woe unto us! ... stretched out! A.J. prints
this sentence in inverted commas, understanding the words as spoken by Israel,

43

5 'Arise, and let us go up by night,
And let us destroy her palaces.'

6 For thus hath the LORD of hosts
said:
Hew ye down her trees,
And cast up a mound against Jeru-
salem;
This is the city to be punished;
Everywhere there is oppression in
the midst of her.

7 As a cistern welleth with her
waters,
So she welleth with her wickedness;
Violence and spoil is heard in her;
Before Me continually is sickness
and wounds.

8 Be thou corrected, O Jerusalem,

5 קוּמוּ וְנַעֲלֶה בַלַּיְלָה
וְנַשְׁחִיתָה אַרְמְנוֹתֶיהָ׃
6 כִּי כֹה אָמַר יְהֹוָה צְבָאוֹת
כִּרְתוּ עֵצָה
וְשִׁפְכוּ עַל־יְרוּשָׁלַם סֹלְלָה
הִיא הָעִיר הָפְקַד
כֻּלָּהּ עֹשֶׁק בְּקִרְבָּהּ׃
7 כְּהָקִיר בֹּור מֵימֶיהָ
כֵּן הֵקֵרָה רָעָתָהּ
חָמָס וָשֹׁד יִשָּׁמַע בָּהּ
עַל־פָּנַי תָּמִיד חֳלִי וּמַכָּה׃
8 הִוָּסְרִי יְרוּשָׁלַם

v. 6. הה׳ רפה v. 7. ביר ק׳

---

not the enemy, and as a lament at night-fall over the destruction accomplished during the day, or an expression of fear that, under cover of darkness, the enemy will work even greater destruction. Metsudath David construes the whole verse as the words of the enemy. The second half is, according to him, a lament of the soldiers that the day is already past and the destruction not yet complete. This interpretation is adopted by most moderns and accords better with the next verse.

5. *by night.* We will not wait until morning for the final assault.

palaces. The Hebrew word may signify 'citadels, strongholds.' Heywood (*Journal of Theological Studies*, XIII, pp. 66ff.) suggests that the meaning of the word is 'streets and their houses.'

6. *hew ye down her trees.* For the erection of bulwarks (cf. Deut. xx. 20).

a mound. Level with the walls of the city, to facilitate the attack.

7. *a cistern.* The translation of A.J. follows the *kethib*, whereas the *kerë* means 'well' (so R.V.). Peake remarks that 'the difference is important. The well is self-fed, whereas the cistern has its water stored within it from without. The point of the former metaphor would be that sin is a product of man's own nature, the latter figure implies that wickedness is an alien element, but is welcomed and kept fresh in man's own heart.'

welleth. The meaning of the verb is uncertain; R.V. margin, 'keepeth fresh,' is probable.

violence and spoil. The phrase may be a cry of alarm (cf. xx. 8).

sickness and wounds. 'Disease produced by want, and deeds of violence' (Streane).

8. The prophet has already predicted the doom of the city. Yet, as so often, he makes a last-minute appeal.

Lest My soul be alienated from
thee,
Lest I make thee desolate,
A land not inhabited.

9 Thus saith the LORD of hosts:
They shall thoroughly glean as a
vine
The remnant of Israel;
Turn again thy hand
As a grape-gatherer upon the
shoots.

10 To whom shall I speak and give
warning,
That they may hear?
Behold, their ear is dull,
And they cannot attend;
Behold, the word of the LORD is
become unto them a reproach,
They have no delight in it.

11 Therefore I am full of the fury of
the LORD,
I am weary with holding in:
Pour it out upon the babes in the
street,

פֶּן־תֵּקַע נַפְשִׁי מִמֵּךְ
פֶּן־אֲשִׂימֵךְ שְׁמָמָה
אֶרֶץ לוֹא נוֹשָׁבָה׃
9 כֹּה אָמַר יְהֹוָה צְבָאוֹת
עוֹלֵל יְעוֹלְלוּ כַגֶּפֶן
שְׁאֵרִית יִשְׂרָאֵל
הָשֵׁב יָדְךָ
כְּבוֹצֵר עַל־סַלְסִלּוֹת׃
10 עַל־מִי אֲדַבְּרָה וְאָעִידָה
וְיִשְׁמָעוּ
הִנֵּה עֲרֵלָה אָזְנָם
וְלֹא יוּכְלוּ לְהַקְשִׁיב
הִנֵּה דְבַר־יְהֹוָה
הָיָה לָהֶם
לְחֶרְפָּה לֹא יַחְפְּצוּ־בוֹ׃
11 וְאֵת חֲמַת יְהֹוָה מָלֵאתִי
נִלְאֵיתִי הָכִיל
שְׁפֹךְ עַל־עוֹלָל בַּחוּץ

v. 10. קמץ בז״ק

alienated. lit. 'pulled out.' God is interwoven with Israel, as it were, but sin will wrench Him away from the people—a striking metaphor expressing God's love on the one hand, and the powerful effect of sin on the other.

9-15 THE PEOPLE'S CORRUPTION

9. *turn again.* This is addressed to the enemy.

as a grape-gatherer. Who seeks to leave nothing behind. So is the enemy bidden to be thorough in spoiling sinful Israel. Duhm and Cornill regard *turn again*, etc.,

as addressed to the prophet who is bidden to search whether any good grapes are concealed under the leaves, i.e. whether there are any righteous who deserve to be saved (cf. v. 1). On this interpretation, verse 10 is the despairing answer of the prophet: the search is vain.

10. *a reproach.* They treat the word of God with derision.

11. *pour it out.* The verb is best parsed as the infinitive (so Rashi), 'to pour out,' i.e. this fury is to be poured out.

in the street. While at play (cf. Zech. viii. 5).

45

And upon the assembly of young
men together;
For even the husband with the
wife shall be taken,
The aged with him that is full of
days.

12 And their houses shall be turned
unto others,
Their fields and their wives together;
For I will stretch out My hand
upon the inhabitants of the
land,
Saith the LORD.

13 For from the least of them even
unto the greatest of them
Every one is greedy for gain;
And from the prophet even unto
the priest
Every one dealeth falsely.

14 They have healed also the hurt of
My people lightly,
Saying: 'Peace, peace,' when
there is no peace.

15 They shall be put to shame because they have committed
abomination;
Yea, they are not at all ashamed,
Neither know they how to blush;

וְעַל סוֹד בַּחוּרִים יַחְדָּו
כִּי־גַם־אִישׁ עִם־אִשָּׁה יִלָּכֵדוּ
זָקֵן עִם־מְלֵא יָמִים׃

12 וְנָסַבּוּ בָתֵּיהֶם לַאֲחֵרִים
שָׂדוֹת וְנָשִׁים יַחְדָּו
כִּי־אַטֶּה אֶת־יָדִי
עַל־יֹשְׁבֵי הָאָרֶץ
נְאֻם־יְהוָה׃

13 כִּי מִקְּטַנָּם וְעַד־גְּדוֹלָם
כֻּלּוֹ בּוֹצֵעַ בָּצַע
וּמִנָּבִיא וְעַד־כֹּהֵן
כֻּלּוֹ עֹשֶׂה שָּׁקֶר׃

14 וַיְרַפְּאוּ
אֶת־שֶׁבֶר עַמִּי עַל־נְקַלָּה
לֵאמֹר שָׁלוֹם ׀ שָׁלוֹם
וְאֵין שָׁלוֹם׃

15 הֹבִישׁוּ כִּי־תוֹעֵבָה עָשׂוּ
גַּם־בּוֹשׁ לֹא־יֵבוֹשׁוּ
גַּם־הַכְלִים לֹא יָדָעוּ

v. 15. קמץ בז״ק

---

taken. Overwhelmed by the catastrophe.

12-15. These verses are largely repeated
in viii. 10-12.

13. *greedy for gain.* They are guilty of
self-seeking even if it entail wrong upon
their neighbour.

14. *they have healed.* The subject is the
prophets and priests.

lightly. Simply by assuring them that all
is well. 'Like faithless physicians they
dismissed their patient without going to
the trouble of examining him properly;
soothing him with the medicine of pleas-
ant-sounding phrases when what was
wanted was the deep-cutting knife of a
thorough-going repentance' (Binns).

15. *they shall be put to shame.* A.V. and
R.V. construe as a question: 'were they
ashamed. . . .?' Preference may perhaps

Therefore they shall fall among
them that fall,
At the time that I punish them
they shall stumble,
Saith the LORD.

לָכֵן יִפְּלוּ בַנֹּפְלִים
בְּעֵת־פְּקַדְתִּים יִכָּשְׁלוּ
אָמַר יְהֹוָה:

16 Thus saith the LORD:
Stand ye in the ways and see,
And ask for the old paths,
Where is the good way, and walk
therein,
And ye shall find rest for your
souls.
But they said: 'We will not walk
therein.'

16 כֹּה אָמַר יְהֹוָה
עִמְדוּ עַל־דְּרָכִים וּרְאוּ
וְשַׁאֲלוּ ׀ לִנְתִבוֹת עוֹלָם
אֵי־זֶה דֶרֶךְ הַטּוֹב וּלְכוּ־בָהּ
וּמִצְאוּ מַרְגּוֹעַ לְנַפְשְׁכֶם
וַיֹּאמְרוּ לֹא נֵלֵךְ:

17 And I set watchmen over you:
'Attend to the sound of the horn,'
But they said: 'We will not
attend.'

17 וַהֲקִמֹתִי עֲלֵיכֶם צֹפִים
הַקְשִׁיבוּ לְקוֹל שׁוֹפָר
וַיֹּאמְרוּ לֹא נַקְשִׁיב:

18 Therefore hear, ye nations,
And know, O congregation, what
is against them.

18 לָכֵן שִׁמְעוּ הַגּוֹיִם
וּדְעִי עֵדָה אֶת־אֲשֶׁר־בָּם:

---

be given to the interpretation of Rashi and Metsudath David: 'They should have been ashamed . . . but in fact are not at all ashamed.'

they shall fall. The leaders of the people will not escape punishment, but will share the fate of those whom they had misguided.

16-21 UNHEEDED WARNINGS

16. *old paths.* 'Take up your position on the public roads, and enquire which of the branching paths is the old established one. It will prove the good path, and that which alone ye may follow with Divine sanction' (Streane). 'True reformers do not claim to be heard on the ground of the new things which they proclaim, but rather because they alone give **due** weight to old truths which the mass

of their contemporaries cannot formally deny, but practically ignore' (W. R. Smith). Cf. xviii. 15.

rest for your souls. Freedom from anxiety.

17. *watchmen.* Prophets who sought to waken you to the dangers of your apostasy from God (cf. Ezek. iii. 17, xxxiii. 7).

the sound of the horn. The purpose of which is to arouse you to reflect upon your actions and whither they are leading you.

18. *congregation.* viz. of the Gentiles. Elsewhere the word *edah* always refers to Israel, but the parallelism with *nations* makes it evident that the Gentiles are here intended.

what is against them. Better '(the evil) that is in them' (Rashi, Kimchi).

47

19 Hear, O earth:
Behold, I will bring evil upon this
people,
Even the fruit of their thoughts,
Because they have not attended
unto My words,
And as for My teaching, they
have rejected it.

20 To what purpose is to Me the
frankincense that cometh from
Sheba,
And the sweet cane, from a far
country?
Your burnt-offerings are not
acceptable,
Nor your sacrifices pleasing unto
Me.

21 Therefore thus saith the LORD:
Behold, I will lay stumblingblocks before this people,
And the fathers and the sons
together shall stumble against
them,
The neighbour and his friend,
and they shall perish.

22 Thus saith the LORD:
Behold, a people cometh from the
north country,

19 שִׁמְעִי הָאָרֶץ
הִנֵּה אָנֹכִי מֵבִיא רָעָה
אֶל־הָעָם הַזֶּה
פְּרִי מַחְשְׁבוֹתָם
כִּי עַל־דְּבָרַי לֹא הִקְשִׁיבוּ
וְתוֹרָתִי וַיִּמְאֲסוּ־בָהּ׃

20 לָמָּה־זֶּה לִי לְבוֹנָה
מִשְּׁבָא תָבוֹא
וְקָנֶה הַטּוֹב מֵאֶרֶץ מֶרְחָק
עֹלוֹתֵיכֶם לֹא לְרָצוֹן
וְזִבְחֵיכֶם לֹא־עָרְבוּ לִי׃

21 לָכֵן כֹּה אָמַר יְהוָה
הִנְנִי נֹתֵן
אֶל־הָעָם הַזֶּה מִכְשֹׁלִים
וְכָשְׁלוּ בָם אָבוֹת וּבָנִים יַחְדָּו
שָׁכֵן וְרֵעוֹ יֹאבֵדוּ׃

22 כֹּה אָמַר יְהוָה
הִנֵּה עַם בָּא מֵאֶרֶץ צָפוֹן

v. 21. ואבדו ק׳

19. the fruit of their thoughts. The results of their wicked deeds, inspired by their evil thoughts.

20. Sacrifice without good deeds is unacceptable to God. There is nothing to suggest that Jeremiah or the other prophets opposed sacrifices as a religious institution; what they denounced was conformity to the demands of the Temple without observance of the moral law.

Sheba. In south-west Arabia, the modern Yemen.

far country. Perhaps India is meant.

21. This verse does not deny free will, which all the pleadings, exhortations and denunciations of the prophet emphatically affirm.

stumblingblocks. This undoubtedly refers to material misfortunes, not to moral lapses.

22-26 THE ENEMY DESCRIBED

22. *the north country.* See on i. 13.

And a great nation shall be roused from the uttermost parts of the earth.

23 They lay hold on bow and spear, They are cruel, and have no compassion; Their voice is like the roaring sea, And they ride upon horses; Set in array, as a man for war, Against thee, O daughter of Zion.

24 'We have heard the fame thereof, Our hands wax feeble, Anguish hath taken hold of us, And pain, as of a woman in travail.'

25 Go not forth into the field, Nor walk by the way; For there is the sword of the enemy, And terror on every side.

26 O daughter of my people, gird thee with sackcloth, And wallow thyself in ashes; Make thee mourning, as for an only son,

וְגוֹי גָּדוֹל
יֵעוֹר מִיַּרְכְּתֵי־אָרֶץ׃
23 קֶשֶׁת וְכִידוֹן יַחֲזִיקוּ
אַכְזָרִי הוּא וְלֹא יְרַחֵמוּ
קוֹלָם כַּיָּם יֶהֱמֶה
וְעַל־סוּסִים יִרְכָּבוּ
עָרוּךְ כְּאִישׁ לַמִּלְחָמָה
עָלַיִךְ בַּת־צִיּוֹן׃
24 שָׁמַעְנוּ אֶת־שָׁמְעוֹ
רָפוּ יָדֵינוּ
צָרָה הֶחֱזִיקַתְנוּ
חִיל כַּיּוֹלֵדָה׃
25 אַל־תֵּצְאִי הַשָּׂדֶה
וּבַדֶּרֶךְ אַל־תֵּלֵכִי
כִּי חֶרֶב לְאֹיֵב
מָגוֹר מִסָּבִיב׃
26 בַּת־עַמִּי חִגְרִי־שָׂק
וְהִתְפַּלְּשִׁי בָאֵפֶר
אֵבֶל יָחִיד עֲשִׂי־לָךְ

v. 25. תצאו ק׳   v. 25. תלכו ק׳   v. 26. קמץ בפשטא

the uttermost parts of the earth. Cf. xxxi. 8 where the phrase is used of Babylon, the land of captivity.

23. *set in array.* Or, 'equipped.'

24. Jeremiah expresses the feelings of his countrymen about the enemy.

fame. i.e. report.

25. *go not forth.* Jeremiah warns them of the danger of going beyond the walls of the city.

and terror. Omit *and* which is absent in the original, the word being in apposition to *the sword of the enemy.* The phrase is characteristic of Jeremiah; cf. xx. 3, 10, xlvi. 5, xlix. 29; cf. also Ps. xxxi. 14.

26. *daughter of my people.* The nation as a whole (cf. iv. 11).

as for an only son. The severest bereavement a Hebrew could suffer (cf. Amos. viii. 10; Zech. xii. 10).

Most bitter lamentation;
For the spoiler shall suddenly
   come upon us.

27 I have made thee a tower and a
   fortress among My people;
That thou mayest know and try
   their way.

28 They are all grievous revolters,
Going about with slanders;
They are brass and iron;
They all of them deal corruptly.

29 The bellows blow fiercely,
The lead is consumed of the fire;
In vain doth the founder refine,
For the wicked are not separated.

מִסְפַּד תַּמְרוּרִים
כִּי פִתְאֹם יָבֹא הַשֹּׁדֵד עָלֵינוּ:
27 בָּחוֹן נְתַתִּיךָ בְעַמִּי מִבְצָר
וְתֵדַע וּבָחַנְתָּ אֶת־דַּרְכָּם:
28 כֻּלָּם סָרֵי סוֹרְרִים
הֹלְכֵי רָכִיל
נְחֹשֶׁת וּבַרְזֶל
כֻּלָּם מַשְׁחִיתִים הֵמָּה:
29 נָחַר מַפֻּחַ
מֵאֵשׁתַּם עֹפָרֶת
לַשָּׁוְא צָרַף צָרוֹף
וְרָעִים לֹא נִתָּקוּ:

v. 29. מאש תם ק'

---

the spoiler. viz. Babylon.

suddenly. In view of Jeremiah's repeated warnings as well as the actual march of events, the invaders' attack could hardly be unexpected. But no matter how much we school ourselves to the thought of disaster, an inner hope makes us incredulous of final destruction, and whenever it comes, it is 'sudden.' Or: all your preparations will avail you nothing. When the invader attacks he will brush aside your defences as though you were caught unprepared.

27–30 GOD HAS REJECTED JUDAH

27. *a tower and a fortress.* The words are spoken by God to Jeremiah: I have made you strong to resist all attacks from the people you denounce; therefore you can fearlessly *try their way,* i.e. pronounce judgment upon their evil (cf. i. 18f.).

and try. Hebrew *ubachanta* from the root *bachan;* the use of the verb, or the idea itself, is suggested by *bachon,* tower, in the first half of the verse.

28. *they are brass and iron.* The meaning is doubtful. A comparison with Ezek. xxii. 18-22 suggests that the point is that they are of inferior metal, as brass and iron are in comparison with silver (from the point of view of value). Rashi suggests: Going about with slanderers (strong as) brass and iron (to inflict injury upon their fellow-men).

29. The mention of brass and iron suggests a further simile. 'In refining, the alloy containing the gold or silver is mixed with lead, and fused in a furnace on a vessel of earth or bone-ash; a current of air is turned upon the molten mass (not upon the *fire*); the lead then oxidizes, and acting as a flux, carries away the alloy, leaving the gold or silver pure (I. Napier, *The Ancient Workers in Metal,* pp. 20, 23). In the case here imagined by the prophet, so inextricably is the alloy mixed with the silver, that, though the bellows blow, and the lead is oxidized by the heat, no purification is effected; only impure silver remains' (Driver). All the efforts of the prophets have proved in vain.

30 Refuse silver shall men call them,
   Because the LORD hath rejected
   them.

בֶּ֤סֶף נִמְאָס֙ קָ֣רְא֣וּ לָהֶ֔ם 30

כִּֽי־מָאַ֥ס יְהֹוָ֖ה בָּהֶֽם׃

7   CHAPTER VII   ז

1. The word that came to Jeremiah
from the LORD, saying: 2. Stand
in the gate of the LORD's house, and
proclaim there this word, and say:
Hear the word of the LORD, all ye
of Judah, that enter in at these
gates to worship the LORD. 3. Thus
saith the LORD of hosts, the God of
Israel:

   Amend your ways and your doings,
and I will cause you to dwell in this
place. 4. Trust ye not in lying words,
saying: 'The temple of the LORD, the
temple of the LORD, the temple of

הַדָּבָר֙ אֲשֶׁר־הָיָ֣ה אֶֽל־ 1

יִרְמְיָ֔הוּ מֵאֵ֥ת יְהֹוָ֖ה לֵאמֹֽר׃

עֲמֹ֗ד בְּשַׁ֙עַר֙ בֵּ֣ית יְהֹוָ֔ה וְקָרָ֤אתָ 2

שָׁ֣ם אֶת־הַדָּבָ֣ר הַזֶּ֔ה וְאָמַרְתָּ֗

שִׁמְע֤וּ דְבַר־יְהֹוָה֙ כָּל־

יְהוּדָ֔ה הַבָּאִים֙ בַּשְּׁעָרִ֔ים

הָאֵ֕לֶּה לְהִֽשְׁתַּחֲוֹ֖ת לַיהֹוָֽה׃

כֹּֽה־אָמַ֞ר יְהֹוָ֤ה צְבָאוֹת֙ אֱלֹהֵ֣י 3

יִשְׂרָאֵ֔ל הֵיטִ֥יבוּ דַרְכֵיכֶ֖ם

וּמַֽעַלְלֵיכֶ֑ם וַאֲשַׁכְּנָ֣ה אֶתְכֶ֔ם

בַּמָּק֖וֹם הַזֶּֽה׃ אַל־תִּבְטְח֣וּ 4

לָכֶ֔ם אֶל־דִּבְרֵ֥י הַשֶּׁ֖קֶר

לֵאמֹ֑ר הֵיכַ֤ל יְהֹוָה֙ הֵיכַ֣ל יְהֹוָ֔ה

---

30. refuse . . . rejected. In the Hebrew,
both words are derived from the same
root.

CHAPTER VII

THE prophecies in chapters vii-x were
delivered at the Temple gates. Scholars
disagree about their date, the reigns of
Josiah and Jehoiakim being the most
favoured.

2-15 CALL FOR AMENDMENT

2. the gate. The eastern gate (Kimchi).
Some identify it with the new gate mentioned in xxvi. 10.

all ye of Judah. It has been suggested
that the occasion was one of the three
pilgrim-feasts when the city was crowded
with visitors.

gates. There were seven in all.

3. in this place. i.e. the land, as defined
in verse 7.

4. the temple of the LORD, etc. The false
prophets maintain that the presence of
the Temple of the Lord is a guarantee
for the safety of the city. 'Jeremiah
assails the popular pride in the Temple
as a deadly superstition. He even writes
as though the ceremonial system of

the LORD, are these.' 5. Nay, but if ye thoroughly amend your ways and your doings; if ye thoroughly execute justice between a man and his neighbour; 6. if ye oppress not the stranger, the fatherless, and the widow, and shed not innocent blood in this place, neither walk after other gods to your hurt; 7. then will I cause you to dwell in this place, in the land

5 הֵיכַל יְהוָה הֵמָּה: כִּי אִם־
הֵיטֵיב תֵּיטִיבוּ אֶת־דַּרְכֵיכֶם
וְאֶת־מַעַלְלֵיכֶם אִם־עָשׂוֹ
תַעֲשׂוּ מִשְׁפָּט בֵּין אִישׁ וּבֵין
6 רֵעֵהוּ: גֵּר יָתוֹם וְאַלְמָנָה לֹא
תַעֲשֹׁקוּ וְדָם נָקִי אַל־תִּשְׁפְּכוּ
בַּמָּקוֹם הַזֶּה וְאַחֲרֵי אֱלֹהִים
אֲחֵרִים לֹא תֵלְכוּ לְרַע לָכֶם:
7 וְשִׁכַּנְתִּי אֶתְכֶם בַּמָּקוֹם הַזֶּה

worship formed no part of Israel's duty and was never enjoined by God, Whose law was purely ethical. To take his expressions and argue that he condemned Temple-sacrifices and priestly ministrations as intrinsically wrong and contrary to God's will is a pedantic interpretation. He is conveying in an extreme and paradoxical manner his sense of the hatefulness of mechanical forms without inward piety, and the futility of attempting to atone for the absence of the latter by lavishness in the former' (Findlay). The threefold repetition of the phrase is for emphasis (cf. xxii. 29; Isa. vi. 3). Rashi cites the explanation of the Targum that it alludes to the three times in the year when the Temple was visited by pilgrims (Deut. xvi. 16).

are these. viz. the Temple buildings to which Jeremiah points in his address.

6. *the stranger.* Special consideration for the stranger, who was (and is) so frequently the object of dislike and active persecution, is a marked feature of the Mosaic legislation (cf. Exod. xxii. 20, xxiii. 9; Deut. xxiv. 17). 'In thirty-six places in the Torah we are commanded not to oppress the stranger' (Talmud). 'This law of shielding the alien from all wrong

is of vital significance in the history of religion. With it alone true Religion begins. The alien was to be protected, not because he was a member of one's family, clan, religious community; but because he was a human being. In the alien, therefore, man discovered the idea of humanity' (Hermann Cohen). In the present passage, justice to the alien is made one of the conditions for Israel's continuing to enjoy the possession of his land; otherwise he would be driven into exile. This is a conception of nationality, dependent on and in the service of a wider humanity, which has never been surpassed and has still to be realized by the peoples of the world.

the fatherless, and the widow. Solicitude for the weak and for those who have lost their natural protector is another distinguishing characteristic of Judaism, upon which, as here taught, the stability of the nation depends. 'No other system of jurisprudence in any country at any time is marked by such humanity in respect to the unfortunate' (Houghton). Noteworthy is its inclusion in this verse with the exhortation to desist from murder and idolatry, showing the great importance attached to it.

shed not innocent blood. By the miscarriage of justice.

that I gave to your fathers, for ever
and ever. 8. Behold, ye trust in
lying words, that cannot profit.
9. Will ye steal, murder, and commit adultery, and swear falsely, and
offer unto Baal, and walk after other
gods whom ye have not known,
10. and come and stand before
Me in this house, whereupon My
name is called, and say: 'We are
delivered,' that ye may do all these
abominations? 11. Is this house,
whereupon My name is called, become a den of robbers in your eyes?
Behold, I, even I, have seen it, saith
the LORD. 12. For go ye now unto
My place which was in Shiloh, where

בָּאָרֶץ אֲשֶׁר נָתַתִּי לַאֲבוֹתֵיכֶם
8 לְמִן־עוֹלָם וְעַד־עוֹלָם: הִנֵּה
אַתֶּם בֹּטְחִים לָכֶם עַל־דִּבְרֵי
9 הַשָּׁקֶר לְבִלְתִּי הוֹעִיל: הֲגָנֹב ׀
רָצֹחַ וְנָאֹף וְהִשָּׁבֵעַ לַשֶּׁקֶר
וְקַטֵּר לַבַּעַל וְהָלֹךְ אַחֲרֵי
אֱלֹהִים אֲחֵרִים אֲשֶׁר לֹא־
10 יְדַעְתֶּם: וּבָאתֶם וַעֲמַדְתֶּם
לְפָנַי בַּבַּיִת הַזֶּה אֲשֶׁר נִקְרָא־
שְׁמִי עָלָיו וַאֲמַרְתֶּם נִצַּלְנוּ
לְמַעַן עֲשׂוֹת אֵת כָּל־
11 הַתּוֹעֵבֹת הָאֵלֶּה: הַמְעָרַת
פָּרִצִים הָיָה הַבַּיִת הַזֶּה אֲשֶׁר־
נִקְרָא שְׁמִי־עָלָיו בְּעֵינֵיכֶם
גַּם אָנֹכִי הִנֵּה רָאִיתִי נְאֻם־
12 יְהֹוָה: כִּי לְכוּ־נָא אֶל־
מְקוֹמִי אֲשֶׁר בְּשִׁילוֹ אֲשֶׁר

v. 10. פתח באתנח

9. will ye steal, etc. The verbs in the
Hebrew are infinitives; render: 'What!
steal,' etc.

10. and say: 'We are delivered.' Through
the mere fact of our presence in the
Temple.

that ye may do all these abominations.
What a distortion of religion to imagine
that the existence of the Temple automatically provides you with security, so
that instead of exercising an ethical and
wholesome influence, it even encourages
you to perpetuate all the evils enumerated! The dire threat in verse 13 follows
logically from this reasoning.

11. den of robbers. Whither you retreat
and in which you take refuge after
criminal exploits!

have seen it. That this is how you regard
the Temple (Rashi). Kimchi explains
more simply: I see into your hearts, and
know that even when you approach My
Temple, you still intend to continue in
your evil ways. Buttenwieser renders:
'Verily, I do look upon it as such.'

12. in Shiloh. In the early period of
Israel's history the tabernacle was
located in Shiloh; but it was destroyed
in the days of Eli, probably after the
battle of Eben-ezer, when the ark was
carried away by the Philistines (1 Sam.

I caused My name to dwell at the first, and see what I did to it for the wickedness of My people Israel. 13. And now, because ye have done all these works, saith the LORD, and I spoke unto you, speaking betimes and often, but ye heard not, and I called you, but ye answered not; 14. therefore will I do unto the house, whereupon My name is called, wherein ye trust, and unto the place which I gave to you and to your fathers, as I have done to Shiloh. 15. And I will cast you out of My sight, as I have cast out all your brethren, even the whole seed of Ephraim.

16. Therefore pray not thou for this people, neither lift up cry nor prayer for them, neither make intercession to Me; for I will not hear thee. 17. Seest thou not what they do in the cities of Judah and in the streets of Jerusalem? 18. The

שִׁכַּנְתִּי שְׁמִי שָׁם בָּרִאשׁוֹנָה
וּרְאוּ אֵת אֲשֶׁר־עָשִׂיתִי לוֹ
מִפְּנֵי רָעַת עַמִּי יִשְׂרָאֵל:

13 וְעַתָּה יַעַן עֲשׂוֹתְכֶם אֶת־כָּל־
הַמַּעֲשִׂים הָאֵלֶּה נְאֻם־יְהֹוָה
וָאֲדַבֵּר אֲלֵיכֶם הַשְׁכֵּם וְדַבֵּר
וְלֹא שְׁמַעְתֶּם וָאֶקְרָא אֶתְכֶם

14 וְלֹא עֲנִיתֶם: וְעָשִׂיתִי לַבַּיִת ׀
אֲשֶׁר נִקְרָא־שְׁמִי עָלָיו
אֲשֶׁר אַתֶּם בֹּטְחִים בּוֹ
וְלַמָּקוֹם אֲשֶׁר־נָתַתִּי לָכֶם
וְלַאֲבוֹתֵיכֶם כַּאֲשֶׁר עָשִׂיתִי

15 לְשִׁלוֹ: וְהִשְׁלַכְתִּי אֶתְכֶם מֵעַל
פָּנָי כַּאֲשֶׁר הִשְׁלַכְתִּי אֶת־כָּל־
אֲחֵיכֶם אֵת כָּל־זֶרַע אֶפְרָיִם:

16 וְאַתָּה אַל־תִּתְפַּלֵּל ׀ בְּעַד־
הָעָם הַזֶּה וְאַל־תִּשָּׂא בַעֲדָם
רִנָּה וּתְפִלָּה וְאַל־תִּפְגַּע־בִּי

17 כִּי־אֵינֶנִּי שֹׁמֵעַ אֹתָךְ: הַאֵינְךָ
רֹאֶה מָה הֵמָּה עֹשִׂים בְּעָרֵי
יְהוּדָה וּבְחֻצוֹת יְרוּשָׁלִָם:

iv. 1ff.). The overthrow of Shiloh is alluded to again in xxvi. 6 (cf. Ps. lxxviii. 60).

13. *and I called you*. To repentance.

15. *Ephraim*. i.e. the ten tribes of the Northern Kingdom.

16-20 JEREMIAH IS NOT TO INTERCEDE FOR THE PEOPLE

17. This verse states the reason why it would be useless for the prophet to pray to God to relent.

children gather wood, and the fathers kindle the fire, and the women knead the dough, to make cakes to the queen of heaven, and to pour out drink-offerings unto other gods, that they may provoke Me. 19. Do they provoke Me? saith the LORD; do they not provoke themselves, to the confusion of their own faces? 20. Therefore thus saith the Lord GOD: Behold, Mine anger and My fury shall be poured out upon this place, upon man, and upon beast, and upon the trees of the field, and upon the fruit of the land; and it shall burn, and shall not be quenched.

21. Thus saith the LORD of hosts,

18 הַבָּנִים מְלַקְּטִים עֵצִים
וְהָאָבוֹת מְבַעֲרִים אֶת־הָאֵשׁ
וְהַנָּשִׁים לָשׁוֹת בָּצֵק לַעֲשׂוֹת
כַּוָּנִים לִמְלֶכֶת הַשָּׁמַיִם וְהַסֵּךְ
נְסָכִים לֵאלֹהִים אֲחֵרִים
19 לְמַעַן הַכְעִסֵנִי׃ הַאֹתִי הֵם
מַכְעִסִים נְאֻם־יְהֹוָה הֲלוֹא
אֹתָם לְמַעַן בֹּשֶׁת פְּנֵיהֶם׃
20 לָכֵן כֹּה־אָמַר ׀ אֲדֹנָי יֱהֹוִה
הִנֵּה אַפִּי וַחֲמָתִי נִתֶּכֶת אֶל־
הַמָּקוֹם הַזֶּה עַל־הָאָדָם
וְעַל־הַבְּהֵמָה וְעַל־עֵץ
הַשָּׂדֶה וְעַל־פְּרִי הָאֲדָמָה
21 וּבָעֲרָה וְלֹא תִכְבֶּה׃ כֹּה
אָמַר יְהֹוָה צְבָאוֹת אֱלֹהֵי

v. 21. הפטרת צו

18. *children . . . fathers . . . and the women.* Young and old, male and female, participate in a form of worship which is an affront to God.

cakes. A special word is used, *kawwanim*, probably of foreign origin, which is found again only in xliv. 19, a description of the same cult.

the queen of heaven. The consonants of the Hebrew word would ordinarily be read as *malkath, the queen of*; but the traditional pointing is *melécheth*, and many Hebrew MSS. insert the letter *aleph* which supports it. The translation should accordingly be 'the work of heaven,' i.e. the heavenly bodies. Some

Jewish commentators think of the sun, as the dominant planet; modern expositors favour the moon or the planet Venus.

that they may provoke Me. They know the futility of idolatry and engage in it deliberately to provoke Me (Metsudath David). To the prophet it was inconceivable that anybody could believe in the reality of an idol.

19. *do they provoke Me?* Their idolatry cannot injure God; it leads to their shame and confusion. 'The wrath of God, though there is in it no vindictiveness for the slight thus placed upon Him, is a consuming fire of moral indignation, which will devour them' (Peake).

55

the God of Israel: Add your burnt-offerings unto your sacrifices, and eat ye flesh. 22. For I spoke not unto your fathers, nor commanded them in the day that I brought them out of the land of Egypt, concerning burnt-offerings or sacrifices; 23. but this thing I commanded them, saying: 'Hearken unto My voice,

יִשְׂרָאֵל עֹלוֹתֵיכֶם סְפוּ עַל־
22 זִבְחֵיכֶם וְאִכְלוּ בָשָׂר: כִּי
לֹא־דִבַּרְתִּי אֶת־אֲבוֹתֵיכֶם
וְלֹא צִוִּיתִים בְּיוֹם הוֹצִיאִ֯י
אוֹתָם מֵאֶרֶץ מִצְרָיִם עַל־
23 דִּבְרֵי עוֹלָה וָזָבַח: כִּי אִם־
אֶת־הַדָּבָר הַזֶּה צִוִּיתִי אוֹתָם
לֵאמֹר שִׁמְעוּ בְקוֹלִי וְהָיִיתִי

v. 22. הוציאי ק'

21-28 FUTILITY OF SACRIFICES WITHOUT MORALITY

21. *add your burnt-offerings*, etc. Burnt-offerings were wholly consumed on the altar, whilst other sacrifices parts were eaten by the priests and offerers. The meaning is: There is no sanctity in offerings brought by guilty men; they are merely *flesh* and so you might as well eat your burnt-offerings too!

22. *for I spoke not*, etc. Sacrifices were only of secondary importance and subordinate to moral conduct. But neither Jeremiah nor the other prophets opposed sacrifices as a religious institution. This is made clear from the whole context of the passage. The question is dealt with from the Jewish standpoint in Hertz, *The Pentateuch and Haftorahs*, Soncino edition, pp. 56off. Some non-Jewish commentators have likewise recognized that Judaism has always given precedence to the moral over the ritual law. 'In general it may be said that obedience to the moral law always ranked first (cf. xi. 4), and sacrifices were, as is here taught, wholly worthless when offered by the immoral. ... The Jews, it may be added, in their public service, read this portion of the prophets along with Lev. vi-viii [as the Haphtarah], thus showing

their belief that the sacrifices are but secondary' (Streane).

in the day . . . Egypt. Most moderns interpret the phrase in such a way that it supports their hypothesis that the sacrificial system of 'the Priestly Code' is post-Mosaic. But the context makes it evident that a contrast is drawn between offerings on the altar and the moral laws enjoined in the Decalogue (verse 9); and it is true that there is no mention of sacrifices in the Ten Commandments. Binns suggests a different rendering of the text: 'I spake not unto your fathers . . . for the sake of (or, on account of) burnt-offerings,' i.e. I did not bring you out of Egypt because I wanted your sacrifices, although these are certainly part of the system of Divine worship. Kimchi observes that the individual was not in fact *commanded* to bring sacrifices. Burnt-offerings and peace-offerings were optional (cf. Lev. i. 2, iii. 1); sin-offerings and guilt-offerings were only required when a transgression had to be expiated. The continual burnt-offerings (cf. Num. xxviii. 3) were obligatory, but upon the community as a whole, not upon the individual.

23. *saying.* What follows is not a verbal quotation but a summary of God's fre-

56

and I will be your God, and ye shall be My people; and walk ye in all the way that I command you, that it may be well with you.' 24. But they hearkened not, nor inclined their ear, but walked in their own counsels, even in the stubbornness of their evil heart, and went backward and not forward, 25. even since the day that your fathers came forth out of the land of Egypt unto this day; and though I have sent unto you all My servants the prophets, sending them daily betimes and often, 26. yet they hearkened not unto Me, nor inclined their ear, but made their neck stiff; they did worse than their fathers.

27. And thou shalt speak all these words unto them, but they will not hearken to thee; thou shalt also call unto them, but they will not answer thee. 28. Therefore thou shalt say unto them:

This is the nation that hath not hearkened

לָכֶם לֵאלֹהִים וְאַתֶּם תִּהְיוּ־
לִי לְעָם וַהֲלַכְתֶּם בְּכָל־
הַדֶּרֶךְ אֲשֶׁר אֲצַוֶּה אֶתְכֶם
24 לְמַעַן יִיטַב לָכֶם: וְלֹא שָׁמְעוּ
וְלֹא־הִטּוּ אֶת־אָזְנָם וַיֵּלְכוּ
בְּמֹעֵצוֹת בִּשְׁרִרוּת לִבָּם הָרָע
וַיִּהְיוּ לְאָחוֹר וְלֹא לְפָנִים:
25 לְמִן־הַיּוֹם אֲשֶׁר יָצְאוּ
אֲבוֹתֵיכֶם מֵאֶרֶץ מִצְרַיִם עַד
הַיּוֹם הַזֶּה וָאֶשְׁלַח אֲלֵיכֶם
אֶת־כָּל־עֲבָדַי הַנְּבִיאִים יוֹם
26 הַשְׁכֵּם וְשָׁלֹחַ: וְלֹוא שָׁמְעוּ
אֵלַי וְלֹא הִטּוּ אֶת־אָזְנָם וַיַּקְשׁוּ
אֶת־עָרְפָּם הֵרֵעוּ מֵאֲבוֹתָם:
27 וְדִבַּרְתָּ אֲלֵיהֶם אֶת־כָּל־
הַדְּבָרִים הָאֵלֶּה וְלֹא יִשְׁמְעוּ
אֵלֶיךָ וְקָרָאתָ אֲלֵיהֶם וְלֹא
יַעֲנוּכָה:
28 וְאָמַרְתָּ אֲלֵיהֶם
זֶה הַגּוֹי אֲשֶׁר לוֹא־שָׁמְעוּ

quent exhortation (cf. Exod. xix. 5; Deut. v. 30).

with you. The obedience which I demand is for your benefit, not Mine (Metsudath David).

24. *backward and not forward.* 'To desert the path of faithfulness and righteousness, no matter under what new or attractive name, is always to go backward' (Hertz).

26. *they did worse than their fathers.* Each generation was more sinful than the preceding.

27. *but they will not hearken to thee.* It was the prophet's heartbreaking experience to know in advance that his call would fall on deaf ears. To minister under such conditions, knowing that one's work would bear fruit only in the distant future, calls for the highest degree of faith and deepest conviction (cf. Isa. vi. 9ff.).

To the voice of the LORD their
　　　God,
Nor received correction;
Faithfulness is perished,
And is cut off from their mouth.
29. Cut off thy hair, and cast it away,
　　And take up a lamentation on the
　　　high hills;
　　For the LORD hath rejected and
　　　forsaken the generation of
　　　His wrath.
30. For the children of Judah have
done that which is evil in My sight,
saith the LORD; they have set their
detestable things in the house whereon My name is called, to defile it.
31. And they have built the high
places of Topheth, which is in the
valley of the son of Hinnom, to burn
their sons and their daughters in the

בְּקוֹל יְהֹוָה אֱלֹהָיו
וְלֹא לָקְחוּ מוּסָר
אָבְדָה הָאֱמוּנָה
וְנִכְרְתָה מִפִּיהֶם׃
29 גָּזִּי נִזְרֵךְ וְהַשְׁלִיכִי
וּשְׂאִי עַל־שְׁפָיִם קִינָה
כִּי מָאַס יְהֹוָה
וַיִּטֹּשׁ אֶת־דּוֹר עֶבְרָתוֹ׃
30 כִּי־עָשׂוּ בְנֵי־יְהוּדָה הָרַע
בְּעֵינַי נְאֻם־יְהֹוָה שָׂמוּ
שִׁקּוּצֵיהֶם בַּבַּיִת אֲשֶׁר־נִקְרָא
31 שְׁמִי־עָלָיו לְטַמְּאוֹ׃ וּבָנוּ
בָּמוֹת הַתֹּפֶת אֲשֶׁר בְּגֵיא בֶן־
הִנֹּם לִשְׂרֹף אֶת־בְּנֵיהֶם וְאֶת־

---

28. *faithfulness* (emunah) *is perished.* The
phrase sums up all their misdeeds. Cf.
the contrast in Hab. ii. 4, *the righteous
shall live by his faith* (*emunah*), where
faith sums up all virtues. For the
definition of *emunah*, see on v. 1.

from their mouth. They have even ceased
pretending (Kimchi).

29-VIII. 3　SIN OF THE PEOPLE AND ITS
PUNISHMENT

In this section the nation's hideous
sin of child-sacrifice is particularized and
their impending doom announced.

29. *cut off thy hair.* As a sign of mourning (cf. Mic. i. 16; Job i. 20). The verb
is feminine and indicates that the nation
or Jerusalem is addressed. The Hebrew
for *hair* is literally 'crown,' and several
commentators interpret: remove the
insignia of thy regal power.

30. *their detestable things.* Their idols;
possibly an allusion to what is narrated
in 2 Kings xxi. 5.

in the house, etc. Such an act of sacrilege
is the crowning insult.

31. *Topheth.* The meaning and etymo-
logy of the word are doubtful. It is now
usually regarded as akin to an Aramaic
word for 'fireplace'; in the Bible it
signifies the pit in which human victims
were burned.

valley of the son of Hinnom. The meaning of *Hinnom* is uncertain. Possibly
the son of Hinnom was the name of the
former owner of the valley where the
rites were practised (cf. ii. 23).

to burn their sons. This was the essential
feature of Molech-worship (cf. xix. 5,
xxxii. 35; Lev. xviii. 21). 'The victims
were placed on the red-hot hands of the

fire; which I commanded not, neither came it into My mind. 32. Therefore, behold, the days come, saith the LORD, that it shall no more be called Topheth, nor The valley of the son of Hinnom, but The valley of slaughter; for they shall bury in Topheth, for lack of room. 33. And the carcasses of this people shall be food for the fowls of the heaven, and for the beasts of the earth; and none shall frighten them away. 34. Then will I cause to cease from the cities of Judah, and from the streets of Jerusalem, the voice of mirth and the voice of gladness, the voice of the bridegroom and the voice of the bride; for the land shall be desolate.

בְּנֵיתֵיהֶם בָּאֵשׁ אֲשֶׁר לֹא צִוִּיתִי
32 וְלֹא עָלְתָה עַל־לִבִּי: לָכֵן
הִנֵּה יָמִים בָּאִים נְאֻם־יְהֹוָה
וְלֹא־יֵאָמֵר עוֹד הַתֹּפֶת וְגֵיא
בֶן־הִנֹּם כִּי אִם־גֵּיא הַהֲרֵגָה
וְקָבְרוּ בְתֹפֶת מֵאֵין מָקוֹם:
33 וְהָיְתָה נִבְלַת הָעָם הַזֶּה
לְמַאֲכָל לְעוֹף הַשָּׁמַיִם
וּלְבֶהֱמַת הָאָרֶץ וְאֵין מַחֲרִיד:
34 וְהִשְׁבַּתִּי | מֵעָרֵי יְהוּדָה
וּמֵחֻצוֹת יְרוּשָׁלַם קוֹל שָׂשׂוֹן
וְקוֹל שִׂמְחָה קוֹל חָתָן וְקוֹל
כַּלָּה כִּי לְחָרְבָּה תִּהְיֶה
הָאָרֶץ:

idol, and their agonizing shrieks were drowned by cymbals and the shouts of the frenzied worshippers' (Thomson).

which I commanded not. The protagonists of human sacrifice deliberately or in ignorance perverted the meaning of such a command as that of Exod. xiii. 2, which they may have cited in support of their terrible act; hence the stern and emphatic repudiation in this clause.

32. *The valley of slaughter.* It will become the scene of their slaughter by the enemy.

for lack of room. The place will acquire such a fearful reputation that, although people would be loath to bury a dead body there, they would be forced to do so

with the slain because all other burial places will be filled.

33. *none shall frighten them away.* Utter desolation will reign, with not a person to drive away the birds of prey from the carcasses. With this verse, cf. the threat in Deut. xxviii. 26. The ancients regarded such treatment of the corpse and the lack of proper burial with the utmost horror.

34. 'Jeremiah had a deep appreciation of the joys which life affords; he was no mere pessimist and the harbinger of woe whose only desire was to make others as miserable as himself' (Binns). With this gloomy picture, cf. xvi. 9 and xxv. 10; but the reverse is pictured in xxxiii. 10f.

8   CHAPTER VIII   ח

1 בְּעֵת הַהִיא נְאָם־־יְהֹוָה
וְהוֹצִיאוּ אֶת־עַצְמוֹת מַלְכֵי־
יְהוּדָה וְאֶת־עַצְמוֹת שָׂרָיו
וְאֶת־עַצְמוֹת הַכֹּהֲנִים וְאֵת ׀
עַצְמוֹת הַנְּבִיאִים וְאֵת עַצְמוֹת
יוֹשְׁבֵי־יְרוּשָׁלָ͏ִם מִקִּבְרֵיהֶם׃
2 וּשְׁטָחוּם לַשֶּׁמֶשׁ וְלַיָּרֵחַ וּלְכֹל ׀
צְבָא הַשָּׁמַיִם אֲשֶׁר אֲהֵבוּם
וַאֲשֶׁר עֲבָדוּם וַאֲשֶׁר הָלְכוּ
אַחֲרֵיהֶם וַאֲשֶׁר דְּרָשׁוּם וַאֲשֶׁר
הִשְׁתַּחֲווּ לָהֶם לֹא יֵאָסְפוּ
וְלֹא יִקָּבֵרוּ לְדֹמֶן עַל־פְּנֵי
3 הָאֲדָמָה יִהְיוּ׃ וְנִבְחַר מָוֶת
מֵחַיִּים לְכֹל הַשְּׁאֵרִית

v. 1. יוציאו ק׳   v. 1. קמץ בטרחא

1. At that time, saith the Lord, they shall bring out the bones of the kings of Judah, and the bones of his princes, and the bones of the priests, and the bones of the prophets, and the bones of the inhabitants of Jerusalem, out of their graves; 2. and they shall spread them before the sun, and the moon, and all the host of heaven, whom they have loved, and whom they have served, and after whom they have walked, and whom they have sought, and whom they have worshipped; they shall not be gathered, nor be buried, they shall be for dung upon the face of the earth. 3. And death shall be chosen rather than life by all the

CHAPTER VIII

VERSES 1-3 continue the denunciation contained in the preceding section.

1. they shall bring out. The subject is Israel's enemies, acting as the instruments of Divine punishment. In addition to leaving the slain unburied, they will violate the graves of those who had been interred.

the priests. Who ministered to Baal.

the prophets. i.e. the false prophets. The actual account of the fall of Jerusalem, as related in chapter xxxix and 2 Kings xxv, does not record the fulfilment of this prediction. It is, however, mentioned in the Apocrypha (Baruch ii. 24f.).

2. and all the host of heaven. The heavenly bodies, which had been worshipped as gods, will look powerless upon the dishonour inflicted on their devotees.

whom they have loved. As gods. In the sight of their deities they will suffer these degradations.

3. death shall be chosen rather than life. In spite of the insults to which the dead will be exposed (Rashi). 'Fortunately, the prophet's worst apprehensions were not realized. Time softened the utter despair of the first exiles. Jeremiah

residue that remain of this evil
family, that remain in all the places
whither I have driven them, saith
the LORD of hosts.

4. Moreover thou shalt say unto
them: Thus saith the LORD:

Do men fall, and not rise up
again?

Doth one turn away, and not return?

5 Why then is this people of Jeru-
salem slidden back
By a perpetual backsliding?
They hold fast deceit,
They refuse to return.

6 I attended and listened,
But they spoke not aright;
No man repenteth him of his
wickedness,

הַנִּשְׁאָרִים מִן־הַמִּשְׁפָּחָה
הָרָעָה הַזֹּאת בְּכָל־הַמְּקֹמוֹת
הַנִּשְׁאָרִים אֲשֶׁר הִדַּחְתִּים שָׁם
נְאֻם יְהוָה צְבָאוֹת:

4 וְאָמַרְתָּ אֲלֵיהֶם
כֹּה אָמַר יְהוָֹה
הֲיִפְּלוּ וְלֹא יָקוּמוּ
אִם־יָשׁוּב וְלֹא יָשׁוּב:

5 מַדּוּעַ שׁוֹבְבָה הָעָם הַזֶּה
יְרוּשָׁלַם מְשֻׁבָה נִצַּחַת
הֶחֱזִיקוּ בַּתַּרְמִית
מֵאֲנוּ לָשׁוּב:

6 הִקְשַׁבְתִּי וָאֶשְׁמָע
לוֹא־כֵן יְדַבֵּרוּ
אֵין אִישׁ נִחָם עַל־רָעָתוֹ

v. 5. קמץ בפשטא   v. 6. פתח באתנח

himself was yet to advise them to build
houses and rear families' (Hertz). Nevertheless, he need not be judged as unduly
pessimistic even when he forebodes ill.
All prophecies are conditional; and the
shock of exile must have been so great
as to bring about the change of mind and
heart which warranted the non-fulfilment
of these dire threats.

family. Obviously the whole people is
meant (see on iii. 14).

that remain in all the places. Most
moderns consider the word *remain* to
be an error of dittography by a copyist.
The correct translation is: 'in all the
places that remain,' which Ehrlich understands as towns and villages in Judea
which are left undestroyed.

4-17   IMPENITENCE WILL BRING
RETRIBUTION

4. It is never too late for them to repent,
no matter how deeply they have fallen
and how far they have strayed from God.

doth one turn away, etc. Kimchi interprets: 'if one turn back (from sin), shall
He not turn back (from His intention to
destroy)?'

5. *deceit.* This may be descriptive of
their disloyalty to God, or a reference to
idolatry the character of which is summed
up as *deceit*.

6. *not aright.* lit. 'not so,' which Ehrlich
explains as: their words give no indication that the people have any intention
of returning to God.

Saying: 'What have I done?'
Every one turneth away in his
    course,
As a horse that rusheth headlong
    in the battle.

7 Yea, the stork in the heaven
Knoweth her appointed times;
And the turtle and the swallow
    and the crane
Observe the time of their coming;
But My people know not
The ordinance of the LORD.

8 How do ye say: 'We are wise,
And the Law of the LORD is with
    us'?
Lo, certainly in vain hath wrought

לֵאמֹר מֶה עָשִׂיתִי

כֻּלֹּה שָׁב בִּמְרֻצוֹתָם

כְּסוּס שׁוֹטֵף בַּמִּלְחָמָה:

7 גַּם־חֲסִידָה בַשָּׁמַיִם

יָדְעָה מוֹעֲדֶיהָ

וְתֹר וְסוֹס וְעָגוּר

שָׁמְרוּ אֶת־עֵת בֹּאָנָה

וְעַמִּי לֹא יָדְעוּ

אֵת מִשְׁפַּט יְהֹוָה:

8 אֵיכָה תֹאמְרוּ חֲכָמִים אֲנַחְנוּ

וְתוֹרַת יְהֹוָה אִתָּנוּ

אָכֵן הִנֵּה לַשֶּׁקֶר עָשָׂה

v. 6. וסיס ק׳   v. 7. במרוצתם ק׳

---

every one . . . battle. As a horse rushes headlong into battle, recking nought that it may lead to its destruction, so do they rush thoughtlessly on their course, sinning and turning away from God.

7. Instinctively migratory birds know the times of their coming and going, which are the natural law of their being; yet the people, though endowed with reason, do not know God's ordinances which are the natural law of their existence.

in the heaven. 'There is peculiar force in the words *in the heaven*, for unlike most other emigrants, the stork voyages by day at a great height in the air' (Tristram). The time of its appearance in the Holy Land is in the month of March and it departs northward in May.

the turtle. 'Its return in spring is one of the most marked epochs in the ornithological calendar' (Tristram).

the swallow. The Hebrew *sis* is to be identified with 'the swift' (*cypselus*). 'In

Palestine, the swallow is only a partial migrant, many remaining through the winter. The swift, on the contrary, is a regular migrant, returning in myriads every spring, and so suddenly, that, while one day not a swift can be seen in the country, on the next they have overspread the whole land' (Tristram).

the crane. 'It only visits the cultivated region (of Palestine) at the time of its spring migration, where a few pairs remain in the marshy plains, as by the waters of Merom, but the greater number pass onwards to the north. In the southern wilderness south of Beersheba, it resorts in immense flocks to certain favourite roosting-places during the winter' (Tristram).

8. *the Law of the LORD is with us.* The people (or their religious leaders) probably denied Jeremiah's charges of apostasy and maintained that they were fulfilling God's Torah.

certainly in vain, etc. The labours of the scribes, who were occupied with the

The vain pen of the scribes.

9 The wise men are ashamed,
  They are dismayed and taken;
  Lo, they have rejected the word of
    the LORD;
  And what wisdom is in them?

10 Therefore will I give their wives
    unto others,
  And their fields to them that shall
    possess them;
  For from the least even unto the
    greatest
  Every one is greedy for gain,
  From the prophet even unto the
    priest
  Every one dealeth falsely.

11 And they have healed the hurt of
    the daughter of My people
    lightly,
  Saying: 'Peace, peace,' when
    there is no peace.

12 They shall be put to shame be-
    cause they have committed
    abomination;
  Yea, they are not at all ashamed,
  Neither know they how to blush;

עֵט שֶׁקֶר סֹפְרִים׃

9 הֹבִישׁוּ חֲכָמִים
חַתּוּ וַיִּלָּכֵדוּ
הִנֵּה בִדְבַר־יְהֹוָה מָאָסוּ
וְחָכְמַת־מֶה לָהֶם׃

10 לָכֵן אֶתֵּן אֶת־נְשֵׁיהֶם
לַאֲחֵרִים
שְׂדוֹתֵיהֶם לְיוֹרְשִׁים
כִּי מִקָּטֹן וְעַד־גָּדוֹל
כֻּלֹּה בֹּצֵעַ בָּצַע
מִנָּבִיא וְעַד־כֹּהֵן
כֻּלֹּה עֹשֶׂה שָּׁקֶר׃

11 וַיְרַפְּאוּ אֶת־שֶׁבֶר בַּת־עַמִּי
עַל־נְקַלָּה
לֵאמֹר שָׁלוֹם ׀ שָׁלוֹם
וְאֵין שָׁלוֹם׃

12 הֹבִישׁוּ כִּי תוֹעֵבָה עָשׂוּ
גַּם־בּוֹשׁ לֹא־יֵבוֹשׁוּ
וְהִכָּלֵם לֹא יָדָעוּ

---

v. 9. קמץ בז״ק   v. 11. חסר א׳   v. 12. קמץ בז״ק

---

writing and the study of the Torah, have
been to no purpose, since ye disregard it
(Kimchi). R.V. renders: 'the false pen
of the scribes hath wrought falsely.'
This may refer to written directions for
guidance in ritual which, the prophet
maintains, are a distortion of the truth.
'Israel now possessed a *Scripture*, recognized by all parties; already the heretics
had learned to entrench themselves
behind corrupted readings or crooked
interpretations' (Findlay).

9. *and taken.* Ensnared by their folly.
All the verbs in the first half of the verse
are prophetic perfect and announce
what will happen to *the wise men.*

what wisdom is in them? No wisdom is
wisdom when its source, the word of
God, is rejected.

10. Verses 10-12 have a close resemblance to vi. 12-15. Repetitions of this
kind occur frequently in this Book.

Therefore shall they fall among them that fall,
In the time of their visitation they shall stumble,
Saith the LORD.

13 I will utterly consume them, saith the LORD;
There are no grapes on the vine,
Nor figs on the fig-tree,
And the leaf is faded;
And I gave them that which they transgress.

14 ' Why do we sit still?
Assemble yourselves, and let us enter into the fortified cities,
And let us be cut off there;
For the LORD our God hath cut us off,
And given us water of gall to drink,
Because we have sinned against the LORD.

15 We looked for peace, but no good came;
And for a time of healing, and behold terror!'

לָכֵן יִפְּלוּ בַנֹּפְלִים
בְּעֵת פְּקֻדָּתָם
יִכָּשְׁלוּ אָמַר יְהֹוָה:
13 ‏אָסֹף אֲסִיפֵם נְאֻם־יְהֹוָה
אֵין עֲנָבִים בַּגֶּפֶן
וְאֵין תְּאֵנִים בַּתְּאֵנָה
וְהֶעָלֶה נָבֵל
וָאֶתֵּן לָהֶם יַעַבְרוּם:
14 עַל־מָה אֲנַחְנוּ יֹשְׁבִים
הֵאָסְפוּ וְנָבוֹא
אֶל־עָרֵי הַמִּבְצָר
וְנִדְּמָה־שָּׁם
כִּי יְהֹוָה אֱלֹהֵינוּ הֲדִמָּנוּ
וַיַּשְׁקֵנוּ מֵי־רֹאשׁ
כִּי חָטָאנוּ לַיהֹוָה:
15 קַוֵּה לְשָׁלוֹם וְאֵין טוֹב
לְעֵת מַרְפֵּה וְהִנֵּה בְעָתָה:

v. 13. ‏הפטרת ט׳ באב v. 15. ‏ה׳ במקום א׳

13. The passage commencing with this verse to ix. 23 is the Haphtarah (prophetic lection) on the ninth of Ab, the anniversary of the destruction of the Temple and the overthrow of the Jewish State.

and I gave them, etc. Better, 'that which I gave them (viz. the Torah) they transgress' (so Rashi). Kimchi renders: 'and what I gave them (viz. the produce of their fields) shall pass away from them (to the enemy)'. This is adopted by A.V. and R.V. and is preferable.

14. *why do we sit still?* So will the inhabitants of the countryside speak when the enemy attacks, with the probable meaning that in the fortified cities they will at least be able to sell their lives dearly. Metsudath David explains: '(The people will say), "*Why . . . cities*," to which the prophet rejoins, "And there (too) we will be cut off"—punishment cannot be escaped, for though destruction will come ostensibly from the enemy, in fact it is *the LORD our God* (Who) *hath cut us off*.'

water of gall. A figure for bitterness; again ix. 14, xxiii. 15.

15. Repeated in the second half of xiv. 19 with very slight variation.

64

16 The snorting of his horses is
    heard from Dan;
    At the sound of the neighing of
    his strong ones
    The whole land trembleth;
    For they are come, and have de-
    voured the land and all that is
    in it,
    The city and those that dwell
    therein.
17 For, behold, I will send serpents,
    basilisks, among you,
    Which will not be charmed;
    And they shall bite you, saith the
    LORD.
18 Though I would take comfort
    against sorrow,
    My heart is faint within me.
19 Behold the voice of the cry of the
    daughter of my people
    From a land far off:
    'Is not the LORD in Zion?
    Is not her King in her?'—
    'Why have they provoked Me
    with their graven images,
    And with strange vanities?'—

מִדָּן נִשְׁמַע נַחְרַת סוּסָיו 16
מִקּוֹל מִצְהֲלוֹת אַבִּירָיו
רָעֲשָׁה כָּל־הָאָרֶץ
וַיָּבוֹאוּ וַיֹּאכְלוּ אֶרֶץ וּמְלוֹאָהּ
עִיר וְיֹשְׁבֵי בָהּ:
כִּי הִנְנִי מְשַׁלֵּחַ בָּכֶם 17
נְחָשִׁים צִפְעֹנִים
אֲשֶׁר אֵין־לָהֶם לָחַשׁ
וְנִשְּׁכוּ אֶתְכֶם נְאֻם־יְהֹוָה:
מַבְלִיגִיתִי עֲלֵי יָגוֹן 18
עָלַי לִבִּי דַוָּי:
הִנֵּה־קוֹל שַׁוְעַת בַּת־עַמִּי 19
מֵאֶרֶץ מַרְחַקִּים
הַיהֹוָה אֵין בְּצִיּוֹן
אִם־מַלְכָּהּ אֵין בָּהּ
מַדּוּעַ הִכְעִסוּנִי
בִּפְסִלֵיהֶם בְּהַבְלֵי נֵכָר:

16. *Dan.* See on iv. 15.

strong ones. The war-horses.

17. *serpents*, etc. Descriptive of the
invading host.

which will not be charmed. No charm will
avail against them; so will the enemy also
be implacable.

18-23 LAMENT OVER THE
PEOPLE'S PLIGHT

18. *though I would take comfort.* lit.
'my source of brightness in,' i.e. 'Oh
that I could find a gleam of brightness in
(this time) of anguish!'

19. *from a land far off.* Jeremiah anticipates the captivity, as though it has
already taken place.

is not the LORD . . . in her? The words of
the exiles: in captivity they acknowledge
the might of God, and ask wonderingly
why Zion has been so degraded.

why have they . . . vanities? God's reply.
Rashi and Metsudath David interpret
the whole verse as spoken by God: Behold, My people are in exile (*a land far
off*); it was necessary for them to go into
captivity, for *is not the LORD in her* Who
could have protected them? But I
(changing from the third person to the
first) did not save them, because *they
provoked Me*, etc.

20 'The harvest is past, the summer
is ended,
And we are not saved.'
21 For the hurt of the daughter of
my people am I seized with
anguish;
I am black, appalment hath taken
hold on me.
22 Is there no balm in Gilead?
Is there no physician there?
Why then is not the health
Of the daughter of my people recovered?
23 Oh that my head were waters,
And mine eyes a fountain of tears,
That I might weep day and night
For the slain of the daughter of
my people!

עָבַר קָצִיר כָּלָה קָיִץ 20
וַאֲנַחְנוּ לוֹא נוֹשָׁעְנוּ ׃
עַל־שֶׁבֶר בַּת־עַמִּי הָשְׁבָּרְתִּי 21
קָדַרְתִּי שַׁמָּה הֶחֱזִקָתְנִי ׃
הַצְרִי אֵין בְּגִלְעָד 22
אִם־רֹפֵא אֵין שָׁם
כִּי מַדּוּעַ לֹא עָלְתָה
אֲרֻכַת בַּת־עַמִּי ׃
מִי־יִתֵּן רֹאשִׁי מַיִם 23
וְעֵינִי מְקוֹר דִּמְעָה
וְאֶבְכֶּה יוֹמָם וָלַיְלָה
אֵת חַלְלֵי בַת־עַמִּי ׃

v. 21. פתח באתנח

20. The verse is possibly a proverbial
saying: time rushes by and yet we are
not saved. R.V. margin agrees with
Kimchi: 'The harvest is past, and the
ingathering of summer fruits is ended.'
One naturally looked forward to these
seasons as providing essential food-
supplies; but they have passed without
leaving provision for the future.

21. *for the hurt . . . seized with anguish.*
A more literal translation would be: 'For
the shattering of the daughter of my
people have I been shattered (in heart).'
It should be noted that although Jeremiah incessantly rebuked and upbraided
the people and foretold the inevitable
catastrophe, he fully identifies himself
with them in their trials.

I am black. i.e. in mourning.

22. *is there no balm in Gilead?* Metaphorical for, are there no prophets and

righteous men among them to heal their
spiritual sickness? The phrase has become proverbial. Gilead was famous for
its balm from early times (cf. Gen. xxxvii.
25). 'Some suppose it was the gum or
juice of the turpentine-tree, which still
abounds in Gilead; the resinous distilla-
tion from it is much celebrated by the
Arabs for its healing virtues' (Thomson).

the health . . . recovered. lit. 'the new
flesh (which grows over a wound) . . .
come up.'

23. In the English Versions this is ix. 1.
It is obviously the climax to the foregoing, and Peake remarks, 'The division
is here very unfortunate.'

oh that my head were waters. Would
that my head were turned into liquid
which I could use as a source of tears!

9   CHAPTER IX   פ

1 Oh that I were in the wilderness,
   In a lodging-place of wayfaring
      men,
   That I might leave my people,
   And go from them!
   For they are all adulterers,
   An assembly of treacherous men.

2 And they bend their tongue, their
      bow of falsehood;
   And they are grown mighty in the
      land, but not for truth;
   For they proceed from evil to evil,
   And Me they know not,
   Saith the LORD.

3 Take ye heed every one of his
      neighbour,
   And trust ye not in any brother;

1 מִי־יִתְּנֵנִי בַמִּדְבָּר
  מְלוֹן אֹרְחִים
  וְאֶעֶזְבָה אֶת־עַמִּי
  וְאֵלְכָה מֵאִתָּם
  כִּי כֻלָּם מְנָאֲפִים
  עֲצֶרֶת בֹּגְדִים׃
2 וַיַּדְרְכוּ אֶת־לְשׁוֹנָם
  קַשְׁתָּם שֶׁקֶר
  וְלֹא לֶאֱמוּנָה גָּבְרוּ בָאָרֶץ
  כִּי מֵרָעָה אֶל־רָעָה ׀ יָצָאוּ
  וְאֹתִי לֹא־יָדָעוּ
  נְאֻם־יְהוָֹה׃
3 אִישׁ מֵרֵעֵהוּ הִשָּׁמֵרוּ
  וְעַל־כָּל־אָח אַל־תִּבְטָחוּ

v. 2. קמץ בתביר   v. 2. קמץ בטרחא

CHAPTER IX

1-8 THE NATION'S CORRUPTION

1. *wilderness . . . lodging-place.* Though
desolate and dreary, these are still better
than the city with its vices, which the
prophet proceeds to enumerate.

an assembly of treacherous men. The
Hebrew word *atsereth* may signify any
'assembly,' as here. It is more usually
the term for a gathering for some religious purpose, e.g. to celebrate a
festival. Malbim accordingly explains:
even when they assemble to pray they
are treacherous.

2. *their tongue, their bow of falsehood.*
R.V. is better: 'and they bend their

tongue (as it were) their bow for falsehood.' As the archer bends his bow to
aim, so do they make their tongue ready
to shoot (and kill) with the arrows of
falsehood.

but not for truth. They have sought and
obtained power, but not to promote law
and justice in the land. For the meaning
of *truth* (*emunah*), see on v. 1.

and Me they know not. All sin is eventually traced back to wilful ignorance of
God (cf. Judg. ii. 10; Hos. iv. 1). Possibly *know* is used in the sense of 'have
regard to' (cf. Ps. i. 6).

3. With this verse, cf. Mic. vii. 5f. 'The
mutual distrust, which had already in the
time of Hezekiah broken up families and
divided the nearest friends, and made a

67

For every brother acteth subtly,
And every neighbour goeth about
　　with slanders.

4 And they deceive every one his
　　neighbour,
And truth they speak not;
They have taught their tongue to
　　speak lies,
They weary themselves to commit
　　iniquity.

5 Thy habitation is in the midst of
　　deceit;
Through deceit they refuse to
　　know Me,
Saith the LORD.

6. Therefore thus saith the LORD
　　of hosts:
Behold, I will smelt them, and try
　　them;
For how else should I do,
Because of the daughter of My
　　people?

כִּי כָל־אָח עָקוֹב יַעְקֹב
וְכָל־רֵעַ רָכִיל יַהֲלֹךְ׃
4 וְאִישׁ בְּרֵעֵהוּ יְהָתֵלּוּ
וֶאֱמֶת לֹא יְדַבֵּרוּ
לִמְּדוּ לְשׁוֹנָם
דַּבֶּר־שֶׁקֶר הַעֲוֵה נִלְאוּ׃
5 שִׁבְתְּךָ בְּתוֹךְ מִרְמָה
בְּמִרְמָה מֵאֲנוּ דַעַת־אוֹתִי
נְאֻם־יְהֹוָה׃
6 לָכֵן כֹּה אָמַר יְהֹוָה צְבָאוֹת
הִנְנִי צוֹרְפָם וּבְחַנְתִּים
כִּי־אֵיךְ אֶעֱשֶׂה
מִפְּנֵי בַת־עַמִּי׃

v. 4. הל׳ דגושה

---

man's worst enemy those of his own household, had now reached the highest degree of intensity' (Stanley).

acteth subtly. With guile; the Hebrew *akob yaakob* is doubtless an allusion to Gen. xxvii. 36.

4. *they have taught their tongue to speak lies.* Man is naturally truthful and upright, and must school himself to falsehood before it comes easily to him. Cf. the Hebrew prayer beginning, 'O my God, the soul which Thou gavest me is pure' (A.D.P.B., p. 5). Ehrlich and others explain the verb *taught* in the sense of 'accustomed.'

they weary themselves to commit iniquity. It is so much easier to live uprightly and obedient to God's will, but they labour and toil in order to sin!

5. *thy habitation.* Addressed to the people as a whole.

through deceit. Knowledge of God, Who is holy and recoils from everything unjust and impure, cannot be reconciled with a life of deceit; therefore they deliberately reject knowledge of Him.

6. *I will smelt them.* As the silver is purified from its dross by smelting, so I will purify the nation by making them pass through the crucible of suffering.

try. i.e. test, to find out whether the dross has been removed.

for how else . . . My people? I have no other choice, says God. I cannot leave them in their sin, for they were intended to be a holy people; nor can I utterly destroy them, for they are My people; hence I must purge them by tribulation (Kimchi).

7 Their tongue is a sharpened arrow,
　　It speaketh deceit;
　　One speaketh peaceably to his neighbour with his mouth,
　　But in his heart he layeth wait for him.

8 Shall I not punish them for these things?
　　Saith the LORD;
　　Shall not My soul be avenged On such a nation as this?

9 For the mountains will I take up a weeping and wailing,
　　And for the pastures of the wilderness a lamentation,
　　Because they are burned up, so that none passeth through,
　　And they hear not the voice of the cattle;
　　Both the fowl of the heavens and the beast
　　Are fled, and gone.

10 And I will make Jerusalem heaps,
　　A lair of jackals;
　　And I will make the cities of Judah a desolation,
　　Without an inhabitant.

7 חֵץ שׁוֹחֵט
לְשׁוֹנָם מִרְמָה דִבֵּר
בְּפִיו שָׁלוֹם אֶת־רֵעֵהוּ יְדַבֵּר
וּבְקִרְבּוֹ יָשִׂים אָרְבּוֹ׃
8 הַעַל־אֵלֶּה לֹא־אֶפְקָד־בָּם
נְאֻם־יְהֹוָה
אִם בְּגוֹי אֲשֶׁר־כָּזֶה
לֹא תִתְנַקֵּם נַפְשִׁי׃
9 עַל־הֶהָרִים אֶשָּׂא בְכִי וָנֶהִי
וְעַל־נְאוֹת מִדְבָּר קִינָה
כִּי נִצְּתוּ מִבְּלִי־אִישׁ עֹבֵר
וְלֹא שָׁמְעוּ קוֹל מִקְנֶה
מֵעוֹף הַשָּׁמַיִם וְעַד־בְּהֵמָה
נָדְדוּ הָלָכוּ׃
10 וְנָתַתִּי אֶת־יְרוּשָׁלַם
לְגַלִּים מְעוֹן תַּנִּים
וְאֶת־עָרֵי יְהוּדָה
אֶתֵּן שְׁמָמָה
מִבְּלִי יוֹשֵׁב׃

v. 7. שחוט ק׳

---

7. *a sharpened arrow.* The *kethib, shochet,* means 'a slaying arrow.' The *kerë, shachut,* signifies 'beaten (with a hammer)'; cf. *beaten gold* (1 Kings x. 16).

8. Repeated substantially from v. 9, 29.

9-15 THE COMING PUNISHMENT

A detailed description of the destruction and desolation which will overtake Judea, and the cause of the catastrophe: the abandonment of God's service for idolatry.

9. *wilderness.* The Hebrew *midbar* here and elsewhere denotes 'land to which cattle is driven to graze' (cf. Exod. iii. 1).

the fowl of the heavens. Even they have fled; cf. iv. 25. The verbs in the verse are prophetic perfects.

10. *Jerusalem . . . the cities of Judah.* Desolation will also overtake the cities, and jackals will haunt the ruins of the buildings.

a lair of jackals. A favourite simile of Jeremiah (cf. x.22, xlix.33, li.37).

11 Who is the wise man, that he may
　　understand this?
　　And who is he to whom the
　　mouth of the LORD hath
　　spoken, that he may declare it?
　　Wherefore is the land perished
　　And laid waste like a wilderness,
　　so that none passeth through?

12 And the LORD saith:
　　Because they have forsaken My
　　law which I set before them,
　　And have not hearkened to My
　　voice, neither walked therein;

13 But have walked after the stub-
　　bornness of their own heart,
　　And after the Baalim, which their
　　fathers taught them.

14 Therefore thus saith the LORD of
　　hosts, the God of Israel:
　　Behold, I will feed them, even
　　this people, with wormwood

11 מִי־הָאִישׁ הֶחָכָם
וְיָבֵן אֶת־זֹאת
וַאֲשֶׁר דִּבֶּר פִּי־יְהֹוָה
אֵלָיו וְיַגִּדָהּ
עַל־מָה אָבְדָה הָאָרֶץ
נִצְּתָה כַמִּדְבָּר מִבְּלִי עֹבֵר:
12 וַיֹּאמֶר יְהֹוָה
עַל־עָזְבָם אֶת־תּוֹרָתִי
אֲשֶׁר נָתַתִּי לִפְנֵיהֶם
וְלֹא־שָׁמְעוּ בְקוֹלִי
וְלֹא־הָלְכוּ בָהּ:
13 וַיֵּלְכוּ אַחֲרֵי שְׁרִרוּת לִבָּם
וְאַחֲרֵי הַבְּעָלִים
אֲשֶׁר לִמְּדוּם אֲבוֹתָם:
14 לָכֵן כֹּה־אָמַר
יְהֹוָה צְבָאוֹת אֱלֹהֵי יִשְׂרָאֵל
הִנְנִי מַאֲכִילָם
אֶת־הָעָם הַזֶּה לַעֲנָה

11. *who is the wise man*, etc. Considering
the frequency with which Jeremiah re-
iterated his message that idolatry must
lead to just such a destruction as is here
described, the question is probably rhetorical and expresses his fervent prayer:
would they were wise enough to understand the cause of their downfall, and
acknowledge the truth of God's warning!
Possibly, too, his words are a tilt against
the false prophets who sought the reasons
for the nation's disasters and their
remedies in anything but the truth.

12. *which I set before them*. Originally

at Sinai and subsequently in the exhortations of the prophets.

therein. viz. in *My law*.

13. *their fathers taught them*. Sin begets
sin; the present generation was suffering,
partly at least, through the evil heritage
they had received from former generations. It is in this sense that Exod. xx. 5
must be understood: the iniquity of the
fathers leads the following generations
to sin, and this naturally brings its
punishment. For *the Baalim*, cf. ii. 23.

14. *wormwood . . . water of gall*. Meta-

And give them water of gall to
drink.

15 I will scatter them also among
the nations,
Whom neither they nor their
fathers have known;
And I will send the sword after
them,
Till I have consumed them.

16 Thus saith the LORD of hosts:
Consider ye, and call for the
mourning women, that they
may come;
And send for the wise women,
that they may come;

17 And let them make haste, and
take up a wailing for us,
That our eyes may run down
with tears,
And our eyelids gush out with
waters.

18 For a voice of wailing is heard out
of Zion:
'How are we undone!
We are greatly confounded, because we have forsaken the
land,
Because our dwellings have cast
us out.'

וְהִשְׁקִיתִים מֵי־רֹאשׁ׃

15 וַהֲפִצוֹתִים בַּגּוֹיִם
אֲשֶׁר לֹא יָדְעוּ הֵמָּה וַאֲבוֹתָם
וְשִׁלַּחְתִּי אַחֲרֵיהֶם אֶת־הַחֶרֶב
עַד כַּלּוֹתִי אוֹתָם׃

16 כֹּה אָמַר יְהֹוָה צְבָאוֹת
הִתְבּוֹנְנוּ
וְקִרְאוּ לַמְקוֹנְנוֹת וּתְבוֹאֶינָה
וְאֶל־הַחֲכָמוֹת שִׁלְחוּ
וְתָבוֹאנָה׃

17 וּתְמַהֵרְנָה וְתִשֶּׂנָה עָלֵינוּ נֶהִי
וְתֵרַדְנָה עֵינֵינוּ דִּמְעָה
וְעַפְעַפֵּינוּ יִזְּלוּ־מָיִם׃

18 כִּי קוֹל נְהִי
נִשְׁמַע מִצִּיּוֹן אֵיךְ שֻׁדָּדְנוּ
בֹּשְׁנוּ מְאֹד כִּי־עָזַבְנוּ אָרֶץ
כִּי הִשְׁלִיכוּ מִשְׁכְּנוֹתֵינוּ׃

v. 17. קמץ בז״ק   v. 18. ‏א׳ חסר‏

phorical for the bitterness of affliction
(see on viii. 14).

15. till I have consumed them. i.e. most
of them (Kimchi).

16-21 WAILING AND LAMENT

16. the mourning women. Professional
mourners; they were generally women
who followed the bier of a dead person
and lamented his death in elegiac
measures. 'This custom continues to the
present day in Judea, that women with

dishevelled locks and bared breasts in
musical utterance invite all to weeping'
(Jerome). Now a whole nation was to be
bewailed!

the wise women. Skilled in lamenting.

18. we have forsaken the land. Involun-
tarily, to go into exile. The verb is prophetic perfect.

our dwellings have cast us out. Or, as
A.V., 'because they (i.e. our enemies)
have cast down our dwellings' (so also
Rashi).

71

19 Yea, hear the word of the LORD,
   O ye women,
And let your ear receive the
   word of His mouth,
And teach your daughters wail-
   ing,
And every one her neighbour
   lamentation:
20 'For death is come up into our
   windows,
It is entered into our palaces,
To cut off the children from the
   street,
And the young men from the
   broad places.—
21 Speak: Thus saith the LORD—
And the carcasses of men fall
As dung upon the open field,
And as the handful after the
   harvestman,
Which none gathereth.'
22 Thus saith the LORD:
Let not the wise man glory in his
   wisdom,

19 כִּי־שְׁמַעְנָה נָשִׁים֙ דְּבַר־יְהֹוָ֔ה
וְתִקַּ֤ח אָזְנְכֶם֙ דְּבַר־פִּ֔יו
וְלַמֵּדְנָה בְנֽוֹתֵיכֶם֙ נֶ֔הִי
וְאִשָּׁ֥ה רְעוּתָ֖הּ קִינָֽה׃
20 כִּי־עָ֤לָה מָ֙וֶת֙ בְּחַלּוֹנֵ֔ינוּ
בָּ֖א בְּאַרְמְנוֹתֵ֑ינוּ
לְהַכְרִ֤ית עוֹלָל֙ מִח֔וּץ
בַּחוּרִ֖ים מֵרְחֹבֽוֹת׃
21 דַּבֵּ֗ר כֹּ֚ה נְאֻם־יְהֹוָ֔ה
וְנָֽפְלָה֙ נִבְלַ֣ת הָֽאָדָ֔ם
כְּדֹ֛מֶן עַל־פְּנֵ֥י הַשָּׂדֶ֖ה
וּכְעָמִ֛יר מֵאַחֲרֵ֥י הַקּוֹצֵ֖ר
וְאֵ֥ין מְאַסֵּֽף׃
22 כֹּ֣ה ׀ אָמַ֣ר יְהֹוָ֗ה
אַל־יִתְהַלֵּ֤ל חָכָם֙ בְּחָכְמָת֔וֹ

19. *receive the word of His mouth.* Con-
ventional phrases of lamentation will not
be used; God will dictate the appropriate
phrases.

20. *death is come up into our windows.*
Though we have erected defences against
the enemy, death has penetrated into
our homes; all our precautions have
proved in vain. Many commentators
understand the reference to be to a fatal
epidemic which resulted from the conditions of the siege.

21. *speak: Thus saith the LORD.* 'The
very abruptness of this break gives it
force and point' (Streane).

which none gathereth. Either through
fear of leaving his hiding place (Metsu-

dath David), or because of the multitude
of the slain and the fewness of the survivors.

22-23 KNOWLEDGE OF GOD IS NEEDED
ABOVE ALL

Neither wisdom, strength nor wealth is
a ground for pride. One may justly be
proud only of knowing and understanding that the Lord is the God of love,
justice and righteousness, and that these
are His prime demands upon His creatures.

22. *the wise man.* Without the knowledge
of God human wisdom is futile. *The
fear of the LORD is the beginning of
wisdom* (Ps. cxi. 10; cf. Prov. ix. 10).

Neither let the mighty man glory
in his might,
Let not the rich man glory in his
riches;
23 But let him that glorieth glory in
this,
That he understandeth, and
knoweth Me,
That I am the LORD who exercise
mercy,
Justice, and righteousness, in the
earth;
For in these things I delight,
Saith the LORD.
24. Behold, the days come, saith
the LORD, that I will punish all them
that are circumcised in their uncircumcision: 25. Egypt, and Judah,
and Edom, and the children of
Ammon, and Moab, and all that
have the corners of their hair polled,
that dwell in the wilderness;

וְאַל־יִתְהַלֵּל הַגִּבּוֹר
בִּגְבוּרָתוֹ
אַל־יִתְהַלֵּל עָשִׁיר בְּעָשְׁרוֹ:
23 כִּי אִם־בְּזֹאת
יִתְהַלֵּל הַמִּתְהַלֵּל
הַשְׂכֵּל וְיָדֹעַ אוֹתִי
כִּי אֲנִי יְהוָה עֹשֶׂה חֶסֶד
מִשְׁפָּט וּצְדָקָה בָּאָרֶץ
כִּי־בְאֵלֶּה חָפַצְתִּי
נְאֻם־יְהוָה:
24 הִנֵּה יָמִים בָּאִים נְאֻם־יְהוָה
וּפָקַדְתִּי עַל־כָּל־מוּל
25 בְּעָרְלָה: עַל־מִצְרַיִם וְעַל־
יְהוּדָה וְעַל־אֱדוֹם וְעַל־בְּנֵי
עַמּוֹן וְעַל־מוֹאָב וְעַל כָּל־
קְצוּצֵי פֵאָה הַיֹּשְׁבִים בַּמִּדְבָּר

v. 23. למדנחאי ומשפט עד כאן

might. The only might of which man may truly boast is the moral strength to withstand temptation. 'Who is mighty? He who subdues his passions' (Aboth).

riches. Wealth cannot deliver a man from his fate, and material riches are inferior to spiritual treasures.

23. *knoweth Me.* 'Having acquired this knowledge, he will then be determined always to seek lovingkindness, judgment and righteousness and thus to imitate the ways of God' (Maimonides).

mercy. Or, 'lovingkindness' (A.V., R.V., Hebrew *chesed*). This precedes *justice and righteousness.* Elsewhere in Scripture it even 'precedes "truth."' Truth,

justice and righteousness must all be spoken and acted in *lovingkindness*; otherwise, they cease to be truth, justice and righteousness' (Hertz).

24-25 GOD'S JUDGMENT WILL EXTEND TO OTHER NATIONS ALSO

24. *circumcised in their uncircumcision.* Though physically circumcised, they are spiritually uncircumcised, their hearts being closed to the understanding and love of God and His teachings.

25. *Egypt,* etc. The nations enumerated apparently practised circumcision.

all that have the corners of their hair polled. i.e. cut away from the temples, forbidden

73

For all the nations are uncircumcised,

But all the house of Israel are uncircumcised in the heart.

כִּי כָל־הַגּוֹיִם עֲרֵלִים
וְכָל־בֵּית יִשְׂרָאֵל
עַרְלֵי־לֵב:

10   CHAPTER X   י

1. Hear ye the word which the LORD speaketh unto you, O house of Israel; 2. thus saith the LORD:

Learn not the way of the nations,
And be not dismayed at the signs of heaven;
For the nations are dismayed at them.

3 For the customs of the peoples are vanity;

For it is but a tree which one cutteth out of the forest,
The work of the hands of the workman with the axe.

1 שִׁמְעוּ אֶת־הַדָּבָר אֲשֶׁר דִּבֶּר
יְהוָה עֲלֵיכֶם בֵּית יִשְׂרָאֵל:
2 כֹּה | אָמַר יְהוָה
אֶל־דֶּרֶךְ הַגּוֹיִם אַל־תִּלְמָדוּ
וּמֵאֹתוֹת הַשָּׁמַיִם אַל־תֵּחָתּוּ
כִּי־יֵחַתּוּ הַגּוֹיִם מֵהֵמָּה:
3 כִּי־חֻקּוֹת הָעַמִּים הֶבֶל הוּא
כִּי־עֵץ מִיַּעַר כְּרָתוֹ
מַעֲשֵׂה יְדֵי־חָרָשׁ בַּמַּעֲצָד:

v. 2. קמץ בז״ק

in Lev. xix. 27 and alluded to again in xxv. 23, xlix. 32. This is probably a reference to certain Arab tribes with whom the practice had some religious significance, as recorded by Herodotus. Rashi and Kimchi render: 'and all that are in the uttermost corners (or, that are separated in the extreme ends) who dwell in the wilderness,' i.e. the Arabian desert to the east of the Holy Land.

for all the nations, etc. The clause is difficult and seems to contradict what precedes. The probable meaning is: although the heathen peoples practised circumcision, they are in God's sight *uncircumcised* since their lives lack spirituality; and similarly the circumcision of the Israelites means nothing to Him in that they are *uncircumcised in the heart.* They will be judged like the heathen peoples.

CHAPTER X

1-16 HELPLESSNESS OF IDOLS

2. *the signs of heaven.* Such as eclipses and meteors, which other nations regarded as portents of evil.

3. *customs.* lit. 'statutes.' *Customs* here denotes religious practices and beliefs. Thus the previous verse tells of their love for astrology, and this verse condemns these beliefs in general as vanity, and proceeds to illustrate this by reference to the absurdity of idol-worship.

vanity. Empty and without content. For the description of the making of an idol which follows, cf. Isa. xl. 19f., xliv. 12ff.

for it is. The subject is the manufactured idol, to be understood from the context.

4 They deck it with silver and with gold,
They fasten it with nails and with hammers, that it move not.

5 They are like a pillar in a garden of cucumbers, and speak not;
They must needs be borne, because they cannot go.
Be not afraid of them, for they cannot do evil,
Neither is it in them to do good.

6 There is none like unto Thee, O LORD;
Thou art great, and Thy name is great in might.

7 Who would not fear Thee, O King of the nations?
For it befitteth Thee;
Forasmuch as among all the wise men of the nations, and in all their royalty,
There is none like unto Thee.

בְּכֶסֶף וּבְזָהָב יְיַפֵּהוּ ⁴
בְּמַסְמְרוֹת וּבְמַקָּבוֹת
יְחַזְּקוּם וְלוֹא יָפִיק:
כְּתֹמֶר מִקְשָׁה הֵמָּה ⁵
וְלֹא יְדַבֵּרוּ
נָשׂוֹא יִנָּשׂוּא כִּי־לֹא יִצְעָדוּ
אַל־תִּירְאוּ מֵהֶם
כִּי־לֹא יָרֵעוּ
וְגַם־הֵיטֵיב אֵין אוֹתָם:
מֵאֵין כָּמוֹךָ יְהֹוָה ⁶
גָּדוֹל אַתָּה
וְגָדוֹל שִׁמְךָ בִּגְבוּרָה:
מִי לֹא יִרָאֲךָ מֶלֶךְ הַגּוֹיִם ⁷
כִּי לְךָ יָאָתָה
כִּי בְכָל־חַכְמֵי הַגּוֹיִם
וּבְכָל־מַלְכוּתָם
מֵאֵין כָּמוֹךָ:

v. 5. כצ״ל

5. *like a pillar in a garden of cucumbers.* This rendering agrees with R.V. margin as against A.V. 'they are as upright as the palm tree,' R.V. 'like a palm tree of turned work,' and is certainly correct. The idol is contemptuously compared to a scarecrow, and the same imagery is found in Baruch vi. 70, 'For as a scarecrow in a garden of cucumbers keepeth nothing: so are their gods of wood, and laid over with silver and gold.'

must needs be borne. In religious processions.

6. *there is none*, etc. Better, 'because there is none . . . (therefore) Thou art great.'

7. *who would not fear Thee . . . ?* Cf. v.22. The Hebrew is difficult. Perhaps verses 7f. should be rendered: 'Who should not fear Thee? . . . yet they are altogether brutish', preferring to worship idols of wood. *Wise men* is literally 'the wise of' and may refer to the images which are reputed to have superhuman wisdom; similarly *their royalty* may indicate the pantheon of heathen worship.

O King of the nations. An affirmation of God's universal rule: He is not a tribal God, but Sovereign over all peoples.

it befitteth Thee. It is proper to reverence Thee.

75

8 But they are altogether brutish
and foolish:
The vanities by which they are
instructed are but a stock;

9 Silver beaten into plates which is
brought from Tarshish,
And gold from Uphaz,
The work of the craftsman and of
the hands of the goldsmith;
Blue and purple is their clothing;
They are all the work of skilful
men.

10 But the LORD God is the true
God,
He is the living God, and the
everlasting King;
At His wrath the earth trembleth,
And the nations are not able to
abide His indignation.

11. Thus shall ye say unto them:
'The gods that have not made the
heavens and the earth, these shall
perish from the earth, and from
under the heavens.'

8 וּבְאַחַת יִבְעֲרוּ וְיִכְסָלוּ
מוּסַר הֲבָלִים עֵץ הוּא׃
9 כֶּסֶף מְרֻקָּע מִתַּרְשִׁישׁ יוּבָא
וְזָהָב מֵאוּפָז
מַעֲשֵׂה חָרָשׁ וִידֵי צוֹרֵף
תְּכֵלֶת וְאַרְגָּמָן לְבוּשָׁם
מַעֲשֵׂה חֲכָמִים כֻּלָּם׃
10 וַיהֹוָה אֱלֹהִים אֱמֶת
הוּא־אֱלֹהִים חַיִּים
וּמֶלֶךְ עוֹלָם
מִקִּצְפּוֹ תִּרְעַשׁ הָאָרֶץ
וְלֹא־יָכִלוּ גוֹיִם זַעְמוֹ׃
11 כִּדְנָה תֵּאמְרוּן לְהוֹם אֱלָהַיָּא
דִּי־שְׁמַיָּא וְאַרְקָא לָא עֲבַדוּ
יֵאבַדוּ מֵאַרְעָא וּמִן־תְּחוֹת
שְׁמַיָּא אֵלֶּה׃

v. 11. פתח באתנח

---

8. *the vanities by which they are instructed.*
lit. 'the instruction of (received from)
vanities.'

are but a stock. 'Is no better than the
idol itself; idolatry is destitute of moral
or spiritual force' (Driver). '*Ex nihilo
nihil fit;* a stream cannot flow above its
source, and from a material idol no moral
or spiritual counsel is to be expected'
(Binns).

9. How the idol is manufactured and
robed.

Tarshish. Probably Tartessus in Spain.
'The mineral products supplied by Tarshish to Tyre, silver, iron, tin and lead
(Ezek. xxvii. 12), were exactly those in
which Spain was rich' (Streane).

Uphaz. Unknown. It is also mentioned
in Dan. x. 5 in a similar connection.
Some ancient versions identified it with
Ophir.

10. In contrast to the falsity of idols, God
is truth; in contrast to their deadness and
powerlessness, He is alive and the King
of the universe.

is the true God. lit. 'is truth.' 'Truth is
the seal of God' (Talmud).   Cf. the
Hebrew New Year liturgy: 'For Thou art
God in truth and Thy word is truth'
(A.D.P.B., p. 242).

11. This verse is in Aramaic.   Rashi
suggests that it is the text of a letter sent
by Jeremiah to Jehoiachin and the other
exiles in Babylon, advising them how to

12 He that hath made the earth by
His power,
That hath established the world
by His wisdom,
And hath stretched out the
heavens by His understanding;
13 At the sound of His giving a
multitude of waters in the
heavens,
When He causeth the vapours to
ascend from the ends of the
earth;
When He maketh lightnings
with the rain,
And bringeth forth the wind out
of His treasuries;
14 Every man is proved to be
brutish, without knowledge,
Every goldsmith is put to shame
by the graven image,
His molten image is falsehood,
and there is no breath in them.
15 They are vanity, a work of delusion;
In the time of their visitation
they shall perish.
16 Not like these is the portion of
Jacob;

עֹשֵׂה אֶרֶץ בְּכֹחוֹ 12
מֵכִין תֵּבֵל בְּחָכְמָתוֹ
וּבִתְבוּנָתוֹ נָטָה שָׁמָיִם:
לְקוֹל תִּתּוֹ הֲמוֹן מַיִם בַּשָּׁמַיִם 13
וַיַּעֲלֶה נְשִׂאִים מִקְצֵה אָרֶץ
בְּרָקִים לַמָּטָר עָשָׂה
וַיּוֹצֵא רוּחַ מֵאֹצְרוֹתָיו:
נִבְעַר כָּל־אָדָם מִדַּעַת 14
הֹבִישׁ כָּל־צֹרֵף מִפֶּסֶל
כִּי שֶׁקֶר נִסְכּוֹ וְלֹא־רוּחַ בָּם:
הֶבֶל הֵמָּה מַעֲשֵׂה תַּעְתֻּעִים 15
בְּעֵת פְּקֻדָּתָם יֹאבֵדוּ:
לֹא־כְאֵלֶּה חֵלֶק יַעֲקֹב 16

v. 13. הארץ ק׳

answer those who sought to seduce them
to idolatry.

the gods. viz. the idols.

12. Verse 11 was a digression interrupt-
ing the sequence of thought, and verse
12 logically follows on verse 10. Kimchi,
on the other hand, regards this verse as
the sequel to verse 11, although the
prophet now reverts to Hebrew: whereas
the gods . . . the heavens, we will serve Him
that hath made the earth by His power.

His wisdom. Cf. Prov. viii. 22-31, where
Wisdom (personified) is represented as
presiding at the Creation.

13. *maketh lightnings with the rain.*
Flashes of lightning pierce the clouds so
that they empty their contents upon the
earth (cf. Ps. cxxxv. 7).

His treasuries. Cf. Job xxxviii. 22.

14. *every man.* Who engages in idol-
worship.

every goldsmith. The maker of the image.

is put to shame. When the powerlessness
of the idol is contrasted with God's
supremacy over the elements.

15. *a work of delusion.* They who put
their trust in idols find themselves de-
luded in a time of emergency.

in the time of their visitation. When God
'visits,' i.e. punishes, the idols and their
worshippers according to their deserts
(cf. Isa. ii. 12, 18).

16. *the portion of Jacob.* viz. God (cf. Ps.
xvi. 5). It is a bold thought: if God
owns Israel as His *inheritance* (second
half of the verse), then Israel can regard
Him in a special sense as his *portion.*

For He is the former of all things,

And Israel is the tribe of His inheritance;

The LORD of hosts is His name.

17 Gather up thy wares from the ground,

O thou that abidest in the siege.

18. For thus saith the LORD: Behold, I will sling out the inhabitants of the land at this time, and will distress them, that they may feel it.

19 Woe is me for my hurt!

My wound is grievous;

But I said: 'This is but a sickness,

And I must bear it.'

20 My tent is spoiled,

And all my cords are broken;

כִּי־יוֹצֵר הַכֹּל הוּא

וְיִשְׂרָאֵל שֵׁבֶט נַחֲלָתוֹ

יְהֹוָה צְבָאוֹת שְׁמוֹ׃

17 אִסְפִּי מֵאֶרֶץ כִּנְעָתֵךְ

יוֹשֶׁבְתִּי בַּמָּצוֹר׃

18 כִּי־כֹה אָמַר יְהֹוָה הִנְנִי קוֹלֵעַ

אֶת־יוֹשְׁבֵי הָאָרֶץ בַּפַּעַם

הַזֹּאת וַהֲצֵרֹתִי לָהֶם לְמַעַן

יִמְצָאוּ׃

19 אוֹי־לִי עַל־שִׁבְרִי

נַחְלָה מַכָּתִי

וַאֲנִי אָמַרְתִּי אַךְ

זֶה חֳלִי וְאֶשָּׂאֶנּוּ׃

20 אָהֳלִי שֻׁדָּד

וְכָל־מֵיתָרַי נִתָּקוּ

v. 17. יושבת ק׳   v. 18. מלעיל   v. 20. קמץ בז״ק

---

all things. The universe and all it contains.

17-25 EXILE IS AT HAND

The prophet laments the imminent fate of the people, and prays to God to remember man's natural weakness of character and temper His punishment accordingly.

17. *gather up thy wares from the ground.* The Hebrew word translated *thy wares* (*kin'athech*) occurs nowhere else. It has been connected with an Arabic verb which means 'to contract, fold the wings,' and the sense of the clause is 'pack thy bundle (to take it) from the land,' since thou art going into captivity.

in the siege. viz. of Jerusalem.

18. *sling out.* For this verb, cf. 1 Sam. xxv. 29.

that they may feel it. lit. 'that they may find.' Rashi and Metsudath David interpret: that they may find their just deserts.

19. The prophet, speaking for the nation, laments his misfortunes.

20. The land is likened to a tent which has now been overthrown. But the most severe disaster is that the children of the nation have gone forth into exile, so that there is none to rebuild the shattered country. Cf. Isa. liv. 2 for the reverse, and see on iv. 20.

My children are gone forth of
me, and they are not;
There is none to stretch forth my
tent any more,
And to set up my curtains.

21 For the shepherds are become
brutish,
And have not inquired of the
LORD;
Therefore they have not pros-
pered,
And all their flocks are scattered.

22 Hark! a report, behold, it cometh,
And a great commotion out of the
north country,
To make the cities of Judah des-
olate,
A dwelling-place of jackals.

23 O LORD, I know that man's way
is not his own;
It is not in man to direct his steps
as he walketh.

24 O LORD, correct me, but in
measure;
Not in Thine anger, lest Thou
diminish me.

25 Pour out Thy wrath upon the
nations that know Thee not,

בָּנַי יְצָאֻנִי וְאֵינָם
אֵין־נֹטֶה עוֹד אָהֳלִי
וּמֵקִים יְרִיעוֹתָי :

21 כִּי נִבְעֲרוּ הָרֹעִים
וְאֶת־יְהֹוָה לֹא דָרָשׁוּ
עַל־כֵּן לֹא הִשְׂכִּילוּ
וְכָל־מַרְעִיתָם נָפוֹצָה:

22 קוֹל שְׁמוּעָה הִנֵּה בָאָה
וְרַעַשׁ גָּדוֹל מֵאֶרֶץ צָפוֹן
לָשׂוּם אֶת־עָרֵי יְהוּדָה
שְׁמָמָה מְעוֹן תַּנִּים:

23 יָדַעְתִּי יְהֹוָה כִּי
לֹא לָאָדָם דַּרְכּוֹ
לֹא־לְאִישׁ הֹלֵךְ
וְהָכִין אֶת־צַעֲדוֹ:

24 יַסְּרֵנִי יְהֹוָה אַךְ בְּמִשְׁפָּט
אַל־בְּאַפְּךָ פֶּן־תַּמְעִטֵנִי:

25 שְׁפֹךְ חֲמָתְךָ
עַל־הַגּוֹיִם אֲשֶׁר לֹא־יְדָעוּךָ

---

21. *the shepherds.* The leaders (cf. ii. 8).

brutish. Foolish. Only because a spirit
of folly had entered into them could they
have neglected to inquire of the Lord.

have not inquired of the LORD. They
refused to be guided by His teachings.

all their flocks are scattered. The people
are suffering through the misguidance
of their leaders. Although the exile had
not yet taken place, the prophet speaks
of it as an accomplished fact.

22. *the north country.* Babylon.

a dwelling-place of jackals. Cf. ix. 10.

23. Man is morally weak and does not
always possess the strength to overcome
temptation and direct his steps aright.
Jeremiah urges this plea on behalf of
his people in mitigation of punishment.

24. *in measure.* lit. 'with judgment,' i.e.
not with excessive severity (cf. xlvi. 28).

25. *the nations that know Thee not.* Even
if Israel has sinned, surely he is not to

And upon the families that call
not on Thy name;
For they have devoured Jacob,
Yea, they have devoured him and
consumed him,
And have laid waste his habitation.

וְעַל מִשְׁפָּחוֹת
אֲשֶׁר בְּשִׁמְךָ לֹא קָרָאוּ
כִּי־אָכְלוּ אֶת־יַעֲקֹב
וַאֲכָלֻהוּ וַיְכַלֻּהוּ
וְאֶת־נָוֵהוּ הֵשַׁמּוּ׃

11   CHAPTER XI   יא

1. The word that came to Jeremiah from the LORD, saying: 2. 'Hear
ye the words of this covenant, and
speak unto the men of Judah, and to

1 הַדָּבָר אֲשֶׁר־הָיָה אֶל־
יִרְמְיָהוּ מֵאֵת יְהֹוָה לֵאמֹר׃
2 שִׁמְעוּ אֶת־דִּבְרֵי הַבְּרִית
הַזֹּאת וְדִבַּרְתָּם אֶל־אִישׁ

be punished more severely than the heathens who have never 'known' (i.e. recognized) God.

families. See on iii. 14.

for they have devoured Jacob. Though the disasters of the people are due to their sins, yet the nations who executed God's judgment were animated by a spirit of vindictiveness and exceeded what He ordained; they should accordingly be punished. The verse is repeated in Ps. lxxix. 6f. with slight variations.

CHAPTER XI

FROM xi. 1 to xii. 6 is an exhortation to the people to be faithful to God's covenant with them and a warning of coming judgments. Two views are held on the date of this passage: (*i*) that it belongs to Jehoiakim's reign, and falls between the prophet's address in the Temple courts and Nebuchadnezzar's victory over Egypt at Carchemish in

605 B.C.E.; (*ii*) that it was delivered soon after the discovery of the Book of the Law by Hilkiah in the reign of Josiah (621 B.C.E.), and is connected with that king's reforms in consequence of the discovery (2 Kings xxiif.). The latter is now generally accepted.

2-8 EXHORTATION TO JUDAH

2. *this covenant.* Which God made with Israel when they left Egypt. The general sense of what is meant by the *covenant* is clear from the following verses: Israel was to be loyal to God's commandments, thereby constituting himself God's people, while He would be Israel's God; and only upon this condition rested the claim to possess the Promised Land. Kimchi refers it to the blessings and curses pronounced in the plains of Moab which are summed up as *the words of the covenant* (Deut. xxviii. 69; note the same phrase in verse 8 of this chapter).

hear ye . . . and speak. The plural of the

the inhabitants of Jerusalem; 3. and
say thou unto them: Thus saith the
LORD, the God of Israel: Cursed be
the man that heareth not the words
of this covenant, 4. which I commanded your fathers in the day that
I brought them forth out of the land
of Egypt, out of the iron furnace,
saying: Hearken to My voice, and
do them, according to all which I
command you; so shall ye be My
people, and I will be your God;
5. that I may establish the oath
which I swore unto your fathers, to
give them a land flowing with milk
and honey, as at this day.' Then
answered I, and said: 'Amen, O
LORD.'

6. And the LORD said unto me:
'Proclaim all these words in the
cities of Judah, and in the streets

יְהוּדָה וְעַל־יֹשְׁבֵי יְרוּשָׁלִָם׃
3 וְאָמַרְתָּ אֲלֵיהֶם כֹּה־אָמַר
יְהֹוָה אֱלֹהֵי יִשְׂרָאֵל אָרוּר
הָאִישׁ אֲשֶׁר לֹא יִשְׁמַע אֶת־
4 דִּבְרֵי הַבְּרִית הַזֹּאת׃ אֲשֶׁר
צִוִּיתִי אֶת־אֲבוֹתֵיכֶם בְּיוֹם
הוֹצִיאִי־אוֹתָם מֵאֶרֶץ־
מִצְרַיִם מִכּוּר הַבַּרְזֶל לֵאמֹר
שִׁמְעוּ בְקוֹלִי וַעֲשִׂיתֶם אוֹתָם
כְּכֹל אֲשֶׁר־אֲצַוֶּה אֶתְכֶם
וִהְיִיתֶם לִי לְעָם וְאָנֹכִי אֶהְיֶה
5 לָכֶם לֵאלֹהִים׃ לְמַעַן הָקִים
אֶת־הַשְּׁבוּעָה אֲשֶׁר־נִשְׁבַּעְתִּי
לַאֲבוֹתֵיכֶם לָתֵת לָהֶם אֶרֶץ
זָבַת חָלָב וּדְבַשׁ כַּיּוֹם הַזֶּה
וָאַעַן וָאֹמַר אָמֵן ׀ יְהֹוָה׃
6 וַיֹּאמֶר יְהֹוָה אֵלַי קְרָא אֶת־
כָּל־הַדְּבָרִים הָאֵלֶּה בְּעָרֵי
יְהוּדָה וּבְחֻצוֹת יְרוּשָׁלִָם׃

verbs denotes Jeremiah and other prophets. 'This verse contains the general
injunction laid upon the prophets as a
class, and is followed by the special
command to Jeremiah' (Streane).

3. *cursed be the man.* A very forceful
opening to the address made necessary
by the recalcitrance of the people.

4. *the iron furnace.* A furnace for smelting iron, i.e. the scene of bitter suffering
(cf. Deut. iv. 20).

do them. The commandments communicated by My voice.

5. *as at this day.* Even as you now enjoy.

amen, O LORD. Spoken in confirmation
of *cursed be,* etc. (verse 3), as in Deut.
xxvii. 15ff.

6. *in the cities of Judah, and in the streets
of Jerusalem.* This was probably a
proverbial expression, meaning throughout the length and breadth of the country.

of Jerusalem, saying: Hear ye the words of this covenant, and do them. 7. For I earnestly forewarned your fathers in the day that I brought them up out of the land of Egypt, even unto this day, forewarning betimes and often, saying: Hearken to My voice. 8. Yet they hearkened not, nor inclined their ear, but walked every one in the stubbornness of their evil heart; therefore I brought upon them all the words of this covenant, which I commanded them to do, but they did them not.'

9. And the LORD said unto me: 'A conspiracy is found among the men of Judah, and among the inhabitants of Jerusalem. 10. They are turned back to the iniquities of their forefathers, who refused to hear My words; and they are gone after other gods to serve them; the house of Israel and the house of Judah have broken My covenant

לֵאמֹר שִׁמְעוּ אֶת־דִּבְרֵי
הַבְּרִית הַזֹּאת וַעֲשִׂיתֶם אוֹתָם:
7 כִּי הָעֵד הַעִדֹתִי בַּאֲבוֹתֵיכֶם
בְּיוֹם הַעֲלוֹתִי אוֹתָם מֵאֶרֶץ
מִצְרַיִם עַד־הַיּוֹם הַזֶּה הַשְׁכֵּם
וְהָעֵד לֵאמֹר שִׁמְעוּ בְּקוֹלִי:
8 וְלֹא שָׁמְעוּ וְלֹא־הִטּוּ אֶת־
אָזְנָם וַיֵּלְכוּ אִישׁ בִּשְׁרִירוּת
לִבָּם הָרָע וָאָבִיא עֲלֵיהֶם
אֶת־כָּל־דִּבְרֵי הַבְּרִית־
הַזֹּאת אֲשֶׁר־צִוִּיתִי לַעֲשׂוֹת
9 וְלֹא עָשׂוּ: וַיֹּאמֶר יְהֹוָה אֵלַי
נִמְצָא־קֶשֶׁר בְּאִישׁ יְהוּדָה
10 וּבְיֹשְׁבֵי יְרוּשָׁלָם: שָׁבוּ עַל־
עֲוֺנֹת אֲבוֹתָם הָרִאשֹׁנִים אֲשֶׁר
מֵאֲנוּ לִשְׁמוֹעַ אֶת־דְּבָרַי
וְהֵמָּה הָלְכוּ אַחֲרֵי אֱלֹהִים
אֲחֵרִים לְעָבְדָם הֵפֵרוּ בֵית־
יִשְׂרָאֵל וּבֵית יְהוּדָה אֶת־
בְּרִיתִי אֲשֶׁר כָּרַתִּי אֶת־

v. 10. מלעיל

7. *betimes.* lit. 'rising early,' i.e. incessantly, at all times (cf. vii. 13 and often in this Book).

8. *yet they hearkened . . . heart.* Repeated substantially from vii. 24.

the words. i.e. the penalties for disobedience announced in the covenant.

9-14 THE EXHORTATION IS IGNORED

Israel's apostasy is so glaring that even the prophet's intercession will be of no avail.

9. *a conspiracy.* So widespread has idolatry become that it is as though the whole people have deliberately conspired to renounce their allegiance to God.

10. *they are turned back.* For a time they discontinued the sins of their forefathers in the wilderness and later, but now they resumed them.

which I made with their fathers.
11. Therefore thus saith the LORD:
Behold, I will bring evil upon them,
which they shall not be able to
escape; and though they shall cry
unto Me, I will not hearken unto
them. 12. Then shall the cities of
Judah and the inhabitants of Jerusalem go and cry unto the gods unto
whom they offer; but they shall not
save them at all in the time of their
trouble. 13. For according to the
number of thy cities are thy gods, O
Judah; and according to the number
of the streets of Jerusalem have ye
set up altars to the shameful thing,
even altars to offer unto Baal.
14. Therefore pray not thou for this
people, neither lift up cry nor prayer
for them; for I will not hear them in
the time that they cry unto Me for
their trouble.'

15 What hath My beloved to do in
My house,

11 אֲבוֹתָם : לָכֵן כֹּה־אָמַר יְהֹוָה
הִנְנִי מֵבִיא אֲלֵיהֶם רָעָה אֲשֶׁר
לֹא־יוּכְלוּ לָצֵאת מִמֶּנָּה
וְזָעֲקוּ אֵלַי וְלֹא אֶשְׁמַע
12 אֲלֵיהֶם : וְהָלְכוּ עָרֵי יְהוּדָה
וְיֹשְׁבֵי יְרוּשָׁלַם וְזָעֲקוּ אֶל־
הָאֱלֹהִים אֲשֶׁר הֵם מְקַטְּרִים
לָהֶם וְהוֹשֵׁעַ לֹא־יוֹשִׁיעוּ לָהֶם
13 בְּעֵת רָעָתָם : כִּי מִסְפַּר עָרֶיךָ
הָיוּ אֱלֹהֶיךָ יְהוּדָה וּמִסְפַּר
חֻצוֹת יְרוּשָׁלַם שַׂמְתֶּם
מִזְבְּחוֹת לַבֹּשֶׁת מִזְבְּחוֹת
14 לְקַטֵּר לַבָּעַל : וְאַתָּה אַל־
תִּתְפַּלֵּל בְּעַד־הָעָם הַזֶּה
וְאַל־תִּשָּׂא בַעֲדָם רִנָּה
וּתְפִלָּה כִּי | אֵינֶנִּי שֹׁמֵעַ בְּעֵת
קָרְאָם אֵלַי בְּעַד רָעָתָם :
15 מֶה לִידִידִי בְּבֵיתִי

---

their forefathers. Kimchi defines as the
generations of Amon, Manasseh and
Ahaz.

11. *I will not hearken.* Although 'the gates
of tears are never shut' (Talmud), that
is only when the tears express true
penitence. Here they will merely cry for
mercy, but not in contrition for their sins.

12. *unto whom they offer.* The use of the
present participle may imply that even
when crying to God, they still practise
idolatry.

13. *for according to the number*, etc. Repeated from ii. 28.

the shameful thing. lit. 'the shame,' the
prophet's contemptuous designation for
Baal.

14. *they cry unto Me.* Even if *they*
prayed I would not hearken, since they
cleave to their iniquity; I will certainly
not accept *thy* prayers on their behalf
(Metsudath David). Cf. vii. 16.

15-17 JUDAH'S INFIDELITY TO GOD

15. *My beloved.* viz. Judah; but now

Seeing she hath wrought lewdness with many,
And the hallowed flesh is passed
from thee ?
When thou doest evil, then thou
rejoicest.

16 The LORD called thy name
A leafy olive-tree, fair with
goodly fruit;
With the noise of a great tumult
He hath kindled fire upon it,
And the branches of it are broken.

17. For the LORD of hosts, that
planted thee, hath pronounced evil
against thee, because of the evil of
the house of Israel and of the house
of Judah, which they have wrought
for themselves in provoking Me by
offering unto Baal.

18 And the LORD gave me knowledge of it, and I knew it;
Then Thou showedst me their
doings.

עֲשׂוֹתָהּ הַמְזִמָּתָה הָרַבִּים
וּבְשַׂר־קֹדֶשׁ יַעַבְרוּ מֵעָלַיִךְ
כִּי רָעָתֵכִי אָז תַּעֲלֹזִי׃
16 זַיִת רַעֲנָן יְפֵה פְרִי־תֹאַר
קָרָא יְהֹוָה שְׁמֵךְ
לְקוֹל ׀ הֲמוּלָּה גְדֹלָה
הִצִּית אֵשׁ עָלֶיהָ
וְרָעוּ דָּלִיּוֹתָיו׃
17 וַיהֹוָה צְבָאוֹת הַנּוֹטֵעַ אוֹתָךְ
דִּבֶּר עָלַיִךְ רָעָה בִּגְלַל רָעַת
בֵּית־יִשְׂרָאֵל וּבֵית יְהוּדָה
אֲשֶׁר עָשׂוּ לָהֶם לְהַכְעִסֵנִי
לְקַטֵּר לַבָּעַל׃
18 וַיהֹוָה הוֹדִיעַנִי וָאֵדָעָה
אָז הִרְאִיתַנִי מַעַלְלֵיהֶם׃

v. 16. דגש אחר שורק

Judah has no right in God's house,
since his conduct is an affront to Him.

seeing . . . with many. The Hebrew is
difficult to translate. The word for
lewdness (mezimmah) may mean 'evil
design' and *with* is not in the original.
The best rendering that can be obtained
from the text is: 'seeing that the multitude perform it, viz. evil scheming.'
Accordingly we have a repetition of the
teaching, already familiar in this Book,
that God will not accept the service of
the Temple as long as the people act
corruptly.

and the hallowed flesh is passed from thee.
lit. 'and as for the holy flesh (i.e. the
offerings) let them pass from upon thee.'
Discontinue the sacrifices which you feel
your duty to bring, since they are of no
use to you and will not avert your doom.

16. *a leafy olive-tree.* Rich in foliage (cf.
Ps. lii. 10). Similar imagery is used of
the nation's prosperity in Hos. xiv. 6ff.

noise of a great tumult. Descriptive of a
storm accompanied by thunder and
lightning.

He hath kindled fire. The prophetic
perfect. Although in His love for His
people God described them as a luxuriant
olive-tree, He finds it necessary to destroy
them.

17. *the house of Israel . . . the house of
Judah.* The branches of the olive-tree.

18-23 A PLOT TO SILENCE JEREMIAH

18. *it.* The punishment which was to
befall the nation.

Thou showedst me. This is an aside,

84

19 But I was like a docile lamb that
is led to the slaughter;
And I knew not that they had
devised devices against me:
'Let us destroy the tree with the
fruit thereof,
And let us cut him off from the
land of the living,
That his name may be no more
remembered.'
20 But, O LORD of hosts, that
judgest righteously,
That triest the reins and the
heart,
Let me see Thy vengeance on
them;
For unto Thee have I revealed
my cause.
21. Therefore thus saith the LORD
concerning the men of Anathoth,
that seek thy life, saying: 'Thou shalt
not prophesy in the name of the

19 וַאֲנִי כְּכֶבֶשׂ אַלּוּף
יוּבַל לִטְבּוֹחַ
וְלֹא־יָדַעְתִּי
כִּי־עָלַי ׀ חָשְׁבוּ מַחֲשָׁבוֹת
נַשְׁחִיתָה עֵץ בְּלַחְמוֹ
וְנִכְרְתֶנּוּ מֵאֶרֶץ חַיִּים
וּשְׁמוֹ לֹא־יִזָּכֵר עוֹד׃
20 וַיהוָה צְבָאוֹת שֹׁפֵט צֶדֶק
בֹּחֵן כְּלָיוֹת וָלֵב
אֶרְאֶה נִקְמָתְךָ מֵהֶם
כִּי אֵלֶיךָ גִּלִּיתִי אֶת־רִיבִי׃
21 לָכֵן כֹּה־אָמַר יְהוָה עַל־
אַנְשֵׁי עֲנָתוֹת הַמְבַקְשִׁים אֶת־
נַפְשְׁךָ לֵאמֹר לֹא תִנָּבֵא בְּשֵׁם

perhaps implying: I could hardly have
credited their evil, hadst Thou not
shown it to me. Kimchi relates the verse
to the plot against Jeremiah's life, thus
linking it with what follows: God gave
me the knowledge of their evil machinations against me. This interpretation is
accepted by most moderns.

19. Jeremiah's predictions had aroused
the enmity of his own townspeople
(verse 21) who plotted to take his life
(cf. xviii. 18).

a docile lamb. The prophet compares
himself to a domesticated pet animal
which is ignorant of the owner's intention to slaughter it.

with the fruit thereof. lit. 'with the bread
thereof'; perhaps a proverbial equivalent
of 'root and branch.'

20. *the reins and the heart.* i.e. the innermost feelings and thoughts.

Thy vengeance. 'He does not desire
personal vengeance, but a vindication of
the cause he has taken up for God'
(Pickering).

on them. The men of Anathoth who were
plotting against him.

for unto Thee, etc. Conscious of his
integrity, Jeremiah commits his cause to
God from Whom nothing is hidden.

21. *thou shalt not prophesy.* When evil
cannot justify itself even by the most
specious reasoning, it falls back upon the
weapon of tyrants in all ages: suppression
of freedom of speech by brute force.
For other instances to silence the prophets, cf. Amos ii. 12, vii. 10ff.; Mic. ii. 6.
The threat in this verse apparently
contradicts verse 19, but it may indicate

LORD, that thou die not by our
hand'; 22. therefore thus saith the
LORD of hosts:

> Behold, I will punish them;
> The young men shall die by the
>   sword,
> Their sons and their daughters
>   shall die by famine;
> 23 And there shall be no remnant
>   unto them;
> For I will bring evil upon the
>   men of Anathoth,
> Even the year of their visitation.

יְהֹוָה וְלֹא תָמֻת בְּיָדֵנוּ:

22 לָכֵן כֹּה אָמַר יְהֹוָה צְבָאוֹת
הִנְנִי פֹקֵד עֲלֵיהֶם
הַבַּחוּרִים יָמֻתוּ בַחֶרֶב
בְּנֵיהֶם וּבְנֹתֵיהֶם יָמֻתוּ בָּרָעָב:

23 וּשְׁאֵרִית לֹא תִהְיֶה לָהֶם
כִּי־אָבִיא רָעָה
אֶל־אַנְשֵׁי עֲנָתוֹת
שְׁנַת פְּקֻדָּתָם:

12	CHAPTER XII	יב

1 Right wouldest Thou be, O LORD,

  Were I to contend with Thee,

  Yet will I reason with Thee:

1 צַדִּיק אַתָּה יְהֹוָה
כִּי אָרִיב אֵלֶיךָ
אַךְ מִשְׁפָּטִים אֲדַבֵּר אוֹתָךְ

a later stage in the conspiracy. The
secret plan to kill him having failed, they
try to close his mouth by menaces.

22. The punishment will take a form
which vindicates the prophet: the invasion he foretold will come to pass, and
in it the sword and famine will take their
toll.

23. The judgment on Jeremiah's birthplace is particularly severe, because he
had the right to expect sympathy and
help from the population.

no remnant. This probably refers to the
families of the conspirators, and not the
entire population. It is recorded that
128 men of Anathoth returned to the
Holy Land from the Babylonian captivity
(Ezra ii. 23).

the year of their visitation. When

Nebuchadnezzar would conquer the
country.

CHAPTER XII

1-6 WHY DO THE WICKED PROSPER?

THE evil which prevailed among the
ruling class and the personal attack upon
him aroused in the prophet's mind this
question. It is apparently the first time
that the problem is raised in the Bible.

1. *right wouldest Thou be.* I know that
in any argument Thou must be right.
A.V. and R.V. have: 'righteous art
Thou,' i.e. God's righteousness is axiomatic; nevertheless the question is suggested: how can it be reconciled with the
prosperity of the wicked?

reason with. lit. 'speak judgments,' i.e.
argue with, or complain unto.

Wherefore doth the way of the wicked prosper?
Wherefore are all they secure that deal very treacherously?

2 Thou hast planted them, yea, they have taken root;
They grow, yea, they bring forth fruit;
Thou art near in their mouth,
And far from their reins.

3 But Thou, O LORD, knowest me,
Thou seest me, and triest my heart toward Thee;
Pull them out like sheep for the slaughter,
And prepare them for the day of slaughter.

4 How long shall the land mourn,
And the herbs of the whole field wither?
For the wickedness of them that dwell therein, the beasts are consumed, and the birds;

מַדּוּעַ דֶּרֶךְ רְשָׁעִים צָלֵחָה
שָׁלוּ כָּל־בֹּגְדֵי בָגֶד:
2 נְטַעְתָּם גַּם־שֹׁרָשׁוּ
יֵלְכוּ גַּם־עָשׂוּ פֶרִי
קָרוֹב אַתָּה בְּפִיהֶם
וְרָחוֹק מִכִּלְיוֹתֵיהֶם:
3 וְאַתָּה יְהוָה יְדַעְתָּנִי
תִּרְאֵנִי וּבָחַנְתָּ לִבִּי אִתָּךְ
הַתִּקֵם כְּצֹאן לְטִבְחָה
וְהַקְדִּשֵׁם לְיוֹם הֲרֵגָה:
4 עַד־מָתַי תֶּאֱבַל הָאָרֶץ
וְעֵשֶׂב כָּל־הַשָּׂדֶה יִבָשׁ
מֵרָעַת יֹשְׁבֵי־בָהּ
סָפְתָה בְהֵמוֹת וָעוֹף

---

the wicked. Some understand the term of the people of Anathoth (cf. verse 6), but it is more probably of general application.

2. *Thou hast planted them.* This figure of fixed tenure and stability is met with frequently in the Bible (cf. 2 Sam. vii. 10, referring to the whole nation; Isa. xl. 24; Ps. i. 3). Their prosperity is not by chance, but due to God's decree.

they grow. For this use of the verb *halach,* lit. 'to go,' cf. Hos. xiv. 7, *his branches shall spread.*

Thou art near, etc. They constantly have the Divine name on their lips, but their simulated piety is sheer hypocrisy (cf. Isa. xxix. 13).

3. *triest my heart.* Therefore Thou knowest that I do not speak hypocritically.

pull them . . . slaughter. This is an impassioned plea for the destruction of his enemies, the men of Anathoth (cf. xi. 21). It raises a moral difficulty; but even the prophets, though intoxicated with God, are portrayed as human beings with their common weaknesses and failings. In his anguish at discovering that his own townspeople, even his own family (verse 6), desire his death, Jeremiah gives way to his outraged feelings and prays for their complete overthrow.

4. *how long shall the land mourn.* The soil is represented as 'mourning' when it does not produce, probably through lack of rain. This is a God-sent punishment for the wickedness of the inhabitants; but the righteous among them have to share the penalty! How long, then, will God tolerate this injustice?

Because they said: 'He seeth not
our end.'

5 'If thou hast run with the footmen,
and they have wearied thee,
Then how canst thou contend
with horses?
And though in a land of peace
thou art secure,
Yet how wilt thou do in the
thickets of the Jordan?

6 For even thy brethren, and the
house of thy father,
Even they have dealt treacherously
with thee,
Even they have cried aloud after
thee;
Believe them not, though they
speak fair words unto thee.'

כִּי אָמְרוּ
לֹא יִרְאֶה אֶת־אַחֲרִיתֵנוּ:
5 כִּי אֶת־רַגְלִים ׀ רַצְתָּה
וַיַּלְאוּךָ
וְאֵיךְ תְּתַחֲרֶה אֶת־הַסּוּסִים
וּבְאֶרֶץ שָׁלוֹם אַתָּה בוֹטֵחַ
וְאֵיךְ תַּעֲשֶׂה בִּגְאוֹן הַיַּרְדֵּן:
6 כִּי גַם־אַחֶיךָ וּבֵית־אָבִיךָ
גַּם־הֵמָּה בָּגְדוּ בָךְ
גַּם־הֵמָּה קָרְאוּ אַחֲרֶיךָ מָלֵא
אַל־תַּאֲמֵן בָּם
כִּי־יְדַבְּרוּ אֵלֶיךָ טוֹבוֹת:

He seeth not our end. The subject is
uncertain. Some understand it as God
Who is unconcerned about their actions
and so they can continue in their evil
ways with impunity. Others refer it to
Jeremiah of whom they say that they will
outlive him and he will not see his predictions fulfilled.

5. GOD'S REPLY. The question remains
unanswered, but God demands faith and
patience, for the prophet's present
difficulties are as nothing compared with
what is yet to come.

the footmen ... with horses? If you find the
opposition of the men of Anathoth too
difficult to bear, how will you stand up
to the enmity of more formidable men,
the leaders of the nation?

a land of peace. The phrase is to be
understood in a comparative sense, a land
cultivated and inhabited, in contrast to
the thickets of the Jordan, i.e. the jungle
along the banks of the river, the haunt of
wild animals.

6. *cried aloud after thee.* They raised a
hue and cry against Jeremiah as though
he were a criminal to be hunted down.

though they speak fair words unto thee.
In xi. 21 they are pictured as threatening
him with death. Probably they varied their
tactics, now threatening, now cajoling.

7-13 DEVASTATION OF THE LAND
THREATENED

A plaintive lament by God that He has
had to surrender His beloved into the
hands of their enemies. Such a fate
would be occasioned by a severe national
disaster, and the date may be the first
capture of Jerusalem in 597 B.C.E. But
the verbs can also be construed as the
prophetic perfect and the passage refer
to a catastrophe in the future, spoken of
as though it had already taken place.
In that case, the passage may be a general
answer to the prophet's questioning: even
though the wicked seem to be secure,
yet the time is approaching when widespread devastation will overtake them.

(handwritten annotations: "Gods lament", "Temple", "defiance", "open hostility", "Babylon")

7 I have forsaken My house,
I have cast off My heritage;
I have given the dearly beloved of
My soul
Into the hand of her enemies.
8 My heritage is become unto Me
As a lion in the forest;
She hath uttered her voice against
Me;
Therefore have I hated her.
9 Is My heritage unto Me as a
speckled bird of prey?
Are the birds of prey against her
round about?
Come ye, assemble all the beasts
of the field,
Bring them to devour.
10 Many shepherds have destroyed
My vineyard,
They have trodden My portion
under foot,

עָזַבְתִּי אֶת־בֵּיתִי ‏7
נָטַשְׁתִּי אֶת־נַחֲלָתִי
נָתַתִּי אֶת־יְדִדוּת נַפְשִׁי
בְּכַף אֹיְבֶיהָ:
הָיְתָה־לִּי נַחֲלָתִי ‏8
כְּאַרְיֵה בַיָּעַר
נָתְנָה עָלַי בְּקוֹלָהּ
עַל־כֵּן שְׂנֵאתִיהָ:
הַעַיִט צָבוּעַ נַחֲלָתִי לִי ‏9
הַעַיִט סָבִיב עָלֶיהָ
לְכוּ אִסְפוּ כָּל־חַיַּת הַשָּׂדֶה
הֵתָיוּ לְאָכְלָה:
רֹעִים רַבִּים שִׁחֲתוּ כַרְמִי ‏10
בֹּסְסוּ אֶת־חֶלְקָתִי

---

7. My house. This probably means the Temple which, however, is identified with the nation, since their fate is interwoven.

the dearly beloved of My soul. Though sinners, they are God's *dearly beloved*; nevertheless justice demands retribution, since God is no respecter of persons.

8. as a lion, etc. 'The open hostility of the people towards the Lord is likened by Him to the angry roar and fierce attack of a lion ranging the forest. He therefore withdraws and leaves it as some savage beast to the solitude that it has made for itself' (Streane).

uttered her voice against Me. Openly expressed defiance.

hated her. The Targum renders 'expelled her,' so as not to conflict with the *dearly beloved* of the preceding verse;

but the clause means that God will treat the nation as though they were the object of His hate.

9. *a speckled bird of prey.* Which incurs the enmity of other birds of prey. Birds are wont to attack other birds of unfamiliar plumage, a habit which was noted by classical writers.

assemble, etc. The words bear a close resemblance to Isa. lvi. 9.

all the beasts of the field. i.e. Babylon and her satellites.

10. *many shepherds.* viz. rulers, but the reference is not clear. It may mean the generals of the enemy as in vi. 3 (so Rashi, Kimchi); or, the leaders of Israel as in ii. 8 who are misleaders and responsible for the plight of the nation.

My vineyard. Figurative of the people (cf. Isa. v. 1ff.).

They have made My pleasant portion
A desolate wilderness.

11 They have made it a desolation,
It mourneth unto Me, being desolate;
The whole land is made desolate,
Because no man layeth it to heart.

12 Upon all the high hills in the wilderness spoilers are come;
For the sword of the LORD devoureth
From the one end of the land even to the other end of the land,
No flesh hath peace.

13 They have sown wheat, and have reaped thorns;
They have put themselves to pain, they profit not;
Be ye then ashamed of your increase,
Because of the fierce anger of the LORD.

נָתְנוּ אֶת־חֶלְקַת חֶמְדָּתִי
לְמִדְבַּר שְׁמָמָה׃

11 שָׂמָהּ לִשְׁמָמָה
אָבְלָה עָלַי שְׁמֵמָה
נָשַׁמָּה כָּל־הָאָרֶץ
כִּי אֵין אִישׁ שָׂם עַל־לֵב׃

12 עַל־כָּל־שְׁפָיִם בַּמִּדְבָּר
בָּאוּ שֹׁדְדִים
anarchy
כִּי חֶרֶב לַיהוָה אֹכְלָה
מִקְצֵה אֶרֶץ
וְעַד־קְצֵה הָאָרֶץ
אֵין שָׁלוֹם לְכָל־בָּשָׂר׃

13 זָרְעוּ חִטִּים וְקֹצִים קָצָרוּ
נֶחְלוּ לֹא יוֹעִלוּ
וּבֹשׁוּ מִתְּבוּאֹתֵיכֶם
מֵחֲרוֹן אַף־יְהוָה׃

v. 11. המ׳ בצרי　v. 13. קמץ בז״ק

11. *unto Me.* lit. 'upon Me,' i.e. to My grief (cf. for the usage, Gen. xlviii. 7).

layeth it to heart. Even now no one troubles about the pending disaster; all shut their ears to My warnings.

12. *the sword of the LORD.* In the hands of the enemy, who is only God's tool. For this mode of thought, cf. Isa. x. 15.

no flesh hath peace. Not only Judah, but other nations will also be torn by war.

13. *they have sown wheat, and have reaped thorns.* It is simplest to understand *they* as referring to Israel: not only has disaster come from without, but from within too; even his crops have disastrously failed and his labour has been in vain.

be ye then ashamed of your increase. For its poverty demonstrates that you are under God's displeasure (cf. xiv. 3f.; Joel i. 11). The verbs are the prophetic perfect.

14-17 FATE OF ISRAEL'S ENEMIES

Although these nations are God's instruments for the execution of His purpose, they will be punished by exile for destroying Israel, because 'benefit is brought through the instrumentality of the virtuous, whilst hurt is brought through the instrumentality of the evil.' Their exile will only be temporary if they repent, but permanent if they persist in their evil ways. Exactly the same prospect is frequently held out to Israel in

14. Thus saith the LORD: As for all Mine evil neighbours, that touch the inheritance which I have caused My people Israel to inherit, behold, I will pluck them up from off their land, and will pluck up the house of Judah from among them. 15. And it shall come to pass, after that I have plucked them up, I will again have compassion on them; and I will bring them back, every man to his heritage, and every man to his land. 16. And it shall come to pass, if they will diligently learn the ways of My people to swear by My name: 'As the LORD liveth,' even as they taught My people to swear by Baal; then shall they be built up in the midst of My people. 17. But if they will not hearken, then will I pluck up that nation, plucking up and destroying it, saith the LORD.

כֹּה ׀ אָמַר יְהֹוָה עַל־כָּל־ 14
שְׁכֵנַי הָרָעִים הַנֹּגְעִים בַּנַּחֲלָה
אֲשֶׁר־הִנְחַלְתִּי אֶת־עַמִּי
אֶת־יִשְׂרָאֵל הִנְנִי נְֹתָשָׁם מֵעַל
אַדְמָתָם וְאֶת־בֵּית יְהוּדָה
אֶתּוֹשׁ מִתּוֹכָם׃ וְהָיָה אַחֲרֵי 15
נָתְשִׁי אוֹתָם אָשׁוּב וְרִחַמְתִּים
וַהֲשִׁבֹתִים אִישׁ לְנַחֲלָתוֹ וְאִישׁ
לְאַרְצוֹ׃ וְהָיָה אִם־לָמֹד 16
יִלְמְדוּ אֶת־דַּרְכֵי עַמִּי
לְהִשָּׁבֵעַ בִּשְׁמִי חַי־יְהֹוָה
כַּאֲשֶׁר לִמְּדוּ אֶת־עַמִּי
לְהִשָּׁבֵעַ בַּבָּעַל וְנִבְנוּ בְּתוֹךְ
עַמִּי׃ וְאִם לֹא יִשְׁמָעוּ וְנָתַשְׁתִּי 17
אֶת־הַגּוֹי הַהוּא נָתוֹשׁ וְאַבֵּד
נְאֻם־יְהֹוָה׃

the Bible, since God is an impartial Judge. From this may be seen how false is the interpretation of 'chosen people,' applied to Israel, as 'favoured people.'

14. *Mine evil neighbours.* viz. Ammon, Moab, etc. In *Mine* God identifies Himself with Israel.

and will pluck up the house of Judah from among them. The clause is difficult, since it implies the deliverance of Judah, not his punishment as the context requires. Perhaps the thought is that as these nations will be uprooted, Israel will thereby be removed from, and no longer be subject to, their evil influence, which was in some measure responsible for his own downfall.

15. *I will again have compassion on them.* The restoration of Moab is foretold in xlviii. 47 and of Ammon in xlix. 6.

16. *to swear by My name.* See on iv. 2.

be built up. Cf. *if thou return to the Almighty, thou shalt be built up* (Job xxii. 23).

in the midst of My people. i.e. as My people will be restored to their land, so will they. *In the midst* further implies a harmonious state of unity and peace, and the passage may well be a Messianic forecast of the peace and friendship which will one day reign among all peoples.

13   CHAPTER XIII   יג

1. Thus said the LORD unto me: *loin cloth* 'Go, and get thee a linen girdle, and put it upon thy loins, and put it not in water.' 2. So I got a girdle according to the word of the LORD, and put it upon my loins.

3. And the word of the LORD came unto me the second time, saying: 4. 'Take the girdle that thou hast gotten, which is upon thy loins, and arise, go to Perath, and hide it there

1 כֹּה־אָמַר יְהֹוָה אֵלַי הָלוֹךְ
וְקָנִיתָ לְּךָ אֵזוֹר פִּשְׁתִּים וְשַׂמְתּוֹ
עַל־מָתְנֶיךָ וּבַמַּיִם לֹא
2 תְבִאֵהוּ: וָאֶקְנֶה אֶת־הָאֵזוֹר
כִּדְבַר יְהֹוָה וָאָשִׂם עַל־מָתְנָי:
3 וַיְהִי דְבַר־יְהֹוָה אֵלַי שֵׁנִית
4 לֵאמֹר: קַח אֶת־הָאֵזוֹר אֲשֶׁר
קָנִיתָ אֲשֶׁר עַל־מָתְנֶיךָ וְקוּם
לֵךְ פְּרָתָה וְטָמְנֵהוּ שָׁם בִּנְקִיק
left

CHAPTER XIII

1-11 SYMBOL OF THE LINEN GIRDLE

AT the command of God, the prophet deposits a linen girdle, after having worn it a short while, in a cavity on the banks of the Euphrates (but see on verse 4). After a long interval he takes it out, only to find it completely rotted and useless. This is 'an acted parable': like a girdle Israel had been closely attached to God, but had proved unworthy of the honour and will be discarded like a soiled garment. Modern commentators differ on the question whether this was actually carried out by the prophet, or whether he saw it in a vision which he then imparted to the people. They are also divided on whether the passage relates to an early period of Jeremiah's ministry, by which time idolatry was already rife, or falls in Jehoiakim's reign (see on verse 18).

1. *a linen girdle.* The Hebrew word *ezor* denotes a loin-cloth rather than what is now understood as a girdle. Linen garments were worn by the priests (Exod. xxviii. 39). Hence the girdle

fittingly symbolized the community which was intended to be *a kingdom of priests and a holy nation* (Exod. xix. 6).

upon thy loins. Emblematic of Israel's close attachment to God (verse 11).

put it not in water. New linen is steeped in water to soften it and make it more comfortable for wearing. 'The symbolic significance is apparently that the linen is to be guarded against contact with the element that will ultimately ruin it. The girdle in this state represents Israel in his unspoiled purity, in the closest union with his God' (Peake).

4. *Perath.* If the Euphrates is meant (though generally this is prefixed by 'the river'), this would necessitate a double journey of about three hundred miles. Some hold that the Hebrew *perathah* means 'to Parah' (cf. Josh. xviii. 23), a town three miles north-east of Anathoth. It is the modern Wadi Farah which 'suits the picture, having a lavish fountain, a broad pool and a stream, all of which soak into the sand and fissured rock of the surrounding desert' (G. A. Smith).

in a cleft of the rock.' 5. So I went, and hid it in Perath, as the LORD commanded me. 6. And it came to pass after many days, that the LORD said unto me: 'Arise, go to Perath, and take the girdle from thence, which I commanded thee to hide there.' 7. Then I went to Perath, and digged, and took the girdle from the place where I had hid it; and, behold, the girdle was marred, it was profitable for nothing. 8. Then the word of the LORD came unto me, saying:

9. Thus saith the LORD: After this manner will I mar the pride of Judah, and the great pride of Jerusalem, 10. even this evil people, that refuse to hear My words, that

5 הַסָּֽלַע : וָאֵלֵךְ וָאֶטְמְנֵהוּ
בִּפְרָת כַּאֲשֶׁר צִוָּה יְהֹוָה
6 אֹתִֽי : וַיְהִי מִקֵּץ יָמִים רַבִּים
וַיֹּאמֶר יְהֹוָה אֵלַי קוּם לֵךְ
פְרָתָה וְקַח מִשָּׁם אֶת־הָאֵזוֹר
אֲשֶׁר צִוִּיתִיךָ לְטָמְנוֹ־שָֽׁם :
7 וָאֵלֵךְ פְּרָתָה וָאֶחְפֹּר וָאֶקַּח
אֶת־הָאֵזוֹר מִן־הַמָּקוֹם
אֲשֶׁר־טְמַנְתִּיו שָׁמָּה וְהִנֵּה
נִשְׁחַת הָאֵזוֹר לֹא יִצְלַח לַכֹּל :
8 וַיְהִי דְבַר־יְהֹוָה אֵלַי לֵאמֹֽר :
9 כֹּה אָמַר יְהֹוָה כָּכָה אַשְׁחִית
אֶת־גְּאוֹן יְהוּדָה וְאֶת־גְּאוֹן
10 יְרוּשָׁלִַם הָרָב : הָעָם הַזֶּה
הָרָע הַמֵּאֲנִים | לִשְׁמוֹעַ אֶת־

They who understand the word as Euphrates mostly regard the incident as visionary. Streane, on the other hand, argues for the actuality of the experience and points out that Jeremiah was away from Jerusalem during the greater part of the later years of Jehoiakim's reign and nothing is recorded of him in that period. This may have been the time when he was on his journey. He also thinks that he then made contact with Nebuchadnezzar, which explains the kindly feelings of the Babylonian king towards him (cf. xxxix. 11f.).

the rock. If the Euphrates is meant, the part referred to 'cannot be anywhere near Babylon, where there are no rocks, but in the upper part of its course, above Carchemish, or even above Samosata, where it still flows between rocky sides' (Driver).

5. *in Perath.* If the river is intended, the meaning must be a place near the Euphrates.

7. *and digged.* He had originally covered it over with earth so that it should not be removed by a person who found it among the rocks.

9. The rotting of the girdle denotes the humbling of Judah's pride as a punishment for his idolatry which rendered the people as useless as the soiled girdle. Alternatively, their pride will be broken as easily as the rotted girdle disintegrates.

the pride. It is unlikely that the word is used here in the sense of arrogance and conceit, but rather their material eminence, their strength and wealth which are the source of their pride.

walk in the stubbornness of their heart, and are gone after other gods to serve them, and to worship them, that it be as this girdle, which is profitable for nothing. 11. For as the girdle cleaveth to the loins of a man, so have I caused to cleave unto Me the whole house of Israel and the whole house of Judah, saith the LORD, that they might be unto Me for a people, and for a name, and for a praise, and for a glory; but they would not hearken.

12. Moreover thou shalt speak unto them this word: Thus saith the LORD, the God of Israel: 'Every bottle is filled with wine'; and when they shall say unto thee: 'Do we not know that every bottle is filled with wine?' 13. Then shalt thou say unto them: Thus saith the LORD: Behold, I will fill all the inhabitants of this land, even the kings that sit upon

דִּבְרֵי הַהֹלְכִים בִּשְׁרִרוּת
לִבָּם וַיֵּלְכוּ אַחֲרֵי אֱלֹהִים
אֲחֵרִים לְעָבְדָם וּלְהִשְׁתַּחֲוֹת
לָהֶם וִיהִי כָּאֵזוֹר הַזֶּה אֲשֶׁר
11 לֹא־יִצְלַח לַכֹּל׃ כִּי כַּאֲשֶׁר
יִדְבַּק הָאֵזוֹר אֶל־מָתְנֵי אִישׁ
כֵּן הִדְבַּקְתִּי אֵלַי אֶת־כָּל־
בֵּית יִשְׂרָאֵל וְאֶת־כָּל־בֵּית
יְהוּדָה נְאֻם־יְהוָה לִהְיוֹת
לִי לְעָם וּלְשֵׁם וְלִתְהִלָּה
וּלְתִפְאָרֶת וְלֹא שָׁמֵעוּ׃
12 וְאָמַרְתָּ אֲלֵיהֶם אֶת־הַדָּבָר
הַזֶּה כֹּה־אָמַר יְהוָה אֱלֹהֵי
יִשְׂרָאֵל כָּל־נֵבֶל יִמָּלֵא יָיִן
וְאָמְרוּ אֵלֶיךָ הֲיָדֹעַ לֹא נֵדַע
כִּי־כָל־נֵבֶל יִמָּלֵא יָיִן׃
13 וְאָמַרְתָּ אֲלֵיהֶם כֹּה־אָמַר
יְהוָה הִנְנִי מְמַלֵּא אֶת־כָּל־
יֹשְׁבֵי הָאָרֶץ הַזֹּאת וְאֶת־
הַמְּלָכִים הַיֹּשְׁבִים לְדָוִד

12-14 PARABLE OF THE WINE-BOTTLE

12. 'We may imagine that the prophet addresses those who were assembled at some festival, and that the sight of the empty jars suggested the words he spoke, which were perhaps a toper's witticism. Just as the drunken revellers scoffed at the simplicity of Isaiah's instruction (cf. Isa. xxviii. 1ff.), fit only for babes and

sucklings, so their successors tell hi successor that they know quite well wha he has to tell them' (Peake).

bottle. Made of earthenware, not c skin (cf. xlviii. 12).

13. *upon David's throne.* David is men tioned probably in order to emphasiz the contrast between them and him, an show how low they have fallen.

David's throne, and the priests, and
the prophets, and all the inhabitants
of Jerusalem, with drunkenness.

14. And I will dash them one against
another, even the fathers and the
sons together, saith the LORD; I will
not pity, nor spare, nor have compassion, that I should not destroy
them.

15 Hear ye, and give ear, be not
    proud;
    For the LORD hath spoken.

16 Give glory to the LORD your
    God,   /
    Before it grow dark,
    And before your feet stumble
    Upon the mountains of twilight,

עַל־־כִּסְאוֹ וְאֶת־הַכֹּהֲנִים
וְאֶת־הַנְּבִיאִים וְאֶת כָּל־
יֹשְׁבֵי יְרוּשָׁלִַם שִׁכָּרוֹן׃

14 וְנִפַּצְתִּים אִישׁ אֶל־אָחִיו
וְהָאָבוֹת וְהַבָּנִים יַחְדָּו נְאֻם־
יְהֹוָה לֹא־אֶחְמוֹל וְלֹא־
אָחוּס וְלֹא אֲרַחֵם מֵהַשְׁחִיתָם׃

15 שִׁמְעוּ וְהַאֲזִינוּ אַל־תִּגְבָּהוּ
כִּי יְהֹוָה דִּבֵּר׃

16 תְּנוּ לַיהֹוָה אֱלֹהֵיכֶם כָּבוֹד
בְּטֶרֶם יַחְשִׁךְ
וּבְטֶרֶם יִתְנַגְּפוּ רַגְלֵיכֶם
עַל־הָרֵי נָשֶׁף

v. 13. קמץ בטרחא

---

he priests. Who were unfaithful to their
igh office.

he prophets. i.e. the false prophets.

ith drunkenness. Not to be understood
terally, but in the sense of mental
ntoxication, confusion and bewilder-
nent, which will lead them to collide with
ach other in their helplessness before the
nemy. For this figure, cf. xxv. 15f.,
lviii. 26. Streane conjectures that the
ate is about 605 B.C.E. when Nebuchad-
ezzar won his victory over Egypt at
Carchemish.

4. *I will dash*. As intoxicated persons
ollide and cause each other to fall, so
vill the confusion sent by God be a
actor in the destruction of the Kingdom.

5-17 THE PEOPLE EXHORTED TO HEED
      THE WARNING

5. *be not proud*. Do not be too proud
o hearken to God's admonition.

16. 'Here Jeremiah flashes before us a
picture of travellers on the mountains,
who ramble with lighthearted confidence,
till suddenly the sky is overspread, and
there is gloom like twilight. They still
move on with stumbling feet, but warned
by their experience, resolve to wait till
the sky clears again. But as they tarry
the gloom deepens till thick darkness
settles down upon them' (Peake).

give glory. By humbling yourselves
before Him, acknowledging your sin and
yielding Him your obedience (cf. Josh.
vii. 19).

before it grow dark. As the mountain
traveller hastens to reach safety before
darkness overtakes him, so let Israel return to God before the darkness of
disaster engulfs him.

the mountains of twilight. i.e. mountains
enveloped in the dusk of twilight.

95

And, while ye look for light,
He turn it into the shadow of
death,
And make it gross darkness.
17 But if ye will not hear it,
My soul shall weep in secret for
your pride;
And mine eye shall weep sore,
and run down with tears,
Because the LORD'S flock is
carried away captive.
18 Say thou unto the king and to
the queen-mother:

וְקִוִּיתֶם לְאוֹר
וְשָׂמָה לְצַלְמָוֶת
יָשִׁית לַעֲרָפֶל׃
17 וְאִם לֹא תִשְׁמָעוּהָ
בְּמִסְתָּרִים תִּבְכֶּה־נַפְשִׁי
מִפְּנֵי גֵוָה
וְדָמֹעַ תִּדְמַע
וְתֵרַד עֵינִי דִּמְעָה
כִּי נִשְׁבָּה עֵדֶר יְהוָה׃
18 אֱמֹר לַמֶּלֶךְ וְלַגְּבִירָה

v. 16. ושית ק׳

---

and, while ye look for light, etc. The very
source whence you hope for salvation
will become the means of your destruction—an allusion to the false hopes they
entertained of help from Egypt (Kimchi).

17. Jeremiah might appear a stern prophet—so harsh that he roused the fierce
hostility of many sections of the people.
But his harshness was motivated by the
driving force of duty, however unpleas-
ant; a yearning love for his people inspired him with deep compassion for
their woes. In a passage of great tenderness the Talmud interprets the verse of
God as the Speaker: 'As a loving father
sorrowing over his son's misdeeds for
which he has had to punish him, so
God weeps in a secret place over Israel's
glory (*sic*) which has been taken from him
and given to others' (Chag. 5b).

for your pride. Either your pride which
will be humbled (Rashi), or your pride
which causes you stubbornly to refuse
to heed God's word.

the LORD'S flock. Though they have
sinned, they are still *the LORD'S flock.*
For the simile, cf. Ps. lxxiv. 1, lxxx. 2.

is carried. The prophetic perfect.

18-19 DIRGE OVER THE KING AND
QUEEN-MOTHER

18. *the king.* Jehoiachin (cf. xxii. 26).

the queen-mother. Nehushta (2 Kings
xxiv. 8). Eastern etiquette attached
great prominence to the queen-mother,
as is shown by the frequency with which
she is specifically named in the Bible
(cf., e.g., 1 Kings xv. 2, 10, xxii. 42).
This prominence would be enhanced in
the present instance, since Jehoiachin
was only eighteen years old. Since kings
usually had many wives, not all of them
of the same status, the identity of a
prince's mother was a matter of importance in the succession to the throne. It
is remarkable that the mother's name is
given only for the kings of Judah, not
those of Israel. An exception was
Jehoram, whose mother is not mentioned
(cf. 2 Kings viii. 16). His wife was
Ahab's daughter (verse 18), and as a true
daughter of Jezebel she may have forced
the queen-mother into the background
who, for this reason, is not named. The
queen-mothers after that are mentioned
for Judah, but not for Israel. This
seems to indicate that their prominence

'Sit ye down low;
For your headtires are come down,
Even your beautiful crown.'

19 The cities of the South are shut up,
And there is none to open them;
Judah is carried away captive all of it;
It is wholly carried away captive.

20 Lift up your eyes, and behold
Them that come from the north;
Where is the flock that was given thee,

הַשְׁפִּילוּ שֵׁבוּ
כִּי יָרַד מַרְאֲשֹׁתֵיכֶם
עֲטֶרֶת תִּפְאַרְתְּכֶם׃

19 עָרֵי הַנֶּגֶב סֻגְּרוּ
וְאֵין פֹּתֵחַ
הָגְלָת יְהוּדָה כֻּלָּהּ
הָגְלָת שְׁלוֹמִים׃

20 שְׂאִי עֵינֵיכֶם וּרְאִי
הַבָּאִים מִצָּפוֹן
אַיֵּה הָעֵדֶר נִתַּן־לָךְ

v. 20. שְׂאוּ ק׳ v. 20. וּרְאוּ ק׳

was confined to Judah, since Judaism has always paid honour to women. The Kingdom of Israel, on the other hand, which came more strongly under the influence of the surrounding peoples, may have held women in less esteem, in conformity with the general ancient attitude.

sit ye down low. Descend from your throne.

your headtires. Your royal dignity will be humbled to the dust.

19. *the cities of the South.* i.e. of the Negeb, the arid region in the south of Judah. Though remote from the invader these cities will not escape his fury, but be rendered desolate, no inhabitants being left in them even to open their gates.

captive all of it. This is a rhetorical exaggeration. The complete captivity did not come until the reign of Zedekiah; nevertheless, the magnitude even of the present disaster warranted such a description. Moreover, Jehoiachin and the princes who were exiled represented the whole nation.

20-27 CONSEQUENCE OF THEIR GUILT

The people's sins are responsible for the disaster. What has now become of the nation? They whose friendship they courted are now their masters. The nation is so deeply dyed with evil, that it is doubtful whether it can ever be clean again.

20. *lift up your eyes.* The *kethib* is feminine singular whereas the *kerë* is masculine plural. In verse 23 M.T. is masculine plural, but in the rest of the passage M.T. is feminine singular. Jerusalem is addressed (cf. verse 27) and insensibly she merges into the nation.

the north. Babylon.

the flock that was given thee. What have you done with the people entrusted to your care? Although Jerusalem, symbolizing the nation, is addressed in the passage as a whole, Metsudath David understands this verse as referring to the king and queen-mother. But king, nation and Jerusalem apparently merge here; furthermore, the nation as an abstract entity is apostrophized in respect of the individuals who compose it.

Thy beautiful flock?

21 What wilt thou say, when He
    shall set the friends over thee
    as head,
    Whom thou thyself hast trained
    against thee?
    Shall not pangs take hold of thee,
    As of a woman in travail?

22 And if thou say in thy heart:
    'Wherefore are these things be-
    fallen me?'—
    For the greatness of thine iniquity
    are thy skirts uncovered,
    And thy heels suffer violence.

23 Can the Ethiopian change his
    skin,
    Or the leopard his spots?
    Then may ye also do good,
    That are accustomed to do evil.

24 Therefore will I scatter them, as
    the stubble that passeth away
    By the wind of the wilderness.

צֹאן תִּפְאַרְתֵּךְ׃

21 מַה־תֹּאמְרִי כִּי־יִפְקֹד עָלַיִךְ
וְאַתְּ לִמַּדְתְּ אֹתָם עָלַיִךְ
אַלֻּפִים לְרֹאשׁ
הֲלוֹא חֲבָלִים יֹאחֱזוּךְ
כְּמוֹ אֵשֶׁת לֵדָה׃

22 וְכִי תֹאמְרִי בִּלְבָבֵךְ
מַדּוּעַ קְרָאֻנִי אֵלֶּה
בְּרֹב עֲוֹנֵךְ נִגְלוּ שׁוּלַיִךְ
נֶחְמְסוּ עֲקֵבָיִךְ׃

23 הֲיַהֲפֹךְ כּוּשִׁי עוֹרוֹ
וְנָמֵר חֲבַרְבֻּרֹתָיו
גַּם־אַתֶּם תּוּכְלוּ לְהֵיטִיב
לִמֻּדֵי הָרֵעַ׃

24 וַאֲפִיצֵם כְּקַשׁ עוֹבֵר
לְרוּחַ מִדְבָּר׃

---

thy beautiful flock. lit. 'the flock of thy beauty,' i.e. the people who constituted thy glory.

21. *the friends.* Those who you thought were your friends, but in fact you have made your masters, viz. the Babylonians.

22. *are thy skirts uncovered.* The figure is apparently taken from the public shaming of a harlot (cf. verse 26; Hos. ii. 12). Israel's unfaithfulness to God is often likened to adultery, and the disasters which will overwhelm the people are described under the imagery of an adulteress' punishment.

and thy heels suffer violence. This would seem to continue the same figure, al-though its exact application is no obvious.

23. The meaning is that they are so steepe in evil that it is almost impossible fc them to return to righteousness. Th passage is deeply pessimistic. Jeremia like the other prophets, being only huma occasionally gives way to the despairin conviction that the people are too fa gone for repentance (cf. Isa. vi. 9ff. Nevertheless, the whole trend of the mission and their repeated calls penitence show that this pessimism is passing mood and not representative their general attitude.

24. Cf. iv. 11f.

25 This is thy lot, the portion
measured unto thee from Me,
Saith the LORD;
Because thou hast forgotten Me,
And trusted in falsehood.

26 Therefore will I also uncover thy
skirts upon thy face,
And thy shame shall appear.

27 Thine adulteries, and thy neighings, the lewdness of thy
harlotry,
On the hills in the field have I
seen thy detestable acts.
Woe unto thee, O Jerusalem!
thou wilt not be made clean!
When shall it ever be?

25 זֶה גֽוֹרָלֵךְ מְנָת־מִדַּיִךְ
מֵאִתִּי נְאֻם־יְהֹוָה
אֲשֶׁר שָׁכַחַתְּ אוֹתִי
וַתִּבְטְחִי בַּשָּׁקֶר:

26 וְגַם־אֲנִי חָשַׂפְתִּי שׁוּלַיִךְ
עַל־פָּנָיִךְ
וְנִרְאָה קְלוֹנֵךְ:

27 נִאֻפַיִךְ וּמִצְהֲלוֹתַיִךְ
זִמַּת זְנוּתֵךְ
עַל־גְּבָעוֹת בַּשָּׂדֶה
רָאִיתִי שִׁקּוּצָיִךְ
אוֹי לָךְ יְרוּשָׁלַם לֹא תִטְהֲרִי
אַחֲרֵי מָתַי עֹד:

14   CHAPTER XIV   יד

1. The word of the LORD that
came to Jeremiah concerning the
droughts.

1 אֲשֶׁר הָיָה דְבַר־יְהֹוָה אֶל־
יִרְמְיָהוּ עַל־דִּבְרֵי הַבַּצָּרוֹת:

---

5. thy lot. i.e. thy fate, punishment.

alsehood. i.e. idolatry (cf. x. 14).

6. Cf. Nahum iii. 5. The subject in
herefore will I also is very emphatic.
After describing what the people had
done, God declares what He will do.

7. thy neighings. Cf. v. 8.

n the hills. Favourite places for the
practice of idolatry (cf. ii. 20).

vhen shall it ever be? lit. 'after how long
et?' A reformation will take place,
ut how long will it be delayed? 'A

weary sigh, but a glimmer of hope'
(Pickering).

CHAPTER XIV

1-6 DROUGHT AND FAMINE

1. concerning the droughts. Apparently a
series of severe droughts is referred to,
whose intensity had so impressed the
people as to make them an extraordinary
occurrence. 'The recent studies in
Central Asia have led to the view that
there are recurring periods of dryness,
which . . . cause frequent famine'
(Flinders Petrie).

2 Judah mourneth, and the gates
　　thereof languish,
　They bow down in black unto the
　　ground;
　And the cry of Jerusalem is gone
　　up.
3 And their nobles send their lads
　　for water:
　They come to the pits, and find
　　no water;
　Their vessels return empty; ˙
　They are ashamed and con-
　　founded, and cover their heads.
4 Because of the ground which is
　　cracked,
　For there hath been no rain in the
　　land,
　The plowmen are ashamed, they
　　cover their heads.
5 Yea, the hind also in the field
　　calveth, and forsaketh her
　　young,
　Because there is no grass.
6 And the wild asses stand on the
　　high hills,
　They gasp for air like jackals;

אָבְלָה יְהוּדָה 2
וּשְׁעָרֶיהָ אֻמְלְלוּ
קָדְרוּ לָאָרֶץ
וְצִוְחַת יְרוּשָׁלַ͏ִם עָלָתָה:
וְאַדִּירֵיהֶם 3
שָׁלְחוּ צְעוֹרֵיהֶם לַמָּיִם
בָּאוּ עַל־גֵּבִים
לֹא־מָצְאוּ מַיִם
שָׁבוּ כְלֵיהֶם רֵיקָם
בֹּשׁוּ וְהָכְלְמוּ וְחָפוּ רֹאשָׁם:
בַּעֲבוּר הָאֲדָמָה חַתָּה 4
כִּי לֹא־הָיָה גֶשֶׁם בָּאָרֶץ
בֹּשׁוּ אִכָּרִים חָפוּ רֹאשָׁם:
כִּי גַם־אַיֶּלֶת בַּשָּׂדֶה 5
יָלְדָה וְעָזוֹב
כִּי לֹא־הָיָה דֶּשֶׁא:
וּפְרָאִים עָמְדוּ עַל־שְׁפָיִם 6
שָׁאֲפוּ רוּחַ כַּתַּנִּים

v. 2. צ׳ זעירא v. 3. צעיריהם ק׳

2. *the gates.* i.e. the cities and their
inhabitants (cf. Deut. xvii. 2).

they bow down in black unto the ground.
In deep distress and mourning.

3. *lads.* i.e. servants.

ashamed and confounded. Disconcerted
and discomfited at their plight.

cover their heads. As a sign of mourning
(cf. 2 Sam. xv. 30).

4. *cracked.* The Hebrew verb may be
translated 'dismayed.'

5. *the hind.* Even the hind, which has
so much affection for her young, for-
sakes them as soon as they are born.

6. *wild asses.* Cf. ii. 24.

they gasp for air. Through heat and
thirst.

like jackals. The Hebrew noun *tannim*
may perhaps be a variant of *tannin*, 'the
crocodile,' which comes out of the water
gasping for air.

Their eyes fail, because there is
  no herbage.

7 Though our iniquities testify
  against us,
  O LORD, work Thou for Thy
  name's sake;
  For our backslidings are many,
  We have sinned against Thee.

8 O Thou hope of Israel,
  The Saviour thereof in time of
  trouble,
  Why shouldest Thou be as a
  stranger in the land,
  And as a wayfaring man that
  turneth aside to tarry for a
  night?

9 Why shouldest Thou be as a man
  overcome,
  As a mighty man that cannot save?
  Yet Thou, O LORD, art in the
  midst of us,
  And Thy name is called upon us;
  Leave us not.

10. Thus saith the LORD unto this
  people:
  Even so have they loved to
  wander,

בָּלוּ עֵינֵיהֶם כִּי־אֵין עֵֽשֶׂב׃

7 אִם־עֲוֺנֵינוּ עָנוּ בָנוּ
יְהֹוָה עֲשֵׂה לְמַעַן שְׁמֶךָ
כִּי־רַבּוּ מְשׁוּבֹתֵינוּ
לְךָ חָטָֽאנוּ׃

8 מִקְוֵה יִשְׂרָאֵל
מוֹשִׁיעוֹ בְּעֵת צָרָה
לָמָּה תִהְיֶה כְּגֵר בָּאָרֶץ
וּכְאֹרֵחַ נָטָה לָלוּן׃

9 לָמָּה תִהְיֶה כְּאִישׁ נִדְהָם
כְּגִבּוֹר לֹא־יוּכַל לְהוֹשִׁיעַ
וְאַתָּה בְקִרְבֵּנוּ יְהֹוָה
וְשִׁמְךָ עָלֵינוּ נִקְרָא
אַל־תַּנִּחֵֽנוּ׃

10 כֹּה־אָמַר יְהֹוָה לָעָם הַזֶּה
כֵּן אָהֲבוּ לָנוּעַ

---

their eyes fail. This may be meant literally, implying the failing of sight through
thirst. But the phrase may idiomatically
express despair caused by hope unful-
filled (cf. Ps. lxix. 4; Lam. iv. 17).

7-9 JEREMIAH INTERCEDES

7. *our iniquities.* He identifies himself
with the nation even in their sinfulness.

work Thou for Thy name's sake. To
preserve Thine honour by proving that
Thou art the Ruler over all, lest the
heathens boast that their gods are greater
than Thou.

our backslidings are many. Therefore
we can only throw ourselves on Thy
mercy.

8. *hope.* Comparing a cognate Arabic
noun, Ehrlich suggests that the meaning
of *mikweh* is 'might.'

as a stranger . . . and as a wayfaring man.
Who have no interest in the welfare of
the people among whom they dwell
temporarily.

9. *overcome.* lit. 'astonished,' taken by
surprise and incapable of meeting an
emergency.

10-12 GOD'S REPLY

10. *even so have they loved to wander.* To
other gods. If I have now abandoned
them, it is because they first abandoned
Me.

They have not refrained their
feet;
Therefore the LORD doth not
accept them,
Now will He remember their
iniquity,
And punish their sins.

11. And the LORD said unto me:
'Pray not for this people for their
good. 12. When they fast, I will
not hear their cry; and when they
offer burnt-offering and meal-offer-
ing, I will not accept them; but
I will consume them by the sword,
and by the famine, and by the
pestilence.' 13. Then said I: 'Ah,
Lord GOD! behold, the prophets say
unto them: Ye shall not see the
sword, neither shall ye have famine;
but I will give you assured peace in
this place.' 14. Then the LORD
said unto me: 'The prophets prophesy lies in My name; I sent them
not, neither have I commanded
them, neither spoke I unto them;

רַגְלֵיהֶם לֹא חָשָׂכוּ
וַיהוָה לֹא רָצָם
עַתָּה יִזְכֹּר עֲוֹנָם
וְיִפְקֹד חַטֹּאתָם:

11 וַיֹּאמֶר יְהוָה אֵלַי אַל־
תִּתְפַּלֵּל בְּעַד־הָעָם הַזֶּה
12 לְטוֹבָה: כִּי יָצֻמוּ אֵינֶנִּי שֹׁמֵעַ
אֶל־רִנָּתָם וְכִי יַעֲלוּ עֹלָה
וּמִנְחָה אֵינֶנִּי רֹצָם כִּי בַּחֶרֶב
וּבָרָעָב וּבַדֶּבֶר אָנֹכִי מְכַלֶּה
13 אוֹתָם: וָאֹמַר אֲהָהּ | אֲדֹנָי
יְהוָה הִנֵּה הַנְּבִאִים אֹמְרִים
לָהֶם לֹא־תִרְאוּ חֶרֶב וְרָעָב
לֹא־יִהְיֶה לָכֶם כִּי־שָׁלוֹם
אֱמֶת אֶתֵּן לָכֶם בַּמָּקוֹם הַזֶּה:
14 וַיֹּאמֶר יְהוָה אֵלַי שֶׁקֶר
הַנְּבִאִים נִבְּאִים בִּשְׁמִי לֹא
שְׁלַחְתִּים וְלֹא צִוִּיתִים וְלֹא
דִבַּרְתִּי אֲלֵיהֶם חֲזוֹן שֶׁקֶר

---

their feet. From pursuing idolatry.
Alternatively, from going to seek foreign
aid instead of relying upon Me (Kimchi).
The first clause may be similarly understood.

doth not accept them. He no longer has
pleasure in them, and therefore rejects
their plea. From *the LORD* to the end
of the verse is quoted from Hos. viii. 13.

12. *when they fast,* etc. Ceremonial forms
of religion will be of no avail.

13-18 A SECOND PLEA AND THE
RESPONSE

13. *assured peace in this place.* 'You
will not be expelled because *this place*
(Jerusalem or Judea as a whole) is under
God's special protection and He will
surely defend it,' such had been the
message of the false prophets. Since the
people had been misled by their religious
guides, they should be treated by God
leniently.

they prophesy unto you a lying vision, and divination, and a thing of nought, and the deceit of their own heart. 15. Therefore thus saith the LORD: As for the prophets that prophesy in My name, and I sent them not, yet they say: Sword and famine shall not be in this land, by sword and famine shall those prophets be consumed; 16. and the people to whom they prophesy shall be cast out in the streets of Jerusalem because of the famine and the sword; and they shall have none to bury them, them, their wives, nor their sons, nor their daughters; for I will pour their evil upon them.'

17. And thou shalt say this word unto them:

Let mine eyes run down with
tears night and day,
And let them not cease;
For the virgin daughter of my
people is broken with a great
breach,
With a very grievous blow.

וְקֶ֫סֶם וֶאֱלִיל֙ וְתַרְמִ֣ת לִבָּ֔ם
15 הֵ֚מָּה מִֽתְנַבְּאִ֖ים לָכֶ֑ם: לָכֵ֗ן
כֹּֽה־אָמַ֣ר יְהֹוָ֗ה עַל־הַנְּבִאִ֡ים
הַנִּבְּאִים֩ בִּשְׁמִ֨י וַאֲנִ֜י לֹֽא־
שְׁלַחְתִּים֙ וְהֵ֣מָּה אֹֽמְרִ֔ים חֶ֣רֶב
וְרָעָ֔ב לֹ֤א יִֽהְיֶה֙ בָּאָ֣רֶץ הַזֹּ֑את
בַּחֶ֤רֶב וּבָֽרָעָב֙ יִתַּ֔מּוּ הַנְּבִאִ֖ים
16 הָהֵֽמָּה: וְהָעָ֣ם אֲשֶׁר־הֵ֡מָּה
נִבְּאִ֣ים לָהֶ֗ם יִֽהְי֤וּ מֻשְׁלָכִים֙
בְּחֻצ֣וֹת יְרֽוּשָׁלִַ֗ם מִפְּנֵ֣י |
הָֽרָעָ֣ב וְהַחֶ֔רֶב וְאֵ֥ין מְקַבֵּ֖ר
לָהֵ֑מָּה הֵ֧מָּה נְשֵׁיהֶ֛ם וּבְנֵיהֶ֖ם
וּבְנֹֽתֵיהֶ֑ם וְשָׁפַכְתִּ֥י עֲלֵיהֶ֖ם
אֶת־רָֽעָתָֽם:
17 וְאָמַרְתָּ֤ אֲלֵיהֶם֙
אֶת־הַדָּבָ֣ר הַזֶּ֔ה
תֵּרַ֤דְנָה עֵינַי֙ דִּמְעָ֔ה
לַ֥יְלָה וְיוֹמָ֖ם
וְאַל־תִּדְמֶ֑ינָה
כִּי֩ שֶׁ֨בֶר גָּד֜וֹל נִשְׁבְּרָ֗ה
בְּתוּלַת֙ בַּת־עַמִּ֔י
מַכָּ֖ה נַחְלָ֥ה מְאֹֽד:

v. 14. ואליל ק' ותרמית ק'

15. *shall those prophets be consumed.* They will be the first to suffer, since they are the prime cause of the coming retribution.

16. *and the people,* etc. Though misled by false prophets, they must be held responsible for their misdeeds.
their evil. The punishment for their evil.

17. *the virgin daughter.* So described

18 If I go forth into the field,
'Then behold the slain with the
    sword!
And if I enter into the city,
Then behold them that are sick
    with famine!
For both the prophet and the
priest are gone about to a land,
and knew it not.

19 Hast Thou utterly rejected
   Judah?
Hath Thy soul loathed Zion?
Why hast Thou smitten us, and
there is no healing for us?
We looked for peace, but no good
   came;
And for a time of healing, and
behold terror!

20 We acknowledge, O LORD, our
   wickedness,
Even the iniquity of our fathers;
For we have sinned against Thee.

21 Do not contemn us, for Thy
name's sake,

18 אִם־יָצָאתִי הַשָּׂדֶה
וְהִנֵּה חַלְלֵי־חֶרֶב
וְאִם בָּאתִי הָעִיר
וְהִנֵּה תַּחֲלוּאֵי רָעָב
כִּי גַם־נָבִיא גַם־כֹּהֵן
סָחֲרוּ אֶל־אֶרֶץ וְלֹא יָדָעוּ׃
19 הֲמָאֹס מָאַסְתָּ אֶת־יְהוּדָה
אִם־בְּצִיּוֹן גָּעֲלָה נַפְשֶׁךָ
מַדּוּעַ הִכִּיתָנוּ וְאֵין לָנוּ מַרְפֵּא
קַוֵּה לְשָׁלוֹם וְאֵין טוֹב
וּלְעֵת מַרְפֵּא וְהִנֵּה בְעָתָה׃
20 יָדַעְנוּ יְהוָה
רִשְׁעֵנוּ עֲוֹן אֲבוֹתֵינוּ
כִּי חָטָאנוּ לָךְ׃
21 אַל־תִּנְאַץ לְמַעַן שִׁמְךָ

---

because no enemy had conquered the
nation heretofore (cf. the phrase 'virgin
soil').

18. *the prophet.* The false prophet.

the priest. The parallelism suggests that
the priest of Baal is meant; but see on
xiii. 13.

are gone about to a land, and knew it not.
The clause is obscure and the meaning
doubtful. Rashi explains: they have gone
to a (foreign) land to seek salvation and
knew (it) not that that very land would
destroy them. 'The comment of Metsudath David is: they travelled about the
country (like a merchant seeking to sell
his wares; cf. R.V. margin 'trafficked'
which is the sense of the Hebrew verb
elsewhere) prophesying and giving counsel on matters of which they were ignorant. Some modern commentators con-
nect with a verb in Syriac, 'they go as
beggars into a land which they knew not.'

19-22 A FURTHER PLEA TO GOD

19. *we looked for peace . . . terror.* This
clause occurred in viii. 15. Perhaps it
was a current saying, reflecting the darkness and despair before the final disaster.

20. *even the iniquity of our fathers.* There
is a long record of disloyalty to God
extending over many generations. It
now reaches its culminating point when
punishment can no longer be withheld
therefore they can only rely upon God's
mercy.

21. *do not contemn us.* There is nothing
corresponding to *us* in the text and the
object of the verb is *the throne.*

for Thy name's sake. Thy name being
'the Merciful One' (Rashi).

Do not dishonour the throne of
Thy glory;
Remember, break not Thy
covenant with us.
22 Are there any among the vanities
of the nations that can cause
rain?
Or can the heavens give showers?
Art not Thou He, O LORD our
God, and do we not wait for
Thee?
For Thou hast made all these
things.

אַל־תְּנַבֵּל כִּסֵּא כְבוֹדֶךָ
זְכֹר אַל־תָּפֵר בְּרִיתְךָ אִתָּנוּ:
22 הֲיֵשׁ בְּהַבְלֵי הַגּוֹיִם מַגְשִׁמִים
וְאִם־הַשָּׁמַיִם יִתְּנוּ רְבִבִים
הֲלֹא אַתָּה־הוּא
יְהֹוָה אֱלֹהֵינוּ וּנְקַוֶּה־לָּךְ
כִּי־אַתָּה עָשִׂיתָ
אֶת־כָּל־אֵלֶּה:

15   CHAPTER XV   טו

1. Then said the LORD unto me:
'Though Moses and Samuel stood
before Me, yet My mind could not
be toward this people; cast them
out of My sight, and let them go
forth. 2. And it shall come to pass,
when they say unto thee: Whither
shall we go forth? then thou shalt

1 וַיֹּאמֶר יְהֹוָה אֵלַי אִם־יַעֲמֹד
מֹשֶׁה וּשְׁמוּאֵל לְפָנַי אֵין נַפְשִׁי
אֶל־הָעָם הַזֶּה שַׁלַּח מֵעַל־
2 פָּנַי וְיֵצֵאוּ: וְהָיָה כִּי־יֹאמְרוּ
אֵלֶיךָ אָנָה נֵצֵא וְאָמַרְתָּ

---

the throne of Thy glory. i.e. Jerusalem,
the site of the Temple (cf. xvii. 12).
On the general thought, see on verse 7.

22. *the vanities.* The false gods.

that can cause rain. Cf. the Talmudic
statement: 'Three keys have not been
entrusted to an agent (but are kept in
God's hand): the keys of birth, rain and
resurrection' (Sanh. 113a). Only the
Creator has that power.

CHAPTER XV

1-9 THE SUFFERING IN STORE

1. *Moses and Samuel.* Both had interceded with God on Israel's behalf, but

only after they had induced Israel to
repent; then He hearkened to their
prayers. Thus when Israel sinned with
the Golden Calf, they first destroyed the
sinners and then Moses said, *And now
I will go up unto the LORD, peradventure
I shall make atonement for your sin* (Exod.
xxxii. 30). Similarly, Samuel first per-
suaded Israel to remove idolatry and
then prayed for them (1 Sam. vii. 2ff.).
You, however (so spoke God to Jeremiah), pray for Israel even before they
have reformed. In such a case not even
Moses and Samuel could succeed (Rashi).

toward this people. To be well-disposed
towards them.

2. *whither shall we go forth?* If denied
God's forgiveness.

tell them: Thus saith the LORD:
Such as are for death, to death; and
such as are for the sword, to the
sword; and such as are for the
famine, to the famine; and such as
are for captivity, to captivity. 3.
And I will appoint over them four
kinds, saith the LORD: the sword to
slay, and the dogs to drag, and the
fowls of the heaven, and the beasts
of the earth, to devour and to
destroy. 4. And I will cause them
to be a horror among all the kingdoms of the earth, because of
Manasseh the son of Hezekiah king
of Judah, for that which he did in
Jerusalem.

5 For who shall have pity upon thee,
     O Jerusalem?
     Or who shall bemoan thee?
     Or who shall turn aside to ask of
     thy welfare?

6 Thou hast cast Me off, saith the
     LORD,
     Thou art gone backward;
     Therefore do I stretch out My
     hand against thee, and destroy
     thee;

אֲלֵיהֶם כֹּה־אָמַר יְהֹוָה
אֲשֶׁר לַמָּוֶת לַמָּוֶת וַאֲשֶׁר
לַחֶרֶב לַחֶרֶב וַאֲשֶׁר לָרָעָב
לָרָעָב וַאֲשֶׁר לַשְּׁבִי לַשֶּׁבִי׃
3 וּפָקַדְתִּי עֲלֵיהֶם אַרְבַּע
מִשְׁפָּחוֹת נְאֻם־יְהֹוָה אֶת־
הַחֶרֶב לַהֲרֹג וְאֶת־הַכְּלָבִים
לִסְחֹב וְאֶת־עוֹף הַשָּׁמַיִם
וְאֶת־בֶּהֱמַת הָאָרֶץ לֶאֱכֹל
4 וּלְהַשְׁחִית׃ וּנְתַתִּים לְזַוְעָה
לְכֹל מַמְלְכוֹת הָאָרֶץ בִּגְלַל
מְנַשֶּׁה בֶן־יְחִזְקִיָּהוּ מֶלֶךְ
יְהוּדָה עַל אֲשֶׁר־עָשָׂה
בִּירוּשָׁלָ͏ִם׃
5 כִּי מִי־יַחְמֹל עָלַיִךְ יְרוּשָׁלַ͏ִם
וּמִי יָנוּד לָךְ
וּמִי יָסוּר לִשְׁאֹל לְשָׁלֹם לָךְ׃
6 אַתְּ נָטַשְׁתְּ אֹתִי
נְאֻם־יְהֹוָה אָחוֹר תֵּלֵכִי
וָאַט אֶת־יָדִי עָלַיִךְ וָאַשְׁחִיתֵךְ

לזעוה ק׳   v. 4.

---

for death. By pestilence (cf. xviii. 21).
to death, etc. Each to the punishment
decreed for him.

3. *kinds.* lit. 'families,' i.e. modes of
punishment. The verse proceeds to
enumerate them: even when slain, they
will be subjected to the further indignity
of having the corpses dragged by dogs

or devoured by wild beasts (cf. xix. **7,**
xxxiv. 20).

4. *because of Manasseh.* i.e. because they
approved of and imitated his wickedness
(Metsudath David).

5. *who shall turn aside . . . welfare?* Who
will take the least trouble even to inquire
after thee?

I am weary with repenting.

7 And I fan them with a fan in the
gates of the land;
I bereave them of children, I
destroy My people,
Since they return not from their
ways.

8 Their widows are increased to Me
above the sand of the seas;
I bring upon them, against the
mother, a chosen one,
Even a spoiler at noonday;

נִלְאֵיתִי הִנָּחֵם׃

7 וָאֶזְרֵם בְּמִזְרֶה בְּשַׁעֲרֵי הָאָרֶץ
שִׁכַּלְתִּי אִבַּדְתִּי אֶת־עַמִּי
מִדַּרְכֵיהֶם לוֹא שָׁבוּ׃

8 עָצְמוּ־לִי אַלְמְנֹתָו
מֵחוֹל יַמִּים
הֵבֵאתִי לָהֶם עַל־אֵם
בָּחוּר שֹׁדֵד בַּצָּהֳרָיִם

v. 8. אלמנותיו ק׳

6. *I am weary with repenting.* An anthropomorphism (cf. Gen. vi. 6). Many
times God decreed Israel's destruction
but relented; He can do so no more.

7. *I fan them with a fan.* Fan is used in
the sense of 'winnow' and 'a winnowing-
fork.' The meaning apparently is that
God will scatter them. 'The mixture of
corn, chaff and broken straw, produced
by threshing, was shaken about with
these two implements (a winnowing-fork
and a shovel), usually in some exposed
spot, when a wind was blowing (generally in the evening, Ruth iii. 2), and the
wind carried away the chaff and the
straw (Ps. i. 4). If, however, the wind
was too violent, it would blow away the
corn as well; hence the point of Jer.
iv. 11' (Driver), and, presumably, of the
present verse. The intention may, on
the other hand, be that God would
separate the grain from the chaff, reject-
ing and destroying the latter, which
represented the sinners; but these were
so numerous as to involve practically the
total destruction of the nation.

in the gates of the land. Even in captivity
they will not be together, but scattered
throughout the cities of the land of exile
(Kimchi).

since they return not. Since is not in the
original and has been added by A.J. (the
R.V. omits it). Rashi interprets: and

yet they return not (in spite of My
chastisement).

8. *their widows are increased to Me,* etc.
The reference is to the crushing defeat
in the days of Ahaz, when Pekah slew
120,000 in one day (2 Chron. xxviii. 6)
(Kimchi).

against the mother, a chosen one (bachur).
The phrase is difficult. There seems no
reason why *the mother* should be singled
out, unless it is an idiom implying every-
body, as we use the phrase 'even women
and children' to denote that none are
exempted. Some Jewish commentators
understand *mother* as figurative of Jerusalem, citing 2 Sam. xx. 19: *seekest thou
to destroy a city and a mother in Israel?*
where *mother* is synonymous with *city*.
Binns, accepting this, paraphrases: 'I
have brought (upon them) against the
metropolis, yea, against the picked
troops which garrison it (for this rendering of *bachur*, cf. 2 Sam. vi. 1), one who
will destroy them.' If *mother* is understood literally, then the best rendering is
R.V.: 'against the mother of the young
men,' on which Peake makes the comment: 'It seems to mean that suddenly,
when all is fair, the destroyer comes upon
the mother of the young warriors who
have fallen on the battlefield and left her
defenceless."

at noonday. See on vi. 4.

I cause anguish and terrors to fall
upon her suddenly.

9 She that hath borne seven lan-
guisheth;
Her spirit droopeth;
Her sun is gone down while it
was yet day,
She is ashamed and confounded;
And the residue of them will I
deliver to the sword before their
enemies,
Saith the LORD.'

10 Woe is me, my mother, that thou
hast borne me
A man of strife and a man of
contention to the whole earth!
I have not lent, neither have men
lent to me;
Yet every one of them doth curse
me.

11. The LORD said: 'Verily I will
release thee for good; verily I will
cause the enemy to make supplication unto thee in the time of evil and

הִפַּ֤לְתִּי עָלֶ֙יהָ֙ פִּתְאֹ֔ם
עִ֖יר וּבֶהָלֽוֹת׃
9 אֻמְלְלָ֞ה יֹלֶ֣דֶת הַשִּׁבְעָ֗ה
נָפְחָ֣ה נַפְשָׁ֔הּ
בָּ֥אָה שִׁמְשָׁ֛הּ בְּעֹ֥ד יוֹמָ֖ם
בּ֣וֹשָׁה וְחָפֵ֑רָה
וּשְׁאֵֽרִיתָ֗ם לַחֶ֤רֶב אֶתֵּן֙
לִפְנֵ֣י אֹֽיְבֵיהֶ֔ם
נְאֻם־יְהֹוָֽה׃
10 אֽוֹי־לִ֣י אִמִּ֔י כִּ֥י יְלִדְתִּ֖נִי
אִ֣ישׁ רִ֑יב
וְאִ֥ישׁ מָד֖וֹן לְכָל־הָאָ֑רֶץ
לֹֽא־נָשִׁ֥יתִי וְלֹא־נָֽשׁוּ־בִ֖י
כֻּלֹּ֥ה מְקַלְלַֽוְנִי׃
11 אָמַ֣ר יְהֹוָ֔ה אִם־לֹ֖א שֵֽׁרוֹתִ֣ךָ
לְט֑וֹב אִם־ל֣וֹא ׀ הִפְגַּ֣עְתִּי
בְךָ֗ בְּעֵ֥ת רָעָ֖ה וּבְעֵ֥ת צָרָ֑ה

v. 9.   v. 11. בא ק׳   שריתך ק׳

---

anguish. The Hebrew *ir* is unusual in
this sense. It occurs in Hos. xi. 9 where
A.J. renders by *fury*. The Oxford Hebrew
Lexicon derives it from the root *ur*,
'to arouse,' and suggests the translation
'excitement.'

9. *she that hath borne seven.* For the
number *seven*, cf. 1 Sam. ii. 5; a woman
with numerous children. Such a woman
should be most happy, but now she is
wretched.

while it was yet day. i.e. in the prime of
life, prematurely.

10-21 JEREMIAH'S LAMENT: GOD'S REPLY

10. *woe is me.* His fearless denunciations
of the people's sins and his dark fore-
bodings about their future had brought
about no reform; their only sequel was
intense bitterness towards him personally. In a mood of depression he bewails
his lot and wishes that he had never been
born.

I have not lent. The moneylender has
always been held in disfavour.

11. *I will release thee.* The reading of the
kerĕ derives from the root *sharah*, 'set

in the time of affliction. 12. Can iron break iron from the north and brass? 13. Thy substance and thy treasures will I give for a spoil without price, and that for all thy sins, even in all thy borders. 14. And I will make thee to pass with thine enemies into a land which thou knowest not; for a fire is kindled in My nostril, which shall burn upon you.'

15 Thou, O LORD, knowest;
  Remember me, and think of me,
    and avenge me of my per-
    secutors;
  Take me not away because of
    Thy long-suffering;
  Know that for Thy sake I have
    suffered taunts.

אֶת־הָאֹיֵב: הֲיָרֹעַ בַּרְזֶל | 12
בַּרְזֶל מִצָּפוֹן וּנְחֹשֶׁת: חֵילְךָ 13
וְאוֹצְרוֹתֶיךָ לָבַז אֶתֵּן לֹא
בִמְחִיר וּבְכָל־חַטֹּאותֶיךָ
וּבְכָל־גְּבוּלֶיךָ: וְהַעֲבַרְתִּי 14
אֶת־אֹיְבֶיךָ בְּאֶרֶץ לֹא יָדָעְתָּ
כִּי־אֵשׁ קָדְחָה בְאַפִּי עֲלֵיכֶם
תּוּקָד:
אַתָּה יָדַעְתָּ יְהֹוָה 15
זָכְרֵנִי וּפָקְדֵנִי
וְהִנָּקֶם לִי מֵרֹדְפַי
אַל־לְאֶרֶךְ אַפְּךָ תִּקָּחֵנִי
דַּע שְׂאֵתִי עָלֶיךָ חֶרְפָּה:

v. 13. מלא ר'   v. 14. נ״א והעבדתי   v. 14. למדנחאי תיקד

---

free.' It is uncertain what the *kethib* represents. The sense of the clause seems to be: in the catastrophe which is approaching God will deliver him.

the enemy. The opponents of Jeremiah are meant. In their distress they will appeal to him to intercede on their behalf. This happened on several occasions; cf. xxi. 1ff., xxxvii. 3, xlii. 1ff.

12. 'The point of the reference to iron from the north is that the best and hardest iron came from the Black Sea' (Peake). This and the following two verses are apparently a digression in which God (or, according to others, the prophet) addresses the people: can your iron break the iron of the north, viz. the armies of Babylon?

13. This and the next verse occur again with variations in xvii. 3f.

without price. You will receive nothing from the enemy for what he takes of your possessions.

even in all thy borders. Because your sins have filled the whole land.

14. *and I will make thee to pass.* Thee does not occur in the text and the object may be *thy substance and thy treasures* of the previous verse. Many Hebrew MSS. and the Targum read here, as in xvii. 4, *I will cause thee to serve.*

for a fire . . . nostril. Identical with Deut. xxxii. 22.

15. The prophet resumes his dialogue with God.

Thou, O LORD, knowest. How I have suffered in carrying out the commission entrusted to me.

take me not away. Let me not perish.

Thy long-suffering. Towards my opponents.

16 Thy words were found, and I did
    eat them;
And Thy words were unto me a
    joy and the rejoicing of my
    heart;
Because Thy name was called on
    me, O LORD God of hosts.

17 I sat not in the assembly of them
    that make merry, nor rejoiced;
I sat alone because of Thy hand;
For Thou hast filled me with
    indignation.

18 Why is my pain perpetual,
And my wound incurable, so that
    it refuseth to be healed?
Wilt Thou indeed be unto me as
    a deceitful brook,
As waters that fail?

19 Therefore thus saith the LORD:
If thou return, and I bring thee
    back,
Thou shalt stand before Me;

16 נִמְצְא֤וּ דְבָרֶ֨יךָ֙ וָאֹ֣כְלֵ֔ם
וַיְהִ֤י דְבָרְךָ֙ לִ֔י
לְשָׂשׂ֖וֹן וּלְשִׂמְחַ֣ת לְבָבִ֑י
כִּֽי־נִקְרָ֤א שִׁמְךָ֙ עָלַ֔י
יְהֹוָ֖ה אֱלֹהֵ֥י צְבָאֽוֹת׃

17 לֹֽא־יָשַׁ֥בְתִּי בְסֽוֹד־מְשַׂחֲקִ֖ים
וָֽאֶעְלֹ֑ז
מִפְּנֵ֤י יָֽדְךָ֙ בָּדָ֣ד יָשַׁ֔בְתִּי
כִּי־זַ֖עַם מִלֵּאתָֽנִי׃

18 לָ֣מָּה הָיָ֤ה כְאֵבִי֙ נֶ֔צַח
וּמַכָּתִ֣י אֲנוּשָׁ֔ה מֵֽאֲנָ֖ה הֵֽרָפֵ֑א
הָי֨וֹ תִֽהְיֶ֥ה לִי֙ כְּמ֣וֹ אַכְזָ֔ב
מַ֖יִם לֹ֥א נֶאֱמָֽנוּ׃

19 לָכֵ֗ן כֹּֽה־אָמַ֣ר יְהֹוָ֔ה
אִם־תָּשׁ֤וּב וַאֲשִֽׁיבְךָ֙
לְפָנַ֣י תַּֽעֲמֹ֔ד

16. *Thy words were found, and I did eat them.* Thy words descended to me in the spirit of prophecy, and I joyfully welcomed them as one has pleasure in eating something tasty (Kimchi). Cf. the symbolism in Ezek. iii. 1ff.

because Thy name was called on me. As a prophet of God, not as a false prophet.

17. *I sat alone . . . indignation.* The prophetic spirit with which God endowed him set him apart. 'I could not rejoice and make merry with the rest,' he says, 'being filled with indignation over the people's sins.'

because of Thy hand. Laid upon the prophet to arouse his special powers (cf. 2 Kings iii. 15; Isa. viii. 11; Ezek. iii. 14).

18. *wilt Thou indeed . . . fail?* The Hebrew does not necessarily imply a question, although it may do so. In that case we have to assume that the question is rhetorical. It may, however, be a positive statement: 'Thou art indeed unto me,' etc. (so Rashi and Kimchi). Such an allegation need not surprise us. The prophet is only human and in his mental anguish momentarily gives way to despair. Even God has seemingly failed him (cf. xvii. 18 where he prays to be saved from despair).

a deceitful brook. A wadi which dries up in the summer; an image of what is unreliable (cf. Job. vi. 15).

19. *if thou return.* Such doubts are sinful; yet if thou wilt repent of them and return to Me, I will receive thee and

And if thou bring forth the
precious out of the vile,
Thou shalt be as My mouth;
Let them return unto thee,
But thou shalt not return unto
them.

20 And I will make thee unto this
people a fortified brazen wall;
And they shall fight against thee,
But they shall not prevail against
thee;
For I am with thee to save thee
and to deliver thee,
Saith the LORD.

21 And I will deliver thee out of the
hand of the wicked,
And I will redeem thee out of the
hand of the terrible.

וְאִם־תּוֹצִיא יָקָר
מִזּוֹלֵל כְּפִי תִהְיֶה
יָשֻׁבוּ הֵמָּה אֵלֶיךָ
וְאַתָּה לֹא־תָשׁוּב אֲלֵיהֶם׃
20 וּנְתַתִּיךָ לָעָם הַזֶּה
לְחוֹמַת נְחֹשֶׁת בְּצוּרָה
וְנִלְחֲמוּ אֵלֶיךָ
וְלֹא־יוּכְלוּ לָךְ
כִּי־אִתְּךָ אֲנִי
לְהוֹשִׁיעֲךָ וּלְהַצִּילֶךָ
נְאֻם־יְהֹוָה׃
21 וְהִצַּלְתִּיךָ מִיַּד רָעִים
וּפְדִתִיךָ מִכַּף עָרִיצִים׃

16   CHAPTER XVI   טז

1. The word of the LORD came also
unto me, saying:
2 Thou shalt not take thee a wife,

1 וַיְהִי דְבַר־יְהֹוָה אֵלַי לֵאמֹר׃
2 לֹא־תִקַּח לְךָ אִשָּׁה

thou shalt stand before Me, enjoying My
favour (Kimchi).

the precious out of the vile. 'He is exhorted to practise the art of the metal
refiner upon himself and remove all
unworthy suspicions as to God's faithfulness, which though mixed with better
thoughts he had just shown to be entertained in his heart' (Streane).

My mouth. My spokesman (cf. Exod.
iv. 16).

let them return, etc. Although you are
one against many, you must persist until

you raise them and not allow them to
drag you down to their level.

20f. A repetition of the substance of i. 18f.

21. *the terrible.* i.e. the influential men
of the kingdom who use their power ruth-
lessly; they are perhaps to be identified
with the *kings of Judah*, etc., in i. 18.

CHAPTER XVI

1-13 JEREMIAH COMMANDED TO
PRACTISE SELF-DENIAL

2. *thou shalt not take thee a wife.* Marriage was regarded as man's natural

Neither shalt thou have sons or daughters in this place.

3. For thus saith the LORD concerning the sons and concerning the daughters that are born in this place, and concerning their mothers that bore them, and concerning their fathers that begot them in this land:

4 They shall die of grievous deaths;

They shall not be lamented, neither shall they be buried,

They shall be as dung upon the face of the ground;

And they shall be consumed by the sword, and by famine;

And their carcasses shall be meat for the fowls of heaven,

And for the beasts of the earth.

5. For thus saith the LORD: Enter not into the house of mourning, neither go to lament, neither bemoan them; for I have taken away My peace from this people, saith the

וְלֹא־יִהְיוּ לְךָ בָּנִים וּבָנוֹת בַּמָּקוֹם הַזֶּה:

3 כִּי־כֹה ׀ אָמַר יְהוָה עַל־ הַבָּנִים וְעַל־הַבָּנוֹת הַיִּלּוֹדִים בַּמָּקוֹם הַזֶּה וְעַל־אִמֹּתָם הַיֹּלְדוֹת אוֹתָם וְעַל־אֲבוֹתָם הַמּוֹלִדִים אוֹתָם בָּאָרֶץ הַזֹּאת:

4 מְמוֹתֵי תַחֲלֻאִים יָמֻתוּ לֹא יִסָּפְדוּ וְלֹא יִקָּבֵרוּ לְדֹמֶן עַל־פְּנֵי הָאֲדָמָה יִהְיוּ וּבַחֶרֶב וּבָרָעָב יִכְלוּ וְהָיְתָה נִבְלָתָם לְמַאֲכָל לְעוֹף הַשָּׁמַיִם וּלְבֶהֱמַת הָאָרֶץ:

5 כִּי־כֹה ׀ אָמַר יְהוָה אַל־ תָּבוֹא בֵּית מַרְזֵחַ וְאַל־תֵּלֵךְ לִסְפּוֹד וְאַל־תָּנֹד לָהֶם כִּי־ אָסַפְתִּי אֶת־שְׁלוֹמִי מֵאֵת הָעָם הַזֶּה נְאֻם־יְהוָֹה אֶת־

---

state (cf. Gen. i. 28, ii. 18). To refrain from marriage for the reason given would make a deep impression on the people.

in this place. Jerusalem, or Judea.

4. *grievous deaths.* lit. 'deaths of diseases,' from epidemics.

they shall not be lamented. So many will be claimed by death that there will be no time or thought for mourning, or even for burying the dead honourably.

5. *mourning.* The word *marzeach* means 'a shrill sound.' It is applied to revelry in Amos. vi. 7, here to 'wailing for the dead.' Judaism commands visits to mourners to comfort them as an act of piety; but the prophet is told not to perform it because houses of mourning will be so numerous.

LORD, even mercy and compassion.
6. Both the great and the small shall
die in this land; they shall not be
buried; neither shall men lament for
them, nor cut themselves, nor make
themselves bald for them; 7. neither
shall men break bread for them in
mourning, to comfort them for the
dead; neither shall men give them
the cup of consolation to drink for
their father or for their mother.
8. And thou shalt not go into the
house of feasting to sit with them,
to eat and to drink. 9. For thus
saith the LORD of hosts, the God of
Israel:

Behold, I will cause to cease out
of this place,
Before your eyes and in your days,
The voice of mirth and the voice
of gladness,
The voice of the bridegroom and
the voice of the bride.

6 הַחֶסֶד וְאֶת־הָרַחֲמִים : וּמֵׄתוּ
גְדֹלִים וּקְטַנִּים בָּאָרֶץ הַזֹּאת
לֹא יִקָּבֵרוּ וְלֹא־יִסְפְּדוּ לָהֶם
וְלֹא יִתְגֹּדַד וְלֹא יִקָּרֵחַ לָהֶם :
7 וְלֹא־יִפְרְסוּ לָהֶם עַל־־
אֵבֶל לְנַחֲמוֹ עַל־מֵת וְלֹא־
יַשְׁקוּ אוֹתָם כּוֹס תַּנְחוּמִים
8 עַל־אָבִיו וְעַל־אִמּוֹ : וּבֵית־
מִשְׁתֶּה לֹא־תָבוֹא לָשֶׁבֶת
9 אוֹתָם לֶאֱכֹל וְלִשְׁתּוֹת : כִּי
כֹה אָמַר יְהֹוָה צְבָאוֹת אֱלֹהֵי
יִשְׂרָאֵל
הִנְנִי מַשְׁבִּית מִן־הַמָּקוֹם הַזֶּה
לְעֵינֵיכֶם וּבִימֵיכֶם
קוֹל שָׂשׂוֹן וְקוֹל שִׂמְחָה
קוֹל חָתָן וְקוֹל כַּלָּה :

6. the great and the small. The nobles
and commoners.

*nor cut themselves, nor make themselves
bald.* Both these mourning practices
were forbidden (Lev. xix. 28; Deut. xiv. 1
and particularly to priests, Lev. xxi. 5).
Nevertheless, in assimilation to heathen
customs, they were commonly practised
in defiance of the law. Now, however,
death would be so widespread that they
would perforce be neglected.

7. *neither shall men break bread for them.*
The noun *bread* is not stated explicitly
but is implicit in the verb used. It was
customary for the friends of mourners to
provide them with their first meal after
the funeral (cf. 2 Sam. iii. 35; Ezek.
xxiv. 17; Hos. ix. 4).

the cup of consolation. A special cup of
wine, so designated, was drunk by the
mourner, in connection with which a
prayer for comfort was added in the
Grace after meals (Keth. 8b; A.D.P.B.,
pp. 282f.).

8. As he was to avoid houses of mourning, so he was to shun houses where
domestic joys, e.g. marriages, were being
celebrated.

9. *before your eyes.* The calamities would
happen in their lifetime. Most of the
verse is repeated from vii. 34.

10. And it shall come to pass, when thou shalt tell this people all these words, and they shall say unto thee: 'Wherefore hath the LORD pronounced all this great evil against us? or what is our iniquity? or what is our sin that we have committed against the LORD our God?' 11. then shalt thou say unto them: 'Because your fathers have forsaken Me, saith the LORD, and have walked after other gods, and have served them, and have worshipped them, and have forsaken Me, and have not kept My law; 12. and ye have done worse than your fathers; for, behold, ye walk every one after the stubbornness of his evil heart, so that ye hearken not unto Me; 13. therefore will I cast you out of this land into a land that ye have not known, neither ye nor your fathers; and there shall ye serve other gods day

10 וְהָיָה כִּי תַגִּיד לָעָם הַזֶּה אֵת
כָּל־הַדְּבָרִים הָאֵלֶּה וְאָמְרוּ
אֵלֶיךָ עַל־מֶה דִבֶּר יְהֹוָה
עָלֵינוּ אֵת כָּל־הָרָעָה
הַגְּדוֹלָה הַזֹּאת וּמֶה עֲוֹנֵנוּ וּמֶה
חַטָּאתֵנוּ אֲשֶׁר חָטָאנוּ לַיהֹוָה
11 אֱלֹהֵינוּ: וְאָמַרְתָּ אֲלֵיהֶם עַל
אֲשֶׁר־עָזְבוּ אֲבוֹתֵיכֶם אוֹתִי
נְאֻם־יְהֹוָה וַיֵּלְכוּ אַחֲרֵי
אֱלֹהִים אֲחֵרִים וַיַּעַבְדוּם
וַיִּשְׁתַּחֲווּ לָהֶם וְאֹתִי עָזָבוּ
וְאֶת־תּוֹרָתִי לֹא שָׁמָרוּ:
12 וְאַתֶּם הֲרֵעֹתֶם לַעֲשׂוֹת
מֵאֲבוֹתֵיכֶם וְהִנְּכֶם הֹלְכִים
אִישׁ אַחֲרֵי שְׁרִרוּת לִבּוֹ־-
הָרָע לְבִלְתִּי שְׁמֹעַ אֵלָי:
13 וְהֵטַלְתִּי אֶתְכֶם מֵעַל הָאָרֶץ
הַזֹּאת עַל־הָאָרֶץ אֲשֶׁר לֹא
יְדַעְתֶּם אַתֶּם וַאֲבוֹתֵיכֶם
וַעֲבַדְתֶּם־שָׁם אֶת־אֱלֹהִים

v. 11. קמץ בז"ק

10. Cf. v. 19, xiii. 22. In spite of the denunciations of the prophets, the people apparently were still unconscious of guilt. To this complacent frame of mind the false prophets had undoubtedly contributed.

12. *ye have done worse than your fathers.* Instead of being warned and deterred by the evil of former generations, they have wandered still farther along the path of apostasy. Their guilt is therefore greater and the penalty more severe.

13. *a land.* lit. 'the land,' appointed for their captivity.

there shall ye serve other gods. The words are ironical. Banished from the Holy Land to a country where idolatry was the religion of the native population, they would have greater facilities to indulge in their partiality for pagan worship.

and night; forasmuch as I will show
you no favour.'

14. Therefore, behold, the days
come, saith the LORD, that it shall no
more be said: 'As the LORD liveth,
that brought up the children of
Israel out of the land of Egypt,'
15. but: 'As the LORD liveth, that
brought up the children of Israel
from the land of the north, and
from all the countries whither He
had driven them'; and I will bring
them back into their land that I gave
unto their fathers.

16. Behold, I will send for many
fishers, saith the LORD, and they
shall fish them; and afterward I will
send for many hunters, and they
shall hunt them from every mountain, and from every hill, and out of
the clefts of the rocks.

17 For Mine eyes are upon all their
ways,

They are not hid from My face;
Neither is their iniquity concealed from Mine eyes.

אַחֲרִים יוֹמָם וָלַיְלָה אֲשֶׁר

14 לֹא־אֶתֵּן לָכֶם חֲנִינָה׃ לָכֵן
הִנֵּה־יָמִים בָּאִים נְאֻם־יְהֹוָה
וְלֹא־יֵאָמֵר עוֹד חַי־יְהֹוָה
אֲשֶׁר הֶעֱלָה אֶת־בְּנֵי יִשְׂרָאֵל

15 מֵאֶרֶץ מִצְרָיִם׃ כִּי אִם־חַי־
יְהֹוָה אֲשֶׁר הֶעֱלָה אֶת־בְּנֵי
יִשְׂרָאֵל מֵאֶרֶץ צָפוֹן וּמִכֹּל
הָאֲרָצוֹת אֲשֶׁר הִדִּיחָם שָׁמָּה
וַהֲשִׁבוֹתִים עַל־אַדְמָתָם

16 אֲשֶׁר נָתַתִּי לַאֲבוֹתָם׃ הִנְנִי
שֹׁלֵחַ לְדַוָּגִים רַבִּים נְאֻם־
יְהֹוָה וְדִיגוּם וְאַחֲרֵי־כֵן
אֶשְׁלַח לְרַבִּים צַיָּדִים וְצָדוּם
מֵעַל כָּל־הַר וּמֵעַל כָּל־
גִּבְעָה וּמִנְּקִיקֵי הַסְּלָעִים׃

17 כִּי עֵינַי עַל־כָּל־דַּרְכֵיהֶם
לֹא נִסְתְּרוּ מִלְּפָנָי
וְלֹא־נִצְפַּן עֲוֹנָם מִנֶּגֶד עֵינָי׃

v. 16. לדיגים ק׳

14-15 BANISHMENT WILL NOT BE FOR EVER

Repeated substantially in xxiii. 7f. The
verses are regarded by moderns as an
interpolation which breaks the connection with verse 16; but it was a frequent practice of the prophets to temper
their denunciations with a word of hope.

The severity of the forthcoming exile
will cause the subsequent redemption to
overshadow even the deliverance from
Egypt.

16-18 THEIR GUILT IS KNOWN TO GOD

16. The rounding up of the population
is graphically described under the imagery of fishing and hunting.

115

18 And first I will recompense their
    iniquity and their sin double;
    Because they have profaned My
    land;
    They have filled Mine inherit-
    ance
    With the carcasses of their
    detestable things and their
    abominations.
19 O LORD, my strength, and my
    stronghold,
    And my refuge, in the day of
    affliction,
    Unto Thee shall the nations come
    From the ends of the earth, and
    shall say:
    'Our fathers have inherited
    nought but lies,
    Vanity and things wherein there
    is no profit.'
20 Shall a man make unto himself
    gods,
    And they are no gods?
21 Therefore, behold, I will cause
    them to know,

18 וְשִׁלַּמְתִּי רִאשׁוֹנָה
מִשְׁנֵה עֲוֹנָם וְחַטָּאתָם
עַל חַלְּלָם אֶת־אַרְצִי
בְּנִבְלַת שִׁקּוּצֵיהֶם
וְתוֹעֲבוֹתֵיהֶם
מָלְאוּ אֶת־נַחֲלָתִי:
19 יְהֹוָה עֻזִּי וּמָעֻזִּי
וּמְנוּסִי בְּיוֹם צָרָה
אֵלֶיךָ גּוֹיִם יָבֹאוּ
מֵאַפְסֵי־אָרֶץ וְיֹאמְרוּ
אַךְ־שֶׁקֶר נָחֲלוּ אֲבוֹתֵינוּ
הֶבֶל וְאֵין־בָּם מוֹעִיל:
20 הֲיַעֲשֶׂה־לּוֹ אָדָם אֱלֹהִים
וְהֵמָּה לֹא אֱלֹהִים:
21 לָכֵן הִנְנִי מוֹדִיעָם

v. 19. הפטרת בחקותי   v. 19. קמץ בז"ק

---

18. *first.* Before I decree their redemption as promised in verses 14f.

double. In great measure (cf. Isa. xl. 2).

profaned My land. Sin profaporofanes the
whole land, not only the person who
commits it.

the carcasses, etc. As dead bodies defile,
so the idols communicate pollution.

19-21 ULTIMATE REPUDIATION OF IDOLS

The mention of the idols makes the
prophet look forward to the time when
not only Israel, but the heathens also,
will disavow them. Then will the unique-
ness of God's might be universally
acknowledged.

19. *unto Thee shall the nations come.*
This Messianic vision is a distinctive
feature of Biblical teaching, and flows
from the exalted concept of the Brother-
hood of Man which will be realized as
the sequel of all nations acknowledging
the one God. It is worthy of note that
the prophet conceived of this conversion
as a spontaneous act brought about
neither by compulsion nor even per-
suasion.

20. *shall a man,* etc. Kimchi construes
the verse as the continuation of the
avowal of the nations. They will say,
'How could we ever have believed the
work of our hands to be a god?'

21. *cause them to know.* viz. those who
do not return to Me.

This once will I cause them to know
My hand and My might;
And they sha!l know that My name is the LORD.

בְּפַעַם הַזֹּאת אֹודִיעֵם
אֶת־יָדִי וְאֶת־גְּבוּרָתִי
וְיָדְעוּ כִּי־שְׁמִי יְהוָה:

17   CHAPTER XVII   יז

1 The sin of Judah is written
With a pen of iron, and with the point of a diamond;
It is graven upon the tablet of their heart,
And upon the horns of your altars.
2 Like the symbols of their sons are their altars,
And their Asherim are by the leafy trees,

1 חַטַּאת יְהוּדָה כְּתוּבָה
בְּעֵט בַּרְזֶל בְּצִפֹּרֶן שָׁמִיר
חֲרוּשָׁה עַל־לוּחַ לִבָּם
וּלְקַרְנֹות מִזְבְּחֹותֵיכֶם:
2 כִּזְכֹּר בְּנֵיהֶם מִזְבְּחֹותָם
וַאֲשֵׁרֵיהֶם עַל־עֵץ רַעֲנָן

this once. On this occasion when My punishment will be so conspicuously severe.

and they shall know that My name is the LORD. They will then be convinced that I am indeed King and Rulcr, able to fulfil My promises and enforce My decrees (Rashi).

CHAPTER XVII

1-4 THE NATION'S SIN IS INDELIBLF

1. Judah's sin is indelibly engraven upon their hardened hearts. Metsudath David connects this verse with the foregoing: though the heathens will one day acknowledge the true God (xvi. 19), Judah is firmly rooted in transgression.

a pen of iron. Used for writing on the hard surface of stones, etc. (cf. Job xix. 24). It and *the point of a diamond* have to be used because of the extreme hardness of the nation's heart.

their heart . . . your altars. Their guilt has penetrated deep into their *heart*, their innermost nature. It is at the same

time openly flaunted, as though you (here, as frequently, Jeremiah changes suddenly to the second person, but many MSS. read 'their') had written it on the horns of your altars.

2. *like . . . their altars.* The phrase is difficult. The Hebrew is literally 'as they remember their children their altars,' which Rashi and Kimchi interpret: even as men remember their sons always and with longing, so is their remembrance of and yearning for their idolatrous altars. The Hebrew can also be translated: 'whilst their children remember their altars' (so A.V., R.V.) which may mean that 'the children will be so well taught in idolatry by their parents that the tendency towards it will on the very smallest provocation rise up in the mind' (Streane).

Asherim. The *asherah* was a pole set up by the altar and served as a pagan symbol. Being associated with a heathen cult, it was forbidden by the Torah. (Deut. xvi. 21).

by the leafy trees, upon the high hills. See on ii. 20.

Upon the high hills.

3 O thou that sittest upon the
   mountain in the field,
   I will give thy substance and all
    thy treasures for a spoil,
   And thy high places, because of
    sin, throughout all thy borders.

4 And thou, even of thyself, shalt
   discontinue from thy heritage
   That I gave thee;
   And I will cause thee to serve
    thine enemies
   In the land which thou knowest
    not;
   For ye have kindled a fire in My
    nostril,
   Which shall burn for ever.

5 Thus saith the LORD:
   Cursed is the man that trusteth in
    man,
   And maketh flesh his arm,
   And whose heart departeth from
    the LORD.

6 For he shall be like a tamarisk in
   the desert,

עַל גִּבְעוֹת הַגְּבֹהוֹת:

3 הֲרָרִי בַשָּׂדֶה
חֵילְךָ כָל־אוֹצְרוֹתֶיךָ
לָבַז אֶתֵּן
בָּמֹתֶיךָ
בְּחַטָּאת בְּכָל־גְּבוּלֶיךָ:

4 וְשָׁמַטְתָּה וּבְךָ מִנַּחֲלָתְךָ
אֲשֶׁר נָתַתִּי לָךְ
וְהַעֲבַדְתִּיךָ אֶת־אֹיְבֶיךָ
בָּאָרֶץ אֲשֶׁר לֹא־יָדָעְתָּ
כִּי־אֵשׁ קְדַחְתֶּם בְּאַפִּי
עַד־עוֹלָם תּוּקָד:

5 כֹּה | אָמַר יְהֹוָה
אָרוּר הַגֶּבֶר
אֲשֶׁר יִבְטַח בָּאָדָם
וְשָׂם בָּשָׂר זְרֹעוֹ
וּמִן־יְהֹוָה יָסוּר לִבּוֹ:

6 וְהָיָה כְּעַרְעָר בָּעֲרָבָה

---

3. *O thou that sittest*, etc. There is
nothing in the text corresponding to
sittest. More literally is A.V. and R.V.,
'O my mountain in the field,' an allusion
to Jerusalem with its lofty elevation.
Kimchi, disregarding the accents, explains: 'O my people who worship idols
on the mountain, in the field will I give
thy substance,' etc., i.e. it will be free to
all to plunder. From *I will give* to the
end of the verse is reproduced with
variants from xv. 13f.

4. *and thou . . . gave thee.* You will lose
hold on your inheritance.

5-8 TRUST IN MAN AND GOD
CONTRASTED

5. *cursed is the man.* Cornill suggests
that *the man* may refer to king Zedekiah
who relied on the support of Egypt in
defiance of God's warnings through
Jeremiah.

maketh flesh his arm. Depends upon
mortal man for support.

from the LORD. As his Helper.

6. *a tamarisk* (arar). 'There can be no
doubt of the identity of this plant with

And shall not see when good
cometh;
But shall inhabit the parched
places in the wilderness,
A salt land and not inhabited.

7 Blessed is the man that trusteth in
the LORD,
And whose trust the LORD is.

8 For he shall be as a tree planted
by the waters,
And that spreadeth out its roots
by the river,
And shall not see when heat
cometh,
But its foliage shall be luxuriant;
And shall not be anxious in the
year of drought,
Neither shall cease from yielding
fruit.

9 The heart is deceitful above all
things,
And it is exceeding weak—who
can know it?

וְלֹא יִרְאֶה כִּי־יָבֹא טוֹב
וְשָׁכַן חֲרֵרִים בַּמִּדְבָּר
אֶרֶץ מְלֵחָה וְלֹא תֵשֵׁב׃

7 בָּרוּךְ הַגֶּבֶר
אֲשֶׁר יִבְטַח בַּיהוָֹה
וְהָיָה יְהוָֹה מִבְטַחוֹ׃

8 וְהָיָה כְּעֵץ ׀ שָׁתוּל עַל־מַיִם
וְעַל־יוּבַל יְשַׁלַּח שָׁרָשָׁיו
וְלֹא יִרְאֶ֯ה כִּי־יָבֹא חֹם
וְהָיָה עָלֵהוּ רַעֲנָן
וּבִשְׁנַת בַּצֹּרֶת לֹא יִדְאָג
וְלֹא יָמִישׁ מֵעֲשׂוֹת פֶּרִי׃

9 עָקֹב הַלֵּב מִכֹּל
וְאָנֻשׁ הוּא מִי יֵדָעֶנּוּ׃

v. 8. ‏ירָאֶה ק׳‏ v. 8. ‏קמץ בז"ק‏

Arabic *arar* which is a dwarf juniper,
growing in the most barren and rocky
parts of the desert. Its gloomy stunted
appearance, with its scale-like leaves
pressed close to its gnarled stem, and
cropped close by the wild goats, gives
great force to the contrast suggested by
the prophet' (Tristram).

shall not see when good cometh. It does
not benefit from the rainfall. 'Its roots
reach down to no water, its leaves are
refreshed by no rain; starved and
stunted, it just hangs on to a miserable
life' (Peake).

9-10 THE HUMAN HEART

These verses have no apparent connection with what precedes and follows.
Duhm and Cornill suggest that they
should logically be attached to verse 14.

Thus in verse 9 Jeremiah confesses to a
consciousness of sin, arrived at only after
very deep probing, without which none—
not even the person himself—can be
aware of his guilt; to which God replies
(verse 10) that He searches the heart and
knows all. That being so, the prophet
prays (verse 14) that God may heal him
of his moral weakness. Kimchi's interpretation is: The prophet, having contrasted trust in man with trust in God,
goes on to say that it is a matter hidden
in one's heart, which is deceitful: one
may profess trust in God with his lips,
whilst in his heart trusting to man. To
this God replies, *I the* LORD *search the
heart.*

9. weak. Or, connecting *anush* with
enosh, 'man': 'and so very human!'
(Hertz).

10 אֲנִי יְהוָה חֹקֵר לֵב

בֹּחֵן כְּלָיוֹת

וְלָתֵת לְאִישׁ כִּדְרָכָו

כִּפְרִי מַעֲלָלָיו:

11 קֹרֵא דָגַר וְלֹא יָלָד

עֹשֶׂה עֹשֶׁר וְלֹא בְמִשְׁפָּט

בַּחֲצִי יָמֹו יַעַזְבֶנּוּ

וּבְאַחֲרִיתוֹ יִהְיֶה נָבָל:

12 כִּסֵּא כָבוֹד מָרוֹם מֵרִאשׁוֹן

מְקוֹם מִקְדָּשֵׁנוּ:

13 מִקְוֵה יִשְׂרָאֵל יְהוָה

10 I the LORD search the heart,
I try the reins,
Even to give every man according
to his ways,
According to the fruit of his
doings.

11 As the partridge that broodeth
over young which she hath not
brought forth,
So is he that getteth riches, and
not by right;
In the midst of his days he shall
leave them,
And at his end he shall be a fool.

12 Thou throne of glory, on high
from the beginning,
Thou place of our sanctuary,

13 Thou hope of Israel, the LORD!

v. 10. כדרכיו ק'. v. 11. קמץ בז"ק. v. 11. ימיו ק'

---

10. *heart . . . reins.* Cf. xi. 20.

even to give, etc. This is an affirmation of the doctrine of Reward and Punishment, and is repeated in xxxii. 19; cf. also Ps. lxii. 13; Job xxxiv. 11. Perhaps *the fruit of his doings* suggests that good or evil automatically produces its sequel as cause and effect.

11 FATE OF THE UNSCRUPULOUS

the partridge. There was in ancient times a popular belief that the partridge sits upon eggs that are not hers. Tristram thinks that it is not true and comments on this verse: 'The partridge lays a very large number of eggs, but she has many enemies—man not the least destructive—who hunt for her nest and rob her of her eggs . . . The meaning of the prophet is, that the man who enriches himself by unjust means shall have as little enjoyment of his ill-gotten wealth, but shall leave it as prematurely as the partridge which commences to sit, but is speedily robbed of her hopes of a brood.

a fool. The Hebrew word *nabal* does not imply weakness of intellect, but lack

of moral understanding and inability to distinguish between right and wrong.

12-13 THEY WHO FORSAKE GOD ARE WITHOUT HOPE

12. *Thou throne of glory,* etc. *Thou* is not in the original. Its addition makes the two verses an invocation to God Who is addressed as the *throne of glory,* a name doubtless suggested by the Temple which was regarded as God's terrestrial throne. A.V. and R.V., less probably, make the verse a reference to Jerusalem: 'A glorious throne, set on high from the beginning, is the place of our sanctuary.'

Thou place of our sanctuary. God is, as it were, the place in which the Temple stands. Cf. 'He is the place of the universe, but the universe is not His place' (Talmud), i.e. the universe is contained in Him, but not He in it.

13. *hope of Israel.* See on xiv. 8.

shall be written in the earth. Not in a material which endures, like marble or metal.

All that forsake Thee shall be
ashamed;
They that depart from Thee shall
be written in the earth,
Because they have forsaken the
LORD,
The fountain of living waters.

14 Heal me, O LORD, and I shall be
healed;
Save me, and I shall be saved;
For Thou art my praise.

15 Behold, they say unto me:
'Where is the word of the LORD?
let it come now.'

16 As for me, I have not hastened
from being a shepherd after
Thee;
Neither have I desired the woeful
day; Thou knowest it;
That which came out of my lips
was manifest before Thee.

17 Be not a ruin unto me;

כָּל־עֹזְבֶיךָ יֵבֹשׁוּ
יְסוּרַי בָּאָרֶץ יִכָּתֵבוּ
כִּי עָזְבוּ
מְקוֹר מַיִם־חַיִּים אֶת־יְהֹוָה׃

14 רְפָאֵנִי יְהֹוָה וְאֵרָפֵא
הוֹשִׁיעֵנִי וְאִוָּשֵׁעָה
כִּי תְהִלָּתִי אָתָּה׃ *

15 הִנֵּה־הֵמָּה אֹמְרִים אֵלָי
אַיֵּה דְבַר־יְהֹוָה יָבוֹא נָא׃

16 וַאֲנִי
לֹא־אַצְתִּי ׀ מֵרֹעֶה אַחֲרֶיךָ
וְיוֹם אָנוּשׁ
לֹא הִתְאַוֵּיתִי אַתָּה יָדָעְתָּ
מוֹצָא שְׂפָתַי נֹכַח פָּנֶיךָ הָיָה׃

17 אַל־תִּהְיֵה־לִי לִמְחִתָּה

v. 13.   v. 14. עד כאן   v. 17. היו״ד בצרי   וסורי ק׳

---

the fountain of living waters. See on ii. 13.

14-18 JEREMIAH PRAYS FOR VINDICATION

Many commentators treat this as a new
section, but verses 12f. may be the introduction to it. Thus the prayer for healing is introduced by the invocation of
God as the *throne of glory* and *the hope
of Israel*; hence it is natural to turn to
Him for healing and salvation.

14. *for Thou art my praise.* In Thee do
I glory that Thou art my Helper and wilt
deliver me from mine enemies.

15. *let it come now.* They deride Jeremiah's prophecies and mockingly ask for
their fulfilment. Perhaps their jibes
momentarily weakened his faith, and it

was to be healed and saved from his
doubts that he prayed in the previous
verse.

16. *from being a shepherd.* The Hebrew
preposition has a privitive force, 'so as
not to be a shepherd': I had no intention
of hastily abandoning the mission entrusted by God to me because of the
suffering it has entailed.

the woeful day. The day of the fulfilment
of the prophecies of woe. He predicted
the direful event not from personal
inclination, but as directed by God.

that which came out of my lips. My en-
treaties that the threatened doom may be
averted.

17. *a ruin.* Let not my loyalty to Thee
be the cause of my ruin.

Thou art my refuge in the day of evil.

18 Let them be ashamed that persecute me, but let not me be ashamed;

Let them be dismayed, but let not me be dismayed;

Bring upon them the day of evil,

And destroy them with double destruction.

19. Thus said the LORD unto me: Go, and stand in the gate of the children of the people, whereby the kings of Judah come in, and by which they go out, and in all the gates of Jerusalem; 20. and say unto them:

Hear ye the word of the LORD, ye kings of Judah, and all Judah, and all the inhabitants of Jerusalem,

מַחְסִי אַתָּה בְּיוֹם רָעָה:

18 יֵבֹשׁוּ רֹדְפַי וְאַל־אֵבֹשָׁה אָנִי
יֵחַתּוּ הֵמָּה וְאַל־אֵחַתָּה אָנִי
הָבִיא עֲלֵיהֶם יוֹם רָעָה
וּמִשְׁנֶה שִׁבָּרוֹן שָׁבְרֵם:

19 כֹּה־אָמַר יְהוָֹה אֵלַי הָלֹךְ
וְעָמַדְתָּ בְּשַׁעַר בְּנֵי־עָם
אֲשֶׁר יָבֹאוּ בוֹ מַלְכֵי יְהוּדָה
וַאֲשֶׁר יֵצְאוּ בוֹ וּבְכֹל שַׁעֲרֵי
20 יְרוּשָׁלָ͏ִם: וְאָמַרְתָּ אֲלֵיהֶם
שִׁמְעוּ דְבַר־יְהוָֹה מַלְכֵי
יְהוּדָה וְכָל־יְהוּדָה וְכָל יֹשְׁבֵי
יְרוּשָׁלָ͏ִם הַבָּאִים בַּשְּׁעָרִים

v. 19. העם ק'

---

18. double destruction. i.e. complete destruction. This verse apparently contradicts verses 16f., yet not necessarily. The prophet has indeed prayed that the people be spared; but he has none the less failed to convince his persecutors of his good intentions or checked their plans against him. So he now prays for their complete discomfiture (cf. xviii. 18-23).

19-27 SABBATH OBSERVANCE WILL RESTORE NATIONAL GLORY

The prophet exhorts the people to observe the Sabbath. Most modern commentators think of this section as detached; but if interpreted in the context, it would be pedantic to urge that Jeremiah has spoken in certain tones of the people's doom as inevitable. As already pointed out, prophecies, no matter how final in tone, are conditional, since God is always ready to receive the repentant sinner. Furthermore, it is

the prophet's duty to indicate the remedy for current evils. It is therefore natural that Jeremiah should stress the importance of the Sabbath, a basic institution of Judaism. The hallowing of the Sabbath, with its intensive spiritual influence, would tend to wean the people from other malpractices and effect a reformation.

19. the children of the people. This probably signifies the laity (the phrase is used in this sense in 2 Chron. xxxv. 5), including the royal house, as distinct from the priests and Levites. This gate would be the entrance most frequently resorted to by them; so Jeremiah was to proclaim his message there first and repeat it in the other gates.

20. ye kings of Judah. Whereas in the previous verse the plural denotes successive kings, here it seems to mean the reigning monarch and the princes of his house.

that enter in by these gates; 21. thus saith the LORD: Take heed for the sake of your souls, and bear no burden on the sabbath day, nor bring it in by the gates of Jerusalem; 22. neither carry forth a burden out of your houses on the sabbath day, neither do ye any work; but hallow ye the sabbath day, as I commanded your fathers; 23. but they hearkened not, neither inclined their ear, but made their neck stiff, that they might not hear, nor receive instruction. 24. And it shall come to pass, if ye diligently hearken unto Me, saith the LORD, to bring in no burden through the gates of this city on the sabbath day, but to hallow the sabbath day, to do no work therein; 25. then shall there enter in by the gates of this city kings and princes sitting upon the

21 הָאֵ֑לֶּה׃ כֹּ֣ה אָמַ֣ר יְהֹוָ֗ה
הִשָּׁמְר֖וּ בְּנַפְשֽׁוֹתֵיכֶ֑ם וְאַל־
תִּשְׂא֤וּ מַשָּׂא֙ בְּי֣וֹם הַשַּׁבָּ֔ת
וַהֲבֵאתֶ֖ם בְּשַׁעֲרֵ֥י יְרוּשָׁלָֽ͏ִם׃
22 וְלֹא־תוֹצִ֨יאוּ מַשָּׂ֤א מִבָּֽתֵּיכֶם֙
בְּי֣וֹם הַשַּׁבָּ֔ת וְכָל־מְלָאכָ֖ה
לֹ֣א תַעֲשׂ֑וּ וְקִדַּשְׁתֶּם֙ אֶת־י֣וֹם
הַשַּׁבָּ֔ת כַּאֲשֶׁ֥ר צִוִּ֖יתִי אֶת־
23 אֲבוֹתֵיכֶֽם׃ וְלֹ֣א שָֽׁמְע֔וּ וְלֹ֥א
הִטּ֖וּ אֶת־אָזְנָ֑ם וַיַּקְשׁוּ֙ אֶת־
עָרְפָּ֔ם לְבִלְתִּ֣י שׁוֹמֵ֔עַ וּלְבִלְתִּ֖י
24 קַ֥חַת מוּסָֽר׃ וְהָיָ֗ה אִם־שָׁמֹ֨עַ
תִּשְׁמְע֤וּן אֵלַי֙ נְאֻם־יְהֹוָ֔ה
לְבִלְתִּ֣י ׀ הָבִ֣יא מַשָּׂ֗א בְּשַׁעֲרֵ֛י
הָעִ֥יר הַזֹּ֖את בְּי֣וֹם הַשַּׁבָּ֑ת
וּלְקַדֵּשׁ֙ אֶת־י֣וֹם הַשַּׁבָּ֔ת
לְבִלְתִּ֥י עֲשֽׂוֹת־ב֖וֹ כָּל־־
25 מְלָאכָֽה׃ וּבָ֣אוּ בְשַׁעֲרֵ֣י הָעִ֣יר
הַזֹּ֗את מְלָכִ֣ים ׀ וְשָׂרִ֗ים

v. 24. שמוע ק׳   v. 23. בו ק׳

21. *for the sake of your souls.* lit. 'in your souls,' which may be the equivalent of 'in your hearts.' A.V. and R.V. translate: 'take heed to yourselves.'

burden. Of merchandise, or more particularly of produce from the agricultural districts.

22. *out of your houses.* Articles brought from the house with which to barter for the produce brought into the city.

23. Cf. vii. 26.

25. *kings and princes.* In a similar passage (xxii. 4) *and princes* is omitted. 'There, however, the address is to the king, here directly to the people, and the effect is increased by the picture of a grand procession of the royal house and their followers, all attending upon the person of the king' (Streane).

sitting. The subject is *kings*, the *princes* surrounding the throne.

throne of David, riding in chariots and on horses, they, and their princes, the men of Judah, and the inhabitants of Jerusalem; and this city shall be inhabited for ever. 26. And they shall come from the cities of Judah, and from the places round about Jerusalem, and from the land of Benjamin, and from the Lowland, and from the mountains, and from the South, bringing burnt-offerings, and sacrifices, and meal-offerings, and frankincense, and bringing sacrifices of thanksgiving, unto the house of the LORD. 27. But if ye will not hearken unto Me to hallow the sabbath day, and not to bear a burden and enter in at the gates of Jerusalem on the sabbath day; then will I kindle a fire in the gates thereof, and it shall devour the palaces of Jerusalem, and it shall not be quenched.

יֹשְׁבִים עַל־כִּסֵּא דָוִד רֹכְבִים
בָּרֶכֶב וּבַסּוּסִים הֵמָּה וְ
וְשָׂרֵיהֶם אִישׁ יְהוּדָה וְיֹשְׁבֵי
יְרוּשָׁלָ͏ִם וְיָשְׁבָה הָעִיר הַזֹּאת
26 לְעוֹלָם׃ וּבָאוּ מֵעָרֵי־יְהוּדָה
וּמִסְּבִיבוֹת יְרוּשָׁלַ͏ִם וּמֵאֶרֶץ
בִּנְיָמִן וּמִן־הַשְּׁפֵלָה וּמִן־
הָהָר וּמִן־הַנֶּגֶב מְבִאִים עוֹלָה
וְזֶבַח וּמִנְחָה וּלְבוֹנָה וּמְבִאֵי
27 תוֹדָה בֵּית יְהוָה׃ וְאִם־לֹא
תִשְׁמְעוּ אֵלַי לְקַדֵּשׁ אֶת־יוֹם
הַשַּׁבָּת וּלְבִלְתִּי שְׂאֵת מַשָּׂא
וּבֹא בְּשַׁעֲרֵי יְרוּשָׁלַ͏ִם בְּיוֹם
הַשַּׁבָּת וְהִצַּתִּי אֵשׁ בִּשְׁעָרֶיהָ
וְאָכְלָה אַרְמְנוֹת יְרוּשָׁלַ͏ִם וְלֹא
תִכְבֶּה׃

---

26. the land of Benjamin. To the north of Judah.

the Lowland. The low hills and valleys stretching down towards the Philistine plain on the west and south-west of Judah.

the mountains. The hilly country south of Jerusalem.

the South. The Negeb (see on xiii. 19).

bringing burnt-offerings, etc. The prophet did not object to sacrifices as such.

and sacrifices. i.e. peace-offerings (Lev. iii. 1ff.).

meal-offerings. Cf. Lev. ii. 1ff.

frankincense. This is not a separate offering, but a compound of spices was sprinkled on the meal-offerings.

sacrifices of thanksgiving. Cf. Lev. vii. 11ff. These were also peace-offerings, perhaps the most highly esteemed of this class of offerings. 'In the time to come all sacrifices will cease, but the sacrifice of thanksgiving will not cease' (Talmud).

27. a fire. A symbol of destruction (cf. xxi. 14, xlix. 27, l. 32). The penalty resembles the refrain in Amos i. 4-ii. 5.

18   CHAPTER XVIII   יח

1. The word which came to Jeremiah from the LORD, saying: 2. 'Arise, and go down to the potter's house, and there I will cause thee to hear My words.' 3. Then I went down to the potter's house, and, behold, he was at his work on the wheels. 4. And whensoever the vessel that he made of the clay was marred in the hand of the potter, he made it again

1 הַדָּבָר אֲשֶׁר הָיָה אֶל־יִרְמְיָהוּ
2 מֵאֵת יְהֹוָה לֵאמֹר: קוּם
וְיָרַדְתָּ בֵּית הַיּוֹצֵר וְשָׁמָּה
3 אַשְׁמִיעֲךָ אֶת־דְּבָרִי: וָאֵרֵד
בֵּית הַיּוֹצֵר וְהִנֵּהוּ עֹשֶׂה
מְלָאכָה עַל־הָאָבְנָיִם:
4 וְנִשְׁחַת הַכְּלִי אֲשֶׁר הוּא עֹשֶׂה
בַּחֹמֶר בְּיַד הַיּוֹצֵר וְשָׁב

v. 3. והנה הוא ק'

CHAPTER XVIII

1-17 THE POTTER AND HIS CLAY

CHAPTERS xviii-xx form a connected section. The familiar sight of the potter at work with his clay suggests to Jeremiah's mind a parallel to the working of God with His people. Chapter xviii describes the process of remaking a misshapen vessel and applies it to the fate of the nation. This is followed by the parable of the broken bottle with special reference to the persecution of the prophet by an official named Passhur. The composition dates from the early years in the reign of Jehoiakim.

2. *go down.* Streane is of the opinion that the command was addressed to Jeremiah while he was on the Temple mount where he delivered the preceding addresses. The verb may only indicate that the potter's house was situated in a lower district of the city.

3. *the wheels.* The Hebrew noun has the dual formation and is literally 'the two stones.' The apparatus consisted of two circular stones; the lower was worked by the feet and connected 'with the upper, which supported the clay, by a

vertical axis. The upper disc rotated when pressure was applied to the pedal.

4. *of the clay.* The Hebrew editions and MSS. vary in the reading between *kachomer*, 'like the clay,' and *bachomer*, 'in (i.e. of) the clay.' The latter is preferable.

was marred. Thomson witnessed such a scene which he describes as follows: 'From some defect in the clay, or because he had taken too little, the potter suddenly changed his mind, crushed his growing jar instantly into a shapeless mass of mud, and beginning anew, fashioned it into a totally different vessel.' The application of the simile is not that the house of Israel is bound to be fashioned ultimately as God wishes, as might be concluded from verse 4, but that God disposes absolutely of the destinies of Israel and every other nation, in the same way that the potter does whatever he pleases with the clay. This is true notwithstanding previous predictions of blessings or disaster, because such are always conditional: the blessings will be forfeited if the people become unworthy of them, whilst the disaster may be averted if the people repent in time. This simile of the potter and his clay has inspired one of the most

another vessel, as seemed good to the potter to make it.

5. Then the word of the LORD came to me, saying: 6. 'O house of Israel, cannot I do with you as this potter? saith the LORD. Behold, as the clay in the potter's hand, so are ye in My hand, O house of Israel. 7. At one instant I may speak concerning a nation, and concerning a kingdom, to pluck up and to break down and to destroy it; 8. but if that nation turn from their evil, because of which I have spoken against it, I repent of the evil that I thought to do unto it. 9. And at one instant I may speak concerning a nation, and concerning a kingdom, to build and to plant it; 10. but if it do evil in My sight, that it hearken not to My voice, then I repent of the good, wherewith I said I would benefit it. 11. Now therefore do thou speak to the men of Judah, and to the inhabitants of Jerusalem, saying: Thus

וַיַּעֲשֵׂהוּ כְּלִי אַחֵר כַּאֲשֶׁר יָשַׁר
בְּעֵינֵי הַיּוֹצֵר לַעֲשׂוֹת: וַיְהִי 5
דְבַר־יְהֹוָה אֵלַי לֵאמֹר:
הֲכַיּוֹצֵר הַזֶּה לֹא־אוּכַל 6
לַעֲשׂוֹת לָכֶם בֵּית יִשְׂרָאֵל
נְאֻם־יְהֹוָה הִנֵּה כַחֹמֶר בְּיַד
הַיּוֹצֵר כֵּן־אַתֶּם בְּיָדִי בֵּית
יִשְׂרָאֵל: רֶגַע אֲדַבֵּר עַל־ 7
גּוֹי וְעַל־מַמְלָכָה לִנְתוֹשׁ
וְלִנְתוֹץ וּלְהַאֲבִיד: וְשָׁב הַגּוֹי 8
הַהוּא מֵרָעָתוֹ אֲשֶׁר דִּבַּרְתִּי
עָלָיו וְנִחַמְתִּי עַל־הָרָעָה
אֲשֶׁר חָשַׁבְתִּי לַעֲשׂוֹת לוֹ:
וְרֶגַע אֲדַבֵּר עַל־גּוֹי וְעַל־ 9
מַמְלָכָה לִבְנוֹת וְלִנְטוֹעַ:
וְעָשָׂה הָרָעָה בְּעֵינַי לְבִלְתִּי 10
שְׁמֹעַ בְּקוֹלִי וְנִחַמְתִּי עַל־
הַטּוֹבָה אֲשֶׁר אָמַרְתִּי לְהֵיטִיב
אוֹתוֹ: וְעַתָּה אֱמָר־נָא אֶל־ 11
אִישׁ יְהוּדָה וְעַל־יוֹשְׁבֵי
יְרוּשָׁלַם לֵאמֹר כֹּה אָמַר יְהֹוָה:

v. 5. ר׳ מלא   v. 10. הרע ק׳

---

beautiful of Hebrew liturgical poems, included in the service on the eve of the Day of Atonement:

Lo! as the potter mouldeth plastic clay
To form his varying fancy doth display;
So in Thy hand, O God of love, are we:
Thy bond regard, let sin be veiled from Thee.

7. *a nation . . . a kingdom.* Although the

moral is ultimately directed to the Kingdom of Judah (verse 11), *nation* and *kingdom* are an assertion of God's Sovereignty over all peoples.

8. *I repent.* An anthropomorphism, signifying not a change of mind (cf. Num. xxiii. 19), but in treatment occasioned by the change in the people's conduct.

saith the LORD: Behold, I frame evil against you, and devise a device against you; return ye now every one from his evil way, and amend your ways and your doings. 12. But they say: There is no hope; but we will walk after our own devices, and we will do every one after the stubbornness of his evil heart.'

13 Therefore thus saith the LORD:
Ask ye now among the nations,
Who hath heard such things;
The virgin of Israel hath done
A very horrible thing.

14 Doth the snow of Lebanon fail
From the rock of the field?

הִנֵּה אָנֹכִי יוֹצֵר עֲלֵיכֶם רָעָה
וְחֹשֵׁב עֲלֵיכֶם מַחֲשָׁבָה שׁוּבוּ
נָא אִישׁ מִדַּרְכּוֹ הָרָעָה
וְהֵיטִיבוּ דַרְכֵיכֶם
12 וּמָעֲלֵיכֶם: וְאָמְרוּ נוֹאָשׁ
כִּי־אַחֲרֵי מַחְשְׁבוֹתֵינוּ נֵלֵךְ
וְאִישׁ שְׁרִרוּת לִבּוֹ־הָרָע
נַעֲשֶׂה:
13 לָכֵן כֹּה אָמַר יְהוָה
שַׁאֲלוּ־נָא בַּגּוֹיִם
מִי שָׁמַע כָּאֵלֶּה
שַׁעֲרֻרִת עָשְׂתָה מְאֹד
בְּתוּלַת יִשְׂרָאֵל:
14 הֲיַעֲזֹב מִצּוּר שָׂדַי שֶׁלֶג לְבָנוֹן

11. *frame.* The verb, *yotser*, is identical with the word for *potter* and is deliberately chosen to suggest the connection.

12. *there is no hope.* It is too late: we have chosen our path and must continue in it. The same expression occurred in ii. 25.

13. *the virgin of Israel.* See on xiv. 17. The people of Israel, like a virgin who keeps herself undefiled for her future husband, should have avoided contamination by foreign worship as the 'betrothed' of God.

a very horrible thing. An action both unnatural and revolting, as the next verse explains.

14. This is a difficult verse. As rendered by A.J., which agrees substantially with A.V. and R.V., the meaning is that Nature pursues her course unchanged,

whereas the nation has unnaturally changed its course. The Jewish commentators interpret the verse differently: shall one forsake the pure water coursing down the rock of the field from the melting snows (in favour of turbid waters), or should clear running water be abandoned for foul, stagnant waters?

doth . . . fail. The summit of Lebanon (lit. 'the white mountain') is clothed with perpetual snow, and nothing occurs to alter this.

the rock of the field. The expression is strange. Emendations of the text have been proposed, but they are not satisfactory. Ehrlich suggests a translation in accordance with the alternative interpretation given above: 'Doth the ice-cold water (literally snow) of Lebanon fail (to stream down) between (literally from) the rocks into the valley (literally field)?'

Or are the strange cold flowing
waters
Plucked up?

15 For My people hath forgotten
Me,
They offer unto vanity;
And they have been made to
stumble in their ways,
In the ancient paths,
To walk in bypaths,
In a way not cast up;

16 To make their land an astonish-
ment,
And a perpetual hissing;
Every one that passeth thereby
shall be astonished,
And shake his head.

17 I will scatter them as with an
east wind
Before the enemy;
I will look upon their back, and
not their face,
In the day of their calamity.

אִם־יִנָּתְשׁוּ מַיִם
זָרִים קָרִים נֹוזְלִים:

15 כִּי־שְׁכֵחֻנִי עַמִּי לַשָּׁוְא יְקַטֵּרוּ
וַיַּכְשִׁלוּם בְּדַרְכֵיהֶם
שְׁבוּלֵי עֹולָם
לָלֶכֶת נְתִיבוֹת
דֶּרֶךְ לֹא סְלוּלָה:

16 לָשׂוּם אַרְצָם
לְשַׁמָּה שְׁרוֹקַת עוֹלָם
כֹּל עֹובֵר עָלֶיהָ
יִשֹּׁם וְיָנִיד בְּרֹאשׁוֹ:

17 כְּרוּחַ־קָדִים אֲפִיצֵם
לִפְנֵי אוֹיֵב
עֹרֶף וְלֹא־פָנִים
אֶרְאֵם בְּיוֹם אֵידָם:

v. 15.   v. 16. שְׁרוּקַת ק׳   שְׁבִילֵי ק׳

the strange cold flowing waters. The best
explanation of this perplexing clause
seems to be that offered by Streane:
'Does the water that percolates through
the rocks, coming from unknown (*strange*)
regions and cold (thus free from much
evaporation), disappear?' The verb rendered *plucked up* (*yinnatheshu*) may by
metathesis be the equivalent of *yinna-
shethu*, 'dried up.' The general sense is:
'Nature is constant in her operations, but
God, the Rock of Israel, is forsaken by
those who used to follow Him' (Streane).

15. *vanity.* i.e. idols.

and they have been made to stumble. lit.,
as A.V. and R.V., 'and they have caused
them to stumble.' The subject may then
be the idols, to be understood from the
general context; or, *they* may simply be

indefinite, in which case the sense
approximates to 'and they (the people)
have stumbled' (so LXX).

the ancient paths. Cf. vi. 16.

a way not cast up. Not properly constructed, but just carelessly trodden out.

16. *to make,* etc. That must be the
inevitable result of abandoning the paths
ordained by God.

hissing. An act indicative of amazement.

17. *an east wind.* The sirocco, a hot
wind which springs up suddenly from the
desert in the east (cf. xiii. 24).

I will look upon their back. When they
flee from before the enemy and not save
them (Rashi). Kimchi and Metsudath
David interpret: 'I will show them (My)

18 Then said they:
'Come, and let us devise devices
  against Jeremiah;
For instruction shall not perish
  from the priest,
Nor counsel from the wise, nor
  the word from the prophet.
Come, and let us smite him with
  the tongue,
And let us not give heed to any
  of his words.'
19 Give heed to me, O LORD,
And hearken to the voice of them
  that contend with me.
20 Shall evil be recompensed for
  good?
For they have digged a pit for
  my soul.
Remember how I stood before
  Thee
To speak good for them,
To turn away Thy wrath from
  them.

18 וַיֹּאמְר֗וּ
לְכ֞וּ וְנַחְשְׁבָ֣ה עַֽל־יִרְמְיָ֘הוּ֒
מַחֲשָׁב֔וֹת
כִּ֣י לֹא־תֹאבַ֤ד תּוֹרָה֙ מִכֹּהֵ֔ן
וְעֵצָה֙ מֵֽחָכָ֔ם וְדָבָ֖ר מִנָּבִ֑יא
לְכוּ֙ וְנַכֵּ֣הוּ בַלָּשׁ֔וֹן
וְאַל־נַקְשִׁ֖יבָה
אֶל־כָּל־דְּבָרָֽיו׃
19 הַקְשִׁ֥יבָה יְהֹוָ֖ה אֵלָ֑י
וּשְׁמַ֖ע לְק֥וֹל יְרִיבָֽי׃
20 הַיְשֻׁלַּ֤ם תַּֽחַת־טוֹבָה֙ רָעָ֔ה
כִּֽי־כָר֥וּ שׁוּחָ֖ה לְנַפְשִׁ֑י
זְכֹ֣ר ׀ עָמְדִ֤י לְפָנֶ֨יךָ֙
לְדַבֵּ֤ר עֲלֵיהֶם֙ טוֹבָ֔ה
לְהָשִׁ֥יב אֶת־חֲמָתְךָ֖ מֵהֶֽם׃

---

back and not (My) face' (so A.V. and R.V. margin), i.e. I will hide My face from their cries, as though the pointing of the verb was *ar'em*.

18-23 JEREMIAH PRAYS FOR PUNISH-
MENT ON HIS ANTAGONISTS

18. they. Jeremiah's enemies.

for instruction shall not perish, etc. This may mean either (*i*) we are not dependent on him for instruction, counsel and prophecy; there are priests, wise men and prophets to guide us, and we can do without him; or (*ii*) his predictions are unwarranted; we, too, are not lacking in wisdom, etc. Ehrlich considers the clause to be not part of what Jeremiah's enemies say, but his own ironical

interjection. His opponents belonged to the three categories mentioned, and so he remarks sarcastically, 'They can do away with me, as they think, without loss. They possess all the instruction, etc., necessary!'

with the tongue. Let us lay charges against him which will encompass his destruction. The text may mean 'with (his) tongue' (so the Peshitta): let us use his own words to bring about his downfall through a charge of treason.

let us not give heed. We can ignore his threatenings of retribution.

20. *for my soul.* i.e. for my life.

to speak good for them. For Jeremiah's intercessions, cf. xiv. 7ff., 21.

21 Therefore deliver up their
children to the famine,
And hurl them to the power of
the sword;
And let their wives be bereaved
of their children, and widows;
And let their men be slain of
death,
And their young men smitten of
the sword in battle.

22 Let a cry be heard from their
houses,
When thou shalt bring a troop
suddenly upon them;
For they have digged a pit to
take me,
And hid snares for my feet.

23 Yet, LORD, Thou knowest
All their counsel against me to
slay me;
Forgive not their iniquity,
Neither blot out their sin from
Thy sight;

21 לָכֵן֩ תֵּ֨ן אֶת־בְּנֵיהֶ֜ם לָרָעָ֗ב
וְהַגִּרֵם֮ עַל־יְדֵי־חֶ֒רֶב֒
וְתִֽהְיֶ֤נָה נְשֵׁיהֶם֙
שַׁכֻּלוֹת֙ וְאַלְמָנ֔וֹת
וְאַ֨נְשֵׁיהֶ֤ם יִֽהְיוּ֙ הֲרֻ֣גֵי מָ֔וֶת
בַּחֽוּרֵיהֶ֕ם
מֻכֵּי־חֶ֖רֶב בַּמִּלְחָמָֽה:

22 תִּשָּׁמַ֤ע זְעָקָה֙ מִבָּ֣תֵּיהֶ֔ם
כִּֽי־תָבִ֧יא עֲלֵיהֶ֛ם
גְּד֖וּד פִּתְאֹ֑ם
כִּֽי־כָר֤וּ שִׁיחָה֙ לְלָכְדֵ֔נִי
וּפַחִ֖ים טָמְנ֥וּ לְרַגְלָֽי:

23 וְאַתָּ֣ה יְ֠הוָה יָדַ֜עְתָּ
אֶת־כָּל־עֲצָתָ֥ם עָלַ֖י לַמָּ֑וֶת
אַל־תְּכַפֵּר֙ עַל־עֲוֺנָ֔ם
וְחַטָּאתָם֙ מִלְּפָנֶ֣יךָ אַל־תֶּ֔מְחִי

שׂוחה ק׳ v. 22.

21ff. The bitter imprecation is not hurled
against the nation as a whole for refusing
to accept his teaching, but is directed
only against his enemies who plotted his
death. 'The prophets were neither
vegetables nor machines but men of like
passions with ourselves' (G. A. Smith).
Even so, the outburst does not represent
Jeremiah at his highest and is uttered in
a moment of exasperation. It should also
be remembered that his anger was
aroused not so much because he was
being personally attacked as for the
reason that his call from God was
defied.

21. *hurl them to the power of the sword.*
lit. 'pour them out upon the hands of the
sword.' The expression occurs again in
Ezek. xxxv. 5; Ps. lxiii. 11 and means
that they should be thrust upon the sword
so that their life-blood is poured out.

their men. The contrast in the next
clause indicates that here are intended
the men who are too old to fight on the
battlefield, and *of death* signifies 'from
pestilence' as in xv. 2.

22. *their houses.* Broken into and plundered by the enemy.

23. *Thou knowest.* Although they
schemed against Jeremiah in secret, their
plot is known to God.

But let them be made to stumble
before Thee;
Deal Thou with them in the
time of Thine anger.

וְֽיִהְי֤וּ מֻכְשָׁלִים֙ לְפָנֶ֔יךָ
בְּעֵ֥ת אַפְּךָ֖ עֲשֵׂ֥ה בָהֶֽם׃

19   CHAPTER XIX   יט

1. Thus said the LORD: Go, and
get a potter's earthen bottle, and
take of the elders of the people, and
of the elders of the priests; 2. and
go forth unto the valley of the son of
Hinnom, which is by the entry of the
gate Harsith, and proclaim there the
words that I shall tell thee; 3. and
say: Hear ye the word of the LORD,
O kings of Judah, and inhabitants of
Jerusalem; thus saith the LORD of
hosts, the God of Israel:

1 כֹּ֣ה אָמַ֣ר יְהֹוָ֗ה הָלֹ֤ךְ וְקָנִ֙יתָ֙
בַּקְבֻּ֣ק יוֹצֵ֣ר חָ֑רֶשׂ וּמִזִּקְנֵ֥י הָעָ֖ם
2 וּמִזִּקְנֵ֣י הַכֹּהֲנִֽים׃ וְיָצָ֗אתָ֙ אֶל־
גֵּ֤יא בֶן־הִנֹּם֙ אֲשֶׁ֣ר פֶּ֔תַח שַׁ֖עַר
הַֽחַרְס֑וּת וְקָרָ֣אתָ שָּׁ֔ם אֶת־
הַדְּבָרִ֖ים אֲשֶׁר־אֲדַבֵּ֥ר
3 אֵלֶֽיךָ׃ וְאָ֣מַרְתָּ֔ שִׁמְע֥וּ דְבַר־
יְהֹוָ֖ה מַלְכֵ֣י יְהוּדָ֑ה וְיֹשְׁבֵ֖י
יְרוּשָׁלָ֑͏ִם כֹּה־אָמַ֞ר יְהֹוָ֣ה
צְבָא֗וֹת אֱלֹהֵ֤י יִשְׂרָאֵל֙ הִנְנִ֞י

v. 23.   'ק הַחַרְסִית   'ק וִיהְיוּ   v. 2.

---

deal . . . anger. The sense is, 'Deal with
them (as Thou dealest with wrongdoers)
in the time of Thy anger.'

CHAPTER XIX

1-13 PARABLE OF THE EARTHEN BOTTLE

IN the parable of the potter and his
clay, the point is the possibility of
remaking a vessel which has not met
with approval; here it is the destruction
of a vessel which proves useless.

1. *take.* Not in the Hebrew, but to be
understood.

the elders of the priests. Their chiefs
(again in 2 Kings xix. 2 and cf. 2 Chron.
xxxvi. 14).

2. *the valley of the son of Hinnom.* See
on vii. 31.

the gate Harsith. Or, 'the gate of
potsherds' (R.V. margin). It was perhaps given that name because fragments
of pottery were cast there as refuse. It
may be identical with *the dung gate*
(Neh. ii. 13). Another explanation is
that fragments were ground there 'as is
done now, on a flat rock with heavy stone
rollers into dust from which cement is
made, used for plastering cisterns. The
place where this is now done is near the
Birket es-Sultan, a pool at the south-
west of the city, in the upper part of
what was probably the ancient valley of
Hinnom' (Driver).

3. *kings.* See on xvii. 20.

Behold, I will bring evil upon this place, which whosoever heareth, his ears shall tingle; 4. because they have forsaken Me, and have estranged this place, and have offered in it unto other gods, whom neither they nor their fathers have known, nor the kings of Judah; and have filled this place with the blood of innocents; 5. and have built the high places of Baal, to burn their sons in the fire for burnt-offerings unto Baal; which I commanded not, nor spoke it, neither came it into My mind. 6. Therefore, behold, the days come, saith the LORD, that this place shall no more be called Topheth, nor The valley of the son of Hinnom, but The valley of slaughter; 7. and I will make void the counsel of Judah and Jerusalem in this place; and I will cause them to fall by the sword before their

מֵבִיא רָעָה עַל־הַמָּקוֹם הַזֶּה
אֲשֶׁר כָּל־שֹׁמְעָהּ תִּצַּלְנָה
אָזְנָיו: יַעַן ׀ אֲשֶׁר עֲזָבֻנִי 4
וַיְנַכְּרוּ אֶת־הַמָּקוֹם הַזֶּה
וַיְקַטְּרוּ־בוֹ לֵאלֹהִים אֲחֵרִים
אֲשֶׁר לֹא־יְדָעוּם הֵמָּה
וַאֲבוֹתֵיהֶם וּמַלְכֵי יְהוּדָה
וּמָלְאוּ אֶת־הַמָּקוֹם הַזֶּה דָּם
נְקִיִּם: וּבָנוּ אֶת־בָּמוֹת הַבַּעַל 5
לִשְׂרֹף אֶת־בְּנֵיהֶם בָּאֵשׁ
עֹלוֹת לַבָּעַל אֲשֶׁר לֹא־צִוִּיתִי
וְלֹא דִבַּרְתִּי וְלֹא עָלְתָה עַל־
לִבִּי: לָכֵן הִנֵּה־יָמִים בָּאִים 6
נְאֻם־יְהוָֹה וְלֹא־יִקָּרֵא
לַמָּקוֹם הַזֶּה עוֹד הַתֹּפֶת וְגֵיא
בֶן־הִנֹּם כִּי אִם־גֵּיא הַהֲרֵגָה:
וּבַקֹּתִי אֶת־עֲצַת יְהוּדָה 7
וִירוּשָׁלִַם בַּמָּקוֹם הַזֶּה
וְהִפַּלְתִּים בַּחֶרֶב לִפְנֵי

---

this place. viz. Jerusalem (so again in verse 4).

his ears shall tingle. As in 1 Sam. iii. 11; 2 Kings xxi. 12.

4. *have estranged this place.* Made it strange to Me by practising hideous rites in it.

innocents. Most probably the children who were sacrificed, as in the next verse. Or, possibly, the allusion is to the blood of innocent people who were murdered (cf. 2 Kings xxi. 16).

5f. Almost identical with vii. 31f., on which see the notes.

5. *of Baal.* Corresponding to *of Topheth* in vii. 31.

7. *make void the counsel.* They will be emptied of counsel which might save them from the enemy. The verb *bakkothi* is connected with *bakbuk, bottle,* in verse 1 and chosen because of it. Modern commentators think that Jeremiah symbolically emptied the vessel as he spoke these words.

enemies, and by the hand of them that seek their life; and their carcasses will I give to be food for the fowls of the heaven, and for the beasts of the earth; 8. and I will make this city an astonishment, and a hissing; every one that passeth thereby shall be astonished and hiss because of all the plagues thereof; 9. and I will cause them to eat the flesh of their sons and the flesh of their daughters, and they shall eat every one the flesh of his friend, in the siege and in the straitness, wherewith their enemies, and they that seek their life, shall straiten them. 10. Then shalt thou break the bottle in the sight of the men that go with thee, 11. and shalt say unto them: Thus saith the LORD of hosts: Even so will I break this people and this city, as one breaketh a potter's vessel, that cannot be made whole again; and they shall bury in Topheth, for want of room

אֹיְבֵיהֶם וּבְיַד מְבַקְשֵׁי נַפְשָׁם
וְנָתַתִּי אֶת־נִבְלָתָם לְמַאֲכָל
לְעוֹף הַשָּׁמַיִם וּלְבֶהֱמַת
8 הָאָרֶץ: וְשַׂמְתִּי אֶת־הָעִיר
הַזֹּאת לְשַׁמָּה וְלִשְׁרֵקָה כֹּל
עֹבֵר עָלֶיהָ יִשֹּׁם וְיִשְׁרֹק עַל־
9 כָּל־מַכֹּתֶהָ: וְהַאֲכַלְתִּים
אֶת־בְּשַׂר בְּנֵיהֶם וְאֵת בְּשַׂר
בְּנֹתֵיהֶם וְאִישׁ בְּשַׂר־רֵעֵהוּ
יֹאכֵלוּ בְּמָצוֹר וּבְמָצוֹק אֲשֶׁר
יָצִיקוּ לָהֶם אֹיְבֵיהֶם וּמְבַקְשֵׁי
10 נַפְשָׁם: וְשָׁבַרְתָּ הַבַּקְבֻּק
לְעֵינֵי הָאֲנָשִׁים הַהֹלְכִים
11 אוֹתָךְ: וְאָמַרְתָּ אֲלֵיהֶם כֹּה־
אָמַר יְהוָה צְבָאוֹת כָּכָה
אֶשְׁבֹּר אֶת־הָעָם הַזֶּה וְאֶת־
הָעִיר הַזֹּאת כַּאֲשֶׁר יִשְׁבֹּר
אֶת־כְּלִי הַיּוֹצֵר אֲשֶׁר
לֹא־יוּכַל לְהֵרָפֵה עוֹד
וּבְתֹפֶת יִקְבְּרוּ מֵאֵין מָקוֹם

v. 11. ה' במקום א'

---

and their carcasses, etc. Based on vii. 33.

8. The verse repeats the substance of xviii. 16.

9. Their desperate straits will reduce them to cannibalism. This verse is derived from Deut. xxviii. 53. The fulfilment of the prediction is recorded in Lam. iv. 10.

10. *shalt thou break the bottle.* It is still

the practice in the East to break a jar near a person and express the hope that he will be similarly broken.

11. *and they shall bury . . . to bury.* Based on vii. 32. The words are omitted in LXX but fit into the context. In the 'breaking' of the nation, the dead will be so numerous that even the unclean site of Topheth will have to be used for their burial.

to bury. 12. Thus will I do unto this place, saith the LORD, and to the inhabitants thereof, even making this city as Topheth; 13. and the houses of Jerusalem, and the houses of the kings of Judah, which are defiled, shall be as the place of Topheth, even all the houses upon whose roofs they have offered unto all the host of heaven, and have poured out drink-offerings unto other gods.

14. Then came Jeremiah from Topheth, whither the LORD had sent him to prophesy; and he stood in the court of the LORD's house, and said to all the people: 15. 'Thus saith the LORD of hosts, the God of Israel: Behold, I will bring upon this city and upon all her towns all the evil that I have pronounced against it; because they have made their neck stiff, that they might not hear My words.'

לִקְבּוֹר: כֵּן־אֶעֱשֶׂה לַמָּקוֹם 12
הַזֶּה נְאֻם־יְהֹוָה וּלְיוֹשְׁבָיו
וְלָתֵת אֶת־הָעִיר הַזֹּאת
כְּתֹפֶת: וְהָיוּ בָתֵּי יְרוּשָׁלַם 13
וּבָתֵּי מַלְכֵי יְהוּדָה כִּמְקוֹם
הַתֹּפֶת הַטְּמֵאִים לְכֹל הַבָּתִּים
אֲשֶׁר קִטְּרוּ עַל־גַּגּוֹתֵיהֶם לְכֹל
צְבָא הַשָּׁמַיִם וְהַסֵּךְ נְסָכִים
לֵאלֹהִים אֲחֵרִים: וַיָּבֹא 14
יִרְמְיָהוּ מֵהַתֹּפֶת אֲשֶׁר שְׁלָחוֹ
יְהֹוָה שָׁם לְהִנָּבֵא וַיַּעֲמֹד
בַּחֲצַר בֵּית־יְהֹוָה וַיֹּאמֶר
אֶל־כָּל־הָעָם: כֹּה־אָמַר 15
יְהֹוָה צְבָאוֹת אֱלֹהֵי יִשְׂרָאֵל
הִנְנִי מֵבִי אֶל־הָעִיר הַזֹּאת
וְעַל־כָּל־עָרֶיהָ אֵת כָּל־
הָרָעָה אֲשֶׁר דִּבַּרְתִּי עָלֶיהָ כִּי
הִקְשׁוּ אֶת־עָרְפָּם לְבִלְתִּי
שְׁמוֹעַ אֶת־דְּבָרָי:

מביא ק' v. 15.

---

12. *as Topheth.* Which is filled with the bones of the victims of human sacrifice (Rashi); or it is a place which had been defiled by Josiah (2 Kings xxiii. 10).

13. *roofs.* In the East the roofs of buildings are flat and used for various purposes (cf. Judg. xvi. 27; 1 Sam. ix. 26; 2 Sam. xi. 2). That idolatry was practised upon them is mentioned in xxxii. 29; 2 Kings xxiii. 12; Zeph. i. 5. Tablets have been found at Ras Shamra (see on ii. 28) containing a ritual text for offerings on the housetops to the heavenly bodies.

14-15 SENTENCE ON JERUSALEM REPEATED

From verse 14 to xx. 6 Jeremiah is spoken of in the third person. The passage may have been inserted from Baruch's memoirs.

14. *from Topheth.* Where he had delivered his prophecy (verse 2). He now presumably returns to the Temple area and repeats God's message of doom.

15. *all her towns.* i.e. the other towns of Judah (cf. xxxiv. 1).

20 CHAPTER XX כ

1. Now Pashhur the son of Immer the priest, who was chief officer in the house of the LORD, heard Jeremiah prophesying these things. 2. Then Pashhur smote Jeremiah the prophet, and put him in the stocks that were in the upper gate of Benjamin, which was in the house of the LORD. 3. And it came to pass on the morrow, that Pashhur brought forth Jeremiah out of the stocks. Then said Jeremiah unto him: 'The LORD hath not called thy name Pashhur, but Magor-missabib.

1 וַיִּשְׁמַע פַּשְׁחוּר בֶּן־אִמֵּר
הַכֹּהֵן וְהוּא־פָקִיד נָגִיד בְּבֵית
יְהֹוָה אֶת־יִרְמְיָהוּ נִבָּא אֶת־
2 הַדְּבָרִים הָאֵלֶּה: וַיַּכֶּה
פַּשְׁחוּר אֵת יִרְמְיָהוּ הַנָּבִיא
וַיִּתֵּן אֹתוֹ עַל־הַמַּהְפֶּכֶת אֲשֶׁר
בְּשַׁעַר בִּנְיָמִן הָעֶלְיוֹן אֲשֶׁר
3 בְּבֵית יְהֹוָה: וַיְהִי מִמָּחֳרָת
וַיֹּצֵא פַשְׁחוּר אֶת־יִרְמְיָהוּ
מִן־הַמַּהְפָּכֶת וַיֹּאמֶר אֵלָיו
יִרְמְיָהוּ לֹא פַשְׁחוּר קָרָא יְהֹוָה
שְׁמֶךָ כִּי אִם־מָגוֹר מִסָּבִיב:

CHAPTER XX

1-6 JEREMIAH ATTACKED BY PASHHUR

1. *Pashhur the son of Immer.* In later times these were apparently family names (Ezra ii. 37f., x. 20); here they are personal names. In xxi. 1 there is mention of Pashhur the son of Malchiah, and in xxxviii. 1 of Gedaliah the son of Pashhur; so the name seems to have been common.

chief officer. lit. 'overseer ruler' which some explain as 'deputy officer.' But Ehrlich agrees with the translation of A.J. on the ground that only the highest official would have dared to insult the prophet. From xxix. 26 it would appear that the duties of these officers was 'the preservation of order in the Temple and the suppression of whatever might seem subversive of it' (Peake).

2. *smote.* Perhaps with *forty stripes* (Deut. xxv. 3).

the stocks. The Hebrew noun *mahpecheth* means literally 'causing distortion', and denotes a pillory which forced the body into a cramped posture. It is mentioned again in xxix. 26, and 2 Chron. xvi. 10 refers to 'house of the stocks' (so lit., A.J. *prison-house*).

upper gate of Benjamin. Since the territory of Benjamin lay to the north of Jerusalem, this gate was on the north side of the Temple. The addition of *which was in the house of the LORD* serves to distinguish it from the city *gate of Benjamin* (xxxvii. 13, xxxviii. 7). The Temple stood on the slope of a hill so that parts of it were *upper* as compared with others (cf. *the upper court*, xxxvi. 10).

3. *Magor-missabib.* i.e. 'terror on every side.' The name is symbolic of the terror which the Babylonians will arouse among the people of Judah.

4. For thus saith the LORD: Behold, I will make thee a terror to thyself, and to all thy friends; and they shall fall by the sword of their enemies, and thine eyes shall behold it; and I will give all Judah into the hand of the king of Babylon, and he shall carry them captive to Babylon, and shall slay them with the sword. 5. Moreover I will give all the store of this city, and all the gains thereof, and all the wealth thereof, yea, all the treasures of the kings of Judah will I give into the hand of their enemies, who shall spoil them, and take them, and carry them to Babylon. 6. And thou, Pashhur, and all that dwell in thy house shall go into captivity; and thou shalt come to Babylon, and there thou shalt die, and there shalt thou be buried, thou, and all thy friends, to whom thou hast prophesied falsely.'

7 O LORD, Thou hast enticed me, and I was enticed,

4 כִּי־כֹה אָמַר יְהֹוָה הִנְנִי נֹתֶנְךָ
לְמָגוֹר לְךָ ׀ וּלְכָל־אֹהֲבֶיךָ
וְנָפְלוּ בְּחֶרֶב אֹיְבֵיהֶם וְעֵינֶיךָ
רֹאוֹת וְאֶת־כָּל־יְהוּדָה אֶתֵּן
בְּיַד מֶלֶךְ־בָּבֶל וְהִגְלָם
5 בָּבֶלָה וְהִכָּם בֶּחָרֶב: וְנָתַתִּי
אֶת־כָּל־חֹסֶן הָעִיר הַזֹּאת
וְאֶת־כָּל־יְגִיעָהּ וְאֶת־כָּל־
יְקָרָהּ וְאֵת כָּל־אוֹצְרוֹת
מַלְכֵי יְהוּדָה אֶתֵּן בְּיַד
אֹיְבֵיהֶם וּבְזָזוּם וּלְקָחוּם
6 וֶהֱבִיאוּם בָּבֶלָה: וְאַתָּה
פַשְׁחוּר וְכֹל יֹשְׁבֵי בֵיתֶךָ תֵּלְכוּ
בַּשֶּׁבִי וּבָבֶל תָּבוֹא וְשָׁם תָּמוּת
וְשָׁם תִּקָּבֵר אַתָּה וְכָל־
אֹהֲבֶיךָ אֲשֶׁר־נִבֵּאתָ לָהֶם
בַּשָּׁקֶר:
7 פִּתִּיתַנִי יְהֹוָה וָאֶפָּת

---

4. *I will make thee a terror.* It has been surmised that Pashhur was a leader of the pro-Egyptian party in Judea, and this fact may account for his fierce opposition to Jeremiah. His policy will result in his being the cause of the *terror* which was coming upon him and his followers.

thine eyes shall behold it. It will happen in his lifetime.

and shall slay them. And is employed in the sense of 'or': he will either take them into captivity or slay them.

5. *the gains thereof.* The wealth acquired from their labours.

6. *and there shalt thou be buried.* This would be regarded as a severe penalty by one who loved his country. The fact that Jeremiah imposed it upon Pashhur seems to indicate that although he was by his wrong policy encompassing the nation's ruin and exile, he was a patriot at heart.

prophesied falsely. He had acted as a prophet, speaking in the name of God without justification (cf. xiv. 14ff.).

7-18 JEREMIAH'S LAMENT OVER HIS UNHAPPY LOT

'We now reach one of the most powerful

Thou hast overcome me, and hast
   prevailed;
I am become a laughing-stock all
   the day,
Every one mocketh me.

8 For as often as I speak, I cry out,
   I cry: 'Violence and spoil';
Because the word of the LORD is
   made
A reproach unto me, and a deri-
   sion, all the day.

9 And if I say: 'I will not make
   mention of Him,
Nor speak any more in His name,'
Then there is in my heart as it
   were a burning fire
Shut up in my bones,
And I weary myself to hold it in,
But cannot.

10 For I have heard the whispering
   of many,
   Terror on every side:
'Denounce, and we will denounce
   him';

חֲזַקְתַּנִי וַתּוּכָל
הָיִיתִי לִשְׂחוֹק כָּל־הַיּוֹם
כֻּלֹּה לֹעֵג לִי׃

8 כִּי־מִדֵּי אֲדַבֵּר אֶזְעָק
חָמָס וָשֹׁד אֶקְרָא
כִּי־הָיָה דְבַר־יְהֹוָה לִי
לְחֶרְפָּה וּלְקֶלֶס כָּל־הַיּוֹם׃

9 וְאָמַרְתִּי לֹא־אֶזְכְּרֶנּוּ
וְלֹא־אֲדַבֵּר עוֹד בִּשְׁמוֹ
וְהָיָה בְלִבִּי כְּאֵשׁ בֹּעֶרֶת
עָצֻר בְּעַצְמֹתָי
וְנִלְאֵיתִי כַּלְכֵל
וְלֹא אוּכָל׃

10 כִּי שָׁמַעְתִּי דִּבַּת רַבִּים
מָגוֹר מִסָּבִיב
הַגִּידוּ וְנַגִּידֶנּוּ

v. 8. קמץ בז״ק

---

and impressive passages in the whole
of the prophetic literature, a passage
which takes us, as no other, not only
into the depths of the prophet's soul,
but into the secrets of the prophetic
consciousness' (Peake).

7. *enticed.* To become Thy messenger.
The verb, as applied here to God,
signifies 'induced' and implies that
jeremiah undertook his mission under a
Divine urge and not to express his
personal feelings.

Thou hast overcome me. More lit.,
'Thou art stronger than I' (so A.V.,
R.V.). God's will prevailed over his
inclination and he acted and spoke
under His compulsion.

mocketh me. Derides my warnings.

8. *violence and spoil.* The burden of his
message presages disaster, and it brings
upon him nought but reproach and
derision.

9. The true prophet follows the Divine
call in spite of himself. An overpowering realization of his mission compels
him to speak words which he would
rather leave unsaid, but they burn
within him until he has given utterance
to them.

10. *the whispering.* The whispered
plotting against him.

terror on every side. He feels himself
surrounded by danger.

denounce, and we will denounce him.
They urge each other to lay false charges

Even of all my familiar friends,
Them that watch for my halting:
'Peradventure he will be enticed,
 and we shall prevail against
 him,
And we shall take our revenge
 on him.'

11 But the LORD is with me as a
 mighty warrior;
Therefore my persecutors shall
 stumble, and they shall not
 prevail;
They shall be greatly ashamed,
 because they have not prospered,
Even with an everlasting confusion which shall never be
 forgotten.

12 But, O LORD of hosts, that triest
 the righteous,
That seest the reins and the
 heart,
Let me see Thy vengeance on
 them;
For unto Thee have I revealed
 my cause.

13 Sing unto the LORD,
Praise ye the LORD;
For He hath delivered the soul
 of the needy
From the hand of evil-doers.

כֹּל אֱנוֹשׁ שְׁלֹמִי
שֹׁמְרֵי צַלְעִי
אוּלַי יְפֻתֶּה וְנוּכְלָה לוֹ
וְנִקְחָה נִקְמָתֵנוּ מִמֶּנּוּ:
11 וַיהוָה אוֹתִי כְּגִבּוֹר עָרִיץ
עַל־כֵּן רֹדְפַי יִכָּשְׁלוּ
וְלֹא יֻכָלוּ
בֹּשׁוּ מְאֹד כִּי־לֹא הִשְׂכִּילוּ
כְּלִמַּת עוֹלָם לֹא תִשָּׁכֵחַ:
12 וַיהוָה צְבָאוֹת בֹּחֵן צַדִּיק
רֹאֶה כְלָיוֹת וָלֵב
אֶרְאֶה נִקְמָתְךָ מֵהֶם
כִּי אֵלֶיךָ גִּלִּיתִי אֶת־רִיבִי:
13 שִׁירוּ לַיהוָה
הַלְלוּ אֶת־יְהוָה
כִּי הִצִּיל אֶת־נֶפֶשׁ אֶבְיוֹן
מִיַּד מְרֵעִים:

against him so that they may then
denounce him collectively.

watch for my halting. They are on the
look out for him to make a false step to
take immediate advantage of it.

enticed. Into an act or outburst of
words which will occasion a charge
against him.

our revenge. For his utterances which
impeded their pro-Egyptian policy.

11. The gloom of his depression is
pierced by the light which comes from
the awareness that God is on his side.

they have not prospered. i.e. they have
failed in their schemes.

12. Almost identical with xi. 20.

13. Having committed his cause to
God, the prophet, in a sudden upsurge
of faith, breaks into praise of Him.
'When the prophet's heart is strengthened,
he feels that the victory is won, for his
worst enemy is his own weakness of
spirit' (Binns).

the soul of the needy. Generally, as his
own experience testifies.

14 Cursed be the day
  Wherein I was born;
  The day wherein **my** mother
    bore me,
  Let it not be blessed.
15 Cursed be the man who brought
    tidings
  To my father, saying:
  'A man-child is born unto thee';
  Making him very glad.
16 And let that man be as the cities
  Which the Lord overthrew, and
    repented not;
  And let him hear a cry in the
    morning,
  And an alarm at noontide;
17 Because He slew me not from
    the womb;
  And so my mother would have
    been my grave,
  And her womb always great.
18 Wherefore came I forth out of
    the womb
  To see labour and sorrow,
  That my days should be con-
    sumed in shame?

14 אָר֣וּר הַיּ֔וֹם
אֲשֶׁ֥ר יֻלַּ֖דְתִּי בּ֑וֹ
י֛וֹם אֲשֶׁר־יְלָדַ֥תְנִי אִמִּ֖י
אַל־יְהִ֥י בָרֽוּךְ׃
15 אָר֣וּר הָאִ֗ישׁ
אֲשֶׁ֨ר בִּשַּׂ֤ר אֶת־אָבִי֙ לֵאמֹ֔ר
יֻֽלַּד־לְךָ֖ בֵּ֣ן זָכָ֑ר
שַׂמֵּ֖חַ שִׂמֳּחָֽהוּ׃
16 וְהָיָה֙ הָאִ֣ישׁ הַה֔וּא כֶּעָרִ֛ים
אֲשֶׁר־הָפַ֥ךְ יְהוָ֖ה וְלֹ֣א נִחָ֑ם
וְשָׁמַ֤ע זְעָקָה֙ בַּבֹּ֔קֶר
וּתְרוּעָ֖ה בְּעֵ֥ת צָהֳרָֽיִם׃
17 אֲשֶׁ֣ר לֹא־מֽוֹתְתַ֥נִי מֵרָ֑חֶם
וַתְּהִי־לִ֤י אִמִּי֙ קִבְרִ֔י
וְרַחְמָ֖הֿ הָרַ֥ת עוֹלָֽם׃
18 לָ֤מָּה זֶּה֙ מֵרֶ֣חֶם יָצָ֔אתִי
לִרְא֥וֹת עָמָ֖ל וְיָג֑וֹן
וַיִּכְל֥וּ בְּבֹ֖שֶׁת יָמָֽי׃

14-18. With this passage, cf. Job iii. 2-
12. The consciousness of his hard lot
again comes to the fore in his mind.

14. *cursed be the day.* There is no
adequate reason for supposing that actual
personality was ascribed to time, so that
it could be blessed or cursed. This is
nothing more than a vehement way of
regretting that he was ever born.

15. *making him very glad.* The language
is probably ironical: the birth of a son

was the occasion of rejoicing to the
father, but how tragic for the son!

16. *the cities.* viz. Sodom and Gomorrah.

and repented not. Once He had decreed
their destruction.

a cry. Of distress from persons attacked
(cf. xviii. 22).

an alarm. Of war (cf. iv. 19).

17. *her womb always great.* lit. 'her womb
an everlasting conception.' Would that
I had never left it to enter the world!

21   CHAPTER XXI   כא

1. The word which came unto Jeremiah from the LORD, when king Zedekiah sent unto him Pashhur the son of Malchiah, and Zephaniah the son of Maaseiah the priest, saying: 2. 'Inquire, I pray thee, of the LORD for us; for Nebuchadrezzar king of Babylon maketh war against us; peradventure the LORD will deal with us according to all His wondrous works, that he may go up from us.' 3. Then said Jeremiah unto them: Thus shall ye say to Zedekiah: 4. Thus saith the LORD, the God of Israel:

Behold, I will turn back the weapons of war that are in your

1 הַדָּבָר אֲשֶׁר־הָיָה אֶל־
יִרְמְיָהוּ מֵאֵת יְהוָה בִּשְׁלֹחַ
אֵלָיו הַמֶּלֶךְ צִדְקִיָּהוּ אֶת־
פַּשְׁחוּר בֶּן־מַלְכִּיָּה וְאֶת־
צְפַנְיָה בֶן־מַעֲשֵׂיָה הַכֹּהֵן
2 לֵאמֹר: דְּרָשׁ־נָא בַעֲדֵנוּ
אֶת־יְהוָה כִּי נְבוּכַדְרֶאצַּר
מֶלֶךְ־בָּבֶל נִלְחָם עָלֵינוּ אוּלַי
יַעֲשֶׂה יְהוָה אוֹתָנוּ כְּכָל־
נִפְלְאֹתָיו וְיַעֲלֶה מֵעָלֵינוּ:
3 וַיֹּאמֶר יִרְמְיָהוּ אֲלֵיהֶם כֹּה
4 תֹאמְרֻן אֶל־צִדְקִיָּהוּ: כֹּה־
אָמַר יְהוָה אֱלֹהֵי יִשְׂרָאֵל הִנְנִי
מֵסֵב אֶת־כְּלֵי הַמִּלְחָמָה

CHAPTER XXI

THIS chapter marks a new division of the Book. In the previous chapters the period was Jehoiakim's reign; now we pass to the siege of Jerusalem in 588 B.C.E. during the reign of Zedekiah, in which the Kingdom of Judah came to an end.

1-7 ZEDEKIAH'S APPEAL TO JEREMIAH

A similar incident is recorded in xxxvii. 3-10. It is possible that Zedekiah appealed twice to Jeremiah at different periods of the siege.

1. *Pashhur the son of Malchiah.* Not the same man mentioned in xx. 1.

Zephaniah. He is referred to again in xxix. 25. xxxvii. 3. In lii. 24, where the

father's name does not appear, it may be a different man who is intended.

2. *inquire.* Not in the sense of seeking information, but to pray on his behalf.

Nebuchadrezzar. This form of the name is usually employed in this Book and approximates more closely to the Babylonian original, Nabukudurri-uzur.

His wondrous works. Such as the one recorded in 2 Kings xix. 35. 'In spite of Jeremiah's warnings about the necessity of right conduct, Zedekiah apparently hoped for some words of comfort indicating Divine intervention' (Pickering).

4. *turn back the weapons.* So that they are an ineffective defence against the besiegers.

hands, wherewith ye fight against the king of Babylon, and against the Chaldeans, that besiege you without the walls, and I will gather them into the midst of this city. 5. And I myself will fight against you with an outstretched hand and with a strong arm, even in anger, and in fury, and in great wrath. 6. And I will smite the inhabitants of this city, both man and beast; they shall die of a great pestilence. 7. And afterward, saith the LORD, I will deliver Zedekiah king of Judah, and his servants, and the people, and such as are left in this city from the pestilence, from the sword, and from the famine, into the hand of Nebuchadrezzar king of Babylon, and into the hand of their enemies, and into the hand of those that seek their life; and he shall smite them with the edge of the sword; he shall not spare them, neither have pity, nor have compassion.

8. And unto this people thou shalt say: Thus saith the LORD: Behold, I

אֲשֶׁר בְּיֶדְכֶם אֲשֶׁר אַתֶּם
נִלְחָמִים בָּם אֶת־מֶלֶךְ בָּבֶל
וְאֶת־הַכַּשְׂדִּים הַצָּרִים
עֲלֵיכֶם מִחוּץ לַחוֹמָה
וְאָסַפְתִּי אוֹתָם אֶל־תּוֹךְ
5 הָעִיר הַזֹּאת: וְנִלְחַמְתִּי אֲנִי
אִתְּכֶם בְּיָד נְטוּיָה וּבִזְרוֹעַ
חֲזָקָה וּבְאַף וּבְחֵמָה וּבְקֶצֶף
6 גָּדוֹל: וְהִכֵּיתִי אֶת־יוֹשְׁבֵי
הָעִיר הַזֹּאת וְאֶת־הָאָדָם
וְאֶת־הַבְּהֵמָה בְּדֶבֶר גָּדוֹל
7 יָמֻתוּ: וְאַחֲרֵי־כֵן נְאֻם־יְהֹוָה
אֶתֵּן אֶת־צִדְקִיָּהוּ מֶלֶךְ־
יְהוּדָה | וְאֶת־עֲבָדָיו | וְאֶת־
הָעָם וְאֶת־הַנִּשְׁאָרִים בָּעִיר
הַזֹּאת מִן־הַדֶּבֶר | מִן־הַחֶרֶב
וּמִן־הָרָעָב בְּיַד נְבוּכַדְרֶאצַּר
מֶלֶךְ־בָּבֶל וּבְיַד אֹיְבֵיהֶם
וּבְיַד מְבַקְשֵׁי נַפְשָׁם וְהִכָּם
לְפִי־חֶרֶב לֹא־יָחוּס עֲלֵיהֶם
8 וְלֹא יַחְמֹל וְלֹא יְרַחֵם: וְאֶל־
הָעָם הַזֶּה תֹּאמַר כֹּה אָמַר
יְהֹוָה הִנְנִי נֹתֵן לִפְנֵיכֶם אֶת־

---

them. The Chaldeans. Others, less probably, understand the word of the weapons.

5. *I myself will fight against you.* By weakening your power of resistance

through disease which I will send as a visitation upon you.

7. *with the edge of the sword.* An idiom meaning 'without quarter.'

set before you the way of life and the way of death. 9. He that abideth in this city shall die by the sword, and by the famine, and by the pestilence; but he that goeth out, and falleth away to the Chaldeans that besiege you, he shall live, and his life shall be unto him for a prey. 10. For I have set My face against this city for evil, and not for good, saith the LORD; it shall be given into the hand of the king of Babylon, and he shall burn it with fire.

11. And unto the house of the king of Judah: Hear ye the word of the LORD; 12. O house of David, thus saith the LORD:

Execute justice in the morning,

דֶּרֶךְ הַחַיִּים וְאֶת־דֶּרֶךְ
9 הַמָּוֶת: הַיֹּשֵׁב בָּעִיר הַזֹּאת
יָמוּת בַּחֶרֶב וּבָרָעָב וּבַדָּבֶר
וְהַיּוֹצֵא וְנָפַל עַל־הַכַּשְׂדִּים
הַצָּרִים עֲלֵיכֶם יְחָיֶה וְהָיְתָה־
10 לּוֹ נַפְשׁוֹ לְשָׁלָל: כִּי־שַׂמְתִּי
פָנַי בָּעִיר הַזֹּאת לְרָעָה וְלֹא
לְטוֹבָה נְאֻם־יְהֹוָה בְּיַד
מֶלֶךְ־בָּבֶל תִּנָּתֵן וּשְׂרָפָהּ
11 בָּאֵשׁ: וּלְבֵית מֶלֶךְ יְהוּדָה
12 שִׁמְעוּ דְּבַר־יְהֹוָה: בֵּית דָּוִד
כֹּה אָמַר יְהֹוָה
דִּינוּ לַבֹּקֶר מִשְׁפָּט

v. 9. וחיה ק׳

8-10 ADVICE TO THE PEOPLE

8. *the way of life*, etc. Reminiscent of Deut. xxx. 15ff. which the prophet doubtless had in mind. *Life* is, however, employed in a different sense: not 'a prosperous existence' but 'escape from death.'

9. *falleth away.* Surrenders.

for a prey. Like a man who hurriedly snatches up his prey, so will one snatch away his life from those who seek to take it. Binns explains differently: 'The figure is of one who goes out in search of spoil, and in the end is glad to return without the loss of his life.'

11-14 A MESSAGE TO THE KING

The verses seem out of place here, but may contain an eleventh-hour appeal for reformation which still might avert or mitigate the impending doom.

11. *king of Judah.* The addition of

'thou shalt say' is to be understood. Alternatively, the translation is: 'and as for the house of the king of Judah,' and the words that follow are directly addressed to them.

12. *execute justice.* This was the demand of all the prophets and makes the Hebrew Bible pre-eminently the Book of social justice and righteousness. 'It was part of the spirit of prophecy to be dumbfounded at human ferocity as at something against nature and reason. In the presence of the iniquities of the world, the heart of the prophets bled as though from a wound of the Divine Spirit, and their cry of indignation re-echoed the wrath of the Deity. Greece and Rome had their rich and poor, just as Israel had in the days of Jeroboam II, and the various classes continued to slaughter one another for centuries; but no voice of justice and pity arose from the fierce tumult. Therefore the words of the prophets

And deliver the spoiled out of
the hand of the oppressor,
Lest My fury go forth like fire,
And burn that none can quench
it,
Because of the evil of your
doings.

13 Behold, I am against thee, O in-
habitant of the valley,
And rock of the plain, saith the
LORD;
Ye that say: 'Who shall come
down against us?
Or who shall enter into our
habitations?'

14 And I will punish you according
to the fruit of your doings,
Saith the LORD;
And I will kindle a fire in her
forest,
And it shall devour all that is
round about her.

וְהַצִּילוּ גָזוּל מִיַּד עוֹשֵׁק
פֶּן־תֵּצֵא כָאֵשׁ חֲמָתִי
וּבָעֲרָה וְאֵין מְכַבֶּה
מִפְּנֵי רֹעַ מַעַלְלֵיהֶם:

13 הִנְנִי אֵלַיִךְ יֹשֶׁבֶת הָעֵמֶק
צוּר הַמִּישֹׁר נְאֻם־יְהֹוָה
הָאֹמְרִים מִי־יֵחַת עָלֵינוּ
וּמִי יָבוֹא בִּמְעוֹנוֹתֵינוּ:

14 וּפָקַדְתִּי עֲלֵיכֶם
כִּפְרִי מַעַלְלֵיכֶם
נְאֻם־יְהֹוָה
וְהִצַּתִּי אֵשׁ בְּיַעְרָהּ
וְאָכְלָה כָּל־סְבִיבֶיהָ:

v. 12. מעלליכם ק׳

have more vitality at the present time,
and answer better to the needs of modern
souls, than all the classic masterpieces of
antiquity' (Darmesteter).

in the morning. An expression denoting
urgency: be swift to execute justice.
Cf. 'The eager are early in the perform-
ance of God's precepts' (Talmud).

deliver the spoiled. Solicitude for the
weak is characteristic of Bible teaching.

and burn that none can quench it. For
other misdeeds there might be palliation;
for social injustice there is none.

13. The reference is obviously to
Jerusalem, but it is difficult to understand the description since the city is
not situated in a *valley* nor upon a *rock.*
Driver suggests that as the noun rendered
plain is commonly used of the tableland
upon which the principal cities of Moab

lay (cf. xlviii. 8, 21), it may be that the
verse was originally written with
reference to some other city and here
applied to Jerusalem. Kimchi explains
that as Jerusalem was on a hill, the
surrounding land was *plain.*

who shall come down against us? This
would indicate an early stage of the
siege, when the people were still confident
in their ability to withstand the invader.

14. *the fruit of your doings.* Jerusalem
may be strongly fortified, but the
misdeeds of the inhabitants will bring
about their undoing.

in her forest. As the word for *habitations*
in verse 13 is used for the lairs of wild
beasts in the forest (Nahum ii. 12;
Ps. civ. 22), the figurative language may
be continued here and *forests* denote the
houses of the city in which the population
resides.

1. Thus said the LORD: Go down to the house of the king of Judah, and speak there this word, 2. and say: Hear the word of the LORD, O king of Judah, that sittest upon the throne of David, thou, and thy servants, and thy people that enter in by these gates. 3. Thus saith the LORD:

Execute ye justice and righteousness, and deliver the spoiled out of the hand of the oppressor; and do no wrong, do no violence, to the stranger, the fatherless, nor the widow, neither shed innocent blood in this place. 4. For if ye do this thing indeed, then shall there enter in by the gates of this house kings

1 כֹּה אָמַר יְהֹוָה רֵד בֵּית־מֶלֶךְ
יְהוּדָה וְדִבַּרְתָּ שָׁם אֶת־
2 הַדָּבָר הַזֶּה: וְאָמַרְתָּ שְׁמַע
דְּבַר־יְהֹוָה מֶלֶךְ יְהוּדָה
הַיֹּשֵׁב עַל־כִּסֵּא דָוִד אַתָּה
וַעֲבָדֶיךָ וְעַמְּךָ הַבָּאִים
3 בַּשְּׁעָרִים הָאֵלֶּה: כֹּה ׀ אָמַר
יְהֹוָה עֲשׂוּ מִשְׁפָּט וּצְדָקָה
וְהַצִּילוּ נָזוּל מִיַּד עָשׁוֹק וְגֵר
יָתוֹם וְאַלְמָנָה אַל־תֹּנוּ אַל־
תַּחְמֹסוּ וְדָם נָקִי אַל־תִּשְׁפְּכוּ
4 בַּמָּקוֹם הַזֶּה: כִּי אִם־עָשׂוֹ
תַּעֲשׂוּ אֶת־הַדָּבָר הַזֶּה וּבָאוּ
בְשַׁעֲרֵי הַבַּיִת הַזֶּה מְלָכִים

CHAPTER XXII

THIS chapter and the following to verse 8 contain a series of judgments upon several kings of Judah, beginning with the reigning monarch. The separate sections were presumably uttered at different periods, and then brought together to form one consecutive passage.

1-9 EXHORTATION TO THE KING OF JUDAH

1. *go down.* From the Temple. The king's palace lay to the south of the Temple and was on lower ground (cf. xxxvi. 10ff.).

2. Cf. xvii. 20.

3. Cf. xxi. 12.

do no wrong. Even by word of mouth

(the Jewish commentators). The defenceless position of the classes mentioned demands special consideration.

do no violence. The prophet is referring to unjust exactions from the people to meet the cost of building luxurious palaces (verses 13ff.).

the stranger. Whereas the nations of antiquity generally looked with suspicion and hostility upon the stranger, the Bible is particularly solicitous for his rights and feelings.

neither shed innocent blood. For an instance of Jehoiakim's guilt in this respect, cf. xxvi. 20ff.

4. *then shall there enter.* Based substantially on xvii. 25.

sitting upon the throne of David,
riding in chariots and on horses, he,
and his servants, and his people.
5. But if ye will not hear these words,
I swear by Myself, saith the LORD,
that this house shall become a
desolation. 6. For thus saith the
LORD concerning the house of the
king of Judah:

> Thou art Gilead unto Me,
> The head of Lebanon;
> Yet surely I will make thee a
> wilderness,
> Cities which are not inhabited.

7 And I will prepare destroyers
> against thee,
> Every one with his weapons;
> And they shall cut down thy
> choice cedars,
> And cast them into the fire.

8. And many nations shall pass by
this city, and they shall say every
man to his neighbour: 'Wherefore
hath the LORD done thus unto this

יֹשְׁבִים לְדָוִד עַל־כִּסְאֹו
רֹכְבִים בָּרֶכֶב וּבַסּוּסִים הוּא
5 וַעֲבָדָיו וְעַמֹּו: וְאִם־לֹא תִשְׁמְעוּ
אֶת־הַדְּבָרִים הָאֵלֶּה בִּי
נִשְׁבַּעְתִּי נְאֻם־יְהֹוָה כִּי־
לְחָרְבָּה יִהְיֶה הַבַּיִת הַזֶּה:
6 כִּי־כֹה ׀ אָמַר יְהֹוָה עַל־בֵּית
מֶלֶךְ יְהוּדָה
גִּלְעָד אַתָּה לִי רֹאשׁ הַלְּבָנֹון
אִם־לֹא אֲשִׁיתְךָ מִדְבָּר
עָרִים לֹא נוֹשָׁבָה:
7 וְקִדַּשְׁתִּי עָלֶיךָ מַשְׁחִתִים
אִישׁ וְכֵלָיו
וְכָרְתוּ מִבְחַר אֲרָזֶיךָ
וְהִפִּילוּ עַל־הָאֵשׁ:
8 וְעָבְרוּ גֹּויִם רַבִּים עַל הָעִיר
הַזֹּאת וְאָמְרוּ אִישׁ אֶל־רֵעֵהוּ
עַל־מֶה עָשָׂה יְהֹוָה כָּכָה

v. 4. נושבו ק' v. 6. ועבדיו ק'

upon the throne of David. lit. 'for (or, of) David upon his throne.' This wording, which differs from that of xvii. 25, emphasizes that David's descendants will reign; the same is implied in *he and his servants.*

and his people. i.e. the king's subjects who will remain in their land and not be driven into captivity.

5. *I swear by Myself.* A most solemn form of oath which occurs in several places (cf. xlix. 13; Gen. xxii. 16; Isa. xlv. 23). A similar expression occurs in li. 14 and Amos vi. 8.

a desolation. By fire (cf. verse 7, xvii. 27).

6. *thou art Gilead . . . Lebanon.* Specified as well-wooded regions. As these might be denuded of trees to provide fuel, so will God bring destruction upon the kingdom if iniquity continues therein.

7. *prepare.* lit. 'sanctify'; see on vi. 4.

choice cedars. An allusion to the princes and leaders, continuing the figure of Gilead and Lebanon.

8f. A reminiscence of Deut. xxix. 23ff. and 1 Kings ix. 8f.

great city?' 9. Then they shall answer: 'Because they forsook the covenant of the Lord their God, and worshipped other gods, and served them.'

10 Weep ye not for the dead,
Neither bemoan him;
But weep sore for him that goeth away,
For he shall return no more,
Nor see his native country.

11. For thus saith the Lord touching Shallum the son of Josiah, king of Judah, who reigned instead of Josiah his father, and who went forth out of this place: He shall not return thither any more; 12. but in the place whither they have led him captive, there shall he die, and he shall see this land no more.

9 לָעִיר הַגְּדוֹלָה הַזֹּאת: וְאָמְרוּ
עַל אֲשֶׁר עָזְבוּ אֶת־בְּרִית
יְהֹוָה אֱלֹהֵיהֶם וַיִּשְׁתַּחֲווּ
לֵאלֹהִים אֲחֵרִים וַיַּעַבְדוּם:
10 אַל־תִּבְכּוּ לְמֵת
וְאַל־תָּנֻדוּ לוֹ
בְּכוּ בָכוֹ לַהֹלֵךְ
כִּי לֹא יָשׁוּב עוֹד
וְרָאָה אֶת־אֶרֶץ מוֹלַדְתּוֹ:
11 כִּי־כֹה אָמַר־יְהֹוָה אֶל־
שַׁלֻּם בֶּן־יֹאשִׁיָּהוּ מֶלֶךְ יְהוּדָה
הַמֹּלֵךְ תַּחַת יֹאשִׁיָּהוּ אָבִיו
אֲשֶׁר יָצָא מִן־הַמָּקוֹם הַזֶּה
12 לֹא־יָשׁוּב שָׁם עוֹד: כִּי
בִּמְקוֹם אֲשֶׁר־הִגְלוּ אֹתוֹ שָׁם
יָמוּת וְאֶת־הָאָרֶץ הַזֹּאת לֹא־
יִרְאֶה עוֹד:

---

9. *they forsook . . . other gods.* Forsaking the covenant of God was not merely a question of a change in ritual, but as is shown by verse 3 a disregard of social justice and righteousness. The violation of right principles of conduct, not only the practice of revolting rites, made idolatry the target of the fiercest denunciations by the prophets.

10-12 THE FATE OF SHALLUM

This king succeeded his father Josiah on the throne. His reign was cut short after three months, when Pharaoh-neco took him prisoner and led him captive to Egypt where he died (2 Kings xxiii. 30ff.).

10. *the dead.* viz. Josiah, who was slain in battle at Megiddo when fighting against Pharaoh-neco. His fate was not as unhappy as his son's; reserve your lamentations for the latter.

goeth away. To Egypt as a prisoner.

he shall return no more, nor see. Better, in accordance with Hebrew idiom, 'he shall never again see.'

11. *Shallum.* From 1 Chron. iii. 15 we see that he is identical with Jehoahaz of 2 Kings. Possibly this was his name before his accession. Rashi, following the Talmud, identifies him with king Zedekiah. Kimchi supposes him to be

13 Woe unto him that buildeth his
house by unrighteousness,
And his chambers by injustice;
That useth his neighbour's service without wages,
And giveth him not his hire;
14 That saith: 'I will build me a
wide house
And spacious chambers,'
And cutteth him out windows,
And it is ceiled with cedar, and
painted with vermilion.
15 Shalt thou reign, because thou
strivest to excel in cedar?
Did not thy father eat and drink,
and do justice and righteousness?
Then it was well with him.
16 He judged the cause of the poor
and needy;
Then it was well.

13 הֹ֣וי בֹּנֶ֤ה בֵיתוֹ֙ בְּלֹא־צֶ֔דֶק
וַעֲלִיּוֹתָ֖יו בְּלֹ֣א מִשְׁפָּ֑ט
בְּרֵעֵ֙הוּ֙ יַעֲבֹ֣ד חִנָּ֔ם
וּפֹעֲל֖וֹ לֹ֥א יִתֶּן־לֽוֹ׃
14 הָאֹמֵ֕ר אֶבְנֶה־לִּי֙ בֵּ֣ית מִדּ֔וֹת
וַעֲלִיּ֖וֹת מְרֻוָּחִ֑ים
וְקָ֤רַֽע לוֹ֙ חַלּוֹנָ֔י
וְסָפ֣וּן בָּאָ֔רֶז וּמָשׁ֖וֹחַ בַּשָּׁשַֽׁר׃
15 הֲתִ֙מְלֹ֔ךְ כִּ֣י אַתָּ֖ה
מְתַחֲרֶ֣ה בָאָ֑רֶז
אָבִ֙יךָ֙ הֲלֹ֣וא אָכַ֣ל וְשָׁתָ֔ה
וְעָשָׂ֛ה מִשְׁפָּ֥ט וּצְדָקָ֖ה
אָ֖ז ט֥וֹב לֽוֹ׃
16 דָּ֛ן דִּין־עָנִ֥י וְאֶבְי֖וֹן
אָ֣ז ט֑וֹב

v. 14. קמץ בז״ק

the same as Jehoiachin, understanding
son of Josiah as 'grandson,' a usage not
uncommon in the Bible. He is then
referred to as *him that goeth away* of the
preceding verse and *the dead* is Jehoiakim.

13-19 DENUNCIATION OF JEHOIAKIM

13. *by unrighteousness.* By methods
contrary to the teachings of the Torah.

chambers. lit. 'upper chambers.' 'The
construction of these without such aid
as is afforded by modern appliances
would naturally cause most difficulty and
so give rise to most dissatisfaction'
(Streane).

without wages. Forced labour was common amongst Oriental kings. The
Hebrew prophets denounced it as an
injustice; not even the king had a right

to demand unpaid services from his
subjects.

14. *windows.* The form of the plural is
unusual in the Hebrew.

vermilion. The word occurs again only
in Ezek. xxiii. 14.

15. *shalt thou reign . . . cedar?* Should
a king think only of surrounding himself
with luxury!

eat and drink, and do justice. Josiah
enjoyed the material comforts of his
regal status, but he also understood and
performed the duties of kingship. Or,
possibly, the meaning is that he was
satisfied with plain living, with ordinary
food and drink, and spent his energies
in dispensing justice.

Is not this to know Me? saith the
   Lord.

17 But thine eyes and thy heart
    Are not but for thy covetousness,
    And for shedding innocent blood,
    And for oppression, and for
       violence, to do it.

18. Therefore thus saith the Lord
   concerning Jehoiakim the son of
   Josiah, king of Judah:
    They shall not lament for him:
    'Ah my brother!' or: 'Ah sister!'
    They shall not lament for him:
    'Ah lord!' or: 'Ah his glory!'

19 He shall be buried with the
    burial of an ass,
    Drawn and cast forth beyond the
    gates of Jerusalem.

הֲלוֹא־הִיא הַדַּעַת אֹתִי
נְאֻם־יְהֹוָה׃

17 כִּי אֵין עֵינֶיךָ וְלִבְּךָ
כִּי אִם־עַל־בִּצְעֶךָ
וְעַל דַּם־הַנָּקִי לִשְׁפּוֹךְ
וְעַל־הָעֹשֶׁק וְעַל־הַמְּרוּצָה
לַעֲשׂוֹת׃

18 לָכֵן כֹּה־אָמַר יְהֹוָה
אֶל־יְהוֹיָקִים בֶּן־יֹאשִׁיָּהוּ
מֶלֶךְ יְהוּדָה
לֹא־יִסְפְּדוּ לוֹ
הוֹי אָחִי וְהוֹי אָחוֹת
לֹא־יִסְפְּדוּ לוֹ
הוֹי אָדוֹן וְהוֹי הֹדֹה׃

19 קְבוּרַת חֲמוֹר יִקָּבֵר
סָחוֹב וְהַשְׁלֵךְ
מֵהָלְאָה לְשַׁעֲרֵי יְרוּשָׁלָ͏ִם׃

16. *is not this to know Me?* To execute justice and righteousness, to protect the poor and the oppressed—that is to know God. The practical aim of religion could not be defined more succinctly.

17. *thy covetousness, and for shedding innocent blood.* One led to the other; innocent people were condemned to death so that the king might confiscate their estates.

18. *'Ah my brother!' or: 'Ah sister!'* The usual form of lamentation (cf. 1 Kings xiii. 30). *'Ah sister!'* which is not applicable here, is added for the sake of parallelism.

'Ah lord!' or: 'Ah his glory!' The lament of non-relatives over the death of a king.

19. *the burial of an ass.* i.e. without burial, the carcass of an animal being left to rot. This prophecy was doubtless fulfilled, an outraged people showing in this manner their relief at the king's death. It is noteworthy that 2 Kings xxiv. 6 merely records that he *slept with his fathers*, without the usual mention of burial.

20-30   THE FATE OF JEHOIACHIN

'The prophet now, as an introduction to his lamentation over the next king

20 Go up to Lebanon, and cry,
And lift up thy voice in Bashan;
And cry from Abarim,
For all thy lovers are destroyed.

21 I spoke unto thee in thy prosperity,
But thou saidst: 'I will not hear.'
This hath been thy manner from thy youth,
That thou hearkenedst not to My voice.

22 The wind shall feed upon all thy shepherds,
And thy lovers shall go into captivity;
Surely then shalt thou be ashamed and confounded
For all thy wickedness.

23 O inhabitant of Lebanon,
That art nestled in the cedars,

20 עֲלִי הַלְּבָנוֹן וּצְעָקִי
וּבַבָּשָׁן תְּנִי קוֹלֵךְ
וְצַעֲקִי מֵעֲבָרִים
כִּי נִשְׁבְּרוּ כָּל־מְאַהֲבָיִךְ:

21 דִּבַּרְתִּי אֵלַיִךְ בְּשַׁלְוֹתַיִךְ
אָמַרְתְּ לֹא אֶשְׁמָע
זֶה דַרְכֵּךְ מִנְּעוּרַיִךְ
כִּי לֹא־שָׁמַעַתְּ בְּקוֹלִי:

22 כָּל־רֹעַיִךְ תִּרְעֶה־רוּחַ
וּמְאַהֲבַיִךְ בַּשְּׁבִי יֵלֵכוּ
כִּי אָז תֵּבֹשִׁי וְנִכְלַמְתְּ
מִכֹּל רָעָתֵךְ:

23 יֹשַׁבְתִּי בַּלְּבָנוֹן
מְקֻנַּנְתְּ בָּאֲרָזִים

v. 20. כצ״ל. v. 23. ישבת ק׳. v. 23. מקננת ק׳

Jehoiachin (Coniah), bewails the consequences of the policy of that king's father Jehoiakim. The people, under the figure of a woman as on former occasions (cf. xxi. 13), is called upon to ascend the heights which the Chaldean hosts would successively pass in their advance southwards upon Jerusalem, viz. Lebanon in the north, the hills of Bashan in the north-east, and Abarim in the south-east' (Streane).

20. go up. Spoken to the people collectively; hence the use of the feminine in the Hebrew.

Abarim. From there, on mount Nebo, Moses viewed the Promised Land which he was not permitted to enter (Num. xxvii. 12; Deut. xxxii. 49).

thy lovers. Egypt and the other nations upon whom Jehoiachin relied for help against the Chaldeans.

destroyed. lit. 'broken'; they proved to be, as foretold, *a bruised reed* (Isa. xxxvi. 6).

21. thy prosperity. The Hebrew is plural: 'thy times of prosperity.'

22. the wind . . . shepherds. 'Render, "the wind shall shepherd all thy shepherds," in order to preserve the word-play in the Hebrew. The shepherds drive the flock before them, but Judah's shepherds, i.e. her rulers (ii. 8), shall be driven by the wind, they shall be hurried into exile' (Peake).

thy lovers. As in verse 20. They, too, will be driven into captivity; where, then, is thy hope?

23. that art nestled in the cedars. Like a bird in its nest among the cedars upon the heights of Lebanon, secure from attack, so had Judah thought herself safe from invasion.

How gracious shalt thou be when
pangs come upon thee,
The pain as of a woman in travail!
24. As I live, saith the LORD, though
Coniah the son of Jehoiakim king of
Judah were the signet upon My
right hand, yet would I pluck thee
thence; 25. and I will give thee into
the hand of them that seek thy life,
and into the hand of them of whom
thou art afraid, even into the hand of
Nebuchadrezzar king of Babylon,
and into the hand of the Chaldeans.
26. And I will cast thee out, and thy
mother that bore thee, into another
country, where ye were not born;
and there shall ye die. 27. But to
the land whereunto they long to
return, thither shall they not return.
28 Is this man Coniah a despised,
broken image?

מַה־נֵּחַ֫נְתְּ בְּבֹא־לָ֥ךְ חֲבָלִ֖ים
חִ֖יל כַּיּוֹלֵדָֽה:
24 חַי־אָ֫נִי נְאֻם־יְהֹוָה֮ כִּ֣י אִם־
יִהְיֶה֩ כָּנְיָ֨הוּ בֶן־יְהוֹיָקִ֥ים מֶ֫לֶךְ
יְהוּדָ֖ה חוֹתָ֛ם עַל־יַ֥ד יְמִינִ֑י
25 כִּ֣י מִשָּׁ֖ם אֶתְּקֶ֑נְךָ: וּנְתַתִּ֗יךָ
בְּיַד֙ מְבַקְשֵׁ֣י נַפְשֶׁ֔ךָ וּבְיַ֕ד
אֲשֶׁר־אַתָּ֥ה יָג֖וֹר מִפְּנֵיהֶ֑ם
וּבְיַ֛ד נְבוּכַדְרֶאצַּ֥ר מֶֽלֶךְ־
בָּבֶ֖ל וּבְיַ֥ד הַכַּשְׂדִּֽים:
26 וְהֵטַלְתִּ֣י אֹתְךָ֗ וְאֶת־אִמְּךָ֙
אֲשֶׁ֣ר יְלָדַ֔תְךָ עַ֖ל הָאָ֣רֶץ
אַחֶ֑רֶת אֲשֶׁ֥ר לֹֽא־יֻלַּדְתֶּ֖ם שָׁ֑ם
27 וְשָׁ֖ם תָּמֽוּתוּ: וְעַל־הָאָ֕רֶץ
אֲשֶׁ֛ר הֵ֥ם מְנַשְּׂאִ֖ים אֶת־נַפְשָׁ֑ם
לָשׁ֣וּב שָׁ֔ם שָׁ֖מָּה לֹ֥א יָשֽׁוּבוּ:
28 הַעֶ֗צֶב נִבְזֶ֤ה נָפוּץ֙
הָאִ֣ישׁ הַזֶּ֔ה כָּנְיָ֑הוּ

how gracious shalt thou be, etc. Spoken
ironically: what grace and favour dost
thou think to find when the pangs come
upon thee, the horrors of invasion? The
LXX, Peshitta and Targum render:
'how wilt thou groan!' as though the
verb were connected with the root
anach. The text is perhaps to be
translated, 'how art thou to be pitied!'

24. *Coniah.* He is also named Jeconiah
(xxiv. 1, etc.) and Jehoiachin (lii. 31, etc.).

the signet upon My right hand. Which,
on account of its use in sealing docu-
ments, is, as it were, part of its wearer.

It may be intended here as the insignia
of royal rank (cf. Gen. xli. 42; Esth.
iii. 10, although in these passages the
Hebrew uses a different noun).

26. *and thy mother that bore thee.* See
on xiii. 18.

there shall ye die. Cf. lii. 31ff.; 2 Kings
xxv. 27ff.

27. *whereunto they long,* etc. This and
the following verses, which assume the
exile to have begun (whereas verses 24-26
speak of it as yet to take place), are
uttered in prophetic anticipation.

Is he a vessel wherein is no
pleasure?
Wherefore are they cast out, he
and his seed,
And are cast into the land which
they know not?

29 O land, land, land,
Hear the word of the LORD.

30 Thus saith the LORD:
Write ye this man childless,
A man that shall not prosper in
his days;
For no man of his seed shall
prosper,
Sitting upon the throne of David,
And ruling any more in Judah.

אִם־כְּלִי אֵין חֵפֶץ בּוֹ
מַדּוּעַ הוּטְלוּ הוּא וְזַרְעוֹ
וְהֻשְׁלְכוּ עַל־הָאָרֶץ
אֲשֶׁר לֹא־יָדָעוּ׃
29 אֶרֶץ אֶרֶץ אָרֶץ
שִׁמְעִי דְּבַר־יְהֹוָה׃
30 כֹּה ׀ אָמַר יְהֹוָה
כִּתְבוּ אֶת־הָאִישׁ הַזֶּה עֲרִירִי
גֶּבֶר לֹא־יִצְלַח בְּיָמָיו
כִּי לֹא יִצְלַח מִזַּרְעוֹ
אִישׁ יֹשֵׁב עַל־כִּסֵּא דָוִד
וּמֹשֵׁל עוֹד בִּיהוּדָה׃

28   CHAPTER XXIII   כג

1 Woe unto the shepherds that
destroy and scatter

1 הוֹי רֹעִים מְאַבְּדִים וּמְפִצִים

---

28. *cast out.* The prophetic perfect.
The sympathetic tone of this verse shows
that, although Jeremiah was constrained
to utter predictions of a dark future, he
was not actuated by personal animosity.

29. *O land, land, land.* The threefold
repetition denotes extreme affection
(cf. vii. 4).

30. *childless.* 1 Chron. iii. 17 records
that he did have children. Since none
succeeded him on the throne (although
Zerubbabel, his grandson, was one of
the leaders of the Return), with respect to
the monarchy he is regarded as childless.
This is implied in the phrase, *for no man
of his seed,* etc.

CHAPTER XXIII

1-8 PROMISE OF AN IDEAL RULER

AFTER the denunciation of the last
kings of Judah, an assurance is given that
a leader will arise after God's heart. He
will rule over a people restored to their
land.

1. *the shepherds.* The national rulers, as
in ii. 8, x. 21, etc.

that destroy and scatter. Under their
evil leadership the people abandoned the
ways of righteousness and incurred exile.
It is noteworthy that in the final analysis
the misdeeds of the people are attributed
to their leaders.

The sheep of My pasture! saith the LORD.

2. Therefore thus saith the LORD, the God of Israel, against the shepherds that feed My people: Ye have scattered My flock, and driven them away, and have not taken care of them; behold, I will visit upon you the evil of your doings, saith the LORD. 3. And I will gather the remnant of My flock out of all the countries whither I have driven them, and will bring them back to their folds; and they shall be fruitful and multiply. 4. And I will set up shepherds over them, who shall feed them; and they shall fear no more, nor be dismayed, neither shall any be lacking, saith the LORD.

5 Behold, the days come, saith the LORD,

אֶת־צֹאן מַרְעִיתִי
נְאֻם־יְהֹוָה:
2 לָכֵן כֹּה־אָמַר יְהֹוָה אֱלֹהֵי
יִשְׂרָאֵל עַל־הָרֹעִים הָרֹעִים
אֶת־עַמִּי אַתֶּם הֲפִצֹתֶם אֶת־
צֹאנִי וַתַּדִּחוּם וְלֹא פְקַדְתֶּם
אֹתָם הִנְנִי פֹקֵד עֲלֵיכֶם אֶת־
רֹעַ מַעַלְלֵיכֶם נְאֻם־יְהֹוָה:
3 וַאֲנִי אֲקַבֵּץ אֶת־שְׁאֵרִית צֹאנִי
מִכֹּל הָאֲרָצוֹת אֲשֶׁר־הִדַּחְתִּי
אֹתָם שָׁם וַהֲשִׁבֹתִי אֶתְהֶן
עַל־נְוֵהֶן וּפָרוּ וְרָבוּ:
4 וַהֲקִמֹתִי עֲלֵיהֶם רֹעִים וְרָעוּם
וְלֹא־יִירְאוּ עוֹד וְלֹא־יֵחַתּוּ
וְלֹא יִפָּקֵדוּ נְאֻם־יְהֹוָה:
5 הִנֵּה יָמִים בָּאִים נְאֻם־יְהֹוָה

---

the sheep. Such a simile could only have arisen among a people with a love for animals. At the same time the phrase *the sheep of My pasture* indicates God's solicitude for His people.

2. *I will visit.* The Hebrew verb, *pakad*, is the same as that translated *taken care* and is intentionally used: as the shepherds failed to look after their flock, God will not be concerned with their welfare.

3. *the remnant.* A warning that the majority would be lost in captivity.

out of all the countries. Egypt, Assyria and Babylon.

4. *they shall fear no more.* The righteous ruler will ensure them tranquillity and safety.

neither shall any be lacking. He will also watch over them that none be lost, unlike sheep carried off by beasts of prey through their shepherd's neglect.

5-8. In contrast to the unhappy past, a Messianic prophecy of hope for the future is spoken.

5. *behold, the days come.* A favourite introduction by Jeremiah to a message of reassurance; it occurs sixteen times in the Book.

That I will raise unto David a
righteous shoot,
And he shall reign as king and
prosper,
And shall execute justice and
righteousness in the land.

6 In his days Judah shall be saved,
And Israel shall dwell safely;
And this is his name whereby he
shall be called,
The LORD is our righteousness.

7. Therefore, behold, the days come,
saith the LORD, that they shall no
more say: 'As the LORD liveth, that
brought up the children of Israel out
of the land of Egypt'; 8. but: 'As the
LORD liveth, that brought up and
that led the seed of the house of
Israel out of the north country, and
from all the countries whither I had
driven them'; and they shall dwell
in their own land.

וַהֲקִמֹתִי לְדָוִד צֶמַח צַדִּיק
וּמָלַךְ מֶלֶךְ וְהִשְׂכִּיל
וְעָשָׂה מִשְׁפָּט וּצְדָקָה בָּאָרֶץ׃

6 בְּיָמָיו תִּוָּשַׁע יְהוּדָה
וְיִשְׂרָאֵל יִשְׁכֹּן לָבֶטַח
וְזֶה־שְּׁמוֹ אֲשֶׁר־יִקְרְאוֹ
יְהוָה ׀ צִדְקֵנוּ׃

7 לָכֵן הִנֵּה־יָמִים בָּאִים נְאֻם־
יְהוָה וְלֹא־יֹאמְרוּ עוֹד חַי־
יְהוָה אֲשֶׁר הֶעֱלָה אֶת־בְּנֵי
8 יִשְׂרָאֵל מֵאֶרֶץ מִצְרָיִם׃ כִּי
אִם־חַי־יְהוָה אֲשֶׁר הֶעֱלָה
וַאֲשֶׁר הֵבִיא אֶת־זֶרַע בֵּית
יִשְׂרָאֵל מֵאֶרֶץ צָפוֹנָה וּמִכֹּל
הָאֲרָצוֹת אֲשֶׁר הִדַּחְתִּים שָׁם
וְיָשְׁבוּ עַל־אַדְמָתָם׃

מלעיל v. 5.

unto David. i.e. to sit upon the throne
once occupied by David.

shoot. Hebrew *tsemach*, the term used
to denote the Messianic king (cf. xxxiii.
15; Zech. iii. 8, vi. 12).

prosper. Better, as R.V., 'deal wisely';
he will carry on a policy which is
prudent and will bring happiness to his
land. It is the same verb as that found
in Isa. lii. 13.

shall execute justice and righteousness.
This sums up the function of an ideal
ruler (cf. 2 Sam. viii. 15, of David).

6. *Israel shall dwell safely.* The exiles
of the Northern Kingdom will also be
redeemed and return to their land.
A reunion of the nation was hoped for
by the prophets (cf. Ezek. xxxvii. 19).

the LORD is our righteousness. Righteousness will distinguish both ruler and
people, the source of that righteousness
being God. It has been maintained that
the name was suggested by that of the
last reigning king, Zedekiah ('the Lord
is righteous'). In view of his character
(*he did that which was evil in the sight of
the LORD,* 2 Kings xxiv. 19), this is
improbable. If Jeremiah had him in
mind, it was only to mark a contrast with
him. Rashi and Metsudath David interpret the name, 'the Lord will justify
(i.e. vindicate) us'; and Kimchi understands the meaning to be, 'the righteousness of the Lord is with us.'

7f. The verses are substantially repeated
from xvi. 14f. 'In the hour of Judah's
downfall, Jeremiah's ardent faith and

9 Concerning the prophets.

My heart within me is broken,

All my bones shake;

I am like a drunken man,

And like a man whom wine hath overcome;

Because of the LORD,

And because of His holy words.

10 For the land is full of adulterers;

For because of swearing the land mourneth,

The pastures of the wilderness are dried up;

And their course is evil,

And their force is not right.

11 For both prophet and priest are ungodly;

9 לַנְּבִאִים

נִשְׁבַּר לִבִּי בְקִרְבִּי

רָחֲפוּ כָּל־עַצְמוֹתַי

הָיִיתִי כְּאִישׁ שִׁכּוֹר

וּכְגֶבֶר עֲבָרוֹ יָיִן

מִפְּנֵי יְהֹוָה

וּמִפְּנֵי דִּבְרֵי קָדְשׁוֹ׃

10 כִּי מְנָאֲפִים מָלְאָה הָאָרֶץ

כִּי־מִפְּנֵי אָלָה אָבְלָה הָאָרֶץ

יָבְשׁוּ נְאוֹת מִדְבָּר

וַתְּהִי מְרוּצָתָם רָעָה

וּגְבוּרָתָם לֹא־כֵן׃

11 כִּי־גַם־נָבִיא גַם־כֹּהֵן חָנֵפוּ

hope saw that it was possible for God to raise from the ruin caused by sin a righteous community secure in the assurance of Divine help' (Pickering).

9-40 DENUNCIATION OF THE PROPHETS

9. like a drunken man. Jeremiah is overcome by God's words concerning the false prophets. The pathos of the verse is most moving. Jeremiah, himself a prophet and charged with God's message, must have felt deeply the offence of the prophets who abused their calling and confirmed the people in their evil ways.

because of the LORD, and because of His holy words. God and His words are alike profaned by the false prophets. For the vices that prevailed in the land they must bear responsibility, because they condoned, if not actually encouraged them.

10. *adulterers.* Probably to be interpreted literally and not figuratively of idol-worshippers.

swearing. Using the Divine name in false oaths. Peake prefers the translation 'the curse' and comments: 'The sin of the people has brought a curse on the land, which has taken the form of a drought.'

the pastures of the wilderness. See on ix. 9.

their force is not right. They utilize their power for wrongful purposes.

11. *both prophet and priest.* Bible critics are fond of asserting that prophets and priests represented two classes mutually antagonistic, the former in particular being violently opposed to the latter. The impartial condemnation of both by Jeremiah shows this to be incorrect. Cf vi. 13.

Yea, in My house have I found
their wickedness,
Saith the LORD.

12 Wherefore their way shall be
unto them as slippery places in
the darkness,
They shall be thrust, and fall
therein;
For I will bring evil upon them,
Even the year of their visitation,
Saith the LORD.

13 And I have seen unseemliness in
the prophets of Samaria:
They prophesied by Baal,
And caused My people Israel to
err.

14 But in the prophets of Jerusalem
I have seen a horrible thing:
They commit adultery, and walk
in lies,
And they strengthen the hands
of evil-doers,
That none doth return from his
wickedness;
They are all of them become unto
Me as Sodom,
And the inhabitants thereof as
Gomorrah.

גַּם־בְּבֵיתִי מָצָאתִי רָעָתָם
נְאֻם־יְהוָה׃

12 לָכֵן יִהְיֶה דַרְכָּם לָהֶם
כַּחֲלַקְלַקּוֹת בָּאֲפֵלָה
יִדַּחוּ וְנָפְלוּ בָהּ
כִּי־אָבִיא עֲלֵיהֶם רָעָה
שְׁנַת פְּקֻדָּתָם
נְאֻם־יְהוָה׃

13 וּבִנְבִיאֵי שֹׁמְרוֹן רָאִיתִי תִפְלָה
הִנַּבְּאוּ בַבַּעַל
וַיַּתְעוּ אֶת־עַמִּי אֶת־יִשְׂרָאֵל׃

14 וּבִנְבִאֵי יְרוּשָׁלַם
רָאִיתִי שַׁעֲרוּרָה
נָאוֹף וְהָלֹךְ בַּשֶּׁקֶר
וְחִזְּקוּ יְדֵי מְרֵעִים
לְבִלְתִּי־שָׁבוּ אִישׁ מֵרָעָתוֹ
הָיוּ־לִי כֻלָּם כִּסְדֹם
וְיֹשְׁבֶיהָ כַּעֲמֹרָה׃

מלעיל v. 12.

---

in My house. The people introduced
idolatrous sacrifices into the Temple,
apparently with the concurrence of the
false prophets (cf. 2 Kings xxi. 5;
Ezek. viii. 6ff.).

12. *slippery places in the darkness.* The
imagery is comparable with that of xiii. 16,
and cf. Ps. xxxv. 6. Hitherto the
corrupt prophets had pursued their evil
course with assurance; but now the way
will be slippery and dark for them so that
they stumble and fall.

even the year of their visitation. Repeated
from xi. 23.

13f. The prophets of Samaria had been
guilty of *unseemliness* in that they openly
practised idolatry. Those in Jerusalem,
however, committed *a horrible thing* by
addiction to adultery and falsehood, even
encouraging the wrong-doers by their bad
example.

14. *all of them.* The inhabitants of
Jerusalem; in the view of Ehrlich, also
of Samaria.

15. Therefore thus saith the LORD
of hosts concerning the prophets:
  Behold, I will feed them with
    wormwood,
  And make them drink the water
    of gall;
  For from the prophets of Jeru-
    salem
  Is ungodliness gone forth into
    all the land.

16 Thus saith the LORD of hosts:
  Hearken not unto the words of
    the prophets that prophesy
    unto you,
  They lead you unto vanity;
  They speak a vision of their own
    heart,
  And not out of the mouth of the
    LORD.

17 They say continually unto them
    that despise Me:
  'The LORD hath said: Ye shall
    have peace';
  And unto every one that walketh
    in the stubbornness of his own
    heart they say:
  'No evil shall come upon you';

18 For who hath stood in the council
    of the LORD,
  That he should perceive and hear
    His word?

15 לָכֵן כֹּה־אָמַר יְהֹוָה צְבָאוֹת
עַל־הַנְּבִאִים
הִנְנִי מַאֲכִיל אוֹתָם לַעֲנָה
וְהִשְׁקִתִים מֵי־רֹאשׁ
כִּי מֵאֵת נְבִיאֵי יְרוּשָׁלַם
יָצְאָה חֲנֻפָּה לְכָל־הָאָרֶץ:

16 כֹּה־אָמַר יְהֹוָה צְבָאוֹת
אַל־תִּשְׁמְעוּ עַל־דִּבְרֵי
הַנְּבִאִים הַנִּבְּאִים לָכֶם
מַהְבִּלִים הֵמָּה אֶתְכֶם
חֲזוֹן לִבָּם יְדַבֵּרוּ
לֹא מִפִּי יְהֹוָה:

17 אֹמְרִים אָמוֹר לִמְנַאֲצַי
דִּבֶּר יְהֹוָה שָׁלוֹם יִהְיֶה לָכֶם
וְכֹל הֹלֵךְ בִּשְׁרִרוּת לִבּוֹ אָמְרוּ
לֹא־תָבוֹא עֲלֵיכֶם רָעָה:

18 כִּי מִי עָמַד בְּסוֹד יְהֹוָה
וְיֵרֶא וְיִשְׁמַע אֶת־דְּבָרוֹ:

15. The first half of the verse is almost
identical with ix. 14. There it is
directed against the people, here against
the priests and prophets.

ungodliness. Condonation of the evils
of the people (Kimchi).

16. *unto vanity.* They buoy you up with
false prophecies of peace. Or, it may
be a denunciation of the general tenor of
their teaching which was empty of
spiritual content

17. *the LORD hath said.* 'The Hebrew is
an expression which does not elsewhere
introduce the words of the Lord. It

therefore seems to be here used by
Jeremiah as characteristic of the false
prophets' (Streane). See on verse 31.
The LXX and Peshitta pointed the
consonants differently to read, 'unto the
despisers of the word of the Lord,'
but M.T. is attested by the Targum.

no evil shall come upon you. Cf. iv. 10,
vi. 14, xiv. 13. The desire to hear such
comforting prophecies was very strong;
the people wanted them (cf. Isa. xxx. 10)
and the false prophets supplied the
popular demand.

18. *for who hath stood . . . word?* A
rhetorical question: surely such corrupt

Who hath attended to His word,
and heard it?

19 Behold, a storm of the LORD is
gone forth in fury,
Yea, a whirling storm;
It shall whirl upon the head of
the wicked.

20 The anger of the LORD shall not
return,
Until He have executed, and till
He have performed the purposes of His heart;
In the end of days ye shall consider it perfectly.

21 I have not sent these prophets,
yet they ran;
I have not spoken to them, yet
they prophesied.

22 But if they have stood in My
council,
Then let them cause My people
to hear My words,
And turn them from their evil
way,

מִי־הִקְשִׁיב דְּבָרִי וַיִּשְׁמָע׃

19 הִנֵּה ׀ סַעֲרַת יְהוָֹה חֵמָה יָצְאָה
וְסַעַר מִתְחוֹלֵל
עַל רֹאשׁ רְשָׁעִים יָחוּל׃

20 לֹא יָשׁוּב אַף־יְהוָֹה
עַד־עֲשֹׂתוֹ וְעַד־הֲקִימוֹ
מְזִמּוֹת לִבּוֹ
בְּאַחֲרִית הַיָּמִים
תִּתְבּוֹנְנוּ בָהּ בִּינָה׃

21 לֹא־שָׁלַחְתִּי אֶת־הַנְּבִאִים
וְהֵם רָצוּ
לֹא־דִבַּרְתִּי אֲלֵיהֶם
וְהֵם נִבָּאוּ׃

22 וְאִם־עָמְדוּ בְּסוֹדִי
וְיַשְׁמִעוּ דְבָרַי אֶת־עַמִּי
וִישִׁבוּם מִדַּרְכָּם הָרָע

ע. 18. דברו ק׳

men as these cannot claim to enjoy God's
confidences!

His word. The *kethib* has 'My word'
which R.V. adopts. The ancient Versions fluctuate between the two readings.

19f. Repeated with slight variations in
xxx. 23f. These verses break the connection of the passage and are spoken
parenthetically: God's intentions are far
different from the peace smoothly promised by these self-styled prophets.

20. *till He have performed.* God's
purposes may be delayed in fulfilment,
but never thwarted by human action.

the end of days. A Messianic phrase:
when God will vindicate His word and
His Kingdom be established on earth
(cf. xlviii. 47, xlix. 39; Isa. ii. 2).

ye shall consider it perfectly. The
Hebrew verb is in the *hithpael* conjugation which usually has a reflexive force.
It might be rendered: 'Ye shall consider
yourselves therein (with) understanding,'
i.e. at present you refuse to recognize
this, but in the end you will know it from
examining yourselves and from your
experience.

21. *they ran.* In eagerness to deliver
messages which they had invented.

22. *stood in My council.* Continuing
verse 18.

and turn them from their evil way. For
they must have learned in *My council*
what I really desire.

And from the evil of their doings.

23 Am I a God near at hand, saith
the LORD,

And not a God afar off?

24 Can any hide himself in secret
places

That I shall not see him? saith
the LORD.

Do not I fill heaven and earth?

Saith the LORD.

25 I have heard what the prophets
have said,

That prophesy lies in My name,
saying:

'I have dreamed, I have
dreamed.'

26 How long shall this be?

Is it in the heart of the prophets
that prophesy lies,

And the prophets of the deceit
of their own heart?

27 That think to cause My people
to forget My name

By their dreams which they tell
every man to his neighbour,

וּמֵרֹעַ מַעַלְלֵיהֶם׃

23 הַאֱלֹהֵי מִקָּרֹב

אָנִי נְאֻם־יְהוָֹה

וְלֹא אֱלֹהֵי מֵרָחֹק׃

24 אִם־יִסָּתֵר אִישׁ בַּמִּסְתָּרִים

וַאֲנִי לֹא־אֶרְאֶנּוּ נְאֻם־יְהוָֹה

הֲלוֹא אֶת־הַשָּׁמַיִם

וְאֶת־הָאָרֶץ אֲנִי מָלֵא

נְאֻם־יְהוָֹה׃

25 שָׁמַעְתִּי

אֵת אֲשֶׁר־אָמְרוּ הַנְּבִאִים

הַנִּבְּאִים בִּשְׁמִי שֶׁקֶר לֵאמֹר

חָלַמְתִּי חָלָמְתִּי׃

26 עַד־מָתַי הֲיֵשׁ

בְּלֵב הַנְּבִאִים נִבְּאֵי הַשָּׁקֶר

וּנְבִיאֵי תַּרְמִת לִבָּם׃

27 הַחֹשְׁבִים

לְהַשְׁכִּיחַ אֶת־עַמִּי שְׁמִי

בַּחֲלוֹמֹתָם

אֲשֶׁר יְסַפְּרוּ אִישׁ לְרֵעֵהוּ

23. *near at hand.* The false prophets accordingly cannot hide from God to escape their punishment.

24. *do not I fill heaven and earth?* The equivalent of 'am I not omnipresent?' so that nobody can avoid My scrutiny.

25. *I have dreamed.* They claimed their dreams to be genuine revelations from God.

26. The verse is difficult. The probable meaning is: How long will they continue to impose upon the people? Can the true word of God reside in the hearts of men who prophesy deceits of their own conceiving?

27. *to forget My name.* To forget that My essence is justice and righteousness, and so confuse Me with Baal whose worship corrupts morality.

As their fathers forgot My name
for Baal.

28 The prophet that hath a dream,
let him tell a dream;
And he that hath My word, let
him speak My word faithfully.
What hath the straw to do with
the wheat?
Saith the Lord.

29 Is not My word like as fire?
Saith the Lord;
And like a hammer that breaketh
the rock in pieces?

30. Therefore, behold, I am against
the prophets, saith the Lord, that
steal My words every one from his
neighbour. 31. Behold, I am against
the prophets, saith the Lord, that
use their tongues and say: 'He
saith.' 32. Behold, I am against
them that prophesy lying dreams,
saith the Lord, and do tell them,
and cause My people to err by their
lies, and by their wantonness; yet

כַּאֲשֶׁר שָׁכְחוּ אֲבוֹתָם
אֶת־שְׁמִי בַּבָּעַל׃
28 הַנָּבִיא אֲשֶׁר־אִתּוֹ חֲלוֹם
יְסַפֵּר חֲלוֹם
וַאֲשֶׁר דְּבָרִי אִתּוֹ
יְדַבֵּר דְּבָרִי אֱמֶת
מַה־לַתֶּבֶן אֶת־הַבָּר
נְאֻם־יְהֹוָה׃
29 הֲלוֹא כֹה דְבָרִי
כָּאֵשׁ נְאֻם־יְהֹוָה
וּכְפַטִּישׁ יְפֹצֵץ סָלַע׃
30 לָכֵן הִנְנִי עַל־הַנְּבִאִים נְאֻם־
יְהֹוָה מְגַנְּבֵי דְבָרַי אִישׁ מֵאֵת
31 רֵעֵהוּ׃ הִנְנִי עַל־הַנְּבִיאִם
נְאֻם־יְהֹוָה הַלֹּקְחִים לְשׁוֹנָם
32 וַיִּנְאֲמוּ נְאֻם׃ הִנְנִי עַל־נִבְּאֵי
חֲלֹמוֹת שֶׁקֶר נְאֻם־יְהֹוָה
וַיְסַפְּרוּם וַיַּתְעוּ אֶת־עַמִּי
בְּשִׁקְרֵיהֶם וּבְפַחֲזוּתָם וְאָנֹכִי

28. Let dreams be strictly distinguished
from true prophecy. The former are
compared with *straw* which contains no
nourishment, the latter with *wheat* which
provides the necessity for life.

29. The Divine word is not an inert
force, but has dynamic power. It sweeps
on and accomplishes its task, smashing
any obstacle in its way as with a hammer.
By that test the burning ardour of true
prophecy may be distinguished from the
complacency of the false.

30. *that steal My words.* They repeat as
their own (but with variations) prophecies
they heard from others who were truly
inspired.

31. *that use their tongues*, etc. That train
their tongues to utter false prophecies
prefaced by the formula *He saith* (*neum*)
which was employed by genuine prophets
(Rashi).

32. *their wantonness.* The noun *pachazuth*
is derived from a root *pachaz* meaning
'to be hasty, unstable.' It may be

I sent them not, nor commanded them; neither can they profit this people at all, saith the LORD.

33. And when this people, or the prophet, or a priest, shall ask thee, saying: 'What is the burden of the LORD?' then shalt thou say unto them: 'What burden! I will cast you off, saith the LORD.' 34. And as for the prophet, and the priest, and the people, that shall say: 'The burden of the LORD,' I will even punish that man and his house. 35. Thus shall ye say every one to his neighbour, and every one to his brother: 'What hath the LORD answered?' and: 'What hath the LORD spoken?' 36. And the burden of the LORD shall ye mention no more; for every man's own word shall be his burden; and would ye pervert the words of the living God, of the LORD of hosts our God? 37. Thus shalt thou say

לֹא־שְׁלַחְתִּים וְלֹא צִוִּיתִים
וְהוֹעֵיל לֹא־יוֹעִילוּ לָעָם־
33 הַזֶּה נְאֻם־יְהֹוָה: וְכִי־
יִשְׁאָלְךָ הָעָם הַזֶּה אוֹ־הַנָּבִיא
אוֹ־כֹהֵן לֵאמֹר מַה־מַשָּׂא
יְהֹוָה וְאָמַרְתָּ אֲלֵיהֶם אֶת־
מַה־מַשָּׂא וְנָטַשְׁתִּי אֶתְכֶם
34 נְאֻם־יְהֹוָה: וְהַנָּבִיא וְהַכֹּהֵן
וְהָעָם אֲשֶׁר יֹאמַר מַשָּׂא יְהֹוָה
וּפָקַדְתִּי עַל־הָאִישׁ הַהוּא
35 וְעַל־בֵּיתוֹ: כֹּה תֹאמְרוּ אִישׁ
עַל־רֵעֵהוּ וְאִישׁ אֶל־אָחִיו
מֶה־עָנָה יְהֹוָה וּמַה־דִּבֶּר
36 יְהֹוָה: וּמַשָּׂא יְהֹוָה לֹא
תִזְכְּרוּ־עוֹד כִּי הַמַּשָּׂא יִהְיֶה
לְאִישׁ דְּבָרוֹ וַהֲפַכְתֶּם אֶת־
דִּבְרֵי אֱלֹהִים חַיִּים יְהֹוָה
37 צְבָאוֹת אֱלֹהֵינוּ: כֹּה תֹאמַר

---

translated, 'their frivolousness,' i.e. their irresponsibility in lightheartedly claiming to be God-inspired.

33. The text is somewhat difficult, but the general sense is, *massa* signifying both *burden* and 'prophecy': When the people jeeringly ask you (Jeremiah), 'What prophecy (burden) have you now? We are sure that your prophecy will be another tiresome burden!' answer them, '*What burden!* It is that God will cast you off, as one casts off a burden.' By an apparently different division and vocalization of the consonants (*attem hammassa*), LXX and Vulgate render,

'Ye are the burden,' but Rashi derived the same interpretation from M.T.

34ff. Since the term *massa* can be so misused, let it no longer be employed in prophetic utterances.

35. *answered.* In response to an inquiry.

36. *for every man's own word shall be his burden.* Peake remarks, 'We should either render "is his burden," i.e. the oracle he utters has no source higher than himself, or "the burden to every man shall be his word," i.e. his profane use of the term "burden" shall be a burden upon him. The former is perhaps preferable.'

to the prophet: 'What hath the LORD answered thee?' and: 'What hath the LORD spoken?' 38. But if ye say: 'The burden of the LORD'; therefore thus saith the LORD: Because ye say this word: 'The burden of the LORD,' and I have sent unto you, saying: 'Ye shall not say: The burden of the LORD'; 39. therefore, behold, I will utterly tear you out, and I will cast you off, and the city that I gave unto you and to your fathers, away from My presence; 40. and I will bring an everlasting reproach upon you, and a perpetual shame, which shall not be forgotten.

אֶל־הַנָּבִיא מֶה־עָנְךָ יְהֹוָה
38 וּמַה־דִּבֶּר יְהֹוָה: וְאִם־מַשָּׂא
יְהֹוָה תֹּאמֵרוּ לָכֵן כֹּה אָמַר
יְהֹוָה יַעַן אֲמָרְכֶם אֶת־הַדָּבָר
הַזֶּה מַשָּׂא יְהֹוָה וָאֶשְׁלַח
אֲלֵיכֶם לֵאמֹר לֹא תֹאמְרוּ
39 מַשָּׂא יְהֹוָה: לָכֵן הִנְנִי וְנָשִׁיתִי
אֶתְכֶם נָשֹׁא וְנָטַשְׁתִּי אֶתְכֶם
וְאֶת־הָעִיר אֲשֶׁר־נָתַתִּי
לָכֶם וְלַאֲבוֹתֵיכֶם מֵעַל פָּנָי:
40 וְנָתַתִּי עֲלֵיכֶם חֶרְפַּת עוֹלָם
וּכְלִמּוּת עוֹלָם אֲשֶׁר לֹא
תִשָּׁכֵחַ:

---

24   CHAPTER XXIV   כד

1. The LORD showed me, and behold two baskets of figs set before the temple of the LORD; after that

1 הִרְאַנִי יְהֹוָה וְהִנֵּה שְׁנֵי דּוּדָאֵי
תְאֵנִים מוּעָדִים לִפְנֵי הֵיכַל
יְהֹוָה אַחֲרֵי הַגְלוֹת

---

37. the prophet. i.e. the man who claims to be a messenger of God.

39. I will utterly tear you out, and I will cast you off. See on verse 33. Kimchi renders the first clause, followed by A.V. and R.V.: 'I will utterly forget you,' I will forget My covenant with you. Some Hebrew MSS. agree with the ancient Versions in pointing the consonant as s instead of sh which changes the sense to, 'I will lift up with a lifting.' This is still a play upon the double meaning of massa. We cannot understand why so dire a punishment was

merited, and have to assume that false prophecy had reached such proportions as to constitute a major crime which endangered the existence as well as the spiritual state of the nation.

CHAPTER XXIV

VISION OF THE TWO BASKETS OF FIGS

ITS message is that contrary to what might be expected, the Judeans who had been exiled, and not those who remained in the Holy Land, would meet with God's favour. No explicit reason is given for this differentiation, but it is

Nebuchadrezzar king of Babylon had carried away captive Jeconiah the son of Jehoiakim, king of Judah, and the princes of Judah, with the craftsmen and smiths, from Jerusalem, and had brought them to Babylon. 2. One basket had very good figs, like the figs that are first-ripe; and the other basket had very bad figs, which could not be eaten, they were so bad. 3. Then said the LORD unto me: 'What seest thou, Jeremiah?' And I said: 'Figs; the good figs, very good; and the bad, very bad, that cannot be eaten, they are so bad.' 4. And the word of the LORD came unto me, saying: 5. 'Thus saith the LORD, the God of Israel: Like these good figs, so will I regard the captives of Judah, whom I have sent out of this place into the land of the Chaldeans, for

נְבוּכַדְרֶאצַּר מֶלֶךְ־בָּבֶל
אֶת־יְכָנְיָהוּ בֶן־יְהוֹיָקִים
מֶלֶךְ־יְהוּדָה וְאֶת־שָׂרֵי יְהוּדָה
וְאֶת־הֶחָרָשׁ וְאֶת־הַמַּסְגֵּר
מִירוּשָׁלַם וַיְבִאֵם בָּבֶל:
2 הַדּוּד אֶחָד תְּאֵנִים טֹבוֹת מְאֹד
כִּתְאֵנֵי הַבַּכֻּרוֹת וְהַדּוּד אֶחָד
תְּאֵנִים רָעוֹת מְאֹד אֲשֶׁר לֹא־
3 תֵאָכַלְנָה מֵרֹעַ: וַיֹּאמֶר יְהֹוָה
אֵלַי מָה־אַתָּה רֹאֶה יִרְמְיָהוּ
וָאֹמַר תְּאֵנִים הַתְּאֵנִים הַטֹּבוֹת
טֹבוֹת מְאֹד וְהָרָעוֹת רָעוֹת
מְאֹד אֲשֶׁר לֹא־תֵאָכַלְנָה
4 מֵרֹעַ: וַיְהִי דְבַר־יְהֹוָה אֵלָי
5 לֵאמֹר: כֹּה־אָמַר יְהֹוָה
אֱלֹהֵי יִשְׂרָאֵל כַּתְּאֵנִים
הַטֹּבוֹת הָאֵלֶּה כֵּן אַכִּיר אֶת־
גָּלוּת יְהוּדָה אֲשֶׁר שִׁלַּחְתִּי
מִן־הַמָּקוֹם הַזֶּה אֶרֶץ כַּשְׂדִּים

---

hinted at in verse 7. The shock of captivity, entailing physical and spiritual uprooting from the Holy Land, had effected a change in the hearts of the exiles who were now ready to know and acknowledge God. Not so those who stayed at home: they remained obdurate and spiritually deaf and blind; hence they were doomed. For a vehement condemnation of those who had not gone into captivity, cf. Ezek. xxii, and for the hopeful future of the exiles, cf. Ezek. xi. 17-20, xx. 37ff.

1. *Jeconiah.* See on xxii. 24.

the craftsmen and smiths. The phrase is repeated in xxix. 2 and 2 Kings xxiv. 14. It is probably idiomatic denoting all skilled artisans.

2. *the figs that are first-ripe.* In June, considered to be a delicacy (cf. Isa. xxviii. 4; Hos. ix. 10).

5. *for good.* To be connected with *will I regard.* God will look favourably upon them.

good. 6. And I will set Mine eyes upon them for good, and I will bring them back to this land; and I will build them, and not pull them down; and I will plant them, and not pluck them up. 7. And I will give them a heart to know Me, that I am the LORD; and they shall be My people, and I will be their God; for they shall return unto Me with their whole heart. 8. And as the bad figs, which cannot be eaten, they are so bad; surely thus saith the LORD: So will I make Zedekiah the king of Judah, and his princes, and the residue of Jerusalem, that remain in this land, and them that dwell in the land of Egypt; 9. I will even make them a horror among all the kingdoms of the earth for evil; a reproach and a proverb, a taunt and a curse, in all places whither I shall drive them. 10. And I will send the sword, the famine, and the pestilence, among them, till they be consumed from off the land that I gave unto them and to their fathers.'

6 לְטוֹבָה: וְשַׂמְתִּי עֵינִי עֲלֵיהֶם
לְטוֹבָה וַהֲשִׁבֹתִים עַל־הָאָרֶץ
הַזֹּאת וּבְנִיתִים וְלֹא אֶהֱרֹס
7 וּנְטַעְתִּים וְלֹא אֶתּוֹשׁ: וְנָתַתִּי
לָהֶם לֵב לָדַעַת אֹתִי כִּי אֲנִי
יְהֹוָה וְהָיוּ־לִי לְעָם וְאָנֹכִי
אֶהְיֶה לָהֶם לֵאלֹהִים כִּי־
יָשֻׁבוּ אֵלַי בְּכָל־לִבָּם:
8 וְכַתְּאֵנִים הָרָעוֹת אֲשֶׁר לֹא־
תֵאָכַלְנָה מֵרֹעַ כִּי־כֹה ׀ אָמַר
יְהֹוָה כֵּן אֶתֵּן אֶת־צִדְקִיָּהוּ
מֶלֶךְ־יְהוּדָה וְאֶת־שָׂרָיו וְאֵת
׀ שְׁאֵרִית יְרוּשָׁלַם הַנִּשְׁאָרִים
בָּאָרֶץ הַזֹּאת וְהַיֹּשְׁבִים בְּאֶרֶץ
9 מִצְרָיִם: וּנְתַתִּים לְזַוְעָה
לְרָעָה לְכֹל מַמְלְכוֹת הָאָרֶץ
לְחֶרְפָּה וּלְמָשָׁל לִשְׁנִינָה
וְלִקְלָלָה בְּכָל־הַמְּקֹמוֹת
10 אֲשֶׁר־אַדִּיחֵם שָׁם: וְשִׁלַּחְתִּי
בָם אֶת־הַחֶרֶב אֶת־הָרָעָב
וְאֶת־הַדָּבֶר עַד־תֻּמָּם מֵעַל
הָאֲדָמָה אֲשֶׁר־נָתַתִּי לָהֶם
וְלַאֲבוֹתֵיהֶם:

v. 9. לזועה ק׳

6. *eyes.* The Hebrew is singular.
7. *for they shall return unto Me.* Theoretical knowledge of God alone is of no value; it must be an activating force which leads man back to Him.

8. *and them that dwell in the land of Egypt.* They fled there when Zedekiah was taken captive to Babylon, in defiance of God's command through Jeremiah.
9. Cf. Deut. xxviii. 37.

25   CHAPTER XXV   כה

1. The word that came to Jeremiah concerning all the people of Judah in the fourth year of Jehoiakim the son of Josiah, king of Judah, that was the first year of Nebuchadrezzar king of Babylon; 2. which Jeremiah the prophet spoke unto all the people of Judah, and to all the inhabitants of Jerusalem, saying:

3. From the thirteenth year of Josiah the son of Amon, king of Judah, even unto this day, these three and twenty years, the word of the LORD hath come unto me, and I have spoken unto you, speaking betimes and often; but ye have not

א הַדָּבָר אֲשֶׁר־הָיָה עַל־־
יִרְמְיָהוּ עַל־כָּל־עַם יְהוּדָה
בַּשָּׁנָה הָרְבִעִית לִיהוֹיָקִים
בֶּן־יֹאשִׁיָּהוּ מֶלֶךְ יְהוּדָה
הִיא הַשָּׁנָה הָרִאשֹׁנִית
לִנְבוּכַדְרֶאצַּר מֶלֶךְ בָּבֶל:
ב אֲשֶׁר דִּבֶּר יִרְמְיָהוּ הַנָּבִיא
עַל־כָּל־עַם יְהוּדָה וְאֶל
כָּל־יֹשְׁבֵי יְרוּשָׁלַם לֵאמֹר:
ג מִן־שְׁלֹשׁ עֶשְׂרֵה שָׁנָה
לְיֹאשִׁיָּהוּ בֶן־אָמוֹן מֶלֶךְ
יְהוּדָה וְעַד ׀ הַיּוֹם הַזֶּה זֶה
שָׁלֹשׁ וְעֶשְׂרִים שָׁנָה הָיָה דְבַר־
יְהוָה אֵלָי וָאֲדַבֵּר אֲלֵיכֶם
אַשְׁכֵּים וְדַבֵּר וְלֹא שְׁמַעְתֶּם:

v. 3. א׳ במקום ה׳

CHAPTER XXV

CHRONOLOGICALLY this chapter precedes the last four chapters which were Jeremiah's reply to Zedekiah's message (cf. xxi. 1f.). We now return to *the fourth year of Jehoiakim . . . that was the first year of Nebuchadrezzar*. The unusual precision of dating suggests the awareness of the prophet that the year was a turning-point in history. Its date is *c.* 604 B.C.E., after the Babylonian victory at Carchemish over Pharaoh-neco, king of Egypt (cf. xlvi. 2). In that victory Jeremiah detected the doom of Judea and of all nations that would not submit to the conqueror. Rashi comments: 'In this year their exile was finally decreed; yet before it was actualled, Jeremiah was bidden to make one more appeal to the people that they might repent and avert their doom.'

1-7 THE PEOPLE'S HEEDLESSNESS OF DIVINE WARNINGS

2. *unto all the people of Judah.* Not merely to the princes and leaders; he appealed to the masses. At this stage he was still free and not in hiding (cf. xxxvi. 1ff.).

3. *these three and twenty years.* Jeremiah received his call in the thirteenth year of Josiah (i. 2) who reigned thirty-one years (2 Kings xxii. 1); so he prophesied for eighteen or nineteen years in that reign. To this must be added the three months of Jehoahaz's reign (2 Kings xxiii. 31) and the three years of Jehoiakim's.

speaking betimes and often. Cf. vii. 13.

hearkened. 4. And the LORD hath sent unto you all His servants the prophets, sending them betimes and often—but ye have not hearkened, nor inclined your ear to hear—

5. saying: 'Return ye now every one from his evil way, and from the evil of your doings, and dwell in the land that the LORD hath given unto you and to your fathers, for ever and ever; 6. and go not after other gods to serve them, and to worship them, and provoke Me not with the work of your hands; and I will do you no hurt.' 7. Yet ye have not hearkened unto Me, saith the LORD; that ye might provoke Me with the work of your hands to your own hurt. 8. Therefore thus saith the LORD of hosts: Because ye have not heard My words, 9. behold, I will send

4 וְשָׁלַ֨ח יְהוָ֤ה אֲלֵיכֶם֙ אֶת־כָּל־
עֲבָדָ֥יו הַנְּבִאִ֖ים הַשְׁכֵּ֣ם וְשָׁלֹ֑חַ
וְלֹ֤א שְׁמַעְתֶּם֙ וְלֹֽא־הִטִּיתֶ֣ם
5 אֶת־אָזְנְכֶ֖ם לִשְׁמֹֽעַ׃ לֵאמֹ֗ר
שֽׁוּבוּ־נָ֞א אִ֣ישׁ מִדַּרְכּ֤וֹ הָרָעָה֙
וּמֵרֹ֣עַ מַֽעַלְלֵיכֶ֔ם וּשְׁבוּ֙ עַל־
הָ֣אֲדָמָ֔ה אֲשֶׁ֨ר נָתַ֧ן יְהוָ֛ה לָכֶ֖ם
וְלַאֲבֽוֹתֵיכֶ֑ם לְמִן־עוֹלָ֖ם
6 וְעַד־עוֹלָֽם׃ וְאַל־תֵּלְכ֗וּ
אַחֲרֵי֙ אֱלֹהִ֣ים אֲחֵרִ֔ים
לְעָבְדָ֖ם וּלְהִשְׁתַּחֲוֺ֣ת לָהֶ֑ם
וְלֹֽא־תַכְעִ֤יסוּ אוֹתִי֙ בְּמַעֲשֵׂ֣ה
7 יְדֵיכֶ֔ם וְלֹ֥א אָרַ֖ע לָכֶֽם׃ וְלֹֽא־
שְׁמַעְתֶּ֥ם אֵלַ֖י נְאֻם־יְהוָ֑ה
לְמַ֗עַן הַכְעִסֵ֛נִי בְּמַעֲשֵׂ֥ה
8 יְדֵיכֶ֖ם לְרַ֥ע לָכֶֽם׃ לָכֵ֗ן כֹּ֤ה
אָמַר֙ יְהוָ֣ה צְבָא֔וֹת יַ֕עַן אֲשֶׁ֥ר
לֹֽא־שְׁמַעְתֶּ֖ם אֶת־דְּבָרָֽי׃
9 הִנְנִ֣י שֹׁלֵ֗חַ וְלָקַחְתִּ֛י אֶת־כָּל־

v. 7. קמץ בטרחא   v. 7. הכעיסני ק׳

4. *and the LORD hath sent.* Ehrlich construes the verb as pluperfect: 'now the Lord had sent,' before Jeremiah began his mission.

5. *saying.* This follows on *speaking* and *sending* in verses 3f.

and dwell. i.e. and, as a consequence, remain in possession of the land.

6. *provoke Me not.* The prophets in giving God's message would naturally say, in His name, 'provoke *Me* not.' There is no necessity to assume a copyist's error for 'provoke Him not,' as some commentators do. M.T. is supported by LXX.

7. *the work of your hands.* The idols; again in xxxii. 30.

to your own hurt. 'To go against the will of God is to court disaster' (Pickering).

8-11 JUDAH WILL BE SUBJECT TO BABYLON SEVENTY YEARS

9. *families.* See on iii. 14.

and take all the families of the north, saith the LORD, and I will send unto Nebuchadrezzar the king of Babylon, My servant, and will bring them against this land, and against the inhabitants thereof, and against all these nations round about; and I will utterly destroy them, and make them an astonishment, and a hissing, and perpetual desolations.

10. Moreover I will cause to cease from among them the voice of mirth and the voice of gladness, the voice of the bridegroom and the voice of the bride, the sound of the mill-stones, and the light of the lamp.

11. And this whole land shall be a desolation, and a waste; and these nations shall serve the king of Babylon seventy years. 12. And it

מִשְׁפְּחוֹת צָפוֹן נְאֻם־יְהֹוָה
וְאֶל־נְבוּכַדְרֶאצַּר מֶלֶךְ־
בָּבֶל עַבְדִּי וַהֲבִאֹתִים עַל־
הָאָרֶץ הַזֹּאת וְעַל־יֹשְׁבֶיהָ
וְעַל כָּל־הַגּוֹיִם הָאֵלֶּה סָבִיב
וְהַחֲרַמְתִּים וְשַׂמְתִּים לְשַׁמָּה
וְלִשְׁרֵקָה וּלְחָרְבוֹת עוֹלָם:
10 וְהַאֲבַדְתִּי מֵהֶם קוֹל שָׂשׂוֹן
וְקוֹל שִׂמְחָה קוֹל חָתָן וְקוֹל
כַּלָּה קוֹל רֵחַיִם וְאוֹר נֵר:
11 וְהָיְתָה כָּל־הָאָרֶץ הַזֹּאת
לְחָרְבָּה וּלְשַׁמָּה וְעָבְדוּ הַגּוֹיִם
הָאֵלֶּה אֶת־מֶלֶךְ בָּבֶל
12 שִׁבְעִים שָׁנָה: וְהָיָה כִמְלֹאות

v. 11. כצ״ל   v. 12. מלא ר׳

My servant. Nebuchadnezzar was unconsciously carrying out God's purposes and therefore could appropriately be described as His *servant* (so again xxvii. 6, xliii. 10; cf. *His anointed* applied to Cyrus, Isa. xlv. 1).

an astonishment, and a hissing. Cf. xviii. 16.

10. *the voice of mirth,* etc. From vii. 34.

the sound of the millstones. Grinding corn, because there will be none to grind. The Talmud (Sanh. 32b) understands it as the powdering of ingredients used to heal the wound caused by circumcision. This interpretation makes it a sequel to *the voice of the bridegroom,* etc. There will be no marriage and no birth.

the light of the lamp. The Talmud refers this to the kindling of lamps at a domestic festivity. The modern interpretation of

the passage is given by Peake: 'The sound of the grinding, which can be heard at a distance in the early morning, is the invariable sign of human life in the East, and even in the poorest home the lamp is indispensable. The deathly stillness when the harsh sound of the mill no longer falls on the ear, and the darkness in which no light glimmers from the cottage, are infallible tokens that the land has been stripped of its inhabitants.'

11. *these nations.* Round about Judea (verse 9).

seventy years. Approximately, reckoned from the fourth year of Jehoiakim (604 B.C.E.) to the return from Babylon (536 B.C.E.).

12-14 THE FATE OF BABYLON

12. The prediction of Babylon's downfall interrupts the continuity of the passage. Nevertheless its insertion here

shall come to pass, when seventy years are accomplished, that I will punish the king of Babylon, and that nation, saith the LORD, for their iniquity, and the land of the Chaldeans; and I will make it perpetual desolations. 13. And I will bring upon that land all My words which I have pronounced against it, even all that is written in this book, which Jeremiah hath prophesied against all the nations. 14. For many nations and great kings shall make bondmen of them also; and I will recompense them according to their deeds, and according to the work of their own hands.

15. For thus saith the LORD, the God of Israel, unto me: Take this cup of the wine of fury at My hand, and cause all the nations, to whom

שִׁבְעִים שָׁנָה אֶפְקֹד עַל־
מֶלֶךְ־בָּבֶל וְעַל־הַגּוֹי הַהוּא
נְאֻם־יְהוָה אֶת־עֲוֹנָם וְעַל־
אֶרֶץ כַּשְׂדִּים וְשַׂמְתִּי אֹתוֹ
13 לְשִׁמְמוֹת עוֹלָם: וְהֵבֵאֹותִי
עַל־הָאָרֶץ הַהִיא אֶת־כָּל־
דְּבָרַי אֲשֶׁר־דִּבַּרְתִּי עָלֶיהָ
אֵת כָּל־הַכָּתוּב בַּסֵּפֶר הַזֶּה
אֲשֶׁר־נִבָּא יִרְמְיָהוּ עַל־כָּל־
14 הַגּוֹיִם: כִּי עָבְדוּ־בָם גַּם־
הֵמָּה גּוֹיִם רַבִּים וּמְלָכִים
גְּדוֹלִים וְשִׁלַּמְתִּי לָהֶם
כְּפָעֳלָם וּכְמַעֲשֵׂה יְדֵיהֶם:
15 כִּי כֹה אָמַר יְהוָה אֱלֹהֵי
יִשְׂרָאֵל אֵלַי קַח אֶת־כּוֹס
הַיַּיִן הַחֵמָה הַזֹּאת מִיָּדִי
וְהִשְׁקִיתָה אֹתוֹ אֶת־כָּל־
הַגּוֹיִם אֲשֶׁר אָנֹכִי שֹׁלֵחַ אוֹתְךָ

v. 13. והבאתי ק'

is natural; it tells how Judah's exile will come to an end through Babylon's collapse (cf. xxix. 10).

13. in this book. In its concluding chapters, from xlvi to the end.

which Jeremiah hath prophesied. The mention of the prophet in the third person can be explained by the fact that the words are part of God's declaration. The LXX ends this verse with in this book, and 'what Jeremiah hath prophesied against the nations' becomes the beginning of a new section containing the prophecies against Elam and other

foreign nations, which in M.T. appear as xlix. 35-39 and xlvi-li.

14. many nations. The Medes and Persians.

great kings. Babylon was subjugated by Persia.

shall make bondmen. The Hebrew verb is the prophetic perfect.

15-29 THE NATIONS MUST DRINK FROM THE CUP OF GOD'S FURY

15. The cup of wine as symbolizing disaster is a frequent figure in the Bible (cf. xiii. 12f., xlix. 12; Isa. li. 17, 22).

I send thee, to drink it. 16. And
they shall drink, and reel to and fro,
and be like madmen, because of the
sword that I will send among them.
—17. Then took I the cup at the
LORD's hand, and made all the
nations to drink, unto whom the
LORD had sent me: 18. Jerusalem,
and the cities of Judah, and the
kings thereof, and the princes
thereof, to make them an appalment,
an astonishment, a hissing, and a
curse; as it is this day; 19. Pharaoh
king of Egypt, and his servants, and
his princes, and all his people;
20. and all the mingled people; and
all the kings of the land of Uz, and
all the kings of the land of the
Philistines, and Ashkelon, and Gaza,

16 אֲלֵיהֶם: וְשָׁתוּ וְהִתְגֹּעֲשׁוּ
וְהִתְהֹלָלוּ מִפְּנֵי הַחֶרֶב אֲשֶׁר
17 אָנֹכִי שֹׁלֵחַ בֵּינֹתָם: וָאֶקַּח
אֶת־הַכּוֹס מִיַּד יְהוָה וָאַשְׁקֶה
אֶת־כָּל־הַגּוֹיִם אֲשֶׁר־שְׁלָחַנִי
18 יְהוָה אֲלֵיהֶם: אֶת־יְרוּשָׁלַ͏ִם
וְאֶת־עָרֵי יְהוּדָה וְאֶת־
מְלָכֶיהָ אֶת־שָׂרֶיהָ לָתֵת אֹתָם
לְחָרְבָּה לְשַׁמָּה לִשְׁרֵקָה
19 וְלִקְלָלָה כַּיּוֹם הַזֶּה: אֶת־
פַּרְעֹה מֶלֶךְ־מִצְרַיִם וְאֶת־
עֲבָדָיו וְאֶת־שָׂרָיו וְאֶת־כָּל־
20 עַמּוֹ: וְאֵת כָּל־הָעֶרֶב וְאֵת
כָּל־מַלְכֵי אֶרֶץ הָעוּץ וְאֵת
כָּל־מַלְכֵי אֶרֶץ פְּלִשְׁתִּים
וְאֶת־אַשְׁקְלוֹן וְאֶת־עַזָּה

16. be like madmen. The terrors of war
will make them frantic.

17. then took I the cup. To be understood symbolically. Possibly he had a
vision in which he did so (Kimchi).

18ff. 'We may perceive a certain system
(south to north) in the enumeration.
After Jerusalem and Judah the prophet
takes in order the furthest south (Egypt),
south-east (Uz), south-west (Philistines),
east (Edom, etc.), west (Tyre, etc.),
east and northwards (Dedan, etc. to the
Medes), and finally the north far and
near' (Streane).

the kings thereof. Jehoiakim, Jehoiachin
and Zedekiah.

as it is this day. The phrase was probably added after the overthrow of
Judah.

19. his princes. 'Perhaps the petty kings
of Egypt who regarded the Pharaoh as
their suzerain' (Peake).

20. all the mingled people. The foreigners
settled in Egypt.

Uz. An Aramean tribe (Lam. iv. 21),
probably east or north-east of Edom, not
far from Egypt.

Ashkelon. About ten miles north of
Gaza.

Gaza. In the south of Judea, a few
miles inland, on the border of Egypt.

and Ekron, and the remnant of
Ashdod; 21. Edom, and Moab, and
the children of Ammon; 22. and all
the kings of Tyre, and all the kings
of Zidon, and the kings of the isle
which is beyond the sea; 23. Dedan,
and Tema, and Buz, and all that
have the corners of their hair polled;
24. and all the kings of Arabia, and
all the kings of the mingled people
that dwell in the wilderness; 25. and
all the kings of Zimri, and all the
kings of Elam, and all the kings of

וְאֶת־עֶקְרוֹן וְאֵת שְׁאֵרִית
21 אַשְׁדּוֹד: אֶת־אֱדוֹם וְאֶת־
22 מוֹאָב וְאֶת־בְּנֵי עַמּוֹן: וְאֵת
כָּל־מַלְכֵי צֹר וְאֵת כָּל־
מַלְכֵי צִידוֹן וְאֵת מַלְכֵי הָאִי
23 אֲשֶׁר בְּעֵבֶר הַיָּם: אֶת־דְּדָן
וְאֶת־תֵּימָא וְאֶת־בּוּז וְאֵת
24 כָּל־קְצוּצֵי פֵאָה: וְאֵת כָּל־
מַלְכֵי עֲרָב וְאֵת כָּל־מַלְכֵי
הָעֶרֶב הַשֹּׁכְנִים בַּמִּדְבָּר:
25 וְאֵת ׀ כָּל־מַלְכֵי זִמְרִי וְאֵת
כָּל־מַלְכֵי עֵילָם וְאֵת כָּל־

Ekron. One of the five cities of the
Philistines, situated on the border of
Judea.

the remnant of Ashdod. Another of the
Philistine cities, thirty-five miles north
of Gaza. The word *remnant* implies
that its inhabitants were either mostly
slain or deported after its capture by the
Egyptian king Psammetichus.

22. Zidon. About twenty miles south
of Beirut. It extended from the slopes
of Lebanon to the coast.

the isle. The coastland, i.e. the Phoeni-
cian colonies along the shores of the
Mediterranean.

23. Dedan. A tribe dwelling south-east
of Edom, descended from Abraham and
Keturah (Gen. xxv. 3), famed as traders
(Ezek. xxvii. 15, 20, xxxviii. 13).

Tema. An Arabian tribe (cf. Gen.
xxv. 15) inhabiting a region towards the
Syrian desert.

Buz. A tribe descended from Nahor,
Abraham's brother (Gen. xxii. 21).

all that have . . . polled. See on ix. 25.

24. Arabia. 'A tribe (or group of
tribes) somewhere in north Arabia;
cf. Isa. xxi. 13. After Old Testament
times it was gradually extended so as to
denote the whole of what we now know
as "Arabia." But in the Old Testament
the rendering "Arabia" suggests far more
than what is really meant' (Driver).

*the mingled people that dwell in the
wilderness.* See on verse 20. Here it
is hardly likely to mean foreigners.
More probably it refers to various
desert tribes perhaps loosely confederated
under one king. If foreigners are meant,
they would be individuals of foreign
tribes living in the midst of peoples
indigenous to certain parts of the
wilderness.

25. Zimri. As the name of a people it
is not found elsewhere. Kimchi conjectures that this Zimri may be Zimran,
one of Abraham's sons by Keturah
(Gen. xxv. 2) who became the ancestor
of a tribe bearing his name.

Elam. East of Babylon, it is now called
Chuzistan.

the Medes; 26. and all the kings of the north, far and near, one with another; and all the kingdoms of the world, which are upon the face of the earth.—And the king of She-shach shall drink after them. 27. And thou shalt say unto them: Thus saith the LORD of hosts, the God of Israel: Drink ye, and be drunken, and spew, and fall, and rise no more, because of the sword which I will send among you. 28. And it shall be, if they refuse to take the cup at thy hand to drink, then shalt thou say unto them: Thus saith the LORD of hosts: Ye shall surely drink. 29. For, lo, I begin to bring evil on the city whereupon My name is

26 מַלְכֵי מָדָי: וְאֵת ׀ כָּל־מַלְכֵי
הַצָּפוֹן הַקְּרֹבִים וְהָרְחֹקִים
אִישׁ אֶל־אָחִיו וְאֵת כָּל־
הַמַּמְלְכוֹת הָאָרֶץ אֲשֶׁר עַל־
פְּנֵי הָאֲדָמָה וּמֶלֶךְ שֵׁשַׁךְ יִשְׁתֶּה
27 אַחֲרֵיהֶם: וְאָמַרְתָּ אֲלֵיהֶם
כֹּה־אָמַר יְהוָֹה צְבָאוֹת אֱלֹהֵי
יִשְׂרָאֵל שְׁתוּ וְשִׁכְרוּ וּקְיוּ וְנִפְלוּ
וְלֹא תָקוּמוּ מִפְּנֵי הַחֶרֶב אֲשֶׁר
28 אָנֹכִי שֹׁלֵחַ בֵּינֵיכֶם: וְהָיָה כִּי
יְמָאֲנוּ לָקַחַת־הַכּוֹס מִיָּדְךָ
לִשְׁתּוֹת וְאָמַרְתָּ אֲלֵיהֶם כֹּה
אָמַר יְהוָֹה צְבָאוֹת שָׁתוֹ
29 תִשְׁתּוּ: כִּי הִנֵּה בָעִיר אֲשֶׁר־
נִקְרָא שְׁמִי עָלֶיהָ אָנֹכִי מֵחֵל

---

26. *all the kings of the north.* 'Put thus vaguely, as dwelling beyond the ken of the Israelitish nation' (Streane).

one with another. To be attached to what precedes: 'near to, or distant from, one another.'

Sheshach. According to Jewish tradition the name is a cypher for Babel on the system whereby the last letter of the alphabet is substituted for the first, the penultimate for the second, and so on. Cf. li. 41 where Babel and Sheshach are parallel synonyms. Another cypher of this kind occurs in li. 1. 'It is employed here either because at the time this verse was inserted it was dangerous to speak of the fall of Babylon in plain language, or because the writer had the apocalyptic fondness for mysterious designations. In view of the freedom with which Babylon is mentioned in prophecies of

its downfall towards the close of the exile, and especially of the use of Babel in the same breath with Sheshach in li. 41, the former motive seems not to have operated. We may accordingly assume that it was chosen with the latter impulse, but also because the name contained in itself a congenial suggestion. To the Hebrew ear the name would suggest "humiliation" ' (Peake).

shall drink after them. His turn will come too, after these have all suffered humiliation and subjugation. Though he was unwittingly acting as God's *servant* (verse 9), he was consciously bent on plunder and dominion, and therefore punishment will befall him.

29. *the city whereupon My name is called.* Jerusalem which housed the Temple bearing God's name (cf. vii. 10).

called, and should ye be utterly
unpunished? Ye shall not be unpunished; for I will call for a sword
upon all the inhabitants of the earth,
saith the LORD of hosts.

30. Therefore prophesy thou
against them all these words, and
say unto them:

'The LORD doth roar from on
   high,
And utter His voice from His
   holy habitation;
He doth mightily roar because of
   His fold;
He giveth a shout, as they that
   tread the grapes, ·
Against all the inhabitants of the
   earth.

31 A noise is come even to the end
   of the earth;
For the LORD hath a controversy
   with the nations,
He doth plead with all flesh;
As for the wicked, He hath given
   them to the sword, ·
Saith the LORD.

32 Thus saith the LORD of hosts:
Behold, evil shall go forth
From nation to nation,

לְהָרַע וְאַתֶּם הִנָּקֵה תִנָּקוּ לֹא
תִנָּקוּ כִּי חֶרֶב אֲנִי קֹרֵא עַל־
כָּל־יֹשְׁבֵי הָאָרֶץ נְאֻם יְהֹוָה
30 צְבָאוֹת: וְאַתָּה תִּנָּבֵא אֲלֵיהֶם
אֵת כָּל־הַדְּבָרִים הָאֵלֶּה
וְאָמַרְתָּ אֲלֵיהֶם
יְהֹוָה מִמָּרוֹם יִשְׁאָג
וּמִמְּעוֹן קָדְשׁוֹ יִתֵּן קוֹלוֹ
שָׁאֹג יִשְׁאַג עַל־נָוֵהוּ
הֵידָד כְּדֹרְכִים יַעֲנֶה
אֶל כָּל־יֹשְׁבֵי הָאָרֶץ:
31 בָּא שָׁאוֹן עַד־קְצֵה הָאָרֶץ
כִּי רִיב לַיהֹוָה בַּגּוֹיִם
נִשְׁפָּט הוּא לְכָל־בָּשָׂר
הָרְשָׁעִים נְתָנָם לַחֶרֶב
נְאֻם־יְהֹוָה:
32 כֹּה אָמַר יְהֹוָה צְבָאוֹת
הִנֵּה רָעָה יֹצֵאת
מִגּוֹי אֶל־גּוֹי

קמץ בפשטא v. 30.

30-38 DIVINE JUDGMENT UPON
       ALL NATIONS
30. *from on high.* From His heavenly
abode.
because of His fold. He roars in grief
over the destruction of Jerusalem and the
Temple (Rashi, Metsudath David).
A.V., 'upon His habitation' and R.V.,
'against His fold' follow Kimchi: He
roars in indignation against it, calling
for its overthrow. This is more suitable
to the context. But the Divine fury is
only directed first against Judah; it then
extends to all mankind.

a shout. Hebrew *hedad*, the exclamation
of grape-treaders (xlviii. 33), but also the
cry of warriors (li. 14).

31. *plead.* The verb *nishpat* is the
niphal conjugation of *shaphat*, 'to judge';
hence the meaning may be, 'He doth
bring Himself into judgment.' Not as
a capricious and cruel tyrant does He
decree all this desolation, but as a
righteous Judge pronouncing sentence
on the guilty.

32. *from nation to nation.* The sense is
either that the evil will visit the nations

And a great storm shall be raised
up
From the uttermost parts of the
earth.

33. And the slain of the LORD shall
be at that day from one end of the
earth even unto the other end of the
earth; they shall not be lamented,
neither gathered, nor buried; they
shall be dung upon the face of the
ground.

34 Wail, ye shepherds, and cry;
And wallow yourselves in the
dust, ye leaders of the flock;
For the days of your slaughter
are fully come,
And I will break you in pieces,
And ye shall fall like a precious
vessel.

35 And the shepherds shall have no
way to flee,
Nor the leaders of the flock to
escape.

36 Hark! the cry of the shepherds,
And the wailing of the leaders of
the flock!
For the LORD despoileth their
pasture.

וְסַעַר גָּדוֹל יֵעוֹר
מִיַּרְכְּתֵי־אָרֶץ:
33 וְהָיוּ חַלְלֵי יְהוָה בַּיּוֹם הַהוּא
מִקְצֵה הָאָרֶץ וְעַד־־קְצֵה
הָאָרֶץ לֹא יִסָּפְדוּ וְלֹא יֵאָסֵפוּ
וְלֹא יִקָּבֵרוּ לְדֹמֶן עַל־פְּנֵי
הָאֲדָמָה יִהְיוּ:
34 הֵילִילוּ הָרֹעִים וְזַעֲקוּ
וְהִתְפַּלְּשׁוּ אַדִּירֵי הַצֹּאן
כִּי־מָלְאוּ יְמֵיכֶם לִטְבוֹחַ
וּתְפוֹצוֹתִיכֶם
וּנְפַלְתֶּם כִּכְלִי חֶמְדָּה:
35 וְאָבַד מָנוֹס מִן־הָרֹעִים
וּפְלֵיטָה מֵאַדִּירֵי הַצֹּאן:
36 קוֹל צַעֲקַת הָרֹעִים
וְיִלְלַת אַדִּירֵי הַצֹּאן
כִּי־שֹׁדֵד יְהוָה
אֶת־מַרְעִיתָם:

v. 34. הפ׳ בחולם ובחירק הת׳

in succession; or that nations will war
with and inflict evil upon each other
from the uttermost parts of the earth.
Cf. vi. 22 where this phrase is parallel to
the *north country*, showing that Babylon
is meant.

33. Either the destruction will be
universal so that there will be none left
to bewail and bury the dead, or the slain
will be too numerous to receive these
attentions.

34. *shepherds.* National rulers.

wallow yourselves. Cf. vi. 26.

and I will break you in pieces. Rashi,
Metsudath David and several ancient
Versions render: 'and your dispersions
(are close at hand).' You will soon go
into exile.

like a precious vessel. Made of fragile
material which is shattered beyond
repair.

35. Cf. Amos ii. 14.

36. Cf. Zech. xi. 3.

37 And the peaceable folds are brought to silence Because of the fierce anger of the LORD.

38 He hath forsaken His covert, as the lion; For their land is become a waste Because of the fierceness of the oppressing sword, And because of His fierce anger.

37 וְנָדַמּוּ נְאוֹת הַשָּׁלוֹם

מִפְּנֵי חֲרוֹן אַף־יְהֹוָה:

38 עָזַב כַּכְּפִיר סֻכּוֹ

כִּי־הָיְתָה אַרְצָם לְשַׁמָּה

מִפְּנֵי חֲרוֹן הַיּוֹנָה

וּמִפְּנֵי חֲרוֹן אַפּוֹ:

---

26   CHAPTER XXVI   כו

1. In the beginning of the reign of Jehoiakim the son of Josiah, king of Judah, came this word from the LORD, saying: 2. 'Thus saith the LORD: Stand in the court of the LORD's house, and speak unto all the cities of Judah, which come to worship in the LORD's house, all the

1 בְּרֵאשִׁית מַמְלְכוּת יְהוֹיָקִים

בֶּן־יֹאשִׁיָּהוּ מֶלֶךְ יְהוּדָה

הָיָה הַדָּבָר הַזֶּה מֵאֵת יְהֹוָה

2 לֵאמֹר: כֹּה אָמַר יְהֹוָה עֲמֹד

בַּחֲצַר בֵּית־יְהֹוָה וְדִבַּרְתָּ

עַל־כָּל־עָרֵי יְהוּדָה הַבָּאִים

לְהִשְׁתַּחֲוֹת בֵּית־יְהֹוָה אֵת

---

37. *are brought to silence.* The peaceful pastoral regions are now reduced to silence because neither man nor flock is there any more.

38. *as the lion.* The section ends with the same simile as the one at its beginning (verse 30). Like a lion which seeks another when its lair is destroyed, so has God abandoned His land now that it is in ruins.

sword. This word is not in the text but is understood from the context. But many Hebrew MSS. agree with LXX and the Targum in reading *hachereb*, 'the sword,' for *charon*, 'the fierceness of,' as in xlvi. 16, l. 16.

CHAPTER XXVI

BEGINNING with this chapter and extending to the end of xlv we have in the main a record of incidents in the life of Jeremiah. Since the prophet is generally referred to in the third person, it is probable that this section of the Book consists of extracts from the memoirs of Jeremiah compiled by Baruch. The present chapter is to be linked with vii and describes the sequel to the address in the Temple.

1-6 DOOM OF THE TEMPLE FORETOLD
1. *in the beginning*, etc. The date is 607 B.C.E.
2. *the court.* The outer court where the people assembled.

words that I command thee to speak unto them; diminish not a word.

3. It may be they will hearken, and turn every man from his evil way; that I may ɾepent Me of the evil, which I purpose to do unto them because of the evil of their doings.

4. And thou shalt say unto them: Thus saith the LORD: If ye will not hearken to Me, to walk in My law, which I have set before you, 5. to hearken to the words of My servants the prophets, whom I send unto you, even sending them betimes and often, but ye have not hearkened; 6. then will I make this house like Shiloh, and will make this city a curse to all the nations of the earth'.

7. So the priests and the prophets and all the people heard Jeremiah speaking these words in the house of the LORD.

8. Now it came to pass, when

כָּל־הַדְּבָרִים אֲשֶׁר צִוִּיתִיךָ
לְדַבֵּר אֲלֵיהֶם אַל־תִּגְרַע
3 דָּבָר: אוּלַי יִשְׁמְעוּ וְיָשֻׁבוּ
אִישׁ מִדַּרְכּוֹ הָרָעָה וְנִחַמְתִּי
אֶל־הָרָעָה אֲשֶׁר אָנֹכִי חֹשֵׁב
לַעֲשׂוֹת לָהֶם מִפְּנֵי רֹעַ
4 מַעַלְלֵיהֶם: וְאָמַרְתָּ אֲלֵיהֶם
כֹּה אָמַר יְהֹוָה אִם־לֹא
תִשְׁמְעוּ אֵלַי לָלֶכֶת בְּתוֹרָתִי
5 אֲשֶׁר נָתַתִּי לִפְנֵיכֶם: לִשְׁמֹעַ
עַל־דִּבְרֵי עֲבָדַי הַנְּבִאִים
אֲשֶׁר אָנֹכִי שֹׁלֵחַ אֲלֵיכֶם
וְהַשְׁכֵּם וְשָׁלֹחַ וְלֹא שְׁמַעְתֶּם:
6 וְנָתַתִּי אֶת־הַבַּיִת הַזֶּה כְּשִׁלֹה
וְאֶת־הָעִיר הַזֹּאתה אֶתֵּן
לִקְלָלָה לְכֹל גּוֹיֵ הָאָרֶץ:
7 וַיִּשְׁמְעוּ הַכֹּהֲנִים וְהַנְּבִאִים
וְכָל־הָעָם אֶת־יִרְמְיָהוּ
מְדַבֵּר אֶת־הַדְּבָרִים הָאֵלֶּה
8 בְּבֵית יְהֹוָה: וַיְהִי | כְּכַלּוֹת

v. 6. יתיר ה׳   v. 6. חסר י׳

diminish not a word. Although the warning you have given to the people will endanger your life.

3. *that I may repent Me.* See on xviii. 8.

4. *My law.* Better, 'My direction,' through the teachings of the prophets, as the next verse shows.

5. *betimes and often.* Cf. vii. 13.

6. *Shiloh.* See on vii. 12.

a curse. i.e. in cursing, people will say, 'May this place become like Jerusalem.' It is easy to appreciate the moral courage necessary to deliver such a message.

7-9 JEREMIAH'S DEATH DEMANDED

7. *the prophets.* The false prophets. The LXX here and in verses 8, 11, 16 adds the word 'false'; but the context makes it clear that these are intended.

Jeremiah had made an end of speaking all that the LORD had commanded him to speak unto all the people, that the priests and the prophets and all the people laid hold on him, saying: 'Thou shalt surely die. 9. Why hast thou prophesied in the name of the LORD, saying: This house shall be like Shiloh, and this city shall be desolate, without an inhabitant?' And all the people were gathered against Jeremiah in the house of the LORD.

10. When the princes of Judah heard these things, they came up from the king's house unto the house of the LORD; and they sat in the entry of the new gate of the LORD's house. 11. Then spoke the priests and the prophets unto the princes and to all the people, saying: 'This man is worthy of death; for he hath prophesied against this city, as ye have heard with your ears.'

יִרְמְיָהוּ לְדַבֵּר אֵת כָּל־
אֲשֶׁר־צִוָּה יְהֹוָה לְדַבֵּר אֶל־
כָּל־הָעָם וַיִּתְפְּשׂוּ אֹתוֹ
הַכֹּהֲנִים וְהַנְּבִיאִים וְכָל־
הָעָם לֵאמֹר מוֹת תָּמוּת׃
9 מַדּוּעַ נִבֵּיתָ בְשֵׁם־יְהֹוָה
לֵאמֹר כְּשִׁלוֹ יִהְיֶה הַבַּיִת הַזֶּה
וְהָעִיר הַזֹּאת תֶּחֱרַב מֵאֵין
יוֹשֵׁב וַיִּקָּהֵל כָּל־הָעָם אֶל־
10 יִרְמְיָהוּ בְּבֵית יְהֹוָה׃ וַיִּשְׁמְעוּ
שָׂרֵי יְהוּדָה אֵת הַדְּבָרִים
הָאֵלֶּה וַיַּעֲלוּ מִבֵּית־הַמֶּלֶךְ
בֵּית יְהֹוָה וַיֵּשְׁבוּ בְּפֶתַח שַׁעַר־
11 יְהֹוָה הֶחָדָשׁ׃ וַיֹּאמְרוּ הַכֹּהֲנִים
וְהַנְּבִיאִים אֶל־הַשָּׂרִים וְאֶל־
כָּל־הָעָם לֵאמֹר מִשְׁפַּט־
מָוֶת לָאִישׁ הַזֶּה כִּי נִבָּא אֶל־
הָעִיר הַזֹּאת כַּאֲשֶׁר שְׁמַעְתֶּם׃

v. 9. כצ״ל

---

8. *thou shalt surely die.* For prophesying falsely in God's name in accordance with the law of Deut. xviii. 20. It was inconceivable to them that such a prediction could be from God.

9. *all the people.* Here, apparently, the mass of the population sided with the priests and prophets, whereas in verse 16 they were sympathetic to Jeremiah. But, as Pickering remarks, 'A crowd is often fickle.'

10-19 IMPEACHMENT AND ACQUITTAL OF JEREMIAH

10. *princes.* The civil rulers.

they came up. See on xxii. 1.

the new gate. Perhaps the same as *the upper gate* of xx. 2, and identical with the one constructed by Jotham (2 Kings xv. 35).

11. *this man is worthy of death.* A paraphrase of the Hebrew which is literally 'judgment of death to this man.'

as ye have heard with your ears. This was true of the people, but not of the princes who had not been in the Temple court when Jeremiah spoke. The words were doubtless addressed directly to the former to whom the accusers turned.

12. Then spoke Jeremiah unto all the princes and to all the people, saying: 'The LORD sent me to prophesy against this house and against this city all the words that ye have heard. 13. Therefore now amend your ways and your doings, and hearken to the voice of the LORD your God; and the LORD will repent Him of the evil that He hath pronounced against you. 14. But as for me, behold, I am in your hand; do with me as is good and right in your eyes. 15. Only know ye for certain that, if ye put me to death, ye will bring innocent blood upon yourselves, and upon this city, and upon the inhabitants thereof; for of a truth the LORD hath sent me unto you to speak all these words in your ears.'

12 בְּאָזְנֵיכֶם׃ וַיֹּאמֶר יִרְמְיָ֫הוּ
אֶל־כָּל־הַשָּׂרִים וְאֶל־כָּל־
הָעָם לֵאמֹר יְהֹוָה שְׁלָחַ֫נִי
לְהִנָּבֵא אֶל־הַבַּ֫יִת הַזֶּה וְאֶל־
הָעִיר הַזֹּאת אֵת כָּל־
הַדְּבָרִים אֲשֶׁר שְׁמַעְתֶּם׃
13 וְעַתָּ֫ה הֵיטִ֫יבוּ דַרְכֵיכֶ֫ם
וּמַעַלְלֵיכֶ֫ם וְשִׁמְעוּ בְּקוֹל
יְהֹוָה אֱלֹהֵיכֶ֫ם וְיִנָּחֵם יְהֹוָה
אֶל־הָרָעָה אֲשֶׁר דִּבֶּר
14 עֲלֵיכֶ֫ם׃ וַאֲנִי הִנְנִי בְיֶדְכֶ֫ם
עֲשׂוּ־לִי כַּטּוֹב וְכַיָּשָׁר
15 בְּעֵינֵיכֶ֫ם׃ אַ֣ךְ ׀ יָדֹ֫עַ תֵּדְעוּ
כִּי אִם־מְמִתִים אַתֶּם אֹתִ֫י
כִּי־דָם נָקִי אַתֶּם֫ נֹתְנִים
עֲלֵיכֶ֫ם וְאֶל־הָעִיר הַזֹּאת
וְאֶל־יֹשְׁבֶ֫יהָ כִּי בֶאֱמֶת שְׁלָחַ֫נִי
יְהֹוָה עֲלֵיכֶ֫ם לְדַבֵּר בְּאָזְנֵיכֶ֫ם
אֵת כָּל־הַדְּבָרִים הָאֵ֫לֶּה׃

12. *the LORD sent me.* 'It is a great scene which here passes before us, in which the prophet's bearing is wholly worthy of himself, and in which we do well to observe his unshaken conviction that his message had been entrusted to him by God Himself' (Peake).

14f. Jeremiah's answer to the charge is sincere and dignified. The acceptance of his plea against the shedding of his innocent blood is evidence that, in spite of the prevailing wickedness, the rulers and people were not utterly depraved.

It also shows that so far as the masses were concerned, their reason for wishing to put Jeremiah to death was not to silence the announcer of woeful tidings, but they sincerely regarded him as an impostor.

14. *as for me.* 'Jeremiah derives courage from the greatness of his cause; his is only a single life; the contest is not really between himself and his accusers, but between good and evil, right and wrong, God and the powers of darkness. He forgets himself in realizing God' (Binns).

16. Then said the princes and all the people unto the priests and to the prophets: 'This man is not worthy of death; for he hath spoken to us in the name of the LORD our God.'

17. Then rose up certain of the elders of the land, and spoke to all the assembly of the people, saying:

18. 'Micah the Morashtite prophesied in the days of Hezekiah king of Judah; and he spoke to all the people of Judah, saying: Thus saith the LORD of hosts:

Zion shall be plowed as a field,
And Jerusalem shall become heaps,
And the mountain of the house as the high places of a forest.

19. Did Hezekiah king of Judah and all Judah put him at all to death? did he not fear the LORD, and entreat the favour of the LORD, and the LORD repented Him of the evil which He had pronounced against them? Thus

16 וַיֹּאמְרוּ הַשָּׂרִים וְכָל־הָעָם אֶל־הַכֹּהֲנִים וְאֶל־הַנְּבִיאִים אֵין־לָאִישׁ הַזֶּה מִשְׁפַּט־מָוֶת כִּי בְּשֵׁם יְהוָה אֱלֹהֵינוּ דִּבֶּר

17 אֵלֵינוּ: וַיָּקֻמוּ אֲנָשִׁים מִזִּקְנֵי הָאָרֶץ וַיֹּאמְרוּ אֶל־כָּל־

18 קְהַל הָעָם לֵאמֹר: מִיכָיה הַמּוֹרַשְׁתִּי הָיָה נִבָּא בִּימֵי חִזְקִיָּהוּ מֶלֶךְ־יְהוּדָה וַיֹּאמֶר אֶל־כָּל־עַם יְהוּדָה לֵאמֹר כֹּה־אָמַר ׀ יְהוָה צְבָאוֹת צִיּוֹן שָׂדֶה תֵחָרֵשׁ וִירוּשָׁלַיִם עִיִּים תִּהְיֶה וְהַר הַבַּיִת לְבָמוֹת יָעַר:

19 הֶהָמֵת הֱמִתֻהוּ חִזְקִיָּהוּ מֶלֶךְ־ יְהוּדָה וְכָל־יְהוּדָה הֲלֹא יָרֵא אֶת־יְהוָה וַיְחַל אֶת־פְּנֵי יְהוָה וַיִּנָּחֶם יְהוָה אֶל־הָרָעָה אֲשֶׁר־דִּבֶּר עֲלֵיהֶם וַאֲנַחְנוּ

v. 18. מיכה ק׳

16. and all the people. They were convinced by Jeremiah's defence.

17. elders of the land. Usually this term connotes men who held an official status in the community; but here it is better understood in its literal sense. These men of advanced age had themselves heard, or been told by their fathers, the statement made by the earlier prophet which corroborated the Divine origin of Jeremiah's words.

18. the Morashtite. A native of Moresheth, a small town near Gath

about twenty-three miles south-west of Jerusalem. It was also known as Moresheth-gath (Micah i. 14).
in the days of Hezekiah. Cf. Micah i. 1.
Zion shall be plowed, etc. Quoted from Micah iii. 12 with the variant iyyim for iyyin. A direct citation of this kind occurs nowhere else in the prophetic literature.

19. fear the LORD. As the effect of Micah's warnings and Jerusalem was then spared; so here is a precedent to be followed in the present instance.

might we procure great evil against our own souls.'

20. And there was also a man that prophesied in the name of the LORD, Uriah the son of Shemaiah of Kiriath-jearim; and he prophesied against this city and against this land according to all the words of Jeremiah; 21. and when Jehoiakim the king, with all his mighty men, and all the princes, heard his words, the king sought to put him to death; but when Uriah heard it, he was afraid, and fled, and went into Egypt; 22. and Jehoiakim the king sent men into Egypt, Elnathan the son of Achbor, and certain men with him, into Egypt; 23. and they fetched forth Uriah out of Egypt, and brought him unto Jehoiakim the

עֹשִׂים רָעָה גְדוֹלָה עַל־
20 נַפְשׁוֹתֵינוּ: וְגַם־אִישׁ הָיָה
מִתְנַבֵּא בְּשֵׁם יְהֹוָה אוּרִיָּהוּ
בֶן־שְׁמַעְיָהוּ מִקִּרְיַת הַיְעָרִים
וַיִּנָּבֵא עַל־הָעִיר הַזֹּאת וְעַל־
הָאָרֶץ הַזֹּאת כְּכֹל דִּבְרֵי
21 יִרְמְיָהוּ: וַיִּשְׁמַע הַמֶּלֶךְ
יְהוֹיָקִם וְכָל־גִּבּוֹרָיו וְכָל־
הַשָּׂרִים אֶת־דְּבָרָיו וַיְבַקֵּשׁ
הַמֶּלֶךְ הֲמִיתוֹ וַיִּשְׁמַע אוּרִיָּהוּ
וַיִּרָא וַיִּבְרַח וַיָּבֹא מִצְרָיִם:
22 וַיִּשְׁלַח הַמֶּלֶךְ יְהוֹיָקִים אֲנָשִׁים
מִצְרָיִם אֶת־אֶלְנָתָן בֶּן־
עַכְבּוֹר וַאֲנָשִׁים אִתּוֹ אֶל־
23 מִצְרָיִם: וַיּוֹצִיאוּ אֶת־אוּרִיָּהוּ
מִמִּצְרַיִם וַיְבִאֻהוּ אֶל־הַמֶּלֶךְ

---

thus might we procure, etc. Better, 'but we are doing great harm to ourselves,' if we condemn Jeremiah to death.

20-23   URIAH SLAIN FOR HIS PROPHECY

The Siphrē maintains that this episode was cited by Jeremiah's accusers as a counter-precedent to that of Micah, to prove that Jeremiah's defence ought not to be accepted. Be that as it may, the incident demonstrates the grave danger incurred by the prophets who were charged with messages of national disaster.

20. *Uriah the son of Shemaiah.* Nothing is known of him apart from what is here recorded.

Kiriath-jearim. Identified with Karyet-el-Enab seven miles north-west of Jerusalem on the road to Jaffa. It was one of the cities of the Gibeonites (Josh. ix. 17), where the ark was deposited for twenty years (1 Sam. vii. 2).

21. *his mighty men.* The military chiefs as distinct from the *princes* who were civilian rulers.

22. *Elnathan the son of Achbor.* Again mentioned in xxxvi. 12, 25. If identical with the Elnathan of 2 Kings xxiv. 8, he was Jehoiachin's grandfather and Jehoiakim's father-in-law. He would be a person of high status to send to Egypt for Uriah's extradition.

23. *they fetched forth Uriah out of Egypt.* There may have been an extradition

king; who slew him with the sword, and cast his dead body into the graves of the children of the people. 24. Nevertheless the hand of Ahikam the son of Shaphan was with Jeremiah, that they should not give him into the hand of the people to put him to death.

יְהוֹיָקִים וַיַּכֵּהוּ בֶּחֶרֶב וַיַּשְׁלֵךְ
אֶת־נִבְלָתוֹ אֶל־קִבְרֵי בְּנֵי
הָעָם׃ אַךְ יַד אֲחִיקָם בֶּן־ 24
שָׁפָן הָיְתָה אֶת־יִרְמְיָהוּ
לְבִלְתִּי תֵּת־אֹתוֹ בְיַד־הָעָם
לַהֲמִיתוֹ׃

---

27   CHAPTER XXVII   כז

1. In the beginning of the reign of Jehoiakim the son of Josiah, king of Judah, came this word unto Jeremiah from the LORD, saying: 2. 'Thus saith the LORD to me: Make thee bands and bars, and put them upon

בְּרֵאשִׁית מַמְלֶכֶת יְהוֹיָקִם 1
בֶּן־יֹאשִׁיָּהוּ מֶלֶךְ יְהוּדָה הָיָה
הַדָּבָר הַזֶּה אֶל־יִרְמְיָה מֵאֵת
יְהֹוָה לֵאמֹר׃ כֹּה־אָמַר יְהֹוָה 2
אֵלַי עֲשֵׂה לְךָ מוֹסֵרוֹת וּמֹטוֹת

v. 1. מלא ר'

---

treaty between Egypt and Judah, such as Rameses II had in the fourteenth century B.C.E. with a Syrian king named Chetta. Or, Jehoiakim, being subject to the overlordship of Pharaoh, made the demand in the interests of national peace and stability.

the graves of the children of the people. The phrase is found again in 2 Kings xxiii. 6. A form of degradation is obviously meant; A.V. and R.V. 'the common people' approximates to the meaning. A common cemetery, as distinct from a family sepulchre, is to be understood. Torczyner identifies this narrative with a passage in Letter XVI of the Lachish Letters.

24. In spite of this precedent, which re-influenced the people against Jeremiah, Ahikam's protection saved him.

Ahikam the son of Shaphan. One of the men sent by Josiah to consult the prophetess Huldah on the Scroll found

in the Temple (2 Kings xxii. 12). He was the father of Gedaliah who was left in charge in Judah after the Babylonian invasion. The son also proved a friend of Jeremiah (xxxix. 14).

CHAPTER XXVII

1-15 THE KING WARNED NOT TO JOIN IN REVOLT AGAINST NEBUCHADNEZZAR

1. *Jehoiakim.* From verses 3 and 12 it would appear that the warning was addressed to Zedekiah, and that is the reading here of the Peshitta and some Hebrew MSS. Retaining the present text, Rashi and Kimchi explain that although the prophecy concerns Zedekiah, it was communicated to Jeremiah at the beginning of Jehoiakim's reign. The plot to rebel happened in 593 B.C.E.

2. *bands and bars.* To form a yoke consisting of wooden bars held together by leather bands. For the symbolism of

thy neck; 3. and send them to the
king of Edom, and to the king of
Moab, and to the king of the children
of Ammon, and to the king of Tyre,
and to the king of Zidon, by the
hand of the messengers that come to
Jerusalem unto Zedekiah king of
Judah; 4. and give them a charge
unto their masters, saying: Thus
saith the LORD of hosts, the God of
Israel: Thus shall ye say unto your
masters: 5. I have made the earth,
the man and the beast that are upon
the face of the earth, by My great
power and by My outstretched arm;
and I give it unto whom it seemeth
right unto Me. 6. And now have
I given all these lands into the hand
of Nebuchadnezzar the king of
Babylon, My servant; and the
beasts of the field also have I given

3 וְשִׁלַּחְתָּם אֶל־מֶלֶךְ אֱדוֹם : וּנְתַתָּם עַל־־צַוְּארֶךָ
וְאֶל־מֶלֶךְ מוֹאָב וְאֶל־מֶלֶךְ
בְּנֵי עַמּוֹן וְאֶל־מֶלֶךְ צֹר וְאֶל־
מֶלֶךְ צִידוֹן בְּיַד מַלְאָכִים
הַבָּאִים יְרוּשָׁלִַם אֶל־־
4 צִדְקִיָּהוּ מֶלֶךְ יְהוּדָה : וְצִוִּיתָ
אֹתָם אֶל־אֲדֹנֵיהֶם לֵאמֹר
כֹּה־אָמַר יְהֹוָה צְבָאוֹת אֱלֹהֵי
יִשְׂרָאֵל כֹּה תֹאמְרוּ אֶל־
5 אֲדֹנֵיכֶם : אָנֹכִי עָשִׂיתִי אֶת־
הָאָרֶץ אֶת־הָאָדָם וְאֶת־
הַבְּהֵמָה אֲשֶׁר עַל־פְּנֵי הָאָרֶץ
בְּכֹחִי הַגָּדוֹל וּבִזְרוֹעִי הַנְּטוּיָה
וּנְתַתִּיהָ לַאֲשֶׁר יָשַׁר בְּעֵינָי :
6 וְעַתָּה אָנֹכִי נָתַתִּי אֶת־
כָּל־הָאֲרָצוֹת הָאֵלֶּה בְּיַד
נְבוּכַדְנֶאצַּר מֶלֶךְ־בָּבֶל
עַבְדִּי וְגַם אֶת־חַיַּת הַשָּׂדֶה

the action, cf. the parallels in 1 Kings xxii. 11 and Ezek. vii. 23.

3. *and send them.* Probably duplicates of the yoke which the prophet himself was to wear.

Edom . . . Zidon. The nations planning to revolt.

the messengers. Their envoys sent to Zedekiah with an invitation to join in the conspiracy.

4. *thus saith the LORD of hosts.* It was not unusual for the Hebrew prophets to

address themselves to foreign nations, and their messages were heard with respect (cf. Judg. iii. 20; 1 Kings xix. 15; Isa. xviii. 2).

5. God's control over the destinies of peoples is justified by His act of creation which called nations and individuals alike into being.

6. *My servant.* See on xxv. 9.

the beasts of the field also. An idiom expressing the all-embracing extent of God's dominion (cf. xxviii. 14; Dan. ii. 38).

him to serve him. 7. And all the
nations shall serve him, and his son,
and his son's son, until the time of
his own land come; and then many
nations and great kings shall make
him their bondman. 8. And it shall
come to pass, that the nation and the
kingdom which will not serve the
same Nebuchadnezzar king of Babylon, and that will not put their neck
under the yoke of the king of
Babylon, that nation will I visit,
saith the LORD, with the sword, and
with the famine, and with the
pestilence, until I have consumed
them by his hand. 9. But as for
you, hearken ye not to your prophets,
nor to your diviners, nor to your
dreams, nor to your soothsayers, nor
to your sorcerers, that speak unto
you, saying: Ye shall not serve the
king of Babylon; 10. for they
prophesy a lie unto you, to remove

7 נָתַ֫תִּי לֽוֹ לְעָבְד֑וֹ וְעָבְד֤וּ אֹתוֹ
כָל־הַגּוֹיִם וְאֶת־בְּנ֖וֹ וְאֶת־
בֶּן־בְּנ֑וֹ עַ֚ד בֹּא־עֵ֣ת אַרְצ֔וֹ
גַּם־ה֔וּא וְעָ֥בְדוּ ב֖וֹ גּוֹיִ֣ם רַבִּ֑ים
8 וּמְלָכִ֖ים גְּדֹלִֽים׃ וְהָיָ֣ה הַגּ֗וֹי
וְהַמַּמְלָכָ֞ה אֲשֶׁ֣ר לֹֽא־יַֽעַבְד֣וּ
אֹתוֹ אֶת־נְבֽוּכַדְנֶאצַּ֣ר מֶֽלֶךְ־
בָּבֶ֔ל וְאֵ֛ת אֲשֶׁ֥ר לֹֽא־יִתֵּ֛ן
אֶת־צַוָּאר֖וֹ בְּעֹ֣ל מֶ֣לֶךְ בָּבֶ֑ל
בַּחֶ֨רֶב וּבָֽרָעָ֤ב וּבַדֶּ֙בֶר֙ אֶפְקֹ֞ד
עַל־הַגּ֤וֹי הַהוּא֙ נְאֻם־יְהֹוָ֔ה
9 עַד־תֻּמִּ֥י אֹתָ֖ם בְּיָד֑וֹ׃ וְאַתֶּ֡ם
אַל־תִּשְׁמְע֣וּ אֶל־נְבִֽיאֵיכֶ֡ם
וְאֶל־קֹֽסְמֵיכֶם֩ וְאֶל־
חֲלֹמֹ֨תֵיכֶ֜ם וְאֶל־עֹֽנְנֵיכֶ֗ם
וְאֶל־כַּשָּׁפֵיכֶ֑ם אֲשֶׁר־הֵ֞ם
אֹֽמְרִ֤ים אֲלֵיכֶם֙ לֵאמֹ֔ר לֹ֥א
10 תַֽעַבְד֖וּ אֶת־מֶ֣לֶךְ בָּבֶֽל׃ כִּ֣י
שֶׁ֔קֶר הֵ֖ם נִבְּאִ֣ים לָכֶ֑ם לְמַ֗עַן
הַרְחִ֤יק אֶתְכֶם֙ מֵעַ֣ל

---

7. *his son, and his son's son.* viz. Evil-
merodach and Belshazzar respectively
(cf. lii. 31; Dan. v. 1, 30). It is doubtful,
however, whether the verse intends to
define the extent of the Chaldean
dynasty; more probably it means a long
time, but not for ever.

8. *famine . . . pestilence.* The usual
concomitants of *the sword.*

9. *your prophets.* Who advise you to
rebel against Nebuchadnezzar.

your diviners, etc. Who assure you of
the success of your conspiracy.

10. *to remove you,* etc. Not that this was
the intention of those who counselled
in favour of the plot; but it would be the
consequence.

you far from your land; and that
I should drive you out and ye
should perish. 11. But the nation
that shall bring their neck under the
yoke of the king of Babylon, and
serve him, that nation will I let
remain in their own land, saith the
LORD; and they shall till it, and
dwell therein.'

12. And I spoke to Zedekiah king
of Judah according to all these
words, saying: 'Bring your necks
under the yoke of the king of
Babylon, and serve him and his
people, and live. 13. Why will ye
die, thou and thy people, by the
sword, by the famine, and by the
pestilence, as the LORD hath spoken
concerning the nation that will not
serve the king of Babylon? 14. And
hearken not unto the words of the
prophets that speak unto you, saying: Ye shall not serve the king of
Babylon, for they prophesy a lie
unto you. 15. For I have not sent
them, saith the LORD, and they
prophesy falsely in My name; that
I might drive you out, and that ye
might perish, ye, and the prophets
that prophesy unto you.'

אַדְמַתְכֶם וְהִדַּחְתִּי אֶתְכֶם
11 וַאֲבַדְתֶּם: וְהַגּוֹי אֲשֶׁר יָבִיא
אֶת־צַוָּארוֹ בְּעֹל מֶלֶךְ־בָּבֶל
וַעֲבָדוֹ וְהִנַּחְתִּיו עַל־אַדְמָתוֹ
נְאֻם־יְהֹוָה וַעֲבָדָהּ וְיָשַׁב בָּהּ:
12 וְאֶל־צִדְקִיָּה מֶלֶךְ־יְהוּדָה
דִּבַּרְתִּי כְּכָל־הַדְּבָרִים
הָאֵלֶּה לֵאמֹר הָבִיאוּ אֶת־
צַוְּארֵיכֶם בְּעֹל מֶלֶךְ בָּבֶל
13 וְעִבְדוּ אֹתוֹ וְעַמּוֹ וִחְיוּ: לָמָּה
תָמוּתוּ אַתָּה וְעַמֶּךָ בַּחֶרֶב
בָּרָעָב וּבַדָּבֶר כַּאֲשֶׁר דִּבֶּר
יְהֹוָה אֶל־הַגּוֹי אֲשֶׁר לֹא־
14 יַעֲבֹד אֶת־מֶלֶךְ בָּבֶל: וְאַל־
תִּשְׁמְעוּ אֶל־דִּבְרֵי הַנְּבִאִים
הָאֹמְרִים אֲלֵיכֶם לֵאמֹר לֹא
תַעַבְדוּ אֶת־מֶלֶךְ בָּבֶל כִּי
15 שֶׁקֶר הֵם נִבְּאִים לָכֶם: כִּי לֹא
שְׁלַחְתִּים נְאֻם־יְהֹוָה וְהֵם
נִבְּאִים בִּשְׁמִי לַשָּׁקֶר לְמַעַן
הַדִּיחִי אֶתְכֶם וַאֲבַדְתֶּם אַתֶּם
וְהַנְּבִאִים הַנִּבְּאִים לָכֶם:

---

11. *their neck.* lit. 'its neck,' *nation*
having the force of 'each nation.'

12. *your necks.* The plural includes the

'princes' or civil rulers who were in
attendance upon the king when Jeremiah
delivered the message to him. For that
reason they are not included in verse 16.

16. Also I spoke to the priests and to all this people, saying: 'Thus saith the LORD: Hearken not to the words of your prophets that prophesy unto you, saying: Behold, the vessels of the LORD's house shall now shortly be brought back from Babylon; for they prophesy a lie unto you. 17. Hearken not unto them; serve the king of Babylon, and live; wherefore should this city become desolate? 18. But if they be prophets, and if the word of the LORD be with them, let them now make intercession to the LORD of hosts, that the vessels which are left in the house of the LORD, and in the house of the king of Judah, and at Jerusalem, go not to Babylon. 19. For thus saith the LORD of hosts concerning the pillars, and concerning the sea, and concerning the bases, and concerning the residue of the vessels that remain in this city, 20. which Nebuchadnezzar king of

16 וְאֶל־הַכֹּהֲנִים וְאֶל־כָּל־
הָעָם הַזֶּה דִּבַּרְתִּי לֵאמֹר כֹּה
אָמַר יְהוָה אַל־תִּשְׁמְעוּ אֶל־
דִּבְרֵי נְבִיאֵיכֶם הַנִּבְּאִים לָכֶם
לֵאמֹר הִנֵּה כְלֵי בֵית־יְהוָה
מוּשָׁבִים מִבָּבֶלָה עַתָּה מְהֵרָה
כִּי שֶׁקֶר הֵמָּה נִבְּאִים לָכֶם:
17 אַל־תִּשְׁמְעוּ אֲלֵיהֶם עִבְדוּ
אֶת־מֶלֶךְ בָּבֶל וִחְיוּ לָמָּה
תִהְיֶה הָעִיר הַזֹּאת חָרְבָּה:
18 וְאִם־נְבִאִים הֵם וְאִם־יֵשׁ
דְּבַר־יְהוָה אִתָּם יִפְגְּעוּ־נָא
בַּיהוָה צְבָאוֹת לְבִלְתִּי־בֹאוּ
הַכֵּלִים ׀ הַנּוֹתָרִים בְּבֵית־
יְהוָה וּבֵית מֶלֶךְ יְהוּדָה
19 וּבִירוּשָׁלִַם בָּבֶלָה: כִּי כֹה
אָמַר יְהוָה צְבָאוֹת אֶל־
הָעַמֻּדִים וְעַל־הַיָּם וְעַל־
הַמְּכֹנוֹת וְעַל יֶתֶר הַכֵּלִים
20 הַנּוֹתָרִים בָּעִיר הַזֹּאת: אֲשֶׁר

16-22 THE WARNING REPEATED TO PRIESTS AND PEOPLE

16. *the vessels of the LORD'S house.* Which were carried away by Nebuchadnezzar to Babylon in the reign of Jehoiachin (cf. 2 Kings xxiv. 13 and note verse 20 of this chapter). The assurance that the holy vessels are to be restored to the Temple would naturally make a strong appeal to the priests and gain their support to a policy of revolt.

18. *let them now make intercession.* If these men are truly endowed with prophecy and called by God, instead of their deluding the people with false hopes, let them pray that fresh disaster will not befall the nation.

19. *the pillars*, etc. Described in 1 Kings vii. 15-39. They were broken up by the Chaldeans and carried to Babylon (lii. 17).

Babylon took not, when he carried away captive Jeconiah the son of Jehoiakim, king of Judah, from Jerusalem to Babylon, and all the nobles of Judah and Jerusalem; 21. yea, thus saith the LORD of hosts, the God of Israel, concerning the vessels that remain in the house of the LORD, and in the house of the king of Judah, and at Jerusalem: 22. They shall be carried to Babylon, and there shall they be, until the day that I remember them, saith the LORD, and bring them up, and restore them to this place.'

לֹא־לְקָחָם נְבוּכַדְנֶאצַּר מֶלֶךְ
בָּבֶל בַּגְלוֹתוֹ אֶת־יְכָנְיָה בֶן־
יְהוֹיָקִים מֶלֶךְ־יְהוּדָה
מִירוּשָׁלַםִ בָּבֶלָה וְאֵת כָּל־
21 חֹרֵי יְהוּדָה וִירוּשָׁלָםִ׃ כִּי כֹה
אָמַר יְהוָֹה צְבָאוֹת אֱלֹהֵי
יִשְׂרָאֵל עַל־הַכֵּלִים
הַנּוֹתָרִים בֵּית יְהוָֹה וּבֵית
מֶלֶךְ־יְהוּדָה וִירוּשָׁלָםִ׃
22 בָּבֶלָה יוּבָאוּ וְשָׁמָּה יִהְיוּ עַד
יוֹם פָּקְדִי אֹתָם נְאֻם־יְהוָֹה
וְהַעֲלִיתִים וַהֲשִׁבֹתִים אֶל־
הַמָּקוֹם הַזֶּה׃

28   CHAPTER XXVIII   כח

1. And it came to pass the same year, in the beginning of the reign of Zedekiah king of Judah, in the fourth year, in the fifth month, that Hananiah the son of Azzur the prophet, who was of Gibeon, spoke

1 וַיְהִי ׀ בַּשָּׁנָה הַהִיא בְּרֵאשִׁית
מַמְלֶכֶת צִדְקִיָּה מֶלֶךְ־
יְהוּדָה בִּשְׁנָת הָרְבִעִית בַּחֹדֶשׁ
הַחֲמִישִׁי אָמַר אֵלַי חֲנַנְיָה בֶן־
עַזּוּר הַנָּבִיא אֲשֶׁר מִגִּבְעוֹן

v. 20. בשנה ק׳   v. 1. יתיר ו׳

22. *until the day that I remember them.* The predicted event happened in the reign of Cyrus (Ezra i. 7ff.).

CHAPTER XXVIII

HANANIAH OPPOSES JEREMIAH

1. *the same year.* As that to which the last chapter relates (see on xxvii. 1).

Hananiah. According to the Talmud (Sanh. 89a), his false predictions arose

from an unwarranted deduction. Having heard Jeremiah foretell the downfall of Elam (xlix. 34ff.), a satellite State of Babylon, he concluded that the prophecy would apply with even greater force to Babylon. Nothing is known of him beyond what is here recorded.

the prophet. This implies that he was recognized as such.

Gibeon. One of the priestly cities

unto me in the house of the LORD, in the presence of the priests and of all the people, saying: 2. 'Thus speaketh the LORD of hosts, the God of Israel, saying: I have broken the yoke of the king of Babylon. 3. Within two full years will I bring back into this place all the vessels of the LORD's house, that Nebuchadnezzar king of Babylon took away from this place, and carried them to Babylon; 4. and I will bring back to this place Jeconiah the son of Jehoiakim, king of Judah, with all the captives of Judah, that went to Babylon, saith the LORD; for I will break the yoke of the king of Babylon.' 5. Then the prophet Jeremiah said unto the prophet Hananiah in the presence of the priests, and in the presence of all the people that stood in the house of the LORD, 6. even the prophet Jeremiah

בְּבֵית יְהֹוָה לְעֵינֵי הַכֹּהֲנִים
2 וְכָל־הָעָם לֵאמֹר: כֹּה־אָמַר
יְהֹוָה צְבָאוֹת אֱלֹהֵי יִשְׂרָאֵל
לֵאמֹר שָׁבַרְתִּי אֶת־עֹל מֶלֶךְ
3 בָּבֶל: בְּעוֹד | שְׁנָתַיִם יָמִים
אֲנִי מֵשִׁיב אֶל־הַמָּקוֹם הַזֶּה
אֶת־כָּל־כְּלֵי בֵּית יְהֹוָה אֲשֶׁר
לָקַח נְבוּכַדְנֶאצַּר מֶלֶךְ־
בָּבֶל מִן־הַמָּקוֹם הַזֶּה וַיְבִיאֵם
4 בָּבֶל: וְאֶת־יְכָנְיָה בֶן־
יְהוֹיָקִים מֶלֶךְ־יְהוּדָה וְאֶת־
כָּל־גָּלוּת יְהוּדָה הַבָּאִים
בָּבֶלָה אֲנִי מֵשִׁיב אֶל־הַמָּקוֹם
הַזֶּה נְאֻם־יְהֹוָה כִּי אֶשְׁבֹּר
5 אֶת־עֹל מֶלֶךְ בָּבֶל: וַיֹּאמֶר
יִרְמְיָה הַנָּבִיא אֶל־חֲנַנְיָה
הַנָּבִיא לְעֵינֵי הַכֹּהֲנִים וּלְעֵינֵי
כָל־הָעָם הָעֹמְדִים בְּבֵית
6 יְהֹוָה: וַיֹּאמֶר יִרְמְיָה הַנָּבִיא

(Josh. xxi. 17), five miles north-west of Jerusalem.

2. *I have broken.* The prophetic perfect referring to the future.

the yoke. The words have an allusion to the symbolic yoke worn by Jeremiah on his neck (cf. verse 10).

3. *within two full years.* i.e. within the near future. 'The wish was too much father of the thought. The sincere but lower type of patriotism which dominated them (the opponents of

Jeremiah), together with the religious conviction that God was on their side, blinded them to the real facts; their enthusiasm led them to discount the odds against them' (Peake).

4. Hananiah contradicts the prediction of Jeremiah in xxii. 24-27.

6. Jeremiah replies that he hopes Hananiah's forecast of the future will be realized, knowing in his heart that events would falsify it.

said: 'Amen! the LORD do so! the
LORD perform thy words which thou
hast prophesied, to bring back the
vessels of the LORD's house, and all
them that are carried away captive,
from Babylon unto this place!
7. Nevertheless hear thou now this
word that I speak in thine ears, and
in the ears of all the people: 8. The
prophets that have been before me
and before thee of old prophesied
against many countries, and against
great kingdoms, of war, and of evil,
and of pestilence. 9. The prophet
that prophesieth of peace, when the
word of the prophet shall come to
pass, then shall the prophet be
known, that the LORD hath truly
sent him.'

10. Then Hananiah the prophet
took the bar from off the prophet
Jeremiah's neck, and broke it.
11. And Hananiah spoke in the
presence of all the people, saying:
'Thus saith the LORD: Even so will
I break the yoke of Nebuchadnezzar

אָמֵן כֵּן יַעֲשֶׂה יְהוָֹה יָקֵם יְהוָֹה
אֶת־דְּבָרֶיךָ אֲשֶׁר נִבֵּאתָ
לְהָשִׁיב כְּלֵי בֵית־יְהוָֹה וְכָל־
הַגּוֹלָה מִבָּבֶל אֶל־הַמָּקוֹם
7 הַזֶּה: אַךְ שְׁמַע־נָא הַדָּבָר
הַזֶּה אֲשֶׁר אָנֹכִי דֹּבֵר בְּאָזְנֶיךָ
8 וּבְאָזְנֵי כָּל־הָעָם: הַנְּבִיאִים
אֲשֶׁר הָיוּ לְפָנַי וּלְפָנֶיךָ מִן־
הָעוֹלָם וַיִּנָּבְאוּ אֶל־אֲרָצוֹת
רַבּוֹת וְעַל־מַמְלָכוֹת גְּדֹלוֹת
לְמִלְחָמָה וּלְרָעָה וּלְדָבֶר:
9 הַנָּבִיא אֲשֶׁר יִנָּבֵא לְשָׁלוֹם
בְּבֹא דְּבַר הַנָּבִיא יִוָּדַע הַנָּבִיא
אֲשֶׁר־שְׁלָחוֹ יְהוָֹה בֶּאֱמֶת:
10 וַיִּקַּח חֲנַנְיָה הַנָּבִיא אֶת־
הַמּוֹטָה מֵעַל צַוַּאר יִרְמְיָה
11 הַנָּבִיא וַיִּשְׁבְּרֵהוּ: וַיֹּאמֶר
חֲנַנְיָה לְעֵינֵי כָל־הָעָם לֵאמֹר
כֹּה אָמַר יְהוָֹה כָּכָה אֶשְׁבֹּר
אֶת־עֹל ׀ נְבֻכַדְנֶאצַּר מֶלֶךְ־

v. 8. חצי הספר בפסוקים 11 .v על נ״א

8f. Jeremiah's argument is as follows:
The fact that a prophet has the courage
to foretell national calamity, well knowing
the unpopularity and even active hatred
which he would thereby incur, is in itself
proof that he is truly conscious of
uttering a Divine message. Otherwise
he would choose the easier way of
pleasing his hearers with the prophecies
which he knows they prefer to hear.

Consequently, if another prophet contradicts him with comforting predictions,
the only proof of the former's genuineness
is the fulfilment of his words.

10. Hananiah makes no verbal reply,
but evidences his disagreement by
breaking the yoke worn by Jeremiah to
express his conviction that the Babylonian yoke would be similarly broken.

king of Babylon from off the neck of all the nations within two full years.' And the prophet Jeremiah went his way. 12. Then the word of the LORD came unto Jeremiah, after that Hananiah the prophet had broken the bar from off the neck of the prophet Jeremiah, saying: 13. 'Go, and tell Hananiah, saying: Thus saith the LORD: Thou hast broken the bars of wood; but thou shalt make in their stead bars of iron. 14. For thus saith the LORD of hosts, the God of Israel: I have put a yoke of iron upon the neck of all these nations, that they may serve Nebuchadnezzar king of Babylon; and they shall serve him; and I have given him the beasts of the field also.' 15. Then said the prophet Jeremiah unto Hananiah the prophet: 'Hear now, Hananiah; the LORD hath not sent thee; but thou makest this people to trust in a lie.

בְּבֶל בְּעוֹד שְׁנָתַיִם יָמִים מֵעַל צַוַּאר כָּל־הַגּוֹיִם וַיֵּלֶךְ יִרְמְיָה

12 הַנָּבִיא לְדַרְכּוֹ: וַיְהִי דְבַר־ יְהֹוָה אֶל־יִרְמְיָה אַחֲרֵי שְׁבוֹר חֲנַנְיָה הַנָּבִיא אֶת־הַמּוֹטָה מֵעַל צַוַּאר יִרְמְיָה הַנָּבִיא

13 לֵאמֹר: הָלוֹךְ וְאָמַרְתָּ אֶל־ חֲנַנְיָה לֵאמֹר כֹּה אָמַר יְהֹוָה מוֹטֹת עֵץ שָׁבָרְתָּ וְעָשִׂיתָ

14 תַחְתֵּיהֶן מֹטוֹת בַּרְזֶל: כִּי כֹה־אָמַר יְהֹוָה צְבָאוֹת אֱלֹהֵי יִשְׂרָאֵל עֹל בַּרְזֶל נָתַתִּי עַל־ צַוַּאר ׀ כָּל־הַגּוֹיִם הָאֵלֶּה לַעֲבֹד אֶת־נְבֻכַדְנֶאצַּר מֶלֶךְ־בָּבֶל וַעֲבָדֻהוּ וְגַם אֶת־

15 חַיַּת הַשָּׂדֶה נָתַתִּי לוֹ: וַיֹּאמֶר יִרְמְיָה הַנָּבִיא אֶל־חֲנַנְיָה הַנָּבִיא שְׁמַע־נָא חֲנַנְיָה לֹא־ שְׁלָחֲךָ יְהֹוָה וְאַתָּה הִבְטַחְתָּ אֶת־הָעָם הַזֶּה עַל־שָׁקֶר:

11. *went his way.* Jeremiah makes no retort to Hananiah, either because he felt it useless to repeat his admonition and left events to justify it; or possibly, the people may have been so convinced by Hananiah's positive tone and infuriated by Jeremiah's prediction, that he endangered his life if he persisted. The former supposition is the more likely.

An interval separates this from the following verses.

13. *thou shalt make in their stead bars of iron.* By breaking the wooden bar, you are imposing a heavier yoke upon the people as the sequel of the revolt to which you incite them.

14. *the beasts of the field.* See on xxvii. 6.

16. Therefore thus saith the LORD: Behold, I will send thee away from off the face of the earth; this year thou shalt die, because thou hast spoken perversion against the LORD.'
17. So Hananiah the prophet died the same year in the seventh month.

16 לָכֵ֗ן כֹּ֚ה אָמַ֣ר יְהֹוָ֔ה הִנְנִ֤י
מְשַׁלֵּֽחֲךָ֙ מֵעַ֣ל פְּנֵ֣י הָֽאֲדָמָ֔ה
הַשָּׁנָ֥ה אַתָּ֖ה מֵ֑ת כִּֽי־סָרָ֥ה
17 דִבַּ֖רְתָּ אֶל־יְהֹוָֽה: וַיָּ֜מָת
חֲנַנְיָ֤ה הַנָּבִיא֙ בַּשָּׁנָ֣ה הַהִ֔יא
בַּחֹ֖דֶשׁ הַשְּׁבִיעִֽי:

29   CHAPTER XXIX   כט

1. Now these are the words of the letter that Jeremiah the prophet sent from Jerusalem unto the residue of the elders of the captivity, and to the priests, and to the prophets, and to all the people, whom Nebuchadnezzar had carried away captive

1 וְאֵ֙לֶּה֙ דִּבְרֵ֣י הַסֵּ֔פֶר אֲשֶׁ֥ר שָׁלַ֖ח
יִרְמְיָ֥ה הַנָּבִ֖יא מִירוּשָׁלָ֑͏ִם אֶל־
יֶ֜תֶר זִקְנֵ֣י הַגּוֹלָ֗ה וְאֶל־
הַכֹּהֲנִים֙ וְאֶל־הַנְּבִיאִים֙ וְאֶל־
כָּל־הָעָ֑ם אֲשֶׁ֥ר הֶגְלָ֖ה

16. *perversion.* You have perverted God's message.

17. *in the seventh month.* Two months later (cf. verse 1).

CHAPTER XXIX

JEREMIAH'S LETTER TO THE EXILES

ALTHOUGH like other prophets Jeremiah had taught that the exile was punishment for the people's sins, now that many inhabitants of Judea were in captivity (the allusion is to those who were carried off with king Jeconiah in 597 B.C.E.), it was his duty to preach hope and encouragement to them. Though he smote his people with verbal castigations, he also healed, reviving the smitten with fresh confidence. But he was at the same time realistic, and deemed it

his duty to warn the people not to delude themselves into thinking that the exile would come to a speedy end, as some false prophets were assuring them. The letter was probably written in 595 B.C.E.

1. *the residue.* The reference is obscure. Is it possible that many elders of the captivity had perished in some disaster not recorded elsewhere ? Duhm conjectured that there may have been an attempt to escape, or resistance had been offered to Babylonian rule which resulted in the death of many of the elders.

elders . . . priests . . . prophets. The enumeration suggests that a form of communal organization had been retained in exile similar to that which existed in Judea. Jeremiah's epistle was an 'open letter' addressed to all sections of the captives.

from Jerusalem to Babylon, 2. after that Jeconiah the king, and the queen-mother, and the officers, and the princes of Judah and Jerusalem, and the craftsmen, and the smiths, were departed from Jerusalem; 3. by the hand of Elasah the son of Shaphan, and Gemariah the son of Hilkiah, whom Zedekiah king of Judah sent unto Babylon to Nebuchadnezzar king of Babylon, saying: 4. Thus saith the LORD of hosts, the God of Israel, unto all the captivity, whom I have caused to be

נְבוּכַדְנֶאצַּר מִירוּשָׁלָם
2 בָּבֶלָה: אַחֲרֵי צֵאת יְכָנְיָה
הַמֶּלֶךְ וְהַגְּבִירָה וְהַסָּרִיסִים
שָׂרֵי יְהוּדָה וִירוּשָׁלַם וְהֶחָרָשׁ
3 וְהַמַּסְגֵּר מִירוּשָׁלָם: בְּיַד
אֶלְעָשָׂה בֶן־שָׁפָן וּגְמַרְיָה בֶן־
חִלְקִיָּה אֲשֶׁר שָׁלַח צִדְקִיָּה
מֶלֶךְ־יְהוּדָה אֶל־
נְבוּכַדְנֶאצַּר מֶלֶךְ בָּבֶל
4 בָּבֶלָה לֵאמֹר: כֹּה־אָמַר יְהֹוָה
צְבָאוֹת אֱלֹהֵי יִשְׂרָאֵל לְכָל־
הַגּוֹלָה אֲשֶׁר־הִגְלֵיתִי

2. *Jeconiah.* See on xxii. 24.

the queen-mother. Nehushta; see on xiii. 18.

the craftsmen, and the smiths. See on xxiv. 1.

were departed. Into exile.

3. *Elasah the son of Shaphan.* Probably the brother of Ahikam the son of Shaphan who protected Jeremiah when the priests and the people demanded his death (xxvi. 24).

Gemariah. The name, but of a different person, occurs again in xxxvi. 10ff.

Hilkiah. Possibly identical with the High Priest of that name mentioned in 2 Kings xxii. 4.

whom Zedekiah . . . sent unto Babylon. The purpose of the mission is not stated. Perhaps it was in connection with the affairs and problems of the exiles; or they bore tribute to the Babylonian king. It hardly seems likely that they were sent for the purpose of delivering Jeremiah's message, though it is not impossible,

since its contents would have the approval of Nebuchadnezzar.

saying. This refers back to the *letter* in verse 1.

4ff. Jeremiah's message contains a direction which was accepted by the Jewish people in subsequent ages. Since the overthrow of the State in 135 C.E., while the Jew never ceased to hope in an ultimate restoration to Zion, he modelled his relations to the country of his birth or domicile upon Jeremiah's advice. So far as he was permitted, he struck roots there, 'building houses and planting gardens,' and fully identifying himself with the interests of the country. Above all, he 'sought the peace of the city,' loyal citizenship being considered by him a religious duty. The fact that Jeremiah could urge this doctrine upon the exiles, while at the same time assuring them of their restoration after seventy years (verse 10), indicates that in his mind no mutually exclusive dual loyalty was involved, but that on the contrary each fortified the other. This, too, has been the attitude of the Jewish people in the Diaspora.

carried away captive from Jerusalem unto Babylon:

5. Build ye houses, and dwell in them, and plant gardens, and eat the fruit of them; 6. take ye wives, and beget sons and daughters; and take wives for your sons, and give your daughters to husbands, that they may bear sons and daughters; and multiply ye there, and be not diminished. 7. And seek the peace of the city whither I have caused you to be carried away captive, and pray unto the LORD for it; for in the peace thereof shall ye have peace.

8. For thus saith the LORD of hosts, the God of Israel: Let not

מִירוּשָׁלַ֫ם בָּבֶ֫לָה: בְּנ֥וּ בָתִּים ⁵
וְשֵׁ֫בוּ וְנִטְע֣וּ גַנּ֔וֹת וְאִכְל֖וּ אֶת־
קְח֤וּ נָשִׁים֙ וְהוֹלִידוּ֙ פְּרִיָ֑ן ⁶
בָּנִ֣ים וּבָנ֔וֹת וּקְח֤וּ לִבְנֵיכֶ֜ם
נָשִׁ֗ים וְאֶת־בְּנֽוֹתֵיכֶם֙ תְּנ֣וּ
לַֽאֲנָשִׁ֔ים וְתֵלַ֣דְנָה בָּנִ֣ים וּבָנ֑וֹת
וּרְבוּ־שָׁ֖ם וְאַל־תִּמְעָֽטוּ:
וְדִרְשׁ֞וּ אֶת־שְׁל֣וֹם הָעִ֗יר ⁷
אֲשֶׁ֨ר הִגְלֵ֤יתִי אֶתְכֶם֙ שָׁ֔מָּה
וְהִתְפַּֽלְל֥וּ בַעֲדָ֖הּ אֶל־יְהֹוָ֑ה
כִּ֣י בִשְׁלוֹמָ֔הּ יִהְיֶ֥ה לָכֶ֖ם
שָׁלֽוֹם: כִּ֣י כֹ֣ה אָמַ֞ר יְהֹוָ֧ה ⁸
צְבָא֛וֹת אֱלֹהֵ֥י יִשְׂרָאֵ֖ל אַל־

---

5. *build ye houses*, etc. The exiles in Babylon did not suffer the restrictions which were imposed upon Jews in many countries in later times. They were permitted to own land and engage in agriculture. It is noteworthy that Jeremiah's advice did not include engaging in commerce, in which direction it is now thought that the ability of Jews chiefly lay. A variety of circumstances, such as the interdict upon their owning land, combined to force them from the soil and drive them into trade. In the first century C.E. Josephus wrote, 'As for ourselves, we neither inhabit a maritime country, nor delight in commerce, nor in such intercourse with other men as arises from it; but the cities we dwell in are remote from the sea, and as we have a fruitful country to dwell in, we take pains in cultivating it' (*Contra Apionem*, i. 12).

6. *take ye wives*, etc. Celibacy is foreign to Judaism, and the duty to propagate the species is regarded as the first of the precepts of the Torah (Gen. i. 28 and see on xvi. 2). From this duty, an indication of Judaism's robust optimism, not even the grief of the exile was to deflect them. The advice also re-enforced the warning that the stay in Babylon would be of long duration.

7. *and pray unto the LORD for it.* Cf. Ezra vi. 10 where Cyrus asked for the prayers of the people and 1 Macc. vii. 33 which tells that a sacrifice was offered in the Temple for the Syrian monarchy. A Rabbi exhorted, 'Pray for the welfare of the government, since but for the fear of it men would swallow each other alive' (Aboth). Similar expressions of loyalty to the State are recorded in Josephus, *The Jewish War*, II, xvii. 3 and *Contra Apionem*, ii. 6. To this day, the prayer for the king (or head of the State) and his advisers is part of the Service on Sabbaths and Festivals (cf. A.D.P.B., p. 153).

your prophets that are in the midst
of you, and your diviners, beguile
you, neither hearken ye to your
dreams which ye cause to be
dreamed. 9. For they prophesy
falsely unto you in My name; I have
not sent them, saith the Lord.

10. For thus saith the Lord: After
seventy years are accomplished for
Babylon, I will remember you, and
perform My good word toward you,
in causing you to return to this
place. 11. For I know the thoughts
that I think toward you, saith the
Lord, thoughts of peace, and not of
evil, to give you a future and a hope.

12. And ye shall call upon Me, and
go, and pray unto Me, and I will

יִשְּׂאוּ לָכֶם נְבִיאֵיכֶם אֲשֶׁר־
בְּקִרְבְּכֶם וְקֹסְמֵיכֶם וְאַל־
תִּשְׁמְעוּ אֶל־חֲלֹמֹתֵיכֶם אֲשֶׁר
9 אַתֶּם מַחְלְמִים: כִּי בְשֶׁקֶר
הֵם נִבְּאִים לָכֶם בִּשְׁמִי לֹא
10 שְׁלַחְתִּים נְאֻם־יְהֹוָה: כִּי־
כֹה אָמַר יְהֹוָה כִּי לְפִי מְלֹאת
לְבָבֶל שִׁבְעִים שָׁנָה אֶפְקֹד
אֶתְכֶם וַהֲקִמֹתִי עֲלֵיכֶם אֶת־
דְּבָרִי הַטּוֹב לְהָשִׁיב אֶתְכֶם
11 אֶל־הַמָּקוֹם הַזֶּה: כִּי אָנֹכִי
יָדַעְתִּי אֶת־הַמַּחֲשָׁבֹת אֲשֶׁר
אָנֹכִי חֹשֵׁב עֲלֵיכֶם נְאֻם־יְהֹוָה
מַחְשְׁבוֹת שָׁלוֹם וְלֹא לְרָעָה
לָתֵת לָכֶם אַחֲרִית וְתִקְוָה:
12 וּקְרָאתֶם אֹתִי וַהֲלַכְתֶּם
וְהִתְפַּלַּלְתֶּם אֵלַי וְשָׁמַעְתִּי

---

8. *which ye cause to be dreamed.* By
asking the professional seers to reveal
the future by means of oracles derived
from dreams.

10. *seventy years.* See on xxv. 11.

for Babylon. The time for her downfall
will then have been reached (see on
xxv. 12).

My good word. My promise of redemption as recorded in xxvii. 22.

11. *for I know.* The *I* is emphatic and
indicates a contrast: however you may
interpret the purpose of the exile, *I know*,
etc.

thoughts of peace . . . to give you a future.
The delay of seventy years is for your
good; it will make you disposed to
return to Me, thereby assuring a future
for you (Metsudath David).

12. Just as predictions of disaster are
conditional upon whether the people
persist in their evil, so are God's promises
of restoration dependent upon penitence.
He will not show favour to Israel simply
because they are His people; it must be
deserved. The characteristic feature of
this passage, as indeed of all the prophecies of redemption, is the conviction
on the part of the prophets that through
suffering Israel would be purged of sin
and thereby earn salvation.

hearken unto you. 13. And ye shall seek Me, and find Me, when ye shall search for Me with all your heart. 14. And I will be found of you, saith the LORD, and I will turn your captivity, and gather you from all the nations, and from all the places whither I have driven you, saith the LORD; and I will bring you back unto the place whence I caused you to be carried away captive. 15. For ye have said: 'The LORD hath raised us up prophets in Babylon.' 16. For thus saith the LORD concerning the king that sitteth upon the throne of David, and concerning all the people

13 אֲלֵיכֶם: וּבִקַּשְׁתֶּם אֹתִי
וּמְצָאתֶם כִּי תִדְרְשֻׁנִי בְּכָל־
14 לְבַבְכֶם: וְנִמְצֵאתִי לָכֶם
נְאֻם־יְהֹוָה וְשַׁבְתִּי אֶת־
שְׁבִיתְכֶם וְקִבַּצְתִּי אֶתְכֶם
מִכָּל־הַגּוֹיִם וּמִכָּל־
הַמְּקוֹמוֹת אֲשֶׁר הִדַּחְתִּי
אֶתְכֶם שָׁם נְאֻם־יְהֹוָה
וַהֲשִׁבֹתִי אֶתְכֶם אֶל־הַמָּקוֹם
אֲשֶׁר־הִגְלֵיתִי אֶתְכֶם מִשָּׁם:
15 כִּי אֲמַרְתֶּם הֵקִים לָנוּ יְהֹוָה
16 נְבִאִים בְּבָבֶלָה: כִּי־כֹה ׀ אָמַר
יְהֹוָה אֶל־הַמֶּלֶךְ הַיּוֹשֵׁב אֶל־
כִּסֵּא דָוִד וְאֶל־כָּל־הָעָם

v. 14. שבותכם ק'   v. 16. נ"א על

---

13. ye shall seek Me, and find Me. 'This is a great pronouncement of Scripture, proclaiming the omnipotence of repentance. But the sinner must *seek* God; i.e. he must feel the "loss" of God, and take active measures to *find* Him and regain His favour. And that search must be with the sinner's whole heart and soul. Sincere repentance always and everywhere secures the Divine mercy. It would be so in the exile, if they sought God with a radical change of heart, and the devotion of the whole being. And indeed it was in the exile that repentant Israel found God, rediscovered the Torah, rediscovered itself' (Hertz, *The Pentateuch*, Soncino ed., p. 762).

14. I will be found of you. The literal translation is probably 'and I will make Myself found unto you': God makes Himself readily accessible to those who seek Him in true repentance; cf. the Talmudic teaching, 'If one comes to cleanse himself (from sin), he is helped (by God)' (Shab. 104a).

turn your captivity. The general sense of the phrase is, 'reverse your fortunes'; here, more particularly, 'restore you to your land.'

15-19. A repeated admonition to the people not to allow themselves to be beguiled. They maintain that God has given them prophets in Babylon who predict a speedy return. So far from this being true, even they who are still in Judea are destined for destruction because they have not yet learned the grim lesson of the misfortune of the present captives and still refuse to hearken to God's word.

15. prophets in Babylon. Who prophesy a return in the near future.

16. the king. Zedekiah.

that dwell in this city, your brethren that are not gone forth with you into captivity; 17. thus saith the LORD of hosts: Behold, I will send upon them the sword, the famine, and the pestilence, and will make them like vile figs, that cannot be eaten, they are so bad. 18. And I will pursue after them with the sword, with the famine, and with the pestilence, and will make them a horror unto all the kingdoms of the earth, a curse, and an astonishment, and a hissing, and a reproach, among all the nations whither I have driven them; 19. because they have not hearkened to My words, saith the LORD, wherewith I sent unto them My servants the prophets, sending them betimes and often; but ye would not hear, saith the LORD. 20. Hear ye therefore the word of the LORD, all ye of the

הַיּוֹשֵׁב בָּעִיר הַזֹּאת אֲחֵיכֶם
אֲשֶׁר לֹא־יָצְאוּ אִתְּכֶם
בַּגּוֹלָה: כֹּה אָמַר יְהוָֹה 17
צְבָאוֹת הִנְנִי מְשַׁלֵּחַ בָּם אֶת־
הַחֶרֶב אֶת־הָרָעָב וְאֶת־
הַדָּבֶר וְנָתַתִּי אוֹתָם כַּתְּאֵנִים
הַשֹּׁעָרִים אֲשֶׁר לֹא־תֵאָכַלְנָה
מֵרֹעַ: וְרָדַפְתִּי אַחֲרֵיהֶם 18
בַּחֶרֶב בָּרָעָב וּבַדָּבֶר וּנְתַתִּים
לְזַוֲעָה לְכֹל מַמְלְכוֹת הָאָרֶץ
לְאָלָה וּלְשַׁמָּה וְלִשְׁרֵקָה
וּלְחֶרְפָּה בְּכָל־הַגּוֹיִם אֲשֶׁר־
הִדַּחְתִּים שָׁם: תַּחַת אֲשֶׁר־ 19
לֹא־שָׁמְעוּ אֶל־דְּבָרַי
נְאֻם־יְהוָה אֲשֶׁר שָׁלַחְתִּי
אֲלֵיהֶם אֶת־עֲבָדַי הַנְּבִאִים
הַשְׁכֵּם וְשָׁלֹחַ וְלֹא שְׁמַעְתֶּם
נְאֻם־יְהוָה: וְאַתֶּם שִׁמְעוּ 20
דְבַר־יְהוָה כָּל־הַגּוֹלָה

v. 18. לזועה ק'

---

this city. Jerusalem.

17. *like vile figs.* Cf. xxiv. 2-10.

18. *whither I have driven them.* The prophetic perfect.

19. *ye would not hear.* 'The sudden change of person is very natural, and yet serves to show up incidentally the scrupulous care with which the Jews have handed down from one to another the letter of the Scriptures. An obvious alteration would have been to turn this second person into the third, but it was retained. Jeremiah desires to show that it was not merely *other* persons who had behaved wickedly, and by thus including the very people whom he was addressing, he prepared the way for the opening words of verse 20' (Streane).

20. *hear ye therefore.* The emphasis is on *ye*: they in Judea have refused to hear; then do *ye* in captivity hear.

captivity, whom I have sent away from Jerusalem to Babylon: 21. Thus saith the LORD of hosts, the God of Israel, concerning Ahab the son of Kolaiah, and concerning Zedekiah the son of Maaseiah, who prophesy a lie unto you in My name: Behold, I will deliver them into the hand of Nebuchadrezzar king of Babylon; and he shall slay them before your eyes; 22. and of them shall be taken up a curse by all the captivity of Judah that are in Babylon, saying: 'The LORD make thee like Zedekiah and like Ahab, whom the king of Babylon roasted in the fire'; 23. because they have wrought vile deeds in Israel, and have committed adultery with their neighbours' wives, and have spoken words in My name falsely, which I commanded them not; but I am He that knoweth, and am witness, saith the LORD.

24. And concerning Shemaiah the Nehelamite thou shalt speak, saying:

אֲשֶׁר־שִׁלַּחְתִּי מִירוּשָׁלַ֫ם
21 בָּבֶֽלָה: כֹּה־אָמַ֞ר יְהוָ֣ה
צְבָאוֹת אֱלֹהֵ֤י יִשְׂרָאֵל֙ אֶל־
אַחְאָ֣ב בֶּן־קוֹלָיָ֔ה וְאֶל־
צִדְקִיָּ֫הוּ בֶן־מַעֲשֵׂיָה֙ הַֽנִּבְּאִ֤ים
לָכֶ֥ם בִּשְׁמִ֖י שָׁ֑קֶר הִנְנִ֣י ׀ נֹתֵ֣ן
אֹתָ֗ם בְּיַד֙ נְבֽוּכַדְרֶאצַּ֣ר
מֶֽלֶךְ־בָּבֶ֔ל וְהִכָּ֖ם לְעֵינֵיכֶֽם:
22 וְלֻקַּ֨ח מֵהֶ֤ם קְלָלָה֙ לְכֹ֣ל גָּל֣וּת
יְהוּדָ֔ה אֲשֶׁ֥ר בְּבָבֶ֖ל לֵאמֹ֑ר
יְשִֽׂמְךָ֤ יְהוָה֙ כְּצִדְקִיָּ֣הוּ וּכְאֶחָ֔ב
אֲשֶׁר־קָלָ֥ם מֶֽלֶךְ־בָּבֶ֖ל
23 בָּאֵֽשׁ: יַ֣עַן אֲשֶׁר֩ עָשׂ֨וּ נְבָלָ֜ה
בְּיִשְׂרָאֵ֗ל וַֽיְנַאֲפוּ֙ אֶת־נְשֵׁ֣י
רֵעֵיהֶ֔ם וַיְדַבְּר֤וּ דָבָר֙ בִּשְׁמִי֙
שֶׁ֔קֶר אֲשֶׁ֖ר ל֣וֹא צִוִּיתִ֑ם וְאָֽנֹכִ֛י
הַיּוֹדֵ֥עַ וָעֵ֖ד נְאֻם־יְהוָֽה:
24 וְאֶל־שְׁמַֽעְיָ֥הוּ הַנֶּחֱלָמִ֖י

v. 23. הַיּוֹדֵעַ ק׳

21. *Ahab . . . Zedekiah.* Nothing more is known of these men.

he shall slay them. They forfeited their lives because they issued messages to the Judeans in exile which were regarded as treason by the Babylonian king.

22. *a curse.* 'Their names would still be on men's lips, no longer as prophets, but in a gruesome formula of imprecation used by exiles to fellow-exiles' (Peake). A play on the name Kolaiah is to be detected: it is connected with *kelalah* (a curse) and the verb *kalah* (to roast).

roasted in the fire. Cf. the punishment in *the burning fiery furnace* designed for

Shadrach and his companions (Dan. iii. 20).

23. *vile deeds.* Hebrew *nebalah*, usually denoting a gross act of immorality (cf. Gen. xxxiv. 7; Deut. xxii. 21). This was a sin against God Who punished them by delivering them into the hand of Nebuchadnezzar as guilty of treasonous utterances, for which they paid the penalty of death by burning.

24. *the Nehelamite.* This may be a place or family name. Neither is otherwise known. Jeremiah's letter aroused bitter indignation in a leading captive who seeks to have him suppressed as a madman.

25. Thus speaketh the LORD of hosts, the God of Israel, saying: Because thou hast sent letters in thine own name unto all the people that are at Jerusalem, and to Zephaniah the son of Maaseiah the priest, and to all the priests, saying: 26. 'The LORD hath made thee priest in the stead of Jehoiada the priest, that there should be officers in the house of the LORD for every man that is mad, and maketh himself a prophet, that thou shouldest put him in the stocks and in the collar. 27. Now therefore, why hast thou not rebuked Jeremiah of Anathoth, who maketh himself a prophet to you, 28. forasmuch as he hath sent unto us in Babylon, saying: The captivity is long; build ye houses, and dwell in them; and plant gardens, and eat the fruit of them?' 29. And Zephaniah the priest read this letter in the ears of Jeremiah the

25 תֹּאמֶר לֵאמֹר : כֹּה־אָמַ֞ר
יְהֹוָה צְבָאוֹת אֱלֹהֵי יִשְׂרָאֵל
לֵאמֹר יַעַן אֲשֶׁר אַתָּה שָׁלַחְתָּ
בְשִׁמְכָה סְפָרִים אֶל־כָּל־
הָעָם אֲשֶׁר בִּירוּשָׁלַ֫ם וְאֶל־
צְפַנְיָה בֶן־מַעֲשֵׂיָה הַכֹּהֵן
וְאֶל־כָּל־הַכֹּהֲנִים לֵאמֹר :
26 יְהֹוָה נְתָנְךָ כֹהֵן תַּחַת יְהוֹיָדָע
הַכֹּהֵן לִהְיוֹת פְּקִדִים בֵּית
יְהֹוָה לְכָל־אִישׁ מְשֻׁגָּע
וּמִתְנַבֵּא וְנָתַתָּה אֹתוֹ אֶל־
הַמַּהְפֶּכֶת וְאֶל־הַצִּינֹק :
27 וְעַתָּה לָמָּה לֹא גָעַרְתָּ
בְיִרְמְיָהוּ הָעֲנְתֹתִי הַמִּתְנַבֵּא
28 לָכֶם : כִּי עַל־כֵּן שָׁלַח אֵלֵינוּ
בָּבֶל לֵאמֹר אֲרֻכָּה הִיא בְּנוּ
בָתִּים וְשֵׁבוּ וְנִטְעוּ גַנּוֹת וְאִכְלוּ
29 אֶת־פְּרִיהֶן : וַיִּקְרָא צְפַנְיָה
הַכֹּהֵן אֶת־הַסֵּפֶר הַזֶּה

v. 25. יתיר ה'

25. *in thine own name.* Without God's authority; this is Jeremiah's indictment. Shemaiah, of course, claimed that he was speaking in God's name.

Zephaniah. See on xxi. 1.

26. *thee.* Zephaniah. Verses 26-28 give the text of Shemaiah's letter.

Jehoiada. He *appointed officers over the house of the LORD* (2 Kings xi. 18) to maintain order there and suppress disturbances.

mad, and maketh himself a prophet. Binns quotes 2 Kings ix. 11, *wherefore came this mad fellow to thee?* and remarks, 'Eastern peoples, even to the present day, look upon madmen as in some sense inspired.'

the stocks. See on xx. 2.

the collar. Which kept the head fixed in the stocks.

29. *read this letter,* etc. Zephaniah was evidently in sympathy with the prophet.

prophet. 30. Then came the word of the LORD unto Jeremiah, saying: 31. Send to all them of the captivity, saying: Thus saith the LORD concerning Shemaiah the Nehelamite: Because that Shemaiah hath prophesied unto you, and I sent him not, and he hath caused you to trust in a lie; 32. therefore thus saith the LORD: Behold, I will punish Shemaiah the Nehelamite, and his seed; he shall not have a man to dwell among this people, neither shall he behold the good that I will do unto My people, saith the LORD; because he hath spoken perversion against the LORD.

30 בְּאָזְנֵי יִרְמְיָהוּ הַנָּבִיא: וַיְהִי
דְבַר־יְהֹוָה אֶל־יִרְמְיָהוּ
31 לֵאמֹר: שְׁלַח עַל־כָּל־
הַגּוֹלָה לֵאמֹר כֹּה אָמַר יְהֹוָה
אֶל־שְׁמַעְיָה הַנֶּחֱלָמִי יַעַן
אֲשֶׁר נִבָּא לָכֶם שְׁמַעְיָה וַאֲנִי
לֹא שְׁלַחְתִּיו וַיַּבְטַח אֶתְכֶם
32 עַל־שָׁקֶר: לָכֵן כֹּה־אָמַר
יְהֹוָה הִנְנִי פֹקֵד עַל־שְׁמַעְיָה
הַנֶּחֱלָמִי וְעַל־זַרְעוֹ לֹא־
יִהְיֶה לוֹ אִישׁ ׀ יוֹשֵׁב ׀ בְּתוֹךְ־
הָעָם הַזֶּה וְלֹא־יִרְאֶה בַטּוֹב
אֲשֶׁר־אֲנִי עֹשֶׂה־לְעַמִּי נְאֻם־
יְהֹוָה כִּי־סָרָה דִבֶּר עַל־
יְהֹוָה:

30　　　CHAPTER XXX　　ל

1. The word that came to Jeremiah from the LORD, saying: 2. 'Thus

1 הַדָּבָר אֲשֶׁר־הָיָה אֶל־
יִרְמְיָהוּ מֵאֵת יְהֹוָה לֵאמֹר:

Or, perhaps he read it as an indictment to Jeremiah who was able to convince him of the genuineness of his prophecy.

32. the good. The restoration of the people to their land. As Shemaiah could not in any case have experienced this event, which was to take place seventy years hence, it must be understood as referring to his descendants. They would be denied the happiness of returning to the ancestral home.

perversion. Hebrew *sarah*; see on xxviii. 16.

CHAPTER XXX
PROMISE OF NATIONAL RESTORATION

THE biographical chapters are interrupted by the insertion of xxx and xxxi which develop the theme of national restoration foretold at the end of the last chapter. In the main they take the exile for granted, and were apparently

speaketh the LORD, the God of
Israel, saying: Write thee all the
words that I have spoken unto thee
in a book. 3. For, lo, the days come,
saith the LORD, that I will turn the
captivity of My people Israel and
Judah, saith the LORD; and I will
cause them to return to the land
that I gave to their fathers, and they
shall possess it.'

4. And these are the words that
the LORD spoke concerning Israel
and concerning Judah. 5. For thus
saith the LORD:

We have heard a voice of trembling,

Of fear, and not of peace.

6 Ask ye now, and see

2 כֹּה־אָמַ֞ר יְהֹוָ֧ה אֱלֹהֵ֛י יִשְׂרָאֵ֖ל
לֵאמֹ֑ר כְּתָב־לְךָ֗ אֵ֣ת כָּל־
הַדְּבָרִ֛ים אֲשֶׁר־דִּבַּ֥רְתִּי
3 אֵלֶ֖יךָ אֶל־סֵֽפֶר׃ כִּ֣י הִנֵּ֣ה
יָמִ֤ים בָּאִים֙ נְאֻם־יְהֹוָ֔ה וְשַׁבְתִּ֗י
אֶת־שְׁב֛וּת עַמִּ֥י יִשְׂרָאֵ֖ל
וִֽיהוּדָה֙ אָמַ֣ר יְהֹוָ֔ה וַהֲשִׁבֹתִ֗ים
אֶל־הָאָ֛רֶץ אֲשֶׁר־נָתַ֥תִּי
4 לַאֲבוֹתָ֖ם וִֽירֵשֽׁוּהָ׃ וְאֵ֣לֶּה
הַדְּבָרִ֗ים אֲשֶׁ֨ר דִּבֶּ֧ר יְהֹוָ֛ה
אֶל־יִשְׂרָאֵ֖ל וְאֶל־יְהוּדָֽה׃
5 כִּי־כֹה֙ אָמַ֣ר יְהֹוָ֔ה
ק֥וֹל חֲרָדָ֖ה שָׁמָ֑עְנוּ
פַּ֖חַד וְאֵ֥ין שָׁלֽוֹם׃
6 שַׁאֲלוּ־נָ֣א וּרְא֗וּ

written after the overthrow of Judah
(verse 18). The prophet had a twofold
duty: (i) to tell of impending disaster
consequent upon national sin; (ii) to
offer comfort and hope for the future
when the catastrophe had occurred.
There is nothing contradictory in the
two tasks; for as he has to be stern with
sinners and impress upon them the
inevitable consequences of their evil, so,
with the same goal of national amend-
ment in view, he reassures the people
that they can be raised from their
degradation since repentance is always
within their power. Passages such as
this demonstrate the falsity of the
popular conception of Jeremiah as a
pessimist. On the contrary, he was a
realistic optimist, clearly seeing the doom
which the Judeans were bringing upon
themselves, and yet certain of their
ultimate recovery.

1-4 INTRODUCTORY

2. *write thee all the words . . . in a book.*
The implication is that the oracle which
follows forms a special and distinct
prophecy, to be written in a separate
book or scroll.

3. *Israel and Judah.* The restoration of
the whole nation of twelve tribes was the
prophetic ideal and hope.

5-9 THE NATION'S YOKE WILL BE BROKEN

5. *we have heard . . . peace.* This is a
quotation of the people's words, a phrase
like 'ye say' being understood before it.
The verse expresses the popular fear
and insecurity. It is followed by words
of Divine assurance.

6. The gestures which the men display
in their anguish are comparable with the
throes of a woman in childbirth.

Whether a man doth travail with
child;
Wherefore do I see every man
With his hands on his loins, as a
woman in travail,
And all faces are turned into
paleness?

7 Alas! for that day is great,
So that none is like it;
And it is a time of trouble unto
Jacob,
But out of it shall he be saved.

8 And it shall come to pass in that
day,
Saith the LORD of hosts,
That I will break his yoke from
off thy neck,
And will burst thy bands;
And strangers shall no more make
him their bondman;

9 But they shall serve the LORD their
God,
And David their king,
Whom I will raise up unto them.

10 Therefore fear thou not, O Jacob
My servant, saith the LORD;

אִם־יֵ֖לֶד זָכָ֑ר
מַדּ֗וּעַ רָאִ֙יתִי֙ כָל־גֶּ֔בֶר
יָדָ֤יו עַל־חֲלָצָיו֙ כַּיֹּ֣ולֵדָ֔ה
וְנֶהֶפְכ֥וּ כָל־פָּנִ֖ים לְיֵרָקֹֽון׃
7 הֹ֗וי כִּ֥י גָדֹ֛ול הַיֹּ֥ום הַה֖וּא
מֵאַ֣יִן כָּמֹ֑הוּ
וְעֵֽת־צָרָ֥ה הִיא֙ לְיַֽעֲקֹ֔ב
וּמִמֶּ֖נָּה יִוָּשֵֽׁעַ׃
8 וְהָיָה֩ בַיֹּ֨ום הַה֜וּא
נְאֻ֣ם ׀ יְהֹוָ֣ה צְבָאֹ֗ות
אֶשְׁבֹּ֤ר עֻלֹּו֙ מֵעַ֣ל צַוָּארֶ֔ךָ
וּמֹוסְרֹותֶ֖יךָ אֲנַתֵּ֑ק
וְלֹא־יַעַבְדוּ־בֹ֥ו עֹ֖וד זָרִֽים׃
9 וְעָ֣בְד֔וּ אֵ֖ת יְהֹוָ֣ה אֱלֹהֵיהֶ֑ם
וְאֵת֙ דָּוִ֣ד מַלְכָּ֔ם
אֲשֶׁ֥ר אָקִ֖ים לָהֶֽם׃
10 וְאַתָּ֞ה אַל־תִּירָ֤א
עַבְדִּ֤י יַֽעֲקֹב֙ נְאֻם־יְהֹוָ֔ה

---

7. *that day is great.* The day ushering
in the final deliverance will be great in
suffering and distress. *Day* in such a
connection means a period of time.
Jacob. A designation often used by the
prophets for the nation of Israel.
shall he be saved. This line strikes the note
of confidence in the future which is
distinctive of the two chapters.

8. The change from the third to the
second person in this verse is not unusual
in Biblical literature.
his yoke. The yoke of *strangers* upon
Israel.
bands. See on xxvii. 2.

9. *the LORD their God, and David their
king.* This is the true corollary to their
no longer serving strangers. They
would reach the highest form of liberty
for them, viz. the service of the LORD.
His Messianic regent on earth would be
a scion of the house of David (cf. Ezek.
xxxiv. 23; Hos. iii. 5).

10-11 GOD IS THEIR REDEEMER

Verse 10 is repeated almost *verbatim* in
xlvi. 27 and verse 11 is echoed in xlvi. 28.

10. *O Jacob My servant.* A designation
of the people frequently used in the
second part of Isaiah.

Neither be dismayed, O Israel;
For, lo, I will save thee from afar,
And thy seed from the land of
   their captivity;
And Jacob shall again be quiet
   and at ease,
And none shall make him afraid.

11 For I am with thee, saith the
   LORD, to save thee;
For I will make a full end of all
   the nations whither I have
   scattered thee,
But I will not make a full end of
   thee;
For I will correct thee in
   measure,
And will not utterly destroy thee.

12 For thus saith the LORD:
Thy hurt is incurable,
And thy wound is grievous.

13 None deemeth of thy wound that
   it may be bound up;

וְאַל־תֵּחַת יִשְׂרָאֵל
כִּי הִנְנִי מוֹשִׁיעֲךָ מֵרָחוֹק
וְאֶת־זַרְעֲךָ מֵאֶרֶץ שִׁבְיָם
וְשָׁב יַעֲקֹב וְשָׁקַט וְשַׁאֲנַן
וְאֵין מַחֲרִיד׃
11 כִּי־אִתְּךָ אֲנִי
נְאֻם־יְהֹוָה לְהוֹשִׁיעֶךָ
כִּי אֶעֱשֶׂה כָלָה בְּכָל־הַגּוֹיִם ׀
אֲשֶׁר הֲפִצוֹתִיךָ שָּׁם
אַךְ אֹתְךָ לֹא־אֶעֱשֶׂה כָלָה
וְיִסַּרְתִּיךָ לַמִּשְׁפָּט
וְנַקֵּה לֹא אֲנַקֶּךָּ׃
12 כִּי כֹה אָמַר יְהֹוָה
אָנוּשׁ לְשִׁבְרֵךְ
נַחְלָה מַכָּתֵךְ׃
13 אֵין־דָּן דִּינֵךְ לְמָזוֹר

---

from afar. The land of exile, no matter
how distant it be.

11. *for I will make a full end of all the
nations.* This judgment is not pronounced in a spirit of partiality or
vindictiveness. Israel alone of all those
peoples possessed the recuperative power
which enabled him to attain, through
exile and suffering, to spiritual and
national regeneration. Not so the others,
and a people that is irremediably corrupt
must sooner or later perish. History
has amply corroborated this prophecy:
the great nations of antiquity, including
those which drove Israel into exile, have
disappeared, whereas he has suffered
'correction' but lives.

I will correct thee in measure. See on
x. 24 for *in measure.* Divine justice

demands that Israel's sin shall not go
unpunished; but he obtains pardon after
being 'corrected.'

12-17 THEY WHO AFFLICTED
ISRAEL WILL BE PUNISHED

The pronouns in this section are in the
feminine as referring to the nation as a
whole.

12. Jeremiah used somewhat similar
language of himself in xv. 18.

13. *none deemeth of thy wound,* etc. A.J.
reproduces the sense: the hurt done to
thee. A.V. and R.V. render more
literally: 'There is none to plead thy
cause, that thou mayest be bound up.'

Thou hast no healing medicines.

14 All thy lovers have forgotten
thee,
They seek thee not;
For I have wounded thee with
the wound of an enemy,
With the chastisement of a cruel
one;
For the greatness of thine
iniquity,
Because thy sins were increased.

15 Why criest thou for thy hurt,
That thy pain is incurable?
For the greatness of thine iniquity, because thy sins were
increased,
I have done these things unto
thee.

16 Therefore all they that devour
thee shall be devoured,
And all thine adversaries, every
one of them, shall go into
captivity;
And they that spoil thee shall be
a spoil,
And all that prey upon thee will
I give for a prey.

17 For I will restore health unto
thee,
And I will heal thee of thy
wounds, saith the LORD;
Because they have called thee an
outcast:
'She is Zion, there is none that
careth for her.'

רְפֻאוֹת תְּעָלָה אֵין לָךְ׃

14 כָּל־מְאַהֲבַיִךְ שְׁכֵחוּךְ
אוֹתָךְ לֹא יִדְרֹשׁוּ
כִּי מַכַּת אוֹיֵב הִכִּיתִיךְ
מוּסַר אַכְזָרִי
עַל רֹב עֲוֺנֵךְ
עָצְמוּ חַטֹּאתָיִךְ׃

15 מַה־תִּזְעַק עַל־שִׁבְרֵךְ
אָנוּשׁ מַכְאֹבֵךְ
עַל ׀ רֹב עֲוֺנֵךְ עָצְמוּ חַטֹּאתַיִךְ
עָשִׂיתִי אֵלֶּה לָךְ׃

16 לָכֵן כָּל־אֹכְלַיִךְ יֵאָכֵלוּ
וְכָל־צָרַיִךְ כֻּלָּם בַּשְּׁבִי יֵלֵכוּ
וְהָיוּ שֹׁאסַיִךְ לִמְשִׁסָּה
וְכָל־בֹּזְזַיִךְ אֶתֵּן לָבַז׃

17 כִּי אַעֲלֶה אֲרֻכָה לָךְ
וּמִמַּכּוֹתַיִךְ אֶרְפָּאֵךְ
נְאֻם־יְהֹוָה
כִּי נִדָּחָה קָרְאוּ לָךְ
צִיּוֹן הִיא דֹּרֵשׁ אֵין לָהּ׃

v. 16. יתיר א׳

---

14. *thy lovers.* See on xxii. 20. When
Israel was still in his country, his allies
proved but broken reeds. Now that he
is in exile, they have forgotten him.

an enemy . . . a cruel one. An anthropomorphism: so severely had they been
smitten, that it might have been thought
that God had become their harsh and
implacable foe.

15. *why criest thou . . . incurable?* The
sufferings have not been without cause;

they are the consequence of national sin
16. *therefore.* Because God's justice ha
gone to the length of afflicting Israel s
severely, his tormentors also will receiv
condign punishment.
and they that spoil thee, etc. On th
principle of measure for measure.
17. *I will restore health unto thee.* Se
on viii. 22.
she is Zion. Ill-wishers connected th
name Zion with *tsiyyah,* 'a desert.'

18 Thus saith the LORD:
Behold, I will turn the captivity
of Jacob's tents,
And have compassion on his
dwelling-places;
And the city shall be builded
upon her own mound,
And the palace shall be inhabited upon its wonted place.
19 And out of them shall proceed
thanksgiving
And the voice of them that make
merry;
And I will multiply them, and
they shall not be diminished,
I will also increase them, and
they shall not dwindle away.
20 Their children also shall be as
aforetime,
And their congregation shall be
established before Me,
And I will punish all that oppress
them.
21 And their prince shall be of
themselves,
And their ruler shall proceed
from the midst of them;
And I will cause him to draw
near, and he shall approach
unto Me;
For who is he that hath pledged
his heart
To approach unto Me? saith the
LORD.

18 כֹּה ׀ אָמַר יְהֹוָה
הִנְנִי־שָׁב שְׁבוּת אָהֳלֵי יַעֲקוֹב
וּמִשְׁכְּנֹתָיו אֲרַחֵם
וְנִבְנְתָה עִיר עַל־תִּלָּהּ
וְאַרְמוֹן עַל־מִשְׁפָּטוֹ יֵשֵׁב:
19 וְיָצָא מֵהֶם תּוֹדָה
וְקוֹל מְשַׂחֲקִים
וְהִרְבִּתִים וְלֹא יִמְעָטוּ
וְהִכְבַּדְתִּים וְלֹא יִצְעָרוּ:
20 וְהָיוּ בָנָיו כְּקֶדֶם
וַעֲדָתוֹ לְפָנַי תִּכּוֹן
וּפָקַדְתִּי עַל כָּל־לֹחֲצָיו:
21 וְהָיָה אַדִּירוֹ מִמֶּנּוּ
וּמשְׁלוֹ מִקִּרְבּוֹ יֵצֵא
וְהִקְרַבְתִּיו וְנִגַּשׁ אֵלַי
כִּי מִי הוּא־זֶה עָרַב אֶת־לִבּוֹ
לָגֶשֶׁת אֵלַי נְאֻם־יְהֹוָה:

v. 18. ר מלא י

18-22 JERUSALEM WILL BE
REBUILT AND HAPPY

18. his dwelling-places. Which are now
desolate.

her own mound. i.e. on the original site.
Cities were often built on hills or mounds
(Hebrew tel), to guard against a sudden
surprise attack. Hence the frequency of
tel' as part of a place name; e.g. Telassar
(2 Kings xix. 12), Tel-abib (Ezek. iii. 15),
Tel-melah and Tel-harsha (Ezra ii. 59).
Driver (Schweich Lectures, p. 41) points
out that a 'tel' was not an ordinary hill,
out raised ground of which the upper
part at least consisted of a mass of ruins.
the palace. Probably an allusion to the
Temple.

19. thanksgiving. Cf. xxxiii. 11.

20. as aforetime. In the Golden Age of
David and Solomon.

shall be established before Me. God will
watch over and guard them.

21. of themselves . . . from the midst of
them. They will no longer be subject to
foreign rule.

I will cause him to draw near. 'This
ruler will stand in the most intimate
relations with God, to Whom indeed he
will act as priest' (Peake).

for who is he, etc. The clause is of
uncertain meaning. A.V. has 'for who
is this that engaged his heart to approach

201

22 And ye shall be My people,
   And I will be your God.

23 Behold, a storm of the LORD is
   gone forth in fury,
   A sweeping storm;
   It shall whirl upon the head of
   the wicked.

24 The fierce anger of the LORD
   shall not return,
   Until He have executed, and till
   He have performed
   The purposes of His heart;
   In the end of days ye shall
   consider it.

25 At that time, saith the LORD,
   Will I be the God of all the
   families of Israel,
   And they shall be My people.

22 וִהְיִיתֶם לִי לְעָם
וְאָנֹכִי אֶהְיֶה לָכֶם לֵאלֹהִים:
23 הִנֵּה | סַעֲרַת יְהֹוָה חֵמָה יָצְאָה
סַעַר מִתְגּוֹרֵר
עַל רֹאשׁ רְשָׁעִים יָחוּל:
24 לֹא יָשׁוּב חֲרוֹן אַף־יְהֹוָה
עַד־עֲשֹׂתוֹ וְעַד־הֲקִימוֹ
מְזִמּוֹת לִבּוֹ
בְּאַחֲרִית הַיָּמִים תִּתְבּוֹנְנוּ בָהּ:
25 בָּעֵת הַהִיא נְאֻם־יְהֹוָה
אֶהְיֶה לֵאלֹהִים
לְכֹל מִשְׁפְּחוֹת יִשְׂרָאֵל
וְהֵמָּה יִהְיוּ־לִי לְעָם:

---

31   CHAPTER XXXI   לא

1 Thus saith the LORD:
   The people that were left of the
   sword
   Have found grace in the wilderness,

1 כֹּה אָמַר יְהֹוָה
מָצָא חֵן בַּמִּדְבָּר
עַם שְׂרִידֵי חָרֶב

---

v. 25. בנ״א כאן תחלת סימן ל״א   v. 1. הפטרה ליום שני של ר״ה

---

unto Me?'; R.V., 'for who is he that
hath had boldness to approach unto
Me?', and the margin gives the literal
equivalent of the Hebrew, 'hath been
surety for his heart.' Basing himself on
the last mentioned, Pickering gives this
interpretation: 'God Himself, Who has
taken the ruler into closest relations, is
the guarantor of this ideal ruler's
character and excellence.' Accordingly
the answer implied in the question is,
'None other than God.'

23-25 GOD'S JUDGMENT WILL BE
   EXECUTED UPON THE WICKED
These verses are almost identical with
xxiii. 19f. The general sense here is

that the punishment of the wicked,
whether of the oppressive nations or of
the sinners in Israel is uncertain, will
precede the restoration of Israel.

25. In the English Version this verse
begins chapter xxxi. It properly rounds
off chapter xxx and belongs there.

families. Clans; the tribes.

CHAPTER XXXI
1-21 PROMISED RESTORATION OF
THE NORTHERN KINGDOM

1. *that were left of the sword.* The
survivors of the carnage which accompanied the overthrow of the Northern

Even Israel, when I go to cause
him to rest.

2 'From afar the LORD appeared
unto me.'
'Yea, I have loved thee with an
everlasting love;
Therefore with affection have I
drawn thee.

3 Again will I build thee, and thou
shalt be built,
O virgin of Israel;
Again shalt thou be adorned with
thy tabrets,
And shalt go forth in the dances
of them that make merry.

4 Again shalt thou plant vineyards
upon the mountains of Samaria;
The planters shall plant, and shall
have the use thereof.

הָלֹ֖וךְ לְהַרְגִּיע֥וֹ יִשְׂרָאֵֽל׃

2 מֵרָח֕וֹק יְהֹוָ֖ה נִרְאָ֣ה לִ֑י
וְאַהֲבַ֤ת עוֹלָם֙ אֲהַבְתִּ֔יךְ
עַל־כֵּ֖ן מְשַׁכְתִּ֥יךְ חָֽסֶד׃

3 ע֤וֹד אֶבְנֵךְ֙ וְֽנִבְנֵ֔ית
בְּתוּלַ֖ת יִשְׂרָאֵ֑ל
ע֚וֹד תַּעְדִּ֣י תֻפַּ֔יִךְ
וְיָצָ֖את בִּמְח֥וֹל מְשַׂחֲקִֽים׃

4 ע֚וֹד תִּטְּעִ֣י כְרָמִ֔ים
בְּהָרֵ֖י שֹֽׁמְר֑וֹן
נָטְע֥וּ נֹטְעִ֖ים וְחִלֵּֽלוּ׃

Kingdom. The use of this phrase discounts the interpretation that the prophet is alluding to the exodus from Egypt.

the wilderness. The land of their exile. They will find favour in God's eyes. The verbs are in the prophetic past, although applying to the future.

Israel. The Ten Tribes of the north.

cause him to rest. When God restores him to his land. An alternative rendering, given in R.V. margin, is: 'When he (Israel) went to find him rest.'

2. *'from afar . . . me.'* 'Yea,' etc. A.J. puts the two clauses into separate inverted commas, thus dividing the verse into two distinct utterances: the people in distant exile proclaim that God appeared to them from afar, from the land of Israel, and God replies that this is so, because *I have loved thee with an everlasting love.* Another possibility is to understand the word 'saying' before *Yea, I have loved thee,* which makes Israel quote the Divine declaration of love.

have I drawn thee. Towards Me in the former relationship which was interrupted by the captivity. Cf. for the use of the verb in this sense, Hos. xi. 4.

3. *build.* Not only literally, but in the more general sense of 'restore thy fortunes' (cf. xii. 16).

O virgin of Israel. Although others have had dominion over thee, yet thou art as beloved to Me as an unsullied virgin.

tabrets. Cf. Exod. xv. 20. Peake well observes, 'This idyllic picture deserves to be made prominent in any estimate of Jeremiah; it is one of many indications that he was no sour and morose enemy of recreation and merriment.'

4. *shall have the use thereof* (chillelu). For the first three years the fruit borne by a tree was termed *orlah,* lit. 'uncircumcised,' i.e. forbidden. In the fourth year it might be eaten, but only as 'holy' food in Jerusalem. But if it was too burdensome to carry, it was redeemed and its value spent there. The verb *chillel* is the technical term for such redemption (cf. Lev. xix. 23-25; Deut. xx. 6; in the last mentioned verse the verb *chillel* occurs).

5 For there shall be a day,
That the watchmen shall call upon
the mount Ephraim:
Arise ye, and let us go up to Zion,
Unto the LORD our God.'

6 For thus saith the LORD:
Sing with gladness for Jacob,
And shout at the head of the
nations;
Announce ye, praise ye, and say:
'O LORD, save Thy people,
The remnant of Israel.'

7 Behold, I will bring them from the
north country,
And gather them from the uttermost parts of the earth,
And with them the blind and the
lame,
The woman with child and her
that travaileth with child together;
A great company shall they
return hither.

8 They shall come with weeping,
And with supplications will I lead
them;

כִּי יֶשׁ־יוֹם 5
קָרְאוּ נֹצְרִים בְּהַר אֶפְרָיִם
קוּמוּ וְנַעֲלֶה צִיּוֹן
אֶל־יְהֹוָה אֱלֹהֵינוּ:

כִּי־כֹה ׀ אָמַר יְהֹוָה 6
רָנּוּ לְיַעֲקֹב שִׂמְחָה
וְצַהֲלוּ בְּרֹאשׁ הַגּוֹיִם
הַשְׁמִיעוּ הַלְלוּ וְאִמְרוּ
הוֹשַׁע יְהֹוָה אֶת־עַמְּךָ
אֵת שְׁאֵרִית יִשְׂרָאֵל:

הִנְנִי מֵבִיא אוֹתָם מֵאֶרֶץ צָפוֹן 7
וְקִבַּצְתִּים מִיַּרְכְּתֵי־אָרֶץ
בָּם עִוֵּר וּפִסֵּחַ
הָרָה וְיֹלֶדֶת יַחְדָּו
קָהָל גָּדוֹל יָשׁוּבוּ הֵנָּה:

בִּבְכִי יָבֹאוּ 8
וּבְתַחֲנוּנִים אוֹבִילֵם

קמץ בסגולתא v. 7.

---

5. the watchmen. Who give the signal for the pilgrimage. Probably there were watch-towers by the cities on the route from Samaria to Jerusalem. As the watchmen saw the procession of pilgrims from the more distant cities approaching, they gave the signal to their own pilgrims to make ready to join the band.

to Zion. An indication that the breach between Samaria and Judea will have been healed, and Jerusalem resume its rightful place as the religious centre of a reunited Israelite nation.

6. praise ye, and say: 'O LORD, save Thy people.' Praise ye (Hebrew hallelu) probably refers to the liturgical recitation of

God's praises in religious worship (cf. Ps. cxviii. 25 which forms part of what is known in the Jewish liturgy as 'Hallel').

7. the north country. See on iii. 12.

the uttermost parts of the earth. All places where the Ten Tribes had been dispersed.

the blind, etc. Even those for whom the journey would be difficult will be brought back.

8. with weeping . . . with supplications. Their redemption will be consummated through the tears and prayers of a penitent people.

I will cause them to walk by
rivers of waters,
In a straight way wherein they
shall not stumble;
For I am become a father to
Israel,
And Ephraim is My first-
born.

9 Hear the word of the LORD, O
ye nations,
And declare it in the isles afar
off, and say:
'He that scattered Israel doth
gather him,
And keep him, as a shepherd
doth his flock.'

10 For the LORD hath ransomed
Jacob,
And He redeemeth him from the
hand of him that is stronger
than he.

11 And they shall come and sing in
the height of Zion,
And shall flow unto the goodness
of the LORD,
To the corn, and to the wine,
and to the oil,
And to the young of the flock
and of the herd;
And their soul shall be as a
watered garden,

אֹולִיכֵם אֶל־נַחֲלֵי מַיִם
בְּדֶרֶךְ יָשָׁר לֹא יִכָּשְׁלוּ בָּהּ
כִּי־הָיִיתִי לְיִשְׂרָאֵל לְאָב
וְאֶפְרַיִם בְּכֹרִי הוּא׃

9 שִׁמְעוּ דְבַר־יְהוָֹה גֹּויִם
וְהַגִּידוּ בָאִיִּים מִמֶּרְחָק
וְאִמְרוּ מְזָרֵה יִשְׂרָאֵל יְקַבְּצֶנּוּ
וּשְׁמָרֹו כְּרֹעֶה עֶדְרֹו׃

10 כִּי־פָדָה יְהוָֹה אֶת־יַעֲקֹב
וּגְאָלֹו מִיַּד חָזָק מִמֶּנּוּ׃

11 וּבָאוּ וְרִנְּנוּ בִמְרֹום־צִיֹּון
וְנָהֲרֹו אֶל־טוּב יְהוָֹה
עַל־דָּגָן וְעַל־תִּירֹשׁ
וְעַל־יִצְהָר
וְעַל־בְּנֵי־צֹאן וּבָקָר
וְהָיְתָה נַפְשָׁם כְּגַן רָוֶה

v. 11. מלעיל

I will cause . . . waters. God will guide
them like a shepherd who leads his flocks
to a river to quench their thirst.

*a father to Israel, and Ephraim is My
first-born.* It is doubtful whether priority
is intended in the clause. The under-
lying thought is rather God's love for
both sections of His people: *Israel*, i.e.
the Kingdom of Judah, and *Ephraim*, a
designation for the Northern Kingdom.
It need not, therefore, be assumed, as
some suppose, that the verse exalts the
tribe of Ephraim over that of Judah.

9. the isles. See on xxv. 22.

He that scattered Israel. The peoples
who drove the two Kingdoms into
captivity acted as God's agents.

as a shepherd doth his flock. A simile

conveying the idea of great tenderness
(cf. Isa. xl. 11).

10. hath ransomed. The prophetic perfect.

from the hand, etc. This is proof that
the redemption is the effect of Divine
intervention.

11. shall flow unto. The verb has been
explained as denoting either that the
population will stream into Jerusalem to
celebrate a feast in gratitude for their
prosperity; or they will return home from
Zion to enjoy their abundance. Ehrlich
suggests that the verb means here 'they
will beam (with joy) at.'

goodness. i.e. the bounty.

as a watered garden. Cf. Isa. lviii. 11.

And they shall not pine any more
at all.

12 Then shall the virgin rejoice in
the dance,
And the young men and the old
together;
For I will turn their mourning
into joy,
And will comfort them, and make
them rejoice from their sorrow.

13 And I will satiate the soul of the
priests with fatness,
And My people shall be satisfied
with My goodness,
Saith the LORD.

14 Thus saith the LORD:
A voice is heard in Ramah,
Lamentation, and bitter weeping,
Rachel weeping for her children;
She refuseth to be comforted for
her children,
Because they are not.

15 Thus saith the LORD:
Refrain thy voice from weeping,

וְלֹא־יוֹסִ֥יפוּ לְדַאֲבָ֖ה עֽוֹד׃

12 אָ֣ז תִּשְׂמַ֤ח בְּתוּלָה֙ בְּמָח֔וֹל
וּבַחֻרִ֥ים וּזְקֵנִ֖ים יַחְדָּ֑ו
וְהָפַכְתִּ֨י אֶבְלָ֤ם לְשָׂשׂוֹן֙
וְנִֽחַמְתִּ֔ים וְשִׂמַּחְתִּ֖ים מִיגוֹנָֽם׃

13 וְרִוֵּיתִ֛י נֶ֥פֶשׁ הַכֹּהֲנִ֖ים דָּ֑שֶׁן
וְעַמִּ֥י אֶת־טוּבִ֖י יִשְׂבָּ֑עוּ
נְאֻם־יְהֹוָֽה׃

14 כֹּ֣ה ׀ אָמַ֣ר יְהֹוָ֗ה
ק֣וֹל בְּרָמָ֤ה נִשְׁמָע֙
נְהִי֙ בְּכִ֣י תַמְרוּרִ֔ים
רָחֵ֖ל מְבַכָּ֣ה עַל־בָּנֶ֑יהָ
מֵאֲנָ֛ה לְהִנָּחֵ֥ם עַל־בָּנֶ֖יהָ
כִּ֥י אֵינֶֽנּוּ׃

15 כֹּ֣ה ׀ אָמַ֣ר יְהֹוָ֗ה
מִנְעִ֤י קוֹלֵךְ֙ מִבֶּ֔כִי

v. 13. קמץ בטרחא

In a country where water is scarce, the
phrase is expressive of the highest good
and contentment.

shall not pine. As they had done in
captivity.

12. The dancing may be a general term
for rejoicing in the happy state of the
land, or apply more particularly to the
vintage festivals.

13. *I will satiate.* So many sacrifices will
be brought that the priests, to whom
belonged *the breast of waving and the
thigh of heaving* (Lev. vii. 34), will have
all their needs abundantly supplied.

the soul. The Hebrew term *nephesh*
frequently denotes the seat of desire, the
appetite.

14. *Ramah.* Between Gibeon and
Beeroth (Josh. xviii. 25), five miles north
of Jerusalem.

Rachel weeping for her children. Rachel,
an ancestress of a section of the Israelite
people, who had so longed for children
as to regard herself as dead without them
(Gen. xxx. 1), now weeps that they are
no more, slain or driven into exile.
Ramah is mentioned because her tomb
was in its vicinity. According to an
ancient Jewish legend, Jacob intentionally buried her there by the road-side,
because he foresaw that his descendants
would pass by on the way to exile and
she would weep and intercede for them.
Rashi and Metsudath David interpret:
'A voice is heard on high': Rachel's
lamentation has ascended to the heights
of heaven.

And thine eyes from tears;
For thy work shall be rewarded,
saith the LORD;
And they shall come back from
the land of the enemy.

16 And there is hope for thy future,
saith the LORD;
And thy children shall return to
their own border.

17 I have surely heard Ephraim
bemoaning himself:
'Thou hast chastised me, and I
was chastised,
As a calf untrained;
Turn Thou me, and I shall be
turned,
For Thou art the LORD my God.

18 Surely after that I was turned,
I repented,
And after that I was instructed,
I smote upon my thigh;
I was ashamed, yea, even con-
founded,

וְעֵינַיִךְ מִדִּמְעָה
כִּי יֵשׁ שָׂכָר לִפְעֻלָּתֵךְ
נְאֻם־יְהֹוָה
וְשָׁבוּ מֵאֶרֶץ אוֹיֵב׃
16 וְיֵשׁ־תִּקְוָה לְאַחֲרִיתֵךְ
נְאֻם־יְהֹוָה
וְשָׁבוּ בָנִים לִגְבוּלָם׃
17 שָׁמוֹעַ שָׁמַעְתִּי
אֶפְרַיִם מִתְנוֹדֵד
יִסַּרְתַּנִי וָאִוָּסֵר
כְּעֵגֶל לֹא לֻמָּד
הֲשִׁבֵנִי וְאָשׁוּבָה
כִּי אַתָּה יְהֹוָה אֱלֹהָי׃
18 כִּי־אַחֲרֵי שׁוּבִי נִחַמְתִּי
וְאַחֲרֵי הִוָּדְעִי
סָפַקְתִּי עַל־יָרֵךְ
בֹּשְׁתִּי וְגַם־נִכְלַמְתִּי

15. *thy work.* i.e. the toil and care spent
in bearing and rearing her children.
Their exile seemed to make all this *work*
futile; but let her take comfort because
they will come back and revive their
national life.

16. *there is hope for thy future.* That has
been the sustaining thought in the long
night of the Jewish dispersion: hope,
amounting to conviction, of a restoration
to Zion.

17. *Ephraim.* The exiled Northern
Kingdom.

*Thou hast chastised me, and I was
chastised.* The people accepted their

chastisement as proof that they had
sinned and as Divine judgment upon
them. They have learned the lesson to
be derived from their experience.

a calf untrained. To wear the yoke,
undisciplined.

turn Thou me. Accordingly they pray
that God would help them to repent.

18. *I was turned.* The parallelism
suggests that the meaning is 'turned
from God.'

I smote upon my thigh. In contrition
(cf. Ezek. xxi. 17).

Because I did bear the reproach
of my youth.'

19 Is Ephraim a darling son unto
Me?

Is he a child that is dandled?

For as often as I speak of him,
I do earnestly remember him
still;

Therefore My heart yearneth for
him,

I will surely have compassion
upon him, saith the LORD.

20 Set thee up waymarks,
Make thee guide-posts;
Set thy heart toward the high-
way,

Even the way by which thou
wentest;

Return, O virgin of Israel,
Return to these thy cities.

21 How long wilt thou turn away
coyly,

כִּי נָשָׂאתִי חֶרְפַּת נְעוּרָי׃

19 הֲבֵן יַקִּיר לִי אֶפְרַיִם

אִם יֶלֶד שַׁעֲשֻׁעִים

כִּי־מִדֵּי דַבְּרִי בּוֹ

זָכֹר אֶזְכְּרֶנּוּ עוֹד

עַל־כֵּן הָמוּ מֵעַי לוֹ

רַחֵם אֲרַחֲמֶנּוּ נְאֻם־יְהֹוָה׃ ·

20 הַצִּיבִי לָךְ צִיֻּנִים

שִׂמִי לָךְ תַּמְרוּרִים

שִׁתִי לִבֵּךְ לַמְסִלָּה

דֶּרֶךְ הָלָכְתְּ

שׁוּבִי בְּתוּלַת יִשְׂרָאֵל

שֻׁבִי אֶל־עָרַיִךְ אֵלֶּה׃

21 עַד־מָתַי תִּתְחַמָּקִין

v. 19. ע״כ .20 v. הלכת ק'

---

the reproach of my youth. The wicked
deeds perpetrated in early nationhood
which are a *reproach* (disgrace).

19. It would be hard to surpass the
tender love which animates this verse.
is Ephraim a darling son unto Me? In
truth Ephraim has not so behaved that
God should regard him as such; yet His
thoughts are constantly turned to him
in yearning and compassion. 'The
picture is of course adapted to human
modes of thought and feeling, and
represents God as acting in the same way
in which a man would, when thinking
upon the ingratitude and rebellion of a
son, whom he nevertheless cannot but
continue to love' (Streane).
a child that is dandled. lit. 'a child of
delights,' one in whom his parent takes
intense pleasure.
earnestly remember him still. God is
mindful of the close relationship which
in the past had existed between them.

heart. lit. 'bowels,' the seat of the
emotions (cf. iv. 19).

20. *waymarks . . . guide-posts.* Mark
well the road you have travelled into
captivity, because by that road you will
return—a figure of speech emphasizing
the certainty of restoration. Binns comments: 'The Israelites are immediately to
begin to prepare for the return by
sending out pioneers to mark out the
way back to Palestine.'

thou wentest. So the *kerë*; but the
kethib means 'I went': wherever Israel
has gone, God has accompanied him
(Rashi).

O virgin of Israel. As in verse 3.
Though thou hast had many masters,
yet art thou beloved to Me as a virgin
bride.

21. *turn away coyly.* This translation is
questionable. The root *chamak* occurs

O thou backsliding daughter?
For the LORD hath created a new
   thing in the earth:
A woman shall court a man.

22 Thus saith the LORD of hosts,
   the God of Israel:
Yet again shall they use this
   speech
In the land of Judah and in the
   cities thereof,
When I shall turn their captivity:
'The LORD bless thee, O habita-
   tion of righteousness,
O mountain of holiness.'

23 And Judah and all the cities
   thereof
Shall dwell therein together:
The husbandmen, and they that
   go forth with flocks.

24 For I have satiated the weary
   soul,
And every pining soul have I
   replenished.

הַבַּת הַשּׁוֹבֵבָה
כִּי־בָרָא יְהֹוָה חֲדָשָׁה בָּאָרֶץ
נְקֵבָה תְּסוֹבֵב גָּבֶר:

22 כֹּה־אָמַר יְהֹוָה צְבָאוֹת
אֱלֹהֵי יִשְׂרָאֵל
עוֹד יֹאמְרוּ אֶת־הַדָּבָר הַזֶּה
בְּאֶרֶץ יְהוּדָה וּבְעָרָיו
בְּשׁוּבִי אֶת־שְׁבוּתָם
יְבָרֶכְךָ יְהֹוָה
נְוֵה־צֶדֶק הַר הַקֹּדֶשׁ:

23 וְיָשְׁבוּ בָהּ
יְהוּדָה וְכָל־עָרָיו יַחְדָּו
אִכָּרִים וְנָסְעוּ בַּעֵדֶר:

24 כִּי הִרְוֵיתִי נֶפֶשׁ עֲיֵפָה
וְכָל־נֶפֶשׁ דָּאֲבָה מִלֵּאתִי:

in Cant. v. 6, *my beloved had turned away*,
and the conjugation used in this verse
suggests 'turn hither and thither' (so
R.V.), expressive of uncertainty of action,
viz. whether to turn to God or not.

a woman shall court a man. Whatever
the meaning of this obscure clause may
be, it must indicate something that is
most unusual (*a new thing in the earth*).
A commonly accepted interpretation is
that, contrary to the normal procedure,
the woman will propose marriage to the
man she loves; and applied to the
context the sense is that Israel (the female)
will seek union with God. Closer to the
Hebrew verb is the explanation: 'a
female (by nature timid) will turn into a
man (i.e. manly in character, the Hebrew
being *geber* which indicates the *strength*
of the male). Hence, Israel will cease to
be hesitant in returning to God but will
be resolute.

22-25 PROMISED RESTORATION OF JUDAH

22. *yet again.* The words presuppose
that the Southern Kingdom is in a state
of desolation.

O habitation of righteousness, etc. Once
more will Judah be recognized as the
home of righteousness and holiness.

O mountain of holiness. The Temple
mount. The phrase is also used of
Jerusalem as a whole. With the verse,
cf. Zech. viii. 3.

23. *Judah . . . cities.* i.e. the population will *dwell therein*, in a land distinguished for righteousness and holiness.

and they that go forth. Kimchi renders:
'and they shall go about with the flocks,'
without fear of marauders.

24. *I have satiated.* The prophetic
perfect.

25 Upon this I awaked, and beheld;
And my sleep was sweet unto me.

26. Behold, the days come, saith the LORD, that I will sow the house of Israel and the house of Judah with the seed of man, and with the seed of beast. 27. And it shall come to pass, that like as I have watched over them to pluck up and to break down, and to overthrow and to destroy, and to afflict; so will I watch over them to build and to plant, saith the LORD.

28 In those days they shall say no more:
'The fathers have eaten sour grapes,
And the children's teeth are set on edge.'

29. But every one shall die for his own iniquity; every man that eateth

25 עַל־זֹאת הֱקִיצֹתִי וָאֶרְאֶה
וּשְׁנָתִי עָרְבָה לִּי׃

26 הִנֵּה יָמִים בָּאִים נְאֻם־יְהֹוָה
וְזָרַעְתִּי אֶת־בֵּית יִשְׂרָאֵל
וְאֶת־בֵּית יְהוּדָה זֶרַע אָדָם

27 וְזֶרַע בְּהֵמָה׃ וְהָיָה כַּאֲשֶׁר
שָׁקַדְתִּי עֲלֵיהֶם לִנְתוֹשׁ
וְלִנְתוֹץ וְלַהֲרֹס וּלְהַאֲבִיד
וּלְהָרֵעַ כֵּן אֶשְׁקֹד עֲלֵיהֶם
לִבְנוֹת וְלִנְטוֹעַ נְאֻם־יְהֹוָה׃

28 בַּיָּמִים הָהֵם לֹא־יֹאמְרוּ עוֹד
אָבוֹת אָכְלוּ בֹסֶר
וְשִׁנֵּי בָנִים תִּקְהֶינָה׃

29 כִּי אִם־אִישׁ בַּעֲוֹנוֹ יָמוּת כָּל־

25. *I.* The speaker is the prophet, who comments upon the vision of the future which he had just experienced. A sleep in which he beheld so glowing a prospect must indeed have been *sweet* to him.

I awaked. The vision came to him while he was in a trance of ecstasy, from which he now awoke.

26-33 A NEW COVENANT TO BE MADE WITH ISRAEL

26. *I will sow*, etc. In contrast to the present state of the land, sparsely populated and with few cattle in the fields, God will, as it were, sow the soil with seed which will produce men and cattle in abundance. Similar imagery is employed in Ezek. xxxvi. 9ff.

27. Cf. i. 10-12 to which the verse may have reference.

28f. The same proverb receives comment in Ezek. xviii. 2-4. No more will it be assumed that children are punished for the sins of their fathers, but there will be acknowledgment that when people are punished, it is for their own sins. This doctrine does not conflict with Exod. xx. 5. As Streane remarks, 'The punishment which succeeded to the accumulated iniquities of *the third and fourth generation* could be averted by repentance (*and showing mercy unto the thousandth generation*, etc.). The commandment, therefore, is in no way opposed to the words *every one shall die for his own iniquity*, words which express that juster view of the sins of *each* generation, younger as well as older, which was to succeed the complaining tone adopted by those blind to their own disobedience, and convinced that they, though innocent, were suffering only for their fathers' faults.'

the sour grapes, his teeth shall be set
on edge.

30. Behold, the days come, saith
the LORD, that I will make a new
covenant with the house of Israel,
and with the house of Judah;
31. not according to the covenant
that I made with their fathers in the
day that I took them by the hand to
bring them out of the land of
Egypt; forasmuch as they broke
My covenant, although I was a lord
over them, saith the LORD. 32. But
this is the covenant that I will make
with the house of Israel after those
days, saith the LORD, I will put
My law in their inward parts, and
in their heart will I write it; and
I will be their God, and they shall

הָאָדָם הָאֹכֵל הַבֹּסֶר תִּקְהֶינָה
30 שִׁנָּיו: הִנֵּה יָמִים בָּאִים נְאֻם־
יְהֹוָה וְכָרַתִּי אֶת־בֵּית יִשְׂרָאֵל
וְאֶת־בֵּית יְהוּדָה בְּרִית
31 חֲדָשָׁה: לֹא כַבְּרִית אֲשֶׁר
כָּרַתִּי אֶת־אֲבוֹתָם בְּיוֹם
הֶחֱזִיקִי בְיָדָם לְהוֹצִיאָם
מֵאֶרֶץ מִצְרָיִם אֲשֶׁר־הֵמָּה
הֵפֵרוּ אֶת־בְּרִיתִי וְאָנֹכִי
32 בָּעַלְתִּי בָם נְאֻם־יְהֹוָה: כִּי
זֹאת הַבְּרִית אֲשֶׁר אֶכְרֹת אֶת־
בֵּית יִשְׂרָאֵל אַחֲרֵי הַיָּמִים
הָהֵם נְאֻם־יְהֹוָה נָתַתִּי אֶת־
תּוֹרָתִי בְּקִרְבָּם וְעַל־לִבָּם
אֶכְתְּבֶנָּה וְהָיִיתִי לָהֶם
לֵאלֹהִים וְהֵמָּה יִהְיוּ־לִי

30. God will make a new covenant
with Israel which, unlike the old, will be
permanent, because it will be inscribed
on their hearts. There is nothing here
to suggest that the new covenant would
differ in nature from the old. No new
revelation is intended, nor was it needed.
The prophet only makes the assertion
that unlike the past, Israel will henceforth remain faithful to God, while He
in turn will never reject him.

31. that I took them by the hand. Like a
loving father guiding the steps of his
young child (cf. Hos. xi. 3).

they . . . I. The Hebrew includes the
pronouns and does not express them
only in the form of the verbs, to
emphasize the contrast: for their part
they broke the covenant, whereas I

remained their lord, their Protector,
faithful to My promise of help.

32. the house of Israel. Here the
designation of the whole nation, both
Judah and Israel (the Northern Kingdom).

after those days. When they return
from exile.

I will put. lit. 'I have put,' the prophetic
perfect.

in their inward parts, and in their heart.
I will no longer be something external
to them, but so deeply ingrained in their
consciousness as to be part of them.
This, indeed, is the aim of all religious
teaching.

I will be . . . they shall be. I is not
emphasized by the addition of the

be My people; 33. and they shall teach no more every man his neighbour, and every man his brother, saying: 'Know the LORD'; for they shall all know Me, from the least of them unto the greatest of them, saith the LORD; for I will forgive their iniquity, and their sin will I remember no more.

34 Thus saith the LORD,
Who giveth the sun for a light by day,
And the ordinances of the moon and of the stars for a light by night,
Who stirreth up the sea, that the waves thereof roar,
The LORD of hosts is His name:

35 If these ordinances depart from before Me,
Saith the LORD,
Then the seed of Israel also shall cease
From being a nation before Me for ever.

36 Thus saith the LORD:
If heaven above can be measured,

33 לְעָם : וְלֹא יְלַמְּדוּ עוֹד אִישׁ
אֶת־רֵעֵהוּ וְאִישׁ אֶת־אָחִיו
לֵאמֹר דְּעוּ אֶת־יְהוָה כִּי
כוּלָּם יֵדְעוּ אוֹתִי לְמִקְטַנָּם
וְעַד־גְּדוֹלָם נְאֻם־יְהוָֹה כִּי
אֶסְלַח לַעֲוֺנָם וּלְחַטָּאתָם לֹא
אֶזְכָּר־עוֹד :

34 כֹּה ׀ אָמַר יְהוָֹה
נֹתֵן שֶׁמֶשׁ לְאוֹר יוֹמָם
חֻקֹּת יָרֵחַ וְכוֹכָבִים
לְאוֹר לָיְלָה :
רֹגַע הַיָּם וַיֶּהֱמוּ גַלָּיו
יְהוָה צְבָאוֹת שְׁמוֹ :

35 אִם־יָמֻשׁוּ הַחֻקִּים הָאֵלֶּה
מִלְּפָנַי
נְאֻם־יְהוָֹה
גַּם זֶרַע יִשְׂרָאֵל יִשְׁבְּתוּ
מִהְיוֹת גּוֹי לְפָנַי כָּל־הַיָּמִים :

36 כֹּה ׀ אָמַר יְהוָֹה
אִם־יִמַּדּוּ שָׁמַיִם מִלְמַעְלָה

v. 33. דגש אחר שורק

---

pronoun but *they* is (see note on preceding verse). The implication is that God will be what He has always been in His relationship to Israel; *they*, on the other hand, will now likewise permanently acknowledge Him and be His people. Permanence is the essence of the new covenant.

33. *I will forgive their iniquity.* This being the obstacle which prevented them from 'knowing' God.

34-39 SURVIVAL OF ISRAEL AS CERTAIN AS NATURE'S LAWS

34. Only God Who created the universe and ordained the laws of Nature could make the declaration that follows.

35. *cease from being a nation.* 'The preservation of the Jews as a separate people is one of the greatest miracles of history' (Binns).

36. *if heaven . . . beneath.* This **is** unthinkable; similarly beyond thought is

And the foundations of the earth
searched out beneath,
Then will I also cast off all the
seed of Israel
For all that they have done, saith
the LORD.

37. Behold, the days come, saith the
LORD, that the city shall be built to
the LORD from the tower of Hananel
unto the gate of the corner. 38. And
the measuring line shall yet go out
straight forward unto the hill Gareb,
and shall turn about unto Goah.
39. And the whole valley of the dead
bodies, and of the ashes, and all the
fields unto the brook Kidron, unto
the corner of the horse gate toward
the east, shall be holy unto the LORD;
it shall not be plucked up, nor
thrown down any more for ever.

וְיֵחָקְרוּ מוֹסְדֵי־אֶרֶץ לְמָטָּה
גַּם־אֲנִי אֶמְאַס
בְּכָל־זֶרַע יִשְׂרָאֵל
עַל־כָּל־אֲשֶׁר עָשׂוּ
נְאֻם־יְהֹוָה:

37 הִנֵּה יָמִים ‏ נְאֻם־יְהֹוָה
וְנִבְנְתָה הָעִיר לַיהֹוָה מִמִּגְדַּל
38 חֲנַנְאֵל עַד־שַׁעַר הַפִּנָּה: וְיָצָא
עוֹד קַוְה הַמִּדָּה נֶגְדּוֹ עַל
39 גִּבְעַת גָּרֵב וְנָסַב גֹּעָתָה: וְכָל־
הָעֵמֶק הַפְּגָרִים ׀ וְהַדֶּשֶׁן וְכָל־
הַשְּׁרֵמוֹת עַד־נַחַל קִדְרוֹן
עַד־פִּנַּת שַׁעַר הַסּוּסִים
מִזְרָחָה קֹדֶשׁ לַיהֹוָה לֹא־
יִנָּתֵשׁ וְלֹא־יֵהָרֵס עוֹד
לְעוֹלָם:

v. 37. באים קרי ולא כתיב v. 38. קו ק׳ v. 39. השדמות ק׳

the complete and final rejection of Israel
by God.

37. come. Inserted in the text by the
kerë but omitted in the *kethib*.

*the tower of Hananel . . . the gate of
the corner.* At the north-east (cf. Neh.
iii. 1, xii. 39) and the north-west (cf.
2 Kings xiv. 13) of the city respectively.
They are both mentioned in Zech. xiv. 10
and describe the ends of the north wall
from east to west.

38. *Gareb . . . Goah.* Nothing is known
of these, but apparently the verse
indicates an extension of the city
boundary on the western side.

39. *the whole valley of the dead bodies,*
etc. The *valley* is that of *the son of*

Hinnom (see on vii. 31), defiled by
human sacrifices, and the Hebrew for
ashes (*deshen*) denotes the consumed fat
of the victims of the hideous rite. Even
this unclean place will be purified by
God and included in the city of Jerusalem.

the brook Kidron. Flowing east of
Jerusalem.

the horse gate. Mentioned in Neh. iii. 28
and located at the south-east corner of
the Temple.

holy unto the LORD. And added to the
city.

it shall not be plucked up, etc. The
permanence of the nation requires the
permanence of their capital.

32   CHAPTER XXXII   לב

1. The word that came to Jeremiah from the LORD in the tenth year of Zedekiah king of Judah, which was the eighteenth year of Nebuchadrezzar. 2. Now at that time the king of Babylon's army was besieging Jerusalem; and Jeremiah the prophet was shut up in the court of the guard, which was in the king of Judah's house. 3. For Zedekiah king of Judah had shut him up, saying:

1 הַדָּבָר אֲשֶׁר־הָיָה אֶל־יִרְמְיָהוּ
מֵאֵת יְהֹוָה בִּשְׁנַת הָעֲשִׂרִית
לְצִדְקִיָּהוּ מֶלֶךְ יְהוּדָה הִיא
הַשָּׁנָה שְׁמֹנֶה־עֶשְׂרֵה שָׁנָה
2 לִנְבוּכַדְרֶאצַּר: וְאָז חֵיל
מֶלֶךְ בָּבֶל צָרִים עַל־
יְרוּשָׁלָ͏ִם וְיִרְמְיָהוּ הַנָּבִיא הָיָה
כָלוּא בַּחֲצַר הַמַּטָּרָה אֲשֶׁר
3 בֵּית־מֶלֶךְ יְהוּדָה: אֲשֶׁר
כְּלָאוֹ צִדְקִיָּהוּ מֶלֶךְ־יְהוּדָה

v. 1. בשנה ק'

CHAPTER XXXII

JEREMIAH PURCHASES A FAMILY ESTATE

THIS chapter records a transaction revealing Jeremiah's faith in a future for his people. Jerusalem was under siege; God had foretold its downfall and the consequent exile of the nation. At such a time of confusion and uncertainty Jeremiah, at God's bidding, purchases an estate in Anathoth from his kinsman, depositing the title-deeds with Baruch, in the firm conviction that the nation would again return to the homeland. This incident alone is sufficient to free Jeremiah from the charge of pessimism. He was a realist and had no doubt about the imminent collapse of the Judean State, but simultaneously his trust in God's word made him confident of rehabilitation.

1-5 INTRODUCTORY

1. *the tenth year of Zedekiah.* The siege of Jerusalem commenced in the ninth year of his reign (xxxix. 1), was raised on receipt of the news that an Egyptian army was advancing (xxxvii. 5), and subsequently resumed. During the interval Jeremiah left Jerusalem to visit his estate in Anathoth, was accused of defection to the Chaldeans and imprisoned in close confinement (xxxvii. 11-15), which imprisonment, however, was relaxed on his petitioning the king (xxxvii. 21). But this chapter describes him as still *shut up in the court of the guard* (verse 2), and is therefore later than the events enumerated. It is apparent that this section of the Book does not follow a strictly chronological order.

which was the eighteenth year of Nebuchadrezzar. Cf. xxv. 1.

2. *the court of the guard.* 'A part of the court surrounding the palace, railed off to guard prisoners in, whom it was not desired to throw into the common dungeon' (Driver). It is referred to again in Neh. iii. 25.

3. Verses 3-5 are a parenthesis to account for Jeremiah's detention.

'Wherefore dost thou prophesy, and say: Thus saith the LORD: Behold, I will give this city into the hand of the king of Babylon, and he shall take it; 4. and Zedekiah king of Judah shall not escape out of the hand of the Chaldeans, but shall surely be delivered into the hand of the king of Babylon, and shall speak with him mouth to mouth, and his eyes shall behold his eyes; 5. and he shall lead Zedekiah to Babylon, and there shall he be until I remember him, saith the LORD; though ye fight with the Chaldeans, ye shall not prosper?'

6. And Jeremiah said: 'The word of the LORD came unto me, saying: 7. Behold, Hanamel, the son of Shallum thine uncle, shall come unto thee, saying: Buy thee my field that is in Anathoth; for the right of redemption is thine to buy it.'

לֵאמֹר מַדּוּעַ אַתָּה נִבָּא לֵאמֹר
כֹּה אָמַר יְהֹוָה הִנְנִי נֹתֵן אֶת־
הָעִיר הַזֹּאת בְּיַד מֶלֶךְ־בָּבֶל
וּלְכָדָהּ: 4 וְצִדְקִיָּהוּ מֶלֶךְ
יְהוּדָה לֹא יִמָּלֵט מִיַּד
הַכַּשְׂדִּים כִּי־הִנָּתֹן יִנָּתֵן בְּיַד
מֶלֶךְ־בָּבֶל וְדִבֶּר־פִּיו עִם־
פִּיו וְעֵינָיו אֶת־עֵינָו תִּרְאֶינָה:
5 וּבָבֶל יוֹלִךְ אֶת־צִדְקִיָּהוּ וְשָׁם
יִהְיֶה עַד־פָּקְדִי אֹתוֹ נְאֻם־
יְהֹוָה כִּי תִלָּחֲמוּ אֶת־
הַכַּשְׂדִּים לֹא תַצְלִיחוּ:
6 וַיֹּאמֶר יִרְמְיָהוּ הָיָה דְבַר־
יְהֹוָה אֵלַי לֵאמֹר: 7 הִנֵּה
חֲנַמְאֵל בֶּן־שַׁלֻּם דֹּדְךָ בָּא
אֵלֶיךָ לֵאמֹר קְנֵה לְךָ אֶת־
שָׂדִי אֲשֶׁר בַּעֲנָתוֹת כִּי לְךָ
8 מִשְׁפַּט הַגְּאֻלָּה לִקְנוֹת: וַיָּבֹא

v. 4. עֵינָיו ק׳   v. 6. הב׳ בקמץ   v. 7. הפטרת בהר סיני

---

wherefore dost thou prophesy, etc. Although his imprisonment in the first place was due to the charge of defection (see on verse 1), his insistence that Jerusalem would fall was a contributory cause. It is noteworthy that he maintained the truth of his prediction when petitioning the king (xxxvii. 19).

5. *until I remember him.* The verb *pakad* is used in both a favourable and unfavourable sense. A.J. rather suggests the former. A.V. and R.V., 'visit him,' follow the Jewish commentators who explain: with the visitation that comes to all men, viz. death.

6-15 WHY JEREMIAH WAS TOLD TO BUY HANAMEL'S LAND

6. *the word of the LORD came unto me.* Repeated from verse 1 because of the lengthy digression which intervenes.

7. *Hanamel, the son of Shallum thine uncle.* The comma printed in A.J. after *Hanamel* (omitted in A.V. and R.V.) is necessary, because *uncle,* as is clear from verses 8f., refers to Shallum, not to Hanamel.

Anathoth. Jeremiah's birthplace (i. 1).

the right of redemption is thine. As nearest kinsman (we must assume that

8. So Hanamel mine uncle's son came to me in the court of the guard according to the word of the LORD, and said unto me: 'Buy my field, I pray thee, that is in Anathoth, which is in the land of Benjamin; for the right of inheritance is thine, and the redemption is thine; buy it for thyself.' Then I knew that this was the word of the LORD. 9. And I bought the field that was in Anathoth of Hanamel mine uncle's son, and weighed him the money, even seventeen shekels of silver. 10. And I subscribed the deed, and sealed it, and called witnesses, and weighed him the money in the balances. 11. So I took the deed of the purchase, both that which was sealed, containing the terms and conditions, and that which was

אֵלַי חֲנַמְאֵל בֶּן־דֹּדִי כִּדְבַר
יְהֹוָה אֶל־חֲצַר הַמַּטָּרָה
וַיֹּאמֶר אֵלַי קְנֵה נָא אֶת־שָׂדִי
אֲשֶׁר־בַּעֲנָתוֹת אֲשֶׁר ׀ בְּאֶרֶץ
בִּנְיָמִין כִּי־לְךָ מִשְׁפַּט הַיְרֻשָּׁה
וּלְךָ הַגְּאֻלָּה קְנֵה־לָךְ וָאֵדַע
9 כִּי דְבַר־יְהֹוָה הוּא׃ וָאֶקְנֶה
אֶת־הַשָּׂדֶה מֵאֵת חֲנַמְאֵל
בֶּן־דֹּדִי אֲשֶׁר בַּעֲנָתֹת
וָאֶשְׁקֲלָה־לּוֹ אֶת־הַכֶּסֶף
שִׁבְעָה שְׁקָלִים וַעֲשָׂרָה
10 הַכָּסֶף׃ וָאֶכְתֹּב בַּסֵּפֶר
וָאֶחְתֹּם וָאָעֵד עֵדִים וָאֶשְׁקֹל
11 הַכֶּסֶף בְּמֹאזְנָיִם׃ וָאֶקַּח אֶת־
סֵפֶר הַמִּקְנָה אֶת־הֶחָתוּם
הַמִּצְוָה וְהַחֻקִּים וְאֶת־הַגָּלוּי׃

Hanamel was childless), Jeremiah had the right of pre-emption, so that the estate might remain in the family (Lev. xxv. 25). This incident (cf. also Ruth iv. 1ff.) is an indication that this law of land-tenure was actually practised.

8. *the right of inheritance is thine.* As next of kin; therefore *the redemption is thine* too.

then I knew . . . the LORD. This does not mean that he had any doubt about the genuineness of *the word of the LORD* which came to him. The phrase goes much deeper and signifies that Jeremiah at once perceived all that lay behind Hanamel's visit and its import for the future of the nation—that the impending disaster would not end the existence of Israel.

9. *seventeen shekels of silver.* lit. 'seven shekels and ten (pieces of) the silver.' The price appears to be very low, but the field may have been small. It should also be borne in mind that the purchase price was determined by the number of years still to run before the end of the Jubilee cycle when the estate would revert to the original owner. There is no suggestion in the text that the land was sold to Jeremiah at 'panic value' due to the political situation.

10. *I subscribed the deed.* lit. 'I wrote in the book,' i.e. set out all the particulars in the document.

11. *both that which was sealed . . . and that which was open.* 'Contracts stamped upon clay tablets have been found in Babylonia, enclosed in an envelope of

open; 12. and I delivered the deed of the purchase unto Baruch the son of Neriah, the son of Mahseiah, in the presence of Hanamel mine uncle['s son], and in the presence of the witnesses that subscribed the deed of the purchase, before all the Jews that sat in the court of the guard. 13. And I charged Baruch before them, saying: 14. 'Thus saith the LORD of hosts, the God of Israel: Take these deeds, this deed of the purchase, both that which is sealed, and this deed which is open, and put them in an earthen vessel; that

12 וָאֶתֵּן אֶת־הַסֵּפֶר הַמִּקְנָה
אֶל־בָּרוּךְ בֶּן־נֵרִיָּה בֶּן־
מַחְסֵיָה לְעֵינֵי חֲנַמְאֵל דֹּדִי
וּלְעֵינֵי הָעֵדִים הַכֹּתְבִים
בְּסֵפֶר הַמִּקְנָה לְעֵינֵי כָּל־
הַיְּהוּדִים הַיֹּשְׁבִים בַּחֲצַר
13 הַמַּטָּרָה: וָאֲצַוֶּה אֶת־בָּרוּךְ
14 לְעֵינֵיהֶם לֵאמֹר: כֹּה־אָמַר
יְהֹוָה צְבָאוֹת אֱלֹהֵי יִשְׂרָאֵל
לָקוֹחַ אֶת־הַסְּפָרִים הָאֵלֶּה
אֵת סֵפֶר הַמִּקְנָה הַזֶּה וְאֵת
הֶחָתוּם וְאֵת סֵפֶר הַגָּלוּי הַזֶּה
וּנְתַתָּם בִּכְלִי־חָרֶשׂ לְמַעַן

---

clay, on the outside of which an exact duplicate of the contract was impressed. If in course of time any disagreement arose, and it was suspected that the outside text had been tampered with, the envelope was broken in the presence of witnesses to see if the inside texts agreed with it or not' (Driver). The *sealed*, accordingly, refers to the inner tablet and the *open* to the outer envelope. 'The Jews had been vassals of Assyria and Babylon for about a century; and, it seems, transference of land was now performed according to the legal procedure of the Sovereign Power' (Hertz).

containing the terms and conditions. A paraphrase of the Hebrew which is literally 'the commandment and the statutes,' evidently used here in a technical sense.

12. Baruch. Jeremiah's amanuensis mentioned now for the first time. To him we owe the compilation of the material of this Book in the main.

Hanamel mine uncle['s son]. The addition in brackets reconciles the Hebrew text with verse 8. It is supported by LXX, Peshitta and several Hebrew MSS., and is accepted by Kimchi. Rashi suggests that this Hanamel may not be the same man as previously mentioned, but this is most improbable. M.T. may be explained on the hypothesis that both father and son bore the same name. In that case the father would have been the next of kin, not Jeremiah; but the father may have been of very advanced age so that from the practical point of view he could not be considered for the purpose of pre-emption. He would, however, be present at the transaction to indicate that he waived his legal claim.

before all the Jews. It was customary to carry out a transfer of this kind with great publicity (cf. Ruth iv. 9).

14. *put them in an earthen vessel.* 'Earthen jars containing such duplicate contracts

they may continue many days.

15. For thus saith the LORD of hosts, the God of Israel: Houses and fields and vineyards shall yet again be bought in this land.'

16. Now after I had delivered the deed of the purchase unto Baruch the son of Neriah, I prayed unto the LORD, saying: 17. 'Ah Lord GOD! behold, Thou hast made the heaven and the earth by Thy great power and by Thy outstretched arm; there is nothing too hard for Thee; 18. who showest mercy unto thousands, and recompensest the iniquity of the fathers into the bosom of their children after them; the great, the mighty God, the LORD of hosts is His name; 19. great in

15 יַעַמְדוּ יָמִים רַבִּים: כִּי כֹה
אָמַר יְהֹוָה צְבָאוֹת אֱלֹהֵי
יִשְׂרָאֵל עוֹד יִקָּנוּ בָתִּים
וְשָׂדוֹת וּכְרָמִים בָּאָרֶץ הַזֹּאת:
16 וָאֶתְפַּלֵּל אֶל־יְהֹוָה אַחֲרֵי
תִתִּי אֶת־סֵפֶר הַמִּקְנָה אֶל־
17 בָּרוּךְ בֶּן־נֵרִיָּה לֵאמֹר: אֲהָהּ
אֲדֹנָי יֱהֹוִה הִנֵּה ׀ אַתָּה עָשִׂיתָ
אֶת־הַשָּׁמַיִם וְאֶת־הָאָרֶץ
בְּכֹחֲךָ הַגָּדוֹל וּבִזְרֹעֲךָ
הַנְּטוּיָה לֹא־יִפָּלֵא מִמְּךָ כָּל־
18 דָּבָר: עֹשֶׂה חֶסֶד לַאֲלָפִים
וּמְשַׁלֵּם עֲוֹן אָבוֹת אֶל־חֵיק
בְּנֵיהֶם אַחֲרֵיהֶם הָאֵל הַגָּדוֹל
הַגִּבּוֹר יְהֹוָה צְבָאוֹת שְׁמוֹ:

---

have been excavated' (Budden and Hastings, *The Local Colour of the Bible*, p. 215).

15. *shall yet again be bought.* By Jews; herein lay the significance of the transaction, which expressed in most forceful manner God's promise of, and Jeremiah's confidence in, national revival.

16-25 REACTION OF DOUBT IN THE PROPHET

The pious men of the Bible are often depicted as subject to human weaknesses. Though imbued with ardent faith, they cannot always escape the chilling winds of scepticism. It is, indeed, this human quality of its heroes that makes the Bible a help and inspiration to those who strive and aspire, fall yet rise again. Such a wave of doubt now passes over Jeremiah, when he contemplates how seemingly opposed his transaction is not

only to the tragic realities of the situation, the city being about to fall, but also to the messages he has so often proclaimed in God's name of the overthrow of the Judean State. In anguish of spirit he prays to God and receives a reassuring answer.

17. *Ah.* The Hebrew particle expresses a cry of anguish.

there is nothing too hard for Thee. And yet! Such is the mixture of faith and doubt which often assails one in the crises of life.

18 *their children after them.* i.e. when the children follow in their father's footsteps, as did Jeremiah's generation (Rashi).

the great, the mighty God. Jeremiah omitted *the awful* from Moses' description of God (cf. Deut. x. 17), because, he

counsel, and mighty in work; whose eyes are open upon all the ways of the sons of men, to give every one according to his ways, and according to the fruit of his doings; 20. who didst set signs and wonders in the land of Egypt, even unto this day, and in Israel and among other men; and madest Thee a name, as at this day; 21. and didst bring forth Thy people Israel out of the land of Egypt with signs, and with wonders, and with a strong hand, and with an outstretched arm, and with great terror; 22. and gavest them this land, which Thou didst swear to their fathers to give them, a land flowing with milk and honey; 23. and they came in, and possessed it; but they hearkened not to Thy voice, neither walked in Thy law; they have done nothing of all that Thou commandedst them to do; therefore Thou hast caused all this evil to befall them; 24. behold the mounds, they are come unto the city

19 גְּדֹל֙ הָ֣עֵצָ֔ה וְרַ֖ב הָעֲלִֽילִיָּ֑ה
אֲשֶׁר־עֵינֶ֣יךָ פְקֻח֗וֹת עַל־
כָּל־דַּרְכֵי֙ בְּנֵ֣י אָדָ֔ם לָתֵ֤ת
לְאִישׁ֙ כִּדְרָכָ֔יו וְכִפְרִ֖י
20 מַעֲלָלָֽיו׃ אֲשֶׁר־שַׂ֠מְתָּ אֹת֨וֹת
וּמֹפְתִ֤ים בְּאֶֽרֶץ־מִצְרַ֨יִם֙ עַד־
הַיּ֣וֹם הַזֶּ֔ה וּבְיִשְׂרָאֵ֖ל וּבָֽאָדָ֑ם
וַתַּֽעֲשֶׂה־לְּךָ֥ שֵׁ֖ם כַּיּ֥וֹם הַזֶּֽה׃
21 וַתֹּצֵ֛א אֶת־עַמְּךָ֥ אֶת־יִשְׂרָאֵ֖ל
מֵאֶ֣רֶץ מִצְרָ֑יִם בְּאֹת֖וֹת
וּבְמ֣וֹפְתִ֔ים וּבְיָ֤ד חֲזָקָה֙
וּבְאֶזְר֣וֹעַ נְטוּיָ֔ה וּבְמוֹרָ֖א
22 גָּדֽוֹל׃ וַתִּתֵּ֤ן לָהֶם֙ אֶת־הָאָ֣רֶץ
הַזֹּ֔את אֲשֶׁר־נִשְׁבַּ֖עְתָּ לַאֲבוֹתָ֑ם
לָתֵ֣ת לָהֶ֔ם אֶ֛רֶץ זָבַ֥ת חָלָ֖ב
23 וּדְבָ֑שׁ׃ וַיָּבֹ֜אוּ וַיִּֽרְשׁ֣וּ אֹתָ֗הּ
וְלֹֽא־שָׁמְע֤וּ בְקוֹלֶ֨ךָ֙ וּבְתֹרוֹתְךָ֣
לֹֽא־הָלָ֔כוּ אֵת֩ כָּל־אֲשֶׁ֨ר
צִוִּ֧יתָה לָהֶ֛ם לַעֲשׂ֖וֹת לֹ֣א עָשׂ֑וּ
וַתַּקְרֵ֣א אֹתָ֔ם אֵ֥ת כָּל־הָרָעָ֖ה
24 הַזֹּֽאת׃ הִנֵּ֣ה הַסֹּלְל֗וֹת בָּ֣אוּ

v. 23. ׳ק ובתורתך v. 23. קמץ בז״ק

---

said, 'With the heathen about to destroy His Temple, where are His awful deeds!' (Talmud, Yoma 69b).

19. *to give every one*, etc. Repeated from xvii. 10.

20. *even unto this day*. The phrase is variously explained as: 'which are re-

membered to this day'; 'which continue to this day'; 'which are still spoken of.'

21. A reminiscence of Deut. iv. 34, xxvi. 8.

22. Cf. xi. 5.

24. *the mounds*. See on vi. 6.

to take it; and the city is given into
the hand of the Chaldeans that fight
against it, because of the sword, and
of the famine, and of the pestilence;
and what Thou hast spoken is come
to pass; and, behold, Thou seest it.
25. Yet Thou hast said unto me, O
Lord GOD: Buy thee the field for
money, and call witnesses; whereas
the city is given into the hand of the
Chaldeans.'

26. Then came the word of the
LORD unto Jeremiah, saying: 27.
'Behold, I am the LORD, the God of
all flesh; is there any thing too hard
for Me? 28. Therefore thus saith
the LORD: Behold, I will give this
city into the hand of the Chaldeans,
and into the hand of Nebuchadrezzar king of Babylon, and he shall
take it; 29. and the Chaldeans, that
fight against this city, shall come

הָעִיר֙ לְלָכְדָ֔הּ וְהָעִ֣יר נִתְּנָ֗ה
בְּיַד֙ הַכַּשְׂדִּ֔ים הַנִּלְחָמִ֖ים
עָלֶ֑יהָ מִפְּנֵ֛י הַחֶ֥רֶב וְהָרָעָ֖ב
וְהַדָּ֑בֶר וַאֲשֶׁ֥ר דִּבַּ֛רְתָּ הָיָ֖ה
וְהִנְּךָ֥ רֹאֶֽה׃ וְאַתָּ֞ה אָמַ֤רְתָּ אֵלַי֙ 25
אֲדֹנָ֣י יְהֹוִ֗ה קְנֵֽה־לְךָ֤ הַשָּׂדֶה֙
בַּכֶּ֔סֶף וְהָעֵ֖ד עֵדִ֑ים וְהָעִ֛יר 26
נִתְּנָ֖ה בְּיַ֥ד הַכַּשְׂדִּֽים׃ וַיְהִי֙
דְבַר־יְהֹוָ֔ה אֶֽל־יִרְמְיָ֖הוּ
לֵאמֹֽר׃ הִנֵּה֙ אֲנִ֣י יְהֹוָ֔ה אֱלֹהֵ֖י 27
כָּל־בָּשָׂ֑ר הֲמִמֶּ֖נִּי יִפָּלֵ֥א כָּל־
דָּבָֽר׃ לָכֵ֗ן כֹּֽה אָמַ֣ר יְהֹוָ֔ה 28
הִנְנִ֣י נֹתֵ֞ן אֶת־הָעִ֤יר הַזֹּאת֙
בְּיַ֣ד הַכַּשְׂדִּ֔ים וּבְיַ֛ד
נְבֽוּכַדְרֶאצַּ֥ר מֶֽלֶךְ־בָּבֶ֖ל
וּלְכָדָֽהּ׃ וּבָ֙אוּ֙ הַכַּשְׂדִּ֔ים 29
הַנִּלְחָמִים֙ עַל־הָעִ֣יר הַזֹּ֔את

v.27. ע״כ

---

is given. The perfect of certainty; the
city had not yet been captured.

the Chaldeans. By this time Chaldea
included the whole of Babylonia,
although originally it was only the
southern part of it.

25. *yet Thou hast said.* 'The two things,
the state of the city and God's command,
are placed side by side that their apparent
inconsistency may be most strikingly
shown' (Streane).

26–44 GOD'S REPLY TO JEREMIAH

27. *is there any thing too hard for Me?*
'One of the great answers—and facts—
of history (cf. Gen. xviii. 14). God gives

back to Jeremiah his own words, *There
is nothing too hard for Thee* (verse 17).
He had come to God with the best
thoughts about Him, and God gives him
the answer that his thoughts are true'
(Hertz).

28–44. After verse 27 gives the words
of God, the prophecy of Jeremiah is
resumed; hence *thus saith the LORD*.

28. *therefore.* Since He is *the God of all
flesh*, it is He Who will deliver the city
into the hands of the enemy, and not the
might of the foe that will lay it low.
Consequently He, too, will have the
power to redeem it when the time comes
(Metsudath David).

and set this city on fire, and burn it, with the houses, upon whose roofs they have offered unto Baal, and poured out drink-offerings unto other gods, to provoke Me. 30. For the children of Israel and the children of Judah have only done that which was evil in My sight from their youth; for the children of Israel have only provoked Me with the work of their hands, saith the LORD. 31. For this city hath been to Me a provocation of Mine anger and of My fury from the day that they built it even unto this day, that I should remove it from before My face; 32. because of all the evil of the children of Israel and of the children of Judah, which they have done to provoke Me, they, their kings, their princes, their priests, and their

וְהִצִּיתוּ אֶת־הָעִיר הַזֹּאת
בָּאֵשׁ וּשְׂרָפוּהָ וְאֵת הַבָּתִּים
אֲשֶׁר קִטְּרוּ עַל־גַּגּוֹתֵיהֶם
לַבַּעַל וְהִסִּכוּ נְסָכִים
לֵאלֹהִים אֲחֵרִים לְמַעַן
הַכְעִסֵנִי: כִּי־הָיוּ בְנֵי־ 30
יִשְׂרָאֵל וּבְנֵי יְהוּדָה אַךְ עֹשִׂים
הָרַע בְּעֵינַי מִנְּעֻרֹתֵיהֶם כִּי
בְנֵי־יִשְׂרָאֵל אַךְ מַכְעִסִים
אֹתִי בְּמַעֲשֵׂה יְדֵיהֶם נְאֻם־
יְהוָה: כִּי עַל־אַפִּי וְעַל־ 31
חֲמָתִי הָיְתָה לִּי הָעִיר הַזֹּאת
לְמִן־הַיּוֹם אֲשֶׁר־בָּנוּ אוֹתָהּ
וְעַד הַיּוֹם הַזֶּה לַהֲסִירָהּ מֵעַל
פָּנָי: עַל כָּל־רָעַת בְּנֵי־ 32
יִשְׂרָאֵל וּבְנֵי יְהוּדָה אֲשֶׁר עָשׂוּ
לְהַכְעִסֵנִי הֵמָּה מַלְכֵיהֶם
שָׂרֵיהֶם כֹּהֲנֵיהֶם וּנְבִיאֵיהֶם

---

29. *upon whose roofs . . . unto Baal.* See on xix. 13. The clause is not parenthetical but an essential part of the oracle, stating the reason for the city's fate.

30. *from their youth.* From the nation's beginnings.

the children of Israel have only provoked Me. Now used in the wider sense of the whole nation, while in the first half of the verse it designated the Northern Kingdom.

the work of their hands. Either their conduct, or manufactured idols.

31. *from the day that they built it.* In fact the Israelites did not build Jerusalem but captured it from the Jebusites. The verb *banah* is sometimes employed for 'enlarging, repairing' (cf. Josh. xix. 50; Judg. xxi. 23), and this seems to be its force in the verse. When Jerusalem passed into the hands of David, many alterations and additions were made, and the clause indicates that period.

32f. These verses recall ii. 26f., vii. 13, 25, xi. 17.

prophets, and the men of Judah, and the inhabitants of Jerusalem. 33. And they have turned unto Me the back, and not the face; and though I taught them, teaching them betimes and often, yet they have not hearkened to receive instruction. 34. But they set their abominations in the house whereupon My name is called, to defile it. 35. And they built the high places of Baal, which are in the valley of the son of Hinnom, to set apart their sons and their daughters unto Molech; which I commanded them not, neither came it into My mind, that they should do this abomination; to cause Judah to sin. 36. And now therefore thus saith the Lord, the God of Israel, concerning this city, whereof ye say: It is given into the hand of the king of Babylon by the sword, and by the famine, and by the pestilence: 37. Behold, I will gather them out of all the countries, whither I have driven them in Mine anger, and in My fury, and in great wrath; and I will bring them back unto this place, and I will cause them to dwell safely; 38. and they shall be My people, and I will be

וְאִישׁ יְהוּדָה וְיֹשְׁבֵי יְרוּשָׁלָ͏ִם׃
33 וַיִּפְנוּ אֵלַי עֹרֶף וְלֹא פָנִים
וְלַמֵּד אֹתָם הַשְׁכֵּם וְלַמֵּד
וְאֵינָם שֹׁמְעִים לָקַחַת מוּסָר׃
34 וַיָּשִׂימוּ שִׁקּוּצֵיהֶם בַּבַּיִת
אֲשֶׁר־נִקְרָא שְׁמִי־עָלָיו
35 לְטַמְּאוֹ׃ וַיִּבְנוּ אֶת־בָּמוֹת
הַבַּעַל אֲשֶׁר ׀ בְּגֵיא בֶן־הִנֹּם
לְהַעֲבִיר אֶת־בְּנֵיהֶם וְאֶת־
בְּנוֹתֵיהֶם לַמֹּלֶךְ אֲשֶׁר לֹא־
צִוִּיתִים וְלֹא עָלְתָה עַל־לִבִּי
לַעֲשׂוֹת הַתּוֹעֵבָה הַזֹּאת לְמַעַן
36 הַחֲטִי אֶת־יְהוּדָה׃ וְעַתָּה
לָכֵן כֹּה־אָמַר יְהוָה אֱלֹהֵי
יִשְׂרָאֵל אֶל־הָעִיר הַזֹּאת
אֲשֶׁר ׀ אַתֶּם אֹמְרִים נִתְּנָה
בְּיַד מֶלֶךְ־בָּבֶל בַּחֶרֶב
37 וּבָרָעָב וּבַדָּבֶר׃ הִנְנִי
מְקַבְּצָם מִכָּל־הָאֲרָצוֹת אֲשֶׁר
הִדַּחְתִּים שָׁם בְּאַפִּי וּבַחֲמָתִי
וּבְקֶצֶף גָּדוֹל וַהֲשִׁבֹתִים אֶל־
הַמָּקוֹם הַזֶּה וְהֹשַׁבְתִּים
38 לָבֶטַח׃ וְהָיוּ לִי לְעָם וַאֲנִי

v. 35. החטיא ק׳

34f. Mainly reproduced from vii. 30f.
35. *Baal . . . Molech.* The two are identified here, the former being a generic term and the latter specifying it.

36-44 THE PROMISE OF RESTORATION.

36. *and now.* A resumption of verse 27.
37. *I have driven them.* The prophetic perfect.
38. None of the prophets looked forward only to physical restoration. The

their God; 39. and I will give them one heart and one way, that they may fear Me for ever; for the good of them, and of their children after them; 40. and I will make an everlasting covenant with them, that I will not turn away from them, to do them good; and I will put My fear in their hearts, that they shall not depart from Me. 41. Yea, I will rejoice over them to do them good, and I will plant them in this land in truth with My whole heart and with My whole soul. 42. For thus saith the LORD: Like as I have brought all this great evil upon this people, so will I bring upon them all the good that I have promised them. 43. And fields shall be bought in this land, whereof ye say:

39 אֶהְיֶה לָהֶם לֵאלֹהִים: וְנָתַתִּי
לָהֶם לֵב אֶחָד וְדֶרֶךְ אֶחָד
לְיִרְאָה אוֹתִי כָּל־הַיָּמִים
לְטוֹב לָהֶם וְלִבְנֵיהֶם
40 אַחֲרֵיהֶם: וְכָרַתִּי לָהֶם בְּרִית
עוֹלָם אֲשֶׁר לֹא־אָשׁוּב
מֵאַחֲרֵיהֶם לְהֵיטִיבִי אוֹתָם
וְאֶת־יִרְאָתִי אֶתֵּן בִּלְבָבָם
41 לְבִלְתִּי סוּר מֵעָלָי: וְשַׂשְׂתִּי
עֲלֵיהֶם לְהֵטִיב אוֹתָם
וּנְטַעְתִּים בָּאָרֶץ הַזֹּאת בֶּאֱמֶת
42 בְּכָל־לִבִּי וּבְכָל־נַפְשִׁי: כִּי־
כֹה אָמַר יְהֹוָה כַּאֲשֶׁר הֵבֵאתִי
אֶל־הָעָם הַזֶּה אֵת כָּל־
הָרָעָה הַגְּדוֹלָה הַזֹּאת כֵּן אָנֹכִי
מֵבִיא עֲלֵיהֶם אֶת־כָּל־
הַטּוֹבָה אֲשֶׁר אָנֹכִי דֹּבֵר
43 עֲלֵיהֶם: וְנִקְנָה הַשָּׂדֶה בָּאָרֶץ
הַזֹּאת אֲשֶׁר | אַתֶּם אֹמְרִים

return was also to be spiritual (cf. xxxi. 32).

39. *one heart and one way.* Expressive of unanimity and singleness of purpose.

40. *I will not turn . . . good.* i.e. I will not cease doing them good.

I will put My fear in their hearts. The clause is to be understood as nothing more than an emphatic assertion that the fear (i.e. awe and reverence, not terror) of God will be as deeply rooted in them

as though He had put it there. It cannot be understood literally, for that would imply loss of free will which is implicit in the ethical teaching of the Bible. A Rabbinical maxim teaches, 'Everything is in the hands of Heaven (God) save the fear of Heaven.'

41. *with My whole heart.* Nowhere else is this phrase applied to God.

42. The same thought as in xxxi. 27.

43. *fields.* The Hebrew is singular and to be distinguished from *fields* in the next

It is desolate, without man or beast; it is given into the hand of the Chaldeans. 44. Men shall buy fields for money, and subscribe the deeds, and seal them, and call witnesses, in the land of Benjamin, and in the places about Jerusalem, and in the cities of Judah, and in the cities of the hill-country, and in the cities of the Lowland, and in the cities of the South; for I will cause their captivity to return, saith the LORD.'

שְׁמָמָה הִיא מֵאֵין אָדָם וּבְהֵמָה
44 נִתְּנָה בְּיַד הַכַּשְׂדִּים: שָׂדוֹת
בַּכֶּסֶף יִקְנוּ וְכָתוֹב בַּסֵּפֶר
וְחָתוֹם וְהָעֵד עֵדִים בְּאֶרֶץ
בִּנְיָמִן וּבִסְבִיבֵי יְרוּשָׁלַם
וּבְעָרֵי יְהוּדָה וּבְעָרֵי הָהָר
וּבְעָרֵי הַשְּׁפֵלָה וּבְעָרֵי הַנֶּגֶב
כִּי־אָשִׁיב אֶת־שְׁבוּתָם נְאֻם־
יְהֹוָה:

33   CHAPTER XXXIII   לג

1. Moreover the word of the LORD came unto Jeremiah the second time, while he was yet shut up in the court of the guard, saying:
2 Thus saith the LORD the Maker thereof,
The LORD that formed it to establish it,

1 וַיְהִי דְבַר־יְהֹוָה אֶל־
יִרְמְיָהוּ שֵׁנִית וְהוּא עוֹדֶנּוּ
עָצוּר בַּחֲצַר הַמַּטָּרָה לֵאמֹר:
2 כֹּה־אָמַר יְהֹוָה עֹשָׂהּ
יְהֹוָה יוֹצֵר אוֹתָהּ לַהֲכִינָהּ

verse which is plural. Here it signifies a rural district as distinct from urban settlements; in verse 44 'estates' are intended.

44. subscribe the deeds. See on verse 10.

the land of Benjamin, etc. See on xvii. 26. 'The several parts of the land are specified in order to make the promise more distinct that it should be possessed again in its entirety' (Streane).

CHAPTER XXXIII

1-13 RENEWED PROMISE OF REDEMPTION
THE futility of resistance to the Chaldeans

is again stressed, and the promise of a return from captivity repeated.

1. *the second time.* The second message must have come soon after the first as the next clause implies.

the court of the guard. See on xxxii. 2.

2. *the Maker thereof.* This is vague; it most likely means, of the universe.

that formed it to establish it. God did not create the world and then retire from it. He proceeded, and continues, to establish it, never withdrawing His Divine Providence; He is ever active in the unfolding of human development.

The LORD is His name:

3 Call unto Me, and I will answer
 thee,
 And will tell thee great things, and
 hidden, which thou knowest
 not.

4. For thus saith the LORD, the God
of Israel, conccrning the houses of
this city, and concerning the houses
of the kings of Judah, which are
broken down for mounds, and for
ramparts; 5. whereon they come to
fight with the Chaldeans, even to fill
them with the dead bodies of men,
whom I have slain in Mine anger
and in My fury, and for all whose
wickedness I have hid My face from
this city: 6. Behold, I will bring it

יְהֹוָה ׀ שְׁמֽוֹ׃

3 קְרָא אֵלַי וְאֶעֱנֶךָּ
וְאַגִּֽידָה לְךָ גְּדֹלוֹת וּבְצֻרוֹת
לֹא יְדַעְתָּֽם׃
4 כִּי כֹה אָמַר יְהֹוָה אֱלֹהֵי
יִשְׂרָאֵל עַל־בָּתֵּי הָעִיר הַזֹּאת
וְעַל־בָּתֵּי מַלְכֵי יְהוּדָה
הַנְּתֻצִים אֶל־הַסֹּֽלְלוֹת וְאֶל־
5 הֶחָֽרֶב׃ בָּאִים לְהִלָּחֵם אֶת־
הַכַּשְׂדִּים וּלְמַלְאָם אֶת־פִּגְרֵי
הָאָדָם אֲשֶׁר־הִכֵּיתִי בְאַפִּי
וּבַחֲמָתִי וַאֲשֶׁר הִסְתַּרְתִּי פָנַי
מֵהָעִיר הַזֹּאת עַל כָּל־
6 רָעָתָֽם׃ הִנְנִי מַֽעֲלֶה־לָּהּ

---

the LORD is His name. The Tetragram-
maton in the text (the Hebrew consonants
being JHWH) denotes God either under
the aspect of eternity (hence some
translate as 'the Eternal') or, according to
the Rabbis, the attribute of mercy.
This gives point to the introduction of
the Name at this point: He is eternal and
looks beyond the present darkness to
future light; He is merciful, and when
the demands of justice have been met by
a period of exile, He will in His mercy
restore Israel to his land and ancient
glory.

3. *call unto Me, and 1 will answer thee.*
God is ever ready to answer man
(Isa. lviii. 9; Ps. cxlv. 18; Job xiii. 22),
but man must first call upon Him;
co-operation is essential.

hidden. The Hebrew *betsuroth* elsewhere
describes 'fortified' cities, difficult of
access; hence 'secret things' which are
beyond man's knowledge. A few
Hebrew MSS. read *netsuroth, hidden
things,* as in Isa. xlviii. 6; but the more
unusual word of M.T. is likely to have
stood in the original text of the present
verse.

4. *mounds.* For the word, see on vi. 6;
but here the *mounds* indicate material
heaped up to reinforce the city walls and
strengthen the defences.

5. *they come.* The subject is the Judean
defenders of the besieged city.

*even to fill them with the dead bodies of
men.* Their resistance, however heroic,
is futile and only adds to the heaps of the
slain.

I have hid My face. In displeasure;
I have withdrawn My protection.

healing and cure, and I will cure them; and I will reveal unto them the abundance of peace and truth. 7. And I will cause the captivity of Judah and the captivity of Israel to return, and will build them, as at the first. 8. And I will cleanse them from all their iniquity, whereby they have sinned against Me; and I will pardon all their iniquities, whereby they have sinned against Me, and whereby they have transgressed against Me. 9. And this city shall be to Me for a name of joy, for a praise and for a glory, before all the nations of the earth, which shall hear all the good that I do unto them, and shall fear and tremble for all the good and for all the peace that I procure unto it.

10. Thus saith the LORD: Yet again there shall be heard in this place, whereof ye say: It is waste, without man and without beast, even in the cities of Judah, and in the streets of Jerusalem, that are desolate, without man and without

אַרְכָה וּמַרְפֵּא וּרְפָאתִ֗ים
וְגִלֵּיתִי לָהֶם עֲתֶרֶת שָׁלוֹם
7 וֶאֱמֶת: וַהֲשִׁבֹתִי אֶת־שְׁבוּת
יְהוּדָה וְאֵת שְׁבוּת יִשְׂרָאֵל
וּבְנִתִים כְּבָרִאשֹׁנָֽה:
8 וְטִהַרְתִּים מִכָּל־עֲוֺנָם אֲשֶׁר
חָטְאוּ־לִי וְסָלַחְתִּי לְכָל־
עֲוֺנֽוֹתֵיהֶם אֲשֶׁר חָטְאוּ־לִי
9 וֶאֲשֶׁר פָּשְׁעוּ בִי: וְהָיְתָה לִי
לְשֵׁם שָׂשׂוֹן לִתְהִלָּה וּלְתִפְאֶרֶת
לְכֹל גּוֹיֵי הָאָרֶץ אֲשֶׁר יִשְׁמְעוּ
אֶת־כָּל־הַטּוֹבָה אֲשֶׁר אָנֹכִי
עֹשֶׂה אוֹתָם וּפָחֲדוּ וְרָגְזוּ עַל
כָּל־הַטּוֹבָה וְעַל כָּל־
הַשָּׁלוֹם אֲשֶׁר אָנֹכִי עֹשֶׂה לָּהּ:
10 כֹּה ׀ אָמַר יְהוָה עוֹד יִשָּׁמַע
בַּמָּקוֹם־הַזֶּה אֲשֶׁר אַתֶּם
אֹמְרִים חָרֵב הוּא מֵאֵין אָדָם
וּמֵאֵין בְּהֵמָה בְּעָרֵי יְהוּדָה
וּבְחֻצוֹת יְרוּשָׁלַ͏ִם הַנְשַׁמּוֹת
מֵאֵין אָדָם וּמֵאֵין יוֹשֵׁב וּמֵאֵין

ע. 8. יתיר ו'

---

6. *cure.* See on viii. 22.

truth. A demonstration of God's faithfulness in the fulfilment of His promise.

7. *as at the first.* Before the Kingdom was split into two after the death of Solomon.

8. Cf. Ezek. xxxvi. 25.

9. *and shall fear and tremble for all the good,* etc. The love which God will display to His people, who acknowledge Him, will make the nations fear His displeasure for not acknowledging Him.

10. *whereof ye say.* i.e. you will, when in captivity, say.

inhabitant and without beast, 11. the
voice of joy and the voice of gladness,
the voice of the bridegroom and the
voice of the bride, the voice of them
that say: 'Give thanks to the LORD
of hosts, for the LORD is good, for
His mercy endureth for ever,' even
of them that bring offerings of
thanksgiving into the house of the
LORD. For I will cause the captivity of the land to return as at the
first, saith the LORD.

12. Thus saith the LORD of hosts:
Yet again shall there be in this place,
which is waste, without man and
without beast, and in all the cities
thereof, a habitation of shepherds
causing their flocks to lie down.
13. In the cities of the hill-country,
in the cities of the Lowland, and in
the cities of the South, and in the
land of Benjamin, and in the places
about Jerusalem, and in the cities of
Judah, shall the flocks again pass
under the hands of him that counteth
them, saith the LORD.

14. Behold, the days come, saith
the LORD, that I will perform that
good word which I have spoken
concerning the house of Israel and

בְּהֵמָה: קוֹל שָׂשׂוֹן וְקוֹל 11
שִׂמְחָה קוֹל חָתָן וְקוֹל כַּלָּה
קוֹל אֹמְרִים הוֹדוּ אֶת־יְהֹוָה
צְבָאוֹת כִּי־טוֹב יְהֹוָה כִּי־
לְעוֹלָם חַסְדּוֹ מְבִאִים תּוֹדָה
בֵּית יְהֹוָה כִּי־אָשִׁיב אֶת־
שְׁבוּת־הָאָרֶץ כְּבָרִאשֹׁנָה
אָמַר יְהֹוָה: כֹּה אָמַר יְהֹוָה 12
צְבָאוֹת עוֹד יִהְיֶה | בַּמָּקוֹם
הַזֶּה הֶחָרֵב מֵאֵין־אָדָם וְעַד־
בְּהֵמָה וּבְכָל־עָרָיו נְוֵה רֹעִים
מַרְבִּצִים צֹאן: בְּעָרֵי הָהָר 13
בְּעָרֵי הַשְּׁפֵלָה וּבְעָרֵי הַנֶּגֶב
וּבְאֶרֶץ בִּנְיָמֵן וּבִסְבִיבֵי
יְרוּשָׁלַם וּבְעָרֵי יְהוּדָה עֹד
תַּעֲבֹרְנָה הַצֹּאן עַל־יְדֵי־
מוֹנֶה אָמַר יְהֹוָה: הִנֵּה יָמִים 14
בָּאִים נְאֻם־יְהֹוָה וַהֲקִמֹתִי
אֶת־הַדָּבָר הַטּוֹב אֲשֶׁר
דִּבַּרְתִּי אֶל־בֵּית יִשְׂרָאֵל

---

11. *the voice of joy*, etc. Contrast vii. 34.

give thanks . . . for ever. A liturgical
refrain used in the Temple services
(cf. Ps. cvi. 1, cxviii. 1, cxxxvi. 1; Ezra
iii. 11).

that bring offerings. Better, 'as they
bring,' etc.

12. *in this place.* Jerusalem.

all the cities thereof. Of Judea.

causing their flocks to lie down. An
idyllic picture of undisturbed peace: the
flocks will lie down without fear of
attack (Kimchi).

13. *the cities of the hill-country*, etc. See
on xvii. 26 and xxxii. 44.

him that counteth them. To see that
none is missing; the old pastoral life of
the country will be restored.

concerning the house of Judah.

15. In those days, and at that time,
Will I cause a shoot of righteousness to grow up unto David;
And he shall execute justice and
righteousness in the land.

16 In those days shall Judah be
saved,
And Jerusalem shall dwell safely;
And this is the name whereby
she shall be called,
The LORD is our righteousness.

17. For thus saith the LORD: There
shall not be cut off unto David a
man to sit upon the throne of the
house of Israel; 18. neither shall
there be cut off unto the priests the
Levites a man before Me to offer
burnt-offerings, and to burn meal-
offerings, and to do sacrifice continually.

19. And the word of the LORD
came unto Jeremiah, saying: 20.
Thus saith the LORD:

If ye can break My covenant with
the day,
And My covenant with the night,
So that there should not be day
and night in their season;

וְעַל־־בֵּית יְהוּדָֽה׃

15 בַּיָּמִים הָהֵם֙ וּבָעֵת הַהִ֔יא
אַצְמִיחַ לְדָוִד צֶמַח צְדָקָה
וְעָשָׂה מִשְׁפָּט וּצְדָקָה בָּאָֽרֶץ׃

16 בַּיָּמִים הָהֵם֙ תִּוָּשַׁע יְהוּדָ֔ה
וִירוּשָׁלַ֖͏ִם תִּשְׁכּוֹן לָבֶ֑טַח
וְזֶה אֲשֶׁר־־יִקְרָא־לָ֖הּ
יְהֹוָ֥ה ׀ צִדְקֵֽנוּ׃

17 כִּי־כֹה אָמַר יְהֹוָ֔ה לֹא־יִכָּרֵת
לְדָוִד אִישׁ יֹשֵׁב עַל־כִּסֵּא
18 בֵית־יִשְׂרָאֵֽל׃ וְלַכֹּהֲנִים֙
הַלְוִיִּם לֹא־יִכָּרֵת אִישׁ מִלְּפָנָ֑י
מַעֲלֶה עוֹלָה וּמַקְטִיר מִנְחָה
19 וְעֹשֶׂה־זֶּבַח כָּל־הַיָּמִֽים׃ וַיְהִי֙
דְּבַר־־יְהֹוָ֔ה אֶל־־יִרְמְיָ֖הוּ
20 לֵאמֹֽר׃ כֹּה אָמַר יְהֹוָ֔ה
אִם־תָּפֵ֙רוּ֙ אֶת־בְּרִיתִי הַיּ֔וֹם
וְאֶת־בְּרִיתִי הַלָּ֑יְלָה
וּלְבִלְתִּי הֱיוֹת יוֹמָם־וָלַ֖יְלָה
בְּעִתָּֽם׃

v. 19. יתיר ו׳

14-22 RESTORATION OF THE MONARCHY
AND PRIESTHOOD

15f. Repeated with variants from xxiii.
5f. Here *the LORD is our righteousness*
is applied to Jerusalem, not to the king.
It will be the watchword, as it were, of
the city's inhabitants (Kimchi).

17. *there shall not be cut off.* Permanently; should his dynasty cease, it

will only be temporarily, to be renewed in
the future (Rashi).

19f. The covenant with David is as
dependable as the sequence of day and
night (cf. Ps. lxxxix. 36-38).

20. *My covenant with the day . . . the
night.* Possibly an allusion to God's
oath after the Flood (Gen. viii. 22).

228

21 Then may also My covenant be broken with David My servant,

That he should not have a son to reign upon his throne;

And with the Levites the priests, My ministers.

22 As the host of heaven cannot be numbered,

Neither the sand of the sea measured;

So will I multiply the seed of David My servant,

And the Levites that minister unto Me.

23. And the word of the LORD came to Jeremiah, saying: 24. 'Considerest thou not what this people have spoken, saying: The two families which the LORD did choose, He hath cast them off? and they contemn My people, that they should be no more a nation before them. 25. Thus saith the LORD: If My covenant be not with day and night, if I have not appointed the ordinances of heaven and earth; 26. then will I also cast away the seed of Jacob, and of David My

21 גַּם־בְּרִיתִי תֻפַר
אֶת־דָּוִד עַבְדִּי
מִהְיוֹת־לוֹ בֵן
מֹלֵךְ עַל־כִּסְאוֹ
וְאֶת־הַלְוִיִּם הַכֹּהֲנִים
מְשָׁרְתָי:

22 אֲשֶׁר לֹא־יִסָּפֵר צְבָא הַשָּׁמַיִם
וְלֹא יִמַּד חוֹל הַיָּם
כֵּן אַרְבֶּה אֶת־זֶרַע דָּוִד עַבְדִּי
וְאֶת־הַלְוִיִּם מְשָׁרְתֵי אֹתִי:

23 וַיְהִי דְּבַר־יְהֹוָה אֶל־יִרְמְיָהוּ
24 לֵאמֹר: הֲלוֹא רָאִיתָ מָה־
הָעָם הַזֶּה דִּבְּרוּ לֵאמֹר שְׁתֵּי
הַמִּשְׁפָּחוֹת אֲשֶׁר בָּחַר יְהֹוָה
בָּהֶם וַיִּמְאָסֵם וְאֶת־עַמִּי
יִנְאָצוּן מִהְיוֹת עוֹד גּוֹי
25 לִפְנֵיהֶם: כֹּה אָמַר יְהֹוָה אִם־
לֹא בְרִיתִי יוֹמָם וָלָיְלָה חֻקּוֹת
26 שָׁמַיִם וָאָרֶץ לֹא־שָׂמְתִּי: גַּם־
זֶרַע יַעֲקוֹב וְדָוִד עַבְדִּי אֶמְאַס

v. 26. מלא ר

21. *My covenant . . . with David.* Cf. 2 Sam. vii. 12-16.

22. *and the Levites.* Perhaps an allusion to Num. xxv. 13.

23-26 THE COVENANT ALSO APPLIED TO THE NATION

24. *this people . . . My people.* The first alludes to the sceptical and faithless section of the nation, the latter to the community as a whole.

two families. Some explain as Israel and Judah; others as the royal house of David and the priesthood.

before them. Rashi interprets this to mean 'in their view.'

25f. A similar assurance is given with regard to the nation as to the monarchy and priesthood (verse 20).

servant, so that I will not take of his seed to be rulers over the seed of Abraham, Isaac, and Jacob; for I will cause their captivity to return, and will have compassion on them.'

מִקַּחַת מִזַּרְעוֹ מֹשְׁלִים אֶל־
זֶרַע אַבְרָהָם יִשְׂחָק וְיַעֲקֹב
כִּי־אָשׁוֹב אֶת־שְׁבוּתָם
וְרִחַמְתִּים׃

34   CHAPTER XXXIV   לד

1. The word which came unto Jeremiah from the LORD, when Nebuchadrezzar king of Babylon, and all his army, and all the kingdoms of the land of his dominion, and all the peoples, fought against Jerusalem, and against all the cities thereof, saying:

2. Thus saith the LORD, the God of Israel: Go, and speak to Zedekiah king of Judah, and tell him: Thus saith the LORD: Behold, I will give this city into the hand of the king of Babylon, and he shall burn it with fire; 3. and thou shalt not escape out of his hand, but shalt surely be taken, and delivered into his hand; and thine eyes shall behold the eyes of the king of Babylon, and

1 הַדָּבָר אֲשֶׁר־הָיָה אֶל־
יִרְמְיָהוּ מֵאֵת יְהוָה
וּנְבוּכַדְרֶאצַּר מֶלֶךְ־בָּבֶל ׀
וְכָל־חֵילוֹ וְכָל־מַמְלְכוֹת
אֶרֶץ מֶמְשֶׁלֶת יָדוֹ וְכָל־
הָעַמִּים נִלְחָמִים עַל־יְרוּשָׁלַם
וְעַל־כָּל־עָרֶיהָ לֵאמֹר׃
2 כֹּה־אָמַר יְהוָֹה אֱלֹהֵי יִשְׂרָאֵל
הָלֹךְ וְאָמַרְתָּ אֶל־צִדְקִיָּהוּ
מֶלֶךְ יְהוּדָה וְאָמַרְתָּ אֵלָיו כֹּה
אָמַר יְהוָֹה הִנְנִי נֹתֵן אֶת־הָעִיר
הַזֹּאת בְּיַד מֶלֶךְ־בָּבֶל
3 וּשְׂרָפָהּ בָּאֵשׁ׃ וְאַתָּה לֹא
תִמָּלֵט מִיָּדוֹ כִּי תָּפֹשׂ תִּתָּפֵשׂ
וּבְיָדוֹ תִּנָּתֵן וְעֵינֶיךָ אֶת־עֵינֵי
מֶלֶךְ־בָּבֶל תִּרְאֶינָה וּפִיהוּ

v. 26. אשיב ק׳

26. **Isaac.** The Hebrew is spelt *yischak* instead of the usual *yitschak*. So again in Amos vii. 9, 16; Ps. cv. 9.

CHAPTER XXXIV

THE biographical section of the Book is resumed and extends to the end of xxxix.

1-7 THE FATE OF JERUSALEM AND ITS KING

1. The verse refers to the siege during the years 588-586 B.C.E.

all the cities thereof. Cf. verse 7.

3. *and thine eyes shall behold.* Cf. xxxii. 4.

he shall speak with thee mouth to mouth, and thou shalt go to Babylon. 4. Yet hear the word of the LORD, O Zedekiah king of Judah: Thus saith the LORD concerning thee: Thou shalt not die by the sword; 5. thou shalt die in peace; and with the burnings of thy fathers, the former kings that were before thee, so shall they make a burning for thee; and they shall lament thee: 'Ah lord!' for I have spoken the word, saith the LORD.

6. Then Jeremiah the prophet spoke all these words unto Zedekiah king of Judah in Jerusalem, 7. when the king of Babylon's army fought against Jerusalem, and against all the cities of Judah that were left, against Lachish and against Azekah; for these alone remained of the cities of Judah as fortified cities.

8. The word that came unto Jeremiah from the LORD, after that

אֶת־פִּיךָ יְדַבֵּר וּבָבֶל תָּבוֹא:

4 אַךְ שְׁמַע דְּבַר־יְהֹוָה צִדְקִיָּהוּ מֶלֶךְ יְהוּדָה כֹּה־אָמַר יְהֹוָה עָלֶיךָ לֹא תָמוּת בֶּחָרֶב:

5 בְּשָׁלוֹם תָּמוּת וּבְמִשְׂרְפוֹת אֲבוֹתֶיךָ הַמְּלָכִים הָרִאשֹׁנִים אֲשֶׁר־הָיוּ לְפָנֶיךָ כֵּן יִשְׂרְפוּ־ לָךְ וְהוֹי אָדוֹן יִסְפְּדוּ־לָךְ כִּי־דָבָר אֲנִי־דִבַּרְתִּי נְאֻם־

6 יְהֹוָה: וַיְדַבֵּר יִרְמְיָהוּ הַנָּבִיא אֶל־צִדְקִיָּהוּ מֶלֶךְ יְהוּדָה אֵת כָּל־הַדְּבָרִים הָאֵלֶּה

7 בִּירוּשָׁלָםִ: וְחֵיל מֶלֶךְ־ בָּבֶל נִלְחָמִים עַל־יְרוּשָׁלַםִ וְעַל כָּל־עָרֵי יְהוּדָה הַנּוֹתָרוֹת אֶל־לָכִישׁ וְאֶל־ עֲזֵקָה כִּי הֵנָּה נִשְׁאֲרוּ בְּעָרֵי

8 יְהוּדָה עָרֵי מִבְצָר: הַדָּבָר אֲשֶׁר־הָיָה אֶל־יִרְמְיָהוּ מֵאֵת

v. 8. הפטרת משפטים

5. *thou shalt die in peace.* i.e. a natural death; he would not die in battle or by the executioner's sword.

with the burnings of thy fathers. The Talmud records that it was the custom to make a funeral pyre of the bed and other articles as a mark of honour to the deceased (Sanh. 52b). Aromatic spices were laid on the bed (cf. 2 Chron. xvi. 14).

'Ah lord!' See on xxii. 18.

7. *Lachish.* About thirty-five miles south-west of Jerusalem.

Azekah. About fifteen miles south-west of Jerusalem. The towns mark the limit of Nebuchadnezzar's advance southwards.

8-22 OATH TO FREE HEBREW SLAVES VIOLATED

The dire peril of the nation had caused a quickening of the national conscience and some effort at repentance. Zedekiah had induced the owners under a solemn oath to free their slaves. When the danger from Babylon had been

the king Zedekiah had made a covenant with all the people that were at Jerusalem, to proclaim liberty unto them; 9. that every man should let his man-servant, and every man his maid-servant, being a Hebrew man or a Hebrew woman, go free; that none should make bondmen of them, even of a Jew his brother; 10. and all the princes and all the people hearkened, that had entered into the covenant to let every one his man-servant, and every one his maid-servant, go free, and not to make bondmen of them any more; they hearkened, and let them go; 11. but afterwards they turned, and caused the servants and the handmaids, whom they had let go free, to return, and brought them into subjection for servants and for handmaids; 12. therefore the word of the LORD came to Jeremiah from the LORD, saying:

יְהֹוָה אַחֲרֵי כְּרֹת הַמֶּ֫לֶךְ
צִדְקִיָּ֫הוּ בְּרִית אֶת־כָּל־
הָעָם אֲשֶׁר בִּירוּשָׁלַ֫ם לִקְרֹא
9 לָהֶם דְּרוֹר: לְשַׁלַּח אִישׁ אֶת־
עַבְדּוֹ וְאִישׁ אֶת־שִׁפְחָתוֹ
הָעִבְרִי וְהָעִבְרִיָּה חָפְשִׁים
לְבִלְתִּי עֲבָד־בָּם בִּיהוּדִי
10 אָחִיהוּ אִישׁ: וַיִּשְׁמְעוּ כָל־
הַשָּׂרִים וְכָל־הָעָם אֲשֶׁר־
בָּאוּ בַבְּרִית לְשַׁלַּח אִישׁ אֶת־
עַבְדּוֹ וְאִישׁ אֶת־שִׁפְחָתוֹ
חָפְשִׁים לְבִלְתִּי עֲבָד־בָּם
11 עוֹד וַיִּשְׁמְעוּ וַיְשַׁלֵּ֫חוּ: וַיָּשׁוּבוּ
אַחֲרֵי־כֵן וַיָּשִׁבוּ אֶת־
הָעֲבָדִים וְאֶת־הַשְּׁפָחוֹת
אֲשֶׁר שִׁלְּחוּ חָפְשִׁים וַיִּכְבְּשׁוּם
12 לַעֲבָדִים וְלִשְׁפָחוֹת: וַיְהִי
דְבַר־יְהֹוָה אֶל־יִרְמְיָ֫הוּ מֵאֵת

יתיר י׳ v. 11.

---

temporarily removed, the masters broke their oath and forcibly retook them. This act of perjury would have the effect of bringing the Babylonians back to attack Judea.

8. *and had made a covenant.* Which was ratified in the most solemn manner (cf. verses 18f.).

unto them. The slaves, mentioned in the next verse. 'The number of Hebrew slaves is explained by the conditions of the time. The old peasant proprietors had been largely exterminated in the

wars; the heavy tribute and taxation had ruined the poorer people; wealth had accumulated in comparatively few hands, and had been employed in luxury and other barren expenditure; so that the poor, seeing no alternative but starvation, had been forced to sell their children and then themselves into slavery' (Peake).

9. *go free.* It is noteworthy that national repentance took the form of respecting the rights of the weakest and most downtrodden of the people. This is characteristic of the Mosaic Code and of Judaism.

13. Thus saith the LORD, the God of Israel: I made a covenant with your fathers in the day that I brought them forth out of the land of Egypt, out of the house of bondage, saying: 14. 'At the end of seven years ye shall let go every man his brother that is a Hebrew, that hath been sold unto thee, and hath served thee six years, thou shalt let him go free from thee'; but your fathers hearkened not unto Me, neither inclined their ear. 15. And ye were now turned, and had done that which is right in Mine eyes, in proclaiming liberty every man to his neighbour; and ye had made a covenant before Me in the house whereon My name is called; 16. but ye turned and profaned My name, and caused every man his servant, and every man his handmaid, whom ye had let go free at their pleasure, to return; and ye brought them into subjection, to be unto you for

13 יְהֹוָה לֵאמֹר: כֹּה־אָמַר יְהֹוָה
אֱלֹהֵי יִשְׂרָאֵל אָנֹכִי כָּרַתִּי
בְרִית אֶת־אֲבוֹתֵיכֶם בְּיוֹם
הוֹצִאִי אוֹתָם מֵאֶרֶץ מִצְרַיִם
14 מִבֵּית עֲבָדִים לֵאמֹר: מִקֵּץ
שֶׁבַע שָׁנִים תְּשַׁלְּחוּ אִישׁ אֶת־
אָחִיו הָעִבְרִי אֲשֶׁר יִמָּכֵר לְךָ
וַעֲבָדְךָ שֵׁשׁ שָׁנִים וְשִׁלַּחְתּוֹ
חָפְשִׁי מֵעִמָּךְ וְלֹא־שָׁמְעוּ
אֲבוֹתֵיכֶם אֵלַי וְלֹא הִטּוּ אֶת־
15 אָזְנָם: וַתָּשֻׁבוּ אַתֶּם הַיּוֹם
וַתַּעֲשׂוּ אֶת־הַיָּשָׁר בְּעֵינַי
לִקְרֹא דְרוֹר אִישׁ לְרֵעֵהוּ
וַתִּכְרְתוּ בְרִית לְפָנַי בַּבַּיִת
אֲשֶׁר־נִקְרָא שְׁמִי עָלָיו:
16 וַתָּשֻׁבוּ וַתְּחַלְּלוּ אֶת־שְׁמִי
וַתָּשִׁבוּ אִישׁ אֶת־עַבְדּוֹ וְאִישׁ
אֶת־שִׁפְחָתוֹ אֲשֶׁר־שִׁלַּחְתֶּם
חָפְשִׁים לְנַפְשָׁם וַתִּכְבְּשׁוּ אֹתָם
לִהְיוֹת לָכֶם לַעֲבָדִים

13. *I made.* The *I* is emphatic and offers the contrast with *ye were now turned* in verse 15 where *ye* is also stressed.

out of the house of bondage. The reason for mentioning this is clear: the exodus, whereby they were liberated from slavery, was an assertion of man's right to freedom. Hence, if the circumstances of the time made the total abolition of slavery impossible, it was at least to be restricted and made only temporary.

14. *seven years.* This includes the year of liberation. Actually the slave's servitude was limited to six years (Exod. xxi. 2; Deut. xv. 12).

15. *and ye.* See on verse 13.

in the house, etc. This suggests that the covenant was solemnly ratified in the Temple.

16. *and profaned My name.* By violating the oath which must have included the Divine name.

servants and for handmaids. 17.
Therefore thus saith the LORD: Ye
have not hearkened unto Me, to
proclaim liberty, every man to his
brother, and every man to his
neighbour; behold, I proclaim for
you a liberty, saith the LORD, unto
the sword, unto the pestilence, and
unto the famine; and I will make
you a horror unto all the kingdoms
of the earth. 18. And I will give
the men that have transgressed My
covenant, that have not performed
the words of the covenant which
they made before Me, when they
cut the calf in twain and passed
between the parts thereof; 19. the
princes of Judah, and the princes of
Jerusalem, the officers, and the
priests, and all the people of the
land, that passed between the parts
of the calf; 20. I will even give them
into the hand of their enemies, and
into the hand of them that seek their
life; and their dead bodies shall be
for food unto the fowls of the
heaven, and to the beasts of the

17 וְלִשְׁפָחֽוֹת׃ לָכֵן כֹּה־אָמַ֣ר
יְהֹוָ֗ה אַתֶּם֙ לֹֽא־שְׁמַעְתֶּם֙ אֵלַ֔י
לִקְרֹ֣א דְר֔וֹר אִ֤ישׁ לְאָחִיו֙ וְאִ֣ישׁ
לְרֵעֵ֔הוּ הִנְנִ֣י קֹרֵ֩א לָכֶ֨ם דְּר֜וֹר
נְאֻם־יְהֹוָ֗ה אֶל־הַחֶ֨רֶב֙ אֶל־
הַדֶּ֣בֶר וְאֶל־הָרָעָ֔ב וְנָתַתִּ֤י
אֶתְכֶם֙ לְזַוָֽעָ֔ה לְכֹ֖ל מַמְלְכ֥וֹת
18 הָאָֽרֶץ׃ וְנָתַתִּ֣י אֶת־הָאֲנָשִׁ֗ים
הָעֹֽבְרִים֙ אֶת־בְּרִתִ֔י אֲשֶׁ֤ר
לֹֽא־הֵקִ֨ימוּ֙ אֶת־דִּבְרֵ֣י
הַבְּרִ֔ית אֲשֶׁ֥ר כָּרְת֖וּ לְפָנָ֑י
הָעֵ֨גֶל֙ אֲשֶׁ֣ר כָּרְת֣וּ לִשְׁנַ֔יִם
19 וַיַּֽעַבְר֖וּ בֵּ֣ין בְּתָרָֽיו׃ שָׂרֵ֨י
יְהוּדָ֜ה וְשָׂרֵ֣י יְרוּשָׁלַ֗ם
הַסָּֽרִסִים֙ וְהַכֹּ֣הֲנִ֔ים וְכֹ֖ל עַ֣ם
הָאָ֑רֶץ הָעֹֽבְרִ֔ים בֵּ֖ין בִּתְרֵ֥י
20 הָעֵֽגֶל׃ וְנָתַתִּ֤י אוֹתָם֙ בְּיַ֣ד
אֹֽיְבֵיהֶ֔ם וּבְיַ֖ד מְבַקְשֵׁ֣י נַפְשָׁ֑ם
וְהָֽיְתָ֤ה נִבְלָתָם֙ לְמַֽאֲכָ֔ל לְע֥וֹף
הַשָּׁמַ֖יִם וּלְבֶֽהֱמַ֥ת הָאָֽרֶץ׃

v. 17. חסר י׳   v. 18. לזעוה ק׳

---

17. *I proclaim for you a liberty.* Spoken
ironically: you will be freed from My
service and protection and fall a prey to
the sword.

18. *when they cut the calf in twain.* This
was the ancient manner of making a
covenant (cf. Gen. xv. 9f.). Its significance was probably that of an implied
oath: may the person who breaks the

covenant be cut in two even as the calf
is divided.

19. *the people of the land.* Sulzberger
has explained the phrase as denoting the
National Council.

20. *their dead bodies,* etc. The severity
of the punishment is an index to the
heinousness of the offence. Not only
will the guilty be slain, but their bodies
will not receive honourable burial.

earth. **21.** And Zedekiah king of
Judah and his princes will I give
into the hand of their enemies, and
into the hand of them that seek their
life, and into the hand of the king of
Babylon's army, that are gone up
from you. **22.** Behold, I will
command, saith the LORD, and cause
them to return to this city; and they
shall fight against it, and take it, and
burn it with fire; and I will make the
cities of Judah a desolation, without
inhabitant.

21 וְאֶת־צִדְקִיָּהוּ מֶלֶךְ־יְהוּדָה
וְאֶת־שָׂרָיו אֶתֵּן בְּיַד אֹיְבֵיהֶם
וּבְיַד מְבַקְשֵׁי נַפְשָׁם וּבְיַד חֵיל
מֶלֶךְ בָּבֶל הָעֹלִים מֵעֲלֵיכֶם:
22 הִנְנִי מְצַוֶּה נְאֻם־יְהֹוָה
וַהֲשִׁבֹתִים אֶל־הָעִיר הַזֹּאת
וְנִלְחֲמוּ עָלֶיהָ וּלְכָדוּהָ
וּשְׂרָפֻהָ בָאֵשׁ וְאֶת־עָרֵי
יְהוּדָה אֶתֵּן שְׁמָמָה מֵאֵין יֹשֵׁב:

---

35   CHAPTER XXXV   לה

1. The word which came unto
Jeremiah from the LORD in the days
of Jehoiakim the son of Josiah, king
of Judah, saying: **2.** 'Go unto the
house of the Rechabites, and speak

1 הַדָּבָר אֲשֶׁר־הָיָה אֶל־
יִרְמְיָהוּ מֵאֵת יְהֹוָה בִּימֵי
יְהוֹיָקִים בֶּן־יֹאשִׁיָּהוּ מֶלֶךְ
2 יְהוּדָה לֵאמֹר: הָלוֹךְ אֶל־
בֵּית הָרֵכָבִים וְדִבַּרְתָּ אוֹתָם

---

21. *that are gone up from you.* The siege
was temporarily broken off by Nebuchadnezzar at the news that an Egyptian army
was advancing against him (xxxvii. 5).
During this lull the slaves were retaken.

22. *cause them to return.* 'As they have
caused their slaves to return (verse 11),
so God will cause their besiegers to
return and consummate the destruction
of the city' (Peake).

CHAPTER XXXV

THE INCIDENT OF THE RECHABITES

1-11 THE FIDELITY OF THE RECHABITES

1. *in the days of Jehoiakim.* This chapter
and the following chronologically precede

xxxii-xxxiv and take us back to the
latter part of Jehoiakim's reign in 598
B.C.E., when the Chaldeans attacked
Judea and forced many of the inhabitants
to take refuge in Jerusalem. These
refugees included the Rechabites, who
were forbidden by their principles to
live in cities.

2. *the house.* i.e. the tribe, as in verses 3,
5, 18.

Rechabites. The descendants of Jonadab
the son of Rechab (verse 6). They were
a nomadic tribe of Kenite descent and
so connected with Jethro, the father-in-

unto them, and bring them into the house of the Lord, into one of the chambers, and give them wine to drink.' 3. Then I took Jaazaniah the son of Jeremiah, the son of Habazziniah, and his brethren, and all his sons, and the whole house of the Rechabites; 4. and I brought them into the house of the Lord, into the chamber of the sons of Hanan the son of Igdaliah, the man of God, which was by the chamber of the princes, which was above the chamber of Maaseiah the son of Shallum, the keeper of the door; 5. and I set before the sons of the house of the Rechabites goblets full of wine, and cups, and I said unto them: 'Drink ye wine.' 6. But they said: 'We will drink no wine; for Ionadab the son of Rechab our

וַהֲבֵאוֹתָם֙ בֵּ֣ית יְהוָ֔ה אֶל־
אַחַ֣ת הַלְּשָׁכ֑וֹת וְהִשְׁקִיתָ֥ אוֹתָ֖ם
3 יָֽיִן: וָאֶקַּ֞ח אֶת־יַאֲזַנְיָ֣ה בֶן־
יִרְמְיָ֗הוּ בֶּן־חֲבַצִּנְיָ֔ה וְאֶת־
אֶחָ֖יו וְאֶת־כָּל־בָּנָ֑יו וְאֵ֖ת
4 כָּל־בֵּ֥ית הָרֵכָבִֽים: וָאָבִ֣א
אֹתָ֣ם בֵּ֣ית יְהוָ֗ה אֶל־לִשְׁכַּ֡ת
בְּנֵ֣י חָנָ֣ן בֶּן־יִגְדַּלְיָהוּ֮ אִ֣ישׁ
הָאֱלֹהִים֒ אֲשֶׁר־אֵ֨צֶל֙ לִשְׁכַּ֣ת
הַשָּׂרִ֔ים אֲשֶׁ֣ר מִמַּ֔עַל לְלִשְׁכַּ֖ת
מַעֲשֵׂיָ֥הוּ בֶן־שַׁלֻּ֖ם שֹׁמֵ֥ר הַסַּֽף:
5 וָאֶתֵּ֞ן לִפְנֵ֣י ׀ בְּנֵ֣י בֵית־
הָרֵכָבִ֗ים גְּבִעִ֛ים מְלֵאִ֥ים יַ֖יִן
וְכֹס֑וֹת וָאֹמַ֥ר אֲלֵיהֶ֖ם שְׁתוּ־
6 יָֽיִן: וַיֹּאמְר֖וּ לֹ֣א נִשְׁתֶּה־יָּ֑יִן
כִּ֣י יוֹנָדָ֣ב בֶּן־רֵכָ֗ב אָבִ֙ינוּ֙ צִוָּ֣ה

פתח בס״פ v. 4.

---

law of Moses who was a Kenite (Judg. i. 16, and cf. 1 Chron. ii. 55).

chambers. These were anterooms in the Temple for storing *the hallowed things* (1 Chron. xxviii. 12), and for the use of priests and Levites.

3. *Jaazaniah.* Probably the head of the tribe. His father, Jeremiah, is, of course, not to be identified with the prophet.

4. *into the house of the LORD.* To give the widest publicity to what was about to take place.

the sons of. It is uncertain whether this is to be understood literally, or 'the disciples of.' Nothing more is recorded of Hanan.

the man of God. The prophet.

Maaseiah. Cf. xxi. 1.

the keeper of the door. More lit. 'of the threshold.' There were three such officers (cf. lii. 24; 2 Kings xxv. 18) who had charge of the funds for the repair of the Temple (2 Kings xii. 10). In lii. 24 they are mentioned alongside *the chief priest* and *the second priest*, which indicates that they were high-placed dignitaries.

5. *goblets.* Large flagons from which the wine was poured into the *cups.*

6. *our father.* Our ancestor. He collaborated with Jehu in the abolition of Baal-worship (2 Kings x. 15ff.).

father commanded us, saying: Ye shall drink no wine, neither ye, nor your sons, for ever; 7. neither shall ye build house, nor sow seed, nor plant vineyard, nor have any; but all your days ye shall dwell in tents, that ye may live many days in the land wherein ye sojourn. 8. And we have hearkened to the voice of Jonadab the son of Rechab our father in all that he charged us, to drink no wine all our days, we, our wives, our sons, nor our daughters; 9. nor to build houses for us to dwell in, neither to have vineyard, or field, or seed; 10. but we have dwelt in tents, and have hearkened, and done according to all that Jonadab our father commanded us. 11. But it came to pass, when Nebuchadrezzar king of Babylon came up against the land, that we said: Come, and let us go to Jerusalem for fear of the army of the Chaldeans, and for fear of the army of the Arameans; so we dwell at Jerusalem.'

12. Then came the word of the LORD unto Jeremiah, saying:

עָלֵינוּ לֵאמֹר לֹא תִשְׁתּוּ־יַיִן
אַתֶּם וּבְנֵיכֶם עַד־עוֹלָם:
7 וּבַיִת לֹא־תִבְנוּ וְזֶרַע לֹא־
תִזְרָעוּ וְכֶרֶם לֹא־תִטָּעוּ וְלֹא
יִהְיֶה לָכֶם כִּי בָּאֳהָלִים תֵּשְׁבוּ
כָּל־יְמֵיכֶם לְמַעַן תִּחְיוּ יָמִים
רַבִּים עַל־פְּנֵי הָאֲדָמָה אֲשֶׁר
8 אַתֶּם גָּרִים שָׁם: וַנִּשְׁמַע בְּקוֹל
יְהוֹנָדָב בֶּן־רֵכָב אָבִינוּ לְכֹל
אֲשֶׁר צִוָּנוּ לְבִלְתִּי שְׁתוֹת־יַיִן
כָּל־יָמֵינוּ אֲנַחְנוּ נָשֵׁינוּ בָּנֵינוּ
9 וּבְנֹתֵינוּ: וּלְבִלְתִּי בְּנוֹת בָּתִּים
לְשִׁבְתֵּנוּ וְכֶרֶם וְשָׂדֶה וָזֶרַע
10 לֹא יִהְיֶה־לָּנוּ: וַנֵּשֶׁב
בָּאֳהָלִים וַנִּשְׁמַע וַנַּעַשׂ כְּכֹל
11 אֲשֶׁר־צִוָּנוּ יוֹנָדָב אָבִינוּ: וַיְהִי
בַּעֲלוֹת נְבוּכַדְרֶאצַּר מֶלֶךְ־
בָּבֶל אֶל־הָאָרֶץ וַנֹּאמֶר בֹּאוּ
וְנָבוֹא יְרוּשָׁלַםִ מִפְּנֵי חֵיל
הַכַּשְׂדִּים וּמִפְּנֵי חֵיל אֲרָם
12 וַנֵּשֶׁב בִּירוּשָׁלָםִ: וַיְהִי דְּבַר־
יְהֹוָה אֶל־יִרְמְיָהוּ לֵאמֹר:

v. 7. קמץ בפשטא   v. 7. קמץ בז"ק

---

ye shall drink no wine. As nomads they were to live a simple life and shun the luxuries of the cities.

11. let us go to Jerusalem. They were forced by circumstances to transgress the law of their tribe not to dwell in cities, but they would not drink wine.

Arameans. Allies of the Chaldeans (2 Kings xxiv. 2).

12-17 MORAL OF THE INCIDENT FOR THE JUDEANS

13. 'Thus saith the LORD of hosts, the God of Israel: Go, and say to the men of Judah and the inhabitants of Jerusalem: Will ye not receive instruction to hearken to My words? saith the LORD. 14. The words of Jonadab the son of Rechab, that he commanded his sons, not to drink wine, are performed, and unto this day they drink none, for they hearken to their father's commandment; but I have spoken unto you, speaking betimes and often, and ye have not hearkened unto Me. 15. I have sent also unto you all My servants the prophets, sending them betimes and often, saying: Return ye now every man from his evil way, and amend your doings, and go not after other gods to serve them, and ye shall dwell in the land which I have given to you and to your fathers; but ye have not inclined your ear, nor hearkened unto Me. 16. Because the sons of Jonadab the son of Rechab have performed the

13 כֹּה־אָמַר יְהֹוָה צְבָאוֹת אֱלֹהֵי
יִשְׂרָאֵל הָלֹךְ וְאָמַרְתָּ לְאִישׁ
יְהוּדָה וּלְיוֹשְׁבֵי יְרוּשָׁלַ͏ִם הֲלוֹא
תִקְחוּ מוּסָר לִשְׁמֹעַ אֶל־
14 דְּבָרַי נְאֻם־יְהֹוָה: הוּקַם
אֶת־דִּבְרֵי יְהוֹנָדָב בֶּן־רֵכָב
אֲשֶׁר־צִוָּה אֶת־בָּנָיו לְבִלְתִּי
שְׁתוֹת־יַיִן וְלֹא שָׁתוּ עַד־הַיּוֹם
הַזֶּה כִּי שָׁמְעוּ אֵת מִצְוַת
אֲבִיהֶם וְאָנֹכִי דִּבַּרְתִּי אֲלֵיכֶם
הַשְׁכֵּם וְדַבֵּר וְלֹא שְׁמַעְתֶּם
15 אֵלָי: וָאֶשְׁלַח אֲלֵיכֶם אֶת־
כָּל־עֲבָדַי הַנְּבִיאִים | הַשְׁכֵּם
וְשָׁלֹחַ | לֵאמֹר שֻׁבוּ־נָא אִישׁ
מִדַּרְכּוֹ הָרָעָה וְהֵיטִיבוּ
מַעַלְלֵיכֶם וְאַל־־תֵּלְכוּ
אַחֲרֵי אֱלֹהִים אֲחֵרִים
לְעָבְדָם וּשְׁבוּ אֶל־הָאֲדָמָה
אֲשֶׁר־נָתַתִּי לָכֶם וְלַאֲבֹתֵיכֶם
וְלֹא הִטִּיתֶם אֶת־אָזְנְכֶם וְלֹא
16 שְׁמַעְתֶּם אֵלָי: כִּי הֵקִימוּ בְּנֵי
יְהוֹנָדָב בֶּן־רֵכָב אֶת־מִצְוַת

נ״א על v. 15.

13. *will ye not receive . . . My words?* i.e. will you not follow this example of loyal obedience?

14. *are performed.* The Hebrew verb rather signifies 'are established,' i.e. have taken a firm hold on the Rechabites.

unto this day. Although about three hundred years have passed since Jonadab instituted the law.

but I have spoken. The pronoun is emphasized in the Hebrew to mark a contrast with Jonadab who was obeyed, whereas God's commands are ignored.

commandment of their father which
he commanded them, but this people
hath not hearkened unto Me;
17. therefore thus saith the LORD,
the God of hosts, the God of Israel:
Behold, I will bring upon Judah and
upon all the inhabitants of Jerusalem
all the evil that I have pronounced
against them; because I have spoken
unto them, but they have not heard,
and I have called unto them, but
they have not answered.'

18. And unto the house of the
Rechabites Jeremiah said: 'Thus
saith the LORD of hosts, the God of
Israel: Because ye have hearkened
to the commandment of Jonadab
your father, and kept all his precepts,
and done according unto all that he
commanded you; 19. therefore thus
saith the LORD of hosts, the God of
Israel: There shall not be cut off
unto Jonadab the son of Rechab a
man to stand before Me for ever.'

אֲבִיהֶם אֲשֶׁר צִוָּם וְהָעָם הַזֶּה
17 לֹא שָׁמְעוּ אֵלָי: לָכֵן כֹּה־
אָמַר יְהֹוָה אֱלֹהֵי צְבָאוֹת
אֱלֹהֵי יִשְׂרָאֵל הִנְנִי מֵבִיא אֶל־
יְהוּדָה וְאֶל כָּל־יוֹשְׁבֵי
יְרוּשָׁלַ͏ִם אֵת כָּל־הָרָעָה אֲשֶׁר
דִּבַּרְתִּי עֲלֵיהֶם יַעַן דִּבַּרְתִּי
אֲלֵיהֶם וְלֹא שָׁמֵעוּ וָאֶקְרָא
18 לָהֶם וְלֹא עָנוּ: וּלְבֵית
הָרֵכָבִים אָמַר יִרְמְיָהוּ כֹּה־
אָמַר יְהֹוָה צְבָאוֹת אֱלֹהֵי
יִשְׂרָאֵל יַעַן אֲשֶׁר שְׁמַעְתֶּם
עַל־מִצְוַת יְהוֹנָדָב אֲבִיכֶם
וַתִּשְׁמְרוּ אֶת־כָּל־מִצְוֺתָיו
וַתַּעֲשׂוּ כְּכֹל אֲשֶׁר־צִוָּה
19 אֶתְכֶם: לָכֵן כֹּה אָמַר יְהֹוָה
צְבָאוֹת אֱלֹהֵי יִשְׂרָאֵל לֹא־
יִכָּרֵת אִישׁ לְיוֹנָדָב בֶּן־רֵכָב
עֹמֵד לְפָנַי כָּל־הַיָּמִים:

---

17. Cf. xix 15.
18-19 THE REWARD OF THE RECHABITES
18. As the disobedience of the Judeans
will involve them in ruin, so the faithfulness of the Rechabites will receive
recognition by God.
19. *to stand before Me for ever.* See on

xv. 19. The phrase elsewhere usually
connotes service in the Temple. It is
uncertain whether such is the intention
here. For the Rabbinical interpretation
and alleged traces of them in subsequent
times, the reader may consult the article
on 'Rechabites' in the Jewish Encyclo-
pædia.

36   CHAPTER XXXVI   לו

1. And it came to pass in the fourth year of Jehoiakim the son of Josiah, king of Judah, that this word came unto Jeremiah from the LORD, saying: 2. 'Take thee a roll of a book, and write therein all the words that I have spoken unto thee against Israel, and against Judah, and against all the nations, from the day I spoke unto thee, from the days of Josiah, even unto this day. 3. It may be that the house of Judah will hear all the evil which I purpose to do unto them; that they may return every man from his evil way, and I

וַיְהִי֙ בַּשָּׁנָ֣ה הָרְבִיעִ֔ת 1
לִֽיהוֹיָקִ֧ים בֶּן־יֹאשִׁיָּ֛הוּ מֶ֥לֶךְ
יְהוּדָ֖ה הָיָ֣ה הַדָּבָ֥ר הַזֶּ֛ה אֶל־
יִרְמְיָ֖הוּ מֵאֵ֥ת יְהוָ֖ה לֵאמֹֽר׃
קַח־לְךָ֮ מְגִלַּת־סֵפֶר֒ וְכָתַבְתָּ֣ 2
אֵלֶ֗יהָ אֵ֣ת כָּל־הַדְּבָרִ֣ים אֲשֶׁר־
דִּבַּ֧רְתִּי אֵלֶ֛יךָ עַל־יִשְׂרָאֵ֥ל
וְעַל־יְהוּדָ֖ה וְעַל־כָּל־הַגּוֹיִ֑ם
מִיּ֞וֹם דִּבַּ֤רְתִּי אֵלֶ֙יךָ֙ מִימֵ֣י
יֹֽאשִׁיָּ֔הוּ וְעַ֖ד הַיּ֥וֹם הַזֶּֽה׃ אוּלַ֣י 3
יִשְׁמְעוּ֙ בֵּ֣ית יְהוּדָ֔ה אֵ֖ת כָּל־
הָ֣רָעָ֔ה אֲשֶׁ֥ר אָֽנֹכִ֖י חֹשֵׁ֑ב
לַעֲשׂ֣וֹת לָהֶ֑ם לְמַ֙עַן֙ יָשׁ֔וּבוּ
אִ֚ישׁ מִדַּרְכּ֣וֹ הָֽרָעָ֔ה וְסָלַחְתִּ֖י

CHAPTER XXXVI

JEREMIAH DICTATES HIS PROPHECIES TO BARUCH

PEAKE describes this as 'one of the most noteworthy chapters of the Book, since it gives us very important information as to the origin of Jeremiah's prophecies in their written form.'

1-8 JEREMIAH COMMANDED TO COMMIT HIS UTTERANCES TO WRITING

1. *in the fourth year of Jehoiakim.* See on xxv. 1.

2. *a roll of a book.* Ancient books were in the form of scrolls, parchment skins being sewn together and attached to wooden rollers. The text was written in columns parallel to the rollers so that the roll was unwound as the reading proceeded.

all the words. According to the Rabbis, the Book of Lamentations is included under the word *all*.

against Israel, and against Judah. Jeremiah's prophecies about Israel consisted only of promises (cf., e.g., iii. 12ff., xxxi. 1ff.) seeing that the Northern Kingdom no longer existed, and threats of further calamity would have been pointless. It is to be noted that the Hebrew preposition *al* may be rendered 'concerning' as well as 'against' and is perhaps to be so understood here.

and against all the nations. Cf. xxv. 15-29, xlvi-li.

3. *it may be,* etc. God does not desire the destruction of the wicked, but their repentance (cf. xviii. 8, xxvi. 3).

may forgive their iniquity and their sin.'

4. Then Jeremiah called Baruch the son of Neriah; and Baruch wrote from the mouth of Jeremiah all the words of the LORD, which He had spoken unto him, upon a roll of a book. 5. And Jeremiah commanded Baruch, saying: 'I am detained, I cannot go into the house of the LORD; 6. therefore go thou, and read in the roll, which thou hast written from my mouth, the words of the LORD in the ears of the people in the LORD's house upon a fast-day; and also thou shalt read them in the ears of all Judah that come out of their cities. 7. It may be they will present their supplication before the LORD, and will return every one from his evil way; for great is the anger and the fury that the LORD hath pronounced against this people.' 8. And Baruch the son of Neriah did according to all that

4 וַיִּקְרָא לַעֲוֺנָם וּלְחַטָּאתָם׃
יִרְמְיָהוּ אֶת־בָּרוּךְ בֶּן־נֵרִיָּה
וַיִּכְתֹּב בָּרוּךְ מִפִּי יִרְמְיָהוּ
אֵת כָּל־דִּבְרֵי יְהֹוָה אֲשֶׁר־
דִּבֶּר אֵלָיו עַל־מְגִלַּת־סֵפֶר׃
5 וַיְצַוֶּה יִרְמְיָהוּ אֶת־בָּרוּךְ
לֵאמֹר אֲנִי עָצוּר לֹא אוּכַל
6 לָבוֹא בֵּית יְהֹוָה׃ וּבָאתָ אַתָּה
וְקָרָאתָ בַמְּגִלָּה אֲשֶׁר־כָּתַבְתָּ
מִפִּי אֶת־דִּבְרֵי יְהֹוָה בְּאָזְנֵי
הָעָם בֵּית יְהֹוָה בְּיוֹם צוֹם
וְגַם בְּאָזְנֵי כָל־יְהוּדָה הַבָּאִים
7 מֵעָרֵיהֶם תִּקְרָאֵם׃ אוּלַי
תִּפֹּל תְּחִנָּתָם לִפְנֵי יְהֹוָה וְיָשֻׁבוּ
אִישׁ מִדַּרְכּוֹ הָרָעָה כִּי־גָדוֹל
הָאַף וְהַחֵמָה אֲשֶׁר־דִּבֶּר
8 יְהֹוָה אֶל־הָעָם הַזֶּה׃ וַיַּעַשׂ

---

4. *Baruch the son of Neriah.* He is first mentioned in xxxii. 12f. as Jeremiah's attendant.

5. *I am detained.* The Hebrew verb *atsur* occurs in xxxiii. 1 and xxxix. 15 in the sense of 'imprisoned'; but it is evident from verse 19 that Jeremiah was free to escape. Hence A.J. renders *detained* (as in 1 Sam. xxi. 8), but R.V. margin 'restrained' is preferable. In all probability Jeremiah was forbidden by the Temple authorities to speak within its precincts after what is related in chapter xx.

6. *upon a fast-day.* Possibly several fast-days were appointed for intercession on

account of the grave position (cf. verse 9) and one of them was to be selected for the reading because a large crowd would be present.

that come out of their cities. On such a day people would come into Jerusalem from other cities to observe the fast there.

7. *present their supplication.* lit. 'their supplication will fall.' When they learn of the fate that threatens them they may be in a repentant mood. Jeremiah had already warned them many times, yet he does not abandon hope of a last-minute change of heart.

8. *did.* As described in detail in verses 9ff.

Jeremiah the prophet commanded him, reading in the book the words of the LORD in the LORD's house.

9. Now it came to pass in the fifth year of Jehoiakim the son of Josiah, king of Judah, in the ninth month, that they proclaimed a fast before the LORD, all the people in Jerusalem, and all the people that came from the cities of Judah unto Jerusalem. 10. Then did Baruch read in the book the words of Jeremiah in the house of the LORD, in the chamber of Gemariah the son of Shaphan the scribe, in the upper court, at the entry of the new gate of the LORD's house, in the ears of all the people. 11. And when Micaiah the son of Gemariah, the son of Shaphan, had heard out of the book all the words of the LORD,

בָּרוּךְ בֶּן־נֵרִיָּה כְּכֹל אֲשֶׁר־
צִוָּהוּ יִרְמְיָהוּ הַנָּבִיא לִקְרֹא
בַסֵּפֶר דִּבְרֵי יְהֹוָה בֵּית יְהֹוָה׃
9 וַיְהִי בַשָּׁנָה הַחֲמִשִׁית
לִיהוֹיָקִים בֶּן־יֹאשִׁיָּהוּ מֶלֶךְ־
יְהוּדָה בַּחֹדֶשׁ הַתְּשִׁעִי קָרְאוּ
צוֹם לִפְנֵי יְהֹוָה כָּל־הָעָם
בִּירוּשָׁלָ͏ִם וְכָל־הָעָם הַבָּאִים
מֵעָרֵי יְהוּדָה בִּירוּשָׁלָ͏ִם׃
10 וַיִּקְרָא בָרוּךְ בַּסֵּפֶר אֶת־
דִּבְרֵי יִרְמְיָהוּ בֵּית יְהֹוָה
בְּלִשְׁכַּת גְּמַרְיָהוּ בֶן־שָׁפָן
הַסֹּפֵר בֶּחָצֵר הָעֶלְיוֹן פֶּתַח
שַׁעַר בֵּית־יְהֹוָה הֶחָדָשׁ בְּאָזְנֵי
11 כָּל־הָעָם׃ וַיִּשְׁמַע מִכָיְהוּ
בֶן־גְּמַרְיָהוּ בֶן־שָׁפָן אֶת־
כָּל־דִּבְרֵי יְהֹוָה מֵעַל־־

9-26 THE ROLL IS READ IN THE TEMPLE AND TO THE KING AND BURNED

9. in the fifth year. About a year elapsed before the scroll was written and read in public.

in the ninth month. Later called Kislew; it corresponds roughly to December. No statutory Jewish fast is held in this month; so the occasion was special. Since no day of the month is specified, Ehrlich suggests that the new moon is meant.

10. in the chamber. i.e. stood by the entrance of this chamber.

Gemariah the son of Shaphan the scribe. The scribe may refer to either the father or the son. Shaphan was a scribe in the days of Josiah (2 Kings xxii. 3, 8). If the father is the Shaphan mentioned in xxvi. 24, then Gemariah was a brother of Ahikam who was friendly disposed towards Jeremiah. He is not the man of that name in xxix. 3.

upper court. Called the *inner court* in 1 Kings vi. 36, vii. 12.

the new gate. See on xxvi. 10.

11. Micaiah. Gemariah was attending a council of *the princes* at the time of the reading and may have instructed his son to report the contents to him.

12. he went down into the king's house, into the scribe's chamber; and, lo, all the princes sat there, even Elishama the scribe, and Delaiah the son of Shemaiah, and Elnathan the son of Achbor, and Gemariah the son of Shaphan, and Zedekiah the son of Hananiah, and all the princes. 13. Then Micaiah declared unto them all the words that he had heard, when Baruch read the book in the ears of the people. 14. Therefore all the princes sent Jehudi the son of Nethaniah, the son of Shelemiah, the son of Cushi, unto Baruch, saying: 'Take in thy hand the roll wherein thou hast read in the ears of the people, and come.' So Baruch the son of Neriah took the roll in his hand, and came unto them. 15. And they said unto him: 'Sit down now, and read it in our ears.' So Baruch read it in their ears. 16. Now it came to pass, when

12 הַסֹּפֵר : וַיֵּרֶד בֵּית־הַמֶּלֶךְ
עַל־לִשְׁכַּת הַסֹּפֵר וְהִנֵּה־שָׁם
כָּל־הַשָּׂרִים יוֹשְׁבִים אֱלִישָׁמָע
הַסֹּפֵר וּדְלָיָהוּ בֶן־שְׁמַעְיָהוּ
וְאֶלְנָתָן בֶּן־עַכְבּוֹר וּגְמַרְיָהוּ
בֶן־שָׁפָן וְצִדְקִיָּהוּ בֶן־חֲנַנְיָהוּ
13 וְכָל־הַשָּׂרִים : וַיַּגֵּד לָהֶם
מִיכָיְהוּ אֵת כָּל־הַדְּבָרִים
אֲשֶׁר שָׁמֵעַ בִּקְרֹא בָרוּךְ
14 בַּסֵּפֶר בְּאָזְנֵי הָעָם : וַיִּשְׁלְחוּ
כָל־הַשָּׂרִים אֶל־בָּרוּךְ אֶת־
יְהוּדִי בֶּן־נְתַנְיָהוּ בֶּן־שֶׁלֶמְיָהוּ
בֶּן־כּוּשִׁי לֵאמֹר הַמְּגִלָּה אֲשֶׁר
קָרָאתָ בָּהּ בְּאָזְנֵי הָעָם קָחֶנָּה
בְיָדְךָ וָלֵךְ וַיִּקַּח בָּרוּךְ בֶּן־
נֵרִיָּהוּ אֶת־הַמְּגִלָּה בְּיָדוֹ וַיָּבֹא
15 אֲלֵיהֶם : וַיֹּאמְרוּ אֵלָיו שֵׁב
נָא וּקְרָאֶנָּה בְּאָזְנֵינוּ וַיִּקְרָא
16 בָרוּךְ בְּאָזְנֵיהֶם : וַיְהִי כְּשָׁמְעָם

12. *he went down.* See on xxii. 1.

even Elishama the scribe. Scribes evidently held high rank. If identical with the Elishama of xli. 1 and 2 Kings xxv. 25, he was of royal blood.

Elnathan the son of Achbor. He was mentioned in xxvi. 22.

all the princes. i.e. the rest of the princes who are unnamed.

14. *Jehudi . . . Cushi.* The names signify 'Jew' and 'Ethiopian' respectively, and it has been conjectured that

Ethiopian descent is implied. This supposition is unnecessary since the prophet Zephaniah had a father named Cushi (Zeph. i. 1) who was of pure Hebrew lineage.

15. *sit down.* The invitation to Baruch to sit in the presence of the princes is an indication of friendly disposition on their part towards him. Some ancient Versions read the verb as *shub* instead of *sheb*, i.e. 'return and read, read again'; but Peake rejects it as the true reading in favour of M.T.

they had heard all the words, they turned in fear one toward another, and said unto Baruch: 'We will surely tell the king of all these words.' 17. And they asked Baruch, saying: 'Tell us now: How didst thou write all these words at his mouth?' 18. Then Baruch answered them: 'He pronounced all these words unto me with his mouth, and I wrote them with ink in the book.' 19. Then said the princes unto Baruch: 'Go, hide thee, thou and Jeremiah; and let no man know where ye are.' 20. And they went in to the king into the court; but they had deposited the roll in the chamber of Elishama the scribe; and they told all the words in the ears of the king. 21. So the king sent Jehudi to fetch the roll; and he

אֶת־כָּל־הַדְּבָרִים פָּחֲדוּ
אִישׁ אֶל־רֵעֵהוּ וַיֹּאמְרוּ אֶל־
בָּרוּךְ הַגֵּיד נַגִּיד לַמֶּלֶךְ אֵת
כָּל־הַדְּבָרִים הָאֵלֶּה: וְאֶת־ 17
בָּרוּךְ שָׁאֲלוּ לֵאמֹר הַגֶּד־נָא
לָנוּ אֵיךְ כָּתַבְתָּ אֶת־כָּל־
הַדְּבָרִים הָאֵלֶּה מִפִּיו: וַיֹּאמֶר 18
לָהֶם בָּרוּךְ מִפִּיו יִקְרָא אֵלַי
אֵת כָּל־הַדְּבָרִים הָאֵלֶּה וַאֲנִי
כֹּתֵב עַל־הַסֵּפֶר בַּדְּיוֹ:
וַיֹּאמְרוּ הַשָּׂרִים אֶל־בָּרוּךְ 19
לֵךְ הִסָּתֵר אַתָּה וְיִרְמְיָהוּ וְאִישׁ
אַל־יֵדַע אֵיפֹה אַתֶּם: וַיָּבֹאוּ 20
אֶל־הַמֶּלֶךְ חָצֵרָה וְאֶת־
הַמְּגִלָּה הִפְקִדוּ בְּלִשְׁכַּת
אֱלִישָׁמָע הַסֹּפֵר וַיַּגִּידוּ בְּאָזְנֵי
הַמֶּלֶךְ אֵת כָּל־הַדְּבָרִים:
וַיִּשְׁלַח הַמֶּלֶךְ אֶת־יְהוּדִי 21
לָקַחַת אֶת־הַמְּגִלָּה וַיִּקָּחֶהָ

16. *we will surely tell the king.* Better, 'we must certainly tell,' etc.; the contents of the document are considered to be of such importance that they feel obliged to let the king know.

17f. Before the matter is reported to the king, the princes make sure that Baruch wrote down the actual words of Jeremiah.

19. *thou and Jeremiah.* Such direful warnings spoken in public during a crisis endangered the life of both the man who

wrote them and the man who delivered them; cf. what happened to Uriah (xxvi. 23).

let no man know where ye are. 'The so-called "Grotto of Jeremiah" near "the Quarries of Solomon" outside the Damascus Gate has been conjectured, owing to its traditional association with his name, to have been their hiding-place' (Streane).

20. *the court.* i.e. the inner court where the king's residence was located.

they had deposited. For safe keeping.

took it out of the chamber of
Elishama the scribe. And Jehudi
read it in the ears of the king, and
in the ears of all the princes that
stood beside the king. 22. Now the
king was sitting in the winter-house
in the ninth month; and the brazier
was burning before him. 23. And
it came to pass, when Jehudi had
read three or four columns, that he
cut it with the penknife, and cast it
into the fire that was in the brazier,
until all the roll was consumed in the
fire that was in the brazier. 24. Yet
they were not afraid, nor rent their
garments, neither the king, nor any
of his servants that heard all these
words. 25. Moreover Elnathan and

מִלִּשְׁכַּת אֱלִישָׁמָע הַסֹּפֵר
וַיִּקְרָאֶהָ יְהוּדִי בְּאָזְנֵי הַמֶּלֶךְ
וּבְאָזְנֵי כָּל־הַשָּׂרִים הָעֹמְדִים
22 מֵעַל הַמֶּלֶךְ: וְהַמֶּלֶךְ יוֹשֵׁב
בֵּית הַחֹרֶף בַּחֹדֶשׁ הַתְּשִׁיעִי
וְאֶת־הָאָח לְפָנָיו מְבֹעָרֶת:
23 וַיְהִי | כִּקְרוֹא יְהוּדִי שָׁלֹשׁ
דְּלָתוֹת וְאַרְבָּעָה יִקְרָעֶהָ
בְּתַעַר הַסֹּפֵר וְהַשְׁלֵךְ אֶל־
הָאֵשׁ אֲשֶׁר אֶל־הָאָח עַד־תֹּם
כָּל־הַמְּגִלָּה עַל־הָאֵשׁ אֲשֶׁר
24 עַל־הָאָח: וְלֹא פָחֲדוּ וְלֹא
קָרְעוּ אֶת־בִּגְדֵיהֶם הַמֶּלֶךְ
וְכָל־עֲבָדָיו הַשֹּׁמְעִים אֵת
25 כָּל־הַדְּבָרִים הָאֵלֶּה: וְגַם

21. *beside the king.* lit. 'above the king';
he was sitting and they were standing.

22. *the winter-house.* The Hebrew *bayith*
sometimes, as here, denotes a section of
a building (cf. Ezek. xlvi. 24, *the boiling-
places*, lit. 'the house of the boilers';
1 Chron. xxviii. 11, *the houses thereof*,
viz. of the Temple). 'In common
parlance the lower apartments are simply
el-beit, the house; the upper is the
alliyeh, which is the summer-house.
Every respectable dwelling has both . . .
If these are on the same storey, then the
external and airy apartment is the
summer-house, and that for winter is
the interior and more sheltered room.
It is rare to meet a family which has an
entirely separate dwelling for summer'
(Thomson).

in the ninth month. At a time of the year
when the king required the warmth
provided in the winter-house.

and the brazier was burning. The LXX
reads *we-esh*, 'and the fire of the brazier,'
for *we-eth* which is the sign of the
accusative. Although the grammatical
construction of M.T. is difficult it is
attested by the Targum.

23. *when Jehudi*, etc. The Hebrew
means that as often as Jehudi read three
or four columns, he cut off that section
of the scroll, which was perhaps too
large to be consigned to the flames as a
whole.

penknife. lit. 'scribe's knife.'

24. *nor rent their garments.* In token of
grief and penitence. Contrast the
behaviour of king Josiah when he heard
the reading of the newly discovered
book of the Law (2 Kings xxii. 11).

Delaiah and Gemariah had entreated the king not to burn the roll; but he would not hear them. 26. And the king commanded Jerahmeel the king's son, and Seraiah the son of Azriel, and Shelemiah the son of Abdeel, to take Baruch the scribe and Jeremiah the prophet; but the LORD hid them.

27. Then the word of the LORD came to Jeremiah, after that the king had burned the roll, and the words which Baruch wrote at the mouth of Jeremiah, saying: 28. 'Take thee again another roll, and write in it all the former words that were in the first roll, which Jehoiakim the king of Judah hath burned. 29. And concerning Jehoiakim king of Judah thou shalt say: Thus saith the LORD: Thou hast burned this roll, saying: Why hast thou written

אֶלְנָתָן וּדְלָיָהוּ וּגְמַרְיָהוּ
הִפְגִּעוּ בַמֶּלֶךְ לְבִלְתִּי שְׂרֹף
אֶת־הַמְּגִלָּה וְלֹא שָׁמַע
26 אֲלֵיהֶם: וַיְצַוֶּה הַמֶּלֶךְ אֶת־
יְרַחְמְאֵל בֶּן־הַמֶּלֶךְ וְאֶת־
שְׂרָיָהוּ בֶן־עַזְרִיאֵל וְאֶת־
שֶׁלֶמְיָהוּ בֶּן־עַבְדְּאֵל לָקַחַת
אֶת־בָּרוּךְ הַסֹּפֵר וְאֵת
יִרְמְיָהוּ הַנָּבִיא וַיַּסְתִּרֵם יְהֹוָה:
27 וַיְהִי דְבַר־יְהֹוָה אֶל־יִרְמְיָהוּ
אַחֲרֵי | שְׂרֹף הַמֶּלֶךְ אֶת־
הַמְּגִלָּה וְאֶת־הַדְּבָרִים אֲשֶׁר
כָּתַב בָּרוּךְ מִפִּי יִרְמְיָהוּ
28 לֵאמֹר: שׁוּב קַח־לְךָ מְגִלָּה
אַחֶרֶת וּכְתֹב עָלֶיהָ אֵת כָּל־
הַדְּבָרִים הָרִאשֹׁנִים אֲשֶׁר הָיוּ
עַל־הַמְּגִלָּה הָרִאשֹׁנָה אֲשֶׁר
שָׂרַף יְהוֹיָקִים מֶלֶךְ־יְהוּדָה:
29 וְעַל־יְהוֹיָקִים מֶלֶךְ־יְהוּדָה
תֹאמַר כֹּה אָמַר יְהֹוָה אַתָּה
שָׂרַפְתָּ אֶת־הַמְּגִלָּה הַזֹּאת
לֵאמֹר מַדּוּעַ כָּתַבְתָּ עָלֶיהָ

---

25. *not to burn the roll.* Perhaps out of respect for Jeremiah.

26. *Jerahmeel the king's son.* This may only mean a member of the royal household (cf. xxxviii. 6; 1 Kings xxii. 26; Zeph. i. 8). Less probable is the explanation that *Hammelech* is a name.

but the LORD hid them. 'Baruch recognizes in these words that it was due to God's watchful care that their retreat was not discovered' (Peake).

27-32 JEREMIAH COMMANDED TO HAVE THE SCROLL REWRITTEN

29. *saying: Why hast thou written,* etc. Jehoiakim had not actually spoken the words to Jeremiah, who was in hiding.

therein, saying: The king of Babylon shall certainly come and destroy this land, and shall cause to cease from thence man and beast?' 30. Therefore thus saith the LORD concerning Jehoiakim king of Judah: He shall have none to sit upon the throne of David; and his dead body shall be cast out in the day to the heat, and in the night to the frost. 31. And I will visit upon him and his seed and his servants their iniquity; and I will bring upon them, and upon the inhabitants of Jerusalem, and upon the men of Judah, all the evil that I have pronounced against them, but they hearkened not.'

32. Then took Jeremiah another roll, and gave it to Baruch the scribe, the son of Neriah; who wrote therein from the mouth of Jeremiah all the words of the book which Jehoiakim king of Judah had burned in the fire; and there were added besides unto them many like words.

לֵאמֹר בֹּא יָבוֹא מֶלֶךְ בָּבֶל
וְהִשְׁחִית אֶת־הָאָרֶץ הַזֹּאת
וְהִשְׁבִּית מִמֶּנָּה אָדָם וּבְהֵמָה:
30 לָכֵן כֹּה־אָמַר יְהוָה עַל־
יְהוֹיָקִים מֶלֶךְ יְהוּדָה לֹא־
יִהְיֶה־לּוֹ יוֹשֵׁב עַל־כִּסֵּא
דָוִד וְנִבְלָתוֹ תִּהְיֶה מֻשְׁלֶכֶת
לַחֹרֶב בַּיּוֹם וְלַקֶּרַח בַּלָּיְלָה:
31 וּפָקַדְתִּי עָלָיו וְעַל־זַרְעוֹ
וְעַל־עֲבָדָיו אֶת־עֲוֹנָם
וְהֵבֵאתִי עֲלֵיהֶם וְעַל־יֹשְׁבֵי
יְרוּשָׁלַם וְאֶל־אִישׁ יְהוּדָה אֵת
כָּל־הָרָעָה אֲשֶׁר־דִּבַּרְתִּי
32 אֲלֵיהֶם וְלֹא שָׁמֵעוּ: וְיִרְמְיָהוּ
לָקַח | מְגִלָּה אַחֶרֶת וַיִּתְּנָהּ
אֶל־בָּרוּךְ בֶּן־נֵרִיָּהוּ הַסֹּפֵר
וַיִּכְתֹּב עָלֶיהָ מִפִּי יִרְמְיָהוּ
אֵת כָּל־דִּבְרֵי הַסֵּפֶר אֲשֶׁר
שָׂרַף יְהוֹיָקִים מֶלֶךְ־יְהוּדָה
בָּאֵשׁ וְעוֹד נוֹסַף עֲלֵיהֶם
דְּבָרִים רַבִּים כָּהֵמָּה:

They express the thought in the king's mind.

30. *he shall have none to sit upon the throne of David.* His son Jehoiachin did in fact reign, but only for three months, a negligible period.

his dead body shall be cast out. See on xxii. 19.

32. *and there were added,* etc. 'This second roll therefore, still preserved to us in the earlier chapters of the Book, is fuller than that which was read in the ears of the people, and which contained briefer extracts from many years of prophecies' (Streane).

37   CHAPTER XXXVII   לֹז

1. **And** Zedekiah the son of Josiah reigned as king, instead of Coniah the son of Jehoiakim, whom Nebuchadrezzar king of Babylon made king in the land of Judah. 2. But neither he, nor his servants, nor the people of the land, did hearken unto the words of the LORD, which He spoke by the prophet Jeremiah.

3. And Zedekiah the king sent Jehucal the son of Shelemiah, and Zephaniah the son of Maaseiah the priest, to the prophet Jeremiah, saying: 'Pray now unto the LORD our God for us.' 4. Now Jeremiah

1 וַיִּמְלָךְ־מֶלֶךְ צִדְקִיָּהוּ בֶן־
יֹאשִׁיָּהוּ תַּחַת כָּנְיָהוּ בֶן־
יְהוֹיָקִים אֲשֶׁר הִמְלִיךְ
נְבוּכַדְרֶאצַּר מֶלֶךְ־בָּבֶל
2 בְּאֶרֶץ יְהוּדָה: וְלֹא שָׁמַע
הוּא וַעֲבָדָיו וְעַם הָאָרֶץ אֶל־
דִּבְרֵי יְהֹוָה אֲשֶׁר דִּבֶּר בְּיַד
3 יִרְמְיָהוּ הַנָּבִיא: וַיִּשְׁלַח
הַמֶּלֶךְ צִדְקִיָּהוּ אֶת־יְהוּכַל
בֶּן־שֶׁלֶמְיָה וְאֶת־צְפַנְיָהוּ
בֶן־מַעֲשֵׂיָה הַכֹּהֵן אֶל־
יִרְמְיָהוּ הַנָּבִיא לֵאמֹר
הִתְפַּלֶּל־נָא בַעֲדֵנוּ אֶל־
4 יְהֹוָה אֱלֹהֵינוּ: וְיִרְמְיָהוּ בָּא

CHAPTER XXXVII

1-10 ZEDEKIAH WARNED THAT THE BABYLONIANS WILL DESTROY JERUSALEM

1. *Zedekiah.* The last two chapters related to the reign of Jehoiakim. The present one treats of two incidents during Zedekiah's reign.

reigned as king. This is an unusual phrase instead of the normal 'reigned.' Because Jehoiachin (Coniah) reigned only three months, he was hardly to be regarded as a *king*; hence by contrast the text explicitly states that Zedekiah reigned *as king* (Kimchi).

whom Nebuchadrezzar, etc. Referring to Zedekiah (cf. 2 Kings xxiv. 17).

2. *the people of the land.* See on xxxiv. 19; but since there is no apparent reason why the National Council should be meant here, it more probably indicates the general population.

3. *Zedekiah the king sent.* For a previous mission of this kind, cf. xxi. 1. The present deputation was sent when the siege had been raised on account of the Egyptian army's approach.

Jehucal. He was not friendly disposed to Jeremiah; in xxxviii. 4 he was one of those who demanded his death.

Zephaniah the son of Maaseiah the priest. He was a member of the earlier mission to Jeremiah (xxi. 1).

pray now. Zedekiah appreciated that Nebuchadnezzar's departure from Jerusalem was only a temporary relief. He therefore requested Jeremiah to intercede with God that the Babylonian king be decisively defeated by Egypt and so cease to be a menace to Judea.

came in and went out among the
people; for they had not put him
into prison. 5. And Pharaoh's army
was come forth out of Egypt; and
when the Chaldeans that besieged
Jerusalem heard tidings of them,
they broke up from Jerusalem.
6. Then came the word of the LORD
unto the prophet Jeremiah, saying:
7. 'Thus saith the LORD, the God of
Israel: Thus shall ye say to the king
of Judah, that sent you unto Me to
inquire of Me: Behold, Pharaoh's
army, which is come forth to help
you, shall return to Egypt into their
own land. 8. And the Chaldeans
shall return, and fight against this
city; and they shall take it, and
burn it with fire. 9. Thus saith the
LORD: Deceive not yourselves, saying: The Chaldeans shall surely
depart from us; for they shall not
depart. 10. For though ye had
smitten the whole army of the
Chaldeans that fight against you,
and there remained but wounded
men among them, yet would they

וַיֵּצֵא בְּתוֹךְ הָעָם וְלֹא־נְתָנוּ
5 אֹתוֹ בֵּית הַכְּלִיא: וְחֵיל
פַּרְעֹה יָצָא מִמִּצְרַיִם וַיִּשְׁמְעוּ
הַכַּשְׂדִּים הַצָּרִים עַל־־
יְרוּשָׁלִַם אֶת־שִׁמְעָם וַיֵּעָלוּ
6 מֵעַל יְרוּשָׁלִָם: וַיְהִי דְּבַר־
יְהֹוָה אֶל־יִרְמְיָהוּ הַנָּבִיא
7 לֵאמֹר: כֹּה־אָמַר יְהֹוָה
אֱלֹהֵי יִשְׂרָאֵל כֹּה תֹאמְרוּ
אֶל־־מֶלֶךְ יְהוּדָה הַשֹּׁלֵחַ
אֶתְכֶם אֵלַי לְדָרְשֵׁנִי הִנֵּה |
חֵיל פַּרְעֹה הַיֹּצֵא לָכֶם
לְעֶזְרָה שָׁב לְאַרְצוֹ מִצְרָיִם:
8 וְשָׁבוּ הַכַּשְׂדִּים וְנִלְחֲמוּ עַל־
הָעִיר הַזֹּאת וּלְכָדֻהָ וּשְׂרָפֻהָ
9 בָאֵשׁ: כֹּה אָמַר יְהֹוָה אַל־
תַּשִּׁאוּ נַפְשֹׁתֵיכֶם לֵאמֹר הָלֹךְ
יֵלְכוּ מֵעָלֵינוּ הַכַּשְׂדִּים כִּי לֹא
10 יֵלֵכוּ: כִּי אִם־הִכִּיתֶם כָּל־
חֵיל כַּשְׂדִּים הַנִּלְחָמִים אִתְּכֶם
וְנִשְׁאֲרוּ־־בָם אֲנָשִׁים
מְדֻקָּרִים אִישׁ בְּאָהֳלוֹ יָקוּמוּ

הכלוא ק' v. 4.

---

4. *came in and went out.* This is
mentioned to account for his arrest
which soon followed.

5. *Pharaoh's army.* He was Pharaoh
Hophra (cf. xliv. 30) who reigned 590-
571 B.C.E. and was an ally of the Judean
king.

7. *shall return to Egypt.* Without having
given any effective help to Judea. The
cause of the Egyptian army's retreat is
not stated; perhaps it was defeated
(cf. Ezek. xxx. 21), or turned back in
fear of the contest without giving battle.

10. *wounded men.* The Hebrew is literally

rise up every man in his tent, and burn this city with fire.'

11. And it came to pass, that when the army of the Chaldeans was broken up from Jerusalem for fear of Pharaoh's army, 12. then Jeremiah went forth out of Jerusalem to go into the land of Benjamin, to receive his portion there, in the midst of the people. 13. And when he was in the gate of Benjamin, a captain of the ward was there, whose name was Irijah, the son of Shelemiah, the son of Hananiah; and he laid hold on Jeremiah the prophet, saying: 'Thou fallest away to the Chaldeans.' 14. Then said Jeremiah: 'It is false; I fall not away to the Chaldeans'·

וְשָׂרְפ֛וּ אֶת־הָעִ֥יר הַזֹּ֖את

11 בָּאֵֽשׁ: וְהָיָ֗ה בְּהֵעָלוֹת֙ חֵ֣יל הַכַּשְׂדִּ֔ים מֵעַ֖ל יְרוּשָׁלַ֑͏ִם מִפְּנֵ֖י

12 חֵ֣יל פַּרְעֹֽה: וַיֵּצֵ֤א יִרְמְיָ֙הוּ֙ מִירוּשָׁלַ֔͏ִם לָלֶ֖כֶת אֶ֣רֶץ בִּנְיָמִ֑ן לַחֲלִ֥ק מִשָּׁ֖ם בְּת֥וֹךְ הָעָֽם:

13 וַיְהִי־ה֗וּא בְּשַׁ֙עַר֙ בִּנְיָמִ֔ן וְשָׁ֙ם בַּ֣עַל פְּקִדֻ֔ת וּשְׁמוֹ֙ יִרְאִיָּ֔ה בֶּן־שֶֽׁלֶמְיָ֖ה בֶּן־חֲנַנְיָ֑ה וַיִּתְפֹּ֞שׂ אֶת־יִרְמְיָ֥הוּ הַנָּבִ֛יא לֵאמֹ֕ר אֶל־הַכַּשְׂדִּ֖ים אַתָּ֥ה

14 נֹפֵֽל: וַיֹּ֤אמֶר יִרְמְיָ֙הוּ֙ שֶׁ֔קֶר אֵינֶ֣נִּי נֹפֵ֖ל עַל־הַכַּשְׂדִּ֑ים

'thrust through' and can be understood as 'slain men' (cf. Lam. iv. 9). The language is a rhetorical exaggeration which emphasizes the inevitableness of the fate in store for Jerusalem. 'An interesting parallel to this prophecy is found in the history of the Indian mutiny. At a time when the British power seemed broken, a native prince sent to his astrologer to inquire what would finally be the issue of the mutiny, and he received the startling reply, "If all the Europeans save one are slain, that one will remain and fight and reconquer" ' (Binns). *every man in his tent.* lit. 'a man in his tent,' which may mean, if only one man out of the many who occupied a tent survived. According to Ehrlich it signifies the severely wounded men who should remain in their tents.

11-15 JEREMIAH IS ARRESTED

12. *to go into the land of Benjamin.* Doubtless his intended destination was his native town of Anathoth (cf. i. 1, xxxii. 8).

to receive his portion there. The meaning of the verb, literally 'to cause to divide,' cannot be determined with certainty. A.J. is as probable as any other translation and presupposes that a relative had died in Anathoth and it was necessary for Jeremiah to be there in connection with the inheritance. What is related in xxxii happened at a later date. Kimchi renders: 'to escape thence into the midst of the people.' He anticipated arrest and attempted to avoid it.

13. *in the gate of Benjamin.* The wall on the north side of the city leading to the territory of Benjamin.

Hananiah. Not to be identified with Jeremiah's opponent in xxviii. 1off. who would hardly have had a grandson grown to manhood.

fallest away to. i.e. art a deserter to. Jeremiah's utterances gave ground for the suspicion.

14. *I fall not away to the Chaldeans.* Although he had counselled submission

but he hearkened not to him; so Irijah laid hold on Jeremiah, and brought him to the princes. 15. And the princes were wroth with Jeremiah, and smote him, and put him in prison in the house of Jonathan the scribe; for they had made that the prison.

16. When Jeremiah was come into the dungeon-house, and into the cells, and Jeremiah had remained there many days; 17. then Zedekiah the king sent, and fetched him; and the king asked him secretly in his house, and said: 'Is there any word from the LORD?' And Jeremiah said: 'There is.' He said also: 'Thou shalt be delivered into the hand of the king of Babylon'. 18. Moreover Jeremiah said unto

וְלֹא שָׁמַע אֵלָיו וַיִּתְפֹּשׂ יִרְאִיָּיה
בְּיִרְמְיָהוּ וַיְבִאֵהוּ אֶל--
15 הַשָּׂרִים: וַיִּקְצְפוּ הַשָּׂרִים
עַל-יִרְמְיָהוּ וְהִכּוּ אֹתוֹ וְנָתְנוּ
אוֹתוֹ בֵּית הָאֵסוּר בֵּית יְהוֹנָתָן
הַסֹּפֵר כִּי-אֹתוֹ עָשׂוּ לְבֵית
16 הַכֶּלֶא: כִּי בָא יִרְמְיָהוּ אֶל-
בֵּית הַבּוֹר וְאֶל-הַחֲנֻיּוֹת
וַיֵּשֶׁב-שָׁם יִרְמְיָהוּ יָמִים
17 רַבִּים: וַיִּשְׁלַח הַמֶּלֶךְ
צִדְקִיָּהוּ וַיִּקָּחֵהוּ וַיִּשְׁאָלֵהוּ
הַמֶּלֶךְ בְּבֵיתוֹ בַּסֵּתֶר וַיֹּאמֶר
הֲיֵשׁ דָּבָר מֵאֵת יְהוָה וַיֹּאמֶר
יִרְמְיָהוּ יֵשׁ וַיֹּאמֶר בְּיַד-מֶלֶךְ
18 בָּבֶל תִּנָּתֵן: וַיֹּאמֶר יִרְמְיָהוּ

to Babylon (cf. xxi. 9), his personal resolve was to remain in Judea and not surrender himself. Hence his repudiation of the charge.

15. the princes were wroth. Their attitude towards Jeremiah was different from that of their predecessors in Jehoiakim's reign (xxvi. 16, xxxvi. 19) who were now exiles in Babylon. These men were 'upstarts who had no experience of government, hot-headed and short-sighted patriots' (Peake). They remembered how Jeremiah had compared them to bad figs (xxiv).

Jonathan the scribe. No reason is given why his house was chosen for the prophet's detention. It has been suggested that the prisons were filled with political opponents.

16. *into the dungeon-house.* From verse 20

it appears that this dungeon was part of Jonathan's house.

many days. During which time the Chaldeans resumed the siege of the city. This event induced Zedekiah to communicate again with Jeremiah.

17. *secretly.* Fearing the resentment of the princes (cf. xxxviii. 5, 24ff.). Nevertheless his action proves his faith in Jeremiah as a true prophet.

there is. 'The horror of confinement in a subterranean prison of an Eastern city. in time of siege can hardly be imagined, yet Jeremiah's faith in God is unshaken; the word of the Lord is still with Jeremiah. Men may forsake God; God does not forsake men' (Pickering).

thou shalt be delivered, etc. Cf. xxxii. 3f., xxxiv. 2f.

king Zedekiah: 'Wherein have I
sinned against thee, or against thy
servants, or against this people, that
ye have put me in prison? 19. Where
now are your prophets that prophesied unto you, saying: The king
of Babylon shall not come against
you, nor against this land? 20. And
now hear, I pray thee, O my lord
the king: let my supplication, I pray
thee, be presented before thee; that
thou cause me not to return to the
house of Jonathan the scribe, lest
I die there.' 21. Then Zedekiah
the king commanded, and they
committed Jeremiah into the court
of the guard, and they gave him
daily a loaf of bread out of the
bakers' street, until all the bread in
the city was spent. Thus Jeremiah
remained in the court of the guard.

אֶל־הַמֶּ֫לֶךְ צִדְקִיָּ֫הוּ מֶה
חָטָ֫אתִי לְךָ֣ וְלַעֲבָדֶ֫יךָ וְלָעָ֣ם
הַזֶּ֗ה כִּי־נְתַתֶּ֥ם אוֹתִ֖י אֶל־־
19 בֵּ֥ית הַכֶּֽלֶא׃ וְאַיֵּ֣ה נְבִֽיאֵיכֶ֗ם
אֲשֶׁר־נִבְּא֤וּ לָכֶם֙ לֵאמֹ֔ר לֹֽא־
יָבֹ֤א מֶֽלֶךְ־בָּבֶל֙ עֲלֵיכֶ֔ם וְעַ֖ל
20 הָאָ֥רֶץ הַזֹּֽאת׃ וְעַתָּ֣ה שְׁמַֽע־־
נָ֣א אֲדֹנִ֣י הַמֶּ֔לֶךְ תִּפָּל־נָ֤א
תְחִנָּתִי֙ לְפָנֶ֔יךָ וְאַל־תְּשִׁבֵ֗נִי
בֵּ֚ית יְהוֹנָתָ֣ן הַסֹּפֵ֔ר וְלֹ֥א אָמ֖וּת
21 שָֽׁם׃ וַיְצַוֶּ֞ה הַמֶּ֣לֶךְ צִדְקִיָּ֗הוּ
וַיַּפְקִ֤דוּ אֶת־־יִרְמְיָ֨הוּ֙ בַּחֲצַ֣ר
הַמַּטָּרָ֔ה וְנָתֹ֨ן ל֥וֹ כִכַּר־לֶ֜חֶם
לַיּ֤וֹם מִחוּץ֙ הָֽאֹפִ֔ים עַד־תֹּ֥ם
כָּל־הַלֶּ֖חֶם מִן־הָעִ֑יר וַיֵּ֙שֶׁב֙
יִרְמְיָ֔הוּ בַּחֲצַ֖ר הַמַּטָּרָֽה׃

---

38   CHAPTER XXXVIII   לח

1. And Shephatiah the son of
Mattan, and Gedaliah the son of
Pashhur, and Jucal the son of

1 וַיִּשְׁמַ֞ע שְׁפַטְיָ֣ה בֶן־מַתָּ֗ן
וּגְדַלְיָ֨הוּ֙ בֶּן־פַּשְׁח֔וּר וְיוּכַ֣ל

19. *that prophesied unto you.* Cf. xxviii.
2ff.
20. *let my supplication*, etc. See on
xxxvi. 7.
21. *court of the guard.* See on xxxii. 2.
the bakers' street. In the East each trade
was usually confined to a particular
street.
until all the bread, etc. Cf. lii. 6.

CHAPTER XXXVIII
1-13 JEREMIAH'S IMPRISONMENT AND ESCAPE

1. *Shephatiah.* He is not mentioned
elsewhere.
Gedaliah the son of Pashhur. Possibly
the same Pashhur who put Jeremiah in
the stocks (xx. 1f.).
Jucal. Identical with Jehucal of xxxvii. 3.

Shelemiah, and Pashhur the son of Malchiah, heard the words that Jeremiah spoke unto all the people, saying: 2. 'Thus saith the LORD: He that remaineth in this city shall die by the sword, by the famine, and by the pestilence; but he that goeth forth to the Chaldeans shall live, and his life shall be unto him for a prey, and he shall live. 3. Thus saith the LORD: This city shall surely be given into the hand of the army of the king of Babylon, and he shall take it.' 4. Then the princes said unto the king: 'Let this man, we pray thee, be put to death; forasmuch as he weakeneth the hands of the men of war that remain in this city, and the hands of all the people, in speaking such words unto them; for this man seeketh not the welfare of this people, but the hurt.' 5. Then Zedekiah the king said: 'Behold, he is in your hand; for the king is not he that can do any thing

בֶּן־שֶׁלֶמְיָהוּ וּפַשְׁחוּר בֶּן־
מַלְכִּיָּה אֶת־הַדְּבָרִים אֲשֶׁר
יִרְמְיָהוּ מְדַבֵּר אֶל־כָּל־
2 הָעָם לֵאמֹר: כֹּה אָמַר יְהֹוָה
הַיֹּשֵׁב בָּעִיר הַזֹּאת יָמוּת
בַּחֶרֶב בָּרָעָב וּבַדָּבֶר וְהַיֹּצֵא
אֶל־הַכַּשְׂדִּים יִחְיֶה וְהָיְתָה־
3 לּוֹ נַפְשׁוֹ לְשָׁלָל וָחָי: כֹּה אָמַר
יְהֹוָה הִנָּתֹן תִּנָּתֵן הָעִיר הַזֹּאת
בְּיַד חֵיל מֶלֶךְ־בָּבֶל וּלְכָדָהּ:
4 וַיֹּאמְרוּ הַשָּׂרִים אֶל־הַמֶּלֶךְ
יוּמַת נָא אֶת־הָאִישׁ הַזֶּה כִּי
עַל־כֵּן הוּא מְרַפֵּא אֶת־יְדֵי
אַנְשֵׁי הַמִּלְחָמָה הַנִּשְׁאָרִים
בָּעִיר הַזֹּאת וְאֵת יְדֵי כָל־
הָעָם לְדַבֵּר אֲלֵיהֶם כַּדְּבָרִים
הָאֵלֶּה כִּי הָאִישׁ הַזֶּה אֵינֶנּוּ
דֹרֵשׁ לְשָׁלוֹם לָעָם הַזֶּה כִּי
5 אִם־לְרָעָה: וַיֹּאמֶר הַמֶּלֶךְ
צִדְקִיָּהוּ הִנֵּה־הוּא בְּיֶדְכֶם
כִּי־אֵין הַמֶּלֶךְ יוּכַל אֶתְכֶם

v. 2. וְחָיָה ק׳

Pashhur the son of Malchiah. Mentioned in xxi. 1.
the words that Jeremiah spoke unto all the people. Jeremiah's transfer to the court of the guard (xxxvii. 21) apparently gave him an opportunity to address the people.
2. What Jeremiah told *all the people* agreed with the message he had sent to king Zedekiah (cf. xxi. 9).
4. *weakeneth the hands.* Discourages.

that remain. Famine and pestilence had already taken toll of the warriors; also, some had deserted to the enemy (cf. verse 19). Doubtless the king's advisers also had in mind those who had been taken captive in Jehoiachin's reign (cf. 2 Kings xxiv. 14ff.).

5. *the king is not,* etc. What a contrast does this confession of weakness make

against you.' 6. Then took they Jeremiah, and cast him into the pit of Malchiah the king's son, that was in the court of the guard; and they let down Jeremiah with cords. And in the pit there was no water, but mire; and Jeremiah sank in the mire.

7. Now when Ebed-melech the Ethiopian, an officer, who was in the king's house, heard that they had put Jeremiah in the pit; the king then sitting in the gate of Benjamin; 8. Ebed-melech went forth out of the king's house, and spoke to the king, saying: 9. 'My lord the king, these men have done evil in all that they have done to Jeremiah the prophet, whom they have cast into the pit; and he is like to die in the place where he is because of the famine;

6 דָּבָ֑ר׃ וַיִּקְח֣וּ אֶֽת־יִרְמְיָ֗הוּ
וַיַּשְׁלִ֨כוּ אֹת֜וֹ אֶל־הַבּ֣וֹר ׀
מַלְכִּיָּ֣הוּ בֶן־הַמֶּ֗לֶךְ אֲשֶׁר֙
בַּחֲצַ֣ר הַמַּטָּרָ֔ה וַיְשַׁלְּח֥וּ אֶת־
יִרְמְיָ֖הוּ בַּחֲבָלִ֑ים וּבַבּ֤וֹר אֵֽין־
מַ֨יִם֙ כִּ֣י אִם־טִ֔יט וַיִּטְבַּ֥ע
7 יִרְמְיָ֖הוּ בַּטִּֽיט׃ וַיִּשְׁמַ֡ע עֶֽבֶד־
מֶ֨לֶךְ הַכּוּשִׁ֜י אִ֣ישׁ סָרִ֗יס וְהוּא֙
בְּבֵ֣ית הַמֶּ֔לֶךְ כִּֽי־נָתְנ֥וּ אֶת־
יִרְמְיָ֖הוּ אֶל־הַבּ֑וֹר וְהַמֶּ֥לֶךְ
8 יוֹשֵׁ֖ב בְּשַׁ֥עַר בִּנְיָמִֽן׃ וַיֵּצֵ֥א
עֶֽבֶד־מֶ֨לֶךְ֙ מִבֵּ֣ית הַמֶּ֔לֶךְ
וַיְדַבֵּ֥ר אֶל־הַמֶּ֖לֶךְ לֵאמֹֽר׃
9 אֲדֹנִ֣י הַמֶּ֗לֶךְ הֵרֵ֜עוּ הָאֲנָשִׁ֤ים
הָאֵ֨לֶּה֙ אֵ֣ת כָּל־אֲשֶׁ֣ר עָשׂ֔וּ
לְיִרְמְיָ֣הוּ הַנָּבִ֗יא אֵ֤ת אֲשֶׁר־
הִשְׁלִ֨יכוּ֙ אֶל־הַבּ֔וֹר וַיָּ֤מָת
תַּחְתָּיו֙ מִפְּנֵ֣י הָֽרָעָ֔ב כִּ֣י אֵ֤ין

with the autocratic power which was normally wielded by an Oriental king! Zedekiah does not explicitly authorize putting Jeremiah to death.

6. *pit.* More exactly a 'cistern' dug underground for the storage of water.

the king's son. Others, including A.V., 'the son of Hammelech' (see on xxxvi. 26). 'The princes did not kill Jeremiah outright, perhaps they shrank with superstitious dread from such a deed; but they hit on a plan which they trusted might achieve their purpose as well' (Peake).

7. *Ebed-melech.* The name means 'king's servant.' As he was an Ethiopian and an alien, he would not be disturbed by Jeremiah's prediction, and apparently had respect for the prophet.

an officer. The Hebrew *saris* is the usual term for 'eunuch' and is here so rendered by A.V. and R.V.; if so, Ebed-melech was an attendant in the royal harem. But the word may have a wider connotation; it is, e.g., applied to Potiphar (Gen. xxxix. 1) who was a married man.

the gate of Benjamin. See on xxxvii. 13.

9. *because of the famine.* Or, 'for hunger' (A.V.).

for there is no more bread in the city.' 10. Then the king commanded Ebed-melech the Ethiopian, saying: 'Take from hence thirty men with thee, and take up Jeremiah the prophet out of the pit, before he die.' 11. So Ebed-melech took the men with him, and went into the house of the king under the treasury, and took thence worn clouts and worn rags, and let them down by cords into the pit to Jeremiah. 12. And Ebed-melech the Ethiopian said unto Jeremiah: 'Put now these worn clouts and rags under thine armholes under the cords.' And Jeremiah did so. 13. So they drew up Jeremiah with the cords, and took

הַלֶּחֶם עוֹד בָּעִיר: וַיְצַוֶּה 10
הַמֶּלֶךְ אֶת־עֶבֶד־מֶלֶךְ הַכּוּשִׁי
לֵאמֹר קַח בְּיָדְךָ מִזֶּה שְׁלֹשִׁים
אֲנָשִׁים וְהַעֲלִיתָ אֶת־יִרְמְיָהוּ
הַנָּבִיא מִן־הַבּוֹר בְּטֶרֶם
יָמוּת: וַיִּקַּח | עֶבֶד־מֶלֶךְ 11
אֶת־הָאֲנָשִׁים בְּיָדוֹ וַיָּבֹא
בֵית־הַמֶּלֶךְ אֶל־תַּחַת
הָאוֹצָר וַיִּקַּח מִשָּׁם בְּלוֹיֵ
הַסְּחָבוֹת וּבְלוֹיֵ מְלָחִים
וַיְשַׁלְּחֵם אֶל־יִרְמְיָהוּ אֶל־
הַבּוֹר בַּחֲבָלִים: וַיֹּאמֶר 12
עֶבֶד־מֶלֶךְ הַכּוּשִׁי אֶל־
יִרְמְיָהוּ שִׂים נָא בְּלוֹאֵי
הַסְּחָבוֹת וְהַמְּלָחִים תַּחַת
אַצִּלוֹת יָדֶיךָ מִתַּחַת
לַחֲבָלִים וַיַּעַשׂ יִרְמְיָהוּ כֵּן:
וַיִּמְשְׁכוּ אֶת־יִרְמְיָהוּ בַּחֲבָלִים 13

v. 11. סחבות ק'

---

there is no more bread in the city. A natural exaggeration in a plea for Jeremiah's immediate release. Ebed-melech meant that the shortage was so great that no one would think of feeding Jeremiah who was hidden away in the pit.

10. *thirty men.* A surprisingly large number. Rashi and Kimchi explain that famine had so weakened the men of the city that thirty men were necessary to haul Jeremiah up. This is not very plausible, and more probably the king wished to forestall an attempt at resistance on the part of the prophet's enemies.

The grammatical construction is unusual and LXX has 'three men' which modern commentators accept; but the Targum agrees with M.T.

11. *under the treasury.* i.e. into a room under the treasury.

worn clouts and worn rags. 'Ebed-melech's thoughtfulness to spare the prophet all needless pain is shown in his provision of rags to save him from being cut by the rope, and then by his letting the rags down to him with ropes that he might not have to grope for them in the mire. The rags he procured from a lumber-room under the treasury' (Peake).

him up out of the pit; and Jeremiah remained in the court of the guard.

14. Then Zedekiah the king sent, and took Jeremiah the prophet unto him into the third entry that was in the house of the LORD; and the king said unto Jeremiah: 'I will ask thee a thing; hide nothing from me.'
15. Then Jeremiah said unto Zedekiah: 'If I declare it unto thee, wilt thou not surely put me to death? and if I give thee counsel, thou wilt not hearken unto me.' 16. So Zedekiah the king swore secretly unto Jeremiah, saying: 'As the LORD liveth, that made us this soul, I will not put thee to death, neither will I give thee into the hand of these men that seek thy life.'

17. Then said Jeremiah unto Zedekiah: 'Thus saith the LORD, the God of hosts, the God of Israel: If thou wilt go forth unto the king of Babylon's princes, then thy soul

וַיַּעֲלוּ אֹתוֹ מִן־הַבּוֹר וַיֵּשֶׁב
יִרְמְיָהוּ בַּחֲצַר הַמַּטָּרָה:
14 וַיִּשְׁלַח הַמֶּלֶךְ צִדְקִיָּהוּ וַיִּקַּח
אֶת־יִרְמְיָהוּ הַנָּבִיא אֵלָיו
אֶל־מָבוֹא הַשְּׁלִישִׁי אֲשֶׁר
בְּבֵית יְהוָה וַיֹּאמֶר הַמֶּלֶךְ
אֶל־יִרְמְיָהוּ שֹׁאֵל אֲנִי אֹתְךָ
דָּבָר אַל־תְּכַחֵד מִמֶּנִּי דָּבָר:
15 וַיֹּאמֶר יִרְמְיָהוּ אֶל־צִדְקִיָּהוּ
כִּי אַגִּיד לְךָ הֲלוֹא הָמֵת
תְּמִיתֵנִי וְכִי אִיעָצְךָ לֹא תִשְׁמַע
16 אֵלָי: וַיִּשָּׁבַע הַמֶּלֶךְ צִדְקִיָּהוּ
אֶל־יִרְמְיָהוּ בַּסֵּתֶר לֵאמֹר
חַי־יְהוָה אֵת אֲשֶׁר עָשָׂה־לָנוּ
אֶת־הַנֶּפֶשׁ הַזֹּאת אִם־
אֲמִיתֶךָ וְאִם־אֶתֶּנְךָ בְּיַד
הָאֲנָשִׁים הָאֵלֶּה אֲשֶׁר
17 מְבַקְשִׁים אֶת־נַפְשֶׁךָ: וַיֹּאמֶר
יִרְמְיָהוּ אֶל־צִדְקִיָּהוּ כֹּה־
אָמַר יְהוָה אֱלֹהֵי צְבָאוֹת
אֱלֹהֵי יִשְׂרָאֵל אִם־יָצֹא תֵצֵא
אֶל־שָׂרֵי מֶלֶךְ־בָּבֶל וְחָיְתָה

כתיב ולא קרי .v. 16

14-28 ZEDEKIAH AGAIN CONSULTS JEREMIAH

14. *the third entry.* This is not mentioned elsewhere. Perhaps it is identical with *the king's entry* of 2 Kings xvi. 18.
15. Aware how weak-minded the king was, Jeremiah feared that he would

again be imperilled by giving unwelcome information.
16. *that made us this soul.* As God gives life, He takes it away; so may He do that to Zedekiah if he is false to his oath.
17. *go forth.* i.e. surrender.
the king of Babylon's princes. Who were

shall live, and this city shall not be burned with fire; and thou shalt live, thou, and thy house; 18. but if thou wilt not go forth to the king of Babylon's princes, then shall this city be given into the hand of the Chaldeans, and they shall burn it with fire, and thou shalt not escape out of their hand.' 19. And Zedekiah the king said unto Jeremiah: 'I am afraid of the Jews that are fallen away to the Chaldeans, lest they deliver me into their hand, and they mock me.' 20. But Jeremiah said: 'They shall not deliver thee. Hearken, I beseech thee, to the voice of the LORD, in that which I speak unto thee; so it shall be well with thee, and thy soul shall live. 21. But if thou refuse to go forth, this is the word that the LORD hath shown me: 22. Behold, all the women that are left in the king of Judah's house shall be brought forth to the king of Babylon's princes, and those women shall say:

Thy familiar friends have set thee on,
And have prevailed over thee;

נַפְשֶׁךָ וְהָעִיר הַזֹּאת לֹא תִשָּׂרֵף
בָּאֵשׁ וְחָיִתָה אַתָּה וּבֵיתֶךָ:
18 וְאִם לֹא תֵצֵא אֶל שָׂרֵי מֶלֶךְ
בָּבֶל וְנִתְּנָה הָעִיר הַזֹּאת בְּיַד
הַכַּשְׂדִּים וּשְׂרָפוּהָ בָּאֵשׁ וְאַתָּה
19 לֹא תִמָּלֵט מִיָּדָם: וַיֹּאמֶר
הַמֶּלֶךְ צִדְקִיָּהוּ אֶל יִרְמְיָהוּ
אֲנִי דֹאֵג אֶת הַיְּהוּדִים אֲשֶׁר
נָפְלוּ אֶל הַכַּשְׂדִּים פֶּן יִתְּנוּ
אֹתִי בְּיָדָם וְהִתְעַלְלוּ בִי:
20 וַיֹּאמֶר יִרְמְיָהוּ לֹא יִתֵּנוּ שְׁמַע
נָא בְּקוֹל יְהֹוָה לַאֲשֶׁר אֲנִי
דֹּבֵר אֵלֶיךָ וְיִיטַב לְךָ וּתְחִי
21 נַפְשֶׁךָ: וְאִם מָאֵן אַתָּה
לָצֵאת זֶה הַדָּבָר אֲשֶׁר הִרְאַנִי
22 יְהֹוָה: וְהִנֵּה כָל הַנָּשִׁים אֲשֶׁר
נִשְׁאֲרוּ בְּבֵית מֶלֶךְ יְהוּדָה
מוּצָאוֹת אֶל שָׂרֵי מֶלֶךְ בָּבֶל
וְהֵנָּה אֹמְרוֹת הִסִּיתוּךָ וְיָכְלוּ
לְךָ אַנְשֵׁי שְׁלֹמֶךָ הָטְבְּעוּ בַבֹּץ

besieging Jerusalem; the king was apparently not there (cf. xxxix. 3, 5).

19. 'Zedekiah shrinks from surrender, lest the Chaldeans deliver him over to the Jews who had deserted and they mishandle him. It was not an imaginary terror. Party spirit no doubt ran high; those who were opposed to the alliance with Egypt and revolt from Babylon would bitterly resent the ruinous policy for which the king had been responsible, and which its real authors had carried through with such high-handed violence towards its opponents' (Peake).

22. *all the women that are left.* The reference is probably to the ladies of the court who survived the invasion, since the next verse mentions the women of the royal household. Taunts and reproaches from such a source would be especially humiliating to the king.

thy familiar friends. lit. 'the men of thy peace,' i.e. the false prophets who

Thy feet are sunk in the mire,
And they are turned away back.

23. And they shall bring out all thy
wives and thy children to the
Chaldeans; and thou shalt not
escape out of their hand, but shalt
be taken by the hand of the king of
Babylon; and thou shalt cause this
city to be burned with fire.'

24. Then said Zedekiah unto
Jeremiah: 'Let no man know of
these words, and thou shalt not die.

25. But if the princes hear that
I have talked with thee, and they
come unto thee, and say unto thee:
Declare unto us now what thou hast
said unto the king; hide it not from
us, and we will not put thee to
death; also what the king said unto
thee; 26. then thou shalt say unto

23 וְאֶת־ נָשֻׁ֖נוּ אָח֑וֹר : רַגְלֶ֔ךָ
כָּל־ נָשֶׁ֙יךָ֙ וְאֶת־בָּנֶ֔יךָ
מֽוֹצִאִים֙ אֶל־הַכַּשְׂדִּ֔ים וְאַתָּ֕ה
לֹא־תִמָּלֵ֖ט מִיָּדָ֑ם כִּ֣י בְיַ֤ד
מֶֽלֶךְ־בָּבֶל֙ תִּתָּפֵ֔שׂ וְאֶת־
הָעִ֥יר הַזֹּ֖את תִּשְׂרֹ֥ף בָּאֵֽשׁ :
24 וַיֹּ֨אמֶר צִדְקִיָּ֜הוּ אֶל־יִרְמְיָ֗הוּ
אִ֥ישׁ אַל־יֵדַ֖ע בַּדְּבָרִֽים־
25 הָאֵ֖לֶּה וְלֹ֥א תָמֽוּת : וְכִֽי־
יִשְׁמְע֣וּ הַשָּׂרִים֮ כִּֽי־דִבַּ֣רְתִּי
אִתָּךְ֒ וּבָ֣אוּ אֵלֶ֗יךָ וְאָמְר֤וּ אֵלֶ֙יךָ֙
הַגִּֽידָה־נָּ֣א לָ֗נוּ מַה־דִּבַּ֙רְתָּ֙
אֶל־הַמֶּ֙לֶךְ֙ אַל־תְּכַחֵ֣ד מִמֶּ֔נּוּ
וְלֹ֖א נְמִיתֶ֑ךָ וּמַה־דִּבֶּ֥ר אֵלֶ֖יךָ
26 הַמֶּֽלֶךְ : וְאָמַרְתָּ֣ אֲלֵיהֶ֔ם

v. 22. חסרי'

---

prophesied peace (i.e. victory) to the
last (Rashi and Kimchi); or the men who
advised thee, as they thought, for thy
welfare. The phrase occurs again in
Obad. 7.

have set thee on. Incited thee to a
suicidal resistance.

thy feet are sunk in the mire. A proverbial phrase with the meaning: you are
caught in difficulties from which you
cannot extricate yourself, like a traveller
whose feet sink in a bog. It is very
probable that the imagery was suggested
to Jeremiah by his personal experience
when his own feet *sank in the mire*
(verse 6, but the noun is different). God
caused him to be drawn out of it, but
that will not happen to the king.

they are turned away back. They (the
feet) no longer march forward to victory

(Kimchi). Another interpretation refers
they to *thy familiar friends*: in your hour
of need they have deserted you.

23. *and thou shalt cause . . . fire.* Better
and literally, 'and thou shalt burn this
city with fire.' By following a policy
against which Jeremiah had persistently
but unsuccessfully warned him, Zedekiah
was responsible for the city being
destroyed by fire.

24. *thou shalt not die.* Not that Zedekiah
would put him to death; but should the
princes come to know of what transpired
at the interview, they would certainly do
so and the king be powerless to save him.

25. *if the princes hear.* As they probably
would, since what happens at a court can
rarely be kept secret.

258

them: I presented my supplication before the king, that he would not cause me to return to Jonathan's house, to die there.' 27. Then came all the princes unto Jeremiah, and asked him; and he told them according to all these words that the king had commanded. So they left off speaking with him; for the matter was not reported. 28. So Jeremiah abode in the court of the guard until the day that Jerusalem was taken.

And it came to pass, when Jerusalem was taken—

מַפִּיל־־אֲנִי תְחִנָּתִי לִפְנֵי
הַמֶּלֶךְ לְבִלְתִּי הֲשִׁיבֵנִי בֵּית
27 יְהוֹנָתָן לָמוּת שָׁם: וַיָּבֹאוּ כָל־
הַשָּׂרִים אֶל־יִרְמְיָהוּ וַיִּשְׁאֲלוּ
אֹתוֹ וַיַּגֵּד לָהֶם כְּכָל־־
הַדְּבָרִים הָאֵלֶּה אֲשֶׁר צִוָּה
הַמֶּלֶךְ וַיַּחֲרִשׁוּ מִמֶּנּוּ כִּי לֹא־
28 נִשְׁמַע הַדָּבָר: וַיֵּשֶׁב יִרְמְיָהוּ
בַּחֲצַר הַמַּטָּרָה עַד־יוֹם
אֲשֶׁר־נִלְכְּדָה יְרוּשָׁלָיִם ׃וְהָיָה
כַּאֲשֶׁר נִלְכְּדָה יְרוּשָׁלָיִם:

39	CHAPTER XXXIX	לט

1. in the ninth year of Zedekiah king of Judah, in the tenth month, came Nebuchadrezzar king of Babylon and all his army against Jerusalem, and besieged it;

1 בַּשָּׁנָה הַתְּשִׁעִית לְצִדְקִיָּהוּ
מֶלֶךְ־יְהוּדָה בַּחֹדֶשׁ הָעֲשִׂרִי
בָּא נְבוּכַדְרֶאצַּר מֶלֶךְ־בָּבֶל
וְכָל־חֵילוֹ אֶל־יְרוּשָׁלַיִם

פסקא באמצע פסוק v. 28.

26. *Jonathan's house.* Where Jeremiah had nearly died in the dungeon (xxxvii. 15). Doubtless the prophet had made that petition of the king in the course of the interview.

27. *according to all these words*, etc. He told them as much of the conversation as the king permitted.

for the matter was not reported. Referring to the political questions and answers in the interview. Jeremiah could not communicate these to the princes, even if he had wished to do so, without betraying a confidence.

28. *and it came to pass . . . taken.* As translated this clause must be connected with xxxix. 1 and commence the next chapter; but for that meaning we should expect the verb *wayyehi* instead of *wehayah.* Metsudath David renders: 'and he (Jeremiah) remained (there) when Jerusalem was taken.'

CHAPTER XXXIX

1-3 FALL OF JERUSALEM

1. *in the ninth*, etc. This and the following verse are in parenthesis. Verses 1-10 are paralleled by lii. 4-16 and 2 Kings xxv. 1-12.

2. in the eleventh year of Zedekiah, in the fourth month, the ninth day of the month, a breach was made in the city—3. that all the princes of the king of Babylon came in, and sat in the middle gate, even Nergal-sarezer, Samgar-nebo, Sarsechim Rab-saris, Nergal-sarezer Rab-mag, with all the residue of the princes of the king of Babylon. 4. And it came to pass, that when Zedekiah the king of Judah and all the men of war saw them, then they fled, and went forth out of the city by night, by the way of the king's garden, by the gate betwixt the two walls; and he went out the way of the Arabah. 5. But the army of the Chaldeans pursued after them, and overtook Zedekiah in the plains of Jericho; and when they had taken

2 וַיָּצֻרוּ עָלֶיהָ בְּעַשְׁתֵּי־עֶשְׂרֵה
שָׁנָה לְצִדְקִיָּהוּ בַּחֹדֶשׁ
הָרְבִיעִי בְּתִשְׁעָה לַחֹדֶשׁ
3 הָבְקְעָה הָעִיר: וַיָּבֹאוּ כֹּל
שָׂרֵי מֶלֶךְ־בָּבֶל וַיֵּשְׁבוּ בְּשַׁעַר
הַתָּוֶךְ נֵרְגַל שַׂרְאֶצֶר סַמְגַּר־
נְבוּ שַׂרְסְכִים רַב־סָרִיס נֵרְגַל
שַׂרְאֶצֶר רַב־מָג וְכָל־
שְׁאֵרִית שָׂרֵי מֶלֶךְ־בָּבֶל:
4 וַיְהִי כַּאֲשֶׁר רָאָם צִדְקִיָּהוּ
מֶלֶךְ־יְהוּדָה וְכֹל אַנְשֵׁי
הַמִּלְחָמָה וַיִּבְרְחוּ וַיֵּצְאוּ
לַיְלָה מִן־הָעִיר דֶּרֶךְ גַּן
הַמֶּלֶךְ בְּשַׁעַר בֵּין הַחֹמֹתָיִם
5 וַיֵּצֵא דֶּרֶךְ הָעֲרָבָה: וַיִּרְדְּפוּ
חֵיל־כַּשְׂדִּים אַחֲרֵיהֶם וַיַּשִּׂגוּ
אֶת־צִדְקִיָּהוּ בְּעַרְבוֹת יְרֵחוֹ

v. 3. כצ״ל בסין

---

2. lii. 6 adds that on this day the supply of food failed.

3. *the middle gate.* Probably, the central (chief) gate in the walls of Jerusalem.

Nergal-sarezer. The name occurs twice, apparently borne by two different men.

Rab-saris . . . Rab-mag. These titles have been identified on the monuments which recent excavations have discovered: Rab-saris (Rabu-sa-resu) 'Chief of the heads,' and Rab-mag (Rab-mugi) 'the king's chief physician' (Irwin, *The Bible, the Scholar and the Spade*, p. 151).

all the residue. i.e. the rest of the princes who are not named.

4-7 FATE OF ZEDEKIAH

4. *by the gate betwixt the two walls.* 'On the south of the city (the *king's garden* was near the pool of Siloam, Neh. iii. 15), probably the *fountain gate* of Neh. ii. 14, iii. 15, xii. 37, the *two walls* (cf. Isa. xxii. 11) being those below this gate along the west side of the east hill of Jerusalem, and the east side of the west hill' (Driver).

the Arabah. The deep valley of the Jordan north of the Dead Sea. Zedekiah was evidently trying to reach Trans-jordan where he may have hoped to find refuge.

5. *the plains of Jericho.* The west side of the Arabah.

him, they brought him up to
Nebuchadrezzar king of Babylon to
Riblah in the land of Hamath, and
he gave judgment upon him. 6.
Then the king of Babylon slew the
sons of Zedekiah in Riblah before
his eyes; also the king of Babylon
slew all the nobles of Judah.
7. Moreover he put out Zedekiah's
eyes, and bound him in fetters, to
carry him to Babylon. 8. And the
Chaldeans burned the king's house,
and the house of the people, with
fire, and broke down the walls of
Jerusalem. 9. Then Nebuzaradan
the captain of the guard carried
away captive into Babylon the
remnant of the people that remained
in the city, the deserters also, that
fell away to him, with the rest of the
people that remained. 10. But

וַיִּקְחוּ אֹתוֹ וַיַּעֲלֻהוּ אֶל־
נְבוּכַדְרֶאצַּר מֶלֶךְ־בָּבֶל
רִבְלָתָה בְּאֶרֶץ חֲמָת וַיְדַבֵּר
6 אִתּוֹ מִשְׁפָּטִים: וַיִּשְׁחַט מֶלֶךְ
בָּבֶל אֶת־בְּנֵי צִדְקִיָּהוּ
בְּרִבְלָה לְעֵינָיו וְאֵת כָּל־חֹרֵי
יְהוּדָה שָׁחַט מֶלֶךְ בָּבֶל:
7 וְאֶת־עֵינֵי צִדְקִיָּהוּ עִוֵּר
וַיַּאַסְרֵהוּ בַּנְחֻשְׁתַּיִם לָבִיא
8 אֹתוֹ בָּבֶלָה: וְאֶת־בֵּית
הַמֶּלֶךְ וְאֶת־בֵּית הָעָם שָׂרְפוּ
הַכַּשְׂדִּים בָּאֵשׁ וְאֶת־חֹמֹת
9 יְרוּשָׁלִַם נָתָצוּ: וְאֵת יֶתֶר הָעָם
הַנִּשְׁאָרִים בָּעִיר וְאֶת־
הַנֹּפְלִים אֲשֶׁר נָפְלוּ עָלָיו וְאֵת
יֶתֶר הָעָם הַנִּשְׁאָרִים הֶגְלָה
נְבוּזַרְאֲדָן רַב־טַבָּחִים בָּבֶל:

כצ״ל v. 7.

Riblah. This lies between the mountain
ranges of Lebanon and Hermon.
he gave judgment upon him. For having
violated his oath of allegiance (Kimchi;
cf. 2 Chron. xxxvi. 13).
6. nobles. The Hebrew word occurred in
xxvii. 20.
7. he put out Zedekiah's eyes. A common
form of punishment in ancient times.
It is mentioned in the Code of Ham-
murabi.

8-10 FATE OF THE POPULATION
OF JERUSALEM
8. the house of the people. The singular is
used in a collective sense, the people's

houses. The Rabbis interpret it as the
synagogue.

9. **Nebuzaradan.** He arrived in Jerusalem a month after the fall of the city
(lii. 12).

the captain of the guard. lit. 'the chief
of the executioners'; the phrase is comparable with that in Gen. xxxix. 1.

that fell away to him. Before the final
capture of the city.

the rest of the people. From the other
cities of Judah.

261

Nebuzaradan the captain of the guard left of the poor of the people, that had nothing, in the land of Judah, and gave them vineyards and fields in that day. 11. Now Nebuchadrezzar king of Babylon gave charge concerning Jeremiah to Nebuzaradan the captain of the guard, saying: 12. 'Take him, and look well to him, and do him no harm; but do unto him even as he shall say unto thee.' 13. So Nebuzaradan the captain of the guard sent, and Nebushazban Rab-saris, and Nergal-sarezer Rab-mag, and all the chief officers of the king of Babylon; 14. they sent, and took Jeremiah out of the court of the guard, and committed him unto Gedaliah the son of Ahikam, the son of Shaphan, that he should carry him home; so he dwelt among the people.

10 וּמִן־הָעָם הַדַּלִּים אֲשֶׁר
אֵין־לָהֶם מְאוּמָה הִשְׁאִיר
נְבוּזַרְאֲדָן רַב־טַבָּחִים בְּאֶרֶץ
יְהוּדָה וַיִּתֵּן לָהֶם כְּרָמִים
11 וִיגֵבִים בַּיּוֹם הַהוּא: וַיְצַו
נְבוּכַדְרֶאצַּר מֶלֶךְ־בָּבֶל
עַל־יִרְמְיָהוּ בְּיַד נְבוּזַרְאֲדָן
12 רַב־טַבָּחִים לֵאמֹר: קָחֶנּוּ
וְעֵינֶיךָ שִׂים עָלָיו וְאַל־תַּעַשׂ
לוֹ מְאוּמָה רָּע כִּי אִם כַּאֲשֶׁר
יְדַבֵּר אֵלֶיךָ כֵּן עֲשֵׂה עִמּוֹ:
13 וַיִּשְׁלַח נְבוּזַרְאֲדָן רַב־
טַבָּחִים וּנְבוּשַׁזְבָּן רַב־סָרִיס
וְנֵרְגַל שַׂרְאֶצֶר רַב־מָג וְכֹל
14 רַבֵּי מֶלֶךְ־בָּבֶל: וַיִּשְׁלְחוּ
וַיִּקְחוּ אֶת־יִרְמְיָהוּ מֵחֲצַר
הַמַּטָּרָה וַיִּתְּנוּ אֹתוֹ אֶל־
גְּדַלְיָהוּ בֶּן־אֲחִיקָם בֶּן־שָׁפָן
לְהוֹצִאֵהוּ אֶל־הַבָּיִת וַיֵּשֶׁב

v. 12. ר׳ דגושה. v. 12. כתיב ולא קרי v. 13. נון זעירא

---

10. *vineyards and fields.* 'The representative of a foreign conqueror restored to the poor the land the possession of which their fathers had lost to the greed of the rich' (Binns).

11-14 NEBUCHADNEZZAR'S FRIENDLY TREATMENT OF JEREMIAH

12. *look well to him.* Nebuchadnezzar's favourable attitude to Jeremiah was doubtless due to the latter's counsel to Zedekiah to submit.

14. *Gedaliah.* He was subsequently appointed governor over the Jews who were left behind (xl. 5).

Ahikam, the son of Shaphan. See on xxvi. 24.

home. Jeremiah's house.

so he dwelt among the people. i.e. he was no longer in confinement and was now free to come and go. This verse anticipates the fuller narrative in the next chapter.

15. Now the word of the LORD came unto Jeremiah, while he was shut up in the court of the guard, saying: 16. 'Go, and speak to Ebed-melech the Ethiopian, saying: Thus saith the LORD of hosts, the God of Israel: Behold, I will bring My words upon this city for evil, and not for good; and they shall be accomplished before thee in that day. 17. But I will deliver thee in that day, saith the LORD; and thou shalt not be given into the hand of the men of whom thou art afraid. 18. For I will surely deliver thee, and thou shalt not fall by the sword, but thy life shall be for a prey unto thee; because thou hast put thy trust in Me, saith the LORD.'

15 בְּתוֹךְ הָעָם: וְאֶל־יִרְמְיָהוּ
הָיָה דְבַר־יְהֹוָה בִּהְיֹתוֹ עָצוּר
16 בַּחֲצַר הַמַּטָּרָה לֵאמֹר: הָלוֹךְ
וְאָמַרְתָּ לְעֶבֶד־מֶלֶךְ הַכּוּשִׁי
לֵאמֹר כֹּה־אָמַר יְהֹוָה
צְבָאוֹת אֱלֹהֵי יִשְׂרָאֵל הִנְנִי
מֵבִי אֶת־דְּבָרַי אֶל־הָעִיר
הַזֹּאת לְרָעָה וְלֹא לְטוֹבָה
וְהָיוּ לְפָנֶיךָ בַּיּוֹם הַהוּא:
17 וְהִצַּלְתִּיךָ בַיּוֹם־הַהוּא נְאֻם־
יְהֹוָה וְלֹא תִנָּתֵן בְּיַד הָאֲנָשִׁים
18 אֲשֶׁר־אַתָּה יָגוֹר מִפְּנֵיהֶם: כִּי
מַלֵּט אֲמַלֶּטְךָ וּבַחֶרֶב לֹא
תִפֹּל וְהָיְתָה לְךָ נַפְשְׁךָ לְשָׁלָל
כִּי־בָטַחְתָּ בִּי נְאֻם־יְהֹוָה:

v. 16. מביא ק׳

15-18 EBED-MELECH'S REWARD

15. came. Better, 'had come,' since this passage is chronologically earlier than the preceding. It is the sequel to xxxviii, and 'probably was postponed till now in order that there might be no break in the narrative of Jeremiah's imprisonment and the capture of the city' (Streane).

16. Ebed-melech the Ethiopian. He had interceded with the king against the harsh conditions of Jeremiah's imprisonment (xxxviii. 7ff.). The present promise was his reward.

before thee. i.e. he will witness their happening.

17. of whom thou art afraid. Either the princes who would have shown hostility to him on account of his intercession on Jeremiah's behalf; or of the invading Chaldean army. Most commentators accept the former.

18. by the sword. i.e. he will not die by violence.

for a prey. See on xxi. 9. The same promise was made to Baruch (xlv. 5).

because thou hast put thy trust in Me. Manifested by his effort to save Jeremiah, the messenger of God, at the risk of his life.

40   CHAPTER XL   מ

1. The word which came to Jeremiah from the LORD, after that Nebuzaradan the captain of the guard had let him go from Ramah, when he had taken him being bound in chains among all the captives of Jerusalem and Judah, that were carried away captive unto Babylon. 2. And the captain of the guard took Jeremiah, and said unto him: 'The LORD thy God pronounced this evil upon this place; 3. and the LORD hath brought it, and done according as He spoke; because ye have sinned against the LORD, and have not hearkened to His voice, therefore

א הַדָּבָר אֲשֶׁר הָיָה אֶל־יִרְמְיָ֫הוּ
מֵאֵת יְהוָה אַחַר ׀ שַׁלַּח אֹתוֹ
נְבוּזַרְאֲדָן רַב־טַבָּחִים מִן־
הָרָמָה בְּקַחְתּוֹ אֹתוֹ וְהוּא־
אָסוּר בָּאזִקִּים בְּתוֹךְ כָּל־
גָּלוּת יְרוּשָׁלַ֫ם וִיהוּדָה
ב הַמֻּגְלִים בָּבֶלָה: וַיִּקַּח רַב־
טַבָּחִים לְיִרְמְיָהוּ וַיֹּאמֶר אֵלָיו
יְהוָה אֱלֹהֶיךָ דִּבֶּר אֶת־
הָרָעָה הַזֹּאת אֶל־הַמָּקוֹם
ג הַזֶּה: וַיָּבֵא וַיַּעַשׂ יְהוָה כַּאֲשֶׁר
דִּבֵּר כִּי־חֲטָאתֶם לַיהוָה
וְלֹא־שְׁמַעְתֶּם בְּקוֹלוֹ וְהָיָה

א׳ נחה .v. 1

CHAPTER XL

CHAPTERS xl-xliv narrate incidents in Jeremiah's life after the fall of Jerusalem.

1-6 JEREMIAH DECIDES TO REMAIN IN JUDEA

1. *the word which came to Jeremiah from the LORD.* But no Divine utterance follows! The clause is to be understood as a general introduction to the whole narrative of events which immediately followed the capture of Jerusalem. The actual *word* comes later in xlii. 7. Streane points out that the close association in the minds of Jews between history and prophecy is attested by the inclusion of the Historical Books of the Bible under the section of Prophets.

Ramah. See on xxxi. 14. This was a halting-place for the captives on the journey to Babylon.

bound in chains. Although Nebuchadnezzar had ordered that the prophet was to be treated with consideration (xxxix. 12), it is easily understood how the command may have been overlooked in the prevailing confusion. At Ramah the mistake was rectified. The Rabbis declare that, on seeing the file of chained prisoners, Jeremiah voluntarily had himself fettered to demonstrate his complete identification with the sorrows of his people.

that were carried away. Better, 'who were being carried away.'

2. *the LORD thy God pronounced this evil upon this place.* This verse and the next contain a statement which sounds strange in the mouth of a heathen. Nevertheless, Jeremiah's preaching, which may well have reached his ears, apparently impressed Nebuzaradan.

this thing is come upon you.
4. And now, behold, I loose thee
this day from the chains which are
upon thy hand. If it seem good
unto thee to come with me into
Babylon, come, and I will look well
unto thee; but if it seem ill unto thee
to come with me into Babylon,
forbear; behold, all the land is
before thee; whither it seemeth good
and right unto thee to go, thither go.
—5. Yet he would not go back.—
Go back then to Gedaliah the son of
Ahikam, the son of Shaphan, whom
the king of Babylon hath made
governor over the cities of Judah,
and dwell with him among the
people; or go wheresoever it seemeth
right unto thee to go.' So the
captain of the guard gave him an
allowance and a present, and let him
go. 6. Then went Jeremiah unto
Gedaliah the son of Ahikam to
Mizpah, and dwelt with him among

4 לָכֶ֖ם אֶת־הַדָּבָ֣ר הַזֶּ֑ה וְעַתָּ֡ה הִנֵּ֣ה
פִתַּחְתִּ֩יךָ֨ הַיּ֜וֹם מִן־הָאזִקִּ֗ים
אֲשֶׁר֙ עַל־יָדֶ֔ךָ אִם־ט֨וֹב
בְּעֵינֶ֜יךָ לָב֧וֹא אִתִּ֣י בָבֶ֗ל בֹּ֚א
וְאָשִׂ֤ים אֶת־עֵינִי֙ עָלֶ֔יךָ וְאִם־
רַ֧ע בְּעֵינֶ֛יךָ לָבֽוֹא־אִתִּ֥י בָבֶ֖ל
חֲדָ֑ל רְאֵה֙ כָּל־הָאָ֣רֶץ לְפָנֶ֔יךָ
אֶל־ט֨וֹב וְאֶל־הַיָּשָׁ֧ר בְּעֵינֶ֛יךָ
5 לָלֶ֥כֶת שָׁ֖מָּה לֵֽךְ׃ וְעוֹדֶ֣נּוּ לֹא־
יָשׁ֗וּב וְשֻׁ֤בָה אֶל־גְּדַלְיָ֨ה בֶן־
אֲחִיקָ֣ם בֶּן־שָׁפָ֡ן אֲשֶׁר֩ הִפְקִ֨יד
מֶֽלֶךְ־בָּבֶ֜ל בְּעָרֵ֣י יְהוּדָ֗ה וְשֵׁ֤ב
אִתּוֹ֙ בְּת֣וֹךְ הָעָ֔ם א֚וֹ אֶל־כָּל־
הַיָּשָׁ֧ר בְּעֵינֶ֛יךָ לָלֶ֖כֶת לֵ֑ךְ
וַיִּתֶּן־ל֧וֹ רַב־טַבָּחִ֛ים אֲרֻחָ֥ה
6 וּמַשְׂאֵ֖ת וַֽיְשַׁלְּחֵֽהוּ׃ וַיָּבֹ֧א
יִרְמְיָ֣הוּ אֶל־גְּדַלְיָ֧ה בֶּן־
אֲחִיקָ֛ם הַמִּצְפָּ֖תָה וַיֵּ֥שֶׁב אִתּוֹ֙

v. 3. הדבר ק׳ א׳ נחה v. 4.

---

4. *I will look well unto thee.* See on
xxxix. 12.

5. *yet he would not go back*, etc. The
Hebrew is grammatically awkward and
forms a broken sentence. Perhaps the
general sense is: Jeremiah interrupted
Nebuzaradan with a remark that he did
not desire to go back (presumably, to
Jerusalem); whereupon the captain of
the guard, understanding from Jeremiah's
demeanour that he did not wish to
accompany him to Babylon, bade him
go to Gedaliah (Kimchi). Rashi, quoting
the Midrash, remarks that while he was

yet undecided, God bade him return to
Gedaliah, this being *the word which came
to Jeremiah from the LORD* (verse 1).

Gedaliah, etc. Cf. xxxix. 14.

an allowance. Of food for the journey.

a present. As a token of esteem.

6. *Mizpah.* Situated on a hill about
four miles north-west of Jerusalem.
Jeremiah did not return to Jerusalem
because, no doubt, he felt that his place
was by the side of Gedaliah to help him
in his difficult task of governorship over
a stricken land.

the people that were left in the land.
7. Now when all the captains of the forces that were in the fields, even they and their men, heard that the king of Babylon had made Gedaliah the son of Ahikam governor in the land, and had committed unto him men, and women, and children, and of the poorest of the land, of them that were not carried away captive to Babylon; 8. then they came to Gedaliah to Mizpah, even Ishmael the son of Nethaniah, and Johanan and Jonathan the sons of Kareah, and Seraiah the son of Tanhumeth, and the sons of Ephai the Netophathite, and Jezaniah the son of the Maacathite, they and their men. 9. And Gedaliah the son of Ahikam the son of Shaphan swore unto them and to their men, saying: 'Fear not to serve the Chaldeans; dwell in the land, and

בְּתוֹךְ הָעָם הַנִּשְׁאָרִים בָּאָרֶץ׃

7 וַיִּשְׁמְעוּ כָל־־שָׂרֵי הַחֲיָלִים אֲשֶׁר בַּשָּׂדֶה הֵמָּה וְאַנְשֵׁיהֶם כִּי־הִפְקִיד מֶלֶךְ־בָּבֶל אֶת־גְּדַלְיָהוּ בֶן־אֲחִיקָם בָּאָרֶץ וְכִי ׀ הִפְקִיד אִתּוֹ אֲנָשִׁים וְנָשִׁים וָטָף וּמִדַּלַּת הָאָרֶץ מֵאֲשֶׁר לֹא־הָגְלוּ בָּבֶלָה׃

8 וַיָּבֹאוּ אֶל־גְּדַלְיָה הַמִּצְפָּתָה וְיִשְׁמָעֵאל בֶּן־נְתַנְיָהוּ וְיוֹחָנָן וְיוֹנָתָן בְּנֵי־קָרֵחַ וּשְׂרָיָה בֶן־תַּנְחֻמֶת וּבְנֵי ׀ עוֹפַי הַנְּטֹפָתִי וִיזַנְיָהוּ בֶּן־הַמַּעֲכָתִי הֵמָּה

9 וְאַנְשֵׁיהֶם׃ וַיִּשָּׁבַע לָהֶם גְּדַלְיָהוּ בֶן־אֲחִיקָם בֶּן־שָׁפָן וּלְאַנְשֵׁיהֶם לֵאמֹר אַל־־תִּירְאוּ מֵעֲבוֹד הַכַּשְׂדִּים שְׁבוּ

v. 8. עיפי ק׳

7-12 GEDALIAH AS GOVERNOR

7. *in the fields.* i.e. in the open country outside the cities. The *captains of the forces* had either fled there, or were leaders of guerilla bands which had not been in the capital during the siege. 'The destruction of the mere buildings in such a place as Jerusalem would not involve the permanent dispersion of the inhabitants, for the rocky neighbourhood in which the town is situated abounds in caves and these would give an easy refuge to the people until they gained an opportunity of rebuilding their dwellings' (Kinglake, *Eothen*).

8. *Ishmael.* He was of royal blood

(cf. xli. 1); he was responsible for Gedaliah's murder.

Johanan. A loyal supporter of Gedaliah who warned him of a plot against his life (verses 13ff.) and led the expedition against Ishmael after the assassination (xli. 11ff.).

the Netophathite. From the village of Netophah, now identified with Beit Nettif to the east of Bethlehem (cf. Neh. vii. 26).

the Maacathite. Maacah was south-east of Hermon.

9. *swore unto them.* i.e. adjured them.

serve the king of Babylon, and it shall be well with you. 10. As for me, behold, I will dwell at Mizpah, to stand before the Chaldeans that may come unto us; but ye, gather ye wine and summer fruits and oil, and put them in your vessels, and dwell in your cities that ye have taken.' 11. Likewise when all the Jews that were in Moab, and among the children of Ammon, and in Edom, and that were in all the countries, heard that the king of Babylon had left a remnant of Judah, and that he had set over them Gedaliah the son of Ahikam, the son of Shaphan; 12. then all the Jews returned out of all places whither they were driven, and came to the land of Judah, to Gedaliah, unto Mizpah, and gathered wine and summer fruits in great abundance.

13. Moreover Johanan the son of

בָּאָרֶץ וְעִבְדוּ אֶת־מֶלֶךְ בָּבֶל
10 וְיִיטַב לָכֶם: וַאֲנִי הִנְנִי יֹשֵׁב
בַּמִּצְפָּה לַעֲמֹד לִפְנֵי
הַכַּשְׂדִּים אֲשֶׁר יָבֹאוּ אֵלֵינוּ
וְאַתֶּם אִסְפוּ יַיִן וָקַיִץ וְשֶׁמֶן
וְשִׂמוּ בִּכְלֵיכֶם וּשְׁבוּ בְּעָרֵיכֶם
11 אֲשֶׁר־תְּפַשְׂתֶּם: וְגַם כָּל־
הַיְּהוּדִים אֲשֶׁר־בְּמוֹאָב |
וּבִבְנֵי־עַמּוֹן וּבֶאֱדוֹם וַאֲשֶׁר
בְּכָל־הָאֲרָצוֹת שָׁמְעוּ כִּי־
נָתַן | מֶלֶךְ־בָּבֶל שְׁאֵרִית
לִיהוּדָה וְכִי הִפְקִיד עֲלֵיהֶם
אֶת־גְּדַלְיָהוּ בֶּן־אֲחִיקָם
12 בֶּן־שָׁפָן: וַיָּשֻׁבוּ כָל־
הַיְּהוּדִים מִכָּל־הַמְּקֹמוֹת
אֲשֶׁר נִדְּחוּ־שָׁם וַיָּבֹאוּ
אֶרֶץ־יְהוּדָה אֶל־גְּדַלְיָהוּ
הַמִּצְפָּתָה וַיַּאַסְפוּ יַיִן וָקַיִץ
13 הַרְבֵּה מְאֹד: וְיוֹחָנָן בֶּן־קָרֵחַ

---

10. *to stand before the Chaldeans.* As your representative, to protect your interests.

gather ye wine and summer fruits. The debacle having taken place in the fifth month (2 Kings xxv. 8), about the beginning of August, the summer's harvest was yet to be gathered. Evidently the Babylonians had not cut down the vines and trees.

your cities that ye have taken. With a

great part of the population deported, those who remained quickly settled in the derelict cities.

11. *in Moab . . . Ammon . . . Edom.* Whither they had fled. 'The fact that a governor of their own nation had been set over such as were left in the land, gave an assurance to those Jews who were waiting in neighbouring nations to see what would be the issue, that they might return and dwell at peace' (Streane).

Kareah, and all the captains of the
forces that were in the fields, came
to Gedaliah to Mizpah, 14. and said
unto him: 'Dost thou know that
Baalis the king of the children of
Ammon hath sent Ishmael the son
of Nethaniah to take thy life?' But
Gedaliah the son of Ahikam believed
them not. 15. Then Johanan the
son of Kareah spoke to Gedaliah in
Mizpah secretly, saying: 'Let me go,
I pray thee, and I will slay Ishmael
the son of Nethaniah, and no man
shall know it; wherefore should he
take thy life, that all the Jews that
are gathered unto thee should be
scattered, and the remnant of Judah
perish?' 16. But Gedaliah the son
of Ahikam said unto Johanan the
son of Kareah: 'Thou shalt not do
this thing; for thou speakest falsely
of Ishmael.'

וְכָל־־שָׂרֵי הַחֲיָלִים אֲשֶׁר
בַּשָּׂדֶה בָּאוּ אֶל־־גְּדַלְיָהוּ
14 הַמִּצְפָּתָה: וַיֹּאמְרוּ אֵלָיו
הֲיָדֹעַ תֵּדַע כִּי בַּעֲלִיס ׀ מֶלֶךְ
בְּנֵי־עַמּוֹן שָׁלַח אֶת־יִשְׁמָעֵאל
בֶּן־־נְתַנְיָה לְהַכֹּתְךָ נָפֶשׁ
וְלֹא־הֶאֱמִין לָהֶם גְּדַלְיָהוּ
15 בֶּן־אֲחִיקָם: וְיוֹחָנָן בֶּן־קָרֵחַ
אָמַר אֶל־־גְּדַלְיָהוּ בַסֵּתֶר
בַּמִּצְפָּה לֵאמֹר אֵלְכָה נָּא
וְאַכֶּה אֶת־־יִשְׁמָעֵאל בֶּן־
נְתַנְיָה וְאִישׁ לֹא יֵדָע לָמָּה
יַכֶּכָּה נֶּפֶשׁ וְנָפֹצוּ כָּל־יְהוּדָה
הַנִּקְבָּצִים אֵלֶיךָ וְאָבְדָה
16 שְׁאֵרִית יְהוּדָה: וַיֹּאמֶר
גְּדַלְיָהוּ בֶן־אֲחִיקָם אֶל־
יוֹחָנָן בֶּן־קָרֵחַ אַל־תַּעַשׂ
אֶת־הַדָּבָר הַזֶּה כִּי־שֶׁקֶר
אַתָּה דֹבֵר אֶל־יִשְׁמָעֵאל:

v. 16. תעשה ק'

13-16 GEDALIAH IGNORES A WARNING OF ISHMAEL'S PLOT

14. *Baalis.* His motive was probably to
hinder the rehabilitation of the country
which Gedaliah had inaugurated, so that
Judea might fall an easy victim to his
own expansionist plans.

Ishmael. Perhaps his jealousy of
Gedaliah and resentment at being passed
over as governor made him a ready tool
in Baalis' hands.

believed them not. It was incredible to
him that for reasons of personal pique

Ishmael, knowing full well that the
assassination of the governor appointed
by Nebuchadnezzar might entail the
destruction of the remnant of Judea,
would nevertheless commit such an act
of treason.

15. *should be scattered.* As was indeed
the effect of Gedaliah's murder.

16. *thou speakest falsely of Ishmael.* It
is evidence of the nobility of Gedaliah's
character that he refused to give credence
to what was told him.

41   CHAPTER XLI   מא

1. Now it came to pass in the seventh month, that Ishmael the son of Nethaniah, the son of Elishama, of the seed royal, and one of the chief officers of the king, and ten men with him, came unto Gedaliah the son of Ahikam to Mizpah; and there they did eat bread together in Mizpah. 2. Then arose Ishmael the son of Nethaniah, and the ten men that were with him, and smote Gedaliah the son of Ahikam the son of Shaphan with the sword, and slew him, whom the king of Babylon had made governor over the land. 3. Ishmael also slew

1 וַיְהִי ׀ בַּחֹדֶשׁ הַשְּׁבִיעִי בָּא
יִשְׁמָעֵאל בֶּן־נְתַנְיָה בֶן־
אֱלִישָׁמָע מִזֶּרַע הַמְּלוּכָה
וְרַבֵּי הַמֶּלֶךְ וַעֲשָׂרָה אֲנָשִׁים
אִתּוֹ אֶל־גְּדַלְיָהוּ בֶן־
אֲחִיקָם הַמִּצְפָּתָה וַיֹּאכְלוּ שָׁם
2 לֶחֶם יַחְדָּו בַּמִּצְפָּה: וַיָּקׇם
יִשְׁמָעֵאל בֶּן־נְתַנְיָה וַעֲשֶׂרֶת
הָאֲנָשִׁים ׀ אֲשֶׁר־הָיוּ אִתּוֹ וַיַּכּוּ
אֶת־גְּדַלְיָהוּ בֶן־אֲחִיקָם בֶּן־
שָׁפָן בַּחֶרֶב וַיָּמֶת אֹתוֹ אֲשֶׁר־
הִפְקִיד מֶלֶךְ־בָּבֶל בָּאָרֶץ:

CHAPTER XLI

1-3 GEDALIAH MURDERED BY ISHMAEL

1. *in the seventh month.* See on xxxvi. 9. Kimchi also considers the new moon to be intended here. In the Jewish calendar the third of the seventh month is observed as the fast of Gedaliah, deferred to that day because the first and second are New Year.

and one of the chief officers. *One* is not in the original. A.V. has 'and the princes of the king, even ten men.' The Hebrew may mean, 'and some of the chief officers' (so Rashi and Kimchi), the *ten men* being of lower rank. Another possibility is to understand the whole as descriptive of Ishmael: 'one of the seed royal and (of) the chief officers.'

they did eat bread together. Gedaliah received them as guests and gave them hospitality. This made the subsequent crime all the more heinous.

2. *and slew him.* Josephus, *Antiquities* X, ix. 4, relates that Gedaliah 'was immersed in his cups to the degree of insensibility, and had fallen asleep,' and while in this helpless condition he was killed. Either this story is true or Gedaliah's retinue must have been too small to protect him. In spite of the warning he had received (xl. 14), Gedaliah's trust in Ishmael was so great that he took no precautions. In the light of Ishmael's subsequent flight, it is not easy to see what his motive was. If it was mere pique at having been passed over for the governorship, he certainly went to extreme lengths to gratify it. It is more likely, perhaps, that he did not contemplate flight at first (see on the next verse), thinking to take Gedaliah's place as governor, either under Nebuchadnezzar or, if Baalis (see on xl. 14) should annex Judea, under him.

whom the king of Babylon had made governor. Kimchi renders: 'because the

all the Jews that were with him, even with Gedaliah, at Mizpah, and the Chaldeans that were found there, even the men of war.

4. And it came to pass the second day after he had slain Gedaliah, and no man knew it, 5. that there came certain men from Shechem, from Shiloh, and from Samaria, even fourscore men, having their beards shaven and their clothes rent, and having cut themselves, with meal-offerings and frankincense in their hand to bring them to the house of

3 וְאֵת כָּל־הַיְּהוּדִים אֲשֶׁר־
הָיוּ אִתּוֹ אֶת־גְּדַלְיָהוּ בַּמִּצְפָּה
וְאֶת־הַכַּשְׂדִּים אֲשֶׁר נִמְצְאוּ־
שָׁם אֵת אַנְשֵׁי הַמִּלְחָמָה הִכָּה
4 יִשְׁמָעֵאל: וַיְהִי בַּיּוֹם הַשֵּׁנִי
לְהָמִית אֶת־גְּדַלְיָהוּ וְאִישׁ לֹא
5 יָדָע: וַיָּבֹאוּ אֲנָשִׁים מִשְּׁכֶם
מִשִּׁלוֹ וּמִשֹּׁמְרוֹן שְׁמֹנִים אִישׁ
מְגֻלְּחֵי זָקָן וּקְרֻעֵי בְגָדִים
וּמִתְגֹּדְדִים וּמִנְחָה וּלְבוֹנָה
בְּיָדָם לְהָבִיא בֵּית יְהֹוָה:

---

king of Babylon had made him governor.' This rendering explicitly makes resentment the motive.

3. *and the Chaldeans.* This deliberate act of provocation seems to be quite senseless, because Nebuchadnezzar would certainly avenge their death, thereby depriving Ishmael of whatever he thought to gain. Possibly it was not part of his original plan. The Chaldeans may have died in defence of the governor; or perhaps Ishmael became panic-stricken after the death of Gedaliah, and to cover up his deed, if only for a short time (cf. *and no man knew it,* verse 4), slew all present. His later conduct (cf. verses 7ff.) makes the second explanation probable. In any event, the soldiers must have been unarmed since so small a force sufficed to overwhelm them.

4-10 FURTHER ATROCITIES OF ISHMAEL

5. *from Shechem, from Shiloh, and from Samaria.* Three towns in what was formerly the Northern Kingdom which had been destroyed nearly 140 years earlier, in 722 B.C.E., and its inhabitants

deported to Assyria (2 Kings xvii. 6). These pilgrims were either descendants of those Jews who were still left after the deportation of the population (cf. 2 Chron. xxxiv. 9 which records that a *remnant* stayed in the country), or Judeans who had settled there.

Shechem. Now the Arab town of Nablus; it lies in a valley between the mountains Gerizim and Ebal.

Shiloh. See on vii. 12.

Samaria. The capital of the former Northern Kingdom.

having their beards shaven, etc. In mourning for the destroyed Temple.

and having cut themselves. Likewise as a sign of mourning (see on xvi. 6).

meal-offerings and frankincense. Doubtless there were no longer facilities to slaughter animals as offerings.

to bring them to the house of the LORD. In its ruins. The Talmud (Meg. 10a) preserves a tradition that sacrifices could be offered in the first Temple even after it was destroyed.

the LORD. 6. And Ishmael the son of Nethaniah went forth from Mizpah to meet them, weeping all along as he went; and it came to pass, as he met them, he said unto them: 'Come to Gedaliah the son of Ahikam.' 7. And it was so, when they came into the midst of the city, that Ishmael the son of Nethaniah slew them, and cast them into the midst of the pit, he, and the men that were with him. 8. But ten men were found among them that said unto Ishmael: 'Slay us not; for we have stores hidden in the field, of wheat, and of barley, and of oil, and of honey.' So he forbore, and slew them not among their brethren. 9. Now the pit wherein Ishmael cast all the dead bodies of the men whom he had slain by the side of Gedaliah was that which Asa the king had made for fear of Baasa king of Israel;

6 וַיֵּצֵא יִשְׁמָעֵאל בֶּן־נְתַנְיָה
לִקְרָאתָם מִן־הַמִּצְפָּה הֹלֵךְ
הָלֹךְ וּבֹכֶה וַיְהִי כִּפְגֹשׁ אֹתָם
וַיֹּאמֶר אֲלֵיהֶם בֹּאוּ אֶל־
7 גְּדַלְיָהוּ בֶּן־אֲחִיקָם: וַיְהִי
כְּבוֹאָם אֶל־תּוֹךְ הָעִיר
וַיִּשְׁחָטֵם יִשְׁמָעֵאל בֶּן־נְתַנְיָה
אֶל־תּוֹךְ הַבּוֹר הוּא וְהָאֲנָשִׁים
8 אֲשֶׁר־אִתּוֹ: וַעֲשָׂרָה אֲנָשִׁים
נִמְצְאוּ־בָם וַיֹּאמְרוּ אֶל־
יִשְׁמָעֵאל אַל־תְּמִתֵנוּ כִּי־
יֶשׁ־לָנוּ מַטְמֹנִים בַּשָּׂדֶה חִטִּים
וּשְׂעֹרִים וְשֶׁמֶן וּדְבָשׁ וַיֶּחְדַּל
וְלֹא הֱמִיתָם בְּתוֹךְ אֲחֵיהֶם:
9 וְהַבּוֹר אֲשֶׁר הִשְׁלִיךְ שָׁם
יִשְׁמָעֵאל אֵת | כָּל־פִּגְרֵי
הָאֲנָשִׁים אֲשֶׁר הִכָּה בְּיַד־
גְּדַלְיָהוּ הוּא אֲשֶׁר עָשָׂה הַמֶּלֶךְ
אָסָא מִפְּנֵי בַּעְשָׁא מֶלֶךְ־

6. *weeping all along as he went.* To gain their sympathy he mourned with them over the destruction of the Temple. In this way he averted suspicion.

come to Gedaliah. To pay respects to him before proceeding to Jerusalem.

7. *slew them.* His motive is not certain. It may have been to keep the assassination of Gedaliah secret as long as possible. Another explanation, suggested by verse 8, was his lust for plunder.

the pit. Cf. verse 9.

8. *stores hidden in the field.* It is a common custom in the East to use 'wells or cisterns for grain. In them the farmers store their crops of all kinds after the grain is threshed and winnowed. These cisterns are cool, perfectly dry, and tight. The top is hermetically sealed with plaster, and covered with a deep bed of earth' (Thomson). The ten men were impelled to conceal their stores because of the unsafe conditions which then obtained.

9. *that which Asa the king had made.* There is no record of this elsewhere in

the same Ishmael the son of Nethaniah filled with them that were
slain. 10. Then Ishmael carried
away captive all the residue of the
people that were in Mizpah, even
the king's daughters, and all the
people that remained in Mizpah,
whom Nebuzaradan the captain of
the guard had committed to
Gedaliah the son of Ahikam;
Ishmael the son of Nethaniah
carried them away captive, and
departed to go over to the children
of Ammon.

11. But when Johanan the son of
Kareah, and all the captains of the
forces that were with him, heard of
all the evil that Ishmael the son of
Nethaniah had done, 12. then they
took all the men, and went to fight
with Ishmael the son of Nethaniah,
and found him by the great waters
that are in Gibeon. 13. Now it
came to pass, that when all the
people that were with Ishmael saw
Johanan the son of Kareah, and all

יִשְׂרָאֵל אֹתוֹ מִלֵּא יִשְׁמָעֵאל
10 בֶּן־נְתַנְיָהוּ חֲלָלִים: וַיִּשְׁבְּ |
יִשְׁמָעֵאל אֶת־כָּל־שְׁאֵרִית
הָעָם אֲשֶׁר בַּמִּצְפָּה אֶת־בְּנוֹת
הַמֶּלֶךְ וְאֶת־כָּל־הָעָם
הַנִּשְׁאָרִים בַּמִּצְפָּה אֲשֶׁר
הִפְקִיד נְבוּזַרְאֲדָן רַב־
טַבָּחִים אֶת־גְּדַלְיָהוּ בֶּן־
אֲחִיקָם וַיִּשְׁבֵּם יִשְׁמָעֵאל
בֶּן־נְתַנְיָה וַיֵּלֶךְ לַעֲבֹר אֶל־
11 בְּנֵי עַמּוֹן: וַיִּשְׁמַע יוֹחָנָן בֶּן־
קָרֵחַ וְכָל־שָׂרֵי הַחֲיָלִים אֲשֶׁר
אִתּוֹ אֵת כָּל־הָרָעָה אֲשֶׁר
עָשָׂה יִשְׁמָעֵאל בֶּן־נְתַנְיָה:
12 וַיִּקְחוּ אֶת־כָּל־הָאֲנָשִׁים
וַיֵּלְכוּ לְהִלָּחֶם עִם־יִשְׁמָעֵאל
בֶּן־נְתַנְיָה וַיִּמְצְאוּ אֹתוֹ אֶל־
13 מַיִם רַבִּים אֲשֶׁר בְּגִבְעוֹן: וַיְהִי
כִּרְאוֹת כָּל־הָעָם אֲשֶׁר אֶת־
יִשְׁמָעֵאל אֶת־יוֹחָנָן בֶּן־קָרֵחַ

---

the Bible; but commentators refer to
1 Kings xv. 22 and 2 Chron. xvi. 6.
Possibly it was a kind of protective moat.

10. *carried away captive.* It seems impossible that he did all this with only
ten men. He must have had a far larger
band, but took only ten with him when
he went to see Gedaliah in order not to
arouse his suspicions.

in Mizpah. Including Jeremiah presumably (cf. xl. 6).

the king's daughters. Not to be interpreted literally, but the princesses in
general.

11-18 JOHANAN RESCUES THE CAPTIVES

12. *Gibeon.* See on xxviii. 1; it was
about a mile north of Mizpah. The
great waters are perhaps identical with
the *pool* mentioned in 2 Sam. ii. 13.

the captains of the forces that were with him, then they were glad. 14. So all the people that Ishmael had carried away captive from Mizpah cast about and returned, and went unto Johanan the son of Kareah. 15. But Ishmael the son of Nethaniah escaped from Johanan with eight men, and went to the children of Ammon.

16. Then took Johanan the son of Kareah, and all the captains of the forces that were with him, all the remnant of the people whom he had recovered from Ishmael the son of Nethaniah, from Mizpah, after that he had slain Gedaliah the son of Ahikam, the men, even the men of war, and the women, and the children, and the officers, whom he had brought back from Gibeon; 17. and they departed, and dwelt in Geruth Chimham, which is by Beth-lehem, to go to enter into Egypt, 18. because of the Chaldeans;

וְאֵת כָּל־שָׂרֵי הַחֲיָלִים אֲשֶׁר
אִתּוֹ וַיִּשְׂמָחוּ: וַיָּסֹבּוּ כָּל־ 14
הָעָם אֲשֶׁר־שָׁבָה יִשְׁמָעֵאל
מִן־הַמִּצְפָּה וַיָּשֻׁבוּ וַיֵּלְכוּ
אֶל־יוֹחָנָן בֶּן־קָרֵחַ:
וְיִשְׁמָעֵאל בֶּן־נְתַנְיָה נִמְלַט 15
בִּשְׁמֹנָה אֲנָשִׁים מִפְּנֵי יוֹחָנָן
וַיֵּלֶךְ אֶל־בְּנֵי עַמּוֹן: וַיִּקַּח 16
יוֹחָנָן בֶּן־קָרֵחַ וְכָל־שָׂרֵי
הַחֲיָלִים אֲשֶׁר־אִתּוֹ אֵת כָּל־
שְׁאֵרִית הָעָם אֲשֶׁר הֵשִׁיב מֵאֵת
יִשְׁמָעֵאל בֶּן־נְתַנְיָה מִן־־
הַמִּצְפָּה אַחַר הִכָּה אֶת־
גְּדַלְיָה בֶּן־אֲחִיקָם גְּבָרִים
אַנְשֵׁי הַמִּלְחָמָה וְנָשִׁים וְטַף
וְסָרִסִים אֲשֶׁר הֵשִׁיב מִגִּבְעוֹן:
וַיֵּלְכוּ וַיֵּשְׁבוּ בְּגֵרוּת כִּמְוֹהָם 17
אֲשֶׁר־אֵצֶל בֵּית לָחֶם לָלֶכֶת
לָבוֹא מִצְרָיִם: מִפְּנֵי 18

v. 17. כמהם ק׳

14. *cast about.* i.e. turned round. While Ishmael's force had been large enough to take this people captive (see on verse 10), it was not sufficiently strong to hold them when deliverance was near.

15. *to the children of Ammon.* Cf. xl. 14.

16. *from Mizpah.* i.e. these persons had been in Mizpah before Ishmael carried them away.

17. *Geruth Chimham.* lit. 'the lodging-place of Chimham.' He was the son of Barzillai the Gileadite, and it is possible that David made a grant of land to Chimham in consideration of services rendered by his father (cf. 2 Sam. xvii. 27ff., xix. 38ff.).

to go to enter into Egypt. Although Jeremiah was consulted on whether they should go to Egypt (xlii), it appears from here (and also perhaps from xliii. 2) that they had already made up their minds. This flight to Egypt was occasioned by the fear that Nebuchadnezzar would take revenge indiscriminately upon the guilty and innocent.

for they were afraid of them, because Ishmael the son of Nethaniah had slain Gedaliah the son of Ahikam, whom the king of Babylon made governor over the land.

הַכַּשְׂדִּים כִּי יָרְאוּ מִפְּנֵיהֶם
כִּי־הִכָּה יִשְׁמָעֵאל בֶּן־נְתַנְיָה
אֶת־גְּדַלְיָהוּ בֶּן־אֲחִיקָם
אֲשֶׁר־הִפְקִיד מֶלֶךְ־בָּבֶל
בָּאָרֶץ:

---

42   CHAPTER XLII   מב

1. Then all the captains of the forces, and Johanan the son of Kareah, and Jezaniah the son of Hoshaiah, and all the people from the least even unto the greatest, came near, 2. and said unto Jeremiah the prophet: 'Let, we pray thee, our supplication be accepted before thee, and pray for us unto the LORD thy God, even for all this remnant; for we are left but a few of many, as thine eyes do behold us; 3. that the LORD thy God may tell us the way wherein we should walk, and the thing that we

1 וַיִּגְּשׁוּ כָּל־שָׂרֵי הַחֲיָלִים וְיוֹחָנָן
בֶּן־קָרֵחַ וִיזַנְיָה בֶּן־הוֹשַׁעְיָה
וְכָל־הָעָם מִקָּטֹן וְעַד־גָּדוֹל:
2 וַיֹּאמְרוּ אֶל־יִרְמְיָהוּ הַנָּבִיא
תִּפָּל־נָא תְחִנָּתֵנוּ לְפָנֶיךָ
וְהִתְפַּלֵּל בַּעֲדֵנוּ אֶל־יְהֹוָה
אֱלֹהֶיךָ בְּעַד כָּל־הַשְּׁאֵרִית
הַזֹּאת כִּי־נִשְׁאַרְנוּ מְעַט
מֵהַרְבֵּה כַּאֲשֶׁר עֵינֶיךָ רֹאוֹת
3 אֹתָנוּ: וְיַגֶּד־לָנוּ יְהֹוָה אֱלֹהֶיךָ
אֶת־הַדֶּרֶךְ אֲשֶׁר־נֵלֶךְ בָּהּ

CHAPTER XLII

IN xlii. 1-xliii. 7 we read that Jeremiah is consulted by his brethren in Judea about migration to Egypt. In spite of his emphatic advice, given in God's name, against the proposal, the people migrate taking the prophet and Baruch with them.

1-6 JEREMIAH ASKED TO SEEK GUIDANCE FROM GOD

1. *Jezaniah the son of Hoshaiah.* Not the same Jezaniah mentioned in xl. 8, but probably identical with Azariah the son of Hoshaiah of xliii. 2. He may have been known by two names which have a similar significance: 'Jah is help' and 'Jah giveth ear' (Jezaniah being abbreviated from Jaazaniah; cf. xxxv. 3).

2. *let . . . our supplication be accepted.* For the idiom, see on xxxvi. 7.

3. *may tell us the way.* As often happens, their desire was not really for guidance, but for Divine confirmation of a decision

should do.' 4. Then Jeremiah the prophet said unto them: 'I have heard you; behold, I will pray unto the LORD your God according to your words; and it shall come to pass, that whatsoever thing the LORD shall answer you, I will declare it unto you; I will keep nothing back from you.' 5. Then they said to Jeremiah: 'The LORD be a true and faithful witness against us, if we do not even according to all the word wherewith the LORD thy God shall send thee to us. 6. Whether it be good, or whether it be evil, we will hearken to the voice of the LORD our God, to whom we send thee; that it may be well with us, when we hearken to the voice of the LORD our God.'

7. And it came to pass after ten days, that the word of the LORD

וְאֶת־הַדָּבָר אֲשֶׁר נַעֲשֶׂה:

4 וַיֹּאמֶר אֲלֵיהֶם יִרְמְיָהוּ הַנָּבִיא
שָׁמַעְתִּי הִנְנִי מִתְפַּלֵּל אֶל־
יְהֹוָה אֱלֹהֵיכֶם כְּדִבְרֵיכֶם
וְהָיָה כָּל־הַדָּבָר אֲשֶׁר־יַעֲנֶה
יְהֹוָה אֶתְכֶם אַגִּיד לָכֶם לֹא־
5 אֶמְנַע מִכֶּם דָּבָר: וְהֵמָּה
אָמְרוּ אֶל־יִרְמְיָהוּ יְהִי יְהֹוָה
בָּנוּ לְעֵד אֱמֶת וְנֶאֱמָן אִם־לֹא
כְּכָל־הַדָּבָר אֲשֶׁר יִשְׁלָחֲךָ
יְהֹוָה אֱלֹהֶיךָ אֵלֵינוּ כֵּן נַעֲשֶׂה:
6 אִם־טוֹב וְאִם־רָע בְּקוֹל |
יְהֹוָה אֱלֹהֵינוּ אֲשֶׁר אֲנוּ שֹׁלְחִים
אֹתְךָ אֵלָיו נִשְׁמָע לְמַעַן אֲשֶׁר
יִיטַב־לָנוּ כִּי נִשְׁמַע בְּקוֹל
7 יְהֹוָה אֱלֹהֵינוּ: וַיְהִי מִקֵּץ
עֲשֶׂרֶת יָמִים וַיְהִי דְבַר־יְהֹוָה

v. 6. אנחנו ק'

which they had already made, viz. to emigrate to Egypt. In his reply Jeremiah showed that he understood that this was the true position (cf. xlii. 17).

4. *I have heard you.* i.e. I will do as you wish.

5. *against us.* May God punish us if we act contrary to His will.

7-22 GOD WARNS AGAINST FLIGHT TO EGYPT

7. *after ten days.* Peake makes the penetrating comment: 'This verse is very important for the insight it gives into the nature of prophecy. Jeremiah does not confuse the Divine revelation with the desires of his heart or the conclusions of his judgment. Otherwise he would not have needed to wait for ten days. His waiting was not that his own mind might be made up, or to still the excitement among the people; for to prolong the suspense, especially when every hour seemed precious, would have been fatal to such an endeavour; nor yet in the hope that new circumstances might guide his decision. It was quite literally because he would not announce as a Divine revelation an answer which he did not definitely know to be such. It was an element in his prophetic gift that he could clearly and sharply distinguish between objective and subjective, between the word of God and the thought of his own heart.'

came unto Jeremiah. 8. Then called
he Johanan the son of Kareah, and
all the captains of the forces that
were with him, and all the people
from the least even to the greatest,
9. and said unto them: 'Thus saith
the LORD, the God of Israel, unto
whom ye sent me to present your
supplication before Him: 10. If ye
will still abide in this land, then
will I build you, and not pull you
down, and I will plant you, and not
pluck you up; for I repent Me of the
evil that I have done unto you.
11. Be not afraid of the king of
Babylon, of whom ye are afraid; be
not afraid of him, saith the LORD;
for I am with you to save you, and to
deliver you from his hand. 12. And
I will grant you compassion, that he
may have compassion upon you, and
cause you to return to your own
land. 13. But if ye say: We will not

8 אֶל־יִרְמְיָהוּ: וַיִּקְרָא אֶל־
יוֹחָנָן בֶּן־קָרֵחַ וְאֶל כָּל־שָׂרֵי
הַחֲיָלִים אֲשֶׁר אִתּוֹ וּלְכָל־
הָעָם לְמִקָּטֹן וְעַד־גָּדוֹל:
9 וַיֹּאמֶר אֲלֵיהֶם כֹּה־אָמַר
יְהֹוָה אֱלֹהֵי יִשְׂרָאֵל אֲשֶׁר
שְׁלַחְתֶּם אֹתִי אֵלָיו לְהַפִּיל
10 תְּחִנַּתְכֶם לְפָנָיו: אִם־שׁוֹב
תֵּשְׁבוּ בָּאָרֶץ הַזֹּאת וּבָנִיתִי
אֶתְכֶם וְלֹא אֶהֱרֹס וְנָטַעְתִּי
אֶתְכֶם וְלֹא אֶתּוֹשׁ כִּי נִחַמְתִּי
אֶל־הָרָעָה אֲשֶׁר עָשִׂיתִי
11 לָכֶם: אַל־תִּירְאוּ מִפְּנֵי מֶלֶךְ
בָּבֶל אֲשֶׁר־אַתֶּם יְרֵאִים
מִפָּנָיו אַל־תִּירְאוּ מִמֶּנּוּ נְאֻם־
יְהֹוָה כִּי־אִתְּכֶם אָנִי לְהוֹשִׁיעַ
אֶתְכֶם וּלְהַצִּיל אֶתְכֶם מִיָּדוֹ:
12 וְאֶתֵּן לָכֶם רַחֲמִים וְרִחַם
אֶתְכֶם וְהֵשִׁיב אֶתְכֶם אֶל־
13 אַדְמַתְכֶם: וְאִם־אֹמְרִים

10. *then will I build you*, etc. Cf. xxiv. 6.

for I repent Me. An anthropomorphism:
God's conduct towards the people would
now be reversed, which in human eyes
indicates regret over the past. In fact,
however, there is no mental change in
God; still less is there regret. Divine
punishment is remedial, not vindictive;
and now that suffering may have been
supposed to convince the people of the

error of their ways, destruction could
give way to reconstruction.

11. *of whom ye are afraid.* They feared
the vengeance of Nebuchadnezzar for
Gedaliah's murder (cf. xli. 18).

12. *I will grant you compassion.* By
withholding the Babylonian king from
violent action against you.

and cause you to return. i.e. those of
you (the word referring to the nation as
a whole) who have been exiled.

abide in this land; so that ye hearken
not to the voice of the LORD your
God; 14. saying: No; but we will go
into the land of Egypt, where we
shall see no war, nor hear the sound
of the horn, nor have hunger of
bread; and there will we abide;
15. now therefore hear ye the word
of the LORD, O remnant of Judah:
Thus saith the LORD of hosts, the
God of Israel: If ye wholly set your
faces to enter into Egypt, and go to
sojourn there; 16. then it shall come
to pass, that the sword, which ye
fear, shall overtake you there in the
land of Egypt, and the famine,
whereof ye are afraid, shall follow
hard after you there in Egypt; and
there ye shall die. 17. So shall it be
with all the men that set their faces
to go into Egypt to sojourn there;
they shall die by the sword, by the
famine, and by the pestilence; and
none of them shall remain or escape
from the evil that I will bring upon

אַתֶּם לֹא נֵשֵׁב בָּאָרֶץ הַזֹּאת
לְבִלְתִּי שְׁמֹעַ בְּקוֹל יְהֹוָה
אֱלֹהֵיכֶם: לֵאמֹר לֹא כִּי אֶרֶץ 14
מִצְרַיִם נָבוֹא אֲשֶׁר לֹא־נִרְאֶה
מִלְחָמָה וְקוֹל שׁוֹפָר לֹא נִשְׁמָע
וְלַלֶּחֶם לֹא־נִרְעָב וְשָׁם נֵשֵׁב:
וְעַתָּה לָכֵן שִׁמְעוּ דְבַר־יְהֹוָה 15
שְׁאֵרִית יְהוּדָה כֹּה־אָמַר
יְהֹוָה צְבָאוֹת אֱלֹהֵי יִשְׂרָאֵל
אִם־אַתֶּם שׂוֹם תְּשִׂמוּן פְּנֵיכֶם
לָבֹא מִצְרַיִם וּבָאתֶם לָגוּר
שָׁם: וְהָיְתָה הַחֶרֶב אֲשֶׁר אַתֶּם 16
יְרֵאִים מִמֶּנָּה שָׁם תַּשִּׂיג אֶתְכֶם
בְּאֶרֶץ מִצְרָיִם וְהָרָעָב אֲשֶׁר־
אַתֶּם | דֹּאֲגִים מִמֶּנּוּ שָׁם יִדְבַּק
אַחֲרֵיכֶם מִצְרַיִם וְשָׁם תָּמֻתוּ:
וְיִהְיוּ כָל־הָאֲנָשִׁים אֲשֶׁר־ 17
שָׂמוּ אֶת־פְּנֵיהֶם לָבוֹא
מִצְרַיִם לָגוּר שָׁם יָמוּתוּ בַּחֶרֶב
בָּרָעָב וּבַדָּבֶר וְלֹא־יִהְיֶה
לָהֶם שָׂרִיד וּפָלִיט מִפְּנֵי
הָרָעָה אֲשֶׁר אֲנִי מֵבִיא

14. *and there will we abide.* Without fear of attack from Babylon. Distance lends enchantment to the scene, and they conjured up a picture of an Egypt at peace and prosperous, for which there was little warrant.

17. *from the evil that I will bring upon them.* Although *I repent Me of the evil that I have done unto you* (verse 10), should you migrate to Egypt in defiance of My command, you prove that you have still not learned to obey Me, and further punishment is necessary.

them. 18. For thus saith the LORD
of hosts, the God of Israel: As Mine
anger and My fury hath been poured
forth upon the inhabitants of Jerusalem, so shall My fury be poured
forth upon you, when ye shall enter
into Egypt; and ye shall be an
execration, and an astonishment, and
a curse, and a reproach; and ye shall
see this place no more. 19. The
LORD hath spoken concerning you,
O remnant of Judah: Go ye not into
Egypt; know certainly that I have
forewarned you this day. 20. For
ye have dealt deceitfully against
your own souls; for ye sent me unto
the LORD your God, saying: Pray
for us unto the LORD our God; and
according unto all that the LORD our
God shall say, so declare unto us,
and we will do it; 21. and I have this
day declared it to you; but ye have
not hearkened to the voice of the
LORD your God in any thing for

18 עֲלֵיהֶ֑ם כִּ֣י כֹ֣ה אָמַ֞ר יְהֹוָ֣ה
צְבָאוֹת֮ אֱלֹהֵ֣י יִשְׂרָאֵל֒ כַּאֲשֶׁר֩
נִתַּ֨ךְ אַפִּ֜י וַחֲמָתִ֗י עַל־יֹשְׁבֵי֙
יְרֽוּשָׁלִַ֔ם כֵּ֣ן תִּתַּ֤ךְ חֲמָתִי֙
עֲלֵיכֶ֔ם בְּבֹאֲכֶ֖ם מִצְרָ֑יִם
וִהְיִיתֶ֞ם לְאָלָ֣ה וּלְשַׁמָּה֙
וְלִקְלָלָ֣ה וּלְחֶרְפָּ֔ה וְלֹא־
תִרְא֣וּ ע֔וֹד אֶת־הַמָּק֖וֹם הַזֶּֽה׃
19 דִּבֶּ֨ר יְהֹוָ֤ה עֲלֵיכֶם֙ שְׁאֵרִ֣ית
יְהוּדָ֔ה אַל־תָּבֹ֖אוּ מִצְרָ֑יִם
יָדֹ֥עַ תֵּדְע֖וּ כִּֽי־הַעִידֹ֥תִי
20 בָכֶ֥ם הַיּֽוֹם׃ כִּ֣י הִתְעֵתֶ֗ם
בְּנַפְשֽׁוֹתֵיכֶם֒ כִּֽי־אַתֶּ֞ם
שְׁלַחְתֶּ֤ם אֹתִי֙ אֶל־יְהֹוָ֣ה
אֱלֹֽהֵיכֶם֙ לֵאמֹ֔ר הִתְפַּלֵּ֣ל
בַּעֲדֵ֗נוּ אֶל־יְהֹוָ֣ה אֱלֹהֵ֔ינוּ
וּכְכֹל֙ אֲשֶׁ֣ר יֹאמַ֔ר יְהֹוָ֥ה
אֱלֹהֵ֖ינוּ כֵּ֥ן הַגֶּד־לָ֖נוּ וְעָשִֽׂינוּ׃
21 וָאַגִּ֨ד לָכֶ֤ם הַיּוֹם֙ וְלֹ֣א שְׁמַעְתֶּ֔ם
בְּק֖וֹל יְהֹוָ֣ה אֱלֹהֵיכֶ֑ם וּלְכֹ֥ל

v. 20. התעיתם ק׳

18. *and ye shall see this place no more.*
These Judeans hoped that their stay in
Egypt would be only temporary, until
Nebuchadnezzar's anger had cooled.

19. Jeremiah has delivered God's direction, but it is evident to him that the
command to remain in Judea is not
acceptable to his hearers; so he adds his
own admonition.

20. *ye have dealt deceitfully against your*

own souls. You practised self-deceit
when you asked for God's guidance,
knowing in your hearts that your course
was already decided. Ehrlich renders:
'Ye have deceived (God) with danger to
your lives.'

21. *in any thing.* lit. 'and in every
thing.' You have not hearkened in this
matter, and indeed in every matter on
which God has sent me to you.

which He hath sent me unto you.
22. Now therefore know certainly
that ye shall die by the sword, by the
famine, and by the pestilence, in the
place whither ye desire to go to
sojourn there.'

22 אֲשֶׁר־שְׁלָחַנִי אֲלֵיכֶם: וְעַתָּה
יָדֹעַ תֵּדְעוּ כִּי בַּחֶרֶב בָּרָעָב
וּבַדֶּבֶר תָּמוּתוּ בַּמָּקוֹם אֲשֶׁר
חֲפַצְתֶּם לָבוֹא לָגוּר שָׁם:

---

43   CHAPTER XLIII   מג

1. And it came to pass, that when
Jeremiah had made an end of
speaking unto all the people all the
words of the LORD their God,
wherewith the LORD their God had
sent him to them, even all these
words, 2. then spoke Azariah the son
of Hoshaiah, and Johanan the son of
Kareah, and all the proud men,
saying unto Jeremiah: 'Thou speakest falsely; the LORD our God hath
not sent thee to say: Ye shall not go
into Egypt to sojourn there; 3. but
Baruch the son of Neriah setteth
thee on against us, to deliver us into
the hand of the Chaldeans, that they
may put us to death, and carry us

1 וַיְהִי כְּכַלּוֹת יִרְמְיָהוּ לְדַבֵּר
אֶל־כָּל־הָעָם אֶת־כָּל־־
דִּבְרֵי יְהֹוָה אֱלֹהֵיהֶם אֲשֶׁר
שְׁלָחוֹ יְהֹוָה אֱלֹהֵיהֶם אֲלֵיהֶם
אֵת כָּל־הַדְּבָרִים הָאֵלֶּה:
2 וַיֹּאמֶר עֲזַרְיָה בֶן־הוֹשַׁעְיָה
וְיוֹחָנָן בֶּן־קָרֵחַ וְכָל־־
הָאֲנָשִׁים הַזֵּדִים אֹמְרִים אֶל־
יִרְמְיָהוּ שֶׁקֶר אַתָּה מְדַבֵּר לֹא
שְׁלָחֲךָ יְהֹוָה אֱלֹהֵינוּ לֵאמֹר
לֹא־תָבֹאוּ מִצְרַיִם לָגוּר שָׁם:
3 כִּי בָּרוּךְ בֶּן־נֵרִיָּה מַסִּית אֹתְךָ
בָּנוּ לְמַעַן תֵּת אֹתָנוּ בְיַד־
הַכַּשְׂדִּים לְהָמִית אֹתָנוּ

CHAPTER XLIII

**1-7 FLIGHT TO EGYPT IN
DEFIANCE OF GOD**

2. *Azariah.* See on xlii. 1.

proud men. Better, 'presumptuous men,'
who were determined to act contrary to
the direction given by Jeremiah.

3. *but Baruch,* etc. Since Jeremiah was
by now an old man, they accused him of
having fallen under Baruch's influence
and expressing his views as a message of
God. To this charge Jeremiah does not
deign to make reply. He appreciates
that the leaders are determined on their
course of action and remonstrance is
useless.

away captives to Babylon.' 4. So Johanan the son of Kareah, and all the captains of the forces, and all the people, hearkened not to the voice of the LORD, to dwell in the land of Judah. 5. But Johanan the son of Kareah, and all the captains of the forces, took all the remnant of Judah, that were returned from all the nations whither they had been driven to sojourn in the land of Judah: 6. the men, and the women, and the children, and the king's daughters, and every person that Nebuzaradan the captain of the guard had left with Gedaliah the son of Ahikam, the son of Shaphan, and Jeremiah the prophet, and Baruch the son of Neriah; 7. and they came into the land of Egypt; for they hearkened not to the voice of the LORD; and they came even to Tahpanhes.

8. Then came the word of the LORD unto Jeremiah in Tahpanhes, saying: 9. 'Take great stones in thy

וּלְהַגְלוֹת אֹתָנוּ בָּבֶל: וְלֹא־ 4
שָׁמַע יוֹחָנָן בֶּן־קָרֵחַ וְכָל־
שָׂרֵי הַחֲיָלִים וְכָל־הָעָם
בְּקוֹל יְהוָה לָשֶׁבֶת בְּאֶרֶץ
יְהוּדָה: וַיִּקַּח יוֹחָנָן בֶּן־קָרֵחַ 5
וְכָל־שָׂרֵי הַחֲיָלִים אֶת כָּל־
שְׁאֵרִית יְהוּדָה אֲשֶׁר־שָׁבוּ
מִכָּל־הַגּוֹיִם אֲשֶׁר נִדְּחוּ־שָׁם
לָגוּר בְּאֶרֶץ יְהוּדָה: אֶת־ 6
הַגְּבָרִים וְאֶת־הַנָּשִׁים וְאֶת־
הַטַּף וְאֶת־בְּנוֹת הַמֶּלֶךְ וְאֵת
כָּל־הַנֶּפֶשׁ אֲשֶׁר הִנִּיחַ
נְבוּזַרְאֲדָן רַב־טַבָּחִים אֶת־
גְּדַלְיָהוּ בֶּן־אֲחִיקָם בֶּן־שָׁפָן
וְאֵת יִרְמְיָהוּ הַנָּבִיא וְאֶת־
בָּרוּךְ בֶּן־נֵרִיָּהוּ: וַיָּבֹאוּ אֶרֶץ 7
מִצְרַיִם כִּי לֹא שָׁמְעוּ בְּקוֹל
יְהוָה וַיָּבֹאוּ עַד־תַּחְפַּנְחֵס:
וַיְהִי דְבַר־יְהוָה אֶל־יִרְמְיָהוּ 8
בְּתַחְפַּנְחֵס לֵאמֹר: קַח בְּיָדְךָ 9

5. *that were returned . . . the land of Judah.* Nearly two months had elapsed between the fall of Jerusalem and the assassination of Gedaliah. It is known that both before the Babylonian invasion and after its success many Judeans had escaped from the doomed city and taken refuge in the surrounding countries of Ammon, Moab and Edom (cf. xl. 11). These may have returned during the two months, and to them the present verse refers. The Hebrew for *they had*

been driven does not necessarily imply compulsory deportation and may well mean voluntary flight.

6. *the king's daughters.* See on xli. 10.

Jeremiah . . . Baruch. They were probably forced to join in the migration, although it is not impossible that they felt it their duty to accompany their brethren to Egypt and be of service to them there.

7. *Tahpanhes.* On the Egyptian frontier; see on ii. 16.

hand, and hide them in the mortar
in the framework, which is at the
entry of Pharaoh's house in Tahpanhes, in the sight of the men of
Judah; 10. and say unto them:
Thus saith the LORD of hosts, the
God of Israel: Behold, I will send
and take Nebuchadrezzar the king
of Babylon, My servant, and will set
his throne upon these stones that
I have hid; and he shall spread his
royal pavilion over them. 11. And
he shall come, and shall smite the
land of Egypt; such as are for death
to death, and such as are for
captivity to captivity, and such as
are for the sword to the sword.
12. And I will kindle a fire in the
houses of the gods of Egypt; and
he shall burn them, and carry them

אֲבָנִים גְּדֹלוֹת וּטְמַנְתָּם בַּמֶּלֶט
בַּמַּלְבֵּן אֲשֶׁר בְּפֶתַח בֵּית־־
פַּרְעֹה בְּתַחְפַּנְחֵס לְעֵינֵי
אֲנָשִׁים יְהוּדִים: וְאָמַרְתָּ   10
אֲלֵיהֶם כֹּה־אָמַר יְהוָה
צְבָאוֹת אֱלֹהֵי יִשְׂרָאֵל הִנְנִי
שֹׁלֵחַ וְלָקַחְתִּי אֶת־־
נְבוּכַדְרֶאצַּר מֶלֶךְ־־בָּבֶל
עַבְדִּי וְשַׂמְתִּי כִסְאוֹ מִמַּעַל
לָאֲבָנִים הָאֵלֶּה אֲשֶׁר טָמָנְתִּי
וְנָטָה אֶת־שַׁפְרוּרוֹ עֲלֵיהֶם:
וּבָאָה וְהִכָּה אֶת־אֶרֶץ   11
מִצְרָיִם אֲשֶׁר לַמָּוֶת לַמָּוֶת
וַאֲשֶׁר לַשְּׁבִי לַשֶּׁבִי וַאֲשֶׁר
לַחֶרֶב לֶחָרֶב: וְהִצַּתִּי אֵשׁ   12
בְּבָתֵּי אֱלֹהֵי מִצְרַיִם וּשְׂרָפָם

v. 10. ׳ובא ק   v. 11. ׳שפרירו ק

8-13 NEBUCHADNEZZAR'S CONQUEST
OF EGYPT FORETOLD

9. *in the mortar in the framework.* The
Egyptologist, Flinders Petrie, who carried
out excavations at Tahpanhes, renders
the Hebrew *malben* by 'pavement.'
His account reads, 'When I came to clear
the fort at Dafneh, there proved to be
but one entry into Pharaoh's house; and
in front of that was a wide paved area on
the north of the fort. It was a place
probably for the external guard, and for
stacking goods, unloading camels, and
such purposes of outdoor life in
Egypt . . . This platform was a place
exactly corresponding to Jeremiah's
detailed account, and the identification of
it is certain.'

10. *My servant.* See on xxv. 9.

will set his throne. When conducting a
campaign against Egypt.

royal pavilion. The strange Hebrew
noun does not occur elsewhere. It is
apparently derived from a root found in
Assyrian meaning, 'to spread out,' and
some commentators have suggested
'carpet,' but A.J. is preferable.

11. *to death.* See on xv. 2.

12. *I will kindle.* The fire will be kindled
by Nebuchadnezzar acting as God's
agent.

burn them. i.e. the images of gold and
silver.

away captives; and he shall fold up
the land of Egypt, as a shepherd
foldeth up his garment; and he shall
go forth from thence in peace.

13. He shall also break the pillars of
Beth-shemesh, that is in the land of
Egypt; and the houses of the gods
of Egypt shall he burn with fire.'

וְשָׁבֵם וְעָטָה אֶת־אֶרֶץ
מִצְרַיִם כַּאֲשֶׁר־יַעֲטֶה הָרֹעֶה
אֶת־בִּגְדוֹ וְיָצָא מִשָּׁם בְּשָׁלוֹם׃
13 וְשִׁבַּר אֶת־מַצְּבוֹת בֵּית שֶׁמֶשׁ
אֲשֶׁר בְּאֶרֶץ מִצְרַיִם וְאֶת־
בָּתֵּי אֱלֹהֵי מִצְרַיִם יִשְׂרֹף
בָּאֵשׁ׃

---

44   CHAPTER XLIV   מד

1. The word that came to Jeremiah
concerning all the Jews that dwelt
in the land of Egypt, that dwelt at

1 הַדָּבָר אֲשֶׁר־הָיָה אֶל־
יִרְמְיָהוּ אֶל כָּל־הַיְּהוּדִים
הַיֹּשְׁבִים בְּאֶרֶץ מִצְרָיִם

---

carry them away captives. The gods
which are not destroyed will form part of
the triumphal procession of the conqueror. This was a common practice in
ancient times.

he shall fold up the land of Egypt. The
figure is of something being rolled up
and taken away. Nebuchadnezzar will
carry Egypt away (i.e. take possession of
it) as easily as a shepherd folds his
garment and walks off. Or, *the land of
Egypt* may signify the spoil of Egypt.

in peace. He will carry away his spoil
unhindered.

13. *Beth-shemesh.* lit. 'house of the
sun.' 'Probably Heliopolis or On. The
reference of the verse is to the temple of
the sun, at the city called by the Greeks
Heliopolis (city of the sun), about six
miles north-east of Cairo. The temple
had in front of it an avenue of obelisks,
one of which remains *in situ.* It was
erected by Thothmes III (*c.* 1500 B.C.E.).
"Cleopatra's Needle," placed on the
Thames Embankment in 1878, is another'
(Streane).

CHAPTER XLIV

JEREMIAH DENOUNCES THE CULT OF THE
QUEEN OF HEAVEN

1-14 IDOLATRY BY EGYPTIAN JEWS
CONDEMNED

1. *the word that came to Jeremiah.* It is
not necessary to assume that this prophecy is considerably later than the
events narrated in the last chapter. The
Jews may have dispersed as soon as they
arrived in Egypt, and quickly formed
communities in the cities named in this
verse. Moreover, there were Jewish
communities in Egypt before the present
immigration. Jeremiah would naturally
take the earliest opportunity of protesting
against heathen practices by his co-
religionists before these became rooted
among the recent settlers, although they
were not new to them (cf. vii. 18). He
hoped that the tragic catastrophe which
they had suffered would recall them to
their senses, and he would prevail upon
them to abandon the pagan rites.

Migdol, and at Tahpanhes, and at
Noph, and in the country of Pathros,
saying: 2. 'Thus saith the LORD of
hosts, the God of Israel: Ye have
seen all the evil that I have brought
upon Jerusalem, and upon all the
cities of Judah; and, behold, this day
they are a desolation, and no man
dwelleth therein; 3. because of their
wickedness which they have committed to provoke Me, in that they
went to offer, and to serve other
gods, whom they knew not, neither
they, nor ye, nor your fathers.
4. Howbeit I sent unto you all My
servants the prophets, sending them
betimes and often, saying: Oh, do
not this abominable thing that I hate.
5. But they hearkened not, nor
inclined their ear to turn from their
wickedness, to forbear offering unto
other gods. 6. Wherefore My fury
and Mine anger was poured forth,
and was kindled in the cities of
Judah and in the streets of Jerusalem; and they are wasted and

הַיְּשְׁבִים בְּמִגְדֹּל וּבְתַחְפַּנְחֵס
וּבְנֹף וּבְאֶרֶץ פַּתְרוֹס לֵאמֹר:
2 כֹּה־אָמַר יְהוָה צְבָאוֹת אֱלֹהֵי
יִשְׂרָאֵל אַתֶּם רְאִיתֶם אֵת כָּל־
הָרָעָה אֲשֶׁר הֵבֵאתִי עַל־
יְרוּשָׁלַםִ וְעַל כָּל־עָרֵי יְהוּדָה
וְהִנָּם חָרְבָּה הַיּוֹם הַזֶּה וְאֵין
3 בָּהֶם יוֹשֵׁב: מִפְּנֵי רָעָתָם אֲשֶׁר
עָשׂוּ לְהַכְעִסֵנִי לָלֶכֶת לְקַטֵּר
לַעֲבֹד לֵאלֹהִים אֲחֵרִים אֲשֶׁר
לֹא יְדָעוּם הֵמָּה אַתֶּם
4 וַאֲבֹתֵיכֶם: וָאֶשְׁלַח אֲלֵיכֶם
אֶת־כָּל־עֲבָדַי הַנְּבִיאִים
הַשְׁכֵּים וְשָׁלֹחַ לֵאמֹר אַל־נָא
תַעֲשׂוּ אֵת דְּבַר־הַתֹּעֵבָה
5 הַזֹּאת אֲשֶׁר שָׂנֵאתִי: וְלֹא
שָׁמְעוּ וְלֹא־הִטּוּ אֶת־אָזְנָם
לָשׁוּב מֵרָעָתָם לְבִלְתִּי קַטֵּר
6 לֵאלֹהִים אֲחֵרִים: וַתִּתַּךְ
חֲמָתִי וְאַפִּי וַתִּבְעַר בְּעָרֵי
יְהוּדָה וּבְחֻצוֹת יְרוּשָׁלָםִ

Migdol. On the north-east border of
Egypt, to the east of Tahpanhes (cf.
Exod. xiv. 2).

Tahpanhes . . . Noph. See on ii. 16.

Pathros. The southern part of what is
now Egypt, formerly claimed by
Ethiopia. It starts a few miles south of

Memphis and extends to Cyrene on the
first cataract.

3. *and to serve.* Omit *and* which is not
in the text.

4. Cf. vii. 25, xxv. 4.

6. *My fury and Mine anger was poured
forth.* Cf. vii. 20, xlii. 18.

desolate, as at this day. 7. Therefore now thus saith the LORD, the God of hosts, the God of Israel: Wherefore commit ye this great evil against your own souls, to cut off from you man and woman, infant and suckling, out of the midst of Judah, to leave you none remaining; 8. in that ye provoke Me with the works of your hands, offering unto other gods in the land of Egypt, whither ye are gone to sojourn; that ye may be cut off, and that ye may be a curse and a reproach among all the nations of the earth? 9. Have ye forgotten the wicked deeds of your fathers, and the wicked deeds of the kings of Judah, and the wicked deeds of their wives, and your own wicked deeds, and the wicked deeds of your wives, which they committed in the land of Judah, and in the streets of Jerusalem? 10. They are not humbled even unto this day, neither have they feared, nor walked in My law, nor in My statutes, that I set before you and before your fathers. 11. Therefore thus saith the LORD of

נַתִּהְיֶינָה לְחָרְבָּה לִשְׁמָמָֽה
7 כַּיּוֹם הַזֶּֽה: וְעַתָּה כֹּה־אָמַר
יְהֹוָה אֱלֹהֵי צְבָאוֹת אֱלֹהֵי
יִשְׂרָאֵל לָמָה אַתֶּם עֹשִׂים רָעָה
גְדוֹלָה אֶל־נַפְשֹׁתֵכֶם
לְהַכְרִית לָכֶם אִישׁ־וְאִשָּׁה
עוֹלֵל וְיוֹנֵק מִתּוֹךְ יְהוּדָה
לְבִלְתִּי הוֹתִיר לָכֶם שְׁאֵרִֽית:
8 לְהַכְעִסֵנִי בְּמַעֲשֵׂי יְדֵיכֶם
לְקַטֵּר לֵאלֹהִים אֲחֵרִים
בְּאֶרֶץ מִצְרַיִם אֲשֶׁר־אַתֶּם
בָּאִים לָגוּר שָׁם לְמַעַן הַכְרִית
לָכֶם וּלְמַעַן הֱיוֹתְכֶם לִקְלָלָה
וּלְחֶרְפָּה בְּכֹל גּוֹיֵי הָאָֽרֶץ:
9 הַשְׁכַחְתֶּם אֶת־רָעוֹת
אֲבוֹתֵיכֶם וְאֶת־רָעוֹת |
מַלְכֵי יְהוּדָה וְאֵת רָעוֹת נָשָׁיו
וְאֵת רָעֹתֵיכֶם וְאֵת רָעֹת
נְשֵׁיכֶם אֲשֶׁר עָשׂוּ בְּאֶרֶץ
10 יְהוּדָה וּבְחֻצוֹת יְרוּשָׁלָֽם: לֹא
דֻכְּאוּ עַד הַיּוֹם הַזֶּה וְלֹא יָרְאוּ
וְלֹא־הָלְכוּ בְתוֹרָתִי וּבְחֻקֹּתַי
אֲשֶׁר־נָתַתִּי לִפְנֵיכֶם וְלִפְנֵי
11 אֲבוֹתֵיכֶֽם: לָכֵן כֹּה־אָמַֽר

---

7. *against your own souls.* i.e. against yourselves, incurring severe penalties.
9. *wives.* Who instigated them to idol-worship (cf. verse 15).

10. *they are not humbled.* The second person is changed to the third for the purpose of including the past generations.
11. *I will set My face.* Cf. xxi. 10.

hosts, the God of Israel: Behold, I will set My face against you for evil, even to cut off all Judah. 12. And I will take the remnant of Judah, that have set their faces to go into the land of Egypt to sojourn there, and they shall all be consumed; in the land of Egypt shall they fall; they shall be consumed by the sword and by the famine; they shall die, from the least even unto the greatest, by the sword and by the famine; and they shall be an execration, and an astonishment, and a curse, and a reproach. 13. For I will punish them that dwell in the land of Egypt, as I have punished Jerusalem, by the sword, by the famine, and by the pestilence; 14. so that none of the remnant of Judah, that are gone into the land of Egypt to sojourn there, shall escape or remain, that they should return into the land of Judah, to which they have a desire to return to dwell there; for none shall return save such as shall escape.'

15. Then all the men who knew

יְהֹוָה צְבָאוֹת אֱלֹהֵי יִשְׂרָאֵל
הִנְנִי שָׂם פָּנַי בָּכֶם לְרָעָה
וּלְהַכְרִית אֶת־כָּל־יְהוּדָה:
12 וְלָקַחְתִּי אֶת־שְׁאֵרִית יְהוּדָה
אֲשֶׁר־שָׂמוּ פְנֵיהֶם לָבוֹא
אֶרֶץ־מִצְרַיִם לָגוּר שָׁם וְתַמּוּ
כֹל בְּאֶרֶץ מִצְרַיִם יִפֹּלוּ
בַּחֶרֶב בָּרָעָב יִתַּמּוּ מִקָּטֹן
וְעַד־גָּדוֹל בַּחֶרֶב וּבָרָעָב
יָמֻתוּ וְהָיוּ לְאָלָה לְשַׁמָּה
13 וְלִקְלָלָה וּלְחֶרְפָּה: וּפָקַדְתִּי
עַל־הַיּוֹשְׁבִים בְּאֶרֶץ מִצְרַיִם
כַּאֲשֶׁר פָּקַדְתִּי עַל־יְרוּשָׁלַ͏ִם
14 בַּחֶרֶב בָּרָעָב וּבַדָּבֶר: וְלֹא
יִהְיֶה פָּלִיט וְשָׂרִיד לִשְׁאֵרִית
יְהוּדָה הַבָּאִים לָגוּר־שָׁם
בְּאֶרֶץ מִצְרַיִם וְלָשׁוּב | אֶרֶץ
יְהוּדָה אֲשֶׁר־הֵמָּה מְנַשְּׂאִים
אֶת־נַפְשָׁם לָשׁוּב לָשֶׁבֶת שָׁם
כִּי לֹא־יָשׁוּבוּ כִּי אִם־
15 פְּלֵטִים: וַיַּעֲנוּ אֶת־יִרְמְיָהוּ
כָל־הָאֲנָשִׁים הַיֹּדְעִים כִּי־

all Judah. i.e. the Judeans who had come to Egypt with the exception of those mentioned in verses 14 and 28.

12. Cf. xlii. 18.

14. *save such as shall escape.* It is significant that even while making so sweeping a prophecy of complete annihilation, the prophet still assumes that some would escape and return, since the connection of the Jews with the Land of Israel could never be finally severed.

that their wives offered unto other gods, and all the women that stood by, a great assembly, even all the people that dwelt in the land of Egypt, in Pathros, answered Jeremiah, saying: 16. 'As for the word that thou hast spoken unto us in the name of the LORD, we will not hearken unto thee. 17. But we will certainly perform every word that is gone forth out of our mouth, to offer unto the queen of heaven, and to pour out drink-offerings unto her, as we have done, we and our fathers, our kings and our princes, in the cities of Judah, and in the streets of Jerusalem; for then had we plenty of food, and were well, and saw no evil. 18. But since we left off to offer to the queen of heaven, and to pour out drink-offerings unto her, we have wanted all things, and have been consumed

מְקַטְּרוֹת נְשֵׁיהֶם֙ לֵאלֹהִ֣ים
אֲחֵרִ֔ים וְכָל־הַנָּשִׁ֗ים
הָעֹמְד֛וֹת קָהָ֥ל גָּד֖וֹל וְכָל־
הָעָ֛ם הַיֹּשְׁבִ֥ים בְּאֶֽרֶץ־
מִצְרַ֖יִם בְּפַתְר֑וֹס לֵאמֹֽר׃

16 הַדָּבָ֞ר אֲשֶׁר־דִּבַּ֧רְתָּ אֵלֵ֛ינוּ
בְּשֵׁ֥ם יְהֹוָ֖ה אֵינֶ֥נּוּ שֹׁמְעִ֖ים

17 אֵלֶֽיךָ׃ כִּ֤י עָשֹׂ֣ה נַעֲשֶׂ֗ה אֶת־
כָּֽל־הַדָּבָ֣ר ׀ אֲשֶׁר־יָצָ֣א
מִפִּ֡ינוּ לְקַטֵּ֣ר לִמְלֶ֣כֶת הַשָּׁמַ֗יִם
וְהַסֵּֽיךְ־לָהּ֙ נְסָכִ֔ים כַּאֲשֶׁ֣ר
עָשִׂ֡ינוּ אֲנַ֣חְנוּ וַאֲבֹתֵ֡ינוּ מְלָכֵ֣ינוּ
וְשָׂרֵ֡ינוּ בְּעָרֵ֣י יְהוּדָ֗ה וּבְחֻצ֣וֹת
יְרוּשָׁלָ֑͏ִם וַנִּשְׂבַּֽע־לֶ֙חֶם֙ וַנִּֽהְיֶ֣ה

18 טוֹבִ֔ים וְרָעָ֖ה לֹ֥א רָאִֽינוּ׃ וּמִן־
אָ֡ז חָדַ֜לְנוּ לְקַטֵּ֣ר לִמְלֶ֣כֶת
הַשָּׁמַ֗יִם וְהַסֵּֽךְ־לָ֖הּ נְסָכִ֑ים
חָסַ֣רְנוּ כֹ֑ל וּבַחֶ֖רֶב וּבָרָעָ֥ב

v. 17. חסר א' v. 18. חסר א'

15-19 THE PROPHET'S ADMONITION
      IS IGNORED

15. *their wives offered unto other gods.*
The cult of the queen of heaven apparently had a special appeal to the women; or perhaps it was confined to them (cf. vii. 18). Although *other gods* are mentioned in general terms, the answer (verse 17) makes it clear that this particular cult is referred to. This may explain why prominence is given to *wives* in verse 9.

17. *every word that is gone forth out of our mouth.* These women had evidently taken a vow to practise this cult.

18. *since we left off.* The allusion is doubtless to Josiah's reforms which swept away the cult (cf. 2 Kings xxiii. 4ff.).

we have wanted all things, etc. They had in mind the disasters which had befallen the nation since Josiah's defeat and death at Megiddo. This passage throws light on their mentality: far from attributing their misfortunes to the judgment of God for their disloyalty to His service, they saw in them the consequence which followed on the abandonment of the pagan cult.

by the sword and by the famine.
19. And is it we that offer to the queen of heaven, and pour out drink-offerings unto her? did we make her cakes in her image, and pour out drink-offerings unto her, without our husbands?'

20. Then Jeremiah said unto all the people, to the men, and to the women, even to all the people that had given him that answer, saying: 21. 'The offering that ye offered in the cities of Judah, and in the streets of Jerusalem, ye and your fathers, your kings and your princes, and the people of the land, did not the LORD remember them, and came it not into His mind? 22. so that the LORD could no longer bear, because of the evil of your doings, and because of the abominations which ye have committed; therefore is your land become a desolation, and an

19 תָּמְנוּ: וְכִי־אֲנַחְנוּ מְקַטְּרִים
לִמְלֶכֶת הַשָּׁמַיִם וּלְהַסֵּךְ לָהּ
נְסָכִים הֲמִבַּלְעֲדֵי אֲנָשֵׁינוּ
עָשִׂינוּ לָהּ כַּוָּנִים לְהַעֲצִבָה
20 וְהַסֵּךְ לָהּ נְסָכִים: וַיֹּאמֶר
יִרְמְיָהוּ אֶל־כָּל־הָעָם עַל־
הַגְּבָרִים וְעַל־הַנָּשִׁים וְעַל־
כָּל־הָעָם הָעֹנִים אֹתוֹ דָּבָר
21 לֵאמֹר: הֲלוֹא אֶת־הַקִּטֵּר
אֲשֶׁר קִטַּרְתֶּם בְּעָרֵי יְהוּדָה
וּבְחֻצוֹת יְרוּשָׁלַם אַתֶּם
וַאֲבוֹתֵיכֶם מַלְכֵיכֶם וְשָׂרֵיכֶם
וְעַם הָאָרֶץ אֹתָם זָכַר יְהֹוָה
22 וַתַּעֲלֶה עַל־לִבּוֹ: וְלֹא־
יוּכַל יְהֹוָה עוֹד לָשֵׂאת מִפְּנֵי
רֹעַ מַעַלְלֵיכֶם מִפְּנֵי הַתּוֹעֵבֹת
אֲשֶׁר עֲשִׂיתֶם וַתְּהִי אַרְצְכֶם

v. 19. הה׳ רפה   v. 19. א׳ חסר

19. This verse is spoken by the women and is their retort to Jeremiah's attack upon them. The first question, like the second, is governed by *without our husbands*. A vow made by a married woman depended for its validity upon the husband's consent and he had the power to annul it (cf. Num. xxx. 7ff.). 'If, then,' the women reply to Jeremiah, 'we have taken part in the worship as the consequence of the vow we made (see on verse 17), do not blame us, but our husbands who approved it!'

her cakes in her image. See on vii. 18.

20-23 JEREMIAH RETORTS THAT IDOLATRY IS THE CAUSE OF THEIR PLIGHT

22. *could no longer bear*. God is long-suffering, but there comes a time when He must punish. That time came after Josiah's reforms which had failed to cleanse the nation of heathenish influences and practices. Sin has been accumulating during the generations until the point was reached when retributive action had to be taken. That punishment had not come sooner, while they were actually practising the rites, was only due to God's forbearance, not to the protection of the queen of heaven.

astonishment, and a curse, without an inhabitant, as at this day. 23. Because ye have offered, and because ye have sinned against the LORD, and have not hearkened to the voice of the LORD, nor walked in His law, nor in His statutes, nor in His testimonies; therefore this evil is happened unto you, as at this day.'

24. Moreover Jeremiah said unto all the people, and to all the women: 'Hear the word of the LORD, all Judah that are in the land of Egypt: 25. Thus saith the LORD of hosts, the God of Israel, saying: Ye and your wives have both spoken with your mouths, and with your hands have fulfilled it, saying: We will surely perform our vows that we have vowed, to offer to the queen of heaven, and to pour out drink-offerings unto her; ye shall surely establish your vows, and surely perform your vows. 26. Therefore hear ye the word of the LORD, all Judah that dwell in the land of Egypt: Behold, I have sworn by

לְחָרְבָּה וּלְשַׁמָּה וְלִקְלָלָה
23 מֵאֵין יוֹשֵׁב כְּהַיּוֹם הַזֶּה: מִפְּנֵי
אֲשֶׁר קִטַּרְתֶּם וַאֲשֶׁר חֲטָאתֶם
לַיהוָה וְלֹא שְׁמַעְתֶּם בְּקוֹל
יְהוָה וּבְתֹרָתוֹ וּבְחֻקֹּתָיו
וּבְעֵדְוֹתָיו לֹא הֲלַכְתֶּם עַל־
כֵּן קָרָאת אֶתְכֶם הָרָעָה הַזֹּאת
24 כַּיּוֹם הַזֶּה: וַיֹּאמֶר יִרְמְיָהוּ
אֶל־כָּל־הָעָם וְאֶל כָּל־
הַנָּשִׁים שִׁמְעוּ דְּבַר־יְהוָה
כָּל־יְהוּדָה אֲשֶׁר בְּאֶרֶץ
25 מִצְרָיִם: כֹּה־אָמַר יְהוָה־
צְבָאוֹת אֱלֹהֵי יִשְׂרָאֵל לֵאמֹר
אַתֶּם וּנְשֵׁיכֶם וַתְּדַבֵּרְנָה
בְּפִיכֶם וּבִידֵיכֶם מִלֵּאתֶם |
לֵאמֹר עָשֹׂה נַעֲשֶׂה אֶת־
נְדָרֵינוּ אֲשֶׁר נָדַרְנוּ לְקַטֵּר
לִמְלֶכֶת הַשָּׁמַיִם וּלְהַסֵּךְ לָהּ
נְסָכִים הָקֵים תָּקִימְנָה אֶת־
נִדְרֵיכֶם וְעָשֹׂה תַעֲשֶׂינָה אֶת־
26 נִדְרֵיכֶם: לָכֵן שִׁמְעוּ דְבַר־
יְהוָה כָּל־יְהוּדָה הַיֹּשְׁבִים
בְּאֶרֶץ מִצְרָיִם הִנְנִי נִשְׁבַּעְתִּי

חסר א' v. 25.

23. Flinders Petrie, excavating at Tahpanhes (see on xliii. 9), discovered a stele which by its characteristic features evidenced heathen worship by Jews.

24–30 JEREMIAH CONCLUDES HIS WARNING

25. *ye shall surely establish*, etc. Spoken ironically. If you insist, then carry on with your rites!

My great name, saith the LORD, that My name shall no more be named in the mouth of any man of Judah in all the land of Egypt, saying: As the Lord GOD liveth. 27. Behold, I watch over them for evil, and not for good; and all the men of Judah that are in the land of Egypt shall be consumed by the sword and by the famine, until there be an end of them. 28. And they that escape the sword shall return out of the land of Egypt into the land of Judah, few in number; and all the remnant of Judah, that are gone into the land of Egypt to sojourn there, shall know whose word shall stand, Mine, or theirs. 29. And this shall be the sign unto you, saith the LORD, that I will punish you in this place, that ye may know that My words shall surely stand against you for evil; 30. thus saith the LORD: Behold, I will give Pharaoh Hophra king of

בִּשְׁמִי הַגָּדוֹל אָמַר יְהֹוָה אִם־
יִהְיֶה עוֹד שְׁמִי נִקְרָא ׀ בְּפִי ׀
כָּל־אִישׁ יְהוּדָה אֹמֵר חַי־
אֲדֹנָי יֱהֹוִה בְּכָל־אֶרֶץ
27 מִצְרָיִם: הִנְנִי שֹׁקֵד עֲלֵיהֶם
לְרָעָה וְלֹא לְטוֹבָה וְתַמּוּ כָל־
אִישׁ יְהוּדָה אֲשֶׁר בְּאֶרֶץ־
מִצְרַיִם בַּחֶרֶב וּבָרָעָב עַד־
28 כְּלוֹתָם: וּפְלִיטֵי חֶרֶב יְשֻׁבוּן
מִן־אֶרֶץ מִצְרַיִם אֶרֶץ יְהוּדָה
מְתֵי מִסְפָּר וְיָדְעוּ כָּל־
שְׁאֵרִית יְהוּדָה הַבָּאִים
לְאֶרֶץ־מִצְרַיִם לָגוּר שָׁם
דְּבַר־מִי יָקוּם מִמֶּנִּי וּמֵהֶם:
29 וְזֹאת לָכֶם הָאוֹת נְאֻם־יְהֹוָה
כִּי־פֹקֵד אֲנִי עֲלֵיכֶם בַּמָּקוֹם
הַזֶּה לְמַעַן תֵּדְעוּ כִּי קוֹם
יָקוּמוּ דְבָרַי עֲלֵיכֶם לְרָעָה:
30 כֹּה ׀ אָמַר יְהֹוָה הִנְנִי נֹתֵן אֶת־
פַּרְעֹה חָפְרַע מֶלֶךְ־מִצְרַיִם

26. *My name shall no more be named.* Because the men of Judah in Egypt will perish.

27. *all the men of Judah.* As the next verse shows, this is not to be pressed too strictly; it merely indicates widespread destruction.

28. *they that escape . . . the land of Judah.* Nevertheless, in course of time a flourishing Jewish community grew in Egypt, worshippers of God and not idolaters. This fact explains the non-fulfilment of the prophecy which is always conditional. By eventually abandoning the idolatrous practices they averted their threatened fate.

29. *the sign.* viz. when you see the overthrow of Pharaoh Hophra you will know that it presages your own doom.

30. *Pharaoh Hophra.* The Greek Apries who reigned from 589 to 570 B.C.E. 'It may be noted that the Hebrew *Hophra*

Egypt into the hand of his enemies,
and into the hand of them that seek
his life; as I gave Zedekiah king of
Judah into the hand of Nebuchadrezzar king of Babylon, his enemy,
and that sought his life.'

בְּיַד אֹיְבָיו וּבְיַד מְבַקְשֵׁי נַפְשׁוֹ
כַּאֲשֶׁר נָתַתִּי אֶת־צִדְקִיָּהוּ
מֶלֶךְ־יְהוּדָה בְּיַד
נְבוּכַדְרֶאצַּר מֶלֶךְ־בָּבֶל
אֹיְבוֹ וּמְבַקֵּשׁ נַפְשׁוֹ :

45   CHAPTER XLV   מה

1. The word that Jeremiah the
prophet spoke unto Baruch the son
of Neriah, when he wrote these
words in a book at the mouth of
Jeremiah, in the fourth year of
Jehoiakim the son of Josiah, king of
Judah, saying: 2. 'Thus saith the
LORD, the God of Israel, concerning
thee, O Baruch:

3 Thou didst say:

Woe is me now!

1 הַדָּבָר אֲשֶׁר דִּבֶּר יִרְמְיָהוּ
הַנָּבִיא אֶל־בָּרוּךְ בֶּן־נֵרִיָּה
בְּכָתְבוֹ אֶת־הַדְּבָרִים הָאֵלֶּה
עַל־סֵפֶר מִפִּי יִרְמְיָהוּ בַּשָּׁנָה
הָרְבִעִית לִיהוֹיָקִים בֶּן־
יֹאשִׁיָּהוּ מֶלֶךְ יְהוּדָה לֵאמֹר :
2 כֹּה־אָמַר יְהוָה אֱלֹהֵי יִשְׂרָאֵל
עָלֶיךָ בָּרוּךְ :
3 אָמַרְתָּ
אוֹי־נָא לִי

---

is very close to the Egyptian Haa-ab-ra
which was pronounced Hoavra. The
Greek form Apries is much less exact'
(Petrie).

that seek his life. Herodotus records
that he was overthrown by the troops
sent by him against Cyrene when they
mutinied. His successor, Amasis,
handed him over to the Egyptians who
strangled him seven years later.

CHAPTER XLV
JEREMIAH'S ANSWER TO BARUCH'S LAMENT

THIS chapter goes back to the fourth
year of the reign of Jehoiakim. It 'is a

supplement to xxxvi. 8; its presen
position, at the end of the biography o
Jeremiah, is due to Baruch's unwilling
ness to introduce a personal element int
the narration' (Pickering). Barucl
bewails his sorrows, occasioned by th
gloomy fate which awaits his belove
country. Jeremiah replies to him i
God's name that he lives in an age wher
he cannot expect *great things* for himsel
seeing that even He is compelled t
destroy His work. Baruch's life, how
ever, will be spared in the debacle.

1. *these words.* viz. the *roll* described i
chapter xxxvi, as the date indicates.

For the LORD hath added sorrow
   to my pain;
I am weary with my groaning,
   And I find no rest.

4. Thus shalt thou say unto him:
   Thus saith the LORD:
   Behold, that which I have built
      will I break down,
   And that which I have planted
      I will pluck up;
   And this in the whole land.

5 And seekest thou great things for
    thyself?
   Seek them not;
for, behold, I will bring evil upon
all flesh, saith the LORD; but thy
life will I give unto thee for a prey
in all places whither thou goest.'

כִּי־יָסַף יְהֹוָה יָגוֹן
עַל־מַכְאֹבִי
יָגַעְתִּי בְּאַנְחָתִי
וּמְנוּחָה לֹא מָצָאתִי:

4 כֹּה | תֹאמַר אֵלָיו
כֹּה אָמַר יְהֹוָה
הִנֵּה אֲשֶׁר־בָּנִיתִי אֲנִי הֹרֵס
וְאֵת אֲשֶׁר־נָטַעְתִּי אֲנִי נֹתֵשׁ
וְאֶת־כָּל־הָאָרֶץ לִי־הִיא:

5 וְאַתָּה תְּבַקֶּשׁ־לְךָ גְדֹלוֹת
אַל־תְּבַקֵּשׁ
כִּי הִנְנִי מֵבִיא רָעָה עַל־כָּל־
בָּשָׂר נְאֻם יְהֹוָה וְנָתַתִּי לְךָ
אֶת־נַפְשְׁךָ לְשָׁלָל עַל כָּל־
הַמְּקֹמוֹת אֲשֶׁר תֵּלֶךְ־שָׁם:

v. 4. במקצת ספרים לא נמצא מלת לי

3. *hath added sorrow to my pain.* For
sorrow we should substitute 'anguish,
anxiety.' Baruch was weighed down by
anxiety about his own future in addition
to pain at the calamities which were foretold for his people.

4. *that which I have built,* etc. Cf. i. 10.
God is about to undo His work; what a
grief it is to Him! But justice demands
that it be done.

and this in the whole land. There are
two readings of the text: 'even all the
land which is Mine,' and 'even all the
land and it is.' If the former is adopted, the
meaning is, 'My own land (of Israel)
it is which will suffer destruction.' The
alternative reading signifies: all the cities
of the land (of Israel) come under this
threat of destruction.

5. *seekest thou great things for thyself?*
In a time when God breaks down what

He has built, it is unfitting that Baruch
should seek personal greatness.
Scripture does not record what form
his aspirations took. According to Rabbinical interpretation, his complaint in
verse 3 was that he had not been granted
the gift of prophecy, as had the disciples
of other great prophets, such as Joshua
and Elisha, the disciples of Moses and
Elijah respectively. He is rebuked and
told that, at such a time, he must expect
no personal aggrandisement, not even of
the spiritual kind. Peake remarks, 'We
may say that what Baruch achieved by
giving to the world his memoirs of
Jeremiah was a far greater thing than his
most soaring ambition had ever con-
templated.'

for a prey. See on xxi. 9. To come
through such disasters alive is all that he
can expect.

whither thou goest. As an exile.

46   CHAPTER XLVI   מו

1. The word of the LORD which came to Jeremiah the prophet concerning the nations.

2. Of Egypt: concerning the army of Pharaoh-neco king of Egypt, which was by the river Euphrates in Carchemish, which Nebuchadrezzar king of Babylon smote in the fourth year of Jehoiakim the son of Josiah, king of Judah.

3 Make ready buckler and shield,
And draw near to battle.

4 Harness the horses, and mount,
ye horsemen,

1 אֲשֶׁ֤ר הָיָה֙ דְבַר־יְהֹוָ֔ה אֶל־
יִרְמְיָ֖הוּ הַנָּבִ֑יא עַל־הַגּוֹיִֽם׃
2 לְמִצְרַ֗יִם עַל־חֵ֨יל פַּרְעֹ֤ה נְכוֹ֙
מֶ֣לֶךְ מִצְרַ֔יִם אֲשֶׁר־הָיָ֖ה עַל־
נְהַר־פְּרָ֣ת בְּכַרְכְּמִ֑שׁ אֲשֶׁ֣ר
הִכָּ֗ה נְבֽוּכַדְרֶאצַּר֙ מֶ֣לֶךְ בָּבֶ֔ל
בִּשְׁנַת֙ הָֽרְבִיעִ֔ית לִיהוֹיָקִ֖ים
בֶּן־יֹֽאשִׁיָּ֖הוּ מֶ֥לֶךְ יְהוּדָֽה׃
3 עִרְכ֤וּ מָגֵן֙ וְצִנָּ֔ה
וּגְשׁ֖וּ לַמִּלְחָמָֽה׃
4 אִסְר֣וּ הַסּוּסִ֗ים
וַֽעֲלוּ֙ הַפָּ֣רָשִׁ֔ים

CHAPTER XLVI

JUDGMENT UPON EGYPT

JEREMIAH felt deeply that he was the eye-witness of world-shattering events. Not only the fate of his own people was hanging in the balance, but likewise the destiny of the surrounding nations. Chapters xlvi-li form a well-defined and separate section with which the prophecies of Jeremiah conclude (cf. li. 64). A similar series of judgments upon contemporary peoples is to be found in other prophets (cf. Isa. xiii-xxiii; Ezek. xxv-xxxii; Amos i. 3-ii. 3).

1. *concerning the nations.* See on i. 5. This verse is the introduction to the whole section to the end of li.

2. *Pharaoh-neco.* He had defeated and slain king Josiah at Megiddo in 608 B.C.E., whose successor, Jehoahaz, he deposed after a reign of only three months, and set Jehoiakim upon the throne (2 Kings xxiii. 29-34). Extending his conquests eastwards, he clashed with Nebuchadnezzar who overthrew him at Carchemish in 605 B.C.E. This decisive victory, which ensured the widespread Babylonian supremacy over neighbouring nations, was the occasion of this oracle.

Carchemish. The Gargamish of the Assyrian inscriptions, a town of great strategic importance. It was situated on the right bank of the Euphrates and was once the capital of the Hittites.

3. *make ready,* etc. A warning to the Egyptians to prepare for a critical contest which would decide the fate of their country. A note of irony is to be detected in the words, since the prophet knew that resistance would prove useless.

buckler and shield. The former was comparatively small and circular in shape; the latter was long and covered the whole body.

4. *harness the horses.* To the chariots; the same verb, lit. 'bind,' as in Exod. xiv. 6.

And stand forth with your helmets;
Furbish the spears, put on the
coats of mail.

5 Wherefore do I see them dis-
mayed and turned backward?
And their mighty ones are beaten
down,
And they are fled apace, and look
not back;
Terror is on every side, saith the
LORD.

6 The swift cannot flee away,
Nor the mighty man escape;
In the north by the river
Euphrates
Have they stumbled and fallen.

7 Who is this like the Nile that
riseth up,
Like the rivers whose waters toss
themselves?

8 Egypt is like the Nile that riseth
up,
And like the rivers whose waters
toss themselves;
And he saith: 'I will rise up,
I will cover the earth,

וְהִתְיַצְּבוּ בְּכוֹבָעִים
מִרְקוּ הָרְמָחִים
לִבְשׁוּ הַסִּרְיֹנֹת׃
5 מַדּוּעַ רָאִיתִי הֵמָּה חַתִּים
נְסֹגִים אָחוֹר
וְגִבּוֹרֵיהֶם יֻכַּתּוּ
וּמָנוֹס נָסוּ וְלֹא הִפְנוּ
מָגוֹר מִסָּבִיב נְאֻם־יְהוָֹה׃
6 אַל־יָנוּס הַקַּל
וְאַל־יִמָּלֵט הַגִּבּוֹר
צָפוֹנָה עַל־יַד נְהַר־פְּרָת
כָּשְׁלוּ וְנָפָלוּ׃
7 מִי־זֶה כַּיְאֹר יַעֲלֶה
כַּנְּהָרוֹת יִתְגָּעֲשׁוּ מֵימָיו׃
8 מִצְרַיִם כַּיְאֹר יַעֲלֶה
וְכַנְּהָרוֹת יִתְגָּעֲשׁוּ מָיִם
וַיֹּאמֶר אֶעֱלֶה אֲכַסֶּה־אֶרֶץ

mount, ye horsemen. Most moderns
prefer the translation, 'mount the steeds.'
stand forth with your helmets. i.e.
wearing your helmets, which were set
upon the head only in actual battle.

5. wherefore do I see, etc. All the
elaborate preparations are made to
withstand the Babylonian army in
accordance with the prophet's advice;
immediately he continues with ironical
surprise that the formidable host of
Egypt is in precipitate flight.
terror is on every side. See on vi. 25.

6. Utter defeat overtakes them; neither

swift retreat nor a brave stand is of avail.

7f. The former onward sweep of the
Egyptian armies, overrunning the
countries of their invasion, is likened to
the irresistible overflowing of the Nile as
its waters inundate the country through
which it flows (cf. Isa. viii. 7f.). What a
contrast to their present helplessness and
dismay!

8. he saith. Pharaoh, or Egypt personified, is the subject.

I will cover the earth. With my waters,
i.e. conquer it.

I will destroy the city and the
inhabitants thereof.'

9 Prance, ye horses, and rush
madly, ye chariots;
And let the mighty men go forth:
Cush and Put, that handle the
shield,
And the Ludim, that handle and
bend the bow.

10 For the Lord GOD of hosts shall
have on that day
A day of vengeance, that He may
avenge Him of His adversaries;
And the sword shall devour and
be satiate,
And shall be made drunk with
their blood;
For the Lord GOD of hosts hath
a sacrifice
In the north country by the river
Euphrates.

11 Go up into Gilead, and take
balm,
O virgin daughter of Egypt;
In vain dost thou use many
medicines;

אֹבִ֫ידָה עִיר וְיֹ֫שְׁבֵי בָֽהּ׃

9 עֲלוּ הַסּוּסִים֩
וְהִתְהֹלְלוּ הָרֶ֫כֶב
וְיֵצְא֣וּ הַגִּבּוֹרִים
כּוּשׁ וּפוּט֙ תֹּֽפְשֵׂי מָגֵן
וְלוּדִ֔ים תֹּֽפְשֵׂי דֹּֽרְכֵי קָֽשֶׁת׃

10 וְֽהַיּ֨וֹם הַה֜וּא
לַֽאדֹנָ֧י יֱהֹוִ֣ה צְבָא֗וֹת
י֤וֹם נְקָמָה֙ לְהִנָּקֵ֣ם מִצָּרָ֔יו
וְאָכְלָ֥ה חֶ֙רֶב֙ וְשָׂבְעָ֔ה
וְרָֽוְתָ֖ה מִדָּמָ֑ם
כִּ֣י זֶ֠בַח לַֽאדֹנָ֨י יֱהֹוִ֧ה צְבָא֛וֹת
בְּאֶ֥רֶץ צָפ֖וֹן אֶל־נְהַר־פְּרָֽת׃

11 עֲלִ֤י גִלְעָד֙ וּקְחִ֣י צֳרִ֔י
בְּתוּלַ֖ת בַּת־מִצְרָ֑יִם
לַשָּׁוְא֙ הרביתי רְפֻא֔וֹת

v. 11. הרבית ק'

---

the city. The singular is used in a
collective sense.

9. *prance, ye horses.* Better, 'advance,'
lit. 'go up.' The verse is probably the
continuation of *he saith* (verse 8).
A.J., which ends the inverted commas
in the preceding verse, understands it as
the ironical urging of the prophet.

Cush and Put . . . and the Ludim.
These were mercenary troops who
formed part of the Egyptian forces.
Cush (the Ethiopians) and Put were
descended from Ham, one of the sons of
Noah (Gen. x. 6). The situation of Put
is uncertain. Some place it on the
north coast of Africa, west of Egypt;
others identify it with 'Punt,' a district
on the Red Sea. The Ludim were also
Africans (Gen. x. 13). These three

peoples are again spoken of as mercenaries in Ezek. xxx. 5.

10. *a day of vengeance.* For the defeat
and death of Josiah at Megiddo (Kimchi).
This event was fresh in Jeremiah's mind,
and the fierceness of the language
expresses a natural human emotion in
the circumstances.

hath a sacrifice. By God's decree a
general 'slaughter' (so the Hebrew may
be translated) will take place (Metsudath
David).

in the north country. At Carchemish.

11. *Gilead.* See on viii. 22.

virgin daughter. Formerly applied to
Jerusalem; see on xiv. 17.

medicines. 'Egyptian knowledge of
medicine is celebrated by Homer

There is no cure for thee.

12 The nations have heard of thy
   shame,
   And the earth is full of thy cry;
   For the mighty man hath
   stumbled against the mighty,
   They are fallen both of them
   together.

13. The word that the LORD spoke
to Jeremiah the prophet, how that
Nebuchadrezzar king of Babylon
should come and smite the land of
Egypt.

14 Declare ye in Egypt, and an-
   nounce in Migdol,
   And announce in Noph and in
   Tahpanhes;
   Say ye: 'Stand forth, and prepare
   thee,
   For the sword hath devoured
   round about thee.'

15 Why is thy strong one overthrown?
   He stood not, because the LORD
   did thrust him down.

תְּעָלָה אֵין לָךְ ׃

12 שָׁמְעוּ גוֹיִם קְלוֹנֵךְ
וְצִוְחָתֵךְ מָלְאָה הָאָרֶץ
כִּי־גִבּוֹר בְּגִבּוֹר כָּשָׁלוּ
יַחְדָּו נָפְלוּ שְׁנֵיהֶם ׃

13 הַדָּבָר אֲשֶׁר דִּבֶּר יְהֹוָה
אֶל־יִרְמְיָהוּ הַנָּבִיא לָבוֹא
נְבוּכַדְרֶאצַּר מֶלֶךְ בָּבֶל
לְהַכּוֹת אֶת־אֶרֶץ מִצְרָיִם ׃

14 הַגִּידוּ בְמִצְרַיִם
וְהַשְׁמִיעוּ בְמִגְדּוֹל
וְהַשְׁמִיעוּ בְנֹף וּבְתַחְפַּנְחֵס
אִמְרוּ הִתְיַצֵּב וְהָכֵן לָךְ
כִּי־אָכְלָה חֶרֶב סְבִיבֶיךָ ׃

15 מַדּוּעַ נִסְחַף אַבִּירֶיךָ
לֹא עָמַד כִּי יְהֹוָה הֲדָפוֹ ׃

v. 12.   v. 13. הפטרת בא קמץ בז״ק

(Odyssey IV. 229). Cyrus and Darius
both sent to Egypt for medical men
(Herodotus III, 1. 132)' (Streane).

12. thy shame. Thy defeat, which puts
thy boasted power to shame.

the mighty man, etc. In the panic of
their flight even their mighty warriors
stumble against one another.

**13. how that Nebuchadrezzar . . . should
come**, etc. This oracle is separate from
the preceding and probably dates from
the time of Jeremiah's residence in
Egypt (cf. xliii. 8ff.; Ezek. xxix. 17ff.).

14. *Egypt.* This is first mentioned
generally and then specific cities are
enumerated.

Migdol. See on xliv. 1.

Noph . . . Tahpanhes. See on ii. 16.

stand forth. The Babylonians have
overrun the neighbouring peoples; let
Egypt prepare for the advance into its
territory.

15. *thy strong one.* The noun is apparently in the plural although the verb
is in the singular. In that case the
meaning is, 'Why are thy strong ones,
every one of them, overthrown?' But
many Hebrew MSS. omit the second *yad*
which makes the noun singular. By
dividing the verb *nischaph* (*overthrown*)
into two words, *nas chaph*, the LXX
reads, 'Why is Apis fled? Thy mighty
one stood not.' Apis was the sacred bull
worshipped at Memphis and called

16 He made many to stumble;
   Yea, they fell one upon another,
   And said: 'Arise, and let us
   return to our own people,
   And to the land of our birth,
   From the oppressing sword.'

17 They cried there: 'Pharaoh king
   of Egypt is but a noise;
   He hath let the appointed time
   pass by.'

18 As I live, saith the King,
   Whose name is the LORD of hosts,
   Surely like Tabor among the
   mountains,
   And like Carmel by the sea, so
   shall he come.

16 הִרְבָּה כּוֹשֵׁל
גַּם־נָפַל אִישׁ אֶל־רֵעֵהוּ
וַיֹּאמְרוּ קוּמָה |
וְנָשֻׁבָה אֶל־עַמֵּנוּ
וְאֶל־אֶרֶץ מוֹלַדְתֵּנוּ
מִפְּנֵי חֶרֶב הַיּוֹנָה׃

17 קָרְאוּ שָׁם
פַּרְעֹה מֶלֶךְ־מִצְרַיִם שָׁאוֹן
הֶעֱבִיר הַמּוֹעֵד׃

18 חַי־אָנִי נְאֻם־הַמֶּלֶךְ
יְהֹוָה צְבָאוֹת שְׁמוֹ
כִּי כְּתָבוֹר בֶּהָרִים
וּכְכַרְמֶל בַּיָּם יָבוֹא׃

Egypt's *strong one*, in the same way that God is described as *the Mighty One of Jacob* (Gen. xlix. 24). The text as rendered in A.J. might therefore be understood, 'Why is thy strong one (the god Apis upon whose protection Egypt relied) overthrown?' The defeat of a people, symbolized by that of their god, is a common idea in the Bible.

16. *they fell one upon another.* The subject may be the mercenary troops or, as some suppose, the foreign traders in Egypt. Either in their panic they each fell over the other as they fled, which makes this a sequel to *stumble*; or, they 'joined with each other' (cf. *thou fallest away to the Chaldeans*, xxxvii. 13, where the verb is used in that sense) *and said*, etc.

17. *there.* On the battlefield, if the subject is the mercenaries, or in Egypt, if it is the foreign traders.

but a noise, Pharaoh's pomp and display of power are but an empty noise

with no reality behind them (so some commentators). *But,* however, is not in the original, and it is doubtful whether *shaon* (the Hebrew for *noise*) is used in this sarcastic way. The meaning may be the reverse: 'Although Pharaoh makes such a tumult, being the king of a great army, yet *he hath let the appointed time pass by*'; either in the sense that he failed to make the necessary preparation while there was time, or, in his cowardice, he refused the challenge to give battle at the time appointed by his generals. Another interpretation is: he let pass the opportunity of securing God's mercy by moral reformation.

18. *like Tabor . . . like Carmel.* As Tabor is conspicuous among mountains, and as Carmel rises prominently by the sea, so will Nebuchadnezzar stand out above former conquerors. 'The metaphor was perhaps suggested to Jeremiah by the flatness of Egypt, which was such a contrast to Palestine' (Peake). Tabor is only 1,800 feet high but rendered

19 O thou daughter that dwellest in
   Egypt,
   Furnish thyself to go into captivity;
   For Noph shall become a desolation,
   And shall be laid waste, without
   inhabitant.
20 Egypt is a very fair heifer;
   But the gadfly out of the north is
   come, it is come.
21 Also her mercenaries in the
   midst of her
   Are like calves of the stall,
   For they also are turned back,
   they are fled away together,
   They did not stand;
   For the day of their calamity is
   come upon them,
   The time of their visitation.
22 The sound thereof shall go like
   the serpent's;

19 כְּלֵי גוֹלָה עֲשִׂי לָךְ
   יוֹשֶׁבֶת בַּת־מִצְרָיִם
   כִּי־נֹף לְשַׁמָּה תִהְיֶה
   וְנִצְּתָה מֵאֵין יוֹשֵׁב׃
20 עֶגְלָה יְפֵה־פִיָּה מִצְרָיִם
   קֶרֶץ מִצָּפוֹן בָּא בָא׃
21 גַּם־שְׂכִרֶיהָ בְקִרְבָּהּ
   כְּעֶגְלֵי מַרְבֵּק
   כִּי־גַם־הֵמָּה הִפְנוּ
   נָסוּ יַחְדָּיו לֹא עָמָדוּ
   כִּי יוֹם אֵידָם בָּא עֲלֵיהֶם
   עֵת פְּקֻדָּתָם׃
22 קוֹלָהּ כַּנָּחָשׁ יֵלֵךְ

conspicuous by the fact that it is situated
in a plain.   Carmel is an impressive
headland on the coast, rising 600 feet
above it. Elijah chose it, perhaps because
of its commanding site, as the scene of
his challenge to Baal (1 Kings xviii. 19ff.).

19. *thou daughter.* Poetically used for
the population.

furnish . . . captivity. lit. 'vessels of
captivity make for thee,' i.e. provide food
and other necessities required for the
journey into captivity.   The same phrase
occurs in Ezek. xii. 3.

20. *a very fair heifer.* i.e. is comparable
to a well-nourished and finely developed
animal.

the gadfly. The foe, stinging her into
flight.   The Hebrew noun *kerets* is not
found elsewhere in the Bible; it is derived
from a root meaning 'to nip.'   A.V. and
R.V., 'destruction,' follow the Jewish
commentators.

out of the north.   From Babylon, to the
north of Egypt.

is come, it is come.   For the repetition of
the verb to convey the idea of certainty,
cf. Ps. xcvi. 13.

21. *her mercenaries.* 'The mercenaries
here mentioned are not those of verse 9,
but the Ionians and Carians, introduced
into his service by Psammetichus, and
retained by his successors.   Hophra did
not send them on the expedition against
Cyrene; they failed to secure him victory
over Amasis (Herodotus II, 152ff.)'
(Peake).

like calves.   Well-fed and vigorous; yet
they proved cowardly and useless in
battle.   Ehrlich explains the comparison
to be that they are alike destined to be
slaughtered.

22. *the sound . . . like the serpent's.*   Or,
'her sound is like that of the serpent as it
goeth' (R.V. margin).   Instead of the
heavy tramp of victorious soldiers, the
sound made by the Egyptian army will be

For they march with an army,
And come against her with axes,
As hewers of wood.

23 They cut down her forest, saith
the LORD,
Though it cannot be searched;
Because they are more than the
locusts,
And are innumerable.

24 The daughter of Egypt is put to
shame;
She is delivered into the hand of
the people of the north.

25. The LORD of hosts, the God of
Israel, saith: Behold, I will punish
Amon of No, and Pharaoh, and
Egypt, with her gods, and her kings;

כִּי־בְחַיִל יֵלֵכוּ
וּבְקַרְדֻּמּוֹת בָּאוּ לָהּ
כְּחֹטְבֵי עֵצִים׃
23 כָּרְתוּ יַעְרָהּ נְאֻם־יְהֹוָה
כִּי לֹא יֵחָקֵר
כִּי רַבּוּ מֵאַרְבֶּה
וְאֵין לָהֶם מִסְפָּר׃
24 הֹבִישָׁה בַּת־מִצְרָיִם
נִתְּנָה בְּיַד עַם־צָפוֹן׃
25 אָמַר יְהֹוָה צְבָאוֹת אֱלֹהֵי
יִשְׂרָאֵל הִנְנִי פוֹקֵד אֶל־אָמוֹן
מִנֹּא וְעַל־פַּרְעֹה וְעַל־
מִצְרַיִם וְעַל־אֱלֹהֶיהָ וְעַל־

---

like that of a serpent stealthily crawling away when it is disturbed. 'The metaphor is all the more appropriate since the serpent holds so conspicuous a place in the royal insignia of Egypt' (Peake).

they march. The subject is the enemy.

with an army. Or, 'with might.'

as hewers of wood. Like a band of woodcutters hewing trees in a forest, so does the enemy cut down the dense population of Egypt.

23. *they cut down.* Ehrlich parses the verb as Piel imperative, an intensive form meaning 'cut down thoroughly.'

her forest. The density of Egypt's inhabitants makes her comparable 'to a *forest . . .* so thick that the only means of finding a way through it is by cutting it down' (Driver).

though it cannot be searched. If *though* is retained, the meaning is: though the

forest is so dense that it cannot be penetrated, i.e. in spite of Egypt's innumerable population, *it* referring to the forest (Egypt). R.V. margin, however, renders: 'for it cannot be searched,' *it* then alluding to the Chaldean army (equals *they* at the beginning of the verse); the Chaldeans cut down the Egyptian host because their army is so numerous that its numbers cannot be counted (so Rashi and Kimchi). The parallelism of the second half of the verse is in favour of the latter interpretation.

because they. viz. the enemy.

locusts. The Hebrew word means 'multiplier' with reference to the vast swarms of the locusts.

25. *Amon of No.* The god Amon worshipped in No, i.e. Thebes, now Luxor, the ancient capital of Upper Egypt (cf. Nahum iii. 8).

L

even Pharaoh, and them that trust
in him; 26. and I will deliver them
into the hand of those that seek
their lives, and into the hand of
Nebuchadrezzar king of Babylon,
and into the hand of his servants;
and afterwards it shall be inhabited,
as in the days of old, saith the LORD.

27 But fear not thou, O Jacob My
    servant,
  Neither be dismayed, O Israel;
  For, lo, I will save thee from afar,
  And thy seed from the land of
    their captivity;
  And Jacob shall again be quiet
    and at ease,
  And none shall make him afraid.
28 Fear not thou, O Jacob My
    servant, saith the LORD,
  For I am with thee;
  For I will make a full end of all
    the nations whither I have
    driven thee,
  But I will not make a full end of
    thee;
  And I will correct thee in
    measure,
  But will not utterly destroy thee.

מַלְכֶיהָ וְעַל־פַּרְעֹה וְעַל

26 הַבֹּטְחִים בּוֹ׃ וּנְתַתִּים בְּיַד

מְבַקְשֵׁי נַפְשָׁם וּבְיַד

נְבוּכַדְרֶאצַּר מֶלֶךְ־בָּבֶל

וּבְיַד עֲבָדָיו וְאַחֲרֵי־כֵן תִּשְׁכֹּן

כִּימֵי־קֶדֶם נְאֻם־יְהוָה׃

27 וְאַתָּה אַל־תִּירָא עַבְדִּי יַעֲקֹב

וְאַל־תֵּחַת יִשְׂרָאֵל

כִּי הִנְנִי מוֹשִׁעֲךָ מֵרָחוֹק

וְאֶת־זַרְעֲךָ מֵאֶרֶץ שִׁבְיָם

וְשָׁב יַעֲקוֹב וְשָׁקַט וְשַׁאֲנָן

וְאֵין מַחֲרִיד׃

28 אַתָּה אַל־תִּירָא

עַבְדִּי יַעֲקֹב נְאֻם־יְהוָה

כִּי אִתְּךָ אָנִי

כִּי אֶעֱשֶׂה כָלָה בְּכָל־הַגּוֹיִם ׀

אֲשֶׁר הִדַּחְתִּיךָ שָׁמָּה

וְאֹתְךָ לֹא־אֶעֱשֶׂה כָלָה

וְיִסַּרְתִּיךָ לַמִּשְׁפָּט

וְנַקֵּה לֹא אֲנַקֶּךָּ׃

v. 27 עד כא׃ מלא ו׳ v. 28.

---

them that trust in him. Egypt's satellites;
or perhaps the Judeans who trusted in
Egypt against Babylon.

26. *and afterwards it shall be inhabited.*
After destruction by Babylon, Egypt
will be restored and repopulated (cf.
Ezek. xxix. 13f.).

27f. Almost identical with xxx. 10f.
As so often happens, the prophet ends
with a message of hope, to a degree
reversing the sombreness of what goes
before. The optimistic outlook springs
from the conviction that Israel's better
self would assert itself before final
destruction overtook him.

47   CHAPTER XLVII   מז

1. The word of the LORD that came to Jeremiah the prophet concerning the Philistines, before that Pharaoh smote Gaza.

2 Thus saith the LORD:
Behold, waters rise up out of the north,
And shall become an overflowing stream,
And they shall overflow the land and all that is therein,
The city and them that dwell therein;
And the men shall cry,
And all the inhabitants of the land shall wail.

3 At the noise of the stamping of the hoofs of his strong ones,
At the rushing of his chariots, at the rumbling of his wheels,
The fathers look not back to their children
For feebleness of hands;

1 אֲשֶׁר הָיָה דְבַר־יְהֹוָה אֶל־
יִרְמְיָהוּ הַנָּבִיא אֶל־פְּלִשְׁתִּים
בְּטֶרֶם יַכֶּה פַרְעֹה אֶת־עַזָּה׃

2 כֹּה ׀ אָמַר יְהֹוָה
הִנֵּה־מַיִם עֹלִים מִצָּפוֹן
וְהָיוּ לְנַחַל שׁוֹטֵף
וְיִשְׁטְפוּ אֶרֶץ וּמְלוֹאָהּ
עִיר וְיֹשְׁבֵי בָהּ
וְזָעֲקוּ הָאָדָם
וְהֵילִל כֹּל יוֹשֵׁב הָאָרֶץ׃

3 מִקּוֹל שַׁעֲטַת פַּרְסוֹת אַבִּירָיו
מֵרַעַשׁ לְרִכְבּוֹ הֲמוֹן גַּלְגִּלָּיו
לֹא־הִפְנוּ אָבוֹת אֶל־בָּנִים
מֵרִפְיוֹן יָדָיִם׃

CHAPTER XLVII
JUDGMENT UPON THE PHILISTINES

1. *before that Pharaoh smote Gaza.* It is not clear to what this refers. Rashi and other Jewish commentators quote the *Seder Olam* as follows: In the tenth year of Zedekiah's reign, while Nebuchadnezzar was besieging Jerusalem, Pharaoh marched from Egypt with a relief force. On the way, however, he was informed that the siege had been raised, whereupon he returned to Egypt, and in the course of his return attacked Gaza. Herodotus (II. 159) records the capture of 'Kadytis,' probably Gaza, by Pharaoh-neco after the battle of Megiddo. In any event, this would not be the same disaster as that mentioned in verse 5 which is described as coming from the north (verse 2), unless it be assumed that the whole prophecy refers to the return of Pharaoh who, on this occasion, would have been coming from the north; but this is unlikely.

Gaza. See on xxv. 20. Its situation on the edge of the Egyptian desert, at the junction of the caravan routes from Egypt and Arabia, made it important from a military as well as a trading point of view.

2. *waters rise up.* Cf. xlvi. 8, where the advance of the Egyptian army is similarly described.

the north. Babylonia.

3. *to their children.* To save them; so intense is the panic that even natural affections are forgotten, and it is each man for himself.

4 Because of the day that cometh
  To spoil all the Philistines,
  To cut off from Tyre and Zidon
  Every helper that remaineth;
  For the LORD will spoil the
    Philistines,
  The remnant of the isle of
    Caphtor.
5 Baldness is come upon Gaza,
  Ashkelon is brought to nought,
    the remnant of their valley;
  How long wilt thou cut thyself?
6 O thou sword of the LORD,
  How long will it be ere thou be
    quiet?
  Put up thyself into thy scabbard,
  Rest, and be still.
7 How canst thou be quiet?
  For the LORD hath given it a
    charge;
  Against Ashkelon, and against the
    sea-shore,
  There hath He appointed it.

עַל־הַיּוֹם הַבָּא 4
לִשְׁדוֹד אֶת־כָּל־פְּלִשְׁתִּים
לְהַכְרִית לְצֹר וּלְצִידוֹן
כֹּל שָׂרִיד עֹזֵר
כִּי־שֹׁדֵד יְהֹוָה אֶת־פְּלִשְׁתִּים
שְׁאֵרִית אִי כַפְתּוֹר׃
בָּאָה קָרְחָה אֶל־עַזָּה 5
נִדְמְתָה אַשְׁקְלוֹן
שְׁאֵרִית עִמְקָם
עַד־מָתַי תִּתְגּוֹדָדִי׃
הוֹי חֶרֶב לַיהֹוָה 6
עַד־אָנָה לֹא תִשְׁקֹטִי
הֵאָסְפִי אֶל־תַּעְרֵךְ
הֵרָגְעִי וָדֹמִּי׃
אֵיךְ תִּשְׁקֹטִי 7
וַיהֹוָה צִוָּה־לָהּ
אֶל־אַשְׁקְלוֹן וְאֶל־חוֹף הַיָּם
שָׁם יְעָדָהּ׃

4. *Tyre and Zidon.* The allies of the Philistines.

the isle of Caphtor. Probably to be identified with Crete (cf. Amos ix. 7). Only a *remnant* of its former population was left after the wars between Egypt and Assyria.

5. *baldness is come upon Gaza.* Gaza is completely razed to the ground, for which baldness is a simile. Or, baldness is mentioned as a symbol of mourning (see on xvi. 6).

Ashkelon. See on xxv. 20.

their valley. G. A. Smith (*The Historical Geography of the Holy Land*, p. 655) explains *valley* as 'the whole Philistine plain.'

6f. The prophet apostrophizes the *sword of the LORD* and appeals to it to cease raging, but admits that it cannot do so because God has charged it to destroy.

7. *the sea-shore.* Philistia.

48   CHAPTER XLVIII   מח

1 Of Moab.

Thus saith the Lord of hosts, the God of Israel:

Woe unto Nebo! for it is spoiled; Kiriathaim is put to shame, it is taken; Misgab is put to shame and dismayed.

2 The praise of Moab is no more; In Heshbon they have devised evil against her: 'Come, and let us cut her off from being a nation.' Thou also, O Madmen, shalt be brought to silence; The sword shall pursue thee.

1 לְמוֹאָב
כֹּה־אָמַר יְהוָֹה צְבָאוֹת
אֱלֹהֵי יִשְׂרָאֵל
הוֹי אֶל־נְבוֹ כִּי שֻׁדָּדָה
הֹבִישָׁה נִלְכְּדָה קִרְיָתַיִם
הֹבִישָׁה הַמִּשְׂגָּב וָחָתָּה׃

2 אֵין עוֹד תְּהִלַּת מוֹאָב
בְּחֶשְׁבּוֹן חָשְׁבוּ עָלֶיהָ רָעָה
לְכוּ וְנַכְרִיתֶנָּה מִגּוֹי
גַּם־מַדְמֵן תִּדֹּמִּי
אַחֲרַיִךְ תֵּלֶךְ חָרֶב׃

CHAPTER XLVIII

JUDGMENT UPON MOAB

THIS chapter has many affinities with other prophetic oracles on Moab, viz. Amos ii. 1-3, Obadiah, Zeph. ii. 8ff. and especially Isa. xvf.

1. *Moab.* The country situated on the tableland east of the Dead Sea.

Nebo. Not the mountain of that name, but the city mentioned in Num. xxxii. 38, built by the Reubenites, where other cities occur which are referred to in this chapter. The Moabite Stone records how it was taken by Mesha, king of Moab (c. 895 B.C.E.). Kiriathaim, Kerioth, Jahzah, Dibon, Aroer, Bozrah (Bezer), Beth-diblathaim, Baal-meon and Horonaim (cf. Num. xxxii. 34-38) are also named on the inscription.

Kiriathaim. Probably Kureyat, ten miles north of the Dead Sea.

Misgab. As a place-name this is unknown. The translation may be 'the high fortress' as in Isa. xxv. 12.

2. *in Heshbon they have devised . . . O Madmen, shalt be brought to silence.* There is a play on the name of each of the cities: *Heshbon* is connected with the verb *chashab*, 'to devise,' and *Madmen* with *damam*, 'to be silent.' Heshbon, one of the chief cities of Moab, lay to the north-east of the Dead Sea, and marked the northern boundary of Moab until the Reubenites claimed the territory lying between it and the Arnon, which flows into the Dead Sea about the middle of its eastern border. Many of the cities mentioned in this chapter as part of Moab were assigned to the Reubenites by Moses (Num. xxxii. 33ff.; Josh. xiii. 15ff.) and proved a source of hostility in the early days (cf. Judg. iii. 12ff.; 1 Sam. xiv. 47); but the sympathy of the prophet with Moab's misfortunes (verse 31; cf. also Isa. xv. 5) is perhaps an indication that Israel had long acquiesced in their seizure. The site of Madmen is unknown; so far as the name is concerned, it may be compared with Madmannah, a city of Judah (Josh. xv. 31) and Madmenah (Isa. x. 31) a Benjamite city.

3 Hark! a cry from Horonaim,
Spoiling and great destruction!

4 Moab is destroyed;
Her little ones have caused a cry
to be heard.

5 For by the ascent of Luhith
With continual weeping shall they
go up;
For in the going down of Horonaim
They have heard the distressing
cry of destruction.

6 Flee, save your lives,
And be like a tamarisk in the
wilderness.

7 For, because thou hast trusted
In thy works and in thy treasures,
Thou also shalt be taken;
And Chemosh shall go forth into
captivity,
His priests and his princes to-
gether.

3 ק֣וֹל צְעָקָ֔ה מֵחֹרֹנָ֑יִם
שֹׁ֖ד וָשֶׁ֥בֶר גָּדֽוֹל׃

4 נִשְׁבְּרָ֖ה מוֹאָ֑ב
הִשְׁמִ֥יעוּ זְּעָקָ֖ה צְעוֹרֶֽיהָ׃

5 כִּ֣י מַעֲלֵ֣ה הַלֻּחוֹת
בִּבְכִ֖י יַֽעֲלֶה־בֶּ֑כִי
כִּ֚י בְּמוֹרַ֣ד חֽוֹרֹנַ֔יִם
צָרֵ֥י צַֽעֲקַת־שֶׁ֖בֶר שָׁמֵֽעוּ׃

6 נֻ֖סוּ מַלְּט֣וּ נַפְשְׁכֶ֑ם
וְתִֽהְיֶ֕ינָה כַּֽעֲרוֹעֵ֖ר בַּמִּדְבָּֽר׃

7 כִּ֠י יַ֣עַן בִּטְחֵ֤ךְ בְּמַֽעֲשַׂ֨יִךְ֙
וּבְא֣וֹצְרוֹתַ֔יִךְ
גַּם־אַ֖תְּ תִּלָּכֵ֑דִי
וְיָצָ֤א כְמִישׁ֙ בַּגּוֹלָ֔ה
כֹּהֲנָ֥יו וְשָׂרָ֖יו יַחְדָּֽו׃

v. 4. צעוריה ק׳ v. 5. הלחית ק׳ v. 7. כמוש ק׳ v. 7. יחדיו ק׳

3. *Horonaim.* This town appears on the Moabite Stone as Horonen. Some scholars maintain that it was in the south of Moab; others, in the north, not far from Heshbon.

4. *her little ones,* etc. For the noun, cf. xiv. 3. Here the word may perhaps be connected with tsa'ar, 'her distressed ones.'

5. With this verse, cf. Isa. xv. 5.

the ascent of Luhith. Between Zoar and Rabbath-Moab.

with continual weeping shall they go up. lit. 'with weeping shall go up weeping,' i.e. one crowd of refugees in tears will succeed another.

6. *be like a tamarisk in the wilderness.* See on xvii. 6. The point is probably: flee to some isolated place; be lonely and

forlorn like the tamarisk, so that you save your lives.

7. *thy works.* The fruit of thy works, viz. flocks and herds; or, thy merchandise. Binns makes the comment, 'Moab and its population depended almost entirely on artificial means for their water supply, a wonderful system of tanks and sluices was necessary before any cultivation was possible. There may be in this verse a reference to these elaborate irrigation *works,* the destruction of which meant the ruin of the country.'

thou also. Not only will your possessions be plundered, but you will be taken captive.

Chemosh. Moab's principal deity (Num. xxi. 29). The downfall of a people was thought also to involve their gods. For a description of idols being carried in a

8 And the spoiler shall come upon
  every city,
And no city shall escape;
The valley also shall perish, and
  the plain shall be destroyed;
As the LORD hath spoken.
9 Give wings unto Moab,
  For she must fly and get away;
And her cities shall become a
  desolation,
Without any to dwell therein.
10 Cursed be he that doeth the work
  of the LORD with a slack hand,
And cursed be he that keepeth
  back his sword from blood.
11 Moab hath been at ease from his
  youth,
And he hath settled on his lees,
And hath not been emptied from
  vessel to vessel,
Neither hath he gone into
  captivity;
Therefore his taste remaineth in
  him,

וְיָבֹא שֹׁדֵד אֶל־כָּל־עִיר 8
וְעִיר לֹא תִמָּלֵט
וְאָבַד הָעֵמֶק וְנִשְׁמַד הַמִּישֹׁר
אֲשֶׁר אָמַר יְהוָה:
תְּנוּ־צִיץ לְמוֹאָב 9
כִּי נָצֹא תֵצֵא
וְעָרֶיהָ לְשַׁמָּה תִהְיֶינָה
מֵאֵין יוֹשֵׁב בָּהֵן:
אָרוּר עֹשֶׂה 10
מְלֶאכֶת יְהוָה רְמִיָּה
וְאָרוּר מֹנֵעַ חַרְבּוֹ מִדָּם:
שַׁאֲנַן מוֹאָב מִנְּעוּרָיו 11
וְשֹׁקֵט הוּא אֶל־שְׁמָרָיו
וְלֹא־הוּרַק מִכְּלִי אֶל־כֶּלִי
וּבַגּוֹלָה לֹא הָלָךְ
עַל־כֵּן עָמַד טַעְמוֹ בּוֹ

triumphal procession, cf. xliii. 12 and
Isa. xlvi. 1f.

8. *the valley.* The valley of the Jordan
towards the Dead Sea.

the plain. The tableland which was the
site of Moab.

9. *wings.* The noun *tsits* is unusual,
although it has this meaning in later
usage. It may have been chosen for its
assonance with the verbs that follow,
natso têtsê.

10. *the work of the LORD.* Moab's
destruction is a Divine decree and must
therefore be executed with zeal. The
vindictive spirit of the verse is called
forth by the bitter experience of Israel at
Moab's hand.

11. *Moab hath been at ease,* etc. 'The
metaphor is well worthy of Jeremiah.
Moab had led a much more settled life
than Israel; it had, of course, suffered
from invasion and foreign dominion, but
not from exile. It had been like wine
suffered to remain on the lees, and not
poured from vessel to vessel. And the
effect of this had been that the quality
of the lees was more and more communicated to the wine. If the wine was
good it was thus improved (cf. Isa. xxv. 6)
but if inferior it deteriorated (cf. Zeph.
i. 12). Moab had suffered by its freedom
from the discipline of removal, its
character had not been enriched by new
experience, it had become more and
more obstinately settled in its native
characteristics, its "taste" and "scent,"
learning nothing, forgetting nothing'
(Peake).

And his scent is not changed.

12 Therefore, behold, the days come,

Saith the LORD,

That I will send unto him them that tilt up,

And they shall tilt him up;

And they shall empty his vessels,

And break their bottles in pieces.

13 And Moab shall be ashamed of Chemosh,

As the house of Israel was ashamed

Of Beth-el their confidence.

14 How say ye: 'We are mighty men,

And valiant men for the war'?

15 Moab is spoiled, and they are gone up into her cities,

And his chosen young men are gone down to the slaughter,

Saith the King,

Whose name is the LORD of hosts.

16 The calamity of Moab is near to come,

And his affliction hasteth fast.

וְרֵיחוֹ לֹא נָמָר׃

12 לָכֵן הִנֵּה־יָמִים בָּאִים

נְאֻם־יְהֹוָה

וְשִׁלַּחְתִּי־לוֹ צֹעִים

וְצֵעֻהוּ

וְכֵלָיו יָרִיקוּ

וְנִבְלֵיהֶם יְנַפֵּצוּ׃

13 וּבֹשׁ מוֹאָב מִכְּמוֹשׁ

כַּאֲשֶׁר־בֹּשׁוּ בֵּית יִשְׂרָאֵל

מִבֵּית אֵל מִבְטֶחָם׃

14 אֵיךְ תֹּאמְרוּ גִּבּוֹרִים אֲנָחְנוּ

וְאַנְשֵׁי־חַיִל לַמִּלְחָמָה׃

15 שֻׁדַּד מוֹאָב וְעָרֶיהָ עָלָה

וּמִבְחַר בַּחוּרָיו יָרְדוּ לַטָּבַח

נְאֻם־הַמֶּלֶךְ

יְהֹוָה צְבָאוֹת שְׁמוֹ׃

16 קָרוֹב אֵיד־מוֹאָב לָבוֹא

וְרָעָתוֹ מִהֲרָה מְאֹד׃

---

12 *them that tilt up.* Instead of the wine being decanted with care so that the lees are not mixed with it, the jars will be broken after the contents are carelessly poured out. In plain language, the Moabites will be driven out as exiles and their land made desolate.

13. *Moab shall be ashamed of Chemosh.* The Moabites will suffer bitter disillusionment for having put trust in their god which had proved helpless to protect them.

Beth-el their confidence. Alluding to the calf set up by Jeroboam at Beth-el when the Northern Kingdom was formed; the fate of the Ten Tribes was captivity in Assyria from which their idol could not save them.

14. Moab had trusted in her strength to spare her the terrors of invasion.

15. *and they are gone up into her cities.* Others render: 'and her cities have gone up' in flame. The former is to be preferred, because the verbs, as in verse 18, are contrasted: as they who came to spoil Moab went up into her cities, the defenders deserted them and took to flight.

16. For the language, cf. Deut. xxxii. 35.

17 Bemoan him, all ye that are
round about him,
And all ye that know his name;
Say: 'How is the strong staff
broken,
The beautiful rod!'

18 O thou daughter that dwellest in
Dibon,
Come down from thy glory, and
sit in thirst;
For the spoiler of Moab is come
up against thee,
He hath destroyed thy strong-
holds.

19 O inhabitant of Aroer,
Stand by the way, and watch;
Ask him that fleeth, and her that
escapeth;
Say: 'What hath been done?'

20 Moab is put to shame, for it is
dismayed;
Wail and cry;
Tell ye it in Arnon,
That Moab is spoiled.

נֻ֤דוּ לוֹ֙ כָּל־סְבִיבָ֔יו 17
וְכֹ֖ל יֹדְעֵ֣י שְׁמ֑וֹ
אִמְר֗וּ אֵיכָ֤ה נִשְׁבַּר֙ מַטֵּה־עֹ֔ז
מַקֵּ֖ל תִּפְאָרָֽה׃
רְדִ֤י מִכָּבוֹד֙ וּשְׁבִ֣י בַצָּמָ֔א 18
יֹשֶׁ֖בֶת בַּת־דִּיבֹ֑ון
כִּֽי־שֹׁדֵ֤ד מוֹאָב֙ עָ֣לָה בָ֔ךְ
שִׁחֵ֖ת מִבְצָרָֽיִךְ׃
אֶל־דֶּ֛רֶךְ עִמְדִ֥י וְצַפִּ֖י 19
יוֹשֶׁ֣בֶת עֲרוֹעֵ֑ר
שַׁאֲלִי־נָ֣ס וְנִמְלָ֔טָה
אִמְרִ֖י מַה־נִּהְיָֽתָה׃
הֹבִ֥ישׁ מוֹאָ֛ב כִּֽי־חַ֖תָּה 20
הֵילִ֣ילִ ׀ וּזְעָ֑קִ
הַגִּ֥ידוּ בְאַרְנ֖וֹן
כִּ֥י שֻׁדַּ֥ד מוֹאָֽב׃

v. 18.   v. 20. הילילו ק׳   v. 20. ושבי ק׳   וזעקו ק׳

17. *round about him.* i.e. peoples in
Moab's vicinity, and *all ye that know his
name* describes the nations which lived
far away but had heard of Moab by repute.
how. Hebrew *echah*, the usual introduction to a lament (cf. Isa. i. 21; Lam. i. 1).
the strong staff . . . the beautiful rod.
The strength and glory of the nation.
18. *daughter . . . Dibon.* i.e. inhabitants of Dibon, now called Diban. It is
four miles north of the Arnon and
thirteen east of the Dead Sea. The
town stands on two hills and possibly
that is why the prophet uses the verb
come down. On the other hand, *come
down from thy glory* is a natural expression which may have no reference to
physical situation. The Moabite Stone
was discovered in Diban in 1868.

sit in thirst. This may be understood
figuratively: you will thirst for all the
things you once enjoyed; or literally: in
your humbled condition as captives, you
will sit on the ground and thirst.

19. *Aroer.* A few miles south-west of
Dibon close to the Arnon. It is not the
Gadite city of that name mentioned in
Num. xxxii. 34, or the Judahite city of
1 Sam. xxx. 28.

20. *for it is dismayed.* In the Hebrew the
verb *is put to shame* is masculine and
is dismayed is feminine. The meaning
may be, 'Moab is put to shame, for it
(Dibon) is dismayed.'

in Arnon. i.e. by the Arnon, on its
banks. This river was the boundary of
Moab (Num. xxi. 13).

21. And judgment is come upon the country of the Plain; upon Holon, and upon Jahzah, and upon Mephaath; 22. and upon Dibon, and upon Nebo, and upon Beth-diblathaim; 23. and upon Kiria-thaim, and upon Beth-gamul, and upon Beth-meon; 24. and upon Kerioth, and upon Bozrah, and upon all the cities of the land of Moab, far or near.

25 The horn of Moab is cut off,

And his arm is broken,

Saith the LORD.

26 Make ye him drunken,

For he magnified himself against the LORD;

21 וּמִשְׁפָּט בָּא אֶל־אֶרֶץ הַמִּישֹׁר
אֶל־חֹלוֹן וְאֶל־יַהְצָה
22 וְעַל־מֵוֹפָעַת׃ וְעַל־דִּיבוֹן
וְעַל־נְבוֹ וְעַל־בֵּית
23 דִּבְלָתָיִם׃ וְעַל קִרְיָתַיִם
וְעַל־בֵּית גָּמוּל וְעַל־בֵּית
24 מְעוֹן׃ וְעַל־קְרִיּוֹת וְעַל־
בָּצְרָה וְעַל כָּל־עָרֵי אֶרֶץ
מוֹאָב הָרְחֹקוֹת וְהַקְּרֹבוֹת׃
25 נִגְדְּעָה קֶרֶן מוֹאָב
וּזְרֹעוֹ נִשְׁבָּרָה
נְאֻם יְהוָה׃
26 הַשְׁכִּירֻהוּ
כִּי עַל־יְהוָה הִגְדִּיל

v. 21. מיפעת ק'

---

21. *the country of the Plain.* i.e. the territory of Moab, an enumeration of whose chief towns follows.

Holon. Still unidentified; it is not the Holon near Hebron (Josh. xv. 51, xxi. 15).

Jahzah. A Levitical city (called Jahaz in Josh. xxi. 36). There Moses defeated the Amorite king Sihon (Num. xxi. 23f.). Its site was probably north-east of Dibon.

Mephaath. Another Levitical city (Josh. xxi. 37).

22. *Dibon.* See on verse 18.

Nebo. See on verse 1.

Beth-diblathaim. lit. 'the house of the two figs.' It is probably not identical with Almon-diblathaim, one of the stages in Israel's journeyings through the wilderness (Num. xxxiii. 46), and its location is unknown.

23. *Kiriathaim.* See on verse 1.

Beth-gamul. Not mentioned elsewhere. Some authorities identify it with Umm el Jemal, south of Bozrah.

Beth-meon. The Baal-meon of Num. xxxii. 38, built by the Gadites; it lies about five miles south-west of Medeba.

24. *Kerioth.* Mentioned in Amos ii. 2. It has been conjecturally identified with Ar of Moab (Num. xxi. 28).

Bozrah. Possibly the Bezer of Deut. iv. 43; Josh. xx. 8, xxi. 36; it lay between Dibon and Aroer. The town of the same name in xlix. 13 was in Edom.

25. *horn.* The symbol of strength, while *arm* signifies dominion.

26. *drunken.* Figurative of bewilderment (cf. xxv. 15).

he magnified himself. See on verses 29f.

And Moab shall wallow in his
vomit,
And he also shall be in derision.

27 For was not Israel a derision
unto thee?
Was he found among thieves?
For as often as thou speakest of
him,
Thou waggest the head.

28 O ye that dwell in Moab,
Leave the cities, and dwell in the
rock;
And be like the dove that maketh
her nest
In the sides of the pit's mouth.

29 We have heard of the pride of
Moab;
He is very proud;
His loftiness, and his pride, and
his haughtiness,
And the assumption of his heart.

30 I know his arrogancy, saith the
LORD,
That it is ill-founded;
His boastings have wrought
nothing well-founded.

וְסָפַק מוֹאָב בְּקִיאוֹ
וְהָיָה לִשְׂחֹק גַּם־הוּא׃
27 וְאִם ׀ לוֹא הַשְּׂחֹק
הָיָה לְךָ יִשְׂרָאֵל
אִם־בְּגַנָּבִים נִמְצָאָה
כִּי־מִדֵּי דְבָרֶיךָ
בּוֹ תִּתְנוֹדָד׃
28 עִזְבוּ עָרִים וְשִׁכְנוּ בַּסֶּלַע
יֹשְׁבֵי מוֹאָב
וִהְיוּ כְיוֹנָה תְּקַנֵּן
בְּעֶבְרֵי פִי־פָחַת׃
29 שָׁמַעְנוּ גְאוֹן־מוֹאָב
גֵּאֶה מְאֹד
גָּבְהוֹ וּגְאוֹנוֹ וְגַאֲוָתוֹ
וְרֻם לִבּוֹ׃
30 אֲנִי יָדַעְתִּי נְאֻם־יְהֹוָה
עֶבְרָתוֹ וְלֹא־כֵן
בַּדָּיו לֹא־כֵן עָשׂוּ׃

נמצא ק׳ v. 27.

---

he also shall be in derision. Just as Israel
had been derided by Moab.

27. *was he found among thieves?* That
Moab treated him with such contempt!
waggest the head. In scorn.

28. *be like the dove*, etc. 'The wild rock-
pigeon invariably selects . . . deep
ravines for its nesting and roosting
place' (Tristram). The Moabites will
now lead a hunted and precarious
existence (cf. iv. 29).

29f. Cf. Isa. xvi. 6. The passage has
a proverbial ring and probably both

Isaiah and Jeremiah were loosely quoting
a current saying about Moab's pride
which was notorious (cf. Isa. xxv. 11;
Zeph. ii. 8ff. *He magnified himself
against the LORD* in verse 26 may also
refer to his inordinate pride).

29. *we have heard.* The subject is
Jeremiah and the Judeans generally.

30. Driver divides the verse differently
and renders: 'I know, saith the Lord,
his wrath; and his boastings are untruth;
they are untruth.' *I* is emphatic, cor-
roborating *we have heard* in the preceding
verse.

31 Therefore will I wail for Moab;
Yea, I will cry out for all Moab;
For the men of Kir-heres shall
my heart moan.

32 With more than the weeping of
Jazer will I weep for thee,
O vine of Sibmah;
Thy branches passed over the
sea,
They reached even to the sea of
Jazer;
Upon thy summer fruits and
upon thy vintage
The spoiler is fallen.

31 עַל־כֵּן עַל־מוֹאָב אֲיֵלִיל
וּלְמוֹאָב כֻּלֹּה אֶזְעָק
אֶל־אַנְשֵׁי קִיר־חֶרֶשׂ יֶהְגֶּה׃

32 מִבְּכִי יַעְזֵר אֶבְכֶּה־לָּךְ
הַגֶּפֶן שִׂבְמָה
נְטִישֹׁתַיִךְ עָבְרוּ יָם
עַד יָם יַעְזֵר נָגָעוּ
עַל־קֵיצֵךְ וְעַל־בְּצִירֵךְ
שֹׁדֵד נָפָל׃

31ff. The strong sympathy of the prophet with Moab should be noted. It is likewise met with in Isaiah and expressed in almost identical words. Evidently there was a close bond between Moab and Judah, notwithstanding the apparently exultant tones of part of this chapter; and this in spite of the fact that when Nebuchadnezzar attacked Judea in Jehoiakim's reign, he was assisted by the Moabites (2 Kings xxiv. 2). It may well be that the prophets, with their sense of universalism, felt this sympathy with the sufferings of the peoples whose downfall they had to announce even where their choice of language suggests satisfaction. A distinction is probably to be drawn between their official utterances, as it were, and their personal feelings.

31. *therefore will I wail.* Isa. xvi. 7 has *therefore shall Moab wail for Moab;* but verse 11 of that chapter reads, *Wherefore my heart moaneth like a harp for Moab, and mine inward parts for Kir-heres.*

the men of (anshë) *Kir-heres.* The reading of the parallel passage in Isa. xvi. 7 is, *the sweet cakes of* (ashishë) *Kir-haraseth.* The version in Jeremiah seems to be a free adaptation of the other. Kir-heres is the modern Kerak, eight miles south of the Dead Sea.

32. Based on Isa. xvi. 8f. with variations.

Jazer . . . Sibmah. The former was ten miles north and the latter two and a half north-west of Heshbon. The district was famed for its vineyards, and remains of wine-presses and vineyard towers have been found in its ruins.

thy branches passed over the sea. Having mentioned the vines, the prophet makes use of a metaphor in which the whole nation is likened to a huge vine, the branches of which (i.e. portions of the nation) go over the sea into captivity (Rashi, Kimchi). In fact, no sea would have to be crossed, but the phrase may be idiomatic for going into captivity. Streane explains that the phrase is 'a hyperbolical metaphor to express the great luxuriance of Sibmah's vines.'

the sea of Jazer. There is no sea (or lake) in the vicinity of Jazer. The phrase may be metaphorical for the sea of corn which grew in the district, although this is not mentioned elsewhere. Perhaps the passage should be rendered, disregarding the accents: 'Thy branches passed over the sea even unto the sea; they reached to Jazer.' The first clause will then be idiomatic, indicating deportation to a great distance.

33 And gladness and joy is taken
   away
   From the fruitful field, and from
   the land of Moab;
   And I have caused wine to cease
   from the winepresses;
   None shall tread with shouting;
   The shouting shall be no shouting.

34 From the cry of Heshbon even
   unto Elealeh,
   Even unto Jahaz have they
   uttered their voice,
   From Zoar even unto Horonaim,
   A heifer of three years old;
   For the Waters of Nimrim also
   Shall be desolate.

35 Moreover I will cause to cease in
   Moab,
   Saith the LORD,
   Him that offereth in the high
   place,
   And him that offereth to his gods.

33 וְנֶאֶסְפָה שִׂמְחָה וָגִיל
מִכַּרְמֶל וּמֵאֶרֶץ מוֹאָב
וְיַיִן מִיקָבִים הִשְׁבַּתִּי
לֹא־יִדְרֹךְ הֵידָד
הֵידָד לֹא הֵידָד:
34 מִזַּעֲקַת חֶשְׁבּוֹן עַד־אֶלְעָלֵה
עַד־יַהַץ נָתְנוּ קוֹלָם
מִצֹּעַר עַד־חֹרֹנַיִם
עֶגְלַת שְׁלִשִׁיָּה
כִּי גַּם־מֵי נִמְרִים
לִמְשַׁמּוֹת יִהְיוּ:
35 וְהִשְׁבַּתִּי לְמוֹאָב
נְאֻם־יְהוָה
מַעֲלֶה בָמָה
וּמַקְטִיר לֵאלֹהָיו:

---

33. Cf. Isa. xvi. 10.

the shouting shall be no shouting. It will
not be the joyous shouting of grape-
treading, but the grim shout of warriors.
The noun *hedad* signifies both sounds
(see on xxv. 30).

34. Cf. Isa. xv. 4-6 of which this verse
is an abbreviation.

Elealeh. About two miles north of
Heshbon (see on verse 2).

even unto Jahaz. 'The sense is that the
cry uttered from Heshbon is heard at
Elealeh, and is even carried on to Jahaz,
a considerable distance south-west.
Again, the wail uttered from Zoar is
borne to Horonaim, both in the south of
the land. Thus the lamentation shall

be caught by one from another and be
universal' (Streane).

a heifer of three years old. Apparently
Moab is likened to a heifer which is fully
grown and developed. It possessed
everything, but now only cries of anguish
are heard (Rashi, Kimchi). The Hebrew
may also mean 'the third Eglath' and is
then to be understood as another place-
name, 'third' distinguishing it from two
other towns called Eglath in that
neighbourhood.

Nimrim. Probably the modern Wadi
Numeirah at the south-east end of the
Dead Sea.

desolate. Dried up because their sources
had been dammed.

35. Cf. Isa. xvi. 12.

36 Therefore my heart moaneth for
Moab like pipes,
And my heart moaneth like pipes
for the men of Kir-heres;
Therefore the abundance that he
hath gotten is perished.

37 For every head is bald,
And every beard clipped;
Upon all the hands are cuttings,
And upon the loins sackcloth.

38 On all the housetops of Moab
and in the broad places thereof
There is lamentation every
where;
For I have broken Moab like a
vessel wherein is no pleasure,
Saith the LORD.

39 'How is it broken down!' wail ye!
'How hath Moab turned the back
with shame!'
So shall Moab become a derision
and a dismay
To all that are round about him.

40 For thus saith the LORD:
Behold, he shall swoop as a
vulture,

עַל־כֵּן לִבִּי לְמוֹאָב 36
כַּחֲלָלִים יֶהֱמֶה
וְלִבִּי אֶל־אַנְשֵׁי קִיר־חֶרֶשׂ
כַּחֲלִילִים יֶהֱמֶה
עַל־כֵּן יִתְרַת עָשָׂה אָבָדוּ:
כִּי כָל־רֹאשׁ קָרְחָה 37
וְכָל־זָקָן גְּרֻעָה
עַל כָּל־יָדַיִם גְּדֻדֹת
וְעַל־מָתְנַיִם שָׂק:
עַל כָּל־גַּגּוֹת מוֹאָב 38
וּבִרְחֹבֹתֶיהָ כֻּלֹּה מִסְפֵּד
כִּי־שָׁבַרְתִּי אֶת־מוֹאָב כִּכְלִי
אֵין־חֵפֶץ בּוֹ
נְאֻם־יְהֹוָה:
אֵיךְ חַתָּה הֵילִילוּ 39
אֵיךְ הִפְנָה־עֹרֶף מוֹאָב בּוֹשׁ
וְהָיָה מוֹאָב לִשְׂחֹק וְלִמְחִתָּה
לְכָל־סְבִיבָיו:
כִּי־כֹה אָמַר יְהֹוָה 40
הִנֵּה כַנֶּשֶׁר יִדְאֶה

---

36. *like pipes.* Used for playing dirges
at funerals.

the men of Kir-heres. As in verse 31.

37f. Cf. Isa. xv. 2f.

37. All display various signs of mourning (see on xvi. 6).

38. *the housetops.* Which were flat and
used for various purposes (see on xix. 13).

40. *he shall swoop.* The subject is the
enemy.

vulture. Cf. xlix. 22 and Deut. xxviii.
49. The simile is apt for the Babylonian

And shall spread out his wings
against Moab.

41 The cities are taken,
And the strongholds are seized,
And the heart of the mighty men
of Moab at that day
Shall be as the heart of a woman
in her pangs.

42 And Moab shall be destroyed
from being a people,
Because he hath magnified himself against the LORD.

43 Terror, and the pit, and the trap,
Are upon thee, O inhabitant of
Moab,
Saith the LORD.

44 He that fleeth from the terror
Shall fall into the pit;
And he that getteth up out of the
pit
Shall be taken in the trap;
For I will bring upon her, even
upon Moab,
The year of their visitation,
saith the LORD.

45 In the shadow of Heshbon the
fugitives
Stand without strength;

וּפָרַ֥שׂ כְּנָפָ֖יו אֶל־מוֹאָֽב׃

41 נִלְכְּדָה֙ הַקְּרִיּ֔וֹת
וְהַמְּצָד֖וֹת נִתְפָּ֑שָׂה
וְֽהָיָ֞ה לֵ֤ב גִּבּוֹרֵ֣י מוֹאָב֙
בַּיּ֣וֹם הַה֔וּא
כְּלֵ֖ב אִשָּׁ֥ה מְצֵרָֽה׃

42 וְנִשְׁמַ֥ד מוֹאָ֖ב מֵעָ֑ם
כִּ֥י עַל־יְהֹוָ֖ה הִגְדִּֽיל׃

43 פַּ֥חַד וָפַ֖חַת וָפָ֑ח
עָלֶ֛יךָ יוֹשֵׁ֥ב מוֹאָ֖ב
נְאֻם־יְהֹוָֽה׃

44 הַנָּ֞יס מִפְּנֵ֤י הַפַּ֙חַד֙
יִפֹּ֣ל אֶל־הַפַּ֔חַת
וְהָעֹלֶה֙ מִן־הַפַּ֔חַת
יִלָּכֵ֖ד בַּפָּ֑ח
כִּֽי־אָבִ֥יא אֵלֶ֛יהָ אֶל־מוֹאָ֖ב
שְׁנַ֥ת פְּקֻדָּתָ֖ם נְאֻם־יְהֹוָֽה׃

45 בְּצֵ֥ל חֶשְׁבּ֖וֹן
עָמְד֥וּ מִכֹּ֖חַ נָסִ֑ים

הנס ק׳   v. 44.

---

empire which 'seemed to those who
witnessed it like the rising of a mighty
eagle, spreading out his vast wings,
feathered with the innumerable colours
of the variegated masses which composed
the Chaldean host, swooping over the
different countries, and striking fear in
his rapid flight' (Stanley).

41. *the cities.* In Hebrew *ha-kerioth*,
with a possible play on *Kerioth* (verse 24).

42. This was completely fulfilled.
After going into exile the Moabites
practically disappeared as a people.

43f. Based in the main upon Isa.
xxiv. 17f.

43. *terror, and the pit, and the trap.* The
assonance of the Hebrew is striking:
pachad wa-phachath wa-phach.

44. *the year of their visitation.* The day
of reckoning for them.

45f. Derived from Num. xxi. 28f.,
xxiv. 17.

45. *without strength.* 'The sense of the
whole verse is that the fugitives of Moab

312

For a fire is gone forth out of
Heshbon,
And a flame from the midst of
Sihon,
And it devoureth the corner of
Moab,
And the crown of the head of the
tumultuous ones.

46 Woe unto thee, O Moab!
The people of Chemosh is un-
done;
For thy sons are taken away
captive,
And thy daughters into captivity.

47 Yet will I turn the captivity of
Moab
In the end of days, saith the
LORD.
Thus far is the judgment of
Moab.

כִּי־אֵשׁ יָצָא מֵחֶשְׁבּוֹן
וְלֶהָבָה מִבֵּין סִיחֹן
וַתֹּאכַל פְּאַת מוֹאָב
וְקָדְקֹד בְּנֵי שָׁאוֹן׃

46 אוֹי־לְךָ מוֹאָב
אָבַד עַם־כְּמוֹשׁ
כִּי־לֻקְּחוּ בָנֶיךָ בַּשֶּׁבִי
וּבְנֹתֶיךָ בַּשִּׁבְיָה׃

47 וְשַׁבְתִּי שְׁבוּת־מוֹאָב
בְּאַחֲרִית הַיָּמִים
נְאֻם־יְהֹוָה
עַד־הֵנָּה מִשְׁפַּט מוֹאָב׃

| | 49 | CHAPTER XLIX | מט |

1 Of the children of Ammon.

Thus saith the LORD:

Hath Israel no sons?

1 לִבְנֵי עַמּוֹן
כֹּה אָמַר יְהֹוָה
הֲבָנִים אֵין לְיִשְׂרָאֵל

v. 45. סבירין יצאה

shall take refuge under the walls of the neighbouring city of the Ammonites, but as they stand there in hopes of aid, there bursts forth from the city on which their only hopes rest a flame kindled by the Chaldean foe, but like that which was in old days kindled in the same place by Sihon the Amorite conqueror. Thus the passage Num. xxi. 28 is quoted with a new application' (Streane).

the tumultuous ones. The Moabite warriors.

46. Chemosh. See on verse 13. The people of Chemosh is synonymous with Moab.

47. turn the captivity. After the long prediction of disaster, the note of comfort is heard, as in the case of Israel. This accords with the universalism of the prophets.

in the end of days. In the days of the Messiah (Kimchi).

thus far . . . Moab. Probably an editorial note by Baruch.

CHAPTER XLIX
1-6 JUDGMENT UPON AMMON

THE Ammonites were Moab's neighbour on the north and of the tribe of Gad on the east.

Hath he no heir?
Why then doth Malcam take
    possession of Gad,
And his people dwell in the cities
    thereof?

2 Therefore, behold, the days come,
    saith the LORD,
That I will cause an alarm of war
    to be heard
Against Rabbah of the children of
    Ammon;
And it shall become a desolate
    mound,
And her daughters shall be burned
    with fire;
Then shall Israel dispossess them
    that did dispossess him,
Saith the LORD.

3 Wail, O Heshbon, for Ai is
    undone;
Cry, ye daughters of Rabbah, gird
    you with sackcloth;

אִם־יוֹרֵשׁ אֵין לוֹ
מַדּוּעַ יָרַשׁ מַלְכָּם אֶת־גָּד
וְעַמּוֹ בְּעָרָיו יָשָׁב׃
2 לָכֵן הִנֵּה יָמִים בָּאִים
נְאֻם־יְהֹוָה
וְהִשְׁמַעְתִּי
אֶל־רַבַּת בְּנֵי־עַמּוֹן
תְּרוּעַת מִלְחָמָה
וְהָיְתָה לְתֵל שְׁמָמָה
וּבְנֹתֶיהָ בָּאֵשׁ תִּצַּתְנָה
וְיָרַשׁ יִשְׂרָאֵל אֶת־יֹרְשָׁיו
אָמַר יְהֹוָה׃
3 הֵילִילִי חֶשְׁבּוֹן כִּי שֻׁדְּדָה־עַי
צְעַקְנָה בְּנוֹת רַבָּה
חֲגֹרְנָה שַׂקִּים

v. 2. פתח באתנח

1. *Malcam.* The Ammonite deity. In
1 Kings xi. 5 the name is pointed
Milcom. The god, as often, is named to
represent the people who worship it.

take possession of Gad. When the
Gadites, together with other peoples on
the east side of the Jordan, were carried
off by Tiglath-pileser (2 Kings xv. 29),
the Ammonites took possession of their
territory. They are denounced for this
action because it was based on the
assumption that the land would never
be occupied again by its owners. The
question is asked of them, 'Although it
is true that the Gadites have been
deported and will die in exile; but will
they not have *heirs* who will return and
claim the land?'

2. *Rabbah.* The Ammonite capital, on
the river Jabbok, fourteen miles north-

east of Heshbon; now Amman the
capital of Transjordan.

her daughters. The less important cities,
again in verse 3 (cf. Num. xxi. 25 where
towns is literally 'daughters').

3. *Heshbon . . . Ai.* Although an Ammonite town Ai is otherwise unknown,
we may assume there was one with the
same name as the town mentioned in
Josh. vii. 2. There is nothing in-
herently improbable in two countries
having cities similarly named. Possibly
the same applies to Heshbon, as we know
that there was a Heshbon in Moab
(xlviii. 2). In that case the meaning is
plain: the fate which overtook Ai will
befall Heshbon in turn. If, however,
the Heshbon of Moab is intended here,
the verse is to be explained: In his march
of conquest Nebuchadnezzar passed

Lament, and run to and fro
  among the folds;
For Malcam shall go into captivity,
His priests and his princes together.
4 Wherefore gloriest thou in the
  valleys,
Thy flowing valley, O backsliding
  daughter?
That didst trust in thy treasures:
'Who shall come unto me?'
5 Behold, I will bring a terror upon
  thee,
Saith the Lord GOD of hosts,
From all that are round about
  thee;
And ye shall be driven out every
  man right forth,
And there shall be none to gather
  up him that wandereth.
6 But afterward I will bring back the
  captivity of the children of
  Ammon,
Saith the LORD.

סְפֹּדְנָה וְהִתְשׁוֹטַטְנָה בַּגְּדֵרֹות
כִּי מַלְכָּם בַּגּוֹלָה יֵלֵךְ
כֹּהֲנָיו וְשָׂרָיו יַחְדָּיו׃
4 מַה־תִּתְהַלְלִי בָּעֲמָקִים
זָב עִמְקֵךְ הַבַּת הַשּׁוֹבֵבָה
הַבֹּטְחָה בְּאֹצְרֹתֶיהָ
מִי יָבֹוא אֵלָי׃
5 הִנְנִי מֵבִיא עָלַיִךְ פַּחַד
נְאֻם־אֲדֹנָי יֱהֹוִה צְבָאֹות
מִכָּל־סְבִיבָיִךְ
וְנִדַּחְתֶּם אִישׁ לְפָנָיו
וְאֵין מְקַבֵּץ לַנֹּדֵד׃
6 וְאַחֲרֵי־כֵן אָשִׁיב
אֶת־שְׁבוּת בְּנֵי־עַמֹּון
נְאֻם־יְהֹוָה׃

---

first through Ammon and then Moab.
Heshbon, city of Moab, is bidden to see
what happened to Ai and lament, because
that will also be her doom. Although
the whole prophecy refers to Ammon,
Heshbon is addressed in order to under-
line the fate of Ai.

among the folds. Where the sheep are
enclosed in the open fields, since the
cities will no longer afford protection.

Malcam shall go into captivity. See on
xliii. 12. The latter part of the verse is
derived from Amos. i. 15.

4. *thy flowing valley.* The expression is
strange. Perhaps it means a well-
watered valley, Rabbah being described
as *the city of waters* (2 Sam. xii. 27).

backsliding. Normally this term refers to
apostasy from the worship of God. In

connection with the Ammonites, who
were heathens, that is inappropriate.
It is to be understood in the sense of
flagrant disregard of the ordinary laws
of humanity and decency (called in
Talmudic literature 'the seven precepts
of the sons of Noah,' Sanh. 56a) obligatory upon all men.

treasures. i.e. ample supplies from the
fertility of the land.

who shall come unto me? She also trusted
in the inaccessible nature of the country
to safeguard her against invasion.

5. *right forth.* Every man will flee
wherever he can, without a thought for
his neighbour; so great will be the terror
(Kimchi).

6. See on xlviii. 47.

7 Of Edom.

Thus saith the LORD of hosts:
Is wisdom no more in Teman?
Is counsel perished from the prudent?
Is their wisdom vanished?

8 Flee ye, turn back, dwell deep,
O inhabitants of Dedan;
For I do bring the calamity of Esau upon him,
The time that I shall punish him.

9 If grape-gatherers came to thee,
Would they not leave some gleaning grapes?
If thieves by night,
Would they not destroy till they had enough?

10 But I have made Esau bare,

7 לֶאֱדוֹם

כֹּה אָמַר יְהוָה צְבָאוֹת
הַאֵין עוֹד חָכְמָה בְּתֵימָן
אָבְדָה עֵצָה מִבָּנִים
נִסְרְחָה חָכְמָתָם:

8 נֻסוּ הָפְנוּ הֶעְמִיקוּ לָשֶׁבֶת
יֹשְׁבֵי דְּדָן
כִּי אֵיד עֵשָׂו הֵבֵאתִי עָלָיו
עֵת פְּקַדְתִּיו:

9 אִם־בֹּצְרִים בָּאוּ לָךְ
לֹא יַשְׁאִרוּ עוֹלֵלוֹת
אִם־גַּנָּבִים בַּלַּיְלָה
הִשְׁחִיתוּ דַיָּם:

10 כִּי־אֲנִי חָשַׂפְתִּי אֶת־עֵשָׂו

7-22 JUDGMENT UPON EDOM

There is close similarity between this section and Obadiah, verses 7, 9, 10a and 14-16 corresponding to Obadiah 8, 5f., 1-4 respectively.

7. *is wisdom no more in Teman?* Has all the wisdom and counsel of Edom vanished that disaster finds her so helpless? Teman was a district in the north of Edom, but the name is sometimes used as a synonym for the whole country (Hab. iii. 3).

8. *turn back.* Turn your backs on your country in flight.

dwell deep. Seek inaccessible and hidden places where the enemy will not be able to find you.

Dedan. See on xxv. 23.

Esau. Edom was the country inhabited by Esau's descendants (cf. Gen. xxxvi. 1). Although Dedan is distinguished from Edom in xxv. 21, 23, they were both parts of Esau's territory.

9f. The general meaning is clear, although the exact rendering is doubtful. According to A.J. the sense is: Surely grape-gatherers leave something over and even thieves destroy only until their rage is satiated; but a clean sweep will be made of Edom. R.V. margin renders: 'If grape-gatherers came to thee, they will leave no gleaning grapes; if thieves by night, they will destroy till they have enough. For I have made Esau bare,' etc. This is preferable: just as grape-gatherers leave nothing behind (it would be pedantic to urge Lev. xix. 10 against this translation) and thieves destroy till they are satisfied, i.e. completely, so have I made a clean sweep of Edom, even of his secret places which might have been expected to escape the attention of raiders.

I have uncovered his secret
places,
And he shall not be able to hide
himself;
His seed is spoiled, and his
brethren,
And his neighbours, and he is
not.

11 Leave thy fatherless children,
I will rear them,
And let thy widows trust in Me.

12. For thus saith the LORD: Behold,
they to whom it pertained not to
drink of the cup shall assuredly
drink; and art thou he that shall
altogether go unpunished? thou
shalt not go unpunished, but thou
shalt surely drink. 13. For I have
sworn by Myself, saith the LORD,
that Bozrah shall become an
astonishment, a reproach, a waste,
and a curse; and all the cities thereof
shall be perpetual wastes.

14 I have heard a message from the
LORD,

גִּלֵּיתִי אֶת־מִסְתָּרָיו
וְנֶחְבָּה לֹא יוּכָל
שֻׁדַּד זַרְעוֹ וְאֶחָיו
וּשְׁכֵנָיו וְאֵינֶנּוּ:
11 עָזְבָה יְתֹמֶיךָ אֲנִי אֲחַיֶּה
וְאַלְמְנֹתֶיךָ עָלַי תִּבְטָחוּ:
12 כִּי־כֹה ׀ אָמַר יְהֹוָה הִנֵּה
אֲשֶׁר־אֵין מִשְׁפָּטָם לִשְׁתּוֹת
הַכּוֹס שָׁתוֹ יִשְׁתּוּ וְאַתָּה הוּא
נָקֹה תִּנָּקֶה לֹא תִנָּקֶה כִּי שָׁתֹה
13 תִשְׁתֶּה: כִּי בִי נִשְׁבַּעְתִּי נְאֻם־
יְהֹוָה כִּי־לְשַׁמָּה לְחָרְפָּה
לְחֹרֶב וְלִקְלָלָה תִּהְיֶה בָצְרָה
וְכָל־עָרֶיהָ תִהְיֶינָה לְחָרְבוֹת
עוֹלָם:
14 שְׁמוּעָה שָׁמַעְתִּי מֵאֵת יְהֹוָה

10. *his secret places.* His hidden retreats
and fastnesses.

his seed is spoiled. The next verse shows
that this is not meant literally in the
sense of total extermination, but rather
as denoting widespread destruction of
young and old.

11. *I will rear them,* etc. A tender verse.
Stern justice demands the suffering
predicted in the previous verses; nevertheless, even when punishing, God does
not abandon His love for His creatures,
and the fatherless and widows who
survive the holocaust may safely be left
to His care. Maybe, too, this is an
exhortation to spare the women and
children from the horrors of war.

12. *they to whom it pertained not to drink,*
etc. Other nations will also be punished

for gloating over Israel's downfall,
although no fraternal ties bound them.
How much more so Edom, who has a
close affinity and blood relationship with
Israel, being descended from Esau,
Jacob's brother! He should have been
grief-stricken and eager to render assistance, instead of rejoicing at and taking
advantage of Israel's catastrophe, and
even intensifying it (cf. Obad. 1, 10-14).
drink of the cup. For the metaphor, see
on xxv. 15.

13. *I have sworn by Myself.* See on
xxii. 5.

Bozrah. See on xlviii. 24. It is usually
identified with Busaireh, twenty miles
south-east of the Dead Sea.

14. *a message . . . an ambassador is sent.*
The message (or, report) is that *an*

And an ambassador is sent
among the nations:
'Gather yourselves together, and
come against her,
And rise up to the battle.'

15 For, behold, I make thee small
among the nations,
And despised among men.

16 Thy terribleness hath deceived
thee,
Even the pride of thy heart,
O thou that dwellest in the clefts
of the rock,
That holdest the height of the
hill;
Though thou shouldest make thy
nest as high as the eagle,
I will bring thee down from
thence, saith the LORD.

17 And Edom shall become an
astonishment;
Every one that passeth by it
Shall be astonished and shall
hiss at all the plagues thereof.

18 As in the overthrow of Sodom
and Gomorrah
And the neighbour cities thereof,
saith the LORD,

וְצִיר בַּגּוֹיִם שָׁלוּחַ
הִתְקַבְּצוּ וּבָאוּ עָלֶיהָ
וְקוּמוּ לַמִּלְחָמָה׃
15 כִּי־הִנֵּה קָטֹן נְתַתִּיךָ בַּגּוֹיִם
בָּזוּי בָּאָדָם׃
16 תִּפְלַצְתְּךָ הִשִּׁיא אֹתָךְ
זְדוֹן לִבֶּךָ
שֹׁכְנִי בְּחַגְוֵי הַסֶּלַע
תֹּפְשִׂי מְרוֹם גִּבְעָה
כִּי־תַגְבִּיהַ כַּנֶּשֶׁר קִנֶּךָ
מִשָּׁם אוֹרִידְךָ נְאֻם־יְהוָה׃
17 וְהָיְתָה אֱדוֹם לְשַׁמָּה
כֹּל עֹבֵר עָלֶיהָ
יִשֹּׁם וְיִשְׁרֹק
עַל־כָּל־מַכּוֹתֶהָ׃
18 כְּמַהְפֵּכַת סְדֹם וַעֲמֹרָה
וּשְׁכֵנֶיהָ אָמַר יְהוָה

---

ambassador is sent, etc. 'The ambassador is any agent, visible or invisible, sent by God. Human powers who wish to stir up war, send human messengers. All things stand at God's command, and whatsoever or whomsoever He employs is a messenger from Him' (Pusey).

15. Edom lost her independence in the second century B.C.E. when she was conquered by John Hyrcanus and became part of Judea. In the rebellion against Rome the Edomites (Idumeans as they were then called) played an important part.

16. *thy terribleness hath deceived thee.* The very strength which Edom at one time enjoyed and made her terrible in the eyes of her neighbours has deceived her and led to her ultimate downfall.

the rock. This may refer to Petra, fifty miles south of the Dead Sea, which 'lay in an amphitheatre of mountains, accessible only through the narrow gorge, called the *Sik*, winding in with precipitous sides from the west; and the mountain sides round Petra, and the ravines about it, contain innumerable rock-hewn cavities, some being tombs but others dwellings, in which the ancient inhabitants lived' (Driver).

17. The language resembles that of xix. 8.

18. *and the neighbour cities thereof.* Cf. Deut. xxix. 22, where Admah and

No man shall abide there,
Neither shall any son of man
dwell therein.

19 Behold, he shall come up like a
 lion from the thickets of the
 Jordan
 Against the strong habitation;
 For I will suddenly make him
 run away from it,
 And whoso is chosen, him will I
 appoint over it;
 For who is like Me? and who will
 appoint Me a time?
 And who is that shepherd that
 will stand before Me?

20 Therefore hear ye the counsel
 of the LORD,
 That He hath taken against
 Edom;
 And His purposes, that He hath
 purposed against the inhabitants of Teman:
 Surely the least of the flock shall
 drag them away,

לֹא־יֵשֵׁב שָׁם אִישׁ
וְלֹא־יָגוּר בָּהּ בֶּן־אָדָם׃

19 הִנֵּה כְּאַרְיֵה יַעֲלֶה
מִגְּאוֹן הַיַּרְדֵּן
אֶל־נְוֵה אֵיתָן
כִּי־אַרְגִּיעָה אֲרִיצֶנּוּ מֵעָלֶיהָ
וּמִי בָחוּר אֵלֶיהָ אֶפְקֹד
כִּי מִי כָמוֹנִי וּמִי יֹעִידֶנִּי
וּמִי־זֶה רֹעֶה
אֲשֶׁר יַעֲמֹד לְפָנָי׃

20 לָכֵן שִׁמְעוּ עֲצַת־יְהוָה
אֲשֶׁר יָעַץ אֶל־אֱדוֹם
וּמַחְשְׁבוֹתָיו אֲשֶׁר חָשַׁב
אֶל־יֹשְׁבֵי תֵימָן
אִם־לֹא יִסְחָבוּם
צְעִירֵי הַצֹּאן

Zeboiim are mentioned as the cities overthrown together with Sodom and Gomorrah (cf. also Gen. x. 19, xix. 24f.). The verse is substantially repeated in l. 40.

19-21. Cf. l. 44-46 where the verses are applied almost *verbatim* to Babylon.

19. *he shall come up.* Edom's enemy and conqueror is the subject.

the thickets of the Jordan. See on xii. 5.

the strong habitation. Edom, which thought herself so strong to withstand attackers.

I will suddenly make him run away. The meaning is obscure and may be: I will make him (the enemy) run away from Edom, not in defeat, but because in one

moment (*suddenly*) he will have overrun and destroyed her, so that he now leaves her for further conquests. Alternatively, the text may be rendered: 'suddenly I will make him run over her.' Both are suggested by Rashi.

who will appoint Me a time? To contend with Me; i.e. who can dispute My will? In former days the commanders of opposing armies mutually arranged the time for battle.

shepherd. i.e. king or leader (cf. iii. 15, vi. 3); which king of Edom can withstand Me? (Kimchi).

20. *the least of the flock.* A nation which is now regarded as weak. The Rabbis apply it to the Persians. Although they became a great Power, at the time when

Surely their habitation shall be
appalled at them.

21 The earth quaketh at the noise
of their fall;
There is a cry, the noise whereof
is heard in the Red Sea.

22 Behold, he shall come up and
swoop down as the vulture,
And spread out his wings against
Bozrah;
And the heart of the mighty men
of Edom at that day
Shall be as the heart of a woman
in her pangs.

23 Of Damascus.
Hamath is ashamed, and Arpad;
For they have heard evil tidings,
they are melted away;
There is trouble in the sea;
It cannot be quiet.

אִם־לֹא־יַשִּׁים
עֲלֵיהֶם נְוֵהֶם׃

21 מִקּוֹל נִפְלָם רָעֲשָׁה הָאָרֶץ
צְעָקָה בְּיַם־סוּף
נִשְׁמַע קוֹלָהּ׃

22 הִנֵּה כַנֶּשֶׁר יַעֲלֶה וְיִדְאֶה
וְיִפְרֹשׂ כְּנָפָיו עַל־בָּצְרָה
וְהָיָה לֵב גִּבּוֹרֵי אֱדוֹם
בַּיּוֹם הַהוּא
כְּלֵב אִשָּׁה מְצֵרָה׃

23 לְדַמֶּשֶׂק
בּוֹשָׁה חֲמָת וְאַרְפָּד
כִּי־שְׁמֻעָה רָעָה שָׁמְעוּ נָמֹגוּ
בַּיָּם דְּאָגָה
הַשְׁקֵט לֹא יוּכָל׃

v. 21. נ"א קולם

Jeremiah spoke they had not attained
their subsequent military strength, and
might with justice be described as *the
least of the flock.*

shall be appalled. The land is personified and represented as being horror-
stricken at the catastrophe which has
befallen the inhabitants.

21. *there is a cry . . . Red Sea.* Streane
comments: 'The Hebrew is purposely
less smooth. "A cry—at the Red Sea is
heard its noise." Edom in its prosperity
extended thither, as we gather from
1 Kings ix. 26.' More probable is the
translation proposed by Ehrlich: 'As the
cry at the Red Sea (when the Egyptians
were overwhelmed there) is the sound
thereof.'

22. Cf. xlviii. 40f.

23-27 JUDGMENT UPON DAMASCUS
23. *Damascus.* The capital of Syria.

Hamath. The modern Hama, on the
Orontes, 110 miles north of Damascus.

is ashamed. i.e. filled with dismay at the
news of Nebuchadnezzar's conquests.

Arpad. Tel Erfad, 95 miles north of
Hamath. These three cities of Syria are
mentioned together in Isa. x. 9 (cf. also
Isa. xxxvi. 19, xxxvii. 13).

melted away. Helpless through fear
(cf. Exod. xv. 15).

there is trouble in the sea. This must be
understood metaphorically, there being
no sea at Damascus. The sense is:
trouble is brewing. For this figure of
the sea as typifying restlessness, cf. Isa.
lvii. 20 where the Hebrew for *it cannot
be quiet* occurs *verbatim.*

24 Damascus is waxed feeble, she
turneth herself to flee,
And trembling hath seized on
her;
Anguish and pangs have taken
hold of her, as of a woman in
travail.

25 'How is the city of praise left
unrepaired,
The city of my joy?'

26 Therefore her young men shall
fall in her broad places,
And all the men of war shall be
brought to silence in that day,
Saith the LORD of hosts.

27 And I will kindle a fire in the wall
of Damascus,
And it shall devour the palaces
of Ben-hadad.

28. Of Kedar, and of the kingdoms
of Hazor, which Nebuchadrezzar
king of Babylon smote.
Thus saith the LORD:
Arise ye, go up against Kedar,

24 רָפְתָה דַמֶּשֶׂק הִפְנְתָה לָנוּס
וְרֶטֶט הֶחֱזִיקָה
צָרָה וַחֲבָלִים
אֲחָזַתָה כַּיּוֹלֵדָה:
25 אֵיךְ לֹא־עֻזְּבָה עִיר תְּהִלָּה
קִרְיַת מְשׂוֹשִׂי:
26 לָכֵן יִפְּלוּ בַחוּרֶיהָ בִּרְחֹבֹתֶיהָ
וְכָל־אַנְשֵׁי הַמִּלְחָמָה יִדַּמּוּ
בַּיּוֹם הַהוּא
נְאֻם יְהֹוָה צְבָאוֹת:
27 וְהִצַּתִּי אֵשׁ בְּחוֹמַת דַּמֶּשֶׂק
וְאָכְלָה אַרְמְנוֹת בֶּן־הֲדָד:
28 לְקֵדָר | וּלְמַמְלְכוֹת חָצוֹר
אֲשֶׁר הִכָּה נְבוּכַדְרֶאצּוֹר
מֶלֶךְ־בָּבֶל
כֹּה אָמַר יְהֹוָה
קוּמוּ עֲלוּ אֶל־קֵדָר

v. 25 ‏תהלת ק׳ יתיר ו׳ v. 28.

25. *how is . . . my joy?* The prophet
puts the sentence into the mouth of a
citizen (or perhaps, the king) of Damascus.
The Hebrew verb translated *unrepaired*
is differently interpreted. Rashi explains: How was it that there was neglect
in fortifying the city's walls? Metsudath
David, taking the verb in its literal sense,
interprets: Why was this famous city not
'forsaken,' i.e. left untouched, by the
Babylonians?

26. *therefore.* Better, 'nevertheless,' i.e.
notwithstanding the question in the
preceding verse.

27. *it shall devour the palaces of Ben-
hadad.* Quoted from Amos i. 4. The

name Ben-hadad was borne by several
kings of Syria (cf. 1 Kings xv. 18, xx. 1;
2 Kings vi. 24, viii. 7, xiii. 3).

28-33 JUDGMENT UPON KEDAR AND HAZOR

28. *Kedar.* See on ii. 10. The name
denominates the nomadic Arabs.

kingdoms of Hazor. Several modern
scholars hold that the word is here
connected with *chatser* 'an unwalled town,
a village,' and denotes Arabs living in
settlements, as distinct from nomads.
The plural *kingdoms* indicates various
tribes which Nebuchadnezzar smote.
This is specifically stated here, Kimchi
suggests, because they had not been

321

And spoil the children of the east.

29 Their tents and their flocks shall
they take,
They shall carry away for themselves their curtains,
And all their vessels, and their
camels;
And they shall proclaim against
them a terror on every side.

30 Flee ye, flit far off, dwell deep,
O ye inhabitants of Hazor, saith
the LORD;
For Nebuchadrezzar king of
Babylon hath taken counsel
against you,
And hath conceived a purpose
against you.

31 Arise, get you up against a
nation that is at ease,
That dwelleth without care, saith
the LORD;
That have neither gates nor bars,
That dwell alone.

32 And their camels shall be a booty,
And the multitude of their cattle
a spoil;

וְשָׁדְדוּ אֶת־בְּנֵי־קֶדֶם׃

29 אָהֳלֵיהֶם וְצֹאנָם יִקָּחוּ
יְרִיעוֹתֵיהֶם וְכָל־כְּלֵיהֶם
וּגְמַלֵּיהֶם יִשְׂאוּ לָהֶם
וְקָרְאוּ עֲלֵיהֶם מָגוֹר מִסָּבִיב׃

30 נֻסוּ נֻּדוּ מְאֹד הֶעְמִיקוּ לָשֶׁבֶת
יֹשְׁבֵי חָצוֹר נְאֻם־יְהֹוָה
כִּי־יָעַץ עֲלֵיכֶם נְבוּכַדְרֶאצַּר
מֶלֶךְ־בָּבֶל עֵצָה
וְחָשַׁב עֲלֵיהֶם מַחֲשָׁבָה׃

31 קוּמוּ עֲלוּ אֶל־גּוֹי שְׁלֵיו
יוֹשֵׁב לָבֶטַח נְאֻם־יְהֹוָה
לֹא־דְלָתַיִם וְלֹא־בְרִיחַ
לוֹ בָּדָד יִשְׁכֹּנוּ׃

32 וְהָיוּ גְמַלֵּיהֶם לָבַז
וַהֲמוֹן מִקְנֵיהֶם לְשָׁלָל

v. 29. עליכם ק׳   v. 30. קמץ בז״ק ק׳

---

previously attacked by the Israelites,
unlike the other peoples named in
Jeremiah's judgment as fated to be
overrun by the Babylonians.

the children of the east. The Arabian
tribes located east of Canaan.

29. tents . . . flocks . . . curtains, etc.
All the terms used in the verse are
appropriate to nomads and villagers.

curtains. The tent-hangings, as in iv. 20.

they shall proclaim against them, etc.
A.J. appears to mean that the Babylonians
will bring havoc upon the inhabitants of
Kedar. The clause may be more probably translated: 'They (the inhabitants)
shall cry out because of them (the
Babylonians), "Terror on every side" '
(so Ehrlich).

30. dwell deep. See on verse 8.

counsel . . . a purpose. He has planned
to conquer you.

31. arise. Addressed to the Babylonians
by God at Whose will they *conceived a
purpose.*

that dwelleth without care, etc. The
Babylonians are encouraged to undertake
this campaign because their opponents
dwelleth without care, i.e. thinking themselves secure from attack they have made
no preparations for defence; *they have
neither gates nor bars,* i.e. they live in
open villages without fortifications and
can be easily overrun; and they *dwell
alone* and have no alliances with neighbouring peoples to come to their aid.

And I will scatter unto all winds
them that have the corners
polled;
And I will bring their calamity
from every side of them, saith
the LORD.

33 And Hazor shall be a dwelling-
place of jackals,
A desolation for ever;
No man shall abide there,
Neither shall any son of man
dwell therein.

34. The word of the LORD that
came to Jeremiah the prophet
concerning Elam in the beginning of
the reign of Zedekiah king of Judah,
saying:

35 Thus saith the LORD of hosts:
Behold, I will break the bow of
Elam,
The chief of their might.

36 And I will bring against Elam the
four winds
From the four quarters of
heaven,
And will scatter them toward all
those winds;

וְזֵרִתִים לְכָל־רוּחַ
קְצוּצֵי פֵאָה
וּמִכָּל־עֲבָרָיו אָבִיא
אֶת־אֵידָם נְאֻם־יְהֹוָה׃
33 וְהָיְתָה חָצוֹר לִמְעוֹן תַּנִּים
שְׁמָמָה עַד־עוֹלָם
לֹא־יֵשֵׁב שָׁם אִישׁ
וְלֹא־יָגוּר בָּהּ בֶּן־אָדָם׃
34 אֲשֶׁר הָיָה דְבַר־יְהֹוָה אֶל־
יִרְמְיָהוּ הַנָּבִיא אֶל־עֵילָם
בְּרֵאשִׁית מַלְכוּת צִדְקִיָּה
מֶלֶךְ־יְהוּדָה לֵאמֹר׃
35 כֹּה אָמַר יְהֹוָה צְבָאוֹת
הִנְנִי שׁוֹבֵר אֶת־קֶשֶׁת עֵילָם
רֵאשִׁית גְּבוּרָתָם׃
36 וְהֵבֵאתִי אֶל־עֵילָם
אַרְבַּע רוּחוֹת
מֵאַרְבַּע קְצוֹת הַשָּׁמַיִם
וְזֵרִתִים לְכֹל הָרֻחוֹת הָאֵלֶּה

32. *the corners polled.* See on ix. 25.

33. *dwelling-place of jackals.* Cf. ix. 10.

dwell. Even temporarily (Metsudath
David).

34-39 JUDGMENT UPON ELAM

34. *Elam.* Now called Chuzistan, a
country east of Babylonia from which it
is separated by the Tigris.

in the beginning of the reign of Zedekiah.

This would be seven or eight years later
than the date assigned to the present
group of prophecies in xlvi. 1f.

35. *the bow.* The Elamites were famous
for their skill in archery (cf. Isa. xxii. 6);
but inasmuch as the same phrase is used
of the Northern Kingdom of Israel
(Hos. i. 5), the phrase may signify nothing
more than 'the military people.'

36. *the four winds.* Attacks will be made
upon Elam from every side.

And there shall be no nation whither the dispersed of Elam shall not come.	וְלֹא־יִהְיֶה הַגּוֹי אֲשֶׁר לֹא־יָבוֹא שָׁם נִדְחֵי עֵילָם:
37 And I will cause Elam to be dismayed before their enemies, And before them that seek their life; And I will bring evil upon them, Even My fierce anger, saith the LORD; And I will send the sword after them, Till I have consumed them;	37 וְהַחְתַּתִּי אֶת־עֵילָם לִפְנֵי אֹיְבֵיהֶם וְלִפְנֵי ׀ מְבַקְשֵׁי נַפְשָׁם וְהֵבֵאתִי עֲלֵיהֶם ׀ רָעָה אֶת־חֲרוֹן אַפִּי נְאֻם־יְהוָה וְשִׁלַּחְתִּי אַחֲרֵיהֶם אֶת־הַחֶרֶב עַד כַּלּוֹתִי אוֹתָם:
38 And I will set My throne in Elam, And will destroy from thence king and princes, saith the LORD.	38 וְשַׂמְתִּי כִסְאִי בְּעֵילָם וְהַאֲבַדְתִּי מִשָּׁם מֶלֶךְ וְשָׂרִים נְאֻם־יְהוָה:
39 But it shall come to pass in the end of days, That I will bring back the captivity of Elam, saith the LORD.	39 וְהָיָה ׀ בְּאַחֲרִית הַיָּמִים אָשׁוּב אֶת־שְׁבִית עֵילָם נְאֻם־יְהוָה:

50   CHAPTER L   נ

1. The word that the LORD spoke   1 הַדָּבָר אֲשֶׁר דִּבֶּר יְהוָה אֶל־

---

v. 36. סבירין יבואו v. 36. עילם ק' v. 39. אשיב ק' v. 39. שבות ק'

---

38. I will set My throne in Elam. A phrase signifying that God will sit in judgment upon the nation. Kimchi interprets metaphorically: the widespread destrucion will prove that God alone is King. The Rabbis, identifying Elam with Persia, refer the fulfilment of this prophecy to the days of Haman: the chain of events which led to the deliverance of the Jews from Haman's machinations, though natural in themselves, was none the less forged by God, whereby He displayed His Sovereignty.

39. See on xlviii. 47.

CHAPTER L

JUDGMENT UPON BABYLON

THE exceptional length of this oracle (l. 1-li. 58) as compared with the judgments pronounced upon other nations is

concerning Babylon, concerning the land of the Chaldeans, by Jeremiah the prophet.

2 Declare ye among the nations and announce,
And set up a standard;
Announce, and conceal not;
Say: 'Babylon is taken,
Bel is put to shame, Merodach is dismayed;
Her images are put to shame, her idols are dismayed.'

3 For out of the north there cometh up a nation against her,
Which shall make her land desolate,
And none shall dwell therein;
They are fled, they are gone, both man and beast.

בָּבֶל אֶל־אֶרֶץ כַּשְׂדִּים בְּיַד
יִרְמְיָהוּ הַנָּבִיא:
2 הַגִּידוּ בַגּוֹיִם וְהַשְׁמִיעוּ
וּשְׂאוּ־נֵס
הַשְׁמִיעוּ אַל־תְּכַחֵדוּ
אִמְרוּ נִלְכְּדָה בָבֶל
הֹבִישׁ בֵּל חַת מְרֹדָךְ
הֹבִישׁוּ עֲצַבֶּיהָ חַתּוּ גִּלּוּלֶיהָ:
3 כִּי עָלָה עָלֶיהָ גּוֹי מִצָּפוֹן
הוּא־יָשִׁית אֶת־אַרְצָהּ לְשַׁמָּה
וְלֹא־יִהְיֶה יוֹשֵׁב בָּהּ
מֵאָדָם וְעַד־בְּהֵמָה
נָדוּ הָלָכוּ:

explained by the prophet's deeper interest in Babylon as his country's conqueror. This explanation also accounts for the sharper and more vindictive tone. It is mere pedantry to urge that Jeremiah regarded Babylon as the agent designated by God for punishing his countrymen. That was true; yet as a patriot he could not but cherish hatred against the ravisher of his land, just as he bewailed his people's fate in spite of having foretold it as just retribution for their sins. His hatred found expression in his joy at Babylon's downfall, a joy further occasioned by the conviction that it was well merited, since 'the virtuous are appointed the agents for reward, whereas the wicked are the agents for retribution' (Talmud).

1. *Babylon . . . the land of the Chaldeans.* Chaldea was originally the southern portion of Babylonia. The Chaldeans gradually became masters of the whole country.

2. *among the nations.* Who had suffered from Babylon's aggressive expansionism.

set up a standard. To summon the people to hear the news.

Bel . . . Merodach. Babylonian deities. The latter is better known as Marduk.

put to shame . . . dismayed. By their inability to protect their devotees from disaster. The language, of course, is figurative, and does not imply that the prophet ascribed any reality to these deities.

3. *out of the north.* An allusion to the Persians. Persia is not geographically north of Babylonia; nevertheless its use is easy to understand. To the Jews *the north* was a phrase of sinister import and became a colloquialism to describe the direction from which invasion by a foreign enemy would come. On the other hand, the reference may be to the Medo-Persian empire, and the Medes lived on the north-west of Babylonia.

4 In those days, and in that time,
saith the LORD,
The children of Israel shall come,
They and the children of Judah
together;
They shall go on their way weep-
ing,
And shall seek the LORD their
God.

5 They shall inquire concerning
Zion
With their faces hitherward:
'Come ye, and join yourselves to
the LORD
In an everlasting covenant that
shall not be forgotten.'

6 My people hath been lost sheep;
Their shepherds have caused them
to go astray,
They have turned them away on
the mountains;
They have gone from mountain
to hill,
They have forgotten their resting-
place.

7 All that found them have devoured
them;
And their adversaries said: 'We
are not guilty';

בַּיָּמִים הָהֵמָּה וּבָעֵת הַהִיא 4
נְאֻם־יְהֹוָה
יָבֹאוּ בְנֵי־יִשְׂרָאֵל
הֵמָּה וּבְנֵי־יְהוּדָה יַחְדָּו
הָלוֹךְ וּבָכוֹ יֵלֵכוּ
וְאֶת־יְהֹוָה אֱלֹהֵיהֶם יְבַקֵּשׁוּ:
צִיּוֹן יִשְׁאָלוּ 5
דֶּרֶךְ הֵנָּה פְנֵיהֶם
בֹּאוּ וְנִלְווּ אֶל־יְהֹוָה
בְּרִית עוֹלָם לֹא תִשָּׁכֵחַ:
צֹאן אֹבְדוֹת הָיָה עַמִּי 6
רֹעֵיהֶם הִתְעוּם
הָרִים שׁוֹבֵבִים
מֵהַר אֶל־גִּבְעָה הָלָכוּ
שָׁכְחוּ רִבְצָם:
כָּל־מוֹצְאֵיהֶם אֲכָלוּם 7
וְצָרֵיהֶם אָמְרוּ לֹא נֶאְשָׁם

v. 5. קמץ בז״ק v. 6. היו ק׳ v. 6. שובבום ק׳ v. 6. קמץ בז״ק

4. Cf. iii. 21-25. The overthrow of
Babylon will arouse a feeling of penitence
within the hearts of the people of Israel,
now reunited by their common suffering.

5. *hitherward*. This is an indication
that Jeremiah was in the Holy Land.

join yourselves to the LORD. The return
would not merely be to the land as a
nation, but to God as a religious community.

an everlasting covenant. Cf. xxxii. 40.

6. *lost sheep*. Better, 'straying sheep'
(see on xxiii. 1).

*they have turned them away on the
mountains.* The parallelism of the first
half of the verse suggests that the

meaning is: they have turned them
adrift on the trackless mountains, i.e.
have led them into spiritual dangers
(idolatry) with none to guide them.
Rashi comments: They have led them to
idolatrous worship which was most
frequently practised on mountains.

from mountain to hill. Either in a literal
sense: they wandered about in search of
pasture without reliable leaders; or
figuratively: they proceeded from idolatry
to idolatry in search of spiritual satisfaction.

their resting-place. lit. 'their crouching,'
i.e. the fold provided for them.

7. *we are not guilty.* Israel is so worth-

Because they have sinned against
the LORD, the habitation of
justice,
Even the LORD, the hope of their
fathers.

8 Flee out of the midst of Babylon,
And go forth out of the land of
the Chaldeans,
And be as the he-goats before the
flocks.

9 For, lo, I will stir up and cause to
come up against Babylon
An assembly of great nations from
the north country;
And they shall set themselves in
array against her,
From thence she shall be taken;
Their arrows shall be as of a
mighty man that maketh childless;
None shall return in vain.

10 And Chaldea shall be a spoil;
All that spoil her shall be
satisfied, saith the LORD.

11 Because ye are glad, because ye
rejoice,
O ye that plunder My heritage,

תַּחַת אֲשֶׁר חָטְאוּ לַיהוָֹה
נְוֵה־צֶדֶק
וּמִקְוֵה אֲבוֹתֵיהֶם יְהוָֹה׃
8 נֻדוּ מִתּוֹךְ בָּבֶל
וּמֵאֶרֶץ כַּשְׂדִּים יֵצֵאוּ
וְהָיוּ כְּעַתּוּדִים לִפְנֵי־צֹאן׃
9 כִּי הִנֵּה אָנֹכִי מֵעִיר
וּמַעֲלֶה עַל־בָּבֶל
קְהַל־גּוֹיִם גְּדֹלִים
מֵאֶרֶץ צָפוֹן
וְעָרְכוּ לָהּ מִשָּׁם תִּלָּכֵד
חִצָּיו כְּגִבּוֹר מַשְׁכִּיל
לֹא יָשׁוּב רֵיקָם׃
10 וְהָיְתָה כַשְׂדִּים לְשָׁלָל
כָּל־שֹׁלְלֶיהָ יִשְׂבָּעוּ
נְאֻם־יְהוָֹה׃
11 כִּי תִשְׂמְחִי כִּי תַעַלְזִי
שֹׁסֵי נַחֲלָתִי

v. 8. צאו ק׳ v. 9. נ״א משכיל v. 10. קמץ בטרחא v. 11. תשמחו ק׳ v. 11. תעלזו ק׳

less that no guilt attaches to one who
destroys him. This plea is refuted in
ii. 3.

because, etc. These are the words of the
prophet explaining the cause of their
bitter experience.

the habitation of justice. A striking
epithet of God. So much is He the
fount of justice, that He is its very
habitation. In xxxi. 22 the phrase is
applied to Jerusalem.

8. *flee,* etc. Hurry back to your own
country.

as the he-goats before the flocks. When a
gate of the enclosure is opened, the he-
goats press forward to pass through first.
Let the Judeans be the first of Babylon's
captive peoples to go into freedom.

9. *an assembly of great nations.* They
are enumerated in li. 27f.

none shall return in vain. If so translated,
the meaning must be that every arrow
will find its mark. Preference is perhaps
to be given to the rendering: '(a warrior)
not returning empty-handed,' without
spoil.

11. *because ye are glad.* The verse may
be understood in two ways. On the

Because ye gambol as a heifer at
grass,
And neigh as strong horses;

12 Your mother shall be sore
ashamed,
She that bore you shall be
confounded;
Behold, the hindermost of the
nations
Shall be a wilderness, a dry land,
and a desert.

13 Because of the wrath of the
LORD it shall not be inhabited,
But it shall be wholly desolate;
Every one that goeth by Babylon
Shall be appalled and hiss at all
her plagues.

14 Set yourselves in array against
Babylon round about,
All ye that bend the bow,
Shoot at her, spare no arrows;
For she hath sinned against the
LORD.

15 Shout against her round about,
she hath submitted herself;

כִּי תָפוּשִׁי כְּעֶגְלָה דָשָׁה
וְתִצְהֲלִי כָּאַבִּרִים:

12 בּוֹשָׁה אִמְּכֶם מְאֹד
חָפְרָה יוֹלַדְתְּכֶם
הִנֵּה אַחֲרִית גּוֹיִם
מִדְבָּר צִיָּה וַעֲרָבָה:

13 מִקֶּצֶף יְהוָֹה לֹא תֵשֵׁב
וְהָיְתָה שְׁמָמָה כֻּלָּהּ
כֹּל עֹבֵר עַל־בָּבֶל
יִשֹּׁם וְיִשְׁרֹק
עַל־כָּל־מַכּוֹתֶיהָ:

14 עִרְכוּ עַל־בָּבֶל ׀ סָבִיב
כָּל־דֹּרְכֵי קֶשֶׁת
יְדוּ אֵלֶיהָ
אַל־תַּחְמְלוּ אֶל־חֵץ
כִּי לַיהוָֹה חָטָאָה:

15 הָרִיעוּ עָלֶיהָ סָבִיב נָתְנָה יָדָהּ

v. 11. תפושׁו ק׳   v. 11. נ״א דשׁא   v. 11. ותצהלו ק׳

---

translation of A.J., it tells the Chaldeans
that what is foretold in verse 12 is the sequel
to their gloating over the plunder carried
away from Judea. Alternatively, the
introductory conjunction may be
rendered 'though,' and the sense will
then be that in spite of the abundance of
spoil gathered from their victims, they
will be brought low and humiliated.
The latter is preferable.

gambol . . . neigh. The first verb describes satiety, the latter the arrogance of
strength. Filled with loot, the Chaldeans
had behaved like the animals named.

12. *your mother.* The city of Babylon,
personified as mother of the inhabitants.

behold, the hindermost of the nations, etc.
A.J. has adopted the translation of A.V.;
but a better sense is derived from R.V.,
'behold, she shall be the hindermost of
the nations, a wilderness,' etc. Babylon
had considered herself the first of nations
in power and glory; she will be reduced to
last place in her devastation.

13. Cf. xviii. 16 where the language is
used of Judea.

14. A summons to the enemy to begin
the attack.

15. *shout.* With battle cries.

she hath submitted herself. lit. 'she hath
given her hand,' i.e. she has capitulated.

Her buttresses are fallen, her
walls are thrown down;
For it is the vengeance of the
LORD, take vengeance upon
her;
As she hath done, do unto her.

16 Cut off the sower from Babylon,
And him that handleth the sickle
in the time of harvest;
For fear of the oppressing sword
they shall turn every one to
his people,
And they shall flee every one to
his own land.

17 Israel is a scattered sheep,
The lions have driven him away;
First the king of Assyria hath
devoured him,
And last this Nebuchadrezzar
king of Babylon hath broken
his bones.

18 Therefore thus saith the LORD of
hosts, the God of Israel:
Behold, I will punish the king of
Babylon and his land,

נָפְלוּ אָשְׁוִיֹּתֶיהָ
נֶהֶרְסוּ חוֹמוֹתֶיהָ
כִּי נִקְמַת יְהֹוָה הִיא הִנָּקְמוּ בָהּ
כַּאֲשֶׁר עָשְׂתָה עֲשׂוּ־לָהּ:
16 כִּרְתוּ זוֹרֵעַ מִבָּבֶל
וְתֹפֵשׂ מַגָּל בְּעֵת קָצִיר
מִפְּנֵי חֶרֶב הַיּוֹנָה
אִישׁ אֶל־עַמּוֹ יִפְנוּ
וְאִישׁ לְאַרְצוֹ יָנֻסוּ:
17 שֶׂה פְזוּרָה יִשְׂרָאֵל
אֲרָיוֹת הִדִּיחוּ
הָרִאשׁוֹן אֲכָלוֹ מֶלֶךְ אַשּׁוּר
וְזֶה הָאַחֲרוֹן עִצְּמוֹ
נְבוּכַדְרֶאצַּר מֶלֶךְ בָּבֶל:
18 לָכֵן כֹּה־אָמַר יְהֹוָה צְבָאוֹת
אֱלֹהֵי יִשְׂרָאֵל
הִנְנִי פֹקֵד אֶל־מֶלֶךְ בָּבֶל
וְאֶל־אַרְצוֹ

v. 15. אשיותיה ק'

buttresses. The Hebrew word is not
found again in the Bible. A.V. 'foundations' is incorrect, the cognate noun in
Arabic meaning 'a supporting pillar.'

her walls are thrown down. 'This was
not done by Cyrus, who entered the city
beneath the walls by the river bed, after
diverting the stream. It therefore points
to the later capture of Babylon by Darius
who "having become master of the place,
destroyed the wall, and tore down all the
gates" (Herodotus III, 159)' (Streane).

vengeance of the LORD. Upon Babylon
for the ill-treatment of God's people.

16. *cut off the sower.* Babylon being left
a wilderness (verse 12), all agricultural
operations come to an end.

they shall turn . . . own land. Quoted
from Isa. xiii. 14, describing the fear
which comes over foreign residents in
Babylon who hurry out of the doomed
country.

17. *first the king of Assyria devoured him.*
A reference to the exile of the Ten Tribes
by Shalmaneser.

hath broken his bones. After the body of
the nation had been weakened by
Assyria's attack.

As I have punished the king of
Assyria.

19 And I will bring Israel back to
his pasture,

And he shall feed on Carmel and
Bashan,

And his soul shall be satisfied
upon the hills of Ephraim and
in Gilead.

20 In those days, and in that time,
saith the LORD,

The iniquity of Israel shall be
sought for, and there shall be
none,

And the sins of Judah, and they
shall not be found;

For I will pardon them whom I
leave as a remnant.

21 Go up against the land of
Merathaim, even against it,

And against the inhabitants of
Pekod;

Waste and utterly destroy after
them, saith the LORD,

And do according to all that I
have commanded thee.

כַּאֲשֶׁר פָּקַדְתִּי
אֶל־מֶלֶךְ אַשּׁוּר׃

19 וְשֹׁבַבְתִּי אֶת־יִשְׂרָאֵל
אֶל־נָוֵהוּ

וְרָעָה הַכַּרְמֶל וְהַבָּשָׁן
וּבְהַר אֶפְרַיִם וְהַגִּלְעָד
תִּשְׂבַּע נַפְשׁוֹ׃

20 בַּיָּמִים הָהֵם וּבָעֵת הַהִיא
נְאֻם־יְהֹוָה

יְבֻקַּשׁ אֶת־עֲוֹן יִשְׂרָאֵל וְאֵינֶנּוּ
וְאֶת־חַטֹּאת יְהוּדָה
וְלֹא תִמָּצֶאינָה

כִּי אֶסְלַח לַאֲשֶׁר אַשְׁאִיר׃

21 עַל־הָאָרֶץ מְרָתַיִם
עֲלֵה עָלֶיהָ

וְאֶל־יוֹשְׁבֵי פְּקוֹד
חֲרֹב וְהַחֲרֵם אַחֲרֵיהֶם
נְאֻם־יְהֹוָה

וַעֲשֵׂה כְּכֹל אֲשֶׁר צִוִּיתִיךָ׃

v. 20. יתיר י׳

---

18. *Assyria.* By this time the land had
been invaded and the power of the nation
shattered.

19. *his pasture.* The Land of Israel in its
earlier dimensions, including even the
territory east of the Jordan.

Carmel. Its name signified fertility (cf.
the Hebrew of iv. 26).

Bashan . . . hills of Ephraim . . . Gilead.
Famous for their forests and herds of
cattle (l. 19; Deut. xxxii. 14; Isa. ii. 13;
Mic. vii. 14; Zech. xi. 2).

20. Cf. xxxi. 33.

21. *go up.* An exhortation to Babylon's
conqueror.

Merathaim . . . Pekod. lit. 'double rebellion . . . visitation.' The destroyer
is bidden to attack Babylon, the country
which had so grievously rebelled against
God, now due to receive punishment.
The names are a play on actual localities.
In south Babylonia there was a place
called *Mat Marratim*, and a Babylonian
people was known as the *Pukudu* (cf.
Ezek. xxiii. 23).

22 Hark! battle is in the land,
   And great destruction.
23 How is the hammer of the whole
   earth
   Cut asunder and broken!
   How is Babylon become
   A desolation among the nations!
24 I have laid a snare for thee, and
   thou art also taken, O Babylon,
   And thou wast not aware;
   Thou art found, and also caught,
   Because thou hast striven against
   the LORD.
25 The LORD hath opened His
   armoury,
   And hath brought forth the
   weapons of His indignation;
   For it is a work that the Lord
   GOD of hosts
   Hath to do in the land of the
   Chaldeans.
26 Come against her from every
   quarter, open her granaries,
   Cast her up as heaps, and destroy
   her utterly;
   Let nothing of her be left.
27 Slay all her bullocks, let them go
   down to the slaughter;

22 קוֹל מִלְחָמָה בָּאָרֶץ
   וְשֶׁבֶר גָּדוֹל׃
23 אֵיךְ נִגְדַּע וַיִּשָּׁבֵר
   פַּטִּישׁ כָּל־הָאָרֶץ
   אֵיךְ הָיְתָה לְשַׁמָּה
   בָּבֶל בַּגּוֹיִם׃
24 יָקֹשְׁתִּי לָךְ וְגַם־נִלְכַּדְתְּ בָּבֶל
   וְאַתְּ לֹא יָדַעַתְּ
   נִמְצֵאת וְגַם־נִתְפַּשְׂתְּ
   כִּי בַיהוָה הִתְגָּרִית׃
25 פָּתַח יְהוָֹה אֶת־אוֹצָרוֹ
   וַיּוֹצֵא אֶת־כְּלֵי זַעְמוֹ
   כִּי־מְלָאכָה הִיא
   לַאדֹנָי יֱהוִֹה צְבָאוֹת
   בְּאֶרֶץ כַּשְׂדִּים׃
26 בֹּאוּ־לָהּ מִקֵּץ
   פִּתְחוּ מַאֲבֻסֶיהָ
   סָלּוּהָ כְמוֹ־עֲרֵמִים
   וְהַחֲרִימוּהָ
   אַל־תְּהִי־לָהּ שְׁאֵרִית׃
27 חִרְבוּ כָּל־פָּרֶיהָ יֵרְדוּ לַטָּבַח

---

23. *the hammer.* Babylon which shattered other nations (cf. li. 20ff.).

24. *thou wast not aware.* Babylon fell by
a surprise attack.

25. *the weapons of His indignation.* The
Persians and Medes who are the weapons
wherewith God wreaks His indignation

upon the Chaldeans (Metsudath David;
cf. Isa. xiii. 5).

26. *cast her up as heaps.* Pile up her
treasures and make an end of them by
carrying them off as spoil or destroying
them.

27. *her bullocks.* Her nobles and princes
(Rashi, Kimchi), or her youthful warriors
(cf. Isa. xxxiv. 7; Ps. xxii. 13).

Woe unto them! for their day is
    come,
The time of their visitation.

28 Hark! they flee and escape out of
    the land of Babylon,
To declare in Zion the vengeance
    of the LORD our God,
The vengeance of His temple.

29 Call together the archers against
    Babylon,
All them that bend the bow;
Encamp against her round about,
Let none thereof escape;
Recompense her according to
    her work,
According to all that she hath
    done, do unto her:
For she hath been arrogant
    against the LORD,
Against the Holy One of Israel.

30 Therefore shall her young men
    fall in her broad places,
And all her men of war shall be
    brought to silence in that day,
Saith the LORD.

31 Behold, I am against thee, O thou
    most arrogant,
Saith the Lord GOD of hosts;
For thy day is come,
The time that I will punish thee.

32 And the most arrogant shall
    stumble and fall,

הוֹי עֲלֵיהֶם כִּי־בָא יוֹמָם
עֵת פְּקֻדָּתָם׃
28 קוֹל נָסִים וּפְלֵטִים
מֵאֶרֶץ בָּבֶל
לְהַגִּיד בְּצִיּוֹן
אֶת־נִקְמַת יְהֹוָה אֱלֹהֵינוּ
נִקְמַת הֵיכָלוֹ׃
29 הַשְׁמִיעוּ אֶל־בָּבֶל ׀ רַבִּים
כָּל־דֹּרְכֵי קֶשֶׁת
חֲנוּ עָלֶיהָ סָבִיב
אַל־יְהִי־ * פְּלֵיטָה
שַׁלְּמוּ־לָהּ כְּפָעֳלָהּ
כְּכֹל אֲשֶׁר עָשְׂתָה עֲשׂוּ־לָהּ
כִּי אֶל־יְהֹוָה זָדָה
אֶל־קְדוֹשׁ יִשְׂרָאֵל׃
30 לָכֵן יִפְּלוּ בַחוּרֶיהָ בִּרְחֹבֹתֶיהָ
וְכָל־אַנְשֵׁי מִלְחַמְתָּהּ יִדַּמּוּ
בַּיּוֹם הַהוּא
נְאֻם־יְהֹוָה׃
31 הִנְנִי אֵלֶיךָ זָדוֹן
נְאֻם־אֲדֹנָי יְהֹוָה צְבָאוֹת
כִּי בָּא יוֹמְךָ
עֵת פְּקַדְתִּיךָ׃
32 וְכָשַׁל זָדוֹן וְנָפַל

v. 29. לה קרי ולא כתיב

28. *they flee.* The Jews who return to
their homeland.

the vengeance of His temple. For having
been burnt by the Chaldeans.

30. Repeated *verbatim* from xlix. **26**
where it applies to Damascus.

31f. Cf. xxi. **13f.**

And none shall raise him up;
And I will kindle a fire in his
cities,
And it shall devour all that are
round about him.

33 Thus saith the LORD of hosts:
The children of Israel and the
children of Judah are op-
pressed together;
And all that took them captives
hold them fast;
They refuse to let them go.

34 Their Redeemer is strong,
The LORD of hosts is His name;
He will thoroughly plead their
cause,
That He may give rest to the
earth,
And disquiet the inhabitants of
Babylon.

35 A sword is upon the Chaldeans,
saith the LORD,
And upon the inhabitants of
Babylon, and upon her princes,
and upon her wise men.

36 A sword is upon the boasters,
and they shall become fools;
A sword is upon her mighty
men, and they shall be dismayed.

37 A sword is upon their horses,
and upon their chariots,

וְאֵין לֹו מְקִים
וְהִצַּתִּי אֵשׁ בְּעָרָיו
וְאָכְלָה כָּל־סְבִיבֹתָיו׃

33 כֹּה אָמַר יְהֹוָה צְבָאֹות
עֲשׁוּקִים בְּנֵי־יִשְׂרָאֵל
וּבְנֵי־יְהוּדָה יַחְדָּו
וְכָל־שֹׁבֵיהֶם הֶחֱזִיקוּ בָם
מֵאֲנוּ שַׁלְּחָם׃

34 גֹּאֲלָם ׀ חָזָק
יְהֹוָה צְבָאֹות שְׁמֹו
רִיב יָרִיב אֶת־רִיבָם
לְמַעַן הִרְגִּיעַ אֶת־הָאָרֶץ
וְהִרְגִּיז לְיֹשְׁבֵי בָבֶל׃

35 חֶרֶב עַל־כַּשְׂדִּים נְאֻם־יְהֹוָה
וְאֶל־יֹשְׁבֵי בָבֶל
וְאֶל־שָׂרֶיהָ וְאֶל־חֲכָמֶיהָ׃

36 חֶרֶב אֶל־הַבַּדִּים וְנֹאָלוּ
חֶרֶב אֶל־גִּבֹּורֶיהָ וָחָתּוּ׃

37 חֶרֶב אֶל־סוּסָיו וְאֶל־רִכְבֹּו

---

34. *their Redeemer*. The Hebrew *goël*
signifies a near kinsman who has the duty
to avenge a murder and act as protector
(cf. Lev. xxv. 25; Num. xxxv. 21).
God is represented as Israel's *goël* Who
will avenge and rescue.

give rest to the earth. As the sequel to
Babylon's downfall.

35. *wise men*. Perhaps the astrologers
who advised the national rulers.

36. *boasters*. A.V. 'liars' follows Rashi

and Kimchi. It probably refers to the
diviners who assured Babylon of permanent domination. The order of these
verses is noteworthy: the princes, wise
men and diviners are the first to fall.
They nourish the spirit and morale of a
people, the imponderable essentials for
a successful war. Accordingly it is
stated that the will to victory will be
destroyed at its source, after which the
demoralization of the army follows as a
matter of course.

וְאֶל־כָּל־הָעֶרֶב

אֲשֶׁר בְּתוֹכָהּ

וְהָיוּ לְנָשִׁים

חֶרֶב אֶל־אוֹצְרֹתֶיהָ וּבֻזָּזוּ׃

38 חֶרֶב אֶל־מֵימֶיהָ וְיָבֵשׁוּ

כִּי אֶרֶץ פְּסִלִים הִיא

וּבָאֵימִים יִתְהֹלָלוּ׃

39 לָכֵן יֵשְׁבוּ צִיִּים אֶת־אִיִּים

וְיָשְׁבוּ בָהּ בְּנוֹת יַעֲנָה

וְלֹא־תֵשֵׁב עוֹד לָנֶצַח

וְלֹא תִשְׁכּוֹן עַד־דּוֹר וָדֹר׃

40 כְּמַהְפֵּכַת אֱלֹהִים

אֶת־סְדֹם וְאֶת־עֲמֹרָה

וְאֶת־שְׁכֵנֶיהָ נְאֻם־יְהֹוָה

לֹא־יֵשֵׁב שָׁם אִישׁ

וְלֹא־יָגוּר בָּהּ בֶּן־אָדָם׃

41 הִנֵּה עַם בָּא מִצָּפוֹן

וְגוֹי גָּדוֹל וּמְלָכִים רַבִּים

יֵעֹרוּ מִיַּרְכְּתֵי־אָרֶץ׃

And upon all the mingled people
that are in the midst of her,
And they shall become as
women;
A sword is upon her treasures,
and they shall be robbed.

38 A drought is upon her waters,
and they shall be dried up;
For it is a land of graven images,
And they are mad upon things of
horror.

39 Therefore the wild-cats with the
jackals shall dwell there,
And the ostriches shall dwell
therein;
And it shall be no more inhabited for ever,
Neither shall it be dwelt in from
generation to generation.

40 As when God overthrew Sodom
and Gomorrah
And the neighbour cities thereof,
saith the LORD;
So shall no man abide there,
Neither shall any son of man
dwell therein.

41 Behold, a people cometh from
the north,
And a great nation, and many
kings
Shall be roused from the uttermost parts of the earth.

---

37. *the mingled people.* This may mean foreign traders or mercenaries (cf. xxv. 20).

38. *drought.* The Hebrew *choreb* (*drought*) has the same consonants as *chereb* (*sword*) in the preceding two verses and was no doubt suggested by it.

her waters. Upon which the commercial prosperity of Babylon depends.

things of horror. The idols, so-called because of their terrifying grotesqueness.

39f. These verses are reminiscent of Isa. xiii. 19-22, while verse 40 is an almost verbal repetition of xlix. 18. 'The ruins of a city are to this day avoided by the Bedawin, who believe that they are the haunt not of wild animals alone but of uncanny creatures' (Peake).

41-43. A repetition of vi. 22-24 with the necessary changes, since there Jerusalem is the subject, while here Babylon is threatened.

41. *a people.* The Persians.

the north. See on verse 3.

many kings. Persia's allies (cf. li. 27f.).

42 They lay hold on bow and spear,
They are cruel, and have no
compassion;
Their voice is like the roaring
sea,
And they ride upon horses;
Set in array, as a man for war,
Against thee, O daughter of
Babylon.

43 The king of Babylon hath heard
the fame of them,
And his hands wax feeble;
Anguish hath taken hold of him,
And pain, as of a woman in
travail.

44 Behold, he shall come up like a
lion from the thickets of the
Jordan
Against the strong habitation;
For I will suddenly make them
run away from it,
And whoso is chosen, him will I
appoint over it;
For who is like Me? and who will
appoint Me a time?
And who is that shepherd that
will stand before Me?

45 Therefore hear ye the counsel of
the LORD,
That He hath taken against
Babylon,
And His purposes, that He hath
purposed against the land of
the Chaldeans:
Surely the least of the flock shall
drag them away,

קֶשֶׁת וְכִידֹן יַחֲזִיקוּ 42
אַכְזָרִי הֵמָּה וְלֹא יְרַחֵמוּ
קוֹלָם כַּיָּם יֶהֱמֶה
וְעַל־סוּסִים יִרְכָּבוּ
עָרוּךְ כְּאִישׁ לַמִּלְחָמָה
עָלַיִךְ בַּת־בָּבֶל ׃

שָׁמַע מֶלֶךְ־בָּבֶל אֶת־שִׁמְעָם 43
וְרָפוּ יָדָיו
צָרָה הֶחֱזִיקַתְהוּ
חִיל כַּיּוֹלֵדָה ׃

הִנֵּה כְּאַרְיֵה יַעֲלֶה 44
מִגְּאוֹן הַיַּרְדֵּן
אֶל־נְוֵה אֵיתָן
כִּי־אַרְגִּעָה אֲרוּצֵם מֵעָלֶיהָ
וּמִי בָחוּר אֵלֶיהָ אֶפְקֹד
כִּי מִי כָמוֹנִי וּמִי יוֹעִדֶנִּי
וּמִי־זֶה רֹעֶה
אֲשֶׁר יַעֲמֹד לְפָנָי ׃

לָכֵן שִׁמְעוּ עֲצַת־יְהוָֹה 45
אֲשֶׁר יָעַץ אֶל־בָּבֶל
וּמַחְשְׁבוֹתָיו אֲשֶׁר חָשַׁב
אֶל־אֶרֶץ כַּשְׂדִּים
אִם־לֹא יִסְחָבוּם
צְעִירֵי הַצֹּאן

אריצם ק׳   v. 44.

44-46. Almost a repetition of xlix. 19-
21; there it applies to Edom, here to
Babylon.
44. *he shall come up.* The subject is
Cyrus; in xlix. 19 it is Nebuchadnezzar.

The language which was used to describe
the latter's overwhelming might is now
applied to his conqueror. Military
power, no matter how seemingly permanent, is but ephemeral.

335

Surely their habitation shall be
  appalled at them,
46 At the noise of the taking of
  Babylon the earth quaketh,
  And the cry is heard among the
  nations.

אִם־לֹא יַשִּׁים עֲלֵיהֶם נָוֶה:

46 מִקּוֹל נִתְפְּשָׂה בָבֶל

נִרְעֲשָׁה הָאָרֶץ

וּזְעָקָה בַּגּוֹיִם נִשְׁמָע:

51   CHAPTER LI   נא

1 Thus saith the LORD:
  Behold, I will raise up against
    Babylon,
  And against them that dwell in
    Leb-kamai, a destroying wind
2 And I will send unto Babylon
    strangers, that shall fan her,
  And they shall empty her land;
  For in the day of trouble they
    shall be against her round about.
3 Let the archer bend his bow
    against her,
  And let him lift himself up against
    her in his coat of mail;

1 כֹּה אָמַר יְהֹוָה

הִנְנִי מֵעִיר עַל־בָּבֶל

וְאֶל־יֹשְׁבֵי לֵב קָמָי

רוּחַ מַשְׁחִית:

2 וְשִׁלַּחְתִּי לְבָבֶל | זָרִים וְזֵרוּהָ

וִיבֹקְקוּ אֶת־אַרְצָהּ

כִּי־הָיוּ עָלֶיהָ מִסָּבִיב

בְּיוֹם רָעָה:

3 אֶל־יִדְרֹךְ יִדְרֹךְ

הַדֹּרֵךְ קַשְׁתּוֹ

וְאֶל־יִתְעַל בְּסִרְיֹנוֹ

v. 3. נ״א אַל—וְאַל   v. 3. כְּתִיב וְלֹא קְרִי

---

46. *the cry.* Of Babylon's anguish.

among the nations. Edom's cry re-
sounded no further than the Red Sea
(xlix. 21); Babylon's, because of her
greater importance, reverberated through
all nations.

CHAPTER LI

1-58 JUDGMENT UPON BABYLON
         CONTINUED

1. *Leb-kamai.* lit. 'the heart of them that
rise up against Me.' According to

tradition, the name is a cypher for
Casdim, Chaldea (see on xxv. 26).

a destroying wind. An allusion to Cyrus.

2. *strangers, that shall fan her.* There is
a play on the words *zarim* (strangers) and
zeruha (*fan her*). For the verb, see on
xv. 7.

3. The verse is difficult, and for *el* and
we-el there is a variant reading *al* and
we-al. The translation of A.J. cannot
be defended. If the reading *el* is
adopted, the verse is an admonition to

And spare ye not her young men,
Destroy ye utterly all her host.

4 And they shall fall down slain in
the land of the Chaldeans,
And thrust through in her streets.

5 For Israel is not widowed, nor
Judah,
Of his God, of the LORD of hosts;
For their land is full of guilt
Against the Holy One of Israel.

6 Flee out of the midst of Babylon,
And save every man his life,
Be not cut off in her iniquity;
For it is the time of the LORD's
vengeance;
He will render unto her a recom-
pense.

7 Babylon hath been a golden cup
in the LORD's hand,

וְאַל־תַּחְמְלוּ אֶל־בַּחֻרֶיהָ
הַחֲרִימוּ כָּל־צְבָאָהּ׃
4 וְנָפְלוּ חֲלָלִים בְּאֶרֶץ כַּשְׂדִּים
וּמְדֻקָּרִים בְּחוּצוֹתֶיהָ׃
5 כִּי לֹא־אַלְמָן
יִשְׂרָאֵל וִיהוּדָה מֵאֱלֹהָיו
מֵיְהֹוָה צְבָאוֹת
כִּי אַרְצָם מָלְאָה אָשָׁם
מִקְּדוֹשׁ יִשְׂרָאֵל׃
6 נֻסוּ ׀ מִתּוֹךְ בָּבֶל
וּמַלְּטוּ אִישׁ נַפְשׁוֹ
אַל־תִּדַּמּוּ בַּעֲוֺנָהּ
כִּי עֵת נְקָמָה הִיא לַיהֹוָה
גְּמוּל הוּא מְשַׁלֵּם לָהּ׃
7 כּוֹס־זָהָב בָּבֶל בְּיַד־יְהֹוָה

the attacking foe to be determined and ruthless: 'Against him that bendeth let the archer bend his bow, and against him that lifteth himself up in his coat of mail' (so A.V.); but the Hebrew is awkwardly expressed if such be the intention. Some of the ancient Versions and several Hebrew MSS. support the variant al which is adopted by R.V., 'Let not the archer bend his bow, and let him not lift himself up.' On this interpretation, the Babylonian soldiers guarding the city are told that resistance is useless. The difficulty in this ex-planation is that the second half of the verse is obviously spoken to the attackers. The best solution is proposed by Ehrlich who accepts the reading al and under-stands the whole verse as addressed to the besieging enemy, connecting it with verse 5: Do not bend the bow or don (lit. 'bring up on oneself') a coat of mail;

there will be no need for you to fight because (as stated in verse 5) God is coming to the rescue of Israel. Do not spare any of the soldiers because (as stated in verse 5) the land is full of guilt.

5. *Israel is not widowed.* Has not lost her Protector. The language is based on the imagery common in the Bible of God as Israel's 'husband.'

their land. viz. of the Chaldeans.

against the Holy One of Israel. The wrongs committed against Israel are sins against Israel's God.

6. *flee.* Addressed to the Judeans (cf. verse 45, l. 8).

the LORD'S vengeance. See on l. 15.

7. *a golden cup.* Cf. xxv. 15f. where Jeremiah was bidden to make the nations drink of God's wrath. Babylon was

That made all the earth drunken;
The nations have drunk of her wine,
Therefore the nations are mad.

8 Babylon is suddenly fallen and destroyed,
Wail for her;
Take balm for her pain,
If so be she may be healed.

9 We would have healed Babylon, but she is not healed;
Forsake her, and let us go every one into his own country;
For her judgment reacheth unto heaven,
And is lifted up even to the skies.

10 The LORD hath brought forth our victory;
Come, and let us declare in Zion
The work of the LORD our God.

11 Make bright the arrows,

מְשַׁכֶּרֶת כָּל־הָאָרֶץ
מִיֵּינָהּ שָׁתוּ גוֹיִם
עַל־כֵּן יִתְהֹלְלוּ גוֹיִם:

8 פִּתְאֹם נָפְלָה בָבֶל וַתִּשָּׁבֵר
הֵילִילוּ עָלֶיהָ
קְחוּ צֳרִי לְמַכְאוֹבָהּ
אוּלַי תֵּרָפֵא:

9 רִפִּאנוּ אֶת־בָּבֶל וְלֹא נִרְפָּתָה
עִזְבוּהָ וְנֵלֵךְ אִישׁ לְאַרְצוֹ
כִּי־נָגַע אֶל־הַשָּׁמַיִם מִשְׁפָּטָהּ
וְנִשָּׂא עַד־שְׁחָקִים:

10 הוֹצִיא יְהֹוָה אֶת־צִדְקֹתֵינוּ
בֹּאוּ וּנְסַפְּרָה בְצִיּוֹן
אֶת־מַעֲשֵׂה יְהֹוָה אֱלֹהֵינוּ:

11 הָבֵרוּ הַחִצִּים

v. 9. חסר א'

God's agent for this purpose (*in the LORD'S hand*). Ehrlich is probably right in understanding the phrase as 'a goblet of gold-coloured wine,' comparing *the golden oil* in Zech. iv. 12. *Golden* possibly typifies the luxury and splendour of the Babylonian empire.

are mad. Cf. xxv. 16. Intoxicated and bereft of their senses, not knowing how to defend themselves.

8. *take balm*, etc. Spoken in sarcasm to the nations under Babylon's sway.

9. *we would have healed Babylon.* 'We must assume that the speakers are foreign residents in Babylon and presumably not captives, since the latter would hail the downfall of the oppressor. They answer the ironical invitation at the end of verse 8. They have been able to find no cure, and must abandon her to her fate, since her guilt and her punishment mount to the skies' (Peake).

her judgment. They recognize that the catastrophe which had overtaken Babylon is in fact retribution for her iniquities.

reacheth unto heaven. Is on a colossal scale.

10. *our victory.* lit. 'our righteousness' (so A.V.). 'Vindication' is the nearest equivalent. In Babylon's overthrow God has demonstrated the rightness of Israel's cause. Nebuchadnezzar exceeded the punishment due to the Judeans for their sins, and he now pays the penalty.

11. *make bright the arrows.* Polishing would increase their power of penetration.

Fill the quivers,

The LORD hath roused the spirit

  of the kings of the Medes;

Because His device is against

  Babylon, to destroy it;

For it is the vengeance of the

  LORD,

The vengeance of His temple.

12 Set up a standard against the

  walls of Babylon,

Make the watch strong,

Set the watchmen, prepare the

  ambushes;

For the LORD hath both devised

  and done

That which He spoke concerning

  the inhabitants of Babylon.

13 O thou that dwellest upon many

  waters,

Abundant in treasures,

Thine end is come,

The measure of thy covetousness.

מִלְאוּ הַשְּׁלָטִים

הֵעִיר יְהֹוָה

אֶת־רוּחַ מַלְכֵי מָדַי

כִּי־עַל־בָּבֶל מְזִמָּתוֹ

לְהַשְׁחִיתָהּ

כִּי־נִקְמַת יְהֹוָה הִיא

נִקְמַת הֵיכָלוֹ׃

12 אֶל־חוֹמֹת בָּבֶל שְׂאוּ־נֵס

הַחֲזִיקוּ הַמִּשְׁמָר

הָקִימוּ שֹׁמְרִים

הָכִינוּ הָאֹרְבִים

כִּי גַּם־זָמַם יְהֹוָה גַּם־עָשָׂה

אֵת אֲשֶׁר־דִּבֶּר

אֶל־יֹשְׁבֵי בָבֶל׃

13 שֹׁכַנְתְּי עַל־מַיִם רַבִּים

רַבַּת אוֹצָרֹת

בָּא קִצֵּךְ

אַמַּת בִּצְעֵךְ׃

v. 13. שכנת ק׳

---

fill the quivers. The Hebrew *shelatim* is of uncertain meaning. The translation *quivers* is given by Rashi; A.V. and R.V. 'shields' follow Kimchi. If the latter is right, the verb *fill* must mean 'gather your bodies behind the shields.' Another rendering proposed is 'armour' which better suits the verb.

the kings. Cyrus and Darius; or the plural is used generically.

the vengeance of His temple. See on l. 28.

12. *make the watch strong.* To cut off any who tried to escape and be on guard against sorties.

13. *many waters.* i.e. the Euphrates and the numerous canals. Babylon relied upon them for defence.

abundant in treasures. Consisting of spoil captured in battle.

the measure of thy covetousness. An alternative rendering is 'the cubit at which thou shalt be cut off,' a metaphor taken from weaving. 'The web of thy destiny is finished. Cf. for the figure Isa. xxxviii. 12, where the word for "cut off" is the same as here' (Driver; Rashi explains similarly).

14 The Lord of hosts hath sworn by
Himself:
Surely I will fill thee with men,
as with the canker-worm,
And they shall lift up a shout
against thee.

15 He that hath made the earth by
His power,
That hath established the world
by His wisdom,
And hath stretched out the
heavens by His discernment;

16 At the sound of His giving a
multitude of waters in the
heavens,
He causeth the vapours to ascend
from the ends of the earth;
He maketh lightnings at the time
of the rain,
And bringeth forth the wind out
of His treasuries;

17 Every man is proved to be
brutish, for the knowledge—
Every goldsmith is put to shame
by the graven image—
That his molten image is falsehood, and there is no breath
in them.

18 They are vanity, a work of
delusion;
In the time of their visitation
they shall perish.

19 The portion of Jacob is not like
these;
For He is the former of all things,
And [Israel] is the tribe of His
inheritance;
The Lord of hosts is His name.

20 Thou art My maul and weapons
of war,

14 נִשְׁבַּע יְהֹוָה צְבָאוֹת בְּנַפְשׁוֹ
כִּי אִם־מִלֵּאתִיךְ אָדָם כַּיֶּלֶק
וְעָנוּ עָלַיִךְ הֵידָד׃

15 עֹשֵׂה אֶרֶץ בְּכֹחוֹ
מֵכִין תֵּבֵל בְּחָכְמָתוֹ
וּבִתְבוּנָתוֹ נָטָה שָׁמָיִם׃

16 לְקוֹל תִּתּוֹ הֲמוֹן מַיִם בַּשָּׁמַיִם
וַיַּעַל נְשִׂאִים מִקְצֵה־אָרֶץ
בְּרָקִים לַמָּטָר עָשָׂה
וַיּוֹצֵא רוּחַ מֵאֹצְרֹתָיו׃

17 נִבְעַר כָּל־אָדָם מִדַּעַת
הֹבִישׁ כָּל־צֹרֵף מִפָּסֶל
כִּי שֶׁקֶר נִסְכּוֹ וְלֹא־רוּחַ בָּם׃

18 הֶבֶל הֵמָּה מַעֲשֵׂה תַּעְתֻּעִים
בְּעֵת פְּקֻדָּתָם יֹאבֵדוּ׃

19 לֹא־כְאֵלֶּה חֵלֶק יַעֲקוֹב
כִּי־יוֹצֵר הַכֹּל הוּא
וְשֵׁבֶט נַחֲלָתוֹ
יְהֹוָה צְבָאוֹת שְׁמוֹ׃

20 מַפֵּץ־אַתָּה לִי כְּלֵי מִלְחָמָה

v. 19. מלא ר׳

14. *sworn by Himself.* See on xxii. 5.

with men. Invading soldiers.

as with the canker-worm. Numerous as
locusts and destructive like them.

a shout. For the Hebrew term *hedad*,
see on xxv. 30.

15-19. This passage is almost a *verbatim*
repetition of x. 12-16, on which see the
notes. It emphasizes how impotent

Babylon's idols are against God, and
therefore the certain fulfilment of His
judgment upon the Chaldeans.

20. *Thou.* Babylon. The present tense
in this verse, and the imperfect (future)
in this and the following verses (21-23)
are all to be understood as referring to
continuous acts in the past: this is the
rôle that Babylon has hitherto played.

maul. A war-club, mace. For the

And with thee will I shatter the nations,
And with thee will I destroy kingdoms;
21 And with thee will I shatter the horse and his rider,
And with thee will I shatter the chariot and him that rideth therein;
22 And with thee will I shatter man and woman,
And with thee will I shatter the old man and the youth,
And with thee will I shatter the young man and the maid;
23 And with thee will I shatter the shepherd and his flock,
And with thee will I shatter the husbandman and his yoke of oxen,
And with thee will I shatter governors and deputies.
24 And I will render unto Babylon and to all the inhabitants of Chaldea
All their evil that they have done in Zion, in your sight,
Saith the LORD.
25 Behold, I am against thee,
O destroying mountain, saith the LORD,
Which destroyest all the earth;
And I will stretch out My hand upon thee,

וְנִפַּצְתִּי בְךָ גּוֹיִם
וְהִשְׁחַתִּי בְךָ מַמְלָכוֹת:
21 וְנִפַּצְתִּי בְךָ סוּס וְרֹכְבוֹ
וְנִפַּצְתִּי בְךָ רֶכֶב וְרֹכְבוֹ:
22 וְנִפַּצְתִּי בְךָ אִישׁ וְאִשָּׁה
וְנִפַּצְתִּי בְךָ זָקֵן וָנָעַר
וְנִפַּצְתִּי בְךָ בָּחוּר וּבְתוּלָה:
23 וְנִפַּצְתִּי בְךָ רֹעֶה וְעֶדְרוֹ
וְנִפַּצְתִּי בְךָ אִכָּר וְצִמְדּוֹ
וְנִפַּצְתִּי בְךָ פַּחוֹת וּסְגָנִים:
24 וְשִׁלַּמְתִּי לְבָבֶל
וּלְכֹל ׀ יוֹשְׁבֵי כַשְׂדִּים
אֵת כָּל־רָעָתָם
אֲשֶׁר־עָשׂוּ בְצִיּוֹן לְעֵינֵיכֶם
נְאֻם יְהֹוָה:
25 הִנְנִי אֵלֶיךָ
הַר הַמַּשְׁחִית נְאֻם־יְהֹוָה
הַמַּשְׁחִית אֶת־כָּל־הָאָרֶץ
וְנָטִיתִי אֶת־יָדִי עָלֶיךָ

figure, cf. l. 23. A similar thought is expressed in Isa. x. 5 where it is applied to Assyria.

23. *governors and deputies.* Hebrew *pachoth u-seganim*, found together again in Ezek. xxiii. 6, 12, 23 where it is translated *governors and rulers.* The former is cognate with 'pasha' and denotes the governor appointed over a province (cf. Hag. i. 1; Ezra v. 6; Neh. v. 14). The latter denotes a subordinate official. In Rabbinical Hebrew it is used for the High Priest's deputy.

24. *in Zion, in your sight.* A comma is rightly placed after *Zion,* as *in your sight* is to be connected with the beginning of the verse : *And I will render . . . in your sight. You* refers to the Judeans who will have the satisfaction of witnessing the downfall of their oppressors.

25. *O destroying mountain.* Though Babylon lay in a plain, she is described as a *mountain* to indicate her towering strength. This figure is continued in the rest of the verse; *roll thee down from the rocks* means that she will be reduced to a lowly level, and *a burnt mountain* that she will be destroyed by fire.

And roll thee down from the
    rocks,
And will make thee a burnt
    mountain.

26 And they shall not take of thee a
    stone for a corner,
Nor a stone for foundations;
But thou shalt be desolate for
    ever, saith the LORD.

27 Set ye up a standard in the land,
Blow the horn among the nations,
Prepare the nations against her,
Call together against her the
    kingdoms of Ararat, Minni,
    and Ashkenaz;
Appoint a marshal against her;
Cause the horses to come up as
    the rough canker-worm.

28 Prepare against her the nations,
    the kings of the Medes,
The governors thereof, and all
    the deputies thereof,

וְגִלְגַּלְתִּ֙יךָ֙ מִן־הַסְּלָעִ֔ים
וּנְתַתִּ֖יךָ לְהַ֥ר שְׂרֵפָֽה׃
26 וְלֹֽא־יִקְח֤וּ מִמְּךָ֙ אֶ֣בֶן לְפִנָּ֔ה
וְאֶ֖בֶן לְמֽוֹסָד֑וֹת
כִּֽי־שִׁמְמ֥וֹת עוֹלָ֖ם
תִּֽהְיֶ֥ה נְאֻם־יְהוָֽה׃
27 שְׂאוּ־נֵ֣ס בָּאָ֗רֶץ
תִּקְע֨וּ שׁוֹפָ֤ר בַּגּוֹיִם֙
קַדְּשׁ֤וּ עָלֶ֙יהָ֙ גּוֹיִ֔ם
הַשְׁמִ֥יעוּ עָלֶ֖יהָ מַמְלְכ֑וֹת
אֲרָרַ֣ט מִנִּ֣י וְאַשְׁכְּנַ֔ז
פִּקְד֥וּ עָלֶ֖יהָ טִפְסָ֑ר
הַעֲלוּ־ס֖וּס כְּיֶ֥לֶק סָמָֽר׃
28 קַדְּשׁ֙וּ עָלֶ֤יהָ גוֹיִם֙
אֶת־מַלְכֵ֣י מָדַ֔י
אֶת־פַּחוֹתֶ֖יהָ
וְאֶת־כָּל־סְגָנֶ֑יהָ

ב״א מלחמה   v. 27.

26. 'The figure of stones, which by the
action of fire have been rendered unfit
for use in building, is continued in this
verse. No empire shall again have
Babylon for its centre. Its position as
a capital city is for ever shattered, and its
glory burnt out' (Streane).

27. *set ye up a standard.* To rally the
nations which will join in the attack upon
Babylon.

prepare. lit. 'sanctify' (see on vi. 4).

Ararat. The Assyrian Urartu, north-
west of Lake Van, a district which
included part of Armenia.

Minni. Occurs on Assyrian inscriptions
as 'Mannai'; not far from Lake Van.

Ashkenaz. Cf. Gen. x. 3; probably near
the two former.

marshal. The Hebrew is *tiphsar*, corresponding to the Assyrian *dupsarru*,
'tablet-writer,' a term for an official.
In Nahum iii. 17 the large number of
such officials is compared with *swarms of
grasshoppers.*

the rough canker-worm. The word for
rough (*samar*) means 'bristling' and the
phrase describes the locusts 'in their third
stage, when their wings are still enveloped
in rough horny cases, which stick up upon
their backs. It is in this stage that they
are so destructive' (Payne Smith).

28. *kings.* See on verse 11.

governors . . . deputies. See on verse 23.

And all the land of his dominion.

29 And the land quaketh and is in pain;
For the purposes of the LORD are performed against Babylon,
To make the land of Babylon a desolation, without inhabitant.

30 The mighty men of Babylon have forborne to fight,
They remain in their strongholds;
Their might hath failed, they are become as women;
Her dwelling-places are set on fire;
Her bars are broken.

31 One post runneth to meet another,
And one messenger to meet another,
To tell the king of Babylon
That his city is taken on every quarter;

32 And the fords are seized,
And the castles they have burned with fire,
And the men of war are affrighted.

33 For thus saith the LORD of hosts, The God of Israel:

וְאֵת כָּל־אֶרֶץ מֶמְשַׁלְתּֽוֹ׃

29 וַתִּרְעַשׁ הָאָרֶץ וַתָּחֹל
כִּי קָמָה עַל־בָּבֶל
מַחְשְׁבוֹת יְהֹוָה
לָשׂוּם אֶת־אֶרֶץ בָּבֶל
לְשַׁמָּה מֵאֵין יוֹשֵֽׁב׃

30 חָדְלוּ גִבּוֹרֵי בָבֶל לְהִלָּחֵם
יָשְׁבוּ בַּמְּצָדוֹת
נָשְׁתָה גְבוּרָתָם הָיוּ לְנָשִׁים
הִצִּיתוּ מִשְׁכְּנֹתֶיהָ
נִשְׁבְּרוּ בְרִיחֶֽיהָ׃

31 רָץ לִקְרַאת־רָץ יָרוּץ
וּמַגִּיד לִקְרַאת מַגִּיד
לְהַגִּיד לְמֶלֶךְ בָּבֶל
כִּי־נִלְכְּדָה עִירוֹ מִקָּצֶֽה׃

32 וְהַמַּעְבָּרוֹת נִתְפָּשׂוּ
וְאֶת־הָאֲגַמִּים שָׂרְפוּ בָאֵשׁ
וְאַנְשֵׁי הַמִּלְחָמָה נִבְהָֽלוּ׃

33 כִּי כֹה אָמַר יְהֹוָה צְבָאוֹת
אֱלֹהֵי יִשְׂרָאֵל

v. 32. קמץ בז״ק

---

all the land of his dominion. The king of Media is to gather men from the peoples over whom he rules.

30. are set on fire. lit. 'they (the enemy) have burnt her dwelling-places' (A.V.).

31. to meet another. The messengers with news of defeat after defeat converge as they approach the king's palace from all sides. Or, as one messenger who has already given his message leaves, he is met by another bringing further tidings of disaster.

32. fords. Modern authorities prefer the translation 'ferries.'

the castles. The rendering of A.J. cannot be defended. Normally agam signifies 'a pool of water'; but since this cannot be 'burned' A.V. and R.V. substitute 'reeds.' A. Cohen (American Journal of Semitic Languages, vol. xl. p. 159) has pointed out that the cognate noun in Arabic means 'thicket' and is found in that sense in Rabbinical Hebrew. Such an interpretation would be suitable here.

The daughter of Babylon is like
a threshing-floor
At the time when it is trodden;
Yet a little while, and the time of
harvest
Shall come for her.

34 Nebuchadrezzar the king of
Babylon hath devoured me,
He hath crushed me,
He hath set me down as an
empty vessel,
He hath swallowed me up like a
dragon,
He hath filled his maw with my
delicacies;
He hath washed me clean.

35 'The violence done to me and to
my flesh be upon Babylon,'
Shall the inhabitant of Zion say;
And: 'My blood be upon the
inhabitants of Chaldea,'
Shall Jerusalem say.

36 Therefore thus saith the LORD:
Behold, I will plead thy cause,
And take vengeance for thee;
And I will dry up her sea,
And make her fountain dry.

37 And Babylon shall become heaps,

בַּת־בָּבֶל כְּגֹרֶן עֵת הִדְרִיכָהּ
עוֹד מְעַט
וּבָאָה עֵת־הַקָּצִיר לָהּ:

34 אֲכָלָנוּ הֲמָמַנּוּ
נְבוּכַדְרֶאצַּר מֶלֶךְ בָּבֶל
הִצִּיגָנוּ כְּלִי רִיק
בְּלָעָנוּ כַּתַּנִּין
מִלָּא כְרֵשׂוֹ מֵעֲדָנָי
הֱדִיחָנוּ:

35 חֲמָסִי וּשְׁאֵרִי עַל־בָּבֶל
תֹּאמַר יֹשֶׁבֶת צִיּוֹן
וְדָמִי אֶל־יֹשְׁבֵי כַשְׂדִּים
תֹּאמַר יְרוּשָׁלָ͏ִם:

36 לָכֵן כֹּה אָמַר יְהֹוָה
הִנְנִי־רָב אֶת־רִיבֵךְ
וְנִקַּמְתִּי אֶת־נִקְמָתֵךְ
וְהַחֲרַבְתִּי אֶת־יַמָּהּ
וְהֹבַשְׁתִּי אֶת־מְקוֹרָהּ:

37 וְהָיְתָה בָבֶל | לְגַלִּים |

v. 34. אכלני ק׳   v. 34. הממני ק׳   v. 34. הציגני ק׳   v. 34. בלעני ק׳   v. 34. הדיחני ק׳

---

33. *at the time . . . trodden.* So has her time come to be trodden down.

the time of harvest shall come for her. The *harvest* will be reaped by the enemy. Babylon will be despoiled. Cf. Isa. xvii. 5; Joel iv. 13.

34. *me.* i.e. Israel.

dragon. The Hebrew *tannin* denotes any great sea monster.

delicacies. National treasures.

he hath washed me clean. He has made a clean sweep of my possessions, leaving me with nothing.

35. *the violence done to me . . . be upon.* The same idiomatic phrase occurs in Gen. xvi. 5, *my wrong be upon thee.*

36. *her sea . . . her fountain.* The allusion may be to the Euphrates or the great reservoir, 420 furlongs in circumference, made by Queen Nitocris, or the lake constructed by Nebuchadnezzar.

A dwelling-place for jackals,
An astonishment, and a hissing,
Without inhabitant.

38 They shall roar together like
young lions;
They shall growl as lions' whelps.

39 With their poison I will prepare
their feast,
And I will make them drunken,
that they may be convulsed,
And sleep a perpetual sleep, and
not wake,
Saith the LORD.

40 I will bring them down like
lambs to the slaughter,
Like rams with he-goats.

41 How is Sheshach taken!
And the praise of the whole earth
seized!
How is Babylon become an
astonishment
Among the nations!

42 The sea is come up upon
Babylon;
She is covered with the multi-
tude of the waves thereof.

43 Her cities are become a desolation,

מְעוֹן־תַּנִּים
שַׁמָּה וּשְׁרֵקָה
מֵאֵין יוֹשֵׁב:

38 יַחְדָּו כַּכְּפִרִים יִשְׁאָגוּ
נָעֲרוּ כְּגוֹרֵי אֲרָיוֹת:

39 בְּחֻמָּם אָשִׁית אֶת־מִשְׁתֵּיהֶם
וְהִשְׁכַּרְתִּים לְמַעַן יַעֲלֹזוּ
וְיָשְׁנוּ שְׁנַת־עוֹלָם וְלֹא יָקִיצוּ
נְאֻם יְהוָה:

40 אוֹרִידֵם כְּכָרִים לִטְבוֹחַ
כְּאֵילִים עִם־עַתּוּדִים:

41 אֵיךְ נִלְכְּדָה שֵׁשַׁךְ
וַתִּתָּפֵשׂ תְּהִלַּת כָּל־הָאָרֶץ
אֵיךְ הָיְתָה לְשַׁמָּה
בָּבֶל בַּגּוֹיִם:

42 עָלָה עַל־בָּבֶל הַיָּם
בַּהֲמוֹן גַּלָּיו נִכְסָתָה:

43 הָיוּ עָרֶיהָ לְשַׁמָּה

38. *they shall roar.* The subject may be the Babylonians: they will cry out in distress as young lions roar when hungry. Alternatively *they* refers to the enemy. The latter is more plausible in itself, but it involves an abrupt change of subject, since the preceding and following verses certainly have reference to the Babylonians. Hence the former is perhaps preferable.

39. *with their poison.* More accurately, 'in their heat' (A.V.) or 'when they are heated' (R.V.), inflamed with desire. While they are revelling and carousing, God will introduce something into their feast which will induce a sleep from which they will never awake. Cf. the story of Belshazzar's banquet (Dan. v.).

40. *lambs . . . rams . . . he-goats.* Typifying the various sections of the population, the last-named representing the leaders (see on l. 8).

41. *Sheshach.* A cryptic name of Babylon (see on xxv. 26).

the praise of the whole earth. Babylon's magnificence and power evoked widespread admiration (cf. Isa. xiii. 19).

42. *the sea.* The flood of enemy troops (cf. xlvi. 7f.).

A dry land, and a desert,
A land wherein no man dwelleth,
Neither doth any son of man
    pass thereby.

44 And I will punish Bel in Babylon,
And I will bring forth out of his
    mouth that which he hath
    swallowed up,
And the nations shall not flow
    any more unto him;
Yea, the wall of Babylon shall
    fall.

45 My people, go ye out of the
    midst of her,
And save yourselves every man
From the fierce anger of the
    LORD.

46 And let not your heart faint,
    neither fear ye,
For the rumour that shall be
    heard in the land;
For a rumour shall come one
    year,
And after that in another year a
    rumour,
And violence in the land, ruler
    against ruler.

47 Therefore, behold, the days
    come,

אֶ֣רֶץ צִיָּ֔ה וַעֲרָבָ֑ה
אֶ֗רֶץ לֹֽא־יֵשֵׁ֤ב בָּהֵן֙ כָּל־אִ֔ישׁ
וְלֹֽא־יַעֲבֹ֥ר בָּהֵ֖ן בֶּן־אָדָֽם׃

44 וּפָקַדְתִּ֥י עַל־בֵּ֖ל בְּבָבֶ֑ל
וְהֹצֵאתִ֤י אֶת־בִּלְעוֹ֙ מִפִּ֔יו
וְלֹֽא־יִנְהֲר֥וּ אֵלָ֛יו ע֖וֹד גּוֹיִ֑ם
גַּם־חוֹמַ֥ת בָּבֶ֖ל נָפָֽלָה׃

45 צְא֤וּ מִתּוֹכָהּ֙ עַמִּ֔י
וּמַלְּט֖וּ אִ֣ישׁ אֶת־נַפְשׁ֑וֹ
מֵחֲר֖וֹן אַף־יְהוָֽה׃

46 וּפֶן־יֵרַ֤ךְ לְבַבְכֶם֙ וְתִֽירְא֔וּ
בַּשְּׁמוּעָ֖ה הַנִּשְׁמַ֣עַת בָּאָ֑רֶץ
וּבָ֤א בַשָּׁנָה֙ הַשְּׁמוּעָ֔ה
וְאַחֲרָ֤יו בַּשָּׁנָה֙ הַשְּׁמוּעָ֔ה
וְחָמָ֣ס בָּאָ֔רֶץ מֹשֵׁ֖ל עַל־מֹשֵֽׁל׃

47 לָכֵן֙ הִנֵּ֣ה יָמִ֣ים בָּאִ֔ים

---

44. *I will punish Bel in Babylon.* For
Bel, cf. l. 2. The nation is identified
with its deity, so that the disaster which
overwhelms the former also involves the
latter, and the despoiling of the nation is
tantamount to depriving its deity of its
ill-gotten wealth.

that which he hath swallowed up. The
riches of conquered peoples.

shall not flow any more unto him. Bel's
impotence having been made manifest,
none will pay it further homage.

the wall of Babylon. Its defence against
attack. With the wall gone, the city is
open to the invader.

45. Cf. verse 6.

46. A picture of the disquiet which will
precede Babylon's final dissolution:
rumour following on rumour and inter-
necine war between her leaders. The
Jews are bidden to remain calm and
confident throughout the anxious period.

and let not your heart faint. More lit.
'and (beware) lest your heart faint.'

one year . . . another year. The in-
ference is that the time of anxiety will be
protracted. 'Four or five years would
be a brief prelude to the downfall of an
empire, and yet it might be a time of
racking suspense, intolerably long to live
through day by day' (Peake).

47. The verse resembles verse 52.

That I will do judgment upon
the graven images of Babylon,
And her whole land shall be
ashamed;
And all her slain shall fall in the
midst of her.

48 Then the heaven and the earth,
and all that is therein,
Shall sing for joy over Babylon;
For the spoilers shall come unto
her
From the north, saith the LORD.

49 As Babylon hath caused the slain
of Israel to fall,
So at Babylon shall fall the slain
of all the land.

50 Ye that have escaped the sword,
Go ye, stand not still;
Remember the LORD from afar,
And let Jerusalem come into your
mind.

51 'We are ashamed, because we
have heard reproach,

וּפָקַדְתִּי עַל־פְּסִילֵי בָבֶל
וְכָל־אַרְצָהּ תֵּבֹושׁ
וְכָל־חֲלָלֶיהָ יִפְּלוּ בְתוֹכָהּ׃
48 וְרִנְּנוּ עַל־בָּבֶל שָׁמַיִם וָאָרֶץ
וְכֹל אֲשֶׁר בָּהֶם
כִּי מִצָּפוֹן
יָבוֹא־לָהּ הַשּׁוֹדְדִים
נְאֻם־יְהֹוָה׃
49 גַּם־בָּבֶל לִנְפֹּל חַלְלֵי יִשְׂרָאֵל
גַּם־לְבָבֶל נָפְלוּ
חַלְלֵי כָל־הָאָרֶץ׃
50 פְּלֵטִים מֵחֶרֶב
הִלְכוּ אַל־תַּעֲמֹדוּ
זִכְרוּ מֵרָחוֹק אֶת־יְהֹוָה
וִירוּשָׁלַ͏ִם
תַּעֲלֶה עַל־לְבַבְכֶם׃
51 בֹּשְׁנוּ כִּי־שָׁמַעְנוּ חֶרְפָּה

v. 48. סבירין יבואו

---

48. *the heaven and the earth.* They are
similarly called upon to rejoice over
Israel's redemption in Isa. xliv. 23.

over Babylon. Over her discomfiture.

from the north. Alluding to the Persians.

49. *as Babylon hath caused,* etc. This
rendering, in which Rashi and Kimchi
concur, assumes that the Hebrew is
elliptical, the equivalent of *hath caused*
being omitted, or that the *kal* conjugation
of the verb is used with the force of the
hiphil. It is preferable to construe
the slain of Israel as vocative: 'Both
Babylon is to fall, O ye slain of Israel,
and at Babylon have fallen' etc. (R.V.
margin, but substituting 'have fallen' for
'shall fall'). As the slain of all the earth

have fallen at Babylon, it is fitting that
now her own shall fall there.

50. The verse is addressed to the
Judeans in Babylon who had survived
the overthrow of their land.

go ye. Back to Judea.

from afar. From Babylon which is
distant from Judea.

let Jerusalem . . . mind. i.e. the hope of
returning there.

51. *we are ashamed,* etc. The answer of
the Judean exiles: they feel keenly the
taunt that their Temple in ruins is
evidence that their God had abandoned
them.

Confusion hath covered our
faces;
For strangers are come
Into the sanctuaries of the LORD's
house.'

52 Wherefore, behold, the days
come, saith the LORD,
That I will do judgment upon
her graven images;
And through all her land the
wounded shall groan.

53 Though Babylon should mount
up to heaven,
And though she should fortify
the height of her strength,
Yet from Me shall spoilers come
unto her, saith the LORD.

54 Hark! a cry from Babylon,
And great destruction from the
land of the Chaldeans!

55 For the LORD spoileth Babylon,
And destroyeth out of her the
great voice;
And their waves roar like many
waters,
The noise of their voice is
uttered;

56 For the spoiler is come upon her,
even upon Babylon,
And her mighty men are taken,
Their bows are shattered;
For the LORD is a God of
recompenses,
He will surely requite.

בָּסְתָה כְלִמָּה פָּנֵינוּ
כִּי בָּאוּ זָרִים
עַל־מִקְדְּשֵׁי בֵּית יְהוָה:
52 לָכֵן הִנֵּה־יָמִים בָּאִים
נְאֻם־יְהוָה
וּפָקַדְתִּי עַל־פְּסִילֶיהָ
וּבְכָל־אַרְצָהּ יֶאֱנֹק חָלָל:
53 כִּי־תַעֲלֶה בָבֶל הַשָּׁמַיִם
וְכִי תְבַצֵּר מְרוֹם עֻזָּהּ
מֵאִתִּי יָבֹאוּ שֹׁדְדִים
לָהּ נְאֻם־יְהוָה:
54 קוֹל זְעָקָה מִבָּבֶל
וְשֶׁבֶר גָּדוֹל מֵאֶרֶץ כַּשְׂדִּים:
55 כִּי־שֹׁדֵד יְהוָה אֶת־בָּבֶל
וְאִבַּד מִמֶּנָּה קוֹל גָּדוֹל
וְהָמוּ גַלֵּיהֶם כְּמַיִם רַבִּים
נִתַּן שְׁאוֹן קוֹלָם:
56 כִּי בָא עָלֶיהָ עַל־בָּבֶל שׁוֹדֵד
וְנִלְכְּדוּ גִּבּוֹרֶיהָ
חִתְּתָה קַשְּׁתוֹתָם
כִּי אֵל גְּמֻלוֹת יְהוָה
שַׁלֵּם יְשַׁלֵּם:

כצ״ל v. 56.

the sanctuaries. The various parts of
the Temple, each of which was a sacred
place.

52. *I will do judgment upon her graven
images.* Thus silencing the reproaches
of the Babylonians.

53. Cf. the language used against Edom

in xlix. 16, and against Babylon in
Isa. xiv. 13ff.

55. *the great voice.* The clamour of the
thronged population.

their waves. Kimchi understands this
of the Chaldeans; but more probably it
refers to the tumult of the attacking
enemy which will drown the noise
within the doomed city.

57 And I will make drunk her
princes and her wise men,
Her governors and her deputies,
and her mighty men;
And they shall sleep a perpetual
sleep, and not wake,
Saith the King, whose name is
the LORD of hosts.

58 Thus saith the LORD of hosts:
The broad walls of Babylon shall
be utterly overthrown,
And her high gates shall be
burned with fire;
And the peoples shall labour for
vanity,
And the nations for the fire;
And they shall be weary.

59. The word which Jeremiah the
prophet commanded Seraiah the son
of Neriah, the son of Mahseiah,
when he went with Zedekiah the

57 וְהִשְׁכַּרְתִּי שָׂרֶיהָ וַחֲכָמֶיהָ
פַּחוֹתֶיהָ וּסְגָנֶיהָ וְגִבּוֹרֶיהָ
וְיָשְׁנוּ שְׁנַת־עוֹלָם וְלֹא יָקִיצוּ
נְאֻם־הַמֶּלֶךְ
יְהוָה צְבָאוֹת שְׁמוֹ׃
58 כֹּה־אָמַר יְהוָה צְבָאוֹת
חֹמוֹת בָּבֶל הָרְחָבָה
עַרְעֵר תִּתְעַרְעָר
וּשְׁעָרֶיהָ הַגְּבֹהִים בָּאֵשׁ יִצַּתּוּ
וְיִגְעוּ עַמִּים בְּדֵי־רִיק
וּלְאֻמִּים בְּדֵי־אֵשׁ
וְיָעֵפוּ׃
59 הַדָּבָר אֲשֶׁר־צִוָּה ׀ יִרְמְיָהוּ
הַנָּבִיא אֶת־שְׂרָיָה בֶן־
נֵרִיָּה בֶּן־מַחְסֵיָה בְּלֶכְתּוֹ
אֶת־צִדְקִיָּהוּ מֶלֶךְ־יְהוּדָה

v. 58. ‏פתח באתנח‎

---

58. *the broad walls of Babylon.* 'According-
ing to Herodotus, the outer wall of
Babylon was 200 royal cubits (about
373 English feet) high, while it was
50 cubits wide. This, however, both
from the nature of the case, and from
the conflicting testimony of other writers,
seems exaggerated. Probably the height
was about 60 or 70 English feet. The
walls may have been 30 or 40 feet wide,
as they allowed a team of four horses
being driven along them' (Streane).
The walls were demolished by Darius.
utterly overthrown. More lit. 'made
bare' (R.V. margin); so completely will
they be razed to the ground that their
foundations will be exposed.
high gates. 'In the circuit of the walls
are a hundred gates, all of brass, with

brazen lintels and side-posts' (Herodotus
I, 179).
the peoples . . . weary. The language
resembles that of Hab. ii. 13. 'Jeremiah
throws light on Habakkuk's meaning,
and at the same time gives it a more
particular application. The fact that
the Chaldean conquests involve nothing
in the end but exhaustion and suffering
to the nations who have to do the
behests of their ambitious rulers is by
Jeremiah applied to the final overthrow
of the Babylonian empire' (Streane).

59-64 JEREMIAH'S INSTRUCTION
TO SERAIAH

59. *the son of Neriah.* Accordingly,
Seraiah was Baruch's brother (cf. xxxii.
12).

king of Judah to Babylon in the fourth year of his reign. Now Seraiah was quartermaster. 60. And Jeremiah wrote in one book all the evil that should come upon Babylon, even all these words that are written concerning Babylon. 61. And Jeremiah said to Seraiah: 'When thou comest to Babylon, then see that thou read all these words, 62. and say: O LORD, Thou hast spoken concerning this place, to cut it off, that none shall dwell therein, neither man nor beast, but that it shall be desolate for ever. 63. And it shall be, when thou hast made an end of reading this book, that thou shalt bind a stone to it, and cast it into

בְּבֶל בִּשְׁנַת הָרְבִעִית לְמָלְכוֹ
וּשְׂרָיָה שַׂר־מְנוּחָה: וַיִּכְתֹּב 60
יִרְמְיָהוּ אֵת כָּל־הָרָעָה
אֲשֶׁר־תָּבוֹא אֶל־בָּבֶל אֶל־
סֵפֶר אֶחָד אֵת כָּל־הַדְּבָרִים
הָאֵלֶּה הַכְּתֻבִים אֶל־בָּבֶל:
וַיֹּאמֶר יִרְמְיָהוּ אֶל־שְׂרָיָה 61
כְּבֹאֲךָ בָבֶל וְרָאִיתָ וְקָרָאתָ
אֵת כָּל־הַדְּבָרִים הָאֵלֶּה:
וְאָמַרְתָּ יְהוָֹה אַתָּה דִבַּרְתָּ 62
אֶל־הַמָּקוֹם הַזֶּה לְהַכְרִיתוֹ
לְבִלְתִּי הֱיוֹת־בּוֹ יוֹשֵׁב
לְמֵאָדָם וְעַד־בְּהֵמָה כִּי־
שִׁמְמוֹת עוֹלָם תִּהְיֶה: וְהָיָה 63
כְּכַלֹּתְךָ לִקְרֹא אֶת־הַסֵּפֶר
הַזֶּה תִּקְשֹׁר עָלָיו אֶבֶן

---

to Babylon. This visit of Zedekiah is not recorded elsewhere. He may have gone to pay homage to Nebuchadnezzar and clear himself from the suspicion of being implicated in the revolt which was then brewing.

in the fourth year of his reign. Cf. xxviii. 1ff. If Hananiah's prophecy of speedy liberation from the Babylonian yoke represented popular hopes and expectations, as it probably did, it would make it all the more necessary for Zedekiah to assure Nebuchadnezzar of his loyalty.

quartermaster. A questionable translation. The commonly accepted explanation is that he was 'prince of the camping place (*menuchah*)' whose duty was to arrange for the king's accommodation while on a journey. Ehrlich offers an

ingenious interpretation: in 1 Kings viii. 56 and 1 Chron. xxii. 9 the noun *menuchah* signifies the opposite of war. Accordingly, Seraiah may here be described as a leader of the peace party in Judea.

60. *in one book.* i.e. on a separate roll of parchment.

61. *then see that thou read.* Better as R.V. margin: 'and shalt see and read,' i.e. thou shalt look at the scroll and read the prophecy. The reading could not have been done in public since it would have been a dangerous thing to do; he was to read it to himself or to a few of the leading Judeans in Babylon.

63. Jeremiah's prophecies were often re-enforced by symbolical action (cf. xiii. 1ff., xix. 1ff., xxvii. 2ff., xliii. 9ff.).

the midst of the Euphrates; 64. and thou shalt say: Thus shall Babylon sink, and shall not rise again because of the evil that I will bring upon her; and they shall be weary.'

Thus far are the words of Jeremiah.

וְהִשְׁלַכְתּוֹ אֶל־תּוֹךְ פְּרָת:

64 וְאָמַרְתָּ כָּכָה תִּשְׁקַע בָּבֶל וְלֹא־תָקוּם מִפְּנֵי הָרָעָה אֲשֶׁר אָנֹכִי מֵבִיא עָלֶיהָ וְיָעֵפוּ עַד־הֵנָּה דִּבְרֵי יִרְמְיָהוּ:

52   CHAPTER LII   נב

1. Zedekiah was one and twenty years old when he began to reign; and he reigned eleven years in Jerusalem; and his mother's name was Hamutal the daughter of Jeremiah of Libnah. 2. And he did that which was evil in the sight of the LORD, according to all that Jehoiakim had done. 3. For through the anger of the LORD did it come to pass in Jerusalem and Judah, until He had cast them out from His presence. And Zedekiah rebelled against the king of Babylon. 4. And it came to pass in the ninth year of his reign, in the tenth month, in the tenth day of

1 בֶּן־עֶשְׂרִים וְאַחַת שָׁנָה צִדְקִיָּהוּ בְמָלְכוֹ וְאַחַת עֶשְׂרֵה שָׁנָה מָלַךְ בִּירוּשָׁלָ͏ִם וְשֵׁם אִמּוֹ חֲמִיטַל בַּת־יִרְמְיָהוּ 2 מִלִּבְנָה: וַיַּעַשׂ הָרַע בְּעֵינֵי יְהוָֹה כְּכֹל אֲשֶׁר־עָשָׂה 3 יְהוֹיָקִים: כִּי עַל־אַף יְהוָֹה הָיְתָה בִּירוּשָׁלַ͏ִם וִיהוּדָה עַד־הִשְׁלִיכוֹ אוֹתָם מֵעַל פָּנָיו וַיִּמְרֹד צִדְקִיָּהוּ בְּמֶלֶךְ בָּבֶל: 4 וַיְהִי בַשָּׁנָה הַתְּשִׁעִית לְמָלְכוֹ בַּחֹדֶשׁ הָעֲשִׂירִי בֶּעָשׂוֹר

חמוטל ק׳   v. 1.

64. *and they shall be weary.* This is the conclusion of verse 58, and is probably to be connected with *thus far*, etc. The oracles of Jeremiah end there, and verses 59-64 are an appendix.

thus far are the words of Jeremiah. This implies that the chapter which follows is not by Jeremiah's hand. It is taken largely from 2 Kings xxiv. 18-xxv. 30.

CHAPTER LII
THE FALL OF JERUSALEM

1. *when he began to reign.* In the year 597 B.C.E.

Hamutal. He was a full brother of Jehoahaz but half brother of Jehoiakim (2 Kings xxiii. 31, 36).

3. *did it come to pass.* The persistence of Zedekiah in his evil ways brought down upon his kingdom this manifestation of God's anger.

4-16. This is paralleled by xxxix. 1-10.

4. *in the tenth month, in the tenth day of the month.* This date marked the beginning of the siege. In commemoration the day was proclaimed a public fast

the month, that Nebuchadrezzar king of Babylon came, he and all his army, against Jerusalem, and encamped against it; and they built forts against it round about. 5. So the city was besieged unto the eleventh year of king Zedekiah. 6. In the fourth month, in the ninth day of the month, the famine was sore in the city, so that there was no bread for the people of the land. 7. Then a breach was made in the city, and all the men of war fled, and went forth out of the city by night by the way of the gate between the two walls, which was by the king's garden—now the Chaldeans were against the city round about—and they went by the way of the Arabah. 8. But the army of the Chaldeans pursued after the king, and overtook Zedekiah in the plains of Jericho; and all his army was scattered from him. 9. Then they took the king, and carried him up unto the king of Babylon to Riblah in the land of Hamath; and he gave

לַחֹדֶשׁ בָּא נְבוּכַדְרֶאצַּר
מֶלֶךְ־בָּבֶל הוּא וְכָל־חֵילוֹ
עַל־יְרוּשָׁלַם וַיַּחֲנוּ עָלֶיהָ
5 וַיִּבְנוּ עָלֶיהָ דָּיֵק סָבִיב: וַתָּבֹא
הָעִיר בַּמָּצוֹר עַד עַשְׁתֵּי־
עֶשְׂרֵה שָׁנָה לַמֶּלֶךְ צִדְקִיָּהוּ:
6 בַּחֹדֶשׁ הָרְבִיעִי בְּתִשְׁעָה
לַחֹדֶשׁ וַיֶּחֱזַק הָרָעָב בָּעִיר
וְלֹא־הָיָה לֶחֶם לְעַם הָאָרֶץ:
7 וַתִּבָּקַע הָעִיר וְכָל־אַנְשֵׁי
הַמִּלְחָמָה יִבְרְחוּ וַיֵּצְאוּ
מֵהָעִיר לַיְלָה דֶּרֶךְ שַׁעַר בֵּין־
הַחֹמֹתַיִם אֲשֶׁר עַל־גַּן הַמֶּלֶךְ
וְכַשְׂדִּים עַל־הָעִיר סָבִיב
8 וַיֵּלְכוּ דֶּרֶךְ הָעֲרָבָה: וַיִּרְדְּפוּ
חֵיל־כַּשְׂדִּים אַחֲרֵי הַמֶּלֶךְ
וַיַּשִּׂיגוּ אֶת־צִדְקִיָּהוּ בְּעַרְבֹת
יְרֵחוֹ וְכָל־חֵילוֹ נָפֹצוּ מֵעָלָיו:
9 וַיִּתְפְּשׂוּ אֶת־הַמֶּלֶךְ וַיַּעֲלוּ
אֹתוֹ אֶל־מֶלֶךְ בָּבֶל רִבְלָתָה
בְּאֶרֶץ חֲמָת וַיְדַבֵּר אִתּוֹ

(cf. Zech. viii. 19) and is still so observed by Jews.

6. in the fourth month, in the ninth day. This day was also instituted as a fast (Zech. viii. 19); but it was later replaced by a fast observed on the seventeenth of the month on which day the walls of the Second Temple were breached by Titus.

the famine. It is graphically described in Lam. ii. 19f., iv. 4, v. 10.

the people of the land. From the description in *Lamentations* it is evident that this term embraces all classes of the population.

7. between the two walls, etc. See on xxxix. 4.

9. Riblah. See on xxxix. 5.

in the land of Hamath. Omitted in 2 Kings xxv. 6.

judgment upon him. 10. And the king of Babylon slew the sons of Zedekiah before his eyes; he slew also all the princes of Judah in Riblah. 11. And he put out the eyes of Zedekiah; and the king of Babylon bound him in fetters, and carried him to Babylon, and put him in prison till the day of his death.

12. Now in the fifth month, in the tenth day of the month, which was the nineteenth year of king Nebuchadrezzar, king of Babylon, came Nebuzaradan the captain of the guard, who stood before the king of Babylon, into Jerusalem; 13. and he burned the house of the LORD, and the king's house; and all the houses of Jerusalem, even every great man's house, burned he with fire. 14. And all the army of the Chaldeans, that were with the captain of the guard, broke down all the walls of Jerusalem

10 מִשְׁפָּטִים: וַיִּשְׁחַט מֶלֶךְ־
בָּבֶל אֶת־בְּנֵי צִדְקִיָּהוּ לְעֵינָיו
וְגַם אֶת־כָּל־שָׂרֵי יְהוּדָה
11 שָׁחַט בְּרִבְלָתָה: וְאֶת־עֵינֵי
צִדְקִיָּהוּ עִוֵּר וַיַּאַסְרֵהוּ
בַנְחֻשְׁתַּיִם וַיְבִאֵהוּ מֶלֶךְ־
בָּבֶל בָּבֶלָה וַיִּתְּנֵהוּ בְבֵית־
הַפְּקֻדֹּת עַד־יוֹם מוֹתוֹ:
12 וּבַחֹדֶשׁ הַחֲמִישִׁי בֶּעָשׂוֹר
לַחֹדֶשׁ הִיא שְׁנַת תְּשַׁע־
עֶשְׂרֵה שָׁנָה לַמֶּלֶךְ
נְבוּכַדְרֶאצַּר מֶלֶךְ־בָּבֶל בָּא
נְבוּזַרְאֲדָן רַב־טַבָּחִים עָמַד
לִפְנֵי מֶלֶךְ־בָּבֶל בִּירוּשָׁלָם:
13 וַיִּשְׂרֹף אֶת־בֵּית־יְהֹוָה וְאֶת־
בֵּית הַמֶּלֶךְ וְאֵת כָּל־בָּתֵּי
יְרוּשָׁלַם וְאֶת־כָּל־בֵּית
14 הַגָּדוֹל שָׂרַף בָּאֵשׁ: וְאֶת־
כָּל־חֹמוֹת יְרוּשָׁלַם סָבִיב

v. 11. בית ק'

---

10. *he slew also . . . Riblah.* Omitted in 2 Kings xxv. 7.

11. *and put him in prison . . . death.* Not included in 2 Kings 'which takes leave of Zedekiah at Riblah, since that record was probably made before anything further could be learned of him' (Streane).

12. *the tenth day of the month.* 2 Kings xxv. 8 has *the seventh day.* The interval of three days may be accounted for as representing the date of Nebuzaradan's

arrival on the scene and the commencement of operations. The Rabbis explained that Nebuzaradan entered the Temple on the seventh, set it on fire on the ninth and it burned until the tenth. Since the destruction of the Second Temple, a fast is kept on the ninth of the month.

the nineteenth year. i.e. 586 B.C.E.

13. *even every great man's house.* Omitted in xxxix. 8; the mansions of the rich.

14. *broke down all the walls of Jerusalem*

round about. 15. Then Nebuzaradan the captain of the guard carried
away captive of the poorest sort of
the people, and the residue of the
people that remained in the city, and
those that fell away, that fell to the
king of Babylon, and the residue of
the multitude. 16. But Nebuzaradan the captain of the guard left of
the poorest of the land to be vine-
dressers and husbandmen. 17. And
the pillars of brass that were in the
house of the LORD, and the bases
and the brazen sea that were in the
house of the LORD, did the Chaldeans break in pieces, and carried
all the brass of them to Babylon.
18. The pots also, and the shovels,

נָתְצוּ כָל־חֵיל כַּשְׂדִּים אֲשֶׁר
15 אֶת־רַב־טַבָּחִים: וּמִדַּלּוֹת
הָעָם וְאֶת־יֶתֶר הָעָם |
הַנִּשְׁאָרִים בָּעִיר וְאֶת־
הַנֹּפְלִים אֲשֶׁר נָפְלוּ אֶל־מֶלֶךְ
בָּבֶל וְאֵת יֶתֶר הָאָמוֹן הֶגְלָה
נְבוּזַרְאֲדָן רַב־טַבָּחִים:
16 וּמִדַּלּוֹת הָאָרֶץ הִשְׁאִיר
נְבוּזַרְאֲדָן רַב־טַבָּחִים
17 לְכֹרְמִים וּלְיֹגְבִים: וְאֶת־
עַמּוּדֵי הַנְּחֹשֶׁת אֲשֶׁר לְבֵית־
יְהוָה וְאֶת־הַמְּכֹנוֹת וְאֶת־יָם
הַנְּחֹשֶׁת אֲשֶׁר בְּבֵית־יְהוָה
שִׁבְּרוּ כַשְׂדִּים וַיִּשְׂאוּ אֶת־
18 כָּל־נְחֻשְׁתָּם בָּבֶלָה: וְאֶת־
הַסִּרוֹת וְאֶת־הַיָּעִים וְאֶת־

round about. 'Jeremiah survived to
behold the sad accomplishment of all his
darkest predictions. He witnessed all
the horrors of the famine, and, when that
had done its work, the triumph of the
enemy. He saw the strongholds of the
city cast down; the palace of Solomon,
the Temple of God, with all its courts,
its roofs of cedar and gold, levelled to
the earth, or committed to the flames;
the sacred vessels, the ark of the covenant
itself, with the cherubim, pillaged by
profane hands. What were the feelings
of a patriotic and religious Jew at this
tremendous crisis, he has left on record
in his unrivalled elegies. Never did city
suffer a more miserable fate, never was
ruined city lamented in language so
exquisitely pathetic' (Milman).

15. *of the poorest sort of the people.* But

not all the inhabitants, as the next verse
makes clear.

that remained in the city. Who had not
been killed in the final attack. This
seems to imply very heavy casualties.

17-23. A description of the sacred
vessels which were carried away. The
account is fuller than that given in
2 Kings xxv. 13-17, and is altogether
absent from the corresponding passage
in chapter xxxix above.

17. *break in pieces.* They were too large
to be carried away whole.

18f. The vessels were of pure gold
(1 Kings vii. 50; cf. Exod. xxv. 29).

18. *the pots.* In which the ashes of the
altar of burnt-offerings were removed
(Exod. xxvii. 3).

and the snuffers, and the basins, and
the pans, and all the vessels of brass
wherewith they ministered, took
they away. 19. And the cups, and
the fire-pans, and the basins, and the
pots, and the candlesticks, and the
pans, and the bowls—that which was
of gold, in gold, and that which was
of silver, in silver—the captain of
the guard took away. 20. The two
pillars, the one sea, and the twelve
brazen bulls that were under the
bases, which king Solomon had
made for the house of the LORD—
the brass of all these vessels was

הַמְזַמְּרוֹת וְאֶת־הַמִּזְרָקֹת־
וְאֶת־הַכַּפּוֹת וְאֵת כָּל־כְּלֵי
הַנְּחֹשֶׁת אֲשֶׁר־יְשָׁרְתוּ בָהֶם
לָקָחוּ: וְאֶת־הַסִּפִּים וְאֶת־ 19
הַמַּחְתֹּת וְאֶת־הַמִּזְרָקוֹת
וְאֶת־הַסִּירוֹת וְאֶת־הַמְּנֹרוֹת
וְאֶת־הַכַּפּוֹת וְאֶת־הַמְנַקִּיוֹת
אֲשֶׁר זָהָב זָהָב וַאֲשֶׁר־כֶּסֶף
כֶּסֶף לָקַח רַב טַבָּחִים:
הָעַמּוּדִים | שְׁנַיִם הַיָּם אֶחָד 20
וְהַבָּקָר שְׁנֵים־עָשָׂר נְחֹשֶׁת
אֲשֶׁר־תַּחַת הַמְּכֹנוֹת אֲשֶׁר
עָשָׂה הַמֶּלֶךְ שְׁלֹמֹה לְבֵית
יְהוָה לֹא־הָיָה מִשְׁקָל
לִנְחֻשְׁתָּם כָּל־הַכֵּלִים

v. 20. כצ״ל כתיב וקרי

shovels. Likewise used in connection
with the altar (Exod. xxvii. 3).

snuffers. For the lamps (Exod. xxv. 38;
Num. iv. 9; 1 Kings vii. 50).

basins. In which the blood of the
sacrifices was caught.

pans. Used in connection with the
incense.

19. cups. Rashi conjectures that they
were jars for receiving (or storing) the
blood, and quotes Exod. xii. 22 where
the Hebrew word rendered basin is the
singular of the noun used here.

basins . . . pots . . . pans. These are
enumerated in the preceding verse;
presumably they were different vessels,
although called by the same name.

the candlesticks. Cf. 1 Kings vii. 49.

bowls. Chalices used in the wine liba-
tions.

that which was of gold . . . in silver.
Idiomatic for 'whether of gold or silver.'

20. two pillars. Cf. 1 Kings vii. 15ff.

the one sea, and the twelve brazen bulls.
Cf. 1 Kings vii. 23ff.

that were under the bases. In Solomon's
Temple the bases were under the lavers,
whilst the bulls supported the sea.
Rashi tries to get over the difficulty by
suggesting that tachath here signifies
'near by.' Metsudath David refers to
2 Kings xvi. 17 where it is narrated how
king Ahaz cut off the borders of the bases,
and removed the laver from off them;
and took down the sea from off the brazen
oxen that were under it, and put it upon a
pavement of stone; and he conjectures

without weight.　21. And as for the pillars, the height of the one pillar was eighteen cubits; and a line of twelve cubits did compass it; and the thickness thereof was four fingers; it was hollow.　22. And a capital of brass was upon it; and the height of the one capital was five cubits, with network and pomegranates upon the capital round about, all of brass; and the second pillar also had like unto these, and pomegranates.　23. And there were ninety and six pomegranates on the outside; all the pomegranates were a hundred upon the network round about.

24. And the captain of the guard took Seraiah the chief priest, and Zephaniah the second priest, and the three keepers of the door; 25. and

21 וְהָעַמּוּדִים שְׁמֹנֶה עֶשְׂרֵה אַמָּה קוֹמָה הָעַמֻּד הָאֶחָד וְחוּט שְׁתֵּים־עֶשְׂרֵה אַמָּה יְסֻבֶּנּוּ וְעָבְיוֹ אַרְבַּע 22 אֶצְבָּעוֹת נָבוּב: וְכֹתֶרֶת עָלָיו נְחֹשֶׁת וְקוֹמַת הַכֹּתֶרֶת הָאַחַת חָמֵשׁ אַמּוֹת וּשְׂבָכָה וְרִמּוֹנִים עַל־הַכּוֹתֶרֶת סָבִיב הַכֹּל נְחֹשֶׁת וְכָאֵלֶּה לָעַמּוּד הַשֵּׁנִי 23 וְרִמּוֹנִים: וַיִּהְיוּ הָרִמֹּנִים תִּשְׁעִים וְשִׁשָּׁה רוּחָה כָּל־הָרִמּוֹנִים מֵאָה עַל־הַשְּׂבָכָה 24 סָבִיב: וַיִּקַּח רַב־טַבָּחִים אֶת־שְׂרָיָה כֹּהֵן הָרֹאשׁ וְאֶת־צְפַנְיָה כֹּהֵן הַמִּשְׁנֶה וְאֶת־ 25 שְׁלֹשֶׁת שֹׁמְרֵי הַסַּף: וּמִן־

v. 21. קומת ק׳

---

that Ahaz set the laver upon the oxen instead of the bases, understanding *tachath* here as 'instead of.'

21. *cubits.* A cubit was eighteen inches.
and the thickness . . . was hollow. This is not mentioned in 1 Kings but cf. 2 Chron. iv. 5 for the thickness.

22. *capital.* The ornamental head of the pillar.

pomegranates. A common form of decoration in the East which also figured upon the High Priest's vestment (Exod. xxviii. 33).

23. Comparing this verse with the parallel account in 1 Kings vii. 20, Rashi concludes that each pillar had two rows each of a hundred pomegranates, but that four of them were hidden owing to

the closeness of the pillars to the wall of the porch.

24-27. This passage is not included in chapter xxxix, but has its parallel in 2 Kings xxv. 18-21.

24. *Seraiah.* In Ezra vii. 1 Ezra is described as *the son of Seraiah*, where *son* probably means 'descendant.'

the chief priest. His ancestry is traced back in a direct descent from Aaron in 1 Chron. v. 29-40. The Hebrew for *chief priest* is not the usual term for 'High Priest,' but that office is doubtless intended.

Zephaniah. See on xxi. 1.

the second priest. Presumably the deputy High Priest.

keepers of the door. See on xxxv. 4.

out of the city he took an officer that was set over the men of war; and seven men of them that saw the king's face, who were found in the city; and the scribe of the captain of the host, who mustered the people of the land; and threescore men of the people of the land, that were found in the midst of the city. 26. And Nebuzaradan the captain of the guard took them, and brought them to the king of Babylon to Riblah. 27. And the king of Babylon smote them, and put them to death at Riblah in the land of Hamath. So Judah was carried away captive out of his land.

28. This is the people whom Nebuchadrezzar carried away captive: in the seventh year three

הָעִיר לָקַח סָרִיס אֶחָד אֲשֶׁר־
הָיָה פָקִיד | עַל־אַנְשֵׁי
הַמִּלְחָמָה וְשִׁבְעָה אֲנָשִׁים
מֵרֹאֵי פְנֵי־הַמֶּלֶךְ אֲשֶׁר־
נִמְצְאוּ בָעִיר וְאֵת סֹפֵר שַׂר
הַצָּבָא הַמַּצְבִּא אֶת־עַם
הָאָרֶץ וְשִׁשִּׁים אִישׁ מֵעַם
הָאָרֶץ הַנִּמְצָאִים בְּתוֹךְ
26 הָעִיר: וַיִּקַּח אוֹתָם נְבוּזַרְאֲדָן
רַב־טַבָּחִים וַיֹּלֶךְ אוֹתָם אֶל־
27 מֶלֶךְ בָּבֶל רִבְלָתָה: וַיַּכֶּה
אוֹתָם מֶלֶךְ בָּבֶל וַיְמִתֵם
בְּרִבְלָה בְּאֶרֶץ חֲמָת וַיִּגֶל
28 יְהוּדָה מֵעַל אַדְמָתוֹ: זֶה הָעָם
אֲשֶׁר הֶגְלָה נְבוּכַדְרֶאצַּר
בִּשְׁנַת־שֶׁבַע יְהוּדִים שְׁלֹשֶׁת

---

25. *an officer.* For the Hebrew *saris*, see on xxxviii. 7.

seven men. 2 Kings xxv. 19 has *five men.* Rashi conjectures that two of these seven were men of lesser importance (cf. Esth. i. 14 where it appears that seven men occupied the position referred to here in the Persian court).

of them that saw the king's face. High officials of the king who acted as his councillors. *Of them* implies that there were more than seven.

who were found in the city. Who had not escaped with the rest.

mustered. Organized for war.

the people of the land . . . the people of the land. Although the phrase is re-peated, the probability is that different meanings are to be attached to each. The first describes the general population of the country, from whom the army would be naturally drawn. The second may refer to a National Council (see on xxxiv. 19).

28-30. Enumeration of the deportees.

28. *in the seventh year.* 2 Kings xxiv. 12 reads *eighth year.* The deportation commenced at the end of the seventh and lasted into the eighth year (Kimchi). Rashi explains that it was the eighth year of Nebuchadnezzar's reign, but only the seventh of his suzerainty over Judea which he reduced to vassalage a year after ascending the throne. See the next note.

thousand Jews and three and twenty;

29. in the eighteenth year of Nebuchadrezzar, from Jerusalem, eight hundred thirty and two persons; 30. in the three and twentieth year of Nebuchadrezzar Nebuzaradan the captain of the guard carried away captive of the Jews seven hundred forty and five persons; all the persons were four thousand and six hundred.

31. And it came to pass in the seven and thirtieth year of the captivity of Jehoiachin king of Judah, in the twelfth month, in the five and twentieth day of the month,

אֲלָפִ֖ים וְעֶשְׂרִ֥ים וּשְׁלֹשָֽׁה׃

29 בִּשְׁנַת֙ שְׁמוֹנֶ֣ה עֶשְׂרֵ֔ה לִנְבֽוּכַדְרֶאצַּ֑ר מִירֽוּשָׁלִַ֗ם נֶ֛פֶשׁ שְׁמֹנֶ֥ה מֵא֖וֹת שְׁלֹשִֽׁים

30 וּשְׁנָֽיִם׃ בִּשְׁנַת֩ שָׁלֹ֨שׁ וְעֶשְׂרִ֜ים לִנְבֽוּכַדְרֶאצַּ֗ר הֶגְלָ֡ה נְבֽוּזַרְאֲדָן֩ רַב־טַבָּחִ֨ים יְהוּדִ֜ים נֶ֗פֶשׁ שְׁבַ֤ע מֵאוֹת֙ אַרְבָּעִ֣ים וַחֲמִשָּׁ֔ה כָּל־נֶ֕פֶשׁ אַרְבַּ֥עַת אֲלָפִ֖ים וְשֵׁ֥שׁ מֵאֽוֹת׃

31 וַיְהִי֩ בִשְׁלֹשִׁ֨ים וָשֶׁ֜בַע שָׁנָ֗ה לְגָלוּת֙ יְהוֹיָכִ֣ן מֶֽלֶךְ־יְהוּדָ֔ה בִּשְׁנֵ֤ים עָשָׂר֙ חֹ֔דֶשׁ בְּעֶשְׂרִ֥ים וַחֲמִשָּׁ֖ה לַחֹ֑דֶשׁ נָשָׂ֡א אֱוִ֣יל

---

three thousand Jews and three and twenty. 2 Kings xxiv. 14 gives the number as 10,000. *Jews* denotes members of the tribe of Judah, whereas the larger number in Kings includes captives of all tribes living in Judea at the time. In this way Rashi seeks to explain the discrepancy in 2 Kings between verses 14 and 16, but it is not very plausible. Although it is quite possible that many of the Northern Kingdom escaped to Judea when the former was overthrown and others of the Ten Tribes may have lived there before then, it is unlikely that they were so numerous, even including the tribe of Benjamin which had always been attached to Judea, that they should furnish more than twice as many captives as the tribe of Judah. Is it possible that 3,000 were deported in the seventh year of his reign and another 7,000 in the *eighth* year (though no break need be assumed), thus making 10,000 in all? A further suggestion is

that the 3,023 deportees were allowed to take their wives and families, which swelled the number to 10,000.

29. *eighteenth year.* Cf. verse 12 and 2 Kings xxv. 8, both of which read *nineteenth year.* The discrepancy may perhaps be explained as suggested in the preceding verse.

30. *in the three and twentieth year.* This third deportation is not recorded in 2 Kings, but we know from Josephus (*Antiquities* X, ix. 7) that in that year Nebuchadnezzar waged war in Syria, Ammon, Moab and Egypt and carried off captives. *Seder Olam* states that Tyre was finally reduced in that year, and the Jews in the countries bordering on the Holy Land were driven into captivity.

31-34. Cf. 2 Kings xxv. 27-30.

31. *in the five and twentieth day of the month.* 2 Kings xxv. 27 has *seven and*

that Evil-merodach king of Babylon,
in the first year of his reign, lifted up
the head of Jehoiachin king of Judah,
and brought him forth out of prison.
32. And he spoke kindly to him, and
set his throne above the throne of
the kings that were with him in
Babylon. 33. And he changed his
prison garments, and did eat bread
before him continually all the days of
his life. 34. And for his allowance,
there was a continual allowance
given him of the king of Babylon,
every day a portion until the day of
his death, all the days of his life.

מְרֹדַךְ מֶלֶךְ בָּבֶל בִּשְׁנַת
מַלְכֻתוֹ אֶת־רֹאשׁ יְהוֹיָכִין
מֶלֶךְ־יְהוּדָה וַיֹּצֵא אֹתוֹ מִבֵּית
32 הַכְּלִיא: וַיְדַבֵּר אִתּוֹ טֹבוֹת
וַיִּתֵּן אֶת־כִּסְאוֹ מִמַּעַל לְכִסֵּא
הַמְּלָכִים אֲשֶׁר אִתּוֹ בְּבָבֶל:
33 וְשִׁנָּה אֵת בִּגְדֵי כִלְאוֹ וְאָכַל
לֶחֶם לְפָנָיו תָּמִיד כָּל־יְמֵי
34 חַיָּו: וַאֲרֻחָתוֹ אֲרֻחַת תָּמִיד
נִתְּנָה־לּוֹ מֵאֵת מֶלֶךְ־בָּבֶל
דְּבַר־יוֹם בְּיוֹמוֹ עַד־יוֹם
מוֹתוֹ כָּל יְמֵי חַיָּו:

v. 31. הכלוא ק׳   v. 32. המלכים ק׳   v. 33. חסר י׳

twentieth. Rashi suggests that Nebuchadnezzar died on the twenty-fifth, was
buried on the twenty-sixth, and the
following day his successor released
Jehoiachin.

Evil-merodach. The name (in the
Babylonian language Amil-Marduk)
means 'servant of Marduk', Babylonia's
chief deity.

lifted up the head. The phrase apparently
means to take cognizance of, whether for
good or for bad (cf. Gen. xl. 13, 19f.).

32. *the kings.* 'Captured kings were
kept at the court of their conqueror to
perpetuate the memory of his triumph
as well as for security against rebellion.
Cf. Judg. i. 7' (Streane).

33. *changed his prison garments.* As was
done to Joseph (Gen. xli. 14).

did eat bread before him. Was admitted
to the privilege of sitting at the king's
table.

34. *all the days of his life.* This clause is
apparently superfluous and may have
been added to avoid closing the Book
with the word *death.* 'The general
object, too, of the paragraph seems to
have been somewhat similar, viz. to leave
the reader with a parting ray of comfort
and encouragement in the thought that
even in exile the Lord remembered His
people and softened the heart of the
heathen tyrant towards David's seed'
(Streanc).

AUTHORITIES QUOTED

Binns, L. E. (Christian Hebraist), *Jeremiah* (Westminster Commentary).
Buttenwieser, M. (Jewish Bible Scholar), *The Prophets of Israel.*
Carlyle, T. (British author).
Cohen, H. (Jewish Philosopher), *Jüdische Schriften.*
Cornill, C. H. (Christian Hebraist), *Das Buch Jeremia erklärt.*
Darmesteter, J. (Jewish Orientalist), *Les Prophètes d'Israél.*
Driver, S. R. (Christian Hebraist), *The Book of the Prophet Jeremiah.*
Duhm, B. (Christian Hebraist), *Jeremia* in Marti's *Kurzer Hand-Commentar zum A.T.*
Ehrlich, A. B. (Biblical Exegete), *Randglossen zur hebräischen Bibel.*
Findlay, G. G. (Christian Bible Scholar), *The Books of the Prophets.*
Herodotus (Greek Historian, 5th century B.C.E.).
Hertz, J. H. (late Chief Rabbi), *The Pentateuch and Haphtorahs.*
Hort, F. J. A. (English Theologian).
Jerome (Christian Translator of the Bible and Commentator, 346-420 C.E.)
Josephus, Flavius (Jewish Historian, 1st century C.E.)
Kimchi, David (1160-1235, Bible Commentator).
Maimonides, Moses (1135-1204, Jewish Philosopher), *Guide for the Perplexed.*
Malbim, M. L. (1809-1879, Jewish Commentator).
Marston, C. (Christian Bible Scholar), *The Bible is True.*
Metsudath David ('Tower of David'), *Commentary on Jeremiah* by David Altschul (17th century).
Midrash, Rabbinic homilies on the Pentateuch, etc.
Milman, H. H. (Christian Historian), *History of the Jews.*
Peake, A. S. (Christian Hebraist), *Jeremiah* (Century Bible).
Peshitta, Syriac translation of the Bible (2nd century C.E.)
Petrie, Flinders (Egyptologist), *Egypt and Israel.*
Philo (Jewish Philosopher in Alexandria, 20 B.C.E.-40 C.E.).
Pickering, B. M. (Christian Hebraist), *Jeremiah* in *A New Commentary on Holy Scripture*, ed. Gore, etc.
Pusey, E. B. (Christian Hebraist), *The Minor Prophets.*
Rashi (Rabbi Solomon ben Isaac, 1040-1105, Bible Commentator).
Schreiner, Olive (South African authoress).
Seder Olam (Early Jewish Historical Chronicle).
Septuagint, Greek translation of the Bible begun in the third century B.C.E.
Siphrë, Ancient Rabbinic Commentary on Numbers and Deuteronomy.
Smith, G. A. (Christian Hebraist), *Jeremiah ; Historical Geography of the Holy Land.*
Smith, Payne (Christian Hebraist), *Jeremiah* (Speaker's Commentary).
Smith, Ryder (Christian Bible Scholar), *The Bible Doctrine of Society.*
Smith, W. R. (Christian Orientalist), *Prophets of Israel.*
Stanley, A. P. (English Ecclesiastical Scholar), *Lectures on the History of the Jewish Church.*
Streane, A. W. (Christian Hebraist), *Jeremiah* (Cambridge Bible).
Sulzberger, M. (Jewish Lawyer and Scholar), *The Am Ha-Arets : The Ancient Hebrew Parliament.*
Talmud, Corpus of Jewish Law and Thought (compiled at the end of the fifth century C.E.).
Targum, Aramaic Translation of the Bible (1st and 2nd centuries C.E.).
Thomson, W. M. (Christian Traveller), *The Land and the Book.*
Torczyner, H. (Jewish Orientalist), *The Lachish Letters.*
Tristram, H. B. (Natural Scientist), *The Natural History of the Bible.*
Vulgate, Latin translation of the Bible (4th century C.E.).

TERMS AND ABBREVIATIONS

A.D.P.B. *Authorized Daily Prayer Book*, ed. S. Singer.

A.J. American-Jewish translation of the Scriptures.

A.V. Authorized Version.

B.C.E. Before the Christian era.

Ber. *Berachoth*, Talmudical tractate.

c. About.

C.E. Common era.

Cf. Compare, refer to.

Chag. *Chagigah*, Talmudical tractate.

ed. Editor, or edited by.

e.g. For example.

etc. Et cetera.

f. Following verse or chapter (plural ff.).

i.e. That is.

kerë. The Hebrew as it is to be read according to the Masoretes.

Keth. *Kethuboth*, Talmudical tractate.

kethib. The Hebrew as it is written according to tradition.

lit. Literally.

LXX. Septuagint (see Authorities Quoted).

Meg. *Megillah*, Talmudical tractate.

MS. Manuscript (plural MSS.).

M.T. Masoretic text.

R.V. Revised Version.

Sanh. *Sanhedrin*, Talmudical tractate.

Shab. *Shabbath*, Talmudical tractate.

sic. Thus (drawing attention to a remarkable reading or statement).

viz. Namely.

I. Names and Subjects

INDEX

II. HEBREW WORDS